# KINSHIP &
# CONSENT

# KINSHIP & CONSENT

## THE JEWISH POLITICAL TRADITION AND ITS CONTEMPORARY USES

### SECOND EDITION
### REVISED AND ENLARGED

EDITED BY

# DANIEL J. ELAZAR

**TRANSACTION PUBLISHERS**
NEW BRUNSWICK (U.S.A.) AND LONDON (U.K.)

Preparation of this book for publication was made possible through the Milken Library of Jewish Public Affairs, funded by the Foundations of the Milken Families.

This book is printed on acid-free paper that meets the American National Standard for Permanence of Paper for Printed Library Materials.

Library of Congress Catalog Number: 96–31952
ISBN: 1–56000–933–0
Printed in the United States of America

Library of Congress Cataloging-in-Publication Data

    Kinship and consent : the Jewish political tradition and its contemporary uses / edited by Daniel J. Elazar—2nd ed., rev. and enl.
        p.   cm.
    Includes bibliographical references and index.
    ISBN 1-56000-933-0 (pbk.  alk. paper)
    1. Judaism and politics—History of doctrines  2. Politics in rabbinical literature. 3. Jews—Politics and government. I. Elazar, Daniel Judah.
BM645.P64K56   1997
296.3'877—dc20
                                              96-31952
                                                CIP

This book is dedicated to Aileen Epstein Whitman and the late Gerson Epstein, two very good friends who helped us launch the first edition of this book and thereby inaugurate the field of Jewish Political Studies.

# Contents

# Preface to the Second Edition

The publication of the first edition of this book was a landmark in the development of Jewish political studies as a field of inquiry. Prior to its appearance, courses in Jewish political studies had been taught at perhaps four universities around the world, two in the United States and two in Israel. With the appearance of the book came the development of other seminars and workshops in the field and within a decade courses in Jewish political studies were being taught at some twenty-five universities in North America, Europe, Israel, and in Australasia. The Kotler Institute held two additional summer seminars dealing with aspects of the field; then in 1980 the Jerusalem Center for Public Affairs established an annual summer workshop that has continued for sixteen years so far. The limited first edition of the book was rapidly sold and went into a second printing which now has also been sold out. The book came to be regularly used in courses on the subject.

In the meantime, research in the field has not only continued but has increased and has become more systematic as scholars have developed a theoretical framework for Jewish political studies, a terminology, and appropriate methodologies. While the original edition has stood the test of time very well, in great part because of the very high quality of the scholars who contributed to it, some of the gaps that then existed in the field have been filled. Hence, the time has come for a new edition. This edition contains five new chapters: "The Concept of the Three *Ketarim*" by Stuart A. Cohen, "The Kehillah" and "The Jewish People as the Classic Diaspora" by the present writer, "The Jewish People and the Kingdom of Heaven" by Ella Belfer, and "The Application of Jewish Public Law in the State of Israel" by Menachem Elon. Other essays have been revised and updated, particularly those by Menachem Elon and Peter Medding. Introductions are provided for each of the four parts, delineating the unifying historical and theoretical developments for each. We hope that the new edition will serve students and scholars in the field even better than the first and continue to provide a link between Jewish political studies and other fields of Jewish study.

This edition was prepared entirely by the Jerusalem Center for Public Affairs. It is part of the Milken Library of Jewish Public Affairs and special thanks for publication support are due the Foundations of the Milken Families. I would also like to express my appreciation to Mark Ami-El, the JCPA's very capable and efficient director of publications, and to Chaya Herskovic, the coordinator of the JCPA's projects in Jewish political studies whose assistance in all of our work related to this volume has been invaluable. Three of the additional chapters were produced for the Workshop on Covenant and the Jewish Political Tradition jointly conducted by the Senator N. M. Paterson Chair of the Department of Political Studies at Bar-Ilan University and the Center for Jewish Community Studies of the JCPA. Meir Kasirer has coordinated the workshop since its beginning. Many thanks are due him as well as to all the participants in the workshop and Bar-Ilan University itself.

Daniel J. Elazar
Jerusalem
Ellul 5756, August 1996

# Preface to the First Edition

The Jews of Israel and the Jewish people as a whole are presently in the process of searching for a usable past. A major part of that search involves the rediscovery of the Jewish political tradition and its application to contemporary conditions in Israel and the diaspora.

The 1975 summer Colloquium of the Institute for Judaism and Contemporary Thought, at Kibbutz Lavi, was devoted to the exploration of Jewish political life and thought from the biblical period to the present in order to ascertain the content and character of the Jewish political tradition and its relevance for our time. The colloquium was organized on the assumption that there is a Jewish political tradition and that it is one worth relating to. Like all of Jewish tradition, its roots are in the Bible, which has provided Jews and the rest of mankind with an important political teaching, principally through the covenant idea and its implications. As a tradition, it is best expressed through the political institutions and behavior of Jewish communities throughout the generations. There are important works in Jewish political thought but, in the manner of Jewish thought, they are essentially commentaries on the reality of Jewish life.

By bringing together scholars and participants in public affairs from Israel and the diaspora—including political and social scientists, Talmudists, historians, philosophers, and students of the Bible—the colloquium brought to bear a wide range of perspectives on the consideration of the various manifestations of the Jewish political tradition today and in the past, such as the relationship between authority and power, patterns of political organization and leadership, the Jewish language of politics, Israel as a Jewish polity and the Jewish views of the ideal polity.

This volume is an outgrowth of the Lavi meeting. It presents the finest fruits of that meeting to a larger public, offering an initial statement regarding the character and content of the Jewish political tradition from the biblical period to the present and suggestions as to the contemporary meaning and manifestations of that tradition. As such, we hope that the book will be an important contribution to contemporary Jewish scholarship and public affairs, one that will stimulate additional scholarly work in the emerging field of Jewish political studies and which will focus public attention on the character, meaning, and importance of the Jewish political tradition for contemporary Jews wherever they may be.

I would like to acknowledge with special thanks Professor Harold Fisch, chairman of the Institute for Judaism and Contemporary Thought and the Board of the Institute, for giving me the opportunity to organize the colloquium under the Institute's auspices. The idea of holding such a colloquium emerged out of discussions among colleagues of the Center for Jewish Community Studies in the late 1960s, but the opportunity did not present itself until Professor Fisch and the Institute Board graciously invited me to organize their 1975 summer meeting. In the interim, Center fellows and associates pursued their work on the subject; they served as the nucleus of the colloquium participants. The fruits of their work were featured prominently at the colloquium itself and represent two-thirds of this volume, or ten of the fifteen chapters included within it. In a real sense then, this book is not only part of the excellent series of explorations of contemporary Jewish issues produced by the Institute for Judaism and Contemporary Thought but is also another product in the continuing work of the Center for Jewish Community Studies, one which reflects its members' efforts to come to grips with the character and content of Jewish political thought and behavior. The Center fellows and associates are identified in the list of contributors.

While the pleasant task of developing the substantive program was given to me, Dr. Menachem Friedman, coordinator of the Institute for Judaism and Contemporary Thought and Senior Lecturer in sociology at Bar-Ilan University, had the far greater burden of organizing the meeting itself. The success of the event was in no small measure due to the way he shouldered that burden. I owe him a great debt of gratitude. Professor Charles S. Liebman, of the Bar-Ilan Department of Political Studies, my good friend and close associate in the work of the Center for Jewish Community Studies was the first link between men and the Institute, on whose board he serves. It was he who made the match that led to the production of this book.

With all my gratitude for the services rendered by others, I know that this project could not have been brought to fruition, either as a seminar or as a book, without the devoted assistance of the staff of the Institute of Local Government and Department of Political Studies of Bar-Ilan University. Moshe Gat, the Institute's assistant, assisted in myriad ways. Sarah Lederhendler, one of the finest secretaries with whom I have ever had the pleasure to work, always seemed to be available when we needed her in the pinch, above and beyond her normal responsibilities. Without her help or that of Judy Cohen, coordinator of the Jerusalem office of the Center for Jewish Community Studies, this book could never have been published. As has been the case almost from the first moment I began my work at Bar-Ilan, Clara Feldman has been my indispensable right arm. There is no enterprise that I have undertaken that has involved my Bar-Ilan office in any way in which she has not demonstrated her critical importance. This project was certainly no exception. I know of no adequate way to acknowledge my debt to her.

Last, but hardly least, very special thanks are due to Aileen and Gerson Epstein for their assistance at a crucial point in bringing this book to publication.

Daniel J. Elazar
Jerusalem
Adar 5737

# Introduction: The Jewish Political Tradition

*Daniel J. Elazar*

At the very end of the sixteenth century, Johannes Althusius, the greatest political theorist of Reformation Protestantism, described politics in the following terms:

> Politics is the art of associating (*consociandi*) men for the purpose of establishing, cultivating, and conserving social life among them. Whence it is called "symbiotics." The subject matter of politics is therefore association (*consociatio*), in which the symbiotes pledge themselves each to the other, by explicit or tacit agreement, to mutual communication of whatever is useful and necessary for the harmonious exercise of social life.

The end of political "symbiotic" man is holy, just, comfortable, and happy symbiosis, a life lacking nothing either necessary or useful.[1]

As a Reformed Protestant, the essential concern of Althusius was to provide a synthesis and adaptation of the biblical political experience with classic political theory, using the Bible to organize political life for his time and make it compatible with Aristotelian political science. Althusius identified himself as a political scientist in those words. His political science was designed to produce a Christian commonwealth, but in that same spirit, he could be seen to pursue the idea of a holy commonwealth for any monotheistic faith. The ancient Israelites of biblical times were his model and their commonwealth the model commonwealth.

Althusius saw the above definition as applying to all of political life. He went on in his magnum opus, *Politica Methodice Digesta*, to apply that definition to the politics of his ideal polity, a Reformed Protestant commonwealth, in the process making allowance for the different possibilities or necessities in political organization of the Holy Roman Empire of his time.

In the middle of the seventeenth century Althusius lost out to his contemporary competitor, Jean Bodin, the theorist of modern statism, and, except for flashes of attention paid him by an occasional dissenter from the modern state system, went into eclipse for three hundred years. He and his ideas have come to the fore once again, early in the postmodern epoch as modern statism gives way to federalism as the dominant paradigm in the world and Althusius' view of the body politic as the *consociatio consociationum* has once again begun to gain the attention of those who are occupied with political theory and its relation to practice.

One political tradition that always operated on the premises embodied in Althusius' thought is the Jewish political tradition, as Althusius well understood. Jews formed a *consociatio consociationum* from their earliest beginnings and continued to maintain their polity with its political tradition in their pre-state period, when they had an in independent state, and throughout the long years of exile. They could well understand Althusius' central principle that "politics is the communication of right in the commonwealth through citizenship and that a polity indicates that communication of right, signifies the manner of administering and regulating the commonwealth, and notes the form and constitution of the commonwealth for which all actions of the citizens are guided."[2]

Althusius goes on, "The symbiotes are co-workers who, by the bond of an associating and uniting agreement, communicate among themselves whatever is appropriate for a comfortable life of soul and body. In other words, they are participants or partners in a common life." Communication or *communicatio* for Althusius means a sharing or making in common. He goes on to state, "This mutual communication, or common enterprise, involves one thing, two services, and three common rights by which the numerous and various needs of each and every symbiote are supplied, the self-sufficiency and mutuality of life in human society are achieved, and social life is established and conserved."[3] All communication takes place within a certain jurisdiction.

One of the features of the paradigm shift from statism to federalism is the shift from the concern for sovereignty to the concern for jurisdiction. Whether ascribing sovereignty to God or forced to recognize the sovereignty of suzereins, the Jewish people always were preoccupied with the question of jurisdiction and indeed helped make that the central question for federal democracy everywhere, first articulating in politics the idea that authority and power were divided among different authorities, each of whom had their sphere of jurisdiction and all of whom were subordinate to the people who empowered them wherever sovereignty was located.

While Althusius never discussed the matter directly, he would have understood how the exploration of the Jewish political tradition was predicated on the recognition of the Jews as a separate people, not merely a religion or a set of moral principles growing out of a religion. The exploration of the Jewish political tradition, then, is an exploration of how the Jews as a people managed to maintain their polity over centuries of independence, exile, and dispersion, and how they animated that polity by communicating their own expressions of political culture and modes of political behavior.

That is the subject of this book, an effort on the part of a significant selection of the greatest scholars in Jewish studies in the first part of the postmodern epoch, whose fields range from Bible to Jewish history, from Jewish law to theology, as well as political science, to begin the exploration of the Jewish people as a polity with its own political tradition. The chapters in this book represent individual cuts into the tradition at critical points. Because not every period in Jewish history has benefitted from the kind of scholarly attention that this book emphasizes, not all are covered. Because the form of the scholarly attention depends to a significant degree on the discipline involved, not every chapter is equally rooted in the terms of political discourse. Nevertheless, together they provide us with a clear-cut introduction to Jewish political studies as a subdiscipline in Jewish studies and begins to enable us to see how it is a subdiscipline of political science.

The Jewish people and its political tradition encompass a span of at least 3300 years and perhaps 500 more. In this span of time Jews have been a tribal polity, an enslaved caste, a simple agrarian republic, a state that was also a regional power, a community in exile, an imperial province, a vassal state, a revolutionary polity, a congeries of dispersed communities bound together by a common law, a set of coreligionists, an ethnic group, and a modern state. Each of these had its own uniqueness. Nevertheless, there are certain threads that seem to run through every one of them that date back to the earliest days of separate Jewish existence. It is the exploration of these threads that is the subject of this volume.

This volume is written with the understanding that the Jews are a people and a culture which, while informed throughout by Judaism as a religion and its value system, still can and should be viewed from that perspective rather than from the more limited perspective of Judaism as a religion. This is the view that Jews have had of themselves throughout their history and which the world unambiguously shared with them until the beginning of the modern epoch. Only in the last two centuries or less have some considered Jews to be members of a religious persuasion and no more.

This latter position was first advanced as a Jewish strategy in Western Europe to achieve their emancipation from the ghettoization imposed on them by the majority Christian society. This position became especially necessary as modernity brought down the divisions in the general society into estates, guilds, and other estate-oriented constructs. With the elimination of medieval society and the emergence of the nation-state, which recognized individual citizens only, in theory without regard to other divisions, most Jews did not want to be left out of the new opportunities that this reclassification offered. Moreover, the Jewish communities lost their informal autonomy as well.

Hence, except for those who remained strictly Orthodox and consequently wished to continue to live in self-contained communities, the Jews as a people sought integration into the new nation-states, which they could do only if they emphasized Judaism as a religious difference rather than Jewishness as a national one. This system worked partially, but in the end the Jews could not survive as a group except by recognizing their corporate character to at least some degree.

Zionism, indeed, emphasized Jewish nationhood to its fullest. The Zionist concession to modernity was to separate nationalism and religion. This, too, was a first time venture and has had mixed success for the same reasons.

Meanwhile, the Jewish political tradition has continued to accept Jewish peoplehood as a fundamental premise and in practice to make such adjustments as have proved to be necessary in Israel and the diaspora. This book speaks out of that approach, which, no matter how one chooses to view it, is fundamental because neat divisions between ethnicity, culture, and religion have proved impossible to maintain in Jewish life, past or present.

The crises of the past few years have generated renewed interest, on the part of Jewish publics in Israel and the diaspora, in the character of the State of Israel as a Jewish state and in the Jewish people as a corporate entity. As a consequence, the modern Jewish search for roots and meaning has been intensified. In the twentieth century, the most practical aspects of this search have involved the restoration of Jewish political independence through the State of Israel and the revival of the sense of Jewish peoplehood throughout the diaspora. It is precisely because contemporary Jewry has moved increasingly towards self-definition in political terms that a significant part of the search for roots and meaning must take place within the political realm.

The Jewish national revival of our times led first to the restoration of Jewish political consciousness, then to the reestablishment of the Jewish polity. The next step in the process is the rediscovery of the Jewish political tradition. This book is based on the premise that there is indeed a Jewish political tradition—with all that it implies in the way of a continuing dialogue regarding proper or acceptable modes of political behavior, institutional forms, and political cultural norms—and is devoted to mustering and examining the evidence to that end.

To suggest that there is a Jewish political tradition is not to suggest that there is a single, uniform, monolithic "Jewish way of politics." A tradition by its very nature is multifaceted, even dialectic in character. Like a river, it has currents within it that are united because they flow within the same banks, and, except for occasional eddies, in the same direction.

A tradition is, in fact, a continuing dialogue based upon a shared set of fundamental questions. For Jews, this dialogue began with the emergence of the Jewish people as an entity, a body politic, early in its history. It has continued ever since, at times—particularly when the Jews have lived independently in their own land—resonating strongly, and at other times less so. The emancipation of the Jews in the modern era nearly brought this dialogue to an end but, precisely at its weakest moment, it was revived as the political dimension of Jewish life became clear once again. After surviving changes of constitution and regime, exile and dispersion, the Jewish political tradition has been nearly lost in our times, precisely on the threshold of renewal of full Jewish political life. Hence, it needs to be recovered by systematic effort so that it may fill a vital and needed role in contemporary Jewish life—both in Israel and in the diaspora.

The enduring foundations of the Jewish political tradition are to be found in the Bible. In one sense, this is because the foundations of all of Jewish tradition are to be found there. In many respects, however, the Jewish political tradition has been more enduringly influenced by the Bible than some other aspects of the Jewish tradition. While all of the tradition has been filtered through the Talmud, the efforts of the sages to diminish the political tradition in the wake of the disastrous Roman wars (the effort, in itself, was a political act of the first magnitude) meant that the tradition was transformed by them into an undifferentiated part of the *halakhic* tradition, so much so that with the revival of explicit political inquiry in the Middle Ages, Jewish thinkers and leaders who otherwise relied on the Talmud for all things went back to biblical sources for ideas with regard to proper political behavior and even institution building. Centuries later, we find an echo of that process in the way that Zionists sought to base on biblical sources their quest for renewed Jewish statehood in the land of Israel.

The revival of political concern among contemporary Jews is only right; it is a reflection—however obscured—of the fundamental truth that the validity of the Jewish teaching can only be fully tested in a political setting, through a polity in which Jews must assume responsibility for the effort to build the "kingdom of heaven"—the good commonwealth—on earth. Accordingly, it becomes vital for Jews to rediscover the Jewish political tradition in order to pursue the Jewish vision at its fullest, and so as to root their institutions, including the State of Israel, more fully within it.

The Jewish political tradition, like the political tradition of any people, is at one and the same time an integral part of the people's overall tradition and a separable expression of the people's culture or civilization. Every political tradition represents shared expectations as to what constitutes justice in public affairs, a common sense of the proper uses of power in the pursuit of political goals, a shared understanding of the reciprocal relationship between power and justice in the body politic, and a common view of the proper relationships between the governors and the governed. It is built around an enduring consensus—a thinking together—on the part of the members of a particular political community or body politic about common questions over generations. The answers to these questions need not be the same for all consenting members of the body politic. Were they the same, we would have a political doctrine, not a tradition, for implicit in the existence of a tradition is a dialectical dimension—a continuing "great debate." A tradition is built around the tension that exists between its different expressions, that remain within the same dialectical framework because they share common questions.

Lest it be assumed otherwise, let it be said at the outset that a political tradition does not simply include the good qualities present in the political life of a people; it includes deficiencies and vices as well as virtues (often, the vices reflect excesses of what otherwise are virtues). While one would hope that the ideals and ends of one's own political tradition would be good (and that is not always the case, by any means), the behavioral dimension of any tradition is necessarily mixed. The way of humanity makes it ever thus. Some political traditions, indeed, are gravely deficient but, while the Jewish political tradition, too, has mixed elements, the authors in this volume argue—explicitly or implicitly—that it is basically a good, even an excellent one, founded on solid premises, emphasizing good ends, and encouraging sound behavior. If the less praiseworthy aspects of Jewish political behavior are underemphasized in these pages, it is not for lack of awareness of them.

What is perhaps most compelling about the need to rediscover the Jewish political tradition is the fact that Jews continue to function in the political arena, in no small measure on the basis of their political tradition, albeit without conscious awareness that they are functioning within a living tradition of their own or any tradition at all. The striking similarities in the structure of Jewish institutions in Israel and the diaspora, present and past, the continuities in the basic characteristics of Jewish political behavior, the persistence of certain fundamental beliefs and practices embedded in Jewish political culture, all attest to the persistence of a Jewish political tradition even if it remains for the most part unrecognized. Were we speaking of the creation of a tradition where none existed, it would be perhaps possible to question the validity of the effort. But since we are speaking of a living phenomenon that is simply unrecognized, the benefits that can be derived from developing a conscious understanding of it are great indeed.

## Some Elements of the Jewish Political Tradition

The Jewish political tradition, like every political tradition, is concerned with power and justice; it differs from the political traditions growing out of classic Greek thought in that it begins with a concern for relationships rather than regimes. It is less concerned with determining the best form of government (in Aristotelian terms, the best constitution) than with establishing the proper relationship between the governors and the governed, power and justice, God and man. This concern for relationships is embodied in the principle of covenant that lies at the root of the Jewish political tradition and also gives the tradition its form. In the Jewish political tradition, as in the Jewish tradition as a whole—all relationships are rooted in the Covenant.

One dimension that is implicit in this covenantal relationship, and which has been explicitly reflected in one way or another throughout Jewish history, is that the polity itself is compounded of several authoritative elements, which, while bound to one another (by covenant), have their own respective integrities. In its classic form, the Jewish polity is an *edah* (meaning an assembly or congregation—a coming together—and perhaps best understood as the Hebrew equivalent of commonwealth), constituted by God and Israel through the Sinai covenant. The powers created by the establishment of this polity are shared by God, the people of Israel in their character as an edah, and those designated as governors by both (e.g., David who is anointed by Samuel in God's name but whose rule is only confirmed after he enters into covenants with the tribal elders of Judah and Israel). The powers are further divided among several governors, for example, the civil leaders, the prophets and the priests—reflected in the tradition as *keter malkhut* (the crown of kingship or rule), *keter torah* (the crown of Torah or Divine teaching), and *keter kehunah* (the crown of the priesthood)—and, later, the householders and the rabbinical leaders.

The result of all this is a separation of powers, not in the modern sense of executive, legislative, and judicial (although the Bible is cognizant of those three basic divisions, cf. Isaiah 33:22—"For the Lord is our Judge, the Lord is our Lawgiver, the Lord is our King; He will save us"), but as an intricate set of power relationships among separate yet linked bodies. The Jewish order of prayer reflects this intricate set of relationships in several ways: in the daily morning service where the heavenly hosts grant (or acknowledge) each other's authority to praise God, and in the blessing after meals when the leader must request authority to take the lead from the others at the table (and, some suggest, from the rabbinical authorities as well), to name but two examples.

Perhaps the best example of all is to be found in the mode of delivery of the priestly blessing in the High Holy Day services. Under Jewish law, those descended from the priestly families are required by God to administer the blessing; theirs is a purely ministerial task in which they have no discretion. When they are called upon to perform this task in the synagogue, a nonpriest (an "Israelite") calls them to it; they respond by asking for reshut (authority) from the congregation, which, in turn, indicates that the authority is really granted by Heaven. The one who called upon them then leads them in the blessing word by word. The "script" is as follows:

ISRAELITE: Cohanim (priests)!
PRIESTS: B'reshut rabbotai (by the authority of the congregation)!
CONGREGATION: B'reshut Shamayim (by the authority of Heaven)! ISRAELITE: Y'varechacha (May you be blessed)...
PRIESTS: Y'varechacha...

This pattern of interlocking authorities is paradigmatic of the Jewish polity; no single person or body has final authority—instead various bodies share powers.

It is in this original sense that the Jewish political tradition is federal (federal: from the Latin *foedus*, meaning covenant) in orientation. Fundamentally, federalism involves the coming together of separate elements to compound a common entity in such a way that their respective integrities are preserved. Appropriately, federal arrangements emphasize relationships as the key to proper structures of a lasting character. For that reason, the variety of structures animated by federal principles is substantial. Jewish history attests to that variety, since the Jewish political tradition has emphasized federal arrangements in the more conventional sense of the term as well. There has hardly been an age when the Jewish *edah* has not been organized on a federal basis, beginning with the tribal confederacy and including the federated kingdom of the tribes, the *politeuma* of the Hellenistic diaspora that stood in federal relationship to the city in which it was located, the several *yeshivot* of Babylonia and their respective communities, the medieval federations of communities, the Council of the Four Lands, the post-emancipation European federations of *cultesgemeinden*, the Latin American federations of country-of-origin communities, and the contemporary North American federations of Jewish functional agencies. And this is not an exhaustive list by any means.

The Jewish political tradition is republican in the original sense of the term—the body politic is held to be *res publica*, a public thing, and not anyone's private preserve. Significantly, the Jewish political tradition in its classic expression has no idea of the state as a reified entity; there are only the varieties of political relationships that create polity. This, too, is a view closely related to federalism. Indeed, the Jewish political tradition does not recognize state sovereignty as such. No state—a human creation—can be sovereign. Classically, only God is sovereign and He entrusts the exercise of His sovereign powers mediated through His Torah-as-constitution to the people as a whole; His priests and prophets as provided through His covenant with Israel.

In the last analysis, the Jewish political tradition is based upon what S. D. Goitein has termed "religious democracy," using the term religious in its original sense of "binding." At the same time, the Jewish political tradition has a strong aristocratic current, again not in the sense of aristocracy as a political structure but as a relationship whereby those who hold powers of government are trustees for both the people and the law, selected on the basis of some qualification to be trustees—Divine sanctification, scholarship, lineage or, de facto, wealth—the particular mix varying according to time and place.

## Exploring the Jewish Political Tradition

The record of the Jewish political tradition is to be found in the Jewish people's sacred and subsidiary texts and in their collective behavior. The exploration of both dimensions is both an intellectual and a practical challenge for contemporary Jews. It is that double interest that requires serious Jews to undertake to explore the Jewish political tradition as fully as possible. On one hand, problems such as the structure of authority and power in the Jewish community, the character of political and communal leadership, political decision making, the ideal polity, all lead to questions that are intellectually interesting and even exciting in and of themselves. At the same time, they all involve very practical challenges for Jews in the process of reconstituting their polity, both in the land of Israel and in the diaspora.

It can even be argued that the survival of a committed Jewry, at least outside of the Orthodox camp, depends in no small measure on the rediscovery of the Jewish political tradition. It is one of the ironies of the postmodern age that, just at the time when all Jews outside of

Israel, over 75 percent of the world Jewish population, have lost all formal corporate political status, the political focus of Jewish identification has suddenly reemerged. The modern era—the three hundred years from the middle of the seventeenth to the middle of the twentieth centuries—was one in which Jews were busy shedding their corporate status and forms of corporate organization. In the process, they also shed the political links that had been part and parcel of Jewish tradition and that had held Jews together as one people even in dispersion. On the intellectual plane, Jews tried to transform those links into theological-cum-ritual ("religious") links of various kinds and, on the practical plane, into social-cum-philanthropic ones. Now, rather suddenly, these various links created by Jewish moderns as the source of Jewish identity and identification have begun to weaken for many Jews. In their place, ironically enough, there has been a rising concern with the political as the focal point of Jewish identity and interest, particularly in the past decade. This is clearly true in the State of Israel. It is also true in the diaspora where Jews are increasingly bound to one another only by formal associational ties that, while not of the old corporate kind, are political in the sense of reflecting such common interests as combatting anti-Semitism, supporting Israel, and maintaining the Jewish right to be different. Jews are suddenly confronting questions of political interest to them as Jews, particularly, but by no means exclusively, relating to Israel. As a result, the political dimension is rapidly emerging as perhaps the only unifying force that can link virtually all Jews at a time when secularization, assimilation, and movement away from tradition are rampant. This curiously ironic state of affairs brings the whole question of the Jewish political tradition into a more central position than it might otherwise have had, although it is an important and compelling question in any event.

It may be asked, why talk about a Jewish political tradition instead of an ideology or set of doctrines? I would suggest that the idea of a Jewish political tradition is particularly important because of the character of Jewish political concerns. Were Jews to derive their political ideas from philosophy (in the classical or technical sense of the term), perhaps it would be appropriate to talk about a Jewish political philosophy, or competing Jewish political philosophies, which would manifest themselves in ideologies derived from philosophies. This is the way of European civilization and, indeed, is characteristic of many peoples who have undergone a revolutionary break with their past which they must ground ideologically. However, Jews derive their framework from *midrash* and *halakhah*, not from philosophy, and are not dependent for their existence on ideology. Hence, they cannot rely upon philosophy to provide a grounding for Jewish political life. (Jews can philosophize, that is, use the tools of philosophy, but only by grounding them in different set of assumptions, methods, and results.)

As in the case of other peoples whose grounding is not philosophic or ideological, tradition in general has always occupied an extremely important role in Jewish life and a political tradition is almost a *sine qua non.* Perhaps a reference to the American example will help clarify this essential point. The Americans are another nonphilosophic and nonideological people. While Americans have, on one level, grappled with philosophic questions and have derived benefit from using the tools of philosophy, their polity was not simply a product of philosophy but was born out of a political persuasion that reflected a common political experience. The persuasion and experience together created an American political tradition. Since its founding, the United States has used its political tradition, particularly as mediated through the decisions of the federal Supreme Court and the actions of political leaders, to provide the framework for considering its own political reality. Similarly, a living Jewish political tradition offers a way to maintain Jewish continuity where there is a common perspective and common experience but no central ideology. The maintenance of a political tradition, then, is the key to the political continuity, which is a necessary part of the continuity of Judaism.

A tradition persists on two levels, the formal and the subliminal. To be a fully living tradition, its bearers must be somewhat conscious that they are part of it and somewhat aware that they are expressing it in their ideas and actions. Yet even under such conditions, a tradition is like the proverbial iceberg—the greater part of it is not a matter of conscious (of self-conscious) articulation but does influence thought and behavior unbeknownst to its bearers. Under the worst conditions, a tradition can survive on the subliminal level in more ways than most people would be likely to notice. For several generations, the Jewish political tradition has survived principally subliminally. Thus, the task before Jews today is to revive the sense of the tradition even more than it is to revive the tradition itself. So the question remains—what must be done, what can be done, to make it a more articulated tradition than it has been in the recent past.

## The Covenant and the Jewish Political Tradition

A major thesis of this volume is that the Jewish political tradition is animated, to a substantial degree, by the covenant, as both idea and reality. Covenant theology has become current enough coin in Jewish circles in the last decade or two, so that the idea itself is hardly foreign even to those who were brought up in a different generation of Jewish intellectual endeavor when that vital aspect of the biblical teaching was overlooked or underemphasized. What is suggested in the following pages is that there is a strong political dimension to the covenant idea, and that covenants themselves have consistently served as the principal instruments for shaping Jewish political institutions and relationships. While not everyone represented in the following pages would accept this formulation, the reader will soon note how the covenant idea, or what the prophet Ezekiel (20:37) referred to as *Masoret HaBrit*—the Covenant bond or tradition—runs through most of the chapters like a common thread.

Like all great ideas, the covenant idea is deceptively simple. The term *brit* (covenant) conveys the sense of a morally grounded perpetual (or at least indeterminately lasting) compact between parties having independent but not necessarily equal status, which establishes certain mutual obligations and a commitment to undertake joint action to achieve defined ends. This action may be limited or comprehensive, under conditions of mutual respect, and in such a way as to protect the fundamental integrity of all parties involved. A covenant is much more than a contract—though our modern system of contracts is related to the covenant idea—because it involves a pledge of loyalty and morally grounded obligation beyond that demanded for mutual advantage, often involving the development of community among the partners.

It is also more than a compact in the sense that God is either a party to it or a witness and guarantor. In its fullest sense, a covenant creates a holy or Divinely sanctioned partnership community based upon a firm, legally defined relationship delineating the authority, power, and integrity of each of the partners but requiring more than a narrow legalistic approach to make the community a real one.

Meir Leibush (Malbim), the Bible commentator, offers us a good summary of the covenantal relationship in his commentary on the covenant between God and Abraham in Genesis 17:

This covenant will be "between Me and thee", meaning that the binding obligation rests on both parties to the covenant, because Abraham also obligated himself to be a partner with God in the act of creation by perfecting what was created and by participating in its improvement. (Meir Leibush Malbim, HaTorah VehaMitzvah, 1, 68)

This covenant idea is of great importance because of what it offers in the way of building relationships. The Bible develops a whole system of relationships based upon covenants, beginning with the covenants between God and mankind, which serve as initial political acts creating the conditions under which regimes can be constituted. The Sinai covenant, for example, transformed the Jewish people from a family of tribes into a body politic which could then proceed to develop its constitution and regime. *Yitro* (Jethro), the Torah portion that describes the Sinai experience, provides us with a clear picture of this process. On one hand, it describes the covenant that institutionalizes the fundamental relationship between God and Israel, which is necessary to actually create the new body politic in which God assumes direct rule over Israel. On the other hand, the actual institutions of the regime are portrayed as coming from distinctly non-Divine, even non-Jewish, sources, partly from the inherited tradition of tribal government and partly from Jethro, Moses' father-in-law, who suggests the way to structure one branch of the national government.

The fact that these two stories are intertwined and placed parallel to one another is of the utmost significance. It suggests that the political basis for the constitution is the covenant, which is more than a social compact. But the covenant does not dictate or establish the form of the regime. Rather, the form of the regime is taken from human sources on the basis of necessity and convenience. This is the pattern of interaction between covenant and regime throughout Jewish history. There is the continuity of the fundamental covenant and the constitution that flows from it, the Torah, with the oral Torah building the body of constitutional law. On the other hand, within the latitude established by the Torah, Jews are free to adopt the form of regime they wish.

The interaction between the two elements is a continuing one. The model of this post-Sinai interaction is to be found in the Book of Joshua, chapter 24, where a covenanting act takes place to confirm the reorganization of the tribal confederacy after the conquest of the land. Subsequent Jewish historical experience brought with it a variety of adaptations of covenantal principles, with a new one for each new era of Jewish political adjustment.

The congregational form itself is a subsidiary product of the covenant idea. Ten male Jews come together and in effect compact among themselves to create a framework (within the larger framework of the Torah) for the conduct of their religious, social, and political life. Even the terminology of congregational organization reflects this orientation. Among Sephardic communities, for example, the articles of agreement that establish congregations are known as *askamot* (articles of agreement)—a term that has an explicitly covenantal derivation and significance.

Significantly, the two great phenomena of twentieth-century Jewry, the reestablishment of a Jewish state in the land of Israel and the establishment of a great Jewish community in North America, represent interesting and important adaptations of the covenant idea. If one looks at the foundation of early institutions and settlements of the new *yishuv* in Eretz Yisrael, one finds that their basis in almost every case was covenantal. Borrowing from the established patterns of congregational *askamot*, they established partnerships and created associations on the basis of formal compacts and constitutional document. This continued to be the standard form of organization in the Jewish *yishuv* even after the British became the occupying power in the country. The *yishuv* was governed internally through a network of covenants and compacts until the emergence of a centralized state in 1948.

In the United States, the organization of all congregations follows the traditional form even though the congregations themselves may be untraditional in their religious practices. Similarly, the organization of social agencies and educational institutions, and their coming together in local Jewish federations or countrywide confederations, is simply another extension of what has been the standard pattern of Jewish organization for several millennia. One might be hard put to prove that, in either the Israeli or the American case, there was a conscious desire to maintain a particular political tradition. Rather, it was a consequence of the shared political culture of the Jews involved that led to the continuation of traditional patterns through new adaptations.

It is more than a little ironic that in the United States, where the government does not care how Jews organize themselves so long as they do not try to go beyond certain fundamental constitutional restrictions, the traditional covenantal pattern has been able to express itself most fully under contemporary conditions, whereas in Israel—where the necessity was felt, as it were, to create an authoritative state on the model of the modern nation-state—this process has run into something of a dead end, stifled by the strong inclination toward centralized control of every aspect of public life brought from their European experiences by the state's molders and shapers. That is precisely why the revival of conscious concern with the Jewish political tradition is so important.

## The Contents of this Volume

Needless to say, a volume such as this can be no more than an introduction to a very large subject. We have tried to touch upon a number of vital themes that need to be addressed in the course of exploration of the Jewish political tradition and its contemporary uses. We do not even claim that we have touched upon all of them by any means, nor that we have treated those included with sufficient comprehensiveness. This is an introduction that tries to combine both breadth and depth in sufficient proportion—a preliminary mapping of the surface coupled with some test bores to see what lies below it. Each chapter is written by a specialist in the field, usually the most renowned, and represents a summary expression of years of research on the part of the author. Hence, the book represents a double synthesis.

The volume is divided into four parts. In part I, we examine the biblical and rabbinic foundations of the Jewish political tradition. In chapter 1, I examine the covenant as the basis of the Jewish political tradition in a broad survey from biblical times to the present, emphasizing the biblical origins of the idea and suggesting ways in which it has persisted as a factor shaping Jewish political thought and behavior in subsequent ages.

In chapter 2, Stuart Cohen describes the structure of the standard Jewish political collective which is parallel to the concept of the Covenant and the federalist tenets derived from this concept. The structure of the Jewish political collective is characterized by a unique division of powers that is discussed in the fourth chapter of *Pirkel Avot* (Ethics of Our Fathers).

This division, which is the basis of the Jewish political collective, reflects both the religious and civil dimensions of Jewish governance. It must be noted that this division of the three *ketarim* accompanies the Jewish people from its beginnings as a nation, although the term itself first appears in the Mishnaic period. According to tradition, the three *ketarim* derive their authority from God, through certain personalities and families. *Keter torah* involves relaying the divine message to the nation, through prophets in the early periods and, later on, through the sages, those who engaged in biblical exegesis, and those who ruled in *halakhic* matters; *keter kehunah* enables the nation to reach its God through the family of Aaron and the priests and today, through certain people appointed by the community; *keter malkhut* involves civil issues of the nation to be dealt with by elders, judges, kings, and administrators.

In chapter 3, Gordon Freeman explores the rabbinic dimension of the foundations of the Jewish political tradition. Freeman sees the rabbinic understanding of the covenant as emphasizing the reciprocal relationship between rulers and ruled. He suggests that this tendency toward reciprocity, which has its origins in the Bible, reaches its full fruition in rabbinic literature. In documenting his view that the covenant concept is largely a manifestation of reciprocity, he reinforces the idea that the Jewish political tradition is primarily concerned with relationships between various actors in the political arena rather than with forms of regimes. Freeman's work is the one piece included in this volume that was not produced in connection with the colloquium. Originally developed for the Workshop on the Covenant Idea and the Jewish Political Tradition sponsored by the Department of Political Studies at Bar-Ilan University and the Center for Jewish Community Studies, it fills an important gap by focusing on the talmudic sources.

The three chapters in part II focus on the theoretical development of the Jewish political tradition. In chapter 4, Bernard Susser and Eliezer Don-Yehiya provide us with a prolegomenon to Jewish political theory, an exploration of the possibilities for Jewish political thought that suggests categories through which it can be explored. After cataloguing possible alternative approaches, Susser and Don-Yehiya suggest that the great issues that have been the focus of political theorizing within the Jewish political tradition include the nature of the ideal polity, the proper Jewish relationship to foreign rule, the principles of operation and organization of the autonomous Jewish community, and the issues surrounding an independent Jewish polity. They then proceed to suggest sources through which Jewish political theory can be explored, and examine the ways in which different Jewish thinkers have explored those sources.

Daniel J. Elazar examines "The Jewish People as the Classic

Diaspora" and how they adapted their existence as a polity to the conditions of dispersion for thousands of years. The chapter provides a historical survey of autonomous Jewish organization in the diaspora from its beginnings to the present and the institutions developed by the Jewish people to maintain their communities and polity. It then turns to the Jewish communities in the modern and postmodern epochs to survey the contemporary Jewish diaspora, its institutions, organizations, and functions. It concludes by drawing some conclusions about the Jewish diaspora and diasporas generally.

In the final chapter of part II, chapter 6, Eliezer Schweid examines the attitude towards the state in modern Jewish thought prior to the emergence of Zionism, that is to say, from Spinoza's radical break with Jewish tradition to the end of the nineteenth century. Focusing on Spinoza, Mendelsohn, Solomon Maimon, Shaul Asher, Shmuel Hirsch, Nahman Krochmal, Shimshon Raphael Hirsch, Heinrich Graetz, Zachariah Frankel, and Shlomo Ludwig Steinheim, Schweid explores both the commonalities in these modern Jewish thinkers' understanding of the Jewish political tradition and the differences in their evaluations of the worth of that tradition as a model and guide for political life under modern conditions. In his exploration, Schweid offers strong evidence of the continuity of Jewish political thought through the era of emancipation. More specifically, he offers a view of the spectrum of attitudes towards the Jewish people as a body politic in a period when Jewish corporate existence was first abandoned in practice and then theoretically rejected by many as well.

Significantly, he traces how others came full circle from Spinoza's rejection of the Jewish vision of the polity as inadequate for the modern state to Steinheim's rejection of the modern state and his renewal of the search for a polity grounded on the traditional Jewish vision.

Schweid suggests that one of the major dilemmas of modern Jewish political thought has been the necessity to respond to the existence of the reified centralized state based upon modern principles of sovereignty which fly in the face of traditional Jewish conceptions of the polity. He points to four key questions that concerned modern Jewish political thinkers in this period: (1) What is the vision of the state in the Torah and traditional Jewish sources? (2) What are the implications of this vision for the views and ways of life of modern Jews? (3) What kind of attitude toward the ways of the modern state is made obligatory by the traditional Jewish vision of the state? (4) What are the changes that need to be and can be made in the traditional vision of the state and in the Jewish way of life, or perhaps in the modern understanding of the state, to adjust the Jewish people to the new reality without causing them to lose their separate identity? While the answers to these questions changed at least partially as a result of the rise of Zionism, the questions themselves remain with us as vital ones in the effort to keep the Jewish political tradition operational in our times.

In part III, we turn to an examination of the institutional dynamics of Jewish political life as a reflection of the continuing Jewish political tradition. Each of the chapters deals with a different period of political transition in Jewish history. In chapter 7, Moshe Weinfeld examines the transition from tribal republic to monarchy in ancient Israel, revealing how the struggle between champions of the *edah*, the Jewish polity of the tribal confederacy, and champions of the monarchy has created a basic tension that has persisted ever since in one form or another as a factor in the Jewish political tradition. His work is built on his earlier explorations of the *edah* as a form of political organization and the introduction of the monarchy as a constitutional revolution.

In chapter 8, which discusses the community, Daniel J. Elazar surveys the history of the autonomous Jewish community in the diaspora—from its beginnings in Babylonia up until the period of the emancipation. This essay serves as an introduction to a series of articles on the constitutional framework and the political activity of the autonomous Jewish communities in the diaspora.

Shlomo Dov Goitein examines political conflict and the uses of power in the world of the Geniza in chapter 9. The 300 years that he reviews represented a period of transition from the rule of the Gaonim over virtually all of world Jewry to the era of the separated, local Jewish communities of medieval Europe. Goitein emphasizes the degree to which the Jewish political organization in the Geniza world was that of a religious democracy. In tracing the character of that religious democracy, he suggests parallels with our own times. Goitein's emphasis on the terminology of the Geniza period is worthy of particular attention. The exploration of Jewish political terminology must necessarily occupy an important place in the study of the Jewish political tradition and Goitein's evidence as to usage of *yeshiva* as the equivalent of *sanhedrin*, and *reshut* (authority) as crucial to determining lines of authority is extremely valuable.

In chapter 10, Menachem Elon focuses on authority and power in the classic *kehilla*, the Jewish community of the Middle Ages to examine the larger issue of authority and power in the Jewish community: the *halakhic* stance of the traditional community and its contemporary implications. As a foremost student of Jewish public law, he examines the great issues confronting legal decision makers in the medieval community, particularly at the time of its foundation, and elucidates them in the perspective of the contemporary effort to restore the great chain of tradition in the realm of Jewish public law, particularly as it applies to problems of government in bodies politic. Elon's description of the fundamental tensions around which medieval Jewish communities developed provides a strong sense of the way in which a political tradition is a dialogue rather than a monolithic stream. The concrete examples that he brings from his sources in the responsa of the time are the raw material for exploring that tradition throughout much of Jewish history since the completion of the Talmud.

In chapter 11, Gerald Blidstein turns to *halakhic* theory to explore the relationship between the individual and the community in the Middle Ages. Blidstein points out that, while the medieval Jewish community was a corporate body with strong organic characteristics, in law it was considered to be an association based upon consent and was so described by the rabbis. This meant that individuals had rights that were not forfeited or transferred by virtue of their association with the community (a doctrine highly reminiscent of the compact theory of the seventeenth-century English political philosophers). In a brilliant synthesis of sources, Blidstein presents an argument thoroughly grounded in the facts. What is particularly important about his effort is that it also demonstrates the use of a methodology for examining Jewish political theory which principally grows out of rabbinical decisions with regard to concrete issues on a case-by-case basis rather than through abstract treatises. The end result of rabbinic application of theory to practice was an integrated system of rights and obligations that provided substantial protection for individuals within the context of a community based upon a combination of kinship and consent.

Peter Medding examines the patterns of political organization and leadership in contemporary Jewish communities in chapter 12, focusing on yet another transitional period, this time our own. He begins by identifying the major issues that have confronted contemporary Jewish communities and the ideologies or persuasions of the forces within

them. Medding then describes some of the conflicts that have animated modern Jewish communities, including the conflict between
established and patrician elements, on the one hand, and the masses of
immigrants on the other, which was a recurring phenomenon of the
communities of immigration: the struggle between the leftist oriented
forces and others in the community; the conflicts between religious
and nonreligious elements; and, of course, the struggle over Zionism—properly treating these as fundamental political issues. He then
turns to the structure of leadership in the community and the dilemmas
of representation in a voluntary setting. Medding concludes with an
examination of the way in which these issues have been handled through
the different organizational frameworks that evolved under modern
conditions.

Part IV explores some of the implications of the Jewish political
tradition for contemporary Jewish life. In chapter 13, Ella Belfer discusses the duplication that exists in the Jewish political conception,
while following the continuity of the convergence of the *theos* as a
supreme system of absolute values, with the *kratos* as the independent
entity of the political system.

In chapter 14, Dan Segre looks at the importance of the Jewish
political tradition as a vehicle for Jewish auto-emancipation in Israel.
He suggests that part of Israel's contemporary moral dilemma is the
fact that Zionism drifted too far from Jewish sources and hence became Jewishly unauthentic, leaving the current generation of Israelis
cut off from the only tradition that can ground them in the Jewish
consciousness that Zionism sought to revive.

In his chapter, he investigates "some of the factors which have so
far hampered the development of a Jewish political thought" in Israel
and speculates on the chances that such a thought might be elaborated
in a modern Jewish polity "not in opposition to but as a possible link
between tradition and modernism." In building his argument, Segre
essentially reviews the subjects covered in the first three parts and
then seeks to apply them to the contemporary conditions of the Jewish
state.

In chapter 15, Peter Medding addresses himself to the Jewish people
as a whole and seeks to develop a general theory of Jewish political
interests and behavior that will explain why modern Jews have behaved politically the way they have and in what direction contemporary Jewish political interests are likely to go. In his analysis, he

examines the relationship between the Jews and the liberal left, and then seeks to define standing Jewish political interests and how they have been expressed in both nonliberal and liberal regimes in the twentieth century. Medding concludes by speculating on the likely impact of Israel on diaspora Jewry's perception of Jewish interests and likely diaspora behavior in response to that perception.

In chapter 17, Charles Liebman looks at the politics of Israel-diaspora relations, focusing on the moral and symbolic elements that he sees as animating that politics. Liebman suggests that "Israel and the diaspora confront and interrelate as two significantly different entities," and hence "the symbolic status and moral claims of each on the other are of particular importance in determining the politics of their relationships." He seeks to examine Israel's moral and symbolic claims on the diaspora, including its claim to moral superiority by virtue of being Zion. He then turns to the diaspora perspective and how it responds to those claims in political terms. Finally, Liebman examines the impact of the foregoing political relationships on the internal communal structure of diaspora Jewry.

Dan Segre strongly emphasized the positive role of *halakhah* in giving shape to the restored Jewish polity in chapter 14. In chapter 18, David Hartman extends that argument by examining *halakhah* as a ground upon which to create a shared political dialogue among contemporary Jews. Hartman begins with Zionism as the source of the now extant framework for Jewish political activism. He then turns to Joseph Ber Soloveichik's idea of the double covenant which links all Jews—the *brit goral*, or covenant of destiny, and the *brit ye'ud*, of the covenant idea. Hartman suggests a political theory of Jewish education that should lead to the revival of the political dimension of *halakhah*, which in turn will make possible a dialogue among contemporary Jews. Hartman's effort to move education in *halakhah* away from the *Kitsur Shulhan Aruch* approach toward that of a larger political concern offers, for him, the possibility of reforging a *halakhically* rooted Jewish people who, in their responses to *halakhah*, will continue the great chain of the Jewish political tradition.

Finally, in an afterword, the present writer attempts to suggest some future directions for the exploration and renewed development of the tradition, both for Jews and humanity as a whole. While the emphasis is on the intellectual and scholarly dimensions, they are designed to lead to practical applications. If it is as yet too early to detail those applications, this book is designed to be at least a modest first step.

## Notes

1. Johannes Althusius, *Politica,* translated by Frederick S. Carney (Indianapolis: Liberty Press, 1995), p. 12.
2. Ibid., chapter 1.
3. Ibid.

# I

# Foundations

# Introduction: The *Edah* as a Classic Republic

The Jewish polity has followed the covenant model since its inception, adapting it to variegated circumstances in which Jews have found themselves over the millennia—as a tribal federation, a federal monarchy, a state with a diaspora, a congress of covenantal communities, a network of regional federations or confederations, or a set of voluntary associations.

The classic Hebrew name for this kind of polity is *edah*. The *edah* is the assembly of all the people constituted as a body politic. *Edah* is often translated as congregation; that term has a religious connotation today that it did not have when it was introduced in sixteenth- and seventeenth-century biblical translations. Then it had a civil meaning as well. It was a "con-gregation"—an institutionalized gathering of people who congregate (come together) at regular times or frequently for common action and decision making.[1]

In Mosaic times *edah* became the Hebrew equivalent of "commonwealth" or "republic," with strong democratic overtones. The idea of the Jewish people as an *edah* has persisted ever since and the term has been used to describe the Jewish body politic in every period to the present. In this respect, the term parallels (and historically precedes) similar phenomena such as the *landesgemeinde* in Switzerland, the Icelandic *althing*, and the town meeting in the United States.

The characteristics of the original *edah* can be summarized as follows:

1. The Torah is the constitution of the *edah*.

2. All members of the *edah*, men, women, and children, participate in constitutional decisions.
3. Political equality exists for those capable of taking full responsibility for Jewish survival.
4. Decisions are made by an assembly that determines its own leaders within the parameters of divine mandate.
5. The *edah* is portable and transcends geography.
6. Nevertheless, for it to function completely, the *edah* needs Eretz Israel.

These basic characteristics have been preserved with such modifications as were necessary over the centuries. Thus, in biblical times, taking full responsibility for Jewish survival meant being able to bear arms. Subsequently, the arms-bearing measure of political equality gave way to one of Torah study. Today the diaspora measure is contributing to the support of Israel, while arms bearing is again the measure in Israel. The principles of assembly, leadership, and decision making have remained the same although modes of assembling, leadership recruitment, and leaders' roles and responsibilities have changed from time to time. The portability of the desert-born *edah* is as notable a characteristic as is its attachment to Zion. The Torah has persisted as the *edah*'s constitution albeit with changing interpretations.

The regime most common in Jewish experience has been the aristocratic republic, in the classic sense of the term—rule by a limited number who take upon themselves an obligation or conceive of themselves as having a special obligation to their people and to God. For Jews, this has been manifested in some combination of a perceived obligation by those of greater status or wealth to utilize their privileged position to help other Jews and by those learned in Torah to serve the will of God by serving the community.

Jewish republicanism is rooted in a democratic foundation based on the equality of all Jews as citizens of the Jewish people. All Jews must participate in the establishment and maintenance of their polity, as demonstrated in the Bible—at Sinai, on the plain of Moab, before Shechem, and elsewhere—in *Sefer HaShtarot*, and in many other sources. Nor is that foundation merely theoretical; even where power may not be exercised on a strictly democratic basis, it is generally exercised in light of democratic norms.

There are problems associated with the use of these terms, but they do help us understand that the Jewish polity often has been governed by a kind of trusteeship. It is a trusteeship because the community is republican, because it is a res publica, a public thing or a commonwealth—a body politic that belongs to its members. The Jewish people is a res publica with a commitment to a teaching and law, which its members are not free simply to alter as they wish but must be maintained to be faithful to principles.

The Western world today takes the republican revolution for granted. Yet the republican revolution was one of the great revolutions of modernity. It is the foundation of modern democratic government. The West pioneered in the idea and practice of republican government. The Jews were among the first many centuries ago. Then came the Greeks and the early Romans. Except for a few outposts, including the Jewish *kehillah*, republicanism died under the realities of imperial Rome and medieval feudalism, replaced by absolutism. In modern times, a revolution was needed to restore the republican principle. Before the republican revolution, the prevailing view was that the state was the private preserve of its governors. When Louis XIV said "I am the state" he was articulating a classic antirepublican position.

The rise and fall of dictators in the Third World today shows the situation in a region that is in transition from prerepublican to republican government. It is no accident that most of the Arab states, after their revolutions in the 1950s and early 1960s, added the word *republic* to their new names, to signify that they sought to be part of the republican revolution. The Islamic world, far more than Europe, held to the notion for centuries that the organs of governance belonged to whomever held power. The people sought to stay clear of involvement with their governors. At best, the ruler was benevolent; he was Harun al-Rashid, who put on a disguise and wandered in the marketplace and, as he saw injustices, rectified them on the spot. He was a benevolent despot, but it was still despotism; it was not a republican government. More often than not, the despotism was just that, hence the postcolonial revolutions in the Arab world and the at least symbolic embracing of republicanism, which, in most Arab states, has yet to become real.

Still, an aristocratic republic always has a darker side in that it has a tendency to degenerate into oligarchy. The history of governance in the Jewish community has been one of swinging between the two poles of aristocratic republicanism and oligarchy. Though this is a perennial problem, the basic aristocratic republicanism of the Jewish polity has worked equally well to prevent absolutism or autocracy.

The Jewish people rarely has had anything like dictatorship and then only locally and de facto under unique circumstances. Jews are notably intractable people, even under conditions of statehood where coercion theoretically has been possible; hence, dictatorship has not been an acceptable regime for Jews.

Nor have Jews in the past had anything like the open society of the kind envisaged by many contemporary Westerners, in which every individual is free to chose his or her own "life-style." One of the reasons for this is that being Jewish and maintaining the Jewish polity has not been simply a matter of survival. It has also been a matter of living up to specific norms based on divine teaching and law, which establish the expectation that private and public life is to be shaped according to that teaching and law.

## The Three Arenas of Jewish Political Organization

From earliest times, the Jewish polity has been organized in three arenas. Besides the *edah*, or national, arena, there are countrywide or regional, and local arenas of organization. The immediately local arena comprises local Jewish communities around the world of varying sizes, under varying forms of communal organization. Whether we are speaking of Yavneh or Saragossa, Mottel or Chicago, the local community remains the basic cell of Jewish communal life. Here the institutions that serve the Jewish community are organized and function.

Beyond the local arena, there is a larger, countrywide arena in which the Jews in particular regions, countries, or states organize for common purposes. The organizational expressions of that arena have included such phenomena as the Resh Galuta (Exilarch) and Yeshivot of Babylonia, the *Vaad Arba Aratzot* (Council of the Four Lands) of late medieval Poland, the State of Israel, the Board of Deputies of British Jewry, and the congeries of "national" (meaning countrywide) organizations of American Jewry framed by the Council of Jewish Federations. Fundraising for Israel, for example, depends on work in local communities but is generally organized in this second arena on a country-by-country basis.

Beyond the second arena, there is the third, that of the Jewish people as a whole: the *edah*. This arena was extremely weak for nearly a millennium but has been given new institutional form within the last century, most particularly in our time. The *edah* is the main focus of the reconstitution of the Jewish people in our time.

This threefold division into separate arenas of governance, once formulated in early Israelite history, has remained a permanent feature of Jewish political life. This is so despite frequent changes in the forms of organization of the several arenas and in the terminology used to describe them.

The Bible delineates the first form in which these three arenas were constituted. The *edah* was constituted by the *shevatim* (*shevet*, tribe), each with its own governmental institutions. Each *shevet* was, in turn, a union of *batei av* (*bet av*, extended household). After the Israelite settlement in Canaan, the most prominent form of local organization was the *ir* (city or township) with its own assembly (*ha'ir*) and council (*sha'ar ha'ir* or *ziknai ha'ir*).

Subsequently, in the local arena, just as the *bet av* gave way to the *ir*, the *ir* gave way to the *kehillah* (local community) wherever the Jewish population was a minority. The *kehillah* became the molecular unit of organization for all postbiblical Jewry, especially because new *kehillot* could be established anywhere by any ten adult Jewish males who so constituted themselves. Although the *kehillah* survives in the diaspora, in contemporary Israel, the local arena is once again governed by comprehensive municipal units—cities or villages.

Similarly, the breakdown of the traditional tribal system (a phenomenon that long preceded the first exile) resulted in the replacement of the *shevet* by the *medinah* (properly rendered as autonomous jurisdiction or province in its original meaning), a regional framework, which embraces a congeries of *kehillot* that it unites in an organizational structure, as in Medinat Yehud (Judea in the Persian Empire). In the diaspora, the term *medinah* became almost interchangeable with *eretz* (country) to describe the intermediate arena, as in Medinat Polin (the organized Jewish community in Poland) or Eretz Lita (the organized Jewish community in late medieval Lithuania). In modern times, the term came to mean a politically sovereign state and is now used only in connection with Medinat Yisrael (the State of Israel).

The term *edah*, as an expression of the widest form of Jewish political association, retained its original usage unimpaired until transformed in colloquial modern Hebrew usage, where it came to denote a country-of-origin group in Israel. Occasionally, it was replaced by such synonyms as *Knesset Yisrael*. The *edah* managed to survive the division of Israel into two kingdoms, the Babylonian exile, and the Roman conquest of Judea by developing new forms of comprehensive organization. During the period of the Second Commonwealth (c. 440 B.C.E.-140 C.E.) and again from the second to the eleventh centuries, it was particularly successful in constructing a fully articulated institutional framework that embraced both Israel and the diaspora. The breakdown of the universal Moslem empire and the consequent demise of the *edah*-wide institutions of Resh Galuta and Gaonate in the middle of the eleventh century left world Jewry bereft of comprehensive institutions other than the *halakhah* itself. From then until the mid-nineteenth century, the *edah* was held together principally by its common Torah and laws as manifested in a worldwide network of rabbinical authorities linked by their communications (responsa) on *halakhic* matters.[2]

## Notes

1.  Daniel J. Elazar and Stuart A. Cohen, *The Jewish Polity: Jewish Political Organization from Biblical Times to the Present* (Bloomington: Indiana University Press, 1985), Introduction; Robert Gordis, "Democratic Origins in Ancient Israel: The Biblical *Edah*" in *Alexander Marx Jubilee Volume* (New York: Jewish Theological Seminary, 1950); Moshe Weinfeld, "The Transition from Tribal Republic to Monarchy in Ancient Israel and Its Impression on Jewish Political History," in Daniel J. Elazar, ed., *Kinship and Consent* (Washington, D.C.: University Press of America, 1983).
2.  Elazar and Cohen, *The Jewish Polity*.

# 1

# Covenant as the Basis of the Jewish Political Tradition

*Daniel J. Elazar*

והבאתי אתכם אל מדבר העמים ונשפטתי אתכם שם פנים אל פנים. כאשר נשפתי
את אבותיכם במדבר ארץ מצרים כן אשפט אתכם נאם ה׳ אלוהים. והעברתי אתכם
תחת השבט והבאתי אתכם במסרת הברית.        (יחזקאל כ:לה–לז)

*I will bring you to the wilderness of the peoples and there will I
plead with you face to face. Just as I pleaded with your fathers
in the wilderness of the land of Egypt, so will I plead with you,
saith the Lord God I will cause you to pass under the rod and
will bring you into the tradition [bond] of the covenant.*
(Ezekiel 20: 35-37)

The thesis of this volume is that there is a Jewish political tradition
whose origins are to be found in the Bible, a tradition that emerged at
the very beginning of the existence of the Jewish people and that has
continued to influence Jewish political and communal life ever since.
The basis of that political tradition is to be found in the biblical idea of
covenant and in the political principles and processes that flow from
it. The biblical political teaching as manifest in the Jewish political
tradition is an important political teaching for Jews and non-Jews alike
and has been so recognized throughout the Western world. At crucial
moments in Western history its influence has been decisive. Nevertheless, after surviving changes of constitution and regime, exile and
dispersion, the Jewish political tradition has been nearly lost in our

times, for Jews as well as non-Jews, precisely at the threshold of the renewal of full Jewish political life, and needs to be recovered by systematic effort so that it may fill a vital and needed role in contemporary Jewish life, both in Israel and in the diaspora.

## The Covenant Idea

In the past two decades, there has been a significant rediscovery of the covenantal basis of Judaism in most if not all contemporary Jewish intellectual circles, and the literature dealing with covenant and its implications has grown accordingly.[1] The thrust of this effort has been theological in character and properly so. Yet the covenant is as much a political as a theological phenomenon. Perhaps it is best described as a theo-political phenomenon, especially in its original biblical form.

Like all great ideas, the covenant idea is at once simple and complex: simple enough to serve as a rallying point for a people, yet sufficiently complex for the entire worldview of the Bible and consequently the essential outlook of all biblically rooted traditions to be built around it.[2] The Hebrew term *brit* signifies a covenant, usually meant to be perpetual between parties having independent but not necessarily equal status, that provides for joint action or obligation to achieve defined ends (limited or comprehensive) under conditions of mutual respect, in such a way as to protect the integrity of all parties involved. A covenant is much more than a contract, though our modern system of contracts is related to the covenant idea, because it involves a moral commitment beyond that demanded for mutual advantage, even involving the development of community among the partners to it. The biblical term *hesed* (often mistranslated as grace, but actually the loving obligation resulting from a covenantal tie) reflects this dimension of the covenantal relationship, adding a dynamic element to the relatively static character of the compact itself (see below). In essence, a covenant creates a partnership based upon a firm, legally defined relationship delineating the authority, power, and integrity of all the partners but which, at the same time, requires them to go beyond the legal definition to fully realize the relationship. In other words, the covenant relationship is to social and political life what Buber's I-Thou relationship is to personal life. Through covenants humans and their institutions are enabled to enter into dialogue and are given (or themselves create) a framework for dialogue.

In its highest form, a covenant community is a community of souls, as expressed in I Samuel 18: "The soul of Jonathan was bound up with the soul of David and Jonathan loved him with all his soul . . . and David and Jonathan made a covenant in their love for each other (which was) like the love of each for his own soul." In that sense, covenantal relationships have been compared to marriages in which the integrity of each partner continues to exist within the community they create. On the other hand, covenants are used in far more limited ways for the long-term resolution of international problems by creating limited but lasting relationships between former or potential enemies, as in Genesis 21 or Joshua 9.

The first covenants of which we are aware were vassal treaties between ancient West Asian (Near Eastern) rulers. Indeed, modern scholars have traced the covenant idea to those treaties and have shown how the classic biblical covenants parallel them in style and structure.[3] Yet the concept as it appears in the Bible, while retaining ancient West Asian forms, is utterly transformed and infused with a new character. The Hebrew language describes the difference succinctly. The relationships in the first instance were between *ba'alei brit* (literally, masters of the covenant), or partners in a particular international agreement, while in the second they involved *bnei brit* (literally, sons of the covenant), or partners in a common entity created by covenant. The transformation was critical, opening up a whole new set of possibilities and relationships, both intellectual and operational.

In essence, the Israelites took the idea and techniques of covenant making from their neighbors but turned them on their head. Mesopotamian and West Semitic covenants were designed to limit previously independent entities by making them vassals, regulating their external behavior but leaving their internal life alone. Israelite covenants function as liberating devices that call into existence new entities. God, by entering into a covenant with humans, accepts a limitation on the exercise of His omnipotence, thus endowing mankind with freedom, but its price is the acceptance of internal reform as well as external obligations. The covenant becomes the framework for mutual obligation and the basis of a new law and politics internally and externally. Consequently both the covenant itself and the ideas or principles that flow from it create and inform a new tradition. In the course of Jewish history, actual covenants and covenantal principles appear and reappear to give the Jewish political tradition both form and content.

In biblical terms, God relates to his universe and the creatures within it, including man, through a system of covenants. We are all familiar with God's covenants with the patriarchs and Israel. Yet the Bible teaches us that God's covenant with Israel must be viewed in the larger context of God's covenant with all men. The Talmud teaches that the beginning of this covenant relationship is implicit in God's relationship to Adam, particularly after man acquires knowledge of good and evil, but the first formal covenant was made with Noah after the flood (Genesis 9). Through Noah, the Talmud teaches that covenant is binding on all people as the basis for universal law.

So pervasive is the covenantal system in the Bible that even God's relationship with the natural order and lower forms of life is frequently portrayed in allegorical terms as a covenantal one (as in Jeremiah 33:25–26), as distinct from the biblical presentation of God's covenants with man as experiential events. From this perspective, *brit* is a term used to capture the Jewish myth of politics, sometimes through real covenants and sometimes symbolically.

Extending the pervasive covenantal relationship between God and man, presented as the only proper one, the Bible necessarily holds that the covenantal relationship is also the only proper basis for political organization, that is, the structured allocating of authority and power among men. In a political sense, biblical covenants take the form of constituting acts that establish the parameters of authority and its division without prescribing the constitutional details of regimes. Thus, the Sinai covenant establishes once and for all God's kingship over Israel and the partnership between God and Israel in *tikun olam* (the reconstruction of the universe). It does not establish any particular political regime. Rather, in the same weekly portion of the Torah (Jethro), it is explicitly pointed out that Moses' political reorganization of the emergent national government of Israel is based upon the highly utilitarian recommendations of Jethro, a Midianite priest far removed from divine authority (Exodus 18:13–26). The interplay is more subtle than that, since the Book of the Covenant, which follows upon the giving of the tablets of the covenant (which is how they are referred to in Hebrew—not as the two tablets or, worse, the Ten Commandments), seems to be presented as God's response to Moses' delegation of power (Exodus 20:19–23, 33). That is to say, as long as Moses himself was the sole judge and interpreter of God's commandments, they did not need to be set down. Specifics could be clarified through the direct and continuing discourse between Moses and God. However, once the power of judging, or interpreting and applying the commandments, was delegated, then a written collection of basic laws was necessary to provide the foundation for those who were not privy to direct communications with the Almighty. The fact that this written collection was explicitly linked to the covenant should speak for itself.

Subsequent to the Sinai covenant, covenants are used to link the governors and the governed under God according to the terms of the great covenant and in light of changing circumstances. The model of such covenants is found in Joshua 24, where Joshua assembles the representatives of the twelve tribes of Israel and the tribal and national officers near Shechem, after the conquest and division of the land, to renew before God the covenant of Moses and reestablish the Israelite confederacy on a landed basis. As in the case of the original, that covenant also established (or reestablished) the basic distribution of authority and powers but did not include a frame of government per se, simply accepting the frame of government established earlier. With the introduction of the monarchy, which represented a major shift in the structure of authority within the nation, a new covenant was made (II Samuel 5:3). Similar covenants were initiated or renewed after every major political change or reform in the biblical period.[5]

While the foregoing examples represent the most important uses of covenantal arrangements in the Bible, the term *brit* and the practice of covenanting involved a wide variety of situations, ranging from what were designed to be lasting or perpetual international treaties to secondary contractual obligations between rulers and ruled. This flexibility of usage is consistent with the biblical worldview which sees the universe as built upon an interlocking and overlapping system of covenantal relationships, each with its own measure of demands and equivalent responses.[6]

Covenantal politics are directed simultaneously toward linking people and communities as partners in common tasks and allowing them space in which to be free. The very idea of a covenant between God and man contains this implication in its most radical form. The omnipotent Deity, by freely covenanting with man, limits his own powers (or "competence" in the European legal usage) to allow man space in which to be free, only requiring of him that he live in accordance with the Law established as normative by the Covenant. The Puritans' recognition of this aspect of the covenantal relationship between God and man in sixteenth- and seventeenth-century Britain and America became the basis of their "federal theology"—inventing the term "federal" to express this theo-political relationship. John Winthrop, the great Puritan governor of Massachusetts, referred to this relationship as "federal liberty," or the freedom to freely obey the law.[9] A century later, in the process of the founding of the United States, the term federal was secularized by the descendents of the Puritans to become simply a political concept.

The ambiguous origins of the Hebrew word *brit* tell us much about this fettered freedom or liberating bondage. Of the two Akkadian words which scholars suggest are related to it, *biritum* means "space between" while *bereiti* means "fetter" or "binding agreement." This notion of dividing and then binding is present in the Hebrew phrase for covenant making, *lichrot brit* (literally, to cut a covenant) and the ceremony that went with that term which in its earliest form involved the halving of an animal and passing between its two parts to symbolically reunite them.[8]

It can be said that, in Jewish tradition, the ties of covenant are the concretization of the relationship of dialogue which, when addressed to God, make man holy and, when addressed to one's fellows, make men human. As the Bible itself makes clear, the covenantal bonds transform what most religions understood as a mystical union into a real one, making life—including political life—possible in an all-too-real world. In many ways, the progress of civilization can be traced as corresponding to the periods in human history when significant groups of people have recognized the covenant idea and sought to concretely apply it to the building of human, political, and social relationships.

Translated into less theological terminology, a covenant-based politics looks toward political arrangements established or, more appropriately, compounded for particular moral purposes, through the linking of separate entities so that each preserves its respective integrity while creating a common association to serve those purposes, broad or limited, for which it was called into being. The purposes range from keeping the peace through permanent but limited alliance of independent entities to forging of a new polity through union of previously separate entities to create a new whole. A covenant-based politics is not simply a symbolic matter; it has to do with very concrete demands for power-sharing and the development of institutionalized forms and processes for so doing.

Whether in its theological form or secularized as the compact theory of the origin of civil society, the covenant idea is one of the two or three fundamental political concepts illuminating the origins and basis of political life. As a major political idea, the covenant principle has manifested itself in a wide variety of ways and conditions, in different places and times, always enduring as a central element in political thought, Jewish and non-Jewish.[9] Ultimately the concrete political embodiment of the covenant model took two forms: the union of families or individuals to form bodies-politic and the federation of bodies-politic to form even more complex political systems. Both forms have manifested themselves in Jewish history. What follows is a brief survey of those manifestations within the Jewish body politic over space and time and then a survey of the ways in which the covenant idea has been applied through the Jewish political tradition. It should be understood from the first that the covenant has consistently manifested itself on three levels: the intellectual, the cultural, and the operational. Here we shall treat all three without necessarily distinguishing between them in so many words at every turn. The reader should be prepared to recognize these three levels and make the requisite distinctions.

### Covenant and Partnership in Jewish Historical Experience

The first biblical covenant explicitly involving Jews is the set of covenants between God and Abraham described in Genesis 15 and 17. They are preconstitutional but provide the preconditions for later developments. While they involve God's promise to one individual only, since that promise explicitly forms the basis for the emergence of a new nation in a land of its own, it sets the stage for the more formally political covenanting at Sinai and subsequently. God's reaffirmation of that covenant in Exodus 6 links those preconstitutional covenants with that of Sinai.

As already suggested, from the political perspective the Sinai covenant is reminiscent of a social compact in that it provides the political and social framework for constitution making but not the constitution itself. The restatement of the Sinai covenant in Deuteronomy is constructed along more explicitly political-legal lines, the pattern characteristic of that book.[10] The Exodus and the Sinai covenant usher in an epoch in Jewish history, the principal political manifestation of which was the tribal federation. During this epoch, the Jewish people clearly began to forge its unique blend of kinship and consent as the basis of its political life, transcending the real or putative links of kinship which characterize tribal society to add the dimension of deliberate consent—one of the outstanding manifestations of the covenant idea—without destroying the people's or the polity's tribal base.[11] The biblical phrase *am v'edah* is a kind of statement of this linkage between kinship and consent. The term *am* (people) reflects a common descent, a kinship, albeit with overtones of a special tie beyond mere kinship; the institutional embodiment of that tie is to be found in the *edah* (the assembly of citizens that met regularly, also used to designate the form of government under the Mosaic covenants), which, as a constituent assembly, is the operational embodiment of the principle of consent.

The political dimensions of the covenant were at their most pronounced at Sinai and in the desert, where the Jewish people acquired a single national constitution and law (in fact, the two were not really separated), which was administered by a combination of tribal and national officers, and which served a federation of tribes, each of which was in itself compounded as a union of families—"houses" in the biblical term. This federation has been describe by some scholars as an amphictyony—a limited confederation for religious purposes built around a common shrine.[12] Whatever elements of amphictyony may have existed in the tribal federation, according to the biblical account, the tribes were more comprehensively linked in a true federation, that is to say, formed around a common constitutional and legal system applied in a noncentralized fashion with power shared among several different institutions and centers.[13]

One major stream in Jewish tradition has consistently viewed the tribal federation as the classical form of Jewish polity (for example, Joshua and Samuel, Ezekiel, the champions of the Elijah tradition, Josephus, Don Isaac Abravanel, and Martin Buber).[14] Moreover, the political model embodied by the tribal confederacy, particularly during its first two generations under Moses and Joshua, must be counted as one of the most influential political models in the Western world while the subsequent history of the tribes during the period of the Judges and on through the attempt to restore the original regime in the days of Samuel, served as the raw material for the debates of political philosophers and constitution makers in the Western world at least as late as the nineteenth century.[15]

The Bible itself offers contradictory assessments as to the success of the tribal confederacy as a polity. What is clear, however, is that its collapse was a result of external forces rather than internal weakness per se. A noncentralized polity based on a loose federation of tribes could not stand up to the assaults of the Philistines. In the process of responding to those assaults, Israel created its own particular brand of what is formally termed a monarchy, but which, in the strict meaning of the term—rule by one—was not that at all because it was limited by specific covenants and the covenant idea generally. According to the biblical account, a limited constitutional monarchy was established and periodically reaffirmed through a covenant between king, people, and God. While under the monarchy a much stronger center of power was created in the polity, other centers and institutions retained real powers as well and at least one, the institution of the prophets, was actually strengthened to counterbalance the king (see chapter 7).[16]

The first such covenant was with David (2 Samuel 5:3; 1 Chronicles 11:3). It introduced a new epoch in Jewish history, one that gave the federation of tribes a common capital with a national government capable of reaching into the lives of every citizen in ways far beyond the limited role of the Judges and Levites in the previous epoch. It seems that, despite the hereditary element introduced by David, his heirs had to be confirmed through covenants with the representatives of the people. Thus, Solomon and the people covenanted with one another before God at the time of the transferring of the Ark of the Covenant (I Kings 8). This was at least so after crises involving a previously reigning monarch who had violated the covenant and thereby cast doubt on the legitimacy of the Davidic house, as in the covenants of Jehoiadah, Josiah, Asa, and Hezekiah.

What was characteristic of this period was the combination of monarchic and tribal (or federal) institutions. David was elevated to the kingship by the tribal leadership speaking in the name of the people. Solomon was reaffirmed by that leadership, and Rehoboam was denied the kingship by ten of the tribes acting in concert when he went to them to establish a similar compact at the beginning of his reign (I Kings 12; II Chronicles 10). Considering his arrogant attitude toward the tribal leadership, it is clear that he was required to go before them by the constitution and did not do so of his own free will. Subsequently, while multitribal institutions disappeared from the southern kingdom because of the dominance of Judah (with the original federal institutions surviving only in the realm of local government), the northern kingdom of Israel maintained them until the very end of its existence.

The disappearance of the tribal federation as a reality after the fall of the northern kingdom can be said to mark the end of the original monarchic epoch in Jewish constitutional history, leading to a search for new political arrangements which culminated in the days of King Josiah when the Book of Deuteronomy became the constitutional basis of the regime (II Kings 22 and 23). The Josianic reform restored the idea that the Israelite polity was based on a tripartite compact between God, Israel, and the king, with God as sovereign and lawgiver represented in day-to-day matters by his prophets (II Chronicles 23:1–2, 21; and 34:29–32). Coming as it did after the reconstitution of the Israelite regime on a nontribal basis, the reform reaffirmed the essentially covenantal basis of the Israelite polity, just in time to strengthen the Jewish will to survive after the destruction of the First Temple.

The prophetic vision of Ezekiel (Chapters 16, 17, 20, 34, 37, 44), which embodies the theo-political aspirations of the exiles in Babylonia, explicitly foresees the restoration of the covenantal polity in its full multitribal form. While the proximate restoration of Jewish rule in Jerusalem (on a home rule basis within the Persian Empire) did not even approach that messianic vision, its political dimension was clearly based on a popular renewal of the covenant at the initiative of Ezra when the people assembled on Succoth to hear the Torah and to assent to its authority, as graphically portrayed in the Bible (Nehemiah 8–10). As at Sinai, the Succoth covenant set the framework for the renewed Jewish polity while the details of the regime were developed subsequently within it. Overall, the regime seems to have been a noncentralized union of families and community-congregations within the framework of the Torah and the developing oral law, whose local and national institutions and leaders were extremely powerful within their respective spheres.

The Succoth covenant was the last of the biblical covenants. The regime it produced survived until the time of the Hasmoneans, and nominally continued to be the basis of the Hasmonean regime as well. It was supplemented by an additional covenant between "the priests, the people, the heads of the nation, and the elders of the land," on one hand, and Simon the Maccabean on the other—whom they designated as "high priest, commander-in-chief and *nasi*" (literally one raised up [to leadership], in modern Hebrew, president)—which was embodied in a covenant document (given in full in I Maccabees 14: 25–49). Even those later Hasmonean rulers who referred to themselves as kings in Greek cautiously continued to refer to themselves as high priests and *nasiim* in Hebrew. In both cases, political covenants confirmed inauguration of new historical epochs for the Jewish people. Characteristic of the first was the abjuration of monarchic leadership in favor of what has been termed theocracy but is better characterized as a nomocracy in which powers of government were shared by priests, *soferim* ("secretaries" as in Secretary of State), and an assembly of family heads and notables. In the second epoch, a central political leader was added to the structure of the regime.

In the immediate postbiblical period, Jewish political thought took two directions which had a vital impact on later generations' view of the covenant idea. Under Hellenistic influences, an attempt was made to reconcile the biblical and philosophical worldviews by recasting the history of ancient Israel and the political teaching of the Bible in Greek modes. Philo and Josephus are the two most prominent exemplars of this effort. The effort was made to satisfy Jews who had come under Hellenistic influences, and to explain Judaism to the non-Jewish world which engulfed it. This tended to substantially reduce the emphasis on the covenant idea, which was not indigenous to Greek thought, in Jewish intellectual circles. It had a lasting influence on our understanding of the Jewish political tradition, precisely because it filtered that tradition through a very powerful and compelling non-Jewish filter. Nevertheless, the continued utilization of the principle shows through in the descriptions of actual political behavior from that period, as in the case of the Maccabean reconstitution.

The epoch initiated by the Hasmonean revolution reached a climax in the destruction of the Second Temple, and came to an end after the failure of the Bar Kochba rebellion. Subsequently, such institutions of national authority as the Jews were able to formally maintain (e.g., the Patriarchate in Israel and the Exilarchate in Babylonia) were formally instituted by the foreign powers holding dominion over them and existed at the sufferance of those powers. One of the struggles of the millennium following the loss of Jewish sovereignty involved the Jews' effort to infuse their own consensual-covenantal dimension into institutions which were designed to rule them hierarchically—precisely because they were forced upon them by foreign powers seeking to keep them in line.[17] This problem is reflected in the Chronicle of Rabbi Natan, which describes how the community acted to assume a role in the appointment of the Exilarch, a position that was actually hereditary: "When he is appointed, if the mind of the community has agreed to appoint him, the two heads of the Yeshivot met with their students and all the heads of the congregation and the elders appoint." In this way the dual principles of consent and power sharing were at least formally maintained.[18]

In the interim, however, the Jews had developed a device through which to maintain their own autonomy and in a covenantal manner to boot, namely the local house of congregation or assembly which is generally known by its Greek name, "synagogue." The congregation-synagogue became a crucial vehicle for Jewish self-expression precisely because it was based upon authentic Jewish political principles and was eminently suited to the wide variety of conditions under which Jews found themselves in their dispersion. As an institution, a congregation could be established anywhere that ten Jewish males came together. Thoroughly portable, it could adapt itself to particular geo-historical conditions to provide the Jews with whatever degree of self-government they were allowed and had the strength to maintain. Thus, in the land of Israel, and later in the small Jewish settlements of the medieval Diaspora, it was usually synonymous with the local community (as the Hebrew name it acquired—*Kahal Kadosh*—indicates), while in the great Hellenistic cities, and later in the great cities of Europe and America, it was perhaps one of several synagogues, sometimes linked within a larger communal framework on a federal or confederal basis and sometimes independent for all intents and purposes.

Every congregation by its very nature came into existence through a compact or covenant between its founders which was extended to those who subsequently became part of it. Although there is some dispute in the *halakhic* literature with regard to the precise legal implications of this, in effect every local Jewish community, as a congregation, was considered to be a kind of partnership based upon a common contractual obligation within the framework of the overall Jewish constitution, namely, the Torah (see chapters 4 and 8). In the Sephardic world, these compacts came to be called *askamot*, perhaps best translated as articles of agreement. The flexibility of this form led to a variety of arrangements depending on local circumstances. In some communities, the entire community was organized as a single congregation with the appropriate governing bodies usually divided along functional lines. On the other extreme, the community as a whole consisted of a loose league of many independent congregations, each of which represented a particular religious point of view or socioeconomic distinction.

The associational model that emerged from this congregational form became the basis for the entire web of Jewish communal organization in the European diaspora. *Sefer Hashtarot* (The Book of Contracts), compiled in the eleventh century by R. Judah HaBarceloni as the era's classic collection of model laws for the governance of the Jewish people, includes a model charter for establishing a community, whose Preamble (an excellent example of the style of covenant documents essentially unchanged since the first ancient Near Eastern vassal covenants) is worth quoting in full:

> We, the elders and leaders of the community of -x-, due to our many sins we have declined and become fewer and weaker, and until only few have been left of many, like a single tree at the mountaintop, and the people of our community have been left with no head or nasi, or head justice or leader, so that they are like sheep without a shepherd and some of our community go about improperly clothed and some speak obscenely and some mix with the gentiles and eat their bread and become like them, so that only in the Jewish name, are they at all different. We have seen and discussed the matter and we agreed in assembly of the entire community, and we all, great and small alike, have gone on to establish this charter in this community.

The model charter continues to describe how the community, by this action, establishes its right to enact ordinances, establish institutions, levy and collect taxes; in short, carry on all the functions of a municipal government.

The principles of community enunciated in the foregoing document are clear. In order for the actions of a community to be legally binding in Jewish law, it had to be duly constituted by its potential members, preferably through a constituent assembly and constitutional document. They must be able to say that "we have discussed the matter," that "we have agreed in assembly of the entire community." If these patterns were not followed, the action would not be valid.

In those cases where communities created intercommunity federations, as in northern France and the Rhineland, the Council of the Communities of Aragon and the Council of the Four Lands, the compacts restored a strong federal element to the overall covenantal base.[19] Within communities, individual *hevrot* (guilds—the term has strong connotations of partnership) were similarly organized as partnerships on a subcommunal basis, usually with some functional orientation.[20]

The great questions of power and authority in the medieval Jewish community were for the most part based upon differences of opinion regarding the implications of this contractual base. So, for example, questions of the apportionment of taxation or the reduction of air rights (so important in densely populated medieval towns) were often related to the issue of whether or not the community was a partnership and, if so, what were the rights of the partners. In essence, the partnership issue was important in all questions of whether decisions could be made by majority vote or required unanimity (see chapter 8).[21] Thus, the Rashba, (R. Shlomo ben Aderet) who, along with Rabbi Meir of Rothenberg, established the constitutional and jurisprudential basis for the medieval Jewish community, responded to a question from the Jewish community of Lerida in fourteenth-century Spain, as follows:

> In all matters of the community, no one part of the community is permitted to do as they please, unless the entire community consents. For the community are as partners in all communal responsibilities and in all communal appointments, such as tax collectors, unless there exist men who have been appointed to deal with communal affairs; those who are called by our sages the seven *tuvei ha'ir*. In most places, nowadays, the important men of the community direct the affairs of the community in consultation and agreement. In general, it is assumed that the individual avoids his own opinion, but if some of the community, even from among those who are not great in wisdom, object, their objection stands. This is certainly so, where the objection is made by some of the men who are normally those to be consulted.

This was qualified in a further response to the Jews of Saragossa:

> The customs of different locales differ in these matters, for there are places where all matters are handled by their elders and advisors, and there are places where even the council can do nothing without the consent of the entire congregation in which there is found the agreement of all, and there are places which appoint for themselves a group of men whose direction they will follow for a given period of time in all matters related to the group.

This is the kind of debate that can only occur in a covenant-created setting where what is at stake is the definition of how much autonomy each partner maintains. The resolution of this issue (and there are opinions on both sides) is less important for our purposes here than the fact that it was an issue at all, that the discussion was not whether there should be rule by one or by the few or by the many, but rather in a system in which the many were assumed to rule, how they were to arrive at their decisions. The fact that many communities did become oligarchies, and a few even fell under autocratic domination, is significant and deserves exploration in its own right as well as in relationship to the theory, but the theory reflected real circumstances, more so than any of the deviations from it in practice. We know this because we find records of the debate not in the esoteric writings of learned men and abstract thinkers but in the responsa of the great sages of those generations, who were forced to adjudicate real disputes.[22]

These questions took on special importance in cases involving the admission of new members to the community, particularly people who wanted to move in from outside in situations where the non-Jewish ruling power made living conditions particularly difficult for the existing Jewish residents.[23] In short, the greater part of Jewish public law in the medieval period had to do with interpreting the meaning of compacts and the rights and obligations of those who came to be party to them, so much so that several historians of the period have suggested that Jewish thought on these matters follows along the same lines as that of Hobbes, Locke, and other seventeenth-century social compact theorists (in this writer's opinion, a correct observation on their part, particularly since both schools flowed from a common source).[24]

With the breakdown of the medieval community, diaspora Jewry had to reorganize itself once again. As the Jewish people ceased to be regarded as a nation among the nations, their polity ceased to be a state within a state. The reorganization was partly forced upon the Jews by the governing authorities of the new nation-states that emerged in the seventeenth century and subsequently, and partly followed internal Jewish initiatives seeking to adjust to the situation. It resulted in the creation of quasi-voluntary communities in the sense that Jews could now choose more easily to cease to be Jews but, if they chose to remain within the Jewish fold, they had to be members of a Jewish community. Legally, these communities were religious associations organized on a membership basis in keeping with the associational or contractual character of modern liberal society. In the Germanies and other Central European countries under Germanic influence, local communities were further federated into countrywide bodies. In France, the centralistic pattern characteristic of modern French society was imposed upon the Jewish community as well, while the Jewries of Great Britain were united just as was the United Kingdom. In short, the tendency for the local Jewish community to take on the organizational characteristics of its host environment was continued, at least in externals. In this case, however, the organizational forms of modern society served to strengthen the contractual character of the communities more often than not. Whatever the formal framework, the associative and increasingly voluntary character of the community maintained the by now traditionally Jewish covenantal base in the forefront, even if the community itself functioned on a reduced basis.[25]

In the New World, the voluntary character of the Jewish community was total from the very first. Even where Jews were not fully admitted into the larger society, they were never required to be members of a Jewish community. While kinship propelled them toward membership, affiliation came only on the basis of active consent. As a result, Jewish institutions were built on an entirely voluntary or associative basis. The initial affiliation of Jews was voluntary and the subsequent linkage among Jewish organizations was even more so.

The Jewish response to New World conditions was to adapt the covenant principle through federative arrangements, generally without any awareness that they were continuing the Jewish political tradition. In the United States, the Jews developed federations of Jewish social service agencies, on the one hand, and federations of congregations on the other.[26] In Canada, they developed a countrywide federation of local communities compounded out of community relations and Zionist bodies.[27] In Latin America, country-of-origin groups formed their own communities, which, over time, confederated with one another to establish citywide or countrywide bodies for limited purposes.[28] Whatever the particular form, characteristic of the whole was the contractual relationship and the institutional structures and processes that flowed from it.

To no small extent, the foundations of the reconstituted Jewish polity in Israel also reflect a continuation of the covenant tradition, although, after 1949, a state structure of the nineteenth-century European model was superimposed on what started as a continuation of older Jewish practice along new lines.[29] The beginnings of modern Jewish resettlement in the land followed the patterns of Jewish "colonization" that existed since the earliest days of the Diaspora adapted to local circumstances. That is to say, Jewish householders banded together to establish pioneering societies to accomplish specific or general tasks, whether construction of new neighborhoods outside the walls of Jerusalem, establishment of agricultural settlements, or the organization of cooperative enterprises. In doing so, the householders compacted together by drawing up articles of agreement reminiscent of those medieval communities or societies organized abroad on the same basis, as pioneering nuclei, as fundraising instrumentalities, or political action groups, finally coming together as the World Zionist Organization, which began as a federation of Zionist societies and rapidly became a federation of ideological movements.

### Figure 1.1: Expressions of the Covenant Idea

| Regime | Political System |
| --- | --- |
| Tribal Confederacy | Confederation of tribes |
| Southern Kingdom (Judah) | Monarchy overlaying union of local communities |
| Northern Kingdom (Israel) | Monarchy overlaying federation of tribes |
| Ezra's Covenantal Community | Union of local community-congregations |
| Hellenistic Politeuma | Loose league of diaspora communities (each the product of a local compact) and Israel |
| Babylonian-Near Eastern Exilarchate/Gaonate | Centralized polity with local home rule and internal division into "camps" based on local links to different authoritative yeshivot |
| Spanish and Rhenish Communities | Communities organized locally by compact which occasionally federated with one another on a regional basis |
| East European Lands | Federated (e.g., Vaad Arba Aratzot) unless prevented from doing so by the non-Jewish authorities |
| Near Eastern-North African Lands | Separated congregation-communities linked locally through leagues |
| Modern Diaspora | Federations or confederations of congregations, camps, and/or functional agencies |
| State of Israel | Centralized parliamentary state superimposed on network of cooperative associations |

The Zionist experience is a classic example of the Jewish use of federative arrangements. Zionism as a whole quickly came to represent the common messianic movement at the cutting edge of modern Jewry. However, in the Jewish fashion, agreement as to general messianic goals was accompanied by sharp disagreement as to the precise character of the goals to be achieved, which led in turn to the development of movements within the Zionist framework that were not only highly competitive on one level, but essentially hostile to one another, since they represented sharply different approaches to solving the Jewish and human problems to which Zionism was directed. Nevertheless, the movements quickly came to recognize the necessity for common action in order to advance both the common and specific elements in their respective goals. The solution was a federation based upon inter- and cross-movement compacts for the sharing of power within the overall Zionist organization—and the division of resources within it. The coalition politics based on the party key, which became characteristic of the World Zionist Organization and, later, the State of Israel, are the principal manifestations of this federative arrangement, the building blocks for all Zionist endeavors.

Parallel to the federation of parties, the Yishuv in Israel constructed federations of settlements and institutions, principally through the Histadrut—General Federation of Labor, which together comprised the "state on the way" of the interwar period.[30] In the process, movements developed that offered their members a comprehensive environment providing them with educational facilities, social services, sports and recreational opportunities, and even military units. The network of charters and compacts forming both provided a constitutional basis for the rebuilding of the land, which culminated in the Declaration of Independence proclaiming the new State of Israel. The content of the Declaration, known as the Scroll of Independence in Hebrew, is in itself of constitutional significance in the traditional way, that is to say, as a founding covenant that sets forth the guidelines within which a constitution can be developed and a regime established, without specifying either.[31]

While the Zionist pioneers relied upon Jewish political tradition, implicitly at least, in nation-building, when it came to state-building, they turned to the European models that they knew, superimposing upon the network of compacts and charters a centralized and highly bureaucratic model of parliamentary democracy. In this respect at least, it is ironic that the communal structure of the Diaspora remains closer to the Jewish political tradition than the new Jewish state. The end result was not a replacement of a covenantal orientation with a bureaucratic one, but a great dysfunctionality between the formal structure and the ways of doing public business rooted in Jewish political culture. The transfer of functions from the parties to the state transformed the former from comprehensive movements—states within a state-in-the-making—into competitors for the rewards that only the state could offer. This led to a network of compacts for the division of those rewards to limit competition and give each party its due share. Interparty compacts also survived in the various electoral blocks formed and reformed in the years since 1948 and in governmental coalition making. The latter actually rest upon signed documents hammered out among the partners. The formal federative framework, as such, continued to persist only in the rural areas through the sectorial and territorial settlement federations such as the several kibbutz and moshav movements and the regional councils. There the gap between structure and practice has been much smaller, with notable results. In sum, where pre-state developments have survived, so too have federative arrangements. Where they have been replaced by post-1948 modes of organization or where such modes of organization have been instituted and have become dominant, only echoes of covenantal arrangements are to be found, by and large in the semiformal substructure that has grown up within the centralized state to make the latter work.

## Applying the Covenant Idea

The foregoing all-too-brief historical survey suggests that the covenant idea has been manifested in the world of action in a variety of ways, reflecting the variety of circumstances to which it has had to be adapted. In addition, the covenant idea has manifested itself through a variety of dimensions. The exploration of these ways and dimensions has hardly begun, and remains a major task in the recovery of the Jewish political tradition. Nevertheless, it is possible to suggest some ways in which the covenant idea has been applied in practice. Here we shall attempt to do so in a suggestive rather than exhaustive way, through the perspective of some of the standard concerns of political science.

*Jewish Political Institutions and Their Organization*

We have already suggested how communities, congregations, and federations all reflect the covenant idea in operation. Figure 1.1 summarizes the various forms of organization that have predominated within the Jewish *edah* since the Exodus and their particular internal character. The overwhelming majority of them were created by compact and many were federal. Even the ones that were not were essentially unions compounded of local communities and/or congregations.[32] In addition, the small congregations and hevrot that represented the first step beyond the family as an organizational unit reflect the same covenantal base. Traditionally, the Jewish people has consisted of a group of families rather than individuals bound together by covenant, thereby accommodating the realms of both kinship and consent.

Of the eleven general patterns of communal organization shown in the figure, only one, the Babylonian-Near Eastern diaspora, was formally organized on a hierarchical basis and only two others, the southern kingdom of Judah after the division of the tribes and contemporary Israel, were centralized arrangements imposed upon an earlier covenantal base in such a way as to formally supersede it. In all the rest, the covenantal framework was carried through from first to last, either directly or in one permutation or another. The Babylonian case (along with that of modern France) represents the hard case in the scheme. The fact that the Talmud was created in Babylonia under the hierarchical conditions that prevailed requires us to consider the implications of that case. What is significant about it is the way in which Jews tried to reintroduce the familiar and by then traditional framework through the back door. Thus, the Talmud discusses appointments to the district courts which, under the hierarchical system, were made by the Exilarch and how the Jewish communities insisted on parallel local appointees as well as local veto powers over the Exilarch's appointees after they appeared on the local scene: "When he (the Exilarch-appointed judge) reaches his destination (a particular community), he chooses two of the important men of the town to sit with him."

Moreover, the establishment of the great Babylonian academies and the struggle between the leaders of those academies and the Exilarch may itself be a reflection of the conflict of traditions, at least with regard to the separation of powers within any particular arena. The *Bereshit Rabbah*, the Midrashic commentary on the Book of Genesis, comments on the verse: "The scepter shall not depart from Judah, nor the ruler's staff from between his legs." According to the *Midrash*, "The scepter . . . " is interpreted as the Exilarchs in Babylon, who rule the people, Israel, with the stick, while "the ruler's staff . . . " are the patriarchs of the family of Rav, who teach the Torah to the populace in the land of Israel. Another explanation of the verse is offered: "The scepter is the Messiah, son of David (Mashiach ben David), who will rule over the kingdom, that is to say, Rome, with a stick. And the ruler's staff are those who teach *halakhah* to Israel." Even after the Messiah comes, there will have to be a separation of powers, for even the *Mashiach* is not to be trusted with all the powers alone. Even if he can rule over Rome, there still must be the great Sanhedrin to teach *halakhah* to Israel.

As a partnership, the Jewish community is clearly republican in its orientation; it is a partnership that is based on the principle that the community is a *res publica*, a public thing, not the private preserve of any man or group, whose leaders are drawn from and are penultimately responsible to the people. Penultimately, not ultimately. Ultimately, all are responsible to God; but penultimately, for matters of this world, leaders are responsible to the people in some way. In fact, much of the internal political history of the Jewish people revolves around the balancing of power among those who are seen as representatives of God's will and those whose authority stems from the people. This fundamental division of powers is crucial to any Jewish polity and is even reflected in modern Israel in the deference shown those recognized as representatives of normative Judaism which goes beyond the demands of coalition politics.

The Jewish community is republican but it is republican in an aristocratic as much as a democratic way. It must be carefully noted that, although the Jewish community has generally attempted to be democratic in its involvement of the people in covenants crucial to its formation and governance, it was not meant to be simply democratic, in the sense that we talk about any person acquiring leadership simply by virtue of some kind of public acclamation. It also seeks to embody the aristocratic ideal because leadership in the Jewish community was and is invariably invested in those able to claim legitimacy on the basis of some authoritative source that stands external to the members of the community, per se. Ideally, the source of authority of the communal leadership is God. According to tradition, it is He who determines what the earthly forms of legitimacy will be, through His covenant with the people and its expression in the Torah. After the days of the Judges, God Himself no longer directly anointed leaders. Consequently, even when Jews were God-fearing, they did not expect God to anoint their leaders, but they did recognize their ultimate responsibility to Him.

This apparent rejection of simple democracy in favor of a kind of federal republicanism is perhaps difficult to appreciate in a democratic era that increasingly equates true democracy with its Jacobin version. Nevertheless, Jews came to the conclusion that the maintenance of the special purpose of the Jewish people necessitated such a stance. While all power must be subject to checks by the people, ultimately the nature of the community is determined by something higher than the people; there is a vision that stands above the simple counting of heads. In practice, this has not always prevented the development of a rabbinic oligarchy supported by claims to Divine favor, but most of the time it has created a framework for power sharing that has prevented autocracy, even in the most autocratic periods of the history of the nations.

### The Covenant Idea in Jewish Political Thought

Classical Jewish sources do not clearly separate political and other teachings. Indeed, the methodological problem of uncovering the Jewish political tradition from within those sources is deserving of extensive treatment in its own right. By and large, standard exegetical techniques (the midrashic method) serve to identify the political ideas contained in those texts and relate them to one another so as to uncover a systematic teaching (see chapter 3).

The covenant idea can be seen to be significant in shaping at least five themes of Jewish political thought: (1) man's stewardship on earth; (2) the special role of Israel among the nations in God's scheme for redemption; (3) the appropriate political regime for the Jewish people; (4) the Jewish conception of the polity as such; and (5) the ideal polity of the messianic age and the political character of the age itself.

The Jewish worldview suggests that man and God are partners in the management of the world. This partnership began when God delegated to Adam the right to name the creatures. Adam, however, was entirely dependent upon God's good will. With Noah, the partnership is regularized through a covenant which is interpreted by the sages as having a political component in the requirement to establish courts of justice, or government, in the world. The Talmudic discussion of the seven Noahide mitzvot is very revealing in that it suggests that six of the seven *mitzvot* were already demanded of Adam, but in effect, the sages teach us, they were not put together into coherent doctrine based upon a formalized relationship between man and God until God covenanted with Noah.[33] The basis of man's relationship with God, the world, and his fellow men remains rooted in the covenant-created partnership.

The special role of Israel among the nations was established by the covenants with Abraham and at Sinai. Through the latter, God assumes direct responsibility for governing His people, a major aspect of their special position as a people set apart (made holy) for exemplary purposes. By and large, this issue is treated by contemporary Jewish thinkers as a theological problem. Yet Moses and the prophets treated it as a political problem first and foremost and there are even echoes of its political character in the Talmud, despite the very real efforts on the part of the Jewish leadership in those centuries to de-emphasize the strictly political dimension of Jewish life in an effort to adjust to the new conditions of exile and relative powerlessness. How does one deal with the problem of "entangling alliances" that were such anathema to the prophets, or with sharing the land with another people so strongly opposed in the Torah and the Book of Joshua except from a perspective that emphasizes the resolution of the political problems involved as a necessary precondition to the attainment of what we term theological goals.

At least as early as the Jews' encounter with Hellenism, the issue of Israel's special role became closely entwined with the question of whether the Jewish people existed simply by virtue of kinship, that is, common descent, or also by virtue of consent, an argument that has carried over into our own times. For those who believe the former, a Jew is set apart from all other men by virtue of his very biology and, even if he strays, is more open to redemption than any non-Jew because of an inherited "Divine spark." This seems to have been the view of Judah Halevi, the Maharal of Prague, and the late Rabbi Kook, among others. On the other hand, there have been those who argued that consent was at least as important as kinship, if not more so in that every Jew has to accept the covenant to be truly part of Israel. This seems to have been the view of Philo and Maimonides, among others. Philo discusses the admission of proselytes on equal terms with those born Jews into the Jewish polity and suggests that the basis of that polity is not common descent but the common heritage of the Torah, that is, common consenting to the commandments of the Torah. Thus, in *De Specialibus Legibus*, Philo says, "The native born Jews obtain the approval of God not because they are members of the God loving polity from birth but because they were not false to the nobility of their birth," while the proselytes obtain God's approval "because they have thought fit to make the passage to piety" (*Spec.* 1, 9, 51). Philo terms such relationships as "kinships of greater dignity and sanctity" (*Spec.* 1, 58, 317).

The latter view is that of most modern Jewish theologians and thinkers, reinforced by the realities of the open society and the general commitment of the moderns to voluntarism. On the other hand, the former view remains strongly that of groups like the Habad Hassidim, which helps explain why, on one hand, they pursue every Jew with equal vigor and, on the other, have an extremely negative attitude toward conversions to Judaism. While one must approach the Talmud cautiously in such matters, in at least one place it suggests that it is the covenant between God and Israel that makes "All Israel responsible for one another." In the larger context, this seems to represent a synthesis between kinship and consent. Certainly the Hebrew term for "responsible" used in the passage, *arevim*, has strong contractual connotations.

The discussion of the appropriate political regime for the Jewish people has been linked with the covenant idea from the first, as illustrated in *Parashat Yithro* (Exodus). As that *parashah* indicates, while the covenant establishes the constitutional grounding of the Jewish people, it does not establish any particular form of government. The Torah itself presents two options—a nomocratic tribal federation ruled by God and led by prophets and judges or one under the leadership of kings. These two options—the first based upon a highly noncentralized regime of locally rooted leaders and the second based upon a court with a bureaucratic—with some variations, remain the principle choices before the Jewish people throughout the biblical period, and may even be seen as prototypes of the choices confronting the Jews as a polity ever since. Subsequently, other variations of those options were developed and instituted through various local compacts (or by outside powers where the Jews were unable to determine their own forms of government).

The struggle between the two options is generally couched in covenantal terms, namely what were the demands of the original covenant at Sinai which established God's direct rule over His people and did God modify those demands by His covenant with David and his house. This debate is one of the great debates in Jewish political thought, manifested in the Talmud, in the medieval world (for example, Maimonides versus Abravanel) and down through modern times (viz. Chaim Herschenson's *Malchi Bakodesh* and Martin Buber's *Kingship of God*).[34] It has also operated on an immediate level in matters regarding the forms of governance, the organization of authority, and the distribution of powers within particular Jewish communities. The responsa literature is replete with references to these two options and seeks to apply them to local situations.[35]

If the Jewish sources do not mandate a particular form of government, they do have a great deal to say about what component elements are necessary for the construction of a good regime. These include both institutions and processes involving such things as the separation of powers and responsibilities, expectations of standards of behavior of political officeholders, and requirements for the protection of individual rights, or, more correctly, privileges, responsibilities, and obligations. In short, an appropriate political structure within the covenantal framework is one that secures both the position of the Torah in the Jewish polity and the liberties (in the classic sense) of the Jewish people.

The lack of emphasis on a particular governmental form is a reflection of the emphasis of the covenantal approach on particular kinds of political relationships—between governors and governed, between components of the polity (or between polities), between God and man. Covenants, after all, are designed to create relationships which are then given form rather than creating forms which are then given content. This emphasis on relationships has been a distinguishing characteristic of the Jewish political tradition from the first, and helps explain why a variety of regimes have proved acceptable to the interpreters of Jewish tradition and also why some forms of regime are simply unacceptable, no matter what.

Every polity is built around certain basic tensions which play a major role in giving it form and in defining its continuing concerns as a polity. Those tensions come on the scene in the course of the very founding of the polity in the first place and are, in all likelihood, inherent in the act of founding, representing unresolved conflicts leading up to the founding or tensions that necessarily result from the founding synthesis. Every generation must grapple with these tensions and work out some *modus vivendi* to manage them so that they are not so exacerbated as to cause the dissolution of the polity in question. At the same time, the tensions are never completely resolved as long as the polity exists. In fact they can be resolved only upon the demise of the polity. Thus, part of the dynamic of every polity is its particular set of tensions and the interaction that occurs between them.

The principal tensions within the Jewish polity are derived from or closely related to the covenant idea. One such tension evolves around the problem of reconciling Divine and popular authority. On one hand, God is the sovereign of the Jewish people and His authority is ultimate and unchallengeable. On the other, for day-to-day matters and even for matters of interpreting Jewish law, authority is vested in humans and, for many such matters, in human majorities. For example, the powers of legal interpretation were entrusted to the Sanhedrin as the ultimate human agency for interpreting the law, and, according to the famous *midrash*, their decisions are by majority rule even when God Himself gives a sign as to the rightness of the minority view. The covenant is perhaps the principal bridge between the two authoritative forces, since it is through the covenant that God has invested human institutions with authoritative roles. Moreover, it is through the various subcovenants that humans have organized their institutions to exercise these roles.

Closely tied in with the question of the appropriate political regime for the Jewish people is the appropriate conception of the polity. Here the covenant idea plays an especially important role. If the Jewish political tradition conveys a clear sense of the existence of polities and their importance, it does not, in its authentic form, have any conception of the state in the modern sense of the term (see chapter 6). The word *medina* appears in the Bible (as do almost all the words that we now take for granted in the Jewish language of politics), where it is used to describe a territorial unit possessing its own political or administrative institutions but clearly not an independent one, in other words, a jurisdiction, whether an administrative district (the usage in *Kings*) or a province (as used in *Esther*). The Bible does not refer to sovereign states because, for it and the Jewish political tradition generally, sovereignty rests only in Heaven. All powers possessed by humans are subsidiary ones, delegated by God to the people or their representatives as variously defined.

In the Jewish political tradition, polities come in all forms, peoples, nations, cities, tribes, kingdoms, empires, and modern states as well. None is considered to be the generic form. The Bible suggests that nations and peoples are generic in the form of polity they choose. As time went on and the Jews experienced a wider variety of political systems, this principle became refined with a new dimension added, namely, that a good polity is in significant ways a partnership of its members. This was a natural outgrowth of the covenant idea.

The elimination of the problem of human sovereignty and absence of any generic form of polity helped reinforce a strong predisposition in Jewish political thought toward the view that all government is a matter of delegated powers. The term *reshut*, which first appears in the Talmud, probably comes closest to encapsulating this concept, reflecting as it does an authority whose powers have been granted by another source. The principle of *reshut* has been institutionalized in Jewish liturgy and ritual as a sign of the equal sharing of God's covenant-granted authority among all Jews. Thus, in the Siddur, the hosts of heaven grant *reshut* to one another to praise God and the leader of the *birkat hamazon* (blessing after the meal) requests *reshut* from his peers (literally stated, his teachers, with the implication that those present are more knowledgeable than he) to lead them in the prayer.

The principle of *reshut* is politically operationalized through *reshuyot* (authorities, as in the sense of the New York Port Authority); among other things, this makes possible overlapping political jurisdictions and structures, each with its own powers or competences, a phenomenon that we already encountered in biblical times as a feature of Jewish governments and which has been a continuing reality of Jewish political life ever since. This theoretical perspective was further reinforced by the long diaspora experience of the Jews, where, in effect, the Jews had obligations to more than one polity simultaneously.

Finally, Jewish political thought has concerned itself with the messianic age and the ideal polity that is to come into existence with the coming of the messiah. Jewish tradition is rather clear on this point. The messianic age will be the age of the realization of God's kingdom upon this earth with all the political implications contained in that phrase. Consequently, a political order will be necessary, but of course it will be the ideal political order. By and large, Jewish equivalents of utopias are directed toward discussion of the messianic polity. Both Isaiah and Ezekiel bring their versions of that polity and talmudic and post-talmudic literature has other such visions.[36] In almost every case, they involve the fulfillment of God's covenant with Israel and the restoration of the tribal federation. All other aspects flow from those two starting points.

The sophistication of the covenant idea in Jewish political thought is perhaps best revealed in the relationship between *brit* and *hesed*. *Brit* represents the structural manifestation of the covenant idea, while *hesed* is its dynamic component. If a *brit* creates a partnership, then hesed is what makes the partnership work.[37]

*Hesed* has been variously translated as "loving-kindness" or "grace." In fact, there is no equivalent term in English that conveys its true meaning (one of the signs of the originality of the idea). Norman Snaith has translated it as "covenant love," but that translation is too theological.[38] *Hesed* really means the obligation of a partner to a covenant to go beyond the narrowly construed contractual demands of the partnership in order to make the relationship between them a truly viable one. It is the Jewish answer to the problem of "narrow legalism." A covenant is, after all, a contract and the tendency in contractual systems is for people to act like lawyers, that is to say, to try to construe the contract as narrowly as possible when defining their obligations and as broadly as possible when defining the obligations of the other parties. That is what narrow legalism is all about. What *hesed* does is to insert into the relationship a more extended dynamic. Through it, Jewish tradition interprets one's contractual obligations broadly rather than narrowly, the broader the better. Thus, *hassidim* have traditionally been those who have defined their obligations vis-à-vis God and their fellow men to include a dimension above and beyond that which is normally required. Jewish history has known three *hassidic* movements identified by that name: the *hassidim* of the Second Temple, those of medieval Ashkenaz, and those who emerged in eighteenth-century Eastern Europe. Each was a unique movement in many ways, but what was common to them all was this sense on the part of the movements' adherents that they were accepting a more broadly construed obligation than that which Israel's covenant with God ordinarily demanded. In essence, they were attempting to fulfill the Talmudic dictum that *lifnim meshurat hadin din hu*, going beyond the law is the law, in their own lives. A *brit* without *hesed* is indeed a narrow thing and, according to Jewish tradition, God himself provides the model of the extension of *hesed* by maintaining His relationship with Israel despite the Jews' repeated violations of the terms of the covenant. That is the finest example of taking the extra step.

### Political Culture and Behavior

The precisely proper combination of *brit* and *hesed* is left to theoretical speculation and the end of days. In the interim, however, the concepts have entered the political culture of the Jewish people to exercise a pronounced, if partial and necessarily flawed, influence on a regular basis. Even in the absence of systematic studies, a reasoned assessment of the evidence can lead us to a certain understanding of the matter. So, for example, as befits a people who see themselves as partners of the Almighty, Jews are not prone to relate to each other (or to others) hierarchically. Quite to the contrary, even the authority of particular leaders is accepted voluntarily on the basis of equality. For most Jews, not even the religious leadership is able to form a permanent elite. Every Jew feels free to recognize his own authoritative interpreters of the Torah. Acceptance of authority in other spheres may involve the recognition of sociological realities—for example, that in a voluntaristic community the wealthy will have more power since they contribute a larger share of the budget—but does not endow the leadership with any special status *per se*. The status exists by consent of the community in both cases.

Melvin Urofsky describes Louis Dembitz Brandeis' reaction to his first serious encounter with still-unassimilated Eastern European Jewish immigrants to the United States as the mediator of the great New York garment workers' strike of 1910.[39]

> While going through the lofts, he heard numerous quarrels between workers and their bosses, and was amazed that they treated each other more like equals than as inferiors and superiors. In one argument an employee shouted at the owner, "Ihr darft sich shemen! Past dos far a Yid?" ("You should be ashamed! Is this worthy of a Jew?"). While another time a machine operator lectured his employer with a quotation from Isaiah: "It is you who have devoured the vineyard, the spoil of the poor is in your houses. What do you mean by crushing My people, by grinding the face of the poor? says the Lord God of hosts."

Brandeis' experience is matched in Israel (or any other Jewish environment) everyday. Jews do not "obey orders." They can be brought to act in a certain way either on the basis of understanding or trade-offs, but not on the basis of commands. Even in the military framework, where there is no problem of obeying immediate commands, the Israel Defense Forces (IDF) has found that it must first inculcate understanding so that it can succeed in commanding. This, indeed, has been IDF doctrine from the first. Behaviorally, this manifests itself in a Jewish conception of leadership that involves leaders actually going first, what in the Israeli army is known as the *acharai* or *follow me* principle. It is no accident that the IDF gains its greatest strength following this principle, just as on a very different level the most influential Jewish leaders in the United States are the big contributors to the annual campaigns—the only American Jewish leaders, who lead by going first and setting the pace.

The operation of this principle can be seen throughout Jewish history. Successful leaders were those who accepted the heavier burdens in whatever direction they desired to lead, else they had no significant influence. It is highly significant that classical Hebrew has no word for obey (there is a modern word created for use in the IDF). Classical Hebrew uses *shamoa*, a term that embraces hearing before acting and implicitly involves the principle of consent. That is to say, an individual—as befits a partner to God's covenant whose integrity and autonomy are established—hears, considers, and decides. He cannot be ordered to do something, but must consent to it. Even the *midrash,* which stands in greatest conflict with the covenant idea, the one describing Israel's acceptance of the Sinai covenant only after God held a mountain over them, still reflects this perspective. According to that *midrash*, God put Israel in a most untenable position, by holding the mountain over them and giving them the choice of agreeing to the covenant or being buried under it, virtually forcing them to consent, but they still had to consent. He did not simply force them to obey, and that is probably the most extreme example (and by no means to be taken as the mainstream view) of a master-servant relationship in classical Jewish thought. Thus, a kind of partnership attitude is a basic datum of Jewish existence. Anyone who attempts to lead, govern, or even work with Jews comes up against it everyday in every way.

The covenantal solution to the problems of Jewish unity can also be seen as cultural and behavioral manifestations of *brit* and hesed. Jewish political thought and culture are characterized by a strong messianic dimension, again as part of the sense that man works in partnership with God to reconstruct or redeem the world. An equally pronounced element in Jewish political culture and behavior has been the conceptualization of the messianic task in different ways, creating a kind of pluralism within Jewish life that manifests itself in the division of Jewry into various movements or camps. It seems that a camp comes into existence when its adherents compact among themselves—implicitly or explicitly—to follow a certain form of Jewish discipline, in effect becoming congregations or covenantal societies within the overall framework of the Jewish people. So it was with the Sadducees, Pharisees, and Essenes in the days of the Second Temple; so it is with contemporary Orthodox, Conservative, and Liberal religious movements; and so it has been with the Zionist parties.

The relationship among camps has been more problematic. Either some linkage has been achieved among them on a federative basis or there has been hostility even to the point of civil war. In the days of the Second Temple, the latter condition prevailed with disastrous consequences for the Jewish people. Since then, there have been moments when a similar result seemed to be in the offing, as in the struggle between Karaites and Rabbanites and later between the Orthodox and the Reformers, but the diaspora situation of the Jewish people in effect prevented them from such suicidal behavior. Twentieth-century Jewry, with all its problems, has implicitly (if not always happily) recognized that the camps are inevitable as long as Jews are free to pursue their respective messianic visions, but has also recognized the necessity for national unity. Thus, in both Israel and the United States, in particular, federative arrangements have been applied to create sufficient unity to undertake common action to protect common interests or advance common goals without interfering with the basic integrity of the camps themselves. Obviously, this involves a continuing process and has left certain continuing problems as well, not the least of which is one inherent in the pursuit of any messianic vision, namely, that there is a limit to the ability of one camp to tolerate another, particularly when they involve grossly contradictory visions and ways of life.

In this respect, twentieth-century Jewry has managed to devise methods that flow out of the Jewish political tradition, even if unawares (one indicator of existence of a Jewish political culture is that such things can happen unawares), that have more or less satisfactorily dealt with a major flash point in Jewish life, one that has brought Jews great grief in the past. Thus, the self-restraint of the overwhelming majority of the various Jewish camps of our times can be looked upon as a signal accomplishment, even if it leads to a certain amount of impatience on the part of those who see their particular messianic vision somehow compromised by the acceptance of various status quo arrangements.

Contractual behavior, if one may so term it, that seems to be endemic to Jewish political culture, is manifested through the series of partnerships that comprise the Jewish community, each of which combines the fundamental autonomy of its members within a bargaining relationship. We have already suggested that leadership under such circumstances has to take on a different character. So, too, decision making becomes principally a matter of negotiation among equals.

At various times in Jewish history, these partnerships have included such phenomena as *shutafim* in the study of Talmud, the kinds of partnerships that S.D. Goitein describes as coming in place of employer-employee relationships in the Egypt of the Geniza, and the cooperative building of contemporary Israel.[40]

It is likely that every society has some kinds of cooperative relationships within it, so that the discovery of such relationships is not definitive, *per se*. It is the prevalence and salience of such relationships that count. In that regard, the Jewish people is one of those societies that stand out in their utilization of partnership devices, all of which also have their roots in the covenant idea.

Political life in Jewish communities and polities has usually involved the following factors: (1) the initial consent of the members to the community's authority and to the authoritative structures and processes of governance within it; (2) a commitment toward participation in communal affairs on the part of a relatively substantial percentage of the citizenry; (3) the utilization of various forms of representation (usually premodern, and only recently modern ones) where direct participation was not feasible; and (4) a system of dispersed decision making with different tasks assigned to different bodies often involving the same individuals wearing many different hats, moving from body to body in their leadership capacities. It is within this framework that links between the covenant idea and the practice of governance in Jewish polities are made.

It is obvious that the sweep of the covenant idea is broad indeed.

This writer is not the first to suggest either its sweep or importance. The many references cited here attest to that. Precisely because of its breadth, the concept requires as much specification as possible. Perhaps the best way to emphasize its specificity is by indicating what would be inconsistent with covenantal relationships, i.e., what is not covenanted. We can begin by excluding the relationship between master and slave (in any form, including political slavery). In that sense, any relationship that denies the fundamental freedom of any of the parties to it is not covenantal. In relation to polities, nonrepublican (in the classic sense of the term: a polity as a *res publica*, a public thing rather than the private preserve of its rulers) relationships are not covenantal.[41]

To suggest that the covenant idea informs a political tradition is not to suggest that it answers all questions, any more than the idea of natural law does in the tradition it informs. What it does do is set the parameters of the debate.

It is always a mistake to underestimate the continuity of culture. Individuals are formed early in their lives by the cultures into which they are born. So, too, is a people. The seeds of whatever Jews are today were planted at the very birth of the Jewish people—when God decided, in His infinite wisdom, to take the Jews in harness, and the Jews, whether because they were foolish or desperate, decided to accept His offer. In sum, when the Jews were formed as a people, they acquired (or already had) certain characteristics that have persisted over time. Despite all the differences, the similarities and elements dating back to or deriving from those original conditions have had an amazing persistence. Jewish culture is permeated with contractual manifestations, symbols, and images. Hardly a page of Jewish text exists without at least one.[42] In the political as well as other realms, the better part of those elements are derived from the covenant.

The question remains: given the political character of the covenant, is a covenantal basis for the Jewish political tradition still valid or even possible given the present secularization of the Jewish and other peoples? The answer to that question can be developed theoretically or empirically. Theoretically it seems neither possible nor valid under such conditions. Empirically, however, the evidence is mixed. Even secular Jews often seem to be striving for just such a relationship within their tradition and few Jews react to it in fully secular ways.

The covenant flourishes as a figure of speech and, it would seem, as the bond which has generated the sense of responsibility Jews have for one another. The behavior of committed Jews of all persuasions in our times would seem to confirm the behavioral reality of the covenant relationship even if the theory behind it needs new clarification.

## Notes

A somewhat different version of the present paper appeared in the *Jewish Journal of Sociology* 20, no. 1 (June 1978): 5–37.

1. See, for example, Arnold Jacob Wolf, ed., *Rediscovering Judaism* (Chicago: Quadrangle Books, 1965), which includes essays by several of the principal North American exponents of this covenant theology, and Jakob J. Petuchowski, *Ever Since Sinai* (New York, 1961). Martin Buber emphasizes the covenant in all of his works. See also Harold Fisch, *Jerusalem and Albion* (New York: Schocken Books, 1964) for an examination of the modern secularization of the covenant idea and John F. A. Taylor, *The Masks of Society, An Inquiry into the Covenants of Civilization* (New York: Appleton-Century-Crofts, 1966) for a contemporary American covenantal perspective. While this article seeks to expound and even shift our understanding of the covenant idea to include and emphasize its political dimension, it also uses theological terminology throughout because the Jewish political tradition of necessity has a theological base just as the European political tradition has a philosophic base. Political theology has declined in importance in the West in recent generations, hence the usages may be somewhat unfamiliar to the reader, but it is nonetheless an old element in political science and legitimate in every respect.
2. See especially Hans Kohn, "Nationalism in Israel and Hellas," in *The Idea of Nationalism* (New York: Macmillan, 1961). From the perspective of the Jewish political tradition, the Bible must be read as a whole work, regardless of the various theories of biblical criticism. What is significant about it is not the extent to which the text in our possession is an edited amalgam but that, as a whole, it presents—and represents—a comprehensive tradition. (See my discussion in the Introduction to this volume.) For a fuller discussion of this problem, see Leo Strauss, *What is Political Philosophy* (Glencoe, Ill.: Free Press, 1959). Strauss applies his perspective in *An Interpretation of Genesis* (Jerusalem and Philadelphia: Center for Jewish Community Studies, 1975).
3. See George Mendenhall, "Covenant Forms in Israelite Tradition," *Biblical Archeologist* 17 (1959): 50–76. For an interesting gloss on Mendenhall, see Moshe Weinfeld, "Berit-Covenant vs. Obligation" in *Biblical* 56, Fasc. 1 (1975): 120–28.
4. The question as to whether or not the choice of regimes is open has been much debated in Jewish tradition. That is to say, is monarchy mandated by the Torah or a matter of choice? For our purposes here we need not determine which view is correct (although this writer believes that the choice is given). The very fact that the question is a perennial one with such distinguished figures as Don Isaac Abravanel opting for the latter view is sufficiently significant to demonstrate the point made here. For a summary of the sources, see Chaim Herschensohn, *Eleh*

*Divrei HaBrit* (Hoboken, N.J., 1918–1921), 3 vols., and *Malchi Bakodesh* (Hoboken, N.J., 1923–1928), 6 vols.

5.  For a fuller discussion of the political institutions of ancient Israel, see Roland de Vaux, *Ancient Israel* (New York: McGraw-Hill, 1965), 2 vols., especially vol. 1, *Social Institutions.*

6.  All biblical usages of the term *brit* have been assembled and classified in *HaMunach "Brit" BaTanach* [The Term "Covenant" in the Bible], a guide published by the Workshop in the Covenant Idea and the Jewish Political Tradition co-sponsored by the Center for Jewish Community Studies, and the Department of Political Studies of Bar-Ilan University.

7.  See Perry Miller, *The New England Mind* (Boston: Beacon Press, 1961), 2 vols., particularly vol. 1, book IV, and appendix B, "The Federal School of Theology."

8.  Moshe Weinfeld, "Covenant" in *Encyclopedia Judaica*, 5: 1012–22. See also Delbert Hillers, *Covenant: The History of a Biblical Idea* (Baltimore: Johns Hopkins Press, 1969) and Ruth Gil, "Brit—HaMunach v'HaMusag" ["Covenant—The Term and the Concept"], an unpublished paper prepared for the Workshop for the Study of the Political Implications of the Covenant Idea. The Hebrew terminology of the Jewish political tradition is especially rich in covenant-related terms, ranging from at least three terms for covenant in the Bible itself to the terminology of contemporary Israeli political life with its emphasis on "compounding" (rather than forming) governments and polities; "consenting" to the conclusions of meetings, etc. Even words like *shalom* that have other manifest meanings have been demonstrated by philologists to contain strong covenantal connotations. The Covenant Workshop has examined these terms in some depth and documentation of their covenantal character can be found in the workshop files.

9.  No comprehensive study of the covenant idea as a political concept, comparable to the several such works on a parallel concept, natural law, presently exists. The Workshop in Israel and a parallel Workshop in Covenant and Politics sponsored by the Center for the Study of Federalism at Temple University in Philadelphia are now at work laying the foundations for such a work. There are, however, studies of various political applications of the covenant idea such as those of Kohn, Hiller, Miller, and Taylor cited above.

10. Rabbi J.D. Soloveichik, among others, treats the two passages as referring to separate covenants, at least for homiletic purposes, in "Lonely Man of Faith," *Tradition* 14, no. 3 (Summer 1974). Since he takes the covenant and basis of Jewish peoplehood seriously, his discussion deserved particular notice even if it is only tangentially political in orientation.

11. See Daniel J. Elazar, "Kinship and Consent in the Jewish Community: Patterns of Continuity in Jewish Communal Life," *Tradition* 14, no. 4 (Fall 1974): 63–79.

12. See Martin Noth, *The History of Israel* (New York: Harper and Row, 1958).

13. The idea that the Torah should be understood as the constitution of the Jewish people is old and oft-recurring, expressed by traditional and modern thinkers, as diverse as Spinoza, who understood the Torah as a political constitution first and foremost, and Mendelsohn, who viewed the political dimension as utterly dispensable. See Benedict Spinoza, *Politico-Theologico Tractate*; Moses Mendelsohn, *Jerusalem*; and Eliezer Schweid, chapter 6 of this volume.

14. See, for example, Martin A. Cohen, "The Role of the Shilonite Priesthood in the United Monarchy of Ancient Israel" in *Hebrew Union College Annual* (Cincinnati: Hebrew Union College, 1965), vol. 36; Josephus's *Antiquities of the Jews*; Abravanel's commentary on *Deuteronomy* and *Samuel*; and Buber's *Kingship of*

*God* (New York: Harper and Row, 1967). Elijah has traditionally been considered an anti-monarchist; the biblical portrayal of him shows him to have a more complex position, supporting Ahab as king but seeking to keep the monarchy tied to the Torah as mediated through the prophets. The reference here is to the tradition rather than to the more complex reality.

15. See, for example, George H. Sabine, *A History of Political Theory* (New York: Henry Holt and Co., 1950), rev. ed.

16. See Norman K. Gottwald, *All the Kingdoms of the Earth* (New York: Harper and Row, 1964). These constitutional and practical issues, such as the relationship between the covenants underlying the tribal federation, God's covenant with David and his house, and the division of powers under the monarchy, are complex and involv ones that require detailed treatment in their own right. They are among the many subjects that deserve to be investigated in the study of the Jewish political tradition and cannot be treated in the space of this chapter.

17. For a description of those efforts, see Michael Avi-Yonah, *The Jews of Palestine, A Political History from the Bar Kokhba War to the Arab Conquest* (New York: Schocken Books, 1976).

18. For a study of power relationships in Babylonian Jewry, see Jacob Neusner, *There They Sat Down* (Nashville and New York: Abingdon Press, 1972).

19. Louis Finkelstein, *Jewish Self-Government in the Middle Ages* (New York: Philipp Feldheim, 1964).

20. Salo W. Baron, *The Jewish Community* (Philadelphia: Jewish Publication Society, 1938–1942), 3 vols.

21. Menachem Elon, chapter 10 in this volume; Irving A. Agus, *Urban Civilization in Pre-Crusade Europe* (New York: Yeshiva University Press, 1968), 2 vols.; and Isidore Epstein, *Studies in the Communal Life of the Jews of Spain* (New York: Hermon Press, 1968). This writer follows Elon in the view that, more often than not, majority rule was the accepted standard, a position entirely consistent with the covenant principle. The more important point is that either position supports the thesis advanced here.

22. Thus, the Workshop in the Covenant Idea and the Jewish Political Tradition, in cooperation with the responsa project at Bar-Ilan, has systematically identified hundreds of practical applications of the word *brit* in the selected responsa presently stored in the project's computer. They are now being classified and analyzed.

23. Gerald Blidstein, chapter 4 in this volume, and *Notes on Hefker Bet-Din in Talmudic and Medieval Law* (Jerusalem: Center for Jewish Community Studies, 1975).

24. Ibid.; Elon, chapter 10 in this volume; Agus, *Urban Civilization*; Epstein, *Studies in the Communal Life.*

25. Daniel J. Elazar, "The Reconstitution of Jewish Communities in the Postwar Period," in *Jewish Journal of Sociology* 11, no. 2 (December 1969): 187–226.

26. Daniel J. Elazar, *Community and Polity: The Organizational Dynamics of American Jewry* (Philadelphia: Jewish Publication Society, 1976).

27. Moshe Davis, "Centres of Jewry in the Western Hemisphere: A Comparative Approach," reprinted in *Five Lectures Delivered at the Third World Congress for Jewish Studies in Jerusalem* (Jerusalem: Hebrew University Institute of Contemporary Jewry, 1964). See also the other lectures reprinted in that pamphlet.

28. Ibid.

29. See Emile Marmorstein, *Heaven at Bay* (London: Oxford University Press, 1969);

and Daniel J. Elazar, *Israel: From Ideological to Territorial Democracy* (New York: General Learning Press, 1970). Eliezer Don-Yehiya of the Covenant Workshop is presently investigating the conscious use of covenant forms and symbols in the development of the Zionist enterprise in Israel. His preliminary findings strongly reinforce the point made in these paragraphs.

30. S. N. Eisenstadt describes this process in *Israeli Society* (New York: Basic Books, 1967).

31. Horace M. Kallen has examined the ideological implications of the Scroll in this way in *Utopians at Bay* (New York: Theodore Herzl Foundation, 1958), pp. 15–19. For a discussion of the scroll's quasi-constitutional character, see Amnon Rubenstein's work in Hebrew, *The Constitutional Law of the State of Israel* (Jerusalem and Tel Aviv: Schocken, 1969), chapter 1.

32. For an understanding of the variety of federal arrangements, and the relationship of union as a constitutional form to those arrangements, see Daniel J. Elazar, *The Ends of Federalism* (Philadelphia: Temple University Center for the Study of Federalism, 1976).

33. See Saul Berman, "Noahide Laws," in *Encyclopedia Judaica*, vol. 12: 1189–91, for a good summary and references to the relevant texts.

34. See Gordon Freeman, chapter 2 in this volume; also Chaim Herschenson, *Malchi Bakodesh*, chapter 11; and Buber, Kingship of God.

35. See the material of the Responsa Literature Information Storage and Retrieval of the Institute for Data Retrieval, Bar-Ilan University, and the files of the Covenant Workshop.

36. See, for example, Stephen Schwarszchild, "A Note on the Nature of the Ideal Society—A Rabbinic Study," in Herbert A. Strauss and Hans G. Reissner, eds., *Jubilee Volume Dedicated to Curt C. Silberman* (New York: American Federation of Jews from Central Europe, 1969).

37. Nelson Glueck documents this in his *Hesed in the Bible* (Cincinnati: Hebrew Union College Press, 1967) without attempting to make the point.

38. Norman H. Snaith, "The Covenant-Love of God," in *The Distinctive Ideas of the Old Testament* (New York: Schocken Books, 1964), chapter 5.

39. Melvin I. Urofsky, "On Louis D. Brandeis," in *Midstream* (January 1975): 42–58.

40. S. D. Goitein, *A Mediterranean Society* (Berkeley and Los Angeles: University of California Press, 1971), vol. 11, *The Community*; and Harry Viteles, *A History of the Cooperative Movement in Israel* (London: Vallentine Mitchell, 1966), 7 vols.

41. There are those who argue that nonvoluntary political associations cannot be covenantal. This writer clearly rejects that position. A state association can be fully covenantal if it is internally constituted on the right principles, i.e., is compounded of free citizens and is linked with other state associations in a federal manner.

42. See, for example, Gordon Freeman, *The Politics of Prayer* (Ramat Gan: Workshop in the Covenant Idea and the Jewish Political Tradition, 1977).

# 2

# The Concept of the Three *Ketarim*: Their Place in Jewish Political Thought and Implications for Studying Jewish Constitutional History

*Stuart A. Cohen*

Jewish political traditions, it has been argued, constitute an integral facet of Jewish civilization in its entirety. They reflect a constant—albeit often implicit—understanding that the validity of Jewish teaching can best find expression in a political setting. They also embody Judaism's commitment to the establishment of the perfect polity. As implemented through the process of covenant *(brit),* and as buttressed by the attribute of loving-kindness *(hesed),* political traditions in effect comprise the vehicles whereby the Congregation of Israel attempts to transpose the kingdom of heaven *(malkhut shamayim*—"the good commonwealth") to earth.

Thus understood, Jewish political traditions are perceived to be utilitarian in intent and dynamic in form. They constitute neither the linear derivatives of a systematic body of political theory nor a monolithic corpus of constitutional doctrine. Rather, they are the products of a continuous political dialogue which, throughout the long course of Jewish history, has been primarily concerned with the practical definition of proper modes of Jewish political conduct and the instrumental application of appropriate forms of internal Jewish government. Only partially has that dialogue been summarized formally, in the occasional comments of Jewish political thinkers. More often, and more fully, it has been articulated in the behavioral dimensions of Jewish public life. That is why its investigation and reconstruction is such an exacting task. The principles underlying Jewish political traditions cannot be distilled from the writings of individual Jewish philosophers—very few of whom have composed reasonably architected statements of political import. Rather, they have to be inferred from the activities and habits of Jewish political practitioners. Ultimately, indeed, they can only be identified by an examination of the instrumental arrangements that have periodically regulated relationships within and between the component segments of the Congregation of the Children of Israel *(adat b'nei yisrael*—otherwise, the *edah)*. It is these that lie at the very root of the Jewish political experience and these that therefore have to be explored in order to understand its evolution.

This chapter is designed as a contribution to that inquiry. Its underlying purpose is to examine the institutional processes whereby the stream of covenantal arrangements that have characterized the various epochs of Jewish constitutional history have been put into effect. Specifically, it seeks to trace the form and structure of the provisions which the Jewish political tradition has made for the exercise of political power and the manner of its distribution. It will attempt to demonstrate that the concept of the three *ketarim* encapsulates the organizational system whereby Jewish polities traditionally—and consistently—distributed authority among and between specific governmental instrumentalities. It will further suggest that a study of the development of the *ketarim* might also facilitate wider historical analyses of the dynamics of Jewish constitutional change.

## Theory in Practice

Fundamental to the argument that follows is the contention that the Jewish political tradition—like all covenantal traditions—demands that power be shared out among properly constituted institutions and officers. It has no sympathy with a system of government in which a single body or group possesses a monopoly of the attributes, prerogatives, and privileges of political authority. A survey of the long history of

Jewish political conduct, as well as a review of the comments passed on the Jewish political tradition by some of its most representative exponents and commentators, reveals this to be a cardinal constitutional axiom. It has made its influence felt in every one of Judaism's constitutional epochs, and in every arena of Jewry's communal organization. In principle, the concentration of power is to be avoided and denigrated; its diffusion among various legitimate (or legitimated) domains of government is to be encouraged and praised. Constitutional omnipotence is occasional and implicitly refused even to God;[1] it is permanently and explicitly denied to man.

One illustration of the Jewish commitment to this rule is provided by the early rabbinic attitude toward the degree of constitutional authority wielded by Moses. The example, as will be readily appreciated, is not chosen at random. Moses is singled out for attention because he is a protagonist of such extraordinary stature and status within the Jewish political tradition. According to the biblical account, not only was he in exceptionally close contact with God. Apart from his successor, Joshua, he was also the only human being ever to be divinely designated *eved adonai* (literally "servant of the Lord," a title which, in constitutional terms, carries with it the designation of "Chief Minister to God"). That is why subsequent commentators found it so difficult to dragoon him into any of the categories conventionally applied to lesser mortals, whose influence over the entire course of Jewish history has been less manifest and less profound.[2] Therein, however, lies the interest of the case. So stringent was the traditional Jewish insistence on the diffusion of political power that not even Moses could be granted the preponderance of authority, which—according to aggadic legend—he blatantly sought. In the words of *Exodus Rabbah* (2:7), "Moses requested that kings and priests should descend from him. Thereupon God said to him: 'Draw not nigh thither' [*al tikrav halom;* Exodus 3:5]; i.e., your sons will not perform sacrifices because the priesthood is already assigned to your brother Aaron . . . .the monarchy is already assigned to David."

What followed, the sources suggest, had to conform to the pattern thus established at an embryonic stage of Jewish constitutional history. As much is emphasized by the rabbinic attitude toward the succession of Joshua, who—although also an *eved adonai*—was clearly in not quite the same category as Moses.[3] The relevant biblical narrative (Numbers 27:15–23) itself intimates that Joshua's authority was not to be as far-ranging as that of Moses; it specifies that at his induction ceremony Joshua, unlike Moses, was commanded to stand before Elazar the High Priest, the custodian of the Urim and Thummim (Numbers 27:21).

Characteristically, commentators of the talmudic era noted this obligation as well as the additional fact that (according to a strict rendering of the text) Moses was instructed to place only one of his hands upon Joshua. Hence the comment, first found in the fourth-century *Sifrei* to this passage, that "Joshua had need of Elazar and Elazar of Joshua."[4] The requirement, we are invited to understand, was not merely functional—in the sense of being the consequence of the manifold tasks that awaited the new leader of the *edah*. It was, rather, constitutional—in the sense of being a symbolic commitment to the survival of the principle of power-sharing arrangements.

To this axiom subsequent rabbinic historiography remained consistently faithful. Accordingly, examples of deviations from the norm were severely castigated; threats to its preservation were stringently denigrated. In some instances, this gave rise to shrewd—and tongue-in-cheek—comments on the political situation prevailing at the time of the redaction of the Talmud (e.g., T.B. *Horayot* 11b: "'The scepter shall not pass from Judah' [Genesis 49:101], this refers to the exilarch of Babylon, who dominates *[rodeh]* Israel with a rod; 'nor the staff from his descendants' *[ibid.],* these are the children of Hillel, who publicly teach the Torah to Israel"). In others it provoked particularistic—perhaps even idiosyncratic—interpretations of Jewish history. A case in point is provided by the treatment accorded to the Hasmonean kingship, a vein of Jewish constitutional history that rabbinic commentators assiduously mined (and to which we ourselves shall have cause to return). Nahmanides (Moses ben Nahman, 1194–1270), to cite only one such source, was in little doubt as to the explanation for the string of tragedies which befell that unfortunate family. Basing himself on eminently respectable sources (T.J. *Horayot* 3:2), he referred explicitly to the principle of the division of powers:

> It is possible that there was an element of sin inherent in their kingship because they were priests and were commanded to reserve their officiation for the needs of the altar. . . . .it was not for them to rule *[limlokh]* but only to perform the service of God. . . . .and R. Hiyya bar Aba explained that the Torah ordained that the priests, levites, and entire tribe of Levi should not have a portion in the kingship—and that is a fitting and proper matter. (Commentary to Genesis 49:10)

The whiff of the manifesto that pervades such comments must not be allowed to conceal their instrumental impulse. The power-sharing principles thus adumbrated were not left in the rarefied sphere of high theory. Such was the unity of conception and execution that they were institutionally fostered throughout the evolutionary course of Jewish constitutional history. A clear line might therefore be traced from the models of constitutional power-sharing described in the Bible to similar arrangements developed under very different political circumstances. The boundaries that (in the traditional view) were supposedly placed on the extent of Joshua's power were not regarded as exceptional. On the contrary, parallel limiting provisions—some of them explicitly derived from such pentateuchal precedents as the limited monarchy of Deuteronomy 17:14–20—were laid down wherever and whenever Jews found themselves confronted with the need to adapt or alter their framework of government to the pressures of unprecedented requirements. One prominent example is provided by the talmudic prohibition against the presence of a *melekh* in the Sanhedrin; another by the convention that the appointment of *dayyanim* in talmudic Babylon be jointly approved by the *resh galuta* (exilarch) and the *rashei yeshivah;* yet a third by the meticulously preserved balance between the *rav rosh* (Rab de la Corte) and the *nagid* in Sephardi communities of the high medieval era; a fourth in the provisions made for joint consultation between the *rashei medinot* and *dayyanei aratzot* in the Va'ad Arba ha-Aratzot (Council of the Four Lands) of sixteenth- and seventeenth-century Polish Jewry.[5] The list suggests that Jews persistently attempted—albeit with varying degrees of success—to divide communal governance in a way that might preserve and foster the federal requirements of their political heritage.

## Modes of Power-Sharing

It would not be difficult to adduce further examples of constitutional power-sharing in Jewish public life. The exercise would undoubtedly be instructive, since each instance possesses intrinsic historical interest. But for present purposes such repetition would probably be superfluous. Unless subjected to further analysis, a mere catalogue of Jewish governmental arrangements would add little to a synoptic understanding of the procedures whereby the appropriate ordinances were initiated and nothing at all to an identification of the procedures whereby they were sustained or modified. In order that these facets of the case might be clarified, attention must therefore be turned elsewhere. Specifically, an examination needs to be made of the forms and structures of the separation of powers which the Jewish political tradition seems most consistently to have favored and to which (as far as the evidence suggests) it most faithfully adhered.

At this point it seems necessary to guard against the intrusion into our discussion of two potentially obstinate red herrings. One is Jesus' injunction to the Pharisees to "Render therefore unto Caesar the things which are Caesar's; and unto God the things that are God's" (Matthew 22:21); the other is Montesquieu's division of the arms of proper government into the three branches known as the executive, the legislative, and the judiciary.[6] These are two familiar formulas, both of which readily come to mind as paradigms for an analysis of the Jewish system of government. Moreover, superficially attractive supports for their adoption as appropriate referents for a study of Jewish attitudes to government can be found in Jewish sources, both classical and postclassical. Montesquieu's division, for instance, might be straitjacketed into the verse: "The Lord our judge, the Lord our lawgiver, the Lord our King—He will save us" (Isaiah 33:22). More explicit, if of slightly less distinguished pedigree, are the props that could be found to support the bifurcate division posited by Jesus. In one frequently quoted passage, for instance, Menahem Ha-Meiri (1249–1316) speaks pointedly of "the leadership" being "generally delivered to two persons, one from the standpoint of the Torah, and he is the high priest; and one for the leadership of the [material] world, and he is the king" *(Beit ha-Behira* on T.B. *Sanhedrin* 18b).

Neither of these formulae can be accepted as a relevant paradigm for the Jewish perspective on the separation of powers. Principally, this is because neither of them complements what we know from sources other than those cited here about Jewish attitudes toward government and its exercise. The classic Christian division into the "two swords" of government, for instance, is most blatantly contradicted by the majoritarian—indeed, virtually unanimous—view of mainstream Jewish thinking, which simply does not abide the division into Church and State to which the paradigm must logically lend itself—and to which, indeed, it has ultimately led in the Western world.[7] The tripartite division suggested by Montesquieu is similarly at odds with the mainstream of the Jewish political tradition, albeit for different reasons. From the Jewish point of view, Montesquieu placed the cart before the horse. His principal concern was with the examination and definition of the major functions of government—which branch was to be responsible for which actions. In his view, a balanced separation of powers constituted a virtually mechanistic guarantee of constitutional freedom, and was therefore an end in itself. ("Liberty does not flourish because men have natural rights or because they revolt if their rulers push them too far; it flourishes because power is so distributed and so organized that whoever is tempted to abuse it finds legal restraints in his way.") Jewish traditions and experience of government, however, suggested a different order of priorities. *How* governmental institutions ought to exercise power became a secondary consideration; *whence* they derive the authority to do so was a subject of prior importance. To put matters another way, the exponents of the Jewish political tradition (over the long haul) considered it proper to tackle the issue of the precise source of constitutional power before getting down to an examination of the appropriate functions of constitutional instruments. It is this which explains why Jewish commentaries addressed themselves to an entire range of questions which Montesquieu (quite rightly, by his own standards) would have considered antecedent to his own concerns: What is the nature of the Jewish people's particular covenantal relationship with God? Within the framework of that covenant, which instrumentalities possess the right to interpret the relationship and make it effective? Whence do they derive the discretionary powers of exegesis and implementation which might enable them to do so?

The answers to these questions, it is here suggested, both reflected and enhanced the covenantal traditions of the Jewish political heritage. In their descriptions of the just governmental system, Jewish sources posit a framework that is both federal in arrangement and consensual in tone. More explicitly, they depict the distribution of political power among three distinct clusters of governmental authority: the sphere of the torah; that of the *kehunah* (priesthood); and that of the *malkhut* (kingship). Each of these domains possesses a distinct franchise, with prerogatives laid down in various sets of law-making enunciations. As thus ordained, the torah constitutes the vehicle whereby God's teachings to Israel are interpreted, specified, and transmitted; the *kehunah,* the conduit whereby God and the *edah* are brought into constant contact and close proximity; the *malkhut,* the legitimately empowered means whereby civic relationships are structured and regulated in accordance with the covenantal stipulations of the divinely ordained constitution. Demarcating these authoritative combinations are divisions not of function but of interest. Their distinctions lie less in the needs they serve than in the perspectives that they bring to bear on Jewish political conduct. Each of these domains is regarded as possessing a distinct focus of interest, an attribute that is reflected in their behavior as separate mediating devices between God and His people. Each *keter,* in effect, acts as a particular prism on the constitution of the Jewish polity. Accordingly, each is entitled to exercise a constitutional check on the others.

## Action and Interaction

References to the tripartite division between the *torah,* the *kehunah,* and the *malkhut* are scattered throughout biblical and rabbinic literature. In the former, the categorization seems sometimes to be implied by the structural arrangement of the text;[8] in the latter it is often referred to obliquely (as in the aggadic passage relating to Moses, quoted above). It is most prominently to be found, however, in sources dating from the talmudic period, where these domains are first specifically referred to as the three *ketarim.*[9]

The timing, it may be suggested, is both significant and neat. It is significant because the term emerged during one of the most convulsive periods of Jewish constitutional history. The first three centuries of the common era span the fall of the Second Commonwealth, the failure of the Bar Kochba revolt, the flowering of rabbinic Judaism, and the rise to authority of the great centers of Jewish government and scholarship in Babylon. Any one of these phenomena might have been expected to necessitate a significant degree of political stock taking. Together, they generated a complete constitutional reappraisal which both summarized the principles of previous constitutional practice and shaped much of the form of subsequent constitutional development. Moreover (as was often the case in Jewish constitutional history), the process was essentially conservative in style. Earlier political modes were not totally abandoned; rather, they were now fully articulated and—in the process—preserved for future adaptation and enhancement.

From that point of view the timing of the use of the term *ketarim* is also neat. Chronologically, the early talmudic period constitutes something of a halfway house in Jewish constitutional development; it stands roughly equidistant from the genesis of the Jewish political tradition (the epoch of the patriarchs) and its present station. The form, structure, and terminology of that critical period can therefore perhaps serve as a benchmark for the study of Jewish constitutional development in its entirety. From it, the historian can delve back for earlier origins and manifestations and reach forward for later derivatives and echoes. Such has been the methodology employed here. No claim is made that during the talmudic era the three *ketarim* had reached their apogee, nor that the balance between them was—from a constitutional perspective—ideal (in many respects, in fact, quite the opposite was the case). Nevertheless, it was during that period of recurrent constitutional crisis that something of an apotheosis was attained, with the claims of each *keter* and its respective instrumentalities being articulated in a particularly pungent form.[10]

An initial examination of those claims reveals two features of immediate relevance; on the one hand, the autonomy of each of the *ketarim;* on the other, the interdependence of the tripartite system as a whole. The first finds expression in those texts that stress the intrinsic "sovereignty" of each *keter* (a concept itself nicely conveyed by the generic title itself, which is literally translated as "crowns"). They depict each as wielding—under God—independent authority within its own sphere of jurisdiction. This is the theme underlying the talmudic insistence that none but the principal instrument of the *keter kehunah* may enter the Holy of Holies; that only officers of the *keter malkhut* can lead the edah into a battle classified as *milhemet reshut;* and that no constitutional interpretation is valid unless it receives the sanction of the accredited representatives of the *keter torah.* No *keter,* is the clear implication, possesses a constitutional right to impinge upon the domain of the others, far less to deprive them of their proper constitutional franchises. As much is indicated by the attested historical circumstances of their creation. According to the classic sources, each *keter* originally derived its authority from a founding covenant of its own with God; the revelation at Sinai established the *keter torah;* the covenant with Aaron called into being the *keter kehunah* (Numbers 25:13); the covenant with the house of David gave institutional form to the *keter malkhut* (Psalms 89:13, Ezekiel 37:24–25). These distinctions were further hallowed by the ordained differences in the internal structures of each *keter.* From the first, each possessed its own network of officers; each, furthermore, instituted its own procedures in order to determine the manner of their legitimate appointment and succession.[11]

Interdependence—the second characteristic of the arrangement here outlined—is no less marked a feature of the ketaric system. Essentially, this principle conveys the idea that no Jewish polity is constitutionally complete unless it contains representatives of all three *ketarim* in one form or another. They are, indeed, the governmental extensions of the three pillars upon which all society must rest; remove any one, and the entire edifice is bound to collapse.[12] They are not, therefore, perceived as severely compartmentalized spheres of jurisdiction, with one (or more) being responsible for matters secular, and the other (or others) for matters religious. On the contrary, what characterizes the system in its entirety—indeed, what transposes it into a system—is the insistence that they must be seen *jointly* to participate in the most crucial areas of Jewish governmental life: judicial as well as legislative, military as well as sacerdotal. That is why authorized officers of all three *ketarim* must combine in order to give constitutional effect to acts of political significance—minor as well as major.[13] The proper Jewish polity, is the implication, is that which contains fully articulated and functioning institutions in all three *ketarim.* The good Jewish polity is that in which, furthermore, the balance between the *ketarim* is both buttressed and respected.

In practice, of course, history rarely obliged by conforming to such neat categorization. Consequently, attested heights of constitutional perfection (as here outlined) were rarely attained. The three *ketarim* can be described as manifestly articulated entities during the ancient periods of independent Jewish statehood. Most obviously was this so during the First Commonwealth. The biblical account suggests that, after an initial period of gestation, the system then settled into what might be described as a "classic" pattern: the prophets constituted the principal instruments of the *keter torah;* the priests those of the *keter kehunah;* and the kings those of the *keter malkhut.* The era of the Second Commonwealth promised to bring about the reemergence of a similar pattern, with the offices being occupied by (respectively) the sages, the priests, and—after the Maccabean revolt—the ethnarch. Even in ancient Israel, however, periods of equilibrium and harmony between the three branches of government were few and far between.

One possible instance is provided by events at the very beginning of the Israelite monarchy, when the Davidic kingship became an established fact of Jewish political life, but not yet an overweening influence over Jewish political development. Another might be sought at the very close of the biblical chronology, when the Ezra-Nehemiah covenant laid down new ground rules for Jewish constitutional expression in circumstances that necessitated a high degree of inter-*keter* cooperation. But even thus to identify brief moments of apparent constitutional equilibrium is to demonstrate the extent to which—even in the classical phase—they were exceptional. The predominant picture of Jewish government was far more turbulent and, for precisely that reason, far more interesting. For the most part, Jewish constitutional history (biblical and postbiblical alike) is shot through with the records of continuous tensions between accredited representatives of the three *ketarim,* few of whom adhered strictly to the boundaries of their prescribed constitutional demesnes, and most of whom sought to attain a preponderance of political power and the preeminence of their own facet of constitutional interpretation. It is these conflicts which, it is here suggested, account for the recurrence of tension that underlay such a large proportion of the intricate gyrations of Jewish politics, both sectional and national.

## Struggles and Their Resolution

Any synoptic examination of Jewish constitutional history from that perspective must begin by noting the fundamental resilience of the tripartite structure of the *ketarim.* For all the vicissitudes of Jewish public life, the basic parameters of the triad seem constantly to have reasserted themselves. Throughout every epoch of Jewish constitutional history, and within virtually every arena of Jewish political organization—in the diaspora as well as in Eretz Israel—each of the *ketarim* can be seen to have found some form of institutional expression. This characteristic is, in retrospect, even more remarkable than the periodic strains that have marked the relationships between representatives of these three domains. Indeed, what has to be noted in this context is not that the *ketarim* were often engaged in struggles for constitutional superiority, but that the struggles were never taken to extremes. If the sources are to be believed, the weapons employed were those of usurpation rather than destruction. Classic Jewish records provide not a single instance of the utter elimination of one *keter* by another (or by a combination of the other two); neither, for that matter, do they indicate a successful attempt on the part of one *keter* to indicate that the existence of any other is either illegitimate or unnecessary. What can be discerned, rather, are numerous examples of a process of co-option. Principal instruments of one *keter* attempted (sometimes, and for limited periods, successfully so) to attain commanding authority within the *edah* by posing as the repositories of two domains. By thus amalgamating prerogatives and wearing, as it were, two crowns, they contrived to neutralize the constitutional influence of the third and subject its officers to their own particular will.

The historical circumstances that generated such shifts in the balance of power between the three *ketarim* can be variously categorized. In some (isolated) instances, the sources indicate that a degree of imbalance must be attributed to God's own will. Such is the case with Moses, the divinely designated *eved adonai,* who combined the principal offices of both the *keter torah* and the *keter malkhut* (and, to boot, ordained the chief officer of the *keter kehunah*—Leviticus 8:12).[14] In a second category, the stimulant to a similar monopoly of power seems to have been more properly foreign, in the sense of being the direct consequence of the actions of a non-Jewish agency. The most blatant example appears to be that of the early talmudic *nasi.* Formally, his seat of authority lay in the *keter torah.* With the approval of the victorious Roman authorities, however, incumbents of this office were also able to straddle the domain of the *keter malkhut*—and thus to acquire a degree of preponderance not recalled since the days of Moses himself.[15]

The most arresting cases of constitutional usurpation, however, were of a third kind: where the stimulants appear to have been primarily— and often exclusively—internal. They are not directly attributable to an *ex machina* agency located beyond the formal confines of the *edah* but to forces and movements at work within one of its component domains. Alterations in the relationships between the *ketarim,* in other words, were in this category allied to changes of institutional command and procedure within individual *ketarim.* The two processes were interdependent, not only because one preceded or succeeded the other, but because they fed upon each other. The relationship was at once both organic and dynamic.

It is true that this structure of relationships has often been obscured.

The attested motives for many of the cases of attempted political usurpation that fall within the present category appear to have been prosaic. A highly personal quest for power—even though occasionally decked out in ideological garb—provided a conventional, but nonetheless viable, explanation for several of the constitutional struggles of Jewish history. Often, in fact, such struggles were depicted as nothing more remarkable than the individual aspirations and ambitions of the *dramatis personae* who stalk the pages of all mainstream Jewish demonologies. But even when due allowance is made for this aspect of human nature,[16] appropriate note might also be taken of the mold into which Jewish constitutional struggles have been invariably cast. Once attention is shifted from the immediate motives of particular episodes to their underlying structure, a recurrent pattern of conflict begins to emerge. Periods of relative constitutional stability, when the balance of power between the three *ketarim* was held more or less stable, seem to have been followed by moments of constitutional crisis, when one *keter* harnessed sufficient strength to assert preponderating claims which necessitated a readjustment of the alignment in its entirety. That readjustment itself held sway for some time, until it was in turn tried, tested, and—if found to be incapable of resisting the aggrandizement of another *keter*—superseded by a new constellation of the forces.

The evolution of this somewhat cyclical pattern can best be illustrated by the examination of various examples, each of which facilitates its analysis step by constitutional step. One striking instance of the *genesis* of the process is provided by the kingship of Solomon; another can be discerned during the reign of Alexander Yannai. Both epochs witnessed the emergence of a particularly strong *keter malkhut*. In both cases, moreover, that *keter* attempted to attain constitutional preponderance by encroaching upon roles that properly belonged to another *keter*. By constructing the Temple, it has been pointed out, Solomon clipped the political wings of the *kohanim* at the same time as he expanded their sacerdotal functions and provided them with economic security—a masterly stroke.[17] Yannai's achievement, although equally important, was considerably less dramatic. It was an accident of birth, which ensured that all Hasmoneans were genetically *kohanim,* that gave him a foot in both domains.

The significance of each of these episodes lies as much in the responses to which they gave rise as in the circumstances from which they evolved. Each was considered to endanger the constitutionally ordained balance between the *ketarim,* and was on those grounds resisted by the *keter,* which felt itself to be dangerously isolated. In the two cases here cited, for example, it was spokesmen for the *keter torah* who recalled the necessity for power-sharing arrangements. During the biblical monarchies the principle was ultimately to be invoked by the *nevi'im,* whose conflicts with the instruments of royal tutelage (*kohanim* included) consequently became endemic (e.g., Amos 7:10–17). During the Maccabean kingship it was enunciated by the Pharisaic sages. Clearly, it was Yannai's usurpation of a second of the three crowns that aroused their ire, quite as much as his rude infringements of the niceties of sacerdotal protocol or the alleged murky circumstances of his mother's past. "Suffice yourself with the *keter malkhut,*" they exhorted him in a classic exposition of the thesis, "and leave the *keter kehunah* to the descendants of Aaron" (T.B. *Kiddushin* 66a).

A range of factors ultimately determined the fate of such constitutional struggles. Hard-and-fast rules are difficult to ascertain, since conditions vary from one constitutional crisis to another, and success was therefore dependent upon the particular political circumstances attendant upon each. In some cases, much depended on the autonomy of the putative arrangement intimated by the aggressive *keter* and its consequent immunity to external interference, whether divine or gentile. (If, to take a very early example, Korah and his entire *edah* are swallowed up by a miraculous earthquake, then there can be no likelihood of the *eved adonai* being easily ousted from his anomalous position. Similarly, there was little hope for a restored and independent *keter malkhut* in Eretz Israel after 135 C.E., when the Roman suzerain restricted its dealings almost entirely to the *nesi'ut.*) More generally, however, the factors determining the fate of a move toward constitutional usurpation seem to have been internal, and to have depended upon the responses of the concerned branches of the Jewish constitutional system itself.

At this level, two other sets of circumstances generally proved to be particularly decisive. One was the cohesiveness of the *keter* which had originally sought to usurp power and to bring about a constitutional realignment. As much is again illustrated by the sequence of events during the biblical and Hasmonean monarchies. In the former case, it was the recurrence of dynastic squabbles within the Judean royal household which enabled Jehoiada, the *kohen gadol,* to reassert his rightful constitutional authority and play a crucial role in the coronation of Joash (as did Hilkiah the *kohen gadol* in the reforms of Josiah). In the latter, it was the internecine strife between Hyrcanus II and Aristobulus II, leading to the intervention of Pompey, which brought about the accession of Herod—who did not share Yannai's pedigree and could not, therefore, possibly continue to function as the principal instrument of the *keter kehunah* as well as the *keter malkhut.*

Equally influential, however, was the response of the *keter* which felt itself to be most threatened by a possible combination of the other two. Here, too, Jewish history provides no infallible recipe for success. In some cases, representatives of threatened *ketarim* attempted to thwart their adversaries by advocating a strategy of entrenchment and conservatism. Such, to quote an early example, was the reaction of the prophet Samuel to the prospect of a mighty *keter malkhut.*[18] Elsewhere, and more successfully, the chosen course was that of reform and flexibility. Threatened *ketarim* managed to survive, not by clinging with gritty determination to their former institutions and procedures, but both by adapting to the new constitutional circumstances and, where and when necessary, by inventing new ones. Such, most notably, was the policy pursued by the *keter torah* during the First and Second Commonwealths in response to the dangerous aggrandizement of the *keter malkhut* and its usurpation of the authority of the *keter kehunah.* In the former case, its response was to adumbrate a distinct "prophetic code," which emphasized the *keter torah's* claims to be the repository of the *edah's* moral conscience. During the Hasmonean monarchy the threat was similarly countered by the formulation of new—and distinctly nonpriestly—rules and procedures for constitutional interpretation and exegesis, and their incorporation into the tradition as the *torah shebe'al peh.*[19] Both developments were far more than the reflexive reactions of spokesmen for popular resistance to royal absolutism (though they were that, too). They were, perhaps above all, attempts to repair infringements of the constitutionally ordained balance of power between the *ketarim* by the invention and application of new mechanisms that might restore some balance to the structure which one keter considered to have been undermined by the actions of another.

It is the hypothesis of the present paper that the pattern thus outlined did not come to an abrupt end with the destruction of the Second Temple. The structure of the three *ketarim* was subsequently preserved, not only in occasional disquisitions of a theoretical nature, but in the practical manifestations of Jewish governmental forms. Not even the heterogeneous nature of diaspora circumstances, it is here contended, entirely obliterated an apparent Jewish commitment to the maintenance of the three *ketarim*. As expressions of governmental forms, they proved to be remarkably persistent and significantly universal. Therein, it might be suggested, lies the intrinsic interest of the paradigm and the possible value of its use as an analytical tool for the study of Jewish constitutional history in its entirety. That history can, indeed, profitably be structured around the fate and fortunes of each of the *ketarim* and can be analyzed from the perspective of their triangular relationships. In this way, observers might be enabled to view Jewish constitutional history not as a record of disparate events but as something approximating to a carefully structured three-legged race in which the participants—even though often out of step and not infrequently tripping each other up—seem generally to be heading toward the same constitutional goal.

## The Influence of Historiography: The Keter Torah

If the essential resilience of the structure of the three *ketarim* seems often to have been obscured, the principal reasons might lie in the nature of Jewish historiography. The vast majority of the surviving records for a study of Jewish constitutional developments derive, almost exclusively, from rabbinic sources. They were compiled by persons who regarded themselves as linear intellectual descendants of the prophets, and hence similarly entitled to serve as the mediators of God's commandments and the interpreters of His constitutional decrees. For precisely that reason, the sources tend to slant matters in such a way as to emphasize the *keter torah's* version of the march of events. That version, indeed, has become something like the "official" Jewish constitutional record. To say that is not to deny that the rabbinic sources do themselves faithfully acknowledge the theoretical rights of the other *ketarim* to an independent form of constitutional expression. Neither is it to disregard the fact that some of the philosophical and kabbalistic literature produced by subsequent generations (such as the *Sefer ha-Hasidim* of the thirteenth-century Hasidei Ashkenaz or the more influential *Zohar* compiled at roughly the same time in Sepharad) also provide glimpses of streams of thought which were at variance with the conventional rabbinic trend. Nevertheless, not until comparatively recently do we begin to possess the range of communal and individual records that might contribute toward a comprehensive interpretation of events from the perspectives of each of the three domains. Until then, the historian is constrained to rely upon sporadic digressions in an area which is for the most part dominated by the vast corpus of halakhic literature at its various levels and in its various literary forms.

It is this circumstance, more than any other, that has contributed to a Jewish version of the "Whig" view of constitutional history. Those segments of the *edah* that are perceived to express sympathy for the claims of the *keter torah* are generally singled out for attention and examined with sympathy; representatives of other attitudes tend to be neglected and their position hardly explored at all. Furthermore, and precisely because the vast majority of Jewish opinions on matters constitutional are to be found in the classic storehouses of halakhic works (the Talmud and its commentaries; the great codes; and the responsa literature), they almost invariably articulate the perspectives of the *keter torah,* by whose representatives they were for the most part compiled. Not only do they insist on the necessity for the full participation of that *keter* in Jewish government (a view that is incontestable), but also on its inherent supremacy (which is far more debatable). Carefully selected biblical verses are subjected to close scrutiny,[20] and then tendentiously set to a purpose that is as avowedly political as manifestly moralistic. They are the props upon which major halakhic authorities of the High Middle Ages supported their contention that the *keter torah* was entitled to be considered the final arbiter of constitutional interpretation.[21] They are also the basis upon which earlier tannaitic sages had constructed a strict hierarchy of three *ketarim*:

It has been found to be said: there are three *ketarim*—the *keter torah,* the *keter kehunah,* and the *keter malkhut.* Aaron merited the *keter kehunah* and took it; David merited the *keter malkhut* and took it; but behold the *keter torah* is not apportioned. This in order not to give an excuse for people to say: "Were the *keter kehunah* and *keter malkhut* still available, I would have merited them and taken them." Behold the *keter torah;* it is an admonition to everybody. For anyone who merits it is considered by God as though he had merited all three. Conversely, anyone who does not merit it is considered by God as though all three *ketarim* were available and he had forfeited them all. And should you say: "Which is the greater?" R. Simeon b. Elazar used to say: "Who is greater, he who anoints the ruler or he who rules *[ha-mamlikh o ha-molekh]?* Obviously the former. . . . ." The entire essence of the other two *ketarim* is derived solely from the strength of the *keter torah;* as it is said: "By me kings reign . . . .by me princes rule" [Prov. 8:15—16]." The Covenant which God entered into with Aaron is greater than that He entered into with David. (*Sifrei* to Numbers, chap. 119)

One striking example of the qualitative imbalance that can be produced by the quantitative discrepancy in the source materials is provided by the *keter torah's* claims to unique continuity. For a large proportion of Jewish history its spokesmen have claimed that they speak for the branch of Jewish government that is not only the most senior of the three but also the one that has been least subject to modifications in structure and form. Ever since mishnaic times (at least) they have claimed to wear a seamless cloak of uninterrupted interpretation and consecutive exegesis, and hence to embody that segment of the polity that has been least subject to disturbance. That, clearly, is the thrust of such historical excursi as Mishnah *Avot* 1:1 ("Moses received the Torah from Sinai and passed it on to Joshua, Joshua to the elders, the elders to the prophets, the prophets to the men of the Great Assembly . . . ."). That, too, is the implication of the various legal formulas which establish rules of halakhic precedence (e.g., *hilkhata ke-vatra'ei*). Such passages are designed to emphasize the perpetuity, as well as the supremacy, of rabbinic discourse. Not surprisingly, therefore, they have been assiduously cited in every one of the constitutional referents and commentaries in whose composition representatives of the *keter torah* have played a commanding role.[22] All proclaim that the thread which linked the talmudic *hakhamim* to Moses continued to stretch, unbroken, down through the *amoraim, savoraim, geonim, posekim*—even to the *gedolei ha-dor* of later eras.

The extent to which such claims are justified in the case of the *keter torah* may, it seems, have been exaggerated. The story of that domain, as has already been indicated, is not one of uninterrupted continuity. Both the First and Second Commonwealths witnessed revolutionary shifts in the persona and institutions of the *keter torah*. Challenges that originated outside its own sphere of constitutional jurisdiction then required its representatives to formulate new forms of constitutional interpretation. These remained distinct from those of the contemporary *keter malkhut* and *keter kehunah*, but they were also noticeably different from those adopted by previous institutions of the *keter torah* itself. The *navi* of the monarchy was not an exact replica of the *ro'eh* of the era of the judges; neither was the *talmid hakham* of the Talmud a carbon copy of the *navi*. (That, it might be argued, is one reason why spokesmen for the *keter torah* during the talmudic era went to such lengths to emphasize that they *were* the legitimate heirs of the prophets' mantle. The difference between the two instrumentalities was too obvious to be passed over in silence.)[23]

Equal note might be taken of the changes that affected the development of the *keter torah* at a later stage, when its claims to continuity and uniformity are less open to question. The shifts, it must be pointed out, were more evolutionary than convulsive; but they are noticeable for all that. The *yeshivot* of the high and late Middle Ages were not the precise equivalents of the earlier recruiting grounds for officers in the *keter torah,* the *metivtot* of Bavel.[24] Neither can the rabbinate of the early modern period, with its strict bureaucracy and heavy formality, be regarded as a replica of the institutional forms fashioned by the *talmidei hakhamim* of talmudic times.[25] Finally, there has been the response of the *keter* to the circumstantial and intellectual challenges of the contemporary age. The postemancipation emergence of modern "schools" of interpretation (the neo-Orthodox, the Conservative, the Reform) seems—from a strictly constitutional perspective—to provide appropriate indices of the continuing vigor of the *keter torah.* That development has, admittedly, produced divisive effects, some of which have brought about the diffusion of the demesne. It has not, however, caused its dissolution. On the contrary, by stimulating the establishment of new "seats" of Jewish learning (the rabbinical seminary, the theological college, and the departments of Jewish studies in the universities), it might be interpreted as a demonstration of the *keter torah's* continuing ability to retain its voice in the Jewish political dialogue of which it forms an integral part.

Be that as it may, a synoptic historical survey suggests that the survival of the *keter torah* (in its various manifestations) need not be regarded as a unique phenomenon in the history of the Jewish political tradition. Indeed, when due account is taken of the potentially destructive pressures exerted on the *keter kehunah* and the *keter malkhut,* it is their resilience that would appear to be the more remarkable. They, too, participated in the Jewish struggle for survival in its constitutional manifestations. Similarly, they both developed characteristics of dynamism and flexibility necessary for their continuity. Hence, each periodically effected multiple changes in its institutional structures and operational procedures. At one level, these took the form of the invention and utilization of a rich variety of terms to describe their principal instruments. At another, they generated more fundamental searches for new means of expression within the original terms of reference. These changes undoubtedly wrought realignments in their individual forms and manifestations. But, notwithstanding the various overlays of terminology and nomenclature, they did not cause their total disappearance. Still less did they precipitate structural alterations of a fundamental character in the system as a whole. Both the *keter kehunah* and the *keter malkhut* continued to articulate the Jewish political tradition's demand for two constitutional perspectives which were independent of the *keter torah*. Both, accordingly, were granted some degree of whatever formal or informal authority the *edah* possessed in the management of its own affairs.

### The Evolution of the Keter Kehunah and Keter Malkhut

It is less difficult to substantiate this thesis in the case of the *keter malkhut* than in the case of the *keter kehunah*. In part, the reasons are functional. In every one of the epochs of Jewish constitutional history there has existed a perceived need for the presence of civic instrumentalities—empowered to participate in the formulation of public policies, the adjudication of communal disputes, and the execution of political requirements. These were functions which no representatives of the *keter torah* ever attempted to fulfill by themselves for any significant length of time. Once the monarchy had received divine sanction, there was no valid precedent for their attempting to do so. *David ha-Melekh,* after all, had been *mashiah adonai* ("the Lord's anointed") and the designated forebear of the Messiah. His direct descendants, therefore, possessed a far more personal claim to partnership in the constitutional framework than did most representatives of the *keter torah*. For precisely that reason, every *nasi* in early talmudic Palestine, like every *resh galuta* in Babylon, stressed his pedigree as *nir le-veit david*.[26] Conventional rabbinic qualifications, which most of them possessed, were not their only criteria of office. The seat of their authority lay in another domain. Hence their claims to independence from (if not precedence over) such representatives of the *keter torah* as the *av bet din* and the *geonim* (respectively).

Subsequent officers of the *keter malkhut* attained equally substantial status. Most significantly was this so during the High Middle Ages, when no single instrumentality of that *keter* was operative at the very broadest level of Jewish communal organization. The centripetal nature of Jewish public life, as expressed by the emergence of the *kehillah* as the virtually autonomous unit of Jewish government, greatly increased the weight of the *keter torah*. Its representatives, operating as a communications network which rested upon halakhic correspondence between individual *posekim,* then constituted the sole means of preserving the unity of the *edah*. Even they, however, did not deny *parnassim, negidim, mishtadlim,* and *shtadlanim* a legitimate share of Jewish communal authority. During the modern era, which witnessed the reemergence of wider civic instrumentalities of the Jewish polity, these rights were further buttressed. The post-emancipation appearance of worldwide Jewish political spokesmen (as first exemplified by Moses Montefiore and Adolphe Cremieux), and subsequently of multicountry Jewish representative organizations (such as the Alliance Israelite Universelle, the Anglo-Jewish Association, B'nai B'rith, and the World Zionist Organization) demonstrated the extent to which the constitutional continuity of the *keter* had been preserved. The occasional overlapping of their claimed franchises was less significant than their collective claim to an authoritative voice in the making of Jewish public policy and their combined representation of interests which were clearly distinguishable from those bespoken by the *keter torah*. The establishment of the State of Israel, whose founding fathers deliberately invoked the slogans and symbols of Jewry's ancient political sovereignty, further underscored this development. Sporadic Israeli claims that the agencies of the state possess a prior right to defend and represent Jewish civic interests throughout the world—however often challenged—are in many respects little more than an atavistic restatement of constitutional principles enunciated at the very dawn of Jewish political history.[27]

The history of the *keter kehunah* is less amenable to linear analysis, principally because, at a particular moment in its history, it was subjected to a more severe crisis than either of the other two *ketarim*. The destruction of the Second Temple (an event that exerted an obviously crucial influence on the entire course of Jewish constitutional development) was for the *keter kehunah* a shock of catastrophic proportions. Admittedly, the weaknesses of this branch of government had long been apparent. Its independence had been undermined by the *keter malkhut* during the biblical monarchy, when *kohanim* were sometimes virtually reduced to the status of royal instrumentalities. Despite the *kehunah's* increased prestige early in the Second Commonwealth (especially under Ezra, himself a priest, and Simon ha-Zaddik, a *kohen gadol*), its principal officers had subsequently suffered from an increasing degree of disrepute, which had already become chronic by the middle generations of the Hasmonean monarchy.[28] Nevertheless, the cessation of the Temple service in 70 c.e. undoubtedly put an end to any hope that the situation might be rectified. At a stroke, the *kohanim* were then deprived of their sacerdotal roles and judicial functions. They were reduced—in fact, if not in name—to the status of fossils, in possession of only marginal constitutional rights and honorific ceremonial duties. Under such circumstances, all attempts to revive the *keter kehunah* in its predestruction form, as a genetically unified and independent branch of Jewish government, were bound to fail.[29] Readjustment, in this case, had necessarily to be a more protracted and complicated process. For a considerable length of time thereafter, accordingly, this *keter* virtually dropped out of sight.

If the Jewish political tradition was to remain true to its own principles, however, this state of vacuum could not long persist. The tradition, to put it baldly, could not suffer the complete disappearance of a domain that addressed constitutional issues from such an important perspective as the ritual dimension of Jewish life. It demanded the continued existence of a recognizable branch of government which would sanctify the polity by helping to bring God's presence into the lives of individual members of the *edah*. From this perspective, the destruction of the Temple merely compelled the domain to seek new instrumental expressions (parallel to the shift in the emphasis of ritual expressions, with the extension of synagogal worship to replace Temple service). It did not ultimately obviate the need for a separate branch of government that would sharpen the *edah's* awareness of the divine and interpret its constitution through such a prism. There was a continued and felt need for a designated and legitimated instrumentality that would help the *edah* to achieve communion with God, and which might attempt to give some metaphysical meaning to His various manifestations.

From a constitutional perspective, these functions could not be performed by the halakhic authorities who adopted the role of spokesmen for the *keter torah*. Their prisms were bound by the strictly codified doctrinal and juridical traditions of their own domain. Instead, they ultimately devolved upon a completely new spectrum of instrumentalities, whose claims to acquired sanctity increasingly came to rest upon the inspirational (and sometimes ecstatic) sources of the spiritual messages that they claimed to embody. Their ultimately philosophical heuristic objectives may not have been very different from those of the scribe-cum-rabbi of the talmudic genre. Like them, they were essentially concerned with a quest for synthesis, through the reconciliation of apparent ambiguities and the resolution of seeming incongruities.[30] Where they differed, however, was in the means whereby the depths of such concerns were explored and mediated. From the point of view of the *keter kehunah,* God and Israel had not merely to be associated by a stream of formal actions whose propriety was established through attested scholarship. They had also to be "married" through emotions and feeling. Godly government, in this sense, necessitated not only the regulating and ritualizing of specific and recurrent modes of behavior. It also required an explicit exploration of the metaphysical dimensions of the concepts upon which such regulations are based.

The distinctions must not, of course, be exaggerated. Intellect and emotion, like scholarship and piety, were never regarded as opposites in the Jewish tradition. Rather, they were perceived as two sides of a coin which—in the most authentic of cases—were combined within the personality of a single individual. Nevertheless, these attributes were sufficiently distinct to be accorded separate designations. It is this, perhaps, which explains the use of a multiplicity of terms to describe the emergence of a range of communal instrumentalities who were collectively considered to fulfill public needs distinct from those satisfied by recognized representatives of the *keter torah* and the *keter malkhut.* The *darshan,* the *moreh horayah,* the *maggid,* the *zaddik*—perhaps even the *shaliah zibbur* and the *hazzan*—provide examples of such roles at the most limited level of communal organization.[31] (The modern communal rabbi of Western communities, who makes extensive use of the moralistic sermon from a pulpit when communicating with his congregants, in many ways epitomizes the type.)[32] Groups and individuals who might be described as pietists and/or speculative thinkers (the *Hasidei Ashkenaz,* the kabbalists, the theologians of the modern era) may be adduced as instances of figures who may be considered to have exerted a wider influence. None can be described as the *functional* descendants of the classical priesthood—most obviously since they do

not perform the ritual services for which that class was solely responsible. Clearly, however, each was also significantly distinct from both
the *posek* of the *halakhah* and the embodiment of Jewish civil government. Their role, rather, has been to serve as interpreters of the Jewish
condition and thus to influence the tone of Jewish government.[33] It was,
in sum, by replacing the sacrament with the word that they kept alive
what has here been described as the essence of the priestly dimension of
the constitution and that they reinforced (or reawakened) the *edah's*
awareness of its presence in the midst of the divine.

## Conclusions

To point to such changes is not, of course, to ignore the unique
circumstances by which each was generated. It is, however, to suggest
that they might also be seen as extensions and expression of a wider
pattern, and thus as evidence of the continuity of Jewish governmental
forms over long periods and across cultural watersheds. It is at this
level that an analysis of the three *ketarim* might facilitate an understanding of the workings of the Jewish political tradition. Through the
three *ketarim,* the multifaceted character of the Jewish people seems to
have found political as well as religious expression in a way that
constitutionalized power sharing. By remaining faithful to that structure, moreover, the Jewish people might traditionally have prevented
their political life from losing all unity of form. On both counts, it is
here suggested, the concept would appear to warrant further investigation. At the very least, it might profitably be employed as an organizational device with whose assistance seemingly disparate elements of
the Jewish constitutional story might be seen to adhere to a recognizable pattern. Furthermore, a study of changes within and between the
*ketarim* might provide observers with a tool of analysis, with whose
help they might measure the forces that have helped to shape the very
texture of Jewish constitutional life.

## Notes

An earlier version of this paper was presented to the Workshop on Studying and
Teaching the Jewish Political Tradition, held in Jerusalem in August 1981 under the
auspices of the Center for Jewish Community Studies. The center, under the direction
of Professor Daniel Elazar, has been in the forefront of Jewish political studies throughout the decade of its existence, and I am grateful for the opportunity to express my

thanks to Professor Elazar and the other fellows and associates of the center for their inspiration and advice. See also D. J. Elazar and S. A. Cohen, *The Jewish Polity: Jewish Political Organization from Biblical Times to the Present* (Bloomington: Indiana University Press, 1985).

1. Hence, Abraham can invoke jurisprudential principles when haggling over the fate of Sodom ("Shall the judge of the entire world not perform justice?"; Genesis 18:25); Moses can refer to basic rights when attempting to avert God's wrath (e.g., Numbers 16:22); the *tannaim* can insist that the *torah* is "not in heaven" (e.g., Talmud Bavli [hereafter T.B.] *Bava Meziah* 59a-b); and the *amoraim* can reject the notion that the covenant was foisted upon an unwilling and virgin people at Sinai (T.B. *Shabbat* 88a and *tosafot*).
2. For one early example of the extent to which Moses was considered to have fulfilled an extraordinarily wide range of constitutional functions, see Philo, *De Sacrificiis Abelis et Caini,* IV, 130, Loeb Classical Library ed., trans. F.H. Colson (London, 1929), vol. 2, p. 189: There he is described as Israel's "captain and leader the High Priest *[sic]* and prophet and friend of God." Talmudic sources, although more precise, are only marginally less extravagant. They refer to Moses as both "king and prophet" (*melekh ve-navi*); e.g., T. B. *Shavu'ot* 15a.
   The designations of David as *eved adonai* in Psalms 18:1 and 36:1 are not manifestly of divine origin. Within the present context they might be understood to be the consequence of a human endeavor to attribute to the founder of the royal dynasty a title which intimated unquestioned constitutional primacy.
3. E.g., T.B. *Bava Batra* 75a; "The elders of that generation said: 'The face of Moses is like the sun; that of Joshua is like the moon.'"
4. Chapter 141. The fact that Moses did, eventually, place *both* of his hands on Joshua (Numbers 27:23) presents an obvious complication and provoked much subsequent rabbinic huffing and puffing (e.g., T.B. *Sanhedrin* 105b and *Numbers Rabbah* 12:9). None of this, however, satisfied the *Malbim* (Meir Loeb ben Jehiel Mikhael, 1809–1879), who restated the obvious: "And then he was commanded to lay on Joshua only one single hand and to bestow upon him only some of his honor" (*Ha-Torah ve-ha-Mitzvah,* Numbers 27:21). For an alternative (non-Jewish) view of this incident, see Thomas Hobbes, *Leviathan,* pt. III, chapter 40.
5. On these instances see, respectively, T.B. *Sanhedrin* 18b, and Maimonides, *Hilkkot Sanhedrin* 2:4; M. Beer, *Reshut ha-Golah be-Bavel bimei ha-Mishnah ve-ha-Talmud* (Tel Aviv, 1970), pp. 106–41; A. Ashtor, *Korot ha-Yehudim bi-Sefarad ha-Muslemit,* 2 vols. (Jerusalem, 1966), vol. 1, pp. 263–65; Y. Baer, *A History of the Jews in Christian Spain,* vol. 1 (Philadelphia, 1961), pp. 212–231; and Y. Heilprin, *Pinkas Va'ad Arbah Aratzot: Lekutei Takkanot, Ketavim ve-Reshumot* (Jerusalem, 1945), introduction. The constitutional position allotted to the *rabbanim rashi'im* and the rabbinical courts in the modern State of Israel—for all its anomalies—can be portrayed as an echo of precisely the same principle.
6. For which the conventional source is *De l'Esprit des Lois,* bk. XI, chap. 6. No attempt is here made to determine whether Montesquieu actually *invented* the notion; that is a scholastic minefield which has already led to the spilling of much ink. Suffice it to say that "this idea was by Montesquieu expounded with greater insight and elaboration than anyone before him; he possessed it more fully than they did, saw fully into its implications and into the conditions, social and psychological, of it being realized. It is his idea by right of conquest." J. Plamenatz, *Man and Society,* vol. 1 (London, 1963), p. 194.

7. See M. Sicker, "Rabbinic Political Thought" (Ph.D. diss., New School for Social Research, 1972), pp. 384–87. This interpretation also points out that a closer study of each of the quotations adduced here suggests that they did not really constitute constitutional comments of the sort which we seek. Rather, they fall into the category of incidental intrusions, each in its own way of intrinsic interest as an indication of the extent to which the Jewish tradition has sporadically managed to pick up occasional statements from other traditions and assimilate them to its own use. They cannot, however, be elevated to the level of comprehensive—and specifically Jewish—statements of political fact or political theory, to which, indeed, they are basically alien.

8. Most notably in the outlines of governmental provisions to be found in Deuteronomy, chapters 17 and 18, wherein, after a general introduction (17:8–13), separate paragraphs are allotted to the appointment and prerogatives of the *melekh* (Deuteronomy 17:14–20), the *kohanim* and *levi'im* (18:1–8), and the *navi* (18:9–22). This division established a form to which, it appears, the Jewish political tradition thereafter remained remarkably faithful. The source is important, since—from the viewpoint of biblical chronology—it provides early evidence for a theory of Jewish civics in conditions of independent statehood. It is also, admittedly, somewhat problematical. Confusion is likely to be engendered by the appearance of the word *yorukhah* (from the same root as *torah*) in juxtaposition to the judicial functions of the priests (17:11). For a discussion of this point that largely does away with the difficulty, see A. Cody, *A History of Old Testament Priesthood* (Rome, 1969), pp. 114–23, esp. p. 119.

   For an explicit exegetical application to these passages of the conceptual framework posited here, see the sixteenth-century commentary *Torat Mosheh* to Deuteronomy 18:1 by Moses Alshekh of Safed, especially par. 6: "Here are the three *ketarim*. . . . ."

9. Of which the most succinct, and probably the best known, is to be found in Mishnah *Avot* 4:13: "Rabbi Simeon said: 'There are three crowns: the crown of *torah*, the crown of *kehunah*, and the crown of *malkut*; but the crown of a good name excels them all.'" The purpose of this particular epigram is manifestly ethical—and that is how it has quite properly been interpreted in the standard commentaries. Nevertheless, the need to acknowledge the heuristic intentions of R. Simeon cannot be transposed into an excuse for ignoring the political realities upon which his statement was based—and which probably rendered it all the more intelligible to his contemporaries. As much was appreciated by the author of *Avot de Rabbi Natan* (chapter 41), as well as by such medievals as Duran and Bartenoro, all of whom did in fact go to some lengths to establish the biblical basis for each of the three *ketarim*. Unfortunately, their efforts have been completely wasted on some other observers, who complain that the original teaching "is only spoiled by laboured interpretations" (R. Travers Herford, *The Ethics of the Fathers* [New York, 1961], p. 113).

   Something of a case might be made for the adoption of an alternative term to that of *ketarim. Zirin* (literally "garlands" or "wreaths"), for instance, might be considered one prospective candidate, not least since it is employed in the Talmud to describe precisely the tripartite division with which we are here concerned (T.B. *Yoma* 72b). Significantly, however, Rashi's commentary on that particular text reverts to the more conventional *ketarim*—and it is in such respectable company that we beg to remain.

10. For an extended analysis, see Stuart A. Cohen, *The Three Crowns: Structure of Communal Politics in Early Rabbinic Jewry* (Cambridge University Press, 1990).

11. As is the case in all political systems, the issue of legitimate succession poses problems of a particularly thorny nature. These are too intricate to be detailed here. Briefly stated, the Jewish political tradition requires that prospective candidates for appointment to governmental office (*minui*) fulfill at least two of the following three criteria: appropriate heredity (*yihus*); popular approval and/or recognition (*haskamah*); and the enactment of a constitutionally recognized ceremony of induction into office (*meshihah*—"anointment"; or *semikhah*—"ordination"). The point to be made here is that the "mix" between these various requirements varies from *keter* to *keter,* with no two *ketarim* demanding identical qualifications. As much is evident, to take but one example, from the deuteronomic passage quoted above: the *melekh,* in that case, derives his power from a process that combines both popular selection and divine approval (in later coronation ceremonies symbolized by both acclamation and *meshihah*); the position of the *kohanim* is made principally dependent on genetic circumstances; the *navi* is "raised up from amongst his brethren" by virtue of his divinely inspired understanding of God's will (which can be given formal recognition within the *keter* by a process of *semikhah,* as in the case of Joshua, who was thus ordained by Moses).

A thorough analysis of this issue—citing classic sources and specifically referring to the differences between the three *ketarim*—is to be found in Moses Sofer, *Responsa Hatam Sofer, Orah Hayyim,* no. 12. I am grateful to Dr. Hildah Nisimi for drawing my attention to this source.

12. E.g., Joshua Falk Katz, *Perishah* to *Tur, Hoshen Mishpat* I, 1a; commentary on *Avot* 1:2.

13. The presence of representatives of all three *ketarim* in such major constitutional actions as the designation of the *melekh* is profusely illustrated in the Bible (e.g., 1 Kings 1). More interesting, because less obviously necessary, is the requirement that any extension of the city limits of Jerusalem, or of the boundaries of the Temple, similarly requires their joint presence. See Mish. *Shavu'ot* 2:2.

14. The fact that the appointee, Aaron, was also his brother, tended further to increase Moses' authority; it also helped to incite the discontent expressed by Korah. See Rashi's commentary to Numbers 16:3.

15. Significant, in this context, is the Talmud's comparison of Moses and R. Judah ha-Nasi, both of whom combined "*torah* and greatness *[gedulah],*" to which Rashi adds: Moses "was superior to all Israel in *malkhut* and *torah,* so was Rabi [Judah ha-Nasi] in the *nesi'ut* and *torah*" (T.B. *Gittin* 59a and *Sanhedrin* 36a).

16. And it is significant that classic Jewish sources do acknowledge the weight that it deserves. "R. Joshua ben Kovsai said: 'All my life I ran away from executive authority [serarah]; now that I wield it, I pour a pot full of boiling water on all who would take it away from me. Just as the pot burns, injures, and sullies—so do I act'" (T.B. *Menahot* 109b, T.J. *Pesahim* 6:1). Contrast this with the apolitical stream of Jewish thought expressed in the injunction to "love work and hate mastery *[rabbanut],* and do not acquaint yourself with government *[reshut]*" (Mish. *Avot* 1:10).

17. Of course, the construction of the Temple essentially culminated a process; it did not set a trend. Solomon's blunt deposition of Abiathar (1 Kings 2:26) had already indicated the balance of forces between the two *ketarim.* See A. Alt, "Formation of the Israelite State in Palestine," in *Essays on Old Testament History and Religion* (Oxford, 1960), p. 218 and fn. 17; Y. Aharoni, *The Land of the Bible* (London, 1966), pp. 268–73; and E. W. Heaton, *Solomon's New Men: The Emergence of Ancient Israel as a Nation State* (London, 1974), pp. 50–51.

18. For which the classic source is 1 Samuel 8:11–18. Within the present context, two points are worthy of note in regard to this passage. The first is the phrase *mishpat ha-melekh,* which may (or may not) be a deliberate echo of Deuteronomy 18:3 (*mishpat ha-kohanim*) possibly designed to contrast the two domains. The second is Samuel's own position. By virtue of his status and activities (and rather ambivalent title: *ro'eh*—"seer"), he may be described as a leader with a foot in both the *keter torah* (as a prophet) and the *keter malkhut* (as a military leader). The fact that, in his youth, he had also ministered at Shiloh might also have left him with residual claims on the *keter kehunah.* The coupling of his name with that of Moses and of Aaron in Psalms 96:6 certainly raises an intriguing question (cf. T.B. *Rosh ha-Shanah* 25a-b).

19. For one view of the political thrust of Pharisaic exegesis, see L. Finkelstein, *New Light from the Prophets* (London, 1969):

> The Mishnah in all its versions was a proclamation of tic authority of the non-priestly scholar as opposed to that of the Temple priests. It was used by the Pharisaic teachers, spiritual heirs of the Prophets and the Men of the Great Synagogue, to show that they, and not the contemporary High Priests, were the authorized interpreters of the Law. (P. 82).

> See also J. Neusner's comment in *A Life of Yohanan ben Zakkai: Ca. 1–80 C.E.,* 2nd ed. (Leiden, 1970), pp. 63–64.

> The sage was not a charismatic leader.....He could not claim authority by reason of a legitimate place in the cult. He did not have any function in the Temple service which might support his demand to direct and interpret the rites. On the contrary the sage's only authentication was his teaching and his own embodiment of the burden of his message. He represented a third force in religion, opposed to the two primary elements of charisma and traditional routine. These two elements were united in the experience of the "Torah."

20. See, for example, the exegesis of Deuteronomy 17:11, 17:18, and 32:7 in such passages as T.B. *Shabbat* 21a—23b, which are themselves amplified in such later commentaries as those of Nahmanides (e.g., to Deuteronomy 17:11). The manner in which these verses are thus examined stands in marked contrast to the treatment accorded to other passages, whose thrust is somewhat different. For a summary of much of this trend, see Abarbanel's commentary on 1 Samuel 8:4–7 in his *Perush al Nevi'im Rishonim,* pp. 202–10.

21. E.g., Maimonides, *Hilkhot Mamrim* 1:1—2, and the sources quoted in M. Elon, *Ha-Mishpat ha-Ivri: Toldotav, Mekorotav, Ekronotav,* 3 vols. (Jerusalem, 1973), pp. 220–21.

22. E.g., Ibn Daud's introduction to his twelfth-century *Sefer ha-Kabbalah,* ed. G. Cohen (Philadelphia, 1966), p. 3:

> The purpose of this Book of Tradition is to provide students with the evidence that all the teachings of our rabbis of blessed memory, namely, the sages of the Mishnah and the Talmud, have been transmitted: each great sage and righteous man having received them from a great sage and righteous man . . . .as far back as the men of the Great Assembly, who received them from the prophets, of blessed memory all.

> See also the introductions to such great codes as those compiled by Maimonides, Asher ben Yehiel, and Joseph Caro (which are all conveniently quoted in Elon, *Mishpat Ivri,* vol. 3).

23. T.B. *Bava Batra* 12a: "From the day that the Holy Temple was destroyed, prophecy was removed from the prophets and given to the sages." See also the com-

mentaries on this passage by the *Perush ha-Kotev* and the *Etz Yosef.* For further evidence, see Elon, *Mishpat Ivri,* p. 225, fn. 15.

24. On which there is a large and growing literature. For recent research in this field, see D. Goodblatt, *Rabbinic Instruction in Sasanian Babylon* (Leiden, 1975); Y. Gafni, *"Yeshivah u-Metivta,"* *Zion* 43 (1978): 12–37; and D. Goodblatt, "Hitpathuyot Hadashot be-Heker Yeshivot Bavel," *Zion* 46 (1981). For an interesting contemporary attempt to seek a direct connection between the geonic *yeshivah* and Moses, see the letters of R. Samuel b. Eli quoted in B. Z. Dinur, *Yisrael ba-Golah,* vol. 1, bk. 2 (Tel Aviv, 1961), p. 119.

25. If, indeed, such an institutional form did then exist. According to one view:

In the world of the sages during the Temple period you find no bureaucratic organization—no system whatsoever of appointment, no promotion, no remuneration, nor even any real arrangements for training or definition of functions. Likewise, there were, of course, no titles; simply the personal name of the sage was used. The titles "rabban" or "rabbi" are of a later time.

E. Urbach, "Jewish Doctrines and Practices in Halakhic and Aggadic Literature," in *Violence and Defense in the Jewish Experience,* ed. S. Baron and G. Wise (Philadelphia, 1977), p. 90.

26. In recognition of which Maimonides noted: "The *rashei galuta* of Babylon replace the *melekh*" (*Hilkhot Sanhedrin* 4:13).

27. C. S. Liebman, *Pressure Without Sanctions: The Influence of World Jewry on Israeli Policy* (Rutherford, N.J., 1977), especially chapter 8, "The Israeli Image of Diaspora Jewry," pp. 216–31; and idem, "Diaspora Influence on Israel: The Ben-Gurion—Blaustein 'Exchange' and Its Aftermath," *Jewish Social Studies* 36 (1974): 278–80.

28. E.g., T.B. *Pesahim* 57a and *Yoma* 81b; cf. earlier notions that the Messiah might be a descendant of Aaron; M. Z. Segal "Moza'oh shel ha-Melekh ha-Mashiah," *Tarbiz* 21 (1950): 133–36.

29. Whether or not any attempts were made remains an intriguing historical question. The thesis that the *kohanim* attempted to reestablish their cohesion and regain their authority was put forward by Buchler (*Kohanim ve-Avodatam*) and Dinur (in his commentary to *Pirkei Avot*). Both of these sources saw indications of this revival in the coup which brought about the deposition of Gamliel II and his replacement by Elazar ben Azariah ha-Kohen. See G. Alon, *Mekharim be-Toldot Yisrael,* vol. 1 (Tel Aviv, 1967), p. 258.

30. J. Neusner, "Max Weber Revisited: Religion and Society in Ancient Judaism," The Eighth Sacks Lecture (Oxford, 1981), esp. pp. 12–18.

31. An office which would once appear to have been of more than marginal importance. The term itself (possibly derived from the Akkadian hazzanu—"governor") is employed in mishnaic texts to describe a Temple of officer (e.g., *Sotah* 7:7–8, Yoma 7: 1–2) and was soon transposed to the synagogue (Tosefta *Megillah* 3:13 and T.J. *Berakhot* 9:4). For the *hazzan's* later participation—often formal—in Jewish communal affairs, see the sources quoted in L. Finkelstein, *Jewish Self-Government in the Middle Ages* (New York, 1936), p. 197, fn. 1; B. Rosensweig, *Ashkenazic Jewry in Transition* (Ontario, 1975), p. 42; and L. Landman, "The Office of the Medieval *Hazzan,*" *Jewish Quarterly Review* 62 (1971–72): 156–87 and 246–76. Discussing one period, Landman notes: "As a result of the educational standards of the cantorate and the fact that they were considered 'the messengers of the community' to intercede with God on the community's behalf, the status of the cantor during the Geonic Age was on a very high level. In some

areas, the *hazzan* was the head of the community."

32. For various discussions of this point, see G. S. Rosenthal (ed.), *The American Rabbi* (New York, 1977), especially A. Kass, "Watchmen for the Community," pp. 9–22; G. S. Rosenthal, "The American Rabbi as Theologian and Philosopher," pp. 77–96; and H. R. Rabinowitz, "The Rabbi as Preacher," pp. 117–40.

33. One recent example is provided by the convention of Holocaust survivors and their children held in Jerusalem in June 1981. The gathering was largely inspired by Elie Wiesel, who in many respects deserved to be regarded as one of the contemporary *edah's* interpreters of its condition and past. By explicitly covenanting to ensure the remembrance of the Holocaust, participants in the gathering—led by Wiesel—undertook to reinforce the place of that experience as a motif of Jewish public life and behavior. The presence of the prime minister of Israel at the closing ceremony of the convention (which was held at the Western Wall) further contributed to the deep symbolic significance of the event, and to its possible reinforcement of the Holocaust syndrome as an influence on Jewish political culture.

# 3

# The Rabbinic Understanding of the Covenant

*Gordon M. Freeman*

The rabbinic understanding of the covenant concept emphasized the reciprocity of the relationship between ruler and ruled. Although the tendency toward reciprocity can be traced to biblical, especially prophetic, sources, it reaches its fruition in rabbinic sources, which will be demonstrated below. That the covenant concept is largely a manifestation of reciprocity, that is, it must understood in terms of a full relationship rather than as a definable concept, is a direct outcome of the organic thought of the rabbis.

This study of rabbinic covenant thought and its political content has been thwarted hitherto by the lack of an adequate model that respects the integrity of the primary texts; usually, the models that have been applied were philosophical, searching for definitions and categories and an integrated system much in the style of the sustained political-philosophic writings of the Greeks. Thus, texts were unsuccessfully pushed into inappropriate models. In fact, the rabbinic texts defy systemization and structural analysis in neat patterns.[1] Lacking such attributes, the study of rabbinic literature for political concepts has largely been ignored.

However, looking at any political phenomenon, one would begin to realize that the philosophic-structural models are really not adequate. Human relationships, including the political, are not definable and cannot be neatly categorized. The use of such analysis ignores the vitality of human relationships since, in order to define or categorize, one has to isolate the phenomenon from everything else. Yet, its life force depends on its connections. Once it is defined, the life has flowed out, and it is no longer the same phenomenon. This study is an attempt to focus on political phenomena in its living and breathing reality rather than as a test tube specimen of dead tissue. For that reason the model that will be used here is organic.

Following Jean Piaget's physiological model where cells, while distinct, have vitality only in their relationships with other cells, this study hopes to demonstrate the application of an organic model on political life as a means of understanding it. Political life, like all life, does not fit into neat niches and categories, nor can it be adequately defined without cutting it off from other objects, relationships, or phenomena. While Piaget applies this model to the study of psychology and learning phenomena, this study applies it to political relationships. In regard to thought, Piaget writes:

> Affective life and cognitive life . . . .are unseparable although distinct. They are unseparable because all interaction with the environment involves both a structuring and a valuation, but they are none the less [sic] distinct since these two aspects of behavior cannot be reduced to one another.[2]

The political actor, whether he be subject or governor, voter or candidate, is separate, yet his political significance has meaning only in his relationship, whether it be action or reaction (or, for that matter, no action) with other actors or political concepts. In the same sense, a political concept, such as, for example, authority, cannot be adequately defined. To understand its significance one must see its relationships to other phenomena, such as the use of power, the role of the ruler and ruled, and so forth.

In the same vein, Piaget emphasizes that as a subject reacts to his environment, he not only changes but the environment changes in reacting to him, so interwoven are the two.[3] So too, in political terms, it is the relationship in its entirety that must be examined between subjects, whether they be people, concepts, or values, since one end of the relationship attains self-understanding through its transactional relationship with something else. The goal of the life form is to maintain its survival, its individuality, which can only be accomplished through its relationships with other life forms. In this sense the political can be understood in terms of how and why persons enter into authority relationships in the social environment and of the specific content and variety of those relationships against differing environments. This organic concept of the political is implicit even in the methods and content of classic Greek philosophers, for, even in his search for the pure form, Plato uses the dialogic method that demonstrates that the question has to have a response in order to attain significance. Aristotle begins his analysis of politics with the family, the most basic social form, but definitely organic since the parent only has significance in terms of his children and vice versa.

The application of the organic model is especially appropriate for rabbinic literature, since the philosophical system simply is not there. One is confronted by seemingly discreet statements with the knowledge that political relationships did indeed exist not only in terms of formal government structure, but more important, in terms of perceptions of the Jewish communities towards authority, power, and a sense of political integrity with shared political goals. The organic model applied to the literature supplies a means of searching for the vital links which explain political relationships. Max Kadushin applies the organic model to rabbinic thought and demonstrates how shared communal values supplied the cohesiveness to the Jewish community. A feeling of consensus in rabbinic literature lasts throughout the many centuries of its development despite cataclysmic historic events and internal schisms,[4] dispersal through many lands and the lack of a national center.[5]

Rabbinic thought, itself, is organic, that is, the understanding of a term or concept is dependent on its context. One idea has no meaning without its relationship to others. The idea changes its nuance as it relates to other ideas or concepts. Without defining, that is, setting limits in a spatial sense, the concepts seem to be living organisms that could not survive without proper nourishment and environmental conditions. Rabbinic thinking was not philosophical or speculative but rather the outcome of religious experience. The object of inquiry was not the object as it existed but rather its significance in its relationship to the perceiver. Experiences of God were temporal in that they were composed of God's relationship to the people in history. These experiences could be national or individual, dramatic or prosaic.

The organic complex was able to express the very relationship the rabbis were experiencing. This complex developed over time and is found in its mature state in rabbinic literature. The complex consisted of concepts "which constituted the mind of the rabbis itself, mental habits so deeply ingrained as to be inseparable from the daily, hourly facts of life they interpreted."[6] The value complex was thus responsible for the very coherence of the community. It was universally shared and understood by all members of the community. To be a member was to be plugged in, so to speak, to the value complex. While communal values were shared by each individual they did not become significant until they were applied to specific situations.[7]

The concepts within the complex are understood in terms of each other:

> All the organic concepts . . . .are integrated with one another and inextricably interweave with each other. Every organic concept possesses its own individuality and cannot be inferred from any other concept . . . .and . . . .the individuality of organic concepts and process of the integration of the organic complex as a whole are not separable, in other words, the wholeness of this organic complex and the particularity of the individual organic concept are mutually interdependent.[8]

The whole influences the parts and the parts influence the whole. There is no hierarchy of parts because each of the parts cannot exist by itself. Nor can the whole exist without the parts.

While a glance at rabbinic literature would indicate the wide divergence of opinion among the rabbis over any given issue, the contradictions are within the conceptual complex, that is, an emphasis of one concept over another.[9] The concept gives significance to experience. In its drive towards concretization, the concept even creates new events. It certainly determines the meaning of any event.[10]

The terms for the various concepts are connotative or suggestive, for "they are not definable and, furthermore, they cannot be made parts of a nicely articulated logical system or arranged in an hierarchical order."[11] They cannot be defined, for the idea embodied in them is not complete until actualized in speech or action.[12]

The concepts represent the value of the community and distinguish it "from all other historic groups."[13] Hence, Kadushin calls them value-concepts which are

> rabbinic terms . . . .(which are noun forms) but they have a different character than other types of terms of concepts . . . .they refer to matters which are not objects, qualities, or relations in sensory experience. Their function is to endow situations or events with significance. These value concepts are related to each other not

logically but organismically. This means that the value concepts are not deduced from one another and that they cannot be placed in a logical order. Instead the coherence or relatedness of the value concepts is such that they interweave dynamically.[14]

The very interpretation of the biblical text was not concerned with the Bible as literature but as a repository of community values.[15]

The rabbinic understanding of the covenant concept is a natural political outcome of the organic model, for it links individuality to relationship. Just how this is accomplished will be demonstrated in part II.

The study of the rabbinic understanding also demonstrates that theology can be a source of political ideas. Leo Strauss distinguishes between political philosophy and political theology. The latter consists of "political teachings which are based on divine revelation. Political philosophy is limited to what is accessible to the unassisted human mind."[16] In this context the sources here examined can be designated as political theology. Divine communication (revelation) is assumed. The rabbis have authority because they participate in the study of God's communicated word. There is no attempt to prove or demonstrate the veracity of this assumption. Yet it is the cornerstone of Jewish thought. It can be demonstrated that even Greek political philosophy is an abstraction from Greek theological and mythological thought.[17] Theology is concerned with the relationship and content of communication between the divine and human elements. In any religion the divine is construed as having some type of authority or at least existing as some kind of authoritative model from human behavior. Or, viewing it from another perspective, human behavior can be perceived as a reflection of divine behavior. The study of myths, legends, and even theological systems that exhibit divine activity can explain and demonstrate human behavior. Such a study can also yield another means of understanding political phenomena. How the divine governs, expresses power and authority, has significance for the men who composed the specific myth, legend, or theology. Rabbinic literature abounds with such legends and certainly has a rich theological content. By extrapolating from such material the community's political reality and goals may be understood. Theology has largely been ignored as a source for political phenomena, yet it can be a legitimate source for the examination of the political.

Finally, the historic environment of the present study demonstrates the use of polemic and its significance for the political. The integrity of the community against a hostile environment is bound to effect the content of its political statements and its urge to survive. That there is a polemical content in most political writing is self-evident, since the writer most often is either defending or attacking however subtle his style. Locke's essay against Filmer's defense of the divine rights of kings, Hobbes' attempt to influence his readers against the decentralization of authority, Plato's argument against the factional interest politics that he saw as tearing apart Athenian society, *The Federalist Papers'* arguments in defense of the proposed constitution are but a few of the many examples of polemical works that have been classics of political philosophy. Similarly, the very choice of covenant terminology and its change by the rabbis exhibit polemical writing.

With the traumatic discovery that reliance on a messianic pretender (Bar Kokhba) to defeat Rome would not succeed in fulfilling Jewish dreams of political independence, the rabbis in the second and third centuries did their best to salvage the saving remnant. These rabbinic leaders were faced with a people, dispersed throughout the world, lacking the religious center of the Temple to unify them. With political hopes dashed, the resulting depression could lead people to seek other means of religious expression. Syncretistic cults, Greek mystery religions, the youthful Christianity, and the various gnostic sects competed for Jewish souls.

The very change in covenant terminology expressed this awareness. In biblical literature the term for covenant was *brit*, a word that may have been derived from either of two roots. Conceivably, it might be a parallel to the similar root in Arabic meaning "to eat." The making of a covenant in the ancient Near East was often accompanied by a covenant meal, a cultic ceremony at which sacrifices were offered to the deity and the covenanting parties partook of the sacrificial offering. The other possible derivation could be from the Hebrew root, "to cut" and/or "to bind." When a covenant was made, the expression was usually stated in terms of "cutting a covenant," which probably refers to the act of cutting the terms of the covenant in some solid object, such as stone, so that the covenant would be permanent, yet binding the parties in a new relationship.[18] In this latter sense, the cutting would demonstrate the individual jurisdiction of each party, while they were bound in an agreement mutually recognizing their separate jurisdictions.

In rabbinic literature the term *brit* was used in a much more limited sense. It had the following four meanings: (1) circumcision; (2) indication of a Jew (*ben brit*) in contrast to a non-Jew; (3) reference to the written Torah as distinct from the oral Torah; also it was used in the context of biblical quotations; (4) use as an expression of the truth of a statement, or that of a fulfillment of a promise (as an oath).

The very multiplicity of the uses of this term as well as the paucity of sources where it is found (in relation to vastness of rabbinic literature), in contrast to the many references to Torah and the giving of the Torah, is significant. That most of the references refer to circumcision might indicate a limitation. One reason there was a reluctance to use *brit* in its pervasive biblical sense could be that Christians claimed that they were the true inheritors of the covenant through the coming of Jesus. We know of sects and Jewish groups that used covenant terminology largely avoided by the rabbis; Torah was substituted in its place. For example, various Jewish sectaries such as the Qumran sect, and the Damascus sect of covenantors used *brit* in their literature. The biblical covenant formulations appear repeatedly in their documents.[19]

The use of covenant in Apocryphal literature, New Testament, and the Septuagint follows a similar pattern.[20] The New Testament uses the Greek word *diatheke* for covenant, which is the exact word used in the Septuagint translation of the Old Testament. The term actually refers to a last will and testament and, like most translations, does not actually fit the word brit *as covenant.*[21] In fact, *diatheke* finds its way into Jewish law as a technical term for a will.[22] The point here is that *diatheke* is not understood as the equivalent of *brit* in rabbinic literature. *Brit* and its Greek "equivalent," *diatheke*, were employed by various sects to demonstrate a renewal of the covenant of Israel, that they were the new Israel, replacing the Jewish people. Because of their sins, the Jews had been punished and rejected by God. It is the new group who now receives God's covenant.

The rabbis were careful in their use of *brit* most frequently referring to circumcision. The claim of those groups, that they were the inheritors of the covenant, was not legitimate because they did not require circumcision. In substituting torah for the covenant term, the rabbis were demonstrating that by their study, interpretation, and application of Torah to life the Jewish people was the only group continuing and living according to the original covenant. The use of *brit* specifically as covenant was no longer necessary, since the covenant had once and for all time bound God and Israel. Even though the Jewish people might have sinned and been punished they were not rejected. The Jews were still bound to the covenant, as God was still bound to his covenant with the Jewish people, the Israel of the Bible. Renewal of the original covenant was not necessary. Covenant, the central concept of rabbinic thought, took on polemical aspects due to historic circumstances. The change of terminology, a radical measure taken by the rabbis, demonstrates its significance to the integrity of the community and its centrality for the body politic.

The study of the rabbinic understanding of covenant then is an appropriate source for political thought. As an organic concept it is a proper means to demonstrate how an organic model can be applied to political thought. As an outcome of theology, the covenant concept can be used to explain how theology can be a source for political ideas. The covenant concept was central to the polemic between groups vying for legitimacy and integrity and, as such, demonstrates its significance as the cohesive concept explaining the purpose of a specific political entity.

This study will attempt to demonstrate that the covenant concept was perceived by rabbinic literature as positing a reciprocal relationship. It was the means of socialization accomplished through participation as an object of study (i.e., Torah study). As the opportunity for participation (and hence socialization) was universal, authority was envisioned as internalizable by each participant (each person could and should become a rabbi, the source of communal authority).

## Reciprocity

The rabbinic understanding of covenant emphasized the reciprocal relationship between authority and people. Usually political language speaks in terms of a ruler-ruled dichotomy. However, such language leaves out the possibility stressed by the rabbis of the ruled to become rulers over themselves. Every relationship has its benefits and costs. People enter a relationship hoping that the benefits will more than offset the costs. In the reciprocal relationship there are no hidden costs. The obligations of membership are explicit. The authority is clear concerning its intention and expectations. Compassion (*hesed* and *rahamim*) is emphasized in order to promote mutual trust. While punishment might be the consequence of disloyalty and rebellion, it is a clear expectation. There is no need to fear the unknown whim of the authority. Fear of the unknown is not a tool used to ensure compliance. In that sense the covenant relationship is open and explicit, that is, it is communicated.

There are two ways of understanding reciprocity. There are rights, claims, and penalties that parties to the agreement accept. On the other hand, there is the trust, love, and mutual expectation of the fulfillment of obligations resulting in security without losing the sense of individuality. The rabbis used the covenant theme to enhance the viability of the community during dangerous times. We have suggested that they were not adverse to its utilization for polemical purposes. But as the leaders of the people they pointed to the opportunity inherent in the covenant relationship, the establishment of the kingdom of heaven on earth which was the crux of the reciprocal relationship. The closer the relationship the stronger the authority of the individual over himself. This might seem paradoxical, for we usually expect the authority to maintain a distance from the governed in order to protect and enhance its powers. In a sort of economy of power, the more power the authority has the less power there is for the governed. Or, if the relationship of the authority with the governed is a close one, we might expect the authority to be either weak or so overwhelming that it engulfs the governed (e.g., "big brother" in George Orwell's *1984*). In rabbinic political thought neither of these tendencies obtain. Since the relationship is mutual and reciprocal when the authority is close and clearly recognizable, not only is its power increased but the power of the individual and community that accepts its rule is increased as well. Power is limited only by the failure of either party to maintain the agreement. The kingdom of heaven comes into being when the relationship becomes completely reciprocal; everyone has authority, and power of one over and against another becomes meaningless.

The intimate relationship between God and Israel is bound by a mutual agreement. This agreement is the Torah-covenant. Both parties to the agreement depend on each other for the full realization of their existence.

Rabbi Shimon ben Elazar said: When the Israelites do God's will, his name is exalted in the world. . . . .When they do not do his will, his name is profaned in the world, as it says, "And they profaned my holy name" ( Ezekiel 36:20).[23]

Rabbi Azariah in the name of Rabbi Y'hudah ben Shimon said: When the Israelites do God's will, they add to the power of God on high. When the Israelites do not do God's will, they, as it were, weaken the great power of God on high.[24]

The relationship between God and Israel can be characterized as inter-dependent. Each influences the other. Each impinges on the other's existence determining the other's existence. Of course Israel's observance or lack of it will result in rewards or punishments; God will determine if he should act on her behalf or not. In doing God's will, in other words, maintaining the covenant, Israel proclaims the legitimacy of his authority to the entire world. Israel demonstrates that God's authority has manifested itself over Israel. The purpose of broadcasting this message universally is to fulfill the ideal that people will recognize that only God's authority has validity.

The receiving of the Torah takes on cosmic significance; the very existence of the world depends on it. The Torah not only is a plan for moral order but the order of nature as well.[25] The creation of the world is understood to be connected to the giving of the Torah. Creation without Torah has no purpose; Torah gives order, predictability and reliability, to creation. But the Torah does not have significance unless it is accepted. Israel, in receiving the Torah, takes on cosmic importance. Israel is the catalyst for the Torah coming into the world so that it can insure the existence of the cosmos: "Rabbi Elazar said: If it were not for the Torah, heaven and earth would not be established, as it is said: 'Without my covenant day and night, the laws of heaven and earth I would not place' (Jeremiah 33:25)."[26]

The Torah, God's blueprint for the creation of the world,[27] has to be accepted by creation or it will return to its primeval form of chaos and confusion (*tohu vavohu*). The world is created on condition that it eventually accepts the Torah in time; that is to say, the entire existence of the world depends on the agreement between creator and created. Without such an explicit acceptance of the agreement the created order of the world could not exist. Nature, then, depends on an explicit agreement and is subservient to Torah. Man determines by his acceptance or rejection of the natural order of the world, which is based on Torah, its very plan. As Torah is continually communicated to man, his fear of nature decreases, for his control over it increases.

Agreements, in order to be sustained, require trust. When all parties to the agreement understand the consequences of it, they predict what will happen, for the Torah's contents are communicated rather than hidden. The fabric of society and the entire creation are based upon trust, which increases as each party experiences the other and realizes that the agreement is being observed. God does not break his agreement since it is his attachment to the world and the very reason for its creation.

Inherent in the idea of agreement is the individuality of each party:

> Rabbi Yishmael says, Generalities were proclaimed at Sinai, and particularities in the tent of meeting. Rabbi Akiba says, Both generalities and particularities were proclaimed at Sinai, repeated in the tent of meeting, and for the third time on the plains of Moab. Consequently, there is not a single commandment written in the Torah in connection with which 48 covenants were not made. Rabbi Shimon ben Y'hudah of K'far Acco said in the name of Rabbi Shimon, "There is not a single commandment written in the Torah in connection with which 48 x 603,550 (number of people) covenants were not made." Rabbi said of the words of Rabbi Shimon ben Y'hudah of K'far Acco who said in the name of Rabbi Shimon, There is no single commandment in the Torah that 48 x 603,550 commandments were not made by 603,550 (people). What is the issue between them? Rabbi Mesharsheya said, the point between them is that of personal responsibility and responsibility for others.[28]

Every single commandment has been given to each person and is binding on everyone because of the individual's experience of receiving the Torah. Each person perceives the event uniquely, depending on his own ability to comprehend it. The collection of individuals becomes a community through the shared experience of the event. Ultimately, the covenant is the responsibility of each individual. However, because he is a member of the community, he is liable for the acts of its individual members. Communal responsibility towards the covenant is the source of its integrity and identity.

The individuality of covenant partners inevitably leads to conflict and struggle. Assimilation of the ego into the divine is dichotomous with an organic covenant concept. Loss of individuality means that there can be no relationship. There is simply no one with whom to relate. God is one, unique, and so is each person created in his image. The relationship between unique persons is the crux of the covenant concept. Just as the individual has no meaning if he stands completely alone and apart, for then he has no one with whom to compare himself, so God cannot have meaning without a world of individuals:

> "Moses went up unto God" (Exodus 19:3). It is written, "You have ascended on high, you have fled captivity captive" (Psalms 68:19). What is the meaning of "You have ascended"? You have been exalted because you did wrestle with angels on high. Another explanation of "You have ascended on high," no creature on high has prevailed as Moses did. Rabbi Berekhiah said, the length of the tablets was six handbreaths; two were, could we speak thus, in the hand of him that called the

world the world into being. Two handbreadths were in the hands of Moses, and two handbreadths separated the two pairs of hands. Another explanation, "You have ascended on high, you have fled captivity, captive." Lest you think that because he captured it, he took it gratis, the psalmist adds, "You have received gifts among men," that is, it was given to him as a prize. Lest you think that he actually paid him money, the psalmist adds, "You have received gifts among men," that is, it was given to him as a prize. Lest you think that he actually paid him money, the psalmist assures that it was the gift; it was given to him as a gift. At that moment the angels wished to attack Moses [because the angels had asked God to give the Torah to them, (see, Shabbat 88b)]. The Holy One Blessed be He made the features of Moses resemble those of Abraham and said to the angels, Are you not ashamed to touch this man to whom you descended from heaven and in whose house you ate? God said to Moses, it is only for the sake of Abraham that the Torah is given to you, as it is said, "You have received gifts among men."[29]

Based on a legend that the angels did not want God to give the Torah to Israel and argued with him, saying that she would not observe it, this statement declares that Moses won the Torah for Israel by contending with the angels and wresting it from them. That he was able to keep it was the prize or gift that he received for winning it.

We might speculate by analyzing this statement in terms of the psychological implications of the authority figure. There is evidently a conflict going on within the authority figure itself whether to take the risk and give the people the opportunity for responsibility. Meanwhile, the people wrest responsibility from authority through force which seems to settle the issue for the authority. By winning they prove themselves capable of and willing to accept responsibility. Unlike the story of Prometheus in Greek mythology where punishment is the consequence of audacity, here reward is given for wresting the Torah from the divine. A parallel Midrash (Midrash on Psalms 8:2, Buber edition, page 73f) adds that the reason God gave to the angels for giving the Torah to man is that man had freedom of choice whereas the angels did not and hence could not be tempted. To make a covenant with angels would not make any sense, for the angels had no choice but to keep God's word.

The closest term in Hebrew for reciprocity is *hesed* (or its equivalent, *g'milut hasadim*), "deeds of loving-kindness," a value that goes beyond the minimum utilitarian aspect of living together in society (which would be closer to the concept of contract). Its purpose is to lead to greater cohesiveness between people. Acts of *g'milut hasadim* include attending a funeral, visiting the sick, helping an orphaned bride. Such acts are to ensure that individuals are mutually concerned for each other. Each person is obligated in a very specific way to others living in the society. When those obligations are fulfilled constantly a trusting relationship results, for each person can know what to expect from his fellows. Herein one can discover the strands of individuals that are woven into a social fabric. Such deeds (along with prayer) replaced the sacrificial cult after the destruction of the Temple, according to Rabban Yohanan ben Zakkai.[30] By acting in such a manner towards each other within the community, the community itself could look forward to God's act of redemption.[31] The word *hesed* refers to "acts in conformity with the covenant between man and God."[32]

"The covenant and the love" (*habrit v'et hahesed*, Deuteronomy 7:12). Rabbi Shimon Ben Halafta said: The matter is like the king who married a lady who brought him two precious ornaments. And the king also added two ornaments, (to match them). But when his wife abandoned her two ornaments, the king abandoned his. After a time she arose and purified herself and brought back her two ornaments, and then the king brought back his two. The king said, the four together shall be made into a crown and shall be put upon the queen's head. So you may find that Abraham gave his descendants two precious ornaments, as it is said: "For I know him that he will command his children after him, and they keep the way of the Lord to do righteousness and justice" (Genesis 18:19). So when the Holy One Blessed be He set up two ornaments to match the other two, namely love and compassion as it is said, "He turned justice into gall and righteousness into hemlock" (Amos 6:12). So God also took his two, as it is said, "I have taken away my peace from this people, even love and compassion" (Jeremiah 16:5). Then Israel arose and purified herself and brought its two back, and God restored his two likewise . . . .(Isaiah 1:27; 54:10). But when Israel brings its two, God gives his two and God says: The four together shall be made into a crown and shall be placed upon Israel's as it is said, "I will betroth you unto me in justice and righteousness and in love and in compassion" (Hosea 2:19).[33]

The Hebrew term *hesed* refers to covenant love, the love relationship between people who make agreements because of their mutual feelings. The word *rahamim* refers to parental love (here translated as compassion), since its root comes from the word *rehem*, which means womb. The verse quoted from Deuteronomy 7:12 places *hesed* together with covenant in parallel which we would expect. The other verses quoted include *hesed* and *rahamim*, so that to the rabbis, *rahamim* was also parallel to covenant. Perhaps the ancient biblical differentiation between these two words for love, *hesed* and *rahamim*, was no longer significant to the rabbis. The usage of the two words simply were regarded as synonymous for love. However, the rabbis regarded the giving of the covenant as an act of love, and Israel's response was to be just and righteous, that is, to act with responsibility:

> Rabbi Y'hoshua ben Hanina said, at first he went to the sons of Esau, he asked them, will you receive the Torah? They said to him: Master of the world, what is written in it? He said to them, You shall not kill. They said to him: Our trust is dependent upon the sword, as it is said, "By your sword you shall live" (Genesis 27:4). We are unable to receive the Torah. After this, he went to the Amonites and Moabites. He said to them: Will you receive the Torah? They said to him: Master of the world what is written in it? He said: You shall not commit adultery or lustful acts. They said to him: They did not come into being except through lust as it is written, "The two daughters of Lot (supposed ancestors of Amon and Moab) conceived through their father" (Genesis 19:36); we are unable to receive the Torah. After that he went to the Ishmaelites. He said to them: Will you receive the Torah? They said to him: Master of the world, what is written in it? He said to them: You shall not steal. They said to him: They cannot live except through stealing and theft, as it is written, "He will be a wild man, his hand will be in everything" (Genesis 16:12). We are unable to receive the Torah. After that he went to Israel. They said, "We will do and listen."[34]

Unlike the nations of the world, Israel did not question the content of the Torah before accepting it. Israel's glory lies in her willingness to listen to God's communication of the Torah, according to the rabbis. This act of trust resulted in the intimate relationship between God and Israel.

Because God chooses Israel through an exclusive relationship, Israel reciprocates by sanctifying God's name.[35] Sanctification of self is a sanctification of God. Holiness is attained by observing the commandments that make Israel unique among nations. The sanctifying act is a confirmation by Israel of this exclusive relationship.

> "And the Lord spoke to Moses, saying, speak unto all the congregation of Israel and say to them, holy shall you be for I the Lord your God am holy." Why was this section of the law to be said before all the congregation? Because the majority of the most important commandments of the Torah are contained in it. "Be holy for I am holy." That is, if you sanctify yourselves, I reckon it as if you sanctified me, and if you do not sanctify yourselves, I regard it as if you did not sanctify me. It does not mean to say, if you did not sanctify me I am not sanctified, and if you do not do so I am not sanctified, for it says, "I am holy." I abide in my holiness whether you sanctify me or not.[36]

God is independent of Israel. Yet God can be sanctified only through Israel. The world will not realize God's sanctity unless Israel acts on it. Holiness or sanctity is a manifestation of the kingdom of heaven. To sanctify it would be an act of legitimizing God's authority. Israel's unique and reciprocal relationship with God is to lead to the rule of God in this world which cannot occur unless "his kingship is received by mankind, for there is no king without a people."[37] God had "concluded this covenant of mutuality with Israel"[38] for the purpose of realizing his kingdom over the entire world.

The Torah must be mutually and eternally binding if the relationship between God and Israel is to exist:

> "Before me" (Exodus 20:3). Why is it said? In order not to give Israel an excuse for saying: Only those who came out from Egypt were commanded not to worship idols. Therefore, it is said, "before me"—just as I am living and enduring forever so also you and your son and your son's sons to the end of generations shall not worship idols.[39]

Although previous generations have covenanted with God the present generation might not feel compelled to give allegiance to his authority. Tacit consent, a solution by later contract theorists, that is, by virtue of living in society they are consenting to the covenant even though it was originally made earlier, solves the problem in a passive sense. To live in a society is to consent to its legitimacy; remaining in the society is regarded as a passive acceptance of the contract. Tacit consent makes sense in the context of Greek philosophy or Roman jurisprudence where *polis* or *imperium*, the form of the state, is an end in itself. If the *polis* or *imperium* dissolves, then consent dissolves as well. But in Jewish thought it is not the form of the state or society that is fundamental but the covenant relationship between persons and authority. Since authority by nature is always present, the very legitimacy of the relationship lies in the existence of authority just as the very existence of the state is the legitimacy of the social contract. The descendents, by virtue of the instruction of their fathers, by receiving the tradition and observing it, constantly renew the relationship.

There is at least one alternative understanding of covenant, that of grace which was held by some of the rabbis (the implications of which will be explained in the conclusion).[40] However, the normative rabbinic understanding of covenant emphasized its reciprocal dimension which fits into the organic mode. Covenant as reciprocal with community and the individual membership in it as well as being reciprocal with the entire cosmos points not only to its all-pervasive character but also to its changing implications depending on the specific relationship that is realized. Seemingly amorphous at first glance, its vitality derives from its concretization in specific events, in statements, and in the participation of those who regarded themselves as members of the community by observing and studying the content of the Torah-covenant. Such participation gave it its living, almost breathing, quality. Realization of the covenant was dependent on the participation of the community. But so reciprocal was the relationship that the reality of the community was dependent on its participation in the covenant.

## Socialization Through Participation

Socialization is the process whereby individuals identify themselves as being part of a social entity. Socialization can be more or less intense: the individual could feel only tangentially part of the community, spend little time or energy in its regard, or he could be identified intensely with it almost to the point of losing his own individuality and assimilating himself into the groups' activities, goals, and personality. The socialization of the individual can be transitory and superficial, for example, the fan at a baseball game; whereas the socialization and identification of the fan is intense during the game it usually loses its power and intensity when the game is over. Socialization can lead to almost complete internalization of social goals and aspirations. The process of socialization can be accomplished through education, indoctrination, mass media, or, less dramatically, by merely living in a specific environment over a period of time, adopting its language, vocabulary, and the syntax of cultural intercommunication. The specification of rewards and punishments is another means used to encourage socialization.

Applying an organic model to socialization, the individual would understand his own significance in terms of his relationship with the social entity. The meaning of his existence would be linked to the intensity, both qualitatively and quantitatively, of his relationship with the social dimension and his self-identification with its goals. Participation is a specific means of socialization, depending on the type of society. Those societies requiring passive acquiescence would not encourage participation as a means of socialization. Participation would most likely occur in a society emphasizing reciprocal relationships, requiring not only active response to its norms but individual application of the norms in specific situations. Such a society would have to allow for flexibility of expression while being secure in the success of the individual's internalization of the social norms.

The Sinai event created a community from disparate individuals who were to be responsible for one another because they agreed to accept the covenant:

> Rabbi Y'hudah (the Prince) says: This proclaims the excellence of Israel, for when they all stood before Mt. Sinai to receive the Torah, they all made up their mind alike to accept the reign of God joyfully. Furthermore, they pledged themselves to one another concerning not only overt acts. The Holy One Blessed be He, revealed himself to them in order to make a covenant with them even in regard to secret acts, for it is said: "The secret things belong to the Lord our God, and the things that are revealed, etc." (Deuteronomy 29:28). They said to him, concerning overt acts, we are ready to make a covenant with you, but we will not make a covenant with you in regard to secret acts, less one of us commits a sin secretly, and the entire community be held responsible for it.[41]

The concern for the terms of the covenant are here elucidated to prevent misunderstanding. An assumption that the people had the power to take exception to the terms of the covenant is emphasized here. The community could not bear the might of God's justice if it was held liable for the secret sins of individuals. It did not want to be responsible for those who did not accept the community norms and values, that is, those who had not been sufficiently socialized.

The covenant binds the nation together to defend itself against the claims and the might of the nations of the world. Like the *polis* for the Greeks and the *imperium* for the Romans, the covenant is the operative ideal that is the quintessence of Israel's being. Unlike the *polis* and the *imperium* the covenant is not limited to a specific place. The covenant relationship establishes the basis of authority, the content of knowledge and the purpose of the community. God is the authority, but he offers the opportunity for partnership to those who fully participate in the relationship. Knowledge of the covenant is the key to full participation.

The mutual interdependence exemplified by communication and commentary, between authority and community, marks the rabbinic concept of government and rule. Everyone who participates in the communication by studying and applying the text to life participates in God's rule. God does not govern from some transcendent place handing down edicts to be obeyed. Rather, the reality of government comes from the active response towards the communicated word.

Communication, in a political context, could be understood as openness and the assumption that decisions are not made arbitrarily.[42] The will of the authority is not only knowable, but it is inherent in the very process of socialization to continue to discover, decipher, and relate to its communication. The obligation to respond completes the act of governing. As the governed progressively know more of the will of authority it becomes its own authority. Each person is ultimately to govern himself by relating to the agreement that binds him to authority. The shared experience of relating to the agreement binds him to others who participate in the same type of endeavor.

Political crises usually cause tears in the social fabric; that is, they threaten the socialization of the individual who might look for alternative societies. Hence, such crises provoke a reexamination not only of the structure of the polity but of its myths, purposes, and direction as well. The political thinker may return to the origins of society and reinterpret its beginnings in order to find new purpose for the existence of the community. Most political thought was a consequence of crises that were provoked by historical circumstances. War, revolution, the introduction of new groups into the society, the strengthening or weakening of existing social classes due to changing economic conditions can cause a profound disorientation of the polity. Under such conditions the old answers and solutions no longer seem appropriate.

One strategy in dealing with such crises is to forge new paths to establish new purposes. Political tradition is abandoned as new forms and ideas are presented (sometimes merely a superficial cover for the "old"). Another strategy is to interpret recent events in the light of ancient traditions. This strategy is especially appropriate when the condition of the community during and after the crisis is so weak that it is necessary to establish continuity and security, and to demonstrate to the people that the old ways are still relevant even though the situation might seem to have changed. Old prophecies and ancient predictions might be revived to explain that what seems new has already been foretold by previous sources. It was the latter strategy that was used by the rabbis. The crisis facing the Jewish people in the second and third centuries was certainly a profound one. The entire structure of the community had been destroyed. Yet the rabbis were able to successfully respond by reinterpreting the communal myth to give purpose and meaning to the new political reality. Using the ancient biblical covenant as a theme they were confronted by the problem that many groups claimed to be the inheritors of that covenant. By changing covenant terminology and using it as a polemic they claimed that their interpretations originated at the same time as the biblical covenant and were exclusively given to their group as an inheritance; by virtue of their traditions of interpretation they were the true Israel.

Through their activity as teachers they could transmit their tradition and embellish it. By making it universally available to all Jews they could encourage the people to share their authority. Education became the means to survival. Since anyone could become a rabbi and study was encouraged, structure was meaningless, for every rabbi was an authority. The control over the curriculum and the careful indoctrination by the rabbis of the community was the means of socialization and the method to prevent anarchy. Although there were schisms, those who remained in the community were socialized by the knowledge they received. Enough flexibility was possible so that a certain amount of dissent was practically institutionalized; both majority and minority opinions were recorded in discussions of Jewish law, and a wide latitude of interpretation was granted in the lore. The basis of the community was to be found in the shared experiences and values that held it together. Each person could participate in the study on the ancient knowledge.

Political knowledge in rabbinic epistemology meant that the connection with the past gave continuity to existence. The promise of the future gave a purpose for existence. The universal availability of power and authority became not only the means to effectuate goals but was a factor in sharing communal responsibility. Participation in study of the communication that bound the community and the response to it (through commentary) was the means of socializing the individual into the communal norms and goals. Having internalized and individualized those norms and goals, the participant gained authority as well.

## The Internalization of Authority

The rabbis envisioned the internalization of authority by each participant through the study of Torah. Most often, authority is regarded as an objective phenomenon, outside the self; someone outside influences the thoughts and behavior of those who acquiesce to it. Certainly, in a theological context, one would expect such objectification of authority. A transcendent, all-powerful God rules over his subjects.

Yet, this model of authority really is one-sided and expresses the viewpoint of the authority towards his subjects. The objectification of authority, strictly defining roles and duties and separating between ruler and ruled, tends to be a means to protect authority rather than an explanation of authority relationships. Applying the organic model we would explain such a relationship first in terms of mutual dependence, that neither ruler nor ruled have significance without the other. Authority is understood as the source of communication. As that communication flows out to those with whom the source relates, authority becomes a shared phenomenon and becomes reciprocal as agreements (covenants) are made that promote mutual survival as well as meaning and significance through their relationship. Although communication begins as a one-sided flow, as the recipients internalize it (in the same way as the proto-internalization by the source) it becomes a two-way flow. Rabbinic covenant thought is concerned with the character of the original source of communication, the authority, God, so that it can understand its own internalized authority:

> Rabbi Menaheman in the name of Rabbi Tanhuma bar Hiyya and Rabbi Mani in the name of Rabbi Yose bar Zevida supported Rabbi Ze'era's interpretation of Exodus 20:7 (that you are not to take upon yourself God's authority as voiced in the Torah if you are not worthy of such authority) by citing another verse, "He that philanders with a woman lacks understanding" (Proverbs 6:32), that is, whenever a man takes on Torah's authority merely to use it, he is no more than a philanderer who uses a woman's body (but does not truly possess her). . . . .According to Rabbi Abbahu, God said: I am called holy and (when you take on Torah's authority you, too, may be called holy but take care). Unless you have all those attributes of mine which I revealed to Moses (Exodus 34: 6–7), You may not take on such authority.[43]

Human authority must be modeled on the authority of God. Power is corruptible when instead of serving the community it is used for self-aggrandizement. Yose bar Zevida[44] and Mani[45] were heads of academies while Tanhuma bar Hiyya was a wealthy man. All of these rabbis, because of their positions, appreciated the use of power. Rule even by the authority of the Torah, could become an opportunity for personal gain. Rabbi Abbahu,[46] who had constant contact with the Roman government, was concerned lest Jewish government become like that of the Romans. The attainment of holiness is to bring recognition of the kingdom of heaven. Specifically it refers to the imitation of God.[47] This statement compares human rule and divine rule. To be a legitimate ruler one must be holy like God.[48] Holiness is attained by adhering to the Torah. This commitment to try to conform with some transcendent force might seem strange at first. However, this phenomenon is pervasive in human thought; only the terminology changes. Nature or history, even the "objectivity" of modem science as a standard to which the human endeavor is to strive, gives direction and discipline to human thought. It seems that humanity attempts to transcend itself. In examining political thought one must try to discover the vision or ideal that is used as a measuring rod by the specific thinker. He might even have a concept of human potential that transcends the present situation as he perceives it. He understands his world and explains political phenomenon in terms of that vision; problems are caused by the failure to internalize that authoritative vision.

God and the rabbis were to be partners in interpreting the Torah and applying it to the community. According to the Midrash God studies Torah and utters the various traditions in the name of their rabbinic authors.[49] Because they shared the act of study with God, their right to interpret the Torah, and thus respond to the communication, and in turn, communicate in their own right, was legitimate.

However, the rabbis had to be accepted by the community in order to be effective. Their claim to authority was based on their exclusive knowledge of the Torah which they were willing to impart. Their program emphasized "loyalty to a way of life based on literature."[50] The criterion for this loyalty was adherence to the Torah. The rabbis had always claimed that their interpretations were authentic. Their sanction was from Sinai, transmitted from one generation to the next. The chain of tradition recounted in Mishnah Avot 1:1 demonstrated that the Torah had passed from Moses ultimately to them. Only the rabbis could claim that their traditions emanated directly from Sinai.

In the ancient world antiquity was a determining factor of authenticity and was probably the motivating factor behind the declarations that all of the Torah, both oral and written, were from Sinai.[51] "The aim of the rabbis . . . .was to find out what God, the sold author of revelation, meant by these particular words, not in a particular moment and for particular persons, but for all men and all time."[52] This aim was repeated in sermons in the synagogue and in lessons in the academies. The people were taught exactly what God required of them by those who possessed that special knowledge.

In sum, the rabbis based their claim to authenticity on the chain of tradition as they understood it. That chain did not include kings and priests. Since the priests had lost their influence with the loss of the Temple ritual, and kings no longer ruled, there was really no one within the community who could effectively oppose their claim. The chain of tradition was also very attractive to the people because it was not exclusive. It was open to anyone who studied Torah. Tales of the humble beginnings of Hillel and Akiba were popular and emphasized that ability alone was the criterion for leadership.

The school became the most significant institution of postbiblical Judaism.[53] Knowledge of the Torah as taught by the rabbis became the source of authority. The rabbis, like Plato, understood the role of education as a means of molding the community. However, in contrast to Plato, their education was not to lead to differentiation between rulers and ruled. The universality of education was to effectuate the biblical vision of a "kingdom of priests" (Exodus 19:6). According to Louis Ginzberg, if it were not for Israel's apostasy before the golden calf there would not have been any need for a specific tribe of priests. All of Israel would have become a universal priesthood.[54] The rabbis took the injunction to be "a kingdom of priests" seriously. "Since they lived in the same purity as the priests, its members claimed holiness equal to those who lived correctly and superior to that of incorrect priests."[55] The Pharisees consciously adopted all the priestly laws of purity and were careful to use only properly tithed products to attain this parity with the priests in the Temple. While achieving this parity the Pharisees also contended for power with the priests. Yet as long as the Temple stood, the priests still maintained their special status since the rabbis could not perform sacrifices in the Temple. After the destruction the priests lost this special function, and the rabbis, by virtue of adopting priestly laws of purity, attained the same status. "The hereditary aristocracy had to give way before the aristocracy of the learned."[56]

Rabban Yohanan ben Zakkai taught that the Temple was not an end in itself. The Temple had represented the "service of God through sacrifice."[57] Now that there was no longer a Temple he taught that what counted were Torah and piety rather than power and national political independence (which the Temple symbolized). Priestly ritual purity was to be universally observed in order to expiate sin everywhere—in the home and in the marketplace. Sacrifice was interpreted in terms of acts of compassion and prayer which could expiate the sin (instead of the actual sin offerings which were no longer possible):[58]

> Rabbi Abdimi from Haifa said: Since the day when the Temple was destroyed prophecy has been taken from the prophets and given to the wise.[59] Is then a wise man not also a prophet? What he meant was this: Although it has been taken from the prophets, it has not been taken from the wise. Amemar said: A wise man is even superior to a prophet as it says, "And a prophet has a heart of wisdom" (Psalms 90:12). Who is compared with whom? Is not the smaller compared with the greater? Abaye said: The proof (that prophecy has not been taken from the wise) is that a great man[60] makes a statement, and the same is then reported in the name of another great man.[61]

The rabbis (the wise) as interpreters of God's word were, in a sense, God's spokesman and were not adverse to confronting God like their prophetic predecessors.[62] Their confidence in the knowledge of God's word led to a wide latitude in their interpretations of the written Torah.[63] According to Travers Herford, "Pharisaism is applied prophecy."[64] The rabbis functioned as a continuation of the prophetic tradition.[65] Where the prophets failed in spreading God's word, the rabbis succeeded through their schools which educated the people in the ways of Torah on a massive scale.[66] Whereas the prophets represented God, the rabbis represented God's word, the Torah, through their thorough knowledge of it.

The rabbis interpreted the Torah, applying it to their situation, and transmitted their traditions to the community. They exercised leadership and influence primarily as teachers and preachers. While their political authority was formalized through ordination, it was dependent on the acceptance and recognition of the people. Usually, the teacher is an external influence on the polity, attempting to exercise his influence on those in power. Here we have a different phenomenon of political leadership. The rabbi, by virtue of his teaching was recognized as the leader. His knowledge was political since he used it as a means of control and discipline. The teacher extended his own knowledge and shared it with his students who, in turn, became teachers themselves. The rabbi was the teacher par excellence since he internalized his own knowledge. He was recognized as the communal authority for he represented the embodiment of the Torah. His students became teachers themselves by internalizing the traditions and myths of the community, in other words, the oral tradition. Continuity which insured the security and integrity of the polity was a consequence of the instruction and indoctrination of communal values. When the teacher had influence (and, therefore, power) and was involved in the decision-making process, he could be a successful authority figure while training students to succeed him.

## Conclusion

The epitome of the rabbinic contribution to political thought is found in the idea that government is a commentary on the original purpose of society. Each person is to transcend himself by becoming his own authority. All those who share this purpose and experience the original intent have this goal in common. The social framework is to allow for maximum interaction without the imposition of the will of one over another. The task of government is accomplished through learning so that each person can internalize this goal, that is, political relationships must be reciprocal.

From this epitome we can extract a number of political themes. The reciprocal relationship emphasized by rabbinic thought is the cornerstone of its understanding of authority and community. This type of relationship distinguishes it from Christian concepts as well. Grace predominated in Christian thought because it explained why God would relate to an imperfect humanity. It was His nature to be gracious by entering history to save mankind who were otherwise doomed. Extrapolated into political thought it led to the concept of the paternal authority figure who would take responsibility for society. Augustine despaired that such a human authority could ever be found outside of the heavenly kingdom and so did the rabbis. Politics was disparaged, for it corrupted the participant. If one enters the political life he cannot come out clean or unsullied. The very process was immoral and tainted. Politics was not the profession for saints. Political thought was then engaged in either finding the proper regime which could corrupt the leader in the least possible way, or ensuring the protection of the citizen against encroachment by the regime on his rights. Even Machiavelli knew his limits. If the government is corrupt or a person's rights are abused, then there is no reason for him to remain in the polity.

The rabbinic solution was to choose reciprocity in preference to grace, which meant that the authority was completely dependent on his constituency. The authority, realizing that his relationship was contingent on recognition and acceptance (an outcome of rabbinic organic thought), had to serve the polity and constantly prove that he was fit to rule. Even God was challenged at times. The check on corruptibility of power was the withdrawal of acceptance. Everyone knew the rule. If promises were broken the consequences were cruel indeed: the dissolution of the polity and the utter insignificance of the authority. He no longer had anyone to rule. Because of the terrible responsibility of the authority, he wanted everyone to share his burden. In that way he was not fully responsible when things went wrong. But the reverse was also true: as each individual shared the authority and fulfilled his promise then surely the kingdom of heaven could be realized.

Participation is emphasized by the rabbis but contrasts with the concept of participation of Athenian democracy. We may learn from Plato's criticism of democracy that it tended towards interest politics and lobbying casting one force against another. Decision making consisted in juggling those forces and interests to come to some sort of synthesis by giving weight to the strongest influence. The interest of a specific group seemed to take precedence over the concern of the polis as a whole. Plato's correction of this system of government which he experienced and detested was to institutionalize authority in the person of the philosopher-king who ruled because of his innate ability and education. His experience in Syracuse failed. It was difficult to establish such a polity and to guarantee that its leader would share his vision of reality.

Participation allows for the wide distribution of political responsibility. The more people involved in making the decisions the less the tendency to cast blame on others. If the citizen shares in the decisions of the polity he has a personal stake in its policy. In Athens, interest and factions destroyed the vision; there was no vision to share by those who participated. Instead each had his own vision which he independently pursued with apparent disregard for the vision of others.

The rabbis must have understood that participation was necessary in order to insure the inclusion of separate views to prevent destructive sectarianism and schismatic breaks. The Jewish community was too weak, too widely scattered and too few in number, especially in Palestine, to withstand groups breaking away and starting their own religions. Yet there had to be some way to prevent factionalism. Participation, they taught, was available to all who were politically socialized, that is, to all those who internalized the goal of the society and participated in studying and interpreting the rabbinic traditions.

Redemption means the fulfillment of the covenant agreement According to Jewish thought, redemption is to be public, historical, and "within the community."[67] It occurs within the visible world. According to the rabbis right action led to redemption. When everyone would keep his agreement, government by men over men would no longer be necessary. "The task of realizing the Kingdom of God was never restricted to the *ecclesia docens*. It always continued to rest with the whole body of believers."[68] The rabbis wanted every person to become a rabbi, that is, participate in the divine communication, to be one's own authority. There was to be, in other words, self rule by each individual in God's kingdom. "And the Lord will be king over all the earth; on that day the Lord will be one and his name one" (Zecharia 14:9).

## Notes

The material in the present chapter is based on the author's unpublished doctoral thesis, "Aspects of Political Thought in the Talmud and Midrash," University of California, Berkeley, 1975. See pp. 121ff of the dissertation on the biblical sources of reciprocity.

1. Louis Ginzberg, "The Religion of the Jews at the Time of Jesus, *Hebrew Union College Annual* 1 (1924): 310.
2. Jean Piaget, *Psychology of Intelligence*, trans. Malcome Piercy and D. E. Berlyne (London: Routledge Kegan Paul, 1947), p. 6.
3. Solomon Schechter, *Aspects of Rabbinic Theology* (New York: Schocken Books, 1961), p. xxii.
4. Ibid.
5. Ibid., xxiii.
6. Max Kadushin, *The Theology of Seder Eliahu, a Study in Organic Thinking* (New York: Bloch Publishing Co., 1932), p. 202.
7. Max Kadushin, *Organic Thinking, a Study in Rabbinic Thought* (New York: The Jewish Theological Seminary, 1938), p. 1.
8. Ibid., p. 184.
9. Kadushin, "Aspects of the Rabbinic Concept of Israel. A Study in the Mekilta," *Hebrew Union College Annual* 19 (1945–1946): 69.
10. Kadushin, *Organic Thinking*, p. 187.
11. Kadushin, *The Rabbinic Mind*, 2nd ed. (New York: Blaidsell Publishing Co., 1965), p. vii and 47.
12. Ibid., pp. 2 and 29ff.
13. Ibid., p. 78.
14. Kadushin, *Workshop and Ethics. A Study in Rabbinic Judaism* (Evanston: Northwestern University Press, 1964), p. vii.

15. Kadushin, *The Rabbinic Mind*, p. 98.

16. Leo Strauss, *What is Political Philosophy?* (Glencoe: The Free Press, 1959), p. 13.

17. Gordon Freeman, "Aspects of Political Thought in the Talmud and Midrash," pp. 18–30.

18. A. Hartom, "B'rit," *Encyclopedia Mikra'it*, II (1954), p. 348.

19. See Solomon Schechter, *Documents of Jewish Sectaries* (New York: Ktav Publishing House, Inc., 1970).

20. Klaus Baltzer, *The Covenant Formulary in Old Testament, Jewish and Early Christian Writings*, trans. David E. Green (Oxford: Basil Blackwell, 1971), pp. 97–172. See also, Boaz Cohen, "Letter and Spirit on Jewish and Roman Law," in *Jubilee Volume*, ed. Moshe Davis and Mordecai M. Kaplan (New York: Jewish Theological Seminary, 1953), p. 111ff on the use of this term in Jewish-Christian polemic. See also Walter Selb, "im Neuen Testament," *Journal of Jewish Studies* 25, no. 1 (February 1974): 183–96 for a detailed exposition of that term and its significance in the New Testament. The writer is indebted to Ilse Schoenholz for translating this article.

21. Delbert R. Hillers, *Covenant: The History of a Biblical Idea* (Baltimore: John Hopkins Press, 1919), p. 181.

22. See Leviticus Rabbah 19 for the use of *diatheke* in context. Natan Ben Yehiel, *Aruch Hashalem*, ed. A. Kohut (New York: Pardes Publishing House, Inc.), III, 55, gives other references for its usage as "will," the usual Greek meaning of this term. See also Reuven Yaron, *Gifts in Contemplation of Death in Jewish and Roman Law* (Oxford: Oxford University Press, 1960), p. 19.

23. Mekhilta, II (Lauterbach Edition), p. 28.

24. Lamentations Rabbah 1:35 on 1:6. See also Sifre 346, 144a on Deuteronomy 33:5; Midrash on Psalms 123:1.

25. The statement uses the phrase *tohu vavohu* (Genesis 1:2) to indicate the primordial state of chaos.

26. Talmud Bavli Pesahim, 68b.; see also T. B. Shabbat 88a; Avodah Zarah 3a; Ruth Rabbah, proem 1.

27. Genesis Rabbah 1:1.

28. T.B. Sota, 37b; Hagigah 6a; Zevahim 115b; see also Mekhilta, II, 297; Exodus Rabbah 5:9.

29. Exodus Rabbah 28:1.

30. Avot D'Rabbi Natan, IV, 34.

31. Jacob Neusner, *A Life of Rabban Yohanan ben Zakkai CA 1–80 C.E.* (Leiden: E.J. Brill, 1962), p. 143.

32. Ibid.

33. Deuteronomy Rabbah 3:9; see also, Song of Songs Rabbah 5:3; Exodus Rabbah 29:3.

34. Pesikta Rabbati: Aseret Hadibrot 21:99 a-b. See also Exodus Rabbah 27:8.

35. Freeman, "Aspects of Political Thought in the Talmud and Midrash," Part 1, p. 49f.

36. Sifra, 89b.

37. Abraham J. Heschel, *Theology of Ancient Judaism* (London and New York: Soncino Press, 1962), vol. I, p. 82. He cites Midrash on Psalms 25:9.

38. Eliezer Berkovitz, "Conversion 'According to Halachah'—What Is It?" *Judaism* 23, no. 4 (Fall 1974): 478.

39. Mekhilta, II, 241. See also Exodus Rabbah 28:6.

40. Freeman, "Aspects of Political thought in the Talmud and Midrash," p. 175ff.
41. Mekhilta, II, 230 (translation revised by present writer). In terms of the period that this statement was made, perhaps as late as the third century (since the name of God used here is the Holy One, Blessed be He, and the author is Rabbi Y'hudah the Prince who lived at that time), one could imagine the concern with secret mystic groups, apocalyptic sects, crypto-Christians, and gnostics who could not be detected. Rabbi Y'hudah, responsible for the community and concerned for the observance of the Torah, realized that secret acts could be harmful to the community but was probably at a loss to know how to deal with them.
42. R. Travers Herford, *The Pharisees* (Boston: Beacon Press, 1962), p. 141f.
43. Pesikta Rabbati IIIa, translated by W.G. Braude, I, 457f. *Sh'rarah* is translated as authority.
44. *Encyclopedia Judaica*, vol. 16, p 150.
45. *Ibid.*, vol. 11, p. 74.
46. *Ibid.*, vol. 1, p. 35. Rabbi Abbahu, who lived in Caesaria, the center of Roman rule and Palestinian Christianity, was learned in mathematics, rhetoric, and Greek. He was held in high esteem by Roman authorities who regarded him as the spokesman for the Jewish people.
47. Freeman, "Aspects of Political Thought in the Talmud and Midrash," p. 48ff.
48. The phraseology used in the text is *t'kabel alecha*, "to accept upon yourself," which is the same as that used for accepting the covenant. To accept rule is to accept a covenant with God which legitimizes authority.
49. T. B. Hagigah 15b. Statement of Rabbah bar Shilo.
50. Moses Hadas, "The First Encounter of Judaism with Europeanism," *The Menorah Treasury*, ed. L. Schwartz (Philadelphia: Jewish Publication Society of America, 1964), p. 47.
51. Salo W. Baron, *A Social and Religious History of the Jews*, vol. 1 (New York and Philadelphia: Columbia University Press and the Jewish Publication Society of America, 1958), p. 161. See T.B. B'rachot 5a, statement by Rabbi Shimon ben Lakish Sanhedrin 21b; Genesis Rabbah 8:2, 57.
52. George F. Moore, "The Idea of Torah in Judaism," *The Menorah Treasury*, ed. L. Schwartz (Philadelphia: The Jewish Publication Society of America, 1964), p. 18.
53. Louis Ginzberg, *Students, Saints and Scholars* (New York and Philadelphia: Meridian Books and the Jewish Publication Society of America, 1958), p. 5.
54. Louis Ginzberg, *The Legends of the Jews*, vol. 3 (Philadelphia: The Jewish Publication Society of America, 1968), p. 187.
55. Max Weber, *Ancient Judaism*, trans. and ed. H. Gerth and D. Martindale (Glencoe: The Free Press, 1952), p. 385.
56. Ibid., p. 391.
57. Jacob Neusner, *From Politics to Piety* (Englewood Cliffs: Prentice Hall. Inc., 1973), p. 146.
58. Ibid., p. 391.
59. *Hakhamim.*
60. Gavra Rabbah.
61. T.B. Bava M'tziah 12a.
62. T.B. Bava M'tziah 58b f.
63. J. Newman, *Halachic Sources from the Beginning to the Ninth Century* (Leiden: E.J. Brill, 1969), p. 5. See in regard to statement in T.B. Gitin 36a concerning Hillel's *prosbul.*
64. R. Travers Herford, *The Pharisees* (Boston: The Beacon Press, 1962), p. 137.

65. Ibid., p. 139.
66. Ginzberg, *Students, Scholars and Saints*, p. 2.
67. Gershom G. Scholem, *The Messianic Idea in Judaism* (New York: Schocken Books, 1972), p. 1.
68. Jacob L. Talmon, *The Unique and the Universal* (London: Secker and Warburg, 1965), p. 78.

# Part II

# Theoretical Development

# Introduction: The Constitutional Dimension of Jewish History

Implicit in the foregoing discussion and otherwise a matter of commonsense knowledge is that the *edah* has gone through periodic regime changes in the course of Jewish history. The key to understanding those changes is to be found in the patterns of constitutional development of the Jewish people and its polity. Indeed, it is possible to suggest that Jewish history can be read as the progression of the generations through a series of historical epochs, each marked by the unfolding and subsequent undoing of its own constitutional synthesis within the overall framework of the Torah, leading in turn to a new epoch and the necessity for a new constitutional synthesis.

It has been the genius of the Jews as *am* and *edah* to keep the flow of generations intact via those periodic reconstitutions, through exile and dispersion. Hence the issue of constitutionalism and constitutional change is central to the study of Jewish political history in its entirety and provides a base for its periodization. Basically, this is because the Jewish constitution has differed from modern constitutions, most significantly because of its all-embracing character. It is not confined to the delineation of the political power of a secular society, but extends into virtually all phases of life. A study of constitutionalism in Jewish history, accordingly, must embrace far more than the record of specific fundamental political laws.

A reconstruction of the communal constitution of any particular period of Jewish history must come to terms with the entire range of communal living during that time and thereby provide a framework that can encompass virtually all aspects of Jewish civilization.[1] The Torah is, in this respect, both an exemplar and a touchstone. It contains all the characteristics of organic and all-embracing law; it has also (for the vast majority of Jewish history and by the vast majority of the Jewish people) been perceived to be of Divine origin. On both counts, the Torah must be regarded as the basic and foremost constitutional document of Jewish history. Its subsequent modifications and/or amplifications must, therefore, be considered to be necessitated by overwhelming pressures for constitutional change.

All subsequent constitutional referents claim, whether explicitly or implicitly, to maintain the traditions embodied in the Torah; but all nevertheless do so in a manner which supplements and redirects the original in line with the pressures of contemporary conditions. The *Mishnah, Gemara,* and the great *halakhic* codes (to cite only a few such documents) thus constitute indices for the identification and analysis of such adjustments and an explanatory device for relating the change from one epoch to another. Indeed, the Torah-as-constitution can be understood as a kind of nucleus to whose original core have been added layers of additional material, each of which becomes compacted onto the original to the point where it is bonded to it permanently and there is no operational difference between earlier and later materials even where it is possible to distinguish between them.

At the same time, the Torah is a uniquely Jewish constitution in that it is first and foremost a teaching, as the word Torah itself indicates. Although binding on Jews through the Sinai covenant, as a teaching it is based on the recognition that, in a covenantal system, its binding character still requires consent. Jews must hearken to their constitutional teaching, and since hearkening begins with hearing, they must be rendered open to hearing. In Jewish tradition, this openness comes as a result of learning, not by nature or grace. This characteristic of the Jewish constitution is reflected, inter alia, in the use of terms which refer to teaching to describe the most important constitutional referents, for example, *Torah, Mishneh Torah* (Deuteronomy), *Mishnah, Gemara, Talmud.*

The idea of Jewish history as constitutional history is not new, just as explicit reference to the Torah as the fundamental constitution of the *edah* is at least as old as Philo and Josephus.[2] Applying this idea in the special way in which the constitution of the Jewish people embraces more than fundamental political law, it is possible to discuss meaningfully constitutions and constitutionalism in Jewish history. Indeed, the principal value of the constitutional approach to the study of Jewish history lies in its ability to provide a framework that can embrace virtually every aspect of Jewish life without either deemphasizing or overemphasizing the political dimension.

What is distinctive about this approach is its deliberate emphasis on the political facet of Jewish history. Accordingly, it is not bound by conventional historiographical categories. Most conspicuously is this so in the thorny matter of chronological divisions. The traditional breakdown into "ancient," "medieval," and "modern" periods is superseded by a more refined typology based on the rhythm of political life; so, too, is the less obtuse (but hardly more helpful) division into standard subperiods: "biblical," "postbiblical," "talmudic," "post-talmudic," "premodern," "modern," and the like.

## Patterns of Constitutional Development

We begin then by distinguishing periods of constitution making and constitutional change in the course of Jewish history on the basis of the Jewish response, or series of connected responses, to challenges from within or without the *edah*. In doing so, we can rely first on recognized constitutional texts and the benchmarks of Jewish political history and constitutional development, noting how they relate to one another. Out of those relationships temporal patterns emerge, with each period representing a particular rhythm of challenge and response. Once that rhythm is identified, the framework within which it moves— and which it modifies—can be identified as well. Each epoch is not only characterized by its constitutional synthesis but also by particular institutional expressions of that synthesis. Each is set off by founding, climactic, and culminating events which set its constitutional agenda, bring that agenda to whatever degree of fruition is achieved, and tie off the epoch's loose ends in such a way as to start the movement toward a new constitutional agenda for a new epoch.

Constitutions are changed or modified only as the necessity for change becomes overwhelming. In the Jewish polity this is particularly true because of the traditionally Divine nature of Jewish fundamental law. Hence, these epochal transitions occur relatively infrequently. By tracing the subsequent constitutional modifications of the Torah which supplemented and redirected the original Torah in line with the demands of later ages, we posit that Jewish history can be divided into fourteen constitutional epochs, each of approximately three centuries' duration and each of which can be seen to possess a distinct political character of its own, as follows:

| | | |
|---|---|---|
| 1. | *Ha-Avot*/The Forefathers | c. 1850–c. 1570 B.C.E. |
| 2. | *Avdut Mizrayim*/Egyptian Bondage | c. 1570–c. 1280 B.C.E. |
| 3. | *Adat Bnei Yisrael*/The Congregation of Israelites | c. 1280–1004 B.C.E. |
| 4. | *Brit ha-Melukhah*/The Federal Monarchy | 1004–721 B.C.E. |
| 5. | *Malkhut Yehudah*/The Kingdom of Judah | 721–440 B.C.E. |
| 6. | *Knesset ha-Gedolah*/The Great Assembly | 440–145 B.C.E. |
| 7. | *Hever ha-Yehudim*/The Jewish Commonwealth | 145 b.c.e.-140 c.e. |
| 8. | *Sanhedrin u-Nesi'ut*/The Sanhedrin and the Patriarchate | 140–429 C.E. |
| 9. | *Ha-Yeshivot ve Rashei ha-Golah*/The Yeshivot and Exilarchs | 429–748 C.E. |
| 10. | *Yeshivot ve-Geonim*/Yeshivot and the Geonim | 748–1038 C.E. |
| 11. | *Ha-Kehillot*/The *Kehillot* | 1038–1348 C.E. |
| 12. | *Ha-Va'adim*/Federations of the *Kehillot* | 1348–1648 C.E. |
| 13. | *Hitagduyot*/Voluntary Associations | 1648–1948 C.E. |
| 14. | *Medinah ve-Am*/State and People | 1948 C.E.-present |

Table II.1 lists the fourteen constitutional epochs of Jewish history as delineated in accordance with the above criteria, also supplying the dates of each epoch, its principal constitutional referents, and dominant events of political significance.

The thirteen epochs that have been completed were remarkably uniform in duration. Each epoch extended over nine historical generations (the years available to mature humans for participation in public affairs), between twenty-five and forty years in length. The shortest epochs were approximately 280 years in length and the longest 320. This seems to indicate rise and decline of historical epochs within a similar general pattern. Each of these epochs corresponds with parallel periods of general history which had their impact on the Jewish people, but what is of the essence in this scheme is the Jewish response to whatever challenges are posed, external as well as internal. Indeed, its

**TABLE II.1**
**The Constitutional Periodization of Jewish History**

| | Epoch | Dates BCE | Constitution | Founding Events | Climactic Events | Culminating Events |
|---|---|---|---|---|---|---|
| 1. | *Ha-Avot/* The Forefathers | c. 1850–c. 1570 | Abraham's covenant | Abraham migrates to Canaan | Jacob becomes Israel | Descent to Egypt |
| 2. | *Avdut Mizrayim/* Egyptian bondage | c. 1570–c. 1280 | Patriarchal covenant as reaffirmed | Settlement in Goshen | Egyptian slavery | Exodus |
| 3. | *Adat Bnei Yisrael* The Congregation of | c. 1280–1004 | Mosaic Torah | Sinai | Gideon rejects kingship | David accepted as king |
| 4. | *Brit Ha-MelukhahN* The Federal Monarchy | 1004–721 | Covenants of kingship | David's kingship | Division of kingdom | Destruction of Israel |
| 5. | *Malkhut Yehudah/* The Kingdom of Judah | 721–440 | Deuteronomy | Judean rule consolidated | Josianic reform | Abortive restoration of monarchy |
| 6. | *Knesset Ha-Gedolah/* The Great Assembly | 440–145 | Ezra/Nehemiah Covenant | Ezra restoration | Shift to Hellenistic world | Hasmonean revolt |
| 7. | *Hever Ha-Yehudim/ml* The Jewish Commonwealth | 145 BCE– 140 CE | Oral tradition (Torah) | Hasmonean kingship | Destruction of Temple | Bar Kochba Rebellion |

**TABLE II.1 (cont.)**

| Epoch | Dates CE | Constitution | Founding Events | Climactic Events | Culminating Events |
|---|---|---|---|---|---|
| 8. *Sanhedrin U-Nesi'ut* The Sanhedrin and the Patriarchate | 140 CE–c. 425 | *Mishnah* | Organization of *Mishnah*/Renewal of Exilarchate | Christian ascendancy established anti-Jewish policy | End of Patriarchate |
| 9. *Ha-Yeshivot ve-Rashei Ha-Golah/* The Yeshivot and Exilarchs | c. 425–c. 750 | *Gemara* | Completion of *Gemara* | Jews come under Islam | Reunification of Jews under Islamic rule |
| 10. *Yeshivot ve-Geonim/* Yeshivot and Geonim | c. 750–1038 | Talmud and codes | *Geonim* and first codes | Last Israel-Babylonian controversy | End of Gaonate |
| 11. *Ha-Kehillot/* The Kehillot | 1038–1348 | Constitutional responsa | Passage of hegemony to Europe | *Kabbalah* in Spain. Reestablishment of Jewish settlement in Jerusalem | Black Death massacres |
| 12. *Ha-Va'adim/* Federations of Kehillot | 1348–1648 | *Arba'ah Turim* | Polish Jewry's charters. Council of Aragonese community | Spanish expulsion and aftermath | Sabbatean movement |
| 13. *Hitagduyot/* Voluntary Associations | 1648–1948 | *Shulhan Arukh* | Rise of Modernism | Emancipation | The Holocaust |
| 14. *Medinah Ve-Am/* State and People | 1948– | ? | Establishment of state of Israel | ? | ? |

emphasis on the internal Jewish rhythm of events is one of the marks of its authenticity. Significantly, the pattern itself is suggested in the Torah, which marks off epochs on a similar basis, ten generations from Adam to Noah (nine preflood and then the generation of the new founding), ten more from Noah to Abraham, 322 years from the birth of Abraham to the death of Jacob, ten generations in Egyptian bondage, and ten more from Moses to David.

## Notes

1. This discussion draws heavily on the political science literature on constitutionalism. Standard works on the subject include James Bryce, *Constitutions* (New York: Oxford University Press, 1905); Carl J. Friedrich, *Constitutional Government and Politics: Nature and Development* (Boston: Ginn and Co., 1937) and "Constitutions and Constitutionalism," in *International Encyclopedia of the Social Sciences*, vol. 3, ed. David L. Sills (New York: MacMillan and Free Press, 1968), pp. 318–26; Charles H. McIlwain, *Constitutionalism, Ancient and Modern* (Ithaca, N.Y.: Cornell University Press, 1947); and M.J.C. Vile, *Constitutionalism and the Separation of Powers* (Oxford: Clarendon Press, 1967). Although otherwise problematic for a system whose origins are in a divine covenant, Hans Kelsen's constitutional theory is particularly helpful in this connection; cf. his *General Theory of Law and State* (New York: Russell and Russell, 1961).

2. Cf. Josephus Flavius, *Antiquities of the Jews*, Book IV, chapter 8, especially paragraphs 196–98 and Philo, *De Specialibus Legibus*, Book IV "De Constitutione Principum." For an analysis of Philo's political thought, with frequent references to Josephus and to classical Jewish sources, see Harry Aystryn Wolfson, *Philo: Foundations of Religious Philosophy in Judaism, Christianity, and Islam*, revised edition, vol. 2 (Cambridge, Mass.: Harvard University Press, 1962), chapter 13, "Political Theory," pp. 322–437.

# 4

# Prolegomena to Jewish Political Theory

*Bernard Susser and Eliezer Don-Yehiya*

Does there exist a Jewish political theory? Were this question asked about Christian or Moslem political theory, the answer would likely be in the affirmative. The vast literature that has accumulated on these subjects dispel whatever doubts may persist. But Jewish political theory hovers in limbo: not sufficiently manifest or systematic to constitute a well-defined discipline, but nevertheless so obviously present at all points that its exclusion is clearly unwarranted. Our aim in the present essay is to set forth methodically and concisely the major features, strategies, and options that any inquiry into Jewish political theory would need to take into account.[1] For the most part we have avoided explicit substantive conclusions and focused on the framework of inquiry, although we are of course conscious that the two can never be fully separated.

Most fundamentally it is imperative to ask at the outset in what sense we use the term "tradition" when we speak of a "tradition" of Jewish political theory. Four possible alternatives are distinguishable and the choice made at this level will necessarily set the parameters and tone for any subsequent exploration. The first alternative, which may be described as minimalist or even trivial, identifies Jewish political theory tout court with political theorizing done by Jews, much as we might speak of Jewish scientists or Jewish linguists.[2] If this arbitrary nexus is held to be the most that can be said about the unity of Jewish political thinking then little argument is required to disqualify the entire enterprise.

A second somewhat more substantive approach views the continuity of Jewish political theorizing in terms of a "Jewish vocabulary of politics," that is, a reservoir of normative texts, formulae, and quotations that are utilized *post facto* to justify and legitimize views and policies whose real origin is unrelated to the Jewish intellectual context. As a cultural and communal island the Jewish ability to adjust, indeed to survive, often depended upon, on the one hand, the capacity for a discriminating and realistic appraisal of political or economic pressures and, on the other, the facility to legitimize imperatives of the moment by resorting to the inexhaustible and multifarious tradition. This alternative relegates Jewish political thinking to the status of an afterthought or, at very best, to the role of a strictly dependent variable whose autonomous leverage is negligible. For example, the wealth of material pertaining to the sources of authority and of political obligation in the autonomous medieval community needs to be approached— if this alternative is accepted—in functionalist historical and not specifically Jewish terms, the Jewish legal vocabulary being only the natural *lingua franca* in which dialogue was conducted. In this sense it could be claimed that Maimonides' political thought is merely classical political theory read right to left; the irreducibly Jewish element adding up to little more than minor glosses and characteristically Jewish terminology. Moreover, following this view, a "tradition" of Jewish political theory can be said to exist only in a formal extrinsic sense because there is no ongoing specifiable context of debate, merely a discontinuous use of a common language by discrete groups reacting to different stimuli.

A third view posits the existence of a solid and enduring Jewish political theory with identifiable differentiae and a coherent context of debate. Just as it would be unthinkable to follow the arguments of Marx, for example, without knowing his Hegelian antecedents, or to follow Hegel without recognizing his debt to Kant—and so on back to Plato—so the Jewish political tradition from Scriptures through the various periods—Hellenistic, Talmudic, Gaonic, medieval, and so forth—represents an independent, influential, continuous, relatively self-determined body of ideas coupled with parameters for debate, extension, and development. The political theory of medieval times is, to be sure, not the political theory of the Talmud or of the Bible but it is an authentic offshoot of the same tree, inconceivable without its predecessors.

A maximalist fourth position, religiously fundamentalist in its more extreme formulations, claims that not only is the intellectual tradition of Jewish political theorizing continuous and coherent but the very ideas themselves exhibit an unchanging regularity and constancy. While the modes of expression, the particular shadings, nuances, and emphases may reflect specific historical concerns, there exists nonetheless a substantive unity that transcends differences, a major theme with harmonizing variations. Advocates of this position contend that the thematic unity has its origin in divine revelation, which, aside from informing Jewish political theorizing with its general constitution and special qualities, also provides for its legitimacy and authority.

There is, of course, nothing essential or necessary about any of these heuristic alternatives—intermediate hybrid positions we suspect would be the most common—nevertheless, a significant line may be drawn dividing the first and second from the third and fourth approaches. The former pair would not encourage or reward, as the latter pair would, a close and systematic study of the sources and texts relating to Jewish political theory.

But whatever decision is taken in this most general of questions it must be recognized that it is precisely in the nature of its sources, texts, and documents that the Jewish tradition of political thinking presents its knottiest and most unique problems. Four different types of sources may be distinguished:

- A political theory that is expressly, systematically, and comprehensively formulated.
- Political ideas scattered in various philosophical and literary sources that require a synoptic and synthetic approach in order to be appreciated as a unified theory.
- Various documents such as responsa, memoranda, correspondence, public charters and agreements, legal discussions and decisions that deal with concrete and operational questions regarding the political system and from which may be deduced a political worldview.
- Political organization and structure itself which reflects political "first principles."

There is, as will become clear below, a significant correlation between the type of source on the one hand and the type of problem entertained on the other.

With only the rarest of exceptions, there do not exist in the Jewish tradition elaborate and systematic treatises on political philosophy comparable to the *Republic, Politics,* or *Leviathan.*[3] Nevertheless, there do exist works of great sophistication and depth that deal fairly methodically with political questions—from Philo to Maimonides to Mendelssohn to Buber. More generally, however, discussion of political questions are imbedded in larger nonpolitical contexts, found in fragments and asides, generally heterogenous, tangential, and implicit. This no doubt accounts for the fitful and scanty attempts to explore the subject.[4] For if scholarship in Western political thought has concentrated on the exposition of texts and the analysis of arguments, the researcher in Jewish political theory is presented with a formidable preliminary task before he can proceed. He must extract, synthesize, and collate from a wide-ranging body of material—from philosophical disquisitions, legal treatises, belle lettristic creations, and so forth—somewhat akin, although on a far larger scale, to studying the political theory of Shakespeare.

The *Locus Classicus* in the Jewish tradition for this type of "anthological approach" and a clear instance of its difficulties is the Bible viewed as a political document. Many Bible scholars and historians have attempted to evince determinate political ideas from the politically relevant texts. But because of the multiplicity and variety of sources as well as the heavy ideological investments scholars bring to the task, the Bible has been seen as justifying every form of government from anarchism to theocracy to liberal democracy. (To what extent, for example, are the scriptural commentaries of a Don Isaac Abravanel or a Martin Buber elucidations of biblical political theory or formulations of the political thought of Abravanel or Martin Buber?)

A further *caveat* needs to be emphasized in the comparison of Western and Jewish political theory. Even after the work of synthesis and collation presents us with a synoptic compendium of theoretical sources it remains eminently clear nonetheless that the discussion of political "first principles" does not constitute the center of gravity for Jewish political theory. Speaking for at least the great span stretching from Talmudic times to the eighteenth century, most Jewish political theorizing was the handmaiden of quotidian life and pressing realities.

Notably, the greater part of political discourse comes in direct response to actual and specific questions posed to celebrated legal scholars. On this level of responsa and legal debate, concern with the ideal state or the philosophical status of the state, or forms of government as a principle, is almost entirely absent. Instead, we encounter questions relating to the obligation of the Jewish community to the regimes under which they lived as well as questions regarding the internal organization and authority of the Jewish community itself. In the latter class are found such staples of Western political theory as the source and nature of the majority's political authority and the protection of minority as well as individual rights, the obligations of the community to the indigent, the many issues surrounding taxation, the proper criteria for leadership, and so on.

In modern terms this constitutes as much an articulation of political culture and tradition as of political theory—somewhat comparable to reconstructing an American Public Philosophy from Supreme Court decisions. So that if the widely scattered sources are less accessible to the researcher they are for all that more reliable and reflective of widely held *Weltanschauungen*. These reality-centered characteristics of Jewish political theorizing resist its succumbing to what is perhaps the major weakness of the History of Ideas orientation of Western political theory, that is, the tendency to study thought *in vacuo*. Even the most fanciful savant would be hard put to dissociate Jewish political ideas from the realities in which they developed.

Parenthetically, it is worth noting that the Jewish tradition of political theorizing is, for the most part, not given to the characteristic Western discussion of the relative merits attached to various forms of government.[5] The focus tends to be on the proper relation between rulers and ruled. There is a perceptible uneasiness with the reified state and a concomitant concern with power as relation. This serves again to reinforce the history-bound practical bent of Jewish political thought.

Jewish political theory invites yet another type of approach. From this very popular perspective the Jewish political tradition constitutes a highly instructive source of prescriptive and experiential wisdom. Whatever position one takes in the debate over historicism, it is nonetheless clear that the abundant records of Jewish national and communal organization, of the responses to crises, of political adaptation and the lack thereof, of successful and unsuccessful national strategies, remain a virtually inexhaustible source for shaping identity and focusing orientation in the present. It is of course true that the very unwieldiness and heterogeneity of the tradition encourage tendentiousness and ideological self-congratulation but this is a general historiographic problem and need not detain us here.

Working our way from speculative to behavioral and experiential perspectives brings us to the most concrete objectification of Jewish political ideas—the study of Jewish political institutions. Whether consciously or not, all societies through their organization, priorities, and procedures inevitably respond to the question: "What is the vocation of man?" In a special sense a political tradition whose defining characteristic is not philosophical expresses itself most articulately on this fundamental issue of human nature and social life through its political institutions. The reconstruction of political theory from political practice—somewhat like studying aesthetics through architecture rather than expressly as philosophy—is a supremely demanding task, but once again its results are likely to be historically anchored as well as representative of more than individual perceptions.

Thus far our prolegomena has catalogued alternative methods and approaches: what are the premises of a Jewish political theory and at what levels may it be approached? We are now ready to turn to the specific questions, the great issues that characterize the Jewish tradition of political theorizing. Four general subjects seem paramount: the ideal polity; the proper relationship to foreign rule; the principles of operation and organization of the autonomous Jewish community; and the proper relationship to an independent Jewish polity. This four-fold distinction may be correlated to the various types of sources enumerated above. Generally speaking, the first and second type of source (the systematic philosophic and "anthological") deal with theoretical questions related to the nature of the ideal polity, with politics *sub specie aetemitatus*, while sources of the third and fourth type (responsa, memoranda, etc., and political institutions) relate mainly to practical operational questions of relatively short-range and programmatic nature.

Classical fascination with the ideal state is duly reflected in Jewish sources although the Jewish concern with messianism and the necessity of God's grace tend to give the issue a somewhat different coloration. In contrast to recent times when Jewish messianism and interest in the ideal state have taken on an activist and programmatic character in both nationalist and socialist movements, prior to the eighteenth century these issues were primarily speculative and normally fragments of larger discussions on the messianic era, the virtues of Mosaic leadership or Davidic monarchy and so on. But, be that as it may, the discussion of the ideal state has a long and interesting history through the Bible, Talmud, Philo, Josephus, Saadia, Maimonides, Judah Halevi, Maharal (Rabbi Judah Loew of Prague), Spinoza, Mendelssohn, Buber, and Kook.

A second area of far less speculative concern was the recurrent and delicate problem of the proper relationship to the non-Jewish powers under whose governance the Jewish communities lived. Here, the limits of political obligation were tested in circumstances quite different from those normally prevailing in the Western sovereign states. While the general doctrine insisted that "the law of the land is the law," (*Dina d'Malchuta Dina*),[6] difficulties involved in such issues as religious observance and personal status (marriage, divorce, and filiation), and of course the traumas of persecution, led to the periodic expansion and contraction of this dictum's validity.

Notably, the rule that "the law of the land is the law" is possessed of a far more discriminating purport than simply to legitimize governmental activity. It entails and often expressly poses the questions of legitimacy and political obligation, of the proper (and improper) areas of governmental intervention, of public law and private religious conscience as well as the omnipresent dilemma of public authority and individual rights.

Probably the richest field of inquiry, in terms of extant documents and records, is the internal organization of the autonomous Jewish community in medieval times. As briefly noted above, the political and para-political questions arising in the hundreds of Jewish communities scattered from Western Europe to the Levant present a digest of the most compelling and essential issues of political thought.[7] Since the autonomous Jewish community was an unprecedented novelty in Jewish history, the legitimate source of its authority and coercive power (if any) was a critical matter that required at least as much political insight and theoretical initiative as it did familiarity with classical sources. One central hotly debated item was, as might be expected, the relative authority of the majority, the minority, and the individual. (One approach contended that a majority decision was not binding upon individuals who opposed it, i.e., communal authority required unanimity.) Public welfare in the form of social services for the destitute and defenseless raised such theoretical problems as the distribution of wealth, the political and economic rights of the needy, the legitimate purposes of taxation and public expenditure and the nature of intercommunal responsibility. Perhaps most delicate of the issues confronting the medieval Jewish community was its right to use the coercive power of the host regime—which normally granted and guaranteed the autonomous legal status of the Jewish community—to force dissidents into conformity with its will.

Our fourth category relates to the independent Jewish state—the monarchies of ancient Israel, the Hasmonean state, and once again in our times the State of Israel. (It should be noted that the State of Israel is in some sense *sui generis* being a Jewish state that does not accept, even formally, the binding nature of the Jewish tradition.) Being less than ideal, more than simply autonomous communally and (at least nominally) unsubjected to foreign rule, the Jewish state presents a unique set of theoretical considerations. The respective domains of religion and state here become a more pressing issue although it never evinces quite the same intense quality as its Western counterpart. Because the Jewish national and religious identity, at least until recently, were inseparable, political conflict over religion and state took place within a single unifying framework that prevented cleavage from leading to total rupture.[8] Nevertheless, clashes between institutionalized religion and public institutions of power, between private religious conscience and public policy, can be traced from Scripture to the State of Israel. In addition to religion and state the issues of legitimacy and political obligation become, in a sense, more compelling in a self-determined sovereign environment that can afford—and often literally invites—such probing questions. A host of other subjects that in nonsovereign periods held interest for only students and scholars, appear in the various Jewish states as living issues on the public political agenda. These include the legitimate purposes and methods of war, the treatment of non-Jewish populations under Jewish governance, religious tolerance, and of course, most generally, the proper political and economic systems to adopt.

The distinction between various frames of reference in Jewish political theory may well be correlated with the substantive differences in approach enumerated above. The discussions relating to Jewish communal life and foreign political rule are apparently influenced by the concrete concern with survival. By contrast, the discussions of the ideal state are more theoretical and speculative and are thus largely freed from the practical and contingent character of operational concerns. From this perspective, an attempt can be made to explain the prevalent differences regarding relationships of individual and society characterizing the two approaches, the practical and the speculative. Practical discussions of Jewish communal affairs are often informed by an orientation, perhaps best described as "organic," with emphasis placed upon the obligation of the individual toward the community, on the individual as part of a whole. On the other hand, the speculative approach shows stronger signs of an "instrumental individualist" perspective; the state appears as a medium to further the spiritual perfection of the individual. While this distinction should not be exaggerated—both approaches may be part of a larger tradition—it more than likely reflects the Jewish community's practical need for unity and solidarity on the one hand and the luxury of "unconditioned" theorizing on the other.[9]

Having specified the great issues, we now need to explore the context of the debate, the differentiae that set the Jewish tradition of political thought apart, endowing it with distinctive parameters, a unique idiom and typical concerns. To be sure, the profile that follows is offered cautiously and tentatively, the authors being fully conscious both of the dangers in compressing a wild grown tradition of millennia into a formal series of attributes, as well as of the arrogance in making Olympian statements such as "Judaism says. . . . ."

In spite of the differences of opinion regarding the interpretation and application of religious principles to the arena of politics, the very recognition of these principles as obligatory and normative was common to virtually all Jewish thinkers up to the middle of the eighteenth century. That is to say, the validity of these principles depended not upon their rationality, their functionality, or even upon their being traditional as such, but rather upon their being divinely revealed.

More specifically, probably the most ubiquitous and defining characteristic of Jewish political theorizing is its legal complexion. In fact the "Torah" itself is seen by thinkers from Josephus and Philo to Mendelssohn and Kant to the present as a divinely inspired *political constitution* and not solely as a system of theological beliefs, cultic practices, and ethical principles. Therefore, more likely than not, issues that in Western hands would take a philosophical, speculative turn, are, in their Jewish treatment, deliberated within the framework of an informing legal system. This is not to say, of course, that philosophical reasoning is absent from the Jewish political tradition—which involves a gross oversimplification—but rather that even the loftiest, most seemingly self-existing philosophical arguments originate in the interstices of the legal code. Jewish philosophical systems represent the scaffolding to the legal structure.

But we are not speaking of "law" in the Western sense of a consultable codex of abstract rules and precedents; notably the term for Jewish law (*halakhah*) has a far more existential, *hic et nunc* ring to it, signifying a way of life rather than juridical categories. Consequently, it is likely that abstract Western conceptions such as "rights" (of the individual or group) receive only casual expression in Jewish sources because the very definition of legal prerogatives and immunities implies such a concept. Furthermore, if law defines relations, duties, and privileges—that is, in Western terms, if the social and political systems are constitutionally specified—political absolutism is *ipso facto* disqualified. This underlying jurisprudential outlook with its affirmation of the legal identity of groups and individuals is manifestly incompatible with etatism.

As opposed to Islam, which is also legal in character, the Jewish tradition, by leaving the authoritative interpretation of law to an independent religious leadership,[10] acts as a restraint upon the executive in a way that Islam with its politically subordinate religious authority does not.[11] But if Judaism does not accept the total integration of religious and political authority—as in Islam—neither does it accept the Christian doctrine of "two swords," one spiritual, the other political. Given the quasi-constitutional nature of religious law, religious authority, despite its independence, is, by definition, political in nature.[12]

Closely allied to the legal character informing Jewish political theorizing is what in Western terms would be classified as a "higher law" tradition. Not that there is any sustained interest in "natural law" in the sense of Cicero, Aquinas, or Locke,[13] but there is, nonetheless, waiting in the wings, a potential appeal to revealed law, to the truth absorbed in the great religious experience, to the divine court of justice against the iniquities of the powers that be. This "higher law" inspired the prophets in the their confrontations with king and community, prompted the Hasmoneans in their struggle with the Hellenizers and, interestingly enough, is at the very center of the *Neturei Karta* (a fundamentalist, anti-modernist, anti-Zionist group) stand against the State of Israel.[14] There is no contradiction between the higher law tradition and the aforementioned dictum "the law of the land is the law," which seemingly points to a doctrine of unmitigated political obligation, because, as a matter of historical fact, the latter rule was severely restricted by many legal and ethico-religious conditions. In fact, these limits in themselves can be seen as indications that "positive" law is judged in the light of a "higher law."[15]

The denial of *human* political sovereignty as implied by the "higher law" tradition finds its most emphatic expression in the "Kingship of God" anarcho-theocratic school that rejects any form of established centralized regime in favor of the direct rule of God.[16] This intellectual tendency, while never dominant since the period of the Judges, has surfaced in various guises throughout Jewish history.[17]

But this emphasis on the limitation of government is not meant to imply that historical Judaism is somehow in the modern "democratic" or "liberal" tradition.[18] The religio-political law does, in fact limit governmental prerogative, but being definitive and transcendent itself it is not open to change or even criticism at human hands. Thus, in place of the absolutism of government Judaism posits the absolutism of the law.[19]

But if there exists a divine imperative that transcends positive law and points to its essential incompleteness, so does Jewish nationhood— even if it does stand with Gibraltar-like firmness at the centripetal hub of the Jewish political tradition—point to a greater reality beyond itself; a universalist vision is rarely very far from the concern with nationhood.[20] Of course, without historical specificity such a statement says both too much and too little; yet not withstanding its historical variability the tension between the poles of universalism and particularism is one of the major defining traits of Jewish political theorizing. And while it is truistic, even platitudinous, to argue that periods of exclusivism and cosmopolitanism alternate with one another, the universal-particular polarity (with temporary dominance of one or the other pole) is a constant or near constant in Jewish history. In periods of exclusiveness, which generally correspond with hostile environmental factors, universalism is pushed into the future as a correlate of messianism—a "utopia" in Mannheim's sense of the word. Periods of well-being and cosmopolitanism tend to relate universalism to the present, to emphasize the universal moral thrust of Judaism—the style of thinking that Mannheim dubs "ideological."

One very interesting if as yet tentative attempt to characterize Jewish political theory identifies the "covenant idea" as uniquely Jewish and as regularly informing the Jewish political tradition.[21] This offshoot of covenant theology sees the concept of agreement and mutuality, whether between equals or between nonequals, as the master thread in the fabric of Jewish political thought. Whether it is the overarching covenantal relationship between God and Israel, the political covenant between the twelve tribes in the desert, the communal federations of medieval times, or the communitarian ideologies of the kibbutz, the underlying factor is regarded as a covenantal consensualism of engaged and responsible partners as well as a repugnance to autocracy. But the very boldness and comprehensiveness of this hypothesis may also be its fundamental weakness. There is a point at which Occam's razor becomes too sharp. Whatever its heuristic qualities, the "covenant thesis" requires further exploration.

One last attribute that relates to the singular convergence of nationality, religion, and political community in Jewish political theorizing remains to be dealt with. With all the acute pressures that may have buffeted other historical fusions, the unity of nationality and religion at least until the eighteenth century was absolute and unquestioned—if we exclude only the efforts of the early Christians who, by their very attempt to separate religion and national identity, announced their intention of leaving the traditional Jewish framework. The third point of our historic triangle alluded to above, the relationship to a sovereign political community, is far more difficult to generalize about successfully because of its historical fluctuations, as we shall see below.

The effects of this coalescence of elements, which in Western political theory are so often fragmented, cannot be overestimated. First, the conception of a national community takes on greater import and multidimensionality because it is the immanent side of a religious community. This community is not only greater than the sum of its individual parts in the Durkheimian sense; it is a sacred, a "charismatic community" hallowed by religious function. Organized as a political community, the religio-national temper suffuses the institutions of power with the consequence that religious and secular authority, the "two swords" of Gelasian doctrine, cannot be compartmentalized nearly so easily as in the West. It is worthy of note that classical

Hebrew has no adequate term for "secular," the closest parallel being what we should call "lay" or simply "not sacred."[23] To a degree surpassing even the *Imperium Sacrum* of Latin Christendom, the Jewish monarchy, or for that matter the autonomous Jewish community of the Middle Ages, were religio-national institutions whose task was not merely to keep the earthly peace so that salvation might be won, or to defend the faith against its enemies, but rather to be symbol, exemplar, and executor of the religio-national will. Once again it is noteworthy that the messiah, the ultimate religion-national leader, is to be a descendant not of any priestly class but of the house of David. Not that this unity betokens some variety of Caesaropapism, but it is equally not to be taken as divided, in Western fashion, into religious and secular authority.

In an interesting sense, this unity, which makes of national interest a religious category, also makes Judaism an inherently political tradition in contrast to Christianity, which confronts political questions, as it were, from without, as a moral spiritual force. The Jewish tradition's religio-national stance entangles it in political realities in a way that Christianity's supranational, transcendent posture does not. To be sure, the definition of national interest is not determined mainly by considerations of national *realpolitik* as perceived by political leaders but is itself molded by moral-religious categories and by religious authorities. We might even speculate that the basic "philosophical" tenor of the Christian political tradition correlates with this universalist character, while the Jewish tradition, with its integral national nexus gravitates to the palpable and situation-bound. Finally, if this religio-national synthesis uniquely enables the embodiment of ideals and abstract virtues into real public institutions, thereby confronting the ideal with "responsibility," it also to some extent weakens the basis of purely religious criticism of national political policy because the two entail and implicate each other so deeply. But this point should not be exaggerated. The critical stance of the prophets and other religious leaders[24] toward the political authorities is sufficient proof of the resilience and latitude of the religious element.[25]

One further word must be addressed to the pre-enlightenment triangle of religion, nation, and state. While religion and nationhood present a monolithic unity throughout, the attitude to political sovereignty is the subject of heated scholarly dispute.[26] Two general schools may be distinguished: those like Roland de Vaux,[27] Salo Baron,[28]

George Foot Moore,[29] and Hermann Cohen,[30] who see Judaism as ambivalent if not generally indifferent or even hostile to statist ideas, and those like Yehezkel Kaufman[31] and Gedaliah Allon,[32] who view political autonomy as a critical ingredient in the Jewish tradition. The subject is far too large for a full treatment here, but there seems little doubt that ideological factors related to the legitimacy of Zionism are relevant to the discussion.[33] Besides, and this is crucial, the multifariousness of Jewish history does not admit of such unequivocal assertions.[34] First, the Jewish attitude to political independence varied greatly from epoch to epoch; second, very authoritative spokesmen, often in the same era, differed profoundly over this basic question; third, a "political" consciousness can take many forms, ranging from simple resistance to an oppressive foreign power to the deliberate desire to establish autonomous political institutions. What seems fair to say is that from its origins up to the middle of the eighteenth century, the Jewish tradition regarding sovereignty was neither radical nor doctrinaire; these ideas should be seen as a continuum reaching from one extreme to the other, in which there is a great clustering at the center and a progressive thinning out as one reaches the poles.

Proceeding historically highlights this variability dramatically. Many different epochs can be distinguished; each evinces its peculiar political personality. Certain periods such as the Davidic monarchy, the resistance to Rome, and the Bar Kochba revolt are highly political in character; others such as much of the Second Temple period and, most notably, from the Bar Kochba revolt down to the middle of the nineteenth century tended to relegate aspirations for political sovereignty to a very theoretical status,[35] leaving them to prayer and to the speculations of mystics, scholars, and utopians.

Once again this seems consonant with the conclusion that if the value of the state never became absolute neither did it ever disappear. Up to the eighteenth century, while religion and national identity were an inseparable unity, the desire for political sovereignty was an oscillating third factor, at times moving to the forefront, at others receding into the background. What may be called the "status quo ante" is therefore a tripartite synthesis in which each element relates to all others forming an integrated moving whole, whose character, particularly the political element, varies from era to era.

Historical changes dislodged, unfastened, and rearranged many of the ideological and material constellations presented above, so that to introduce the historical element is necessarily to disturb the neat symmetry of our categories and attributes. Perhaps the most unsettling of these transformations began in the eighteenth century when the Jewish enlightenment dissolved the unity of even so firmly fused elements as nationality and religion, to say nothing of the attitude to political sovereignty, and set into a flurry of motion the many intellectual satellites that orbited this erstwhile union. Universalism, the legalist tradition, messianism, to mention only a few, lost their assured slots in the consensual order and the "status quo ante" was replaced by a myriad of new combinations, revisions, and reformulations. Our three staples—religion, nation, and the state—are alternately torn asunder, rejected in their entirety, forged into new combinations, and vindicated in their traditional relationship; in William Butler Yeats' words, "things fall apart; the center cannot hold."

The upheaval initiated by the enlightenment left little of the historical consensus intact so that whatever unity Jewish political theory may have possessed prior to the eighteenth century, it forfeits, in marked degree, thereafter. It is difficult to speak of *Jewish political theory* as such but rather of its many heirs and its various faces. Taking nationality, religion, political sovereignty, and universalism as key ingredients in the "status quo ante," at least eight prototypical, ideal type permutations can be distinguished for the period from the enlightenment to the present: the assimilationist, classical Reform Judaism, diaspora nationalism, non-Zionist Orthodoxy, religious Zionism, non-religious Zionism, secular Zionism, and Israeli non-Zionist secularism.

The assimilationist, whether he turns to universalism or to another particular nationalism, rejects every variant of Jewish identification so Jewish political theory is *ipso facto* ruled out. Jewish categories may persist subliminally as has been so often argued in regard to Jewish socialists, but the vagueness of these associations makes for historiographical impressionism rather than systematic political theory.

Classical reform Judaism, which severs the traditional fusion of religious and national existence by making of Judaism a nonparticularist faith on the style of Christianity, gains in universalism what it loses in political sovereignty and nationalism. Its socio-political sensibility is characterized therefore by the moral voice of high principle (indeed a "higher law" in the classical sense), a voice that generally spoke in the political idiom of liberalism and humanitarianism.

Diaspora nationalism retained the tension between nationalism and universalism while excluding political aspirations as well as transvaluing religious practice into ethnic ethos. Jewish statelessness was, in their view, the highest form of national self-expression since it rose above tribalism and the nation-state—political "normalization" they feared would rob Jews of their special sensitivities, spirituality and universalism, to a pure distillate of the national genius unencumbered by the corruptions of power. The political perspective associated with diaspora nationalism is a cosmopolitan nationalism; the Jewish "abnormality" of being "a people whose home is the entire world" situating them ideally to be a "light unto the peoples."[36]

Non-Zionist Orthodoxy claims to be the authentic successor of the "status quo ante,"[37] retaining the historical symmetry of ideas that characterized Jewish tradition. Whatever the substantive truth of this claim there is a significant sense in which non-Zionist Orthodoxy represents a "conservative" rather than a "traditional" position if we understand by traditionalism that unself-conscious, taken-for-granted assimilation of accepted life patterns in a conducive environment and by conservatism the self-conscious, ideologically articulated vindication of threatened and endangered value systems. As such, non-Zionist Orthodoxy betrays its history-bound character and belies its claim to seamless continuity with Jewish tradition. Politically it has emphasized the religious definition of nationality and has tended to make of political sovereignty and universalism messianic categories. The rejection of Western culture and society makes for an insular outlook with concerns that normally do not extend far beyond the horizons of the community.

The religious Zionists present what is perhaps the broadest range of identifications; religion, nation, and state are for them strictly indissociable and each is a necessary condition for the complete fulfillment of the others. Considerably more open to Western influences than the non-Zionist Orthodox, particularly in their activist style of nationalism, more politically cosmopolitan although not necessarily more universalist, it is clear that they too show unmistakable signs of having refashioned the "status quo ante" in a new image. Their political orientation has much in common with mystical nationalism in the European mode—ranging from Barres to Peguy—although the special religio-national integration sets it apart nevertheless.

Nonreligious Zionism[38] places its strongest accents on nationalism and political sovereignty, although the religious tradition, if not its metaphysical claims, is recognized as critical for the national-political identity. Hence, its religious posture is quite unprecedented: the attempt to convert Judaism into a "civil religion,"[39] which underpins national solidarity and strengthens communal integration, but does not involve discomfiting confessional responsibility or strenuous cultic observance. Judaism's religio-national synthesis renders it particularly vulnerable to such transvaluation, because it has always been more a way of life than a confession, and a new category of religious affiliation describing perhaps the larger part of the Israeli populace—the affective-traditional—attests to its quantitative success. Politically, it exhibits great heterogeneity with right- and left-wing versions although an Israel-centered Jewish nationalism is common to them all.

Secular Zionism entails a thoroughgoing rejection of all but the most general Jewish values and symbols in which Jewish peculiarities are generally seen as stepping stones to universal human concerns. Its political orientation involves a commitment to Jewish national renaissance often accompanied by socialist egalitarianism and universalism, sometimes by a cosmopolitan liberalism. It should be added that the "civil" religious pressures of recent years have seriously undermined this position.

Israeli non-Zionist secularism is, in many ways, the ideological alter ego to our first category, the assimilationists. They too reject all variants of Jewish identification, most notably those asserting the Jewish character of Israel. As "Hebrews," Canaanites,"[40] or "Israelis," they are secular and deny all ties to Jewish history or the diaspora, seeing Israel as just another Middle Eastern Semitic state. Here, "Israeli" or "Hebrew" territorial and political nationalism replaces Jewish cultural and religious nationalism.

Yet with all the ideological atomization and heterogeneity of the last two hundred years, it is nevertheless true that the tradition remains influential[41] and that even in rejection there is often a dialectical tie to antecedents—the negations reflecting the rejected source in mirror image. Paradoxically, the tradition remains an influential point of orientation for those most firmly set against it. The Jewish political tradition is therefore not merely of historical interest; it continues to live both in its upholders and its detractors.

# Notes

1. While there is a large literature that deals with Jewish political thought from historical, theological, or legal perspectives, as political thought per se it has been dramatically neglected. (At a recent seminar Professor D. Segre noted that the *Encyclopedia Judaica* had no reference to it at all.) A general discussion of Jewish political studies can be found in Daniel J. Elazar, "Jewish Political Studies as a Field of Inquiry," *Jewish Social Studies* 36, no. 3–4 (1974): 220–33.

2. A view of this sort is held by the Israeli philosopher-scientist Yeshayahu Leibowitz:

   It is difficult to say that one of the many positions expressed in Jewish sources regarding the problem of the individual and society represents the Jewish point of view. Each is the point of view of certain Jews. Each of these points of view is common to certain Jews and certain non-Jews and does not draw on specifically Jewish sources. There is no Jewish morality, no Jewish policy, no Jewish social philosophy. Both Jews and non-Jews differ regarding these questions and the dividing line does not pass between Jews and non-Jews, but rather passes between human beings and human beings. ("Individual and Society from the Jewish Point of View," *Judaism, the Jewish People and the State of Israel* [Hebrew] [Jerusalem, 1975], pp. 315–16)

3. Notably, those Jewish authors who dealt with political questions systematically derived much of their inspiration from non-Jewish sources: Philo from Hellenistic philosophy, Maimonides from the classical tradition and Mendelssohn from eighteenth-century European thought. Spinoza, if he is to be counted a Jewish thinker, clearly derived the bulk of his inspiration from non-Jewish sources.

4. Lerner and Mahdi explain the dearth of literature in the following way:

   We tend to assume that the particular form of expression that political philosophy takes is that which is most familiar to us: there will be a book wholly or largely devoted to systematic discussions of forms of government, law, justice and so forth. We think of the *Leviathan* or the *Social Contract*. We are not accustomed to looking for an author's political philosophy in the interstices, so to speak, of his work—especially if his work takes the form of a commentary of yet another work, or a resume . . . .or if his work seems largely concerned with religious and doctrinal questions arising from revealed religion. (Lerner and Mahdi, eds., *Medieval Political Philosophy* [ New York: Free Press of Glencoe], 1963)

   See also Ralph Lerner, "Moses Maimonides," in *History of Political Philosophy*, 2nd ed., ed. Leo Strauss and Joseph Cropsey (Chicago: Rand McNally, 1972), pp. 203–205.

5. It is most difficult to find a single defining characteristic of Jewish speculations on forms of government, perhaps because government is generally viewed instrumentally, i.e., in its capacity for furthering religious life, and not as an end in itself. Moreover, the stress is squarely on the relationship between rulers and ruled rather than on the institutional structure of power.

6. See Shmuel Shiloh, *Dina de Malchuta Dina* (Hebrew) (Jerusalem: Academic Press, 1975). See also Leo Landman, *Jewish Law in the Diaspora: Confrontation and Accommodation* (Philadelphia: Dropsie, 1968).

7. Western political theory is almost exclusively state-oriented. Perhaps because of

its long history of statelessness the Jewish political tradition (particularly in the Middle Ages) does not normally concern itself with the state in Weber's sense of the term. Nevertheless the central political questions of power, authority, legitimacy, communal organization, civic obligation, and so on are dealt with constantly. Interestingly, the modern political science research approaches such as systems analysis, functionalism, and communications theory are entirely opposite to the study of the autonomous Jewish community because they focus on the "political system" rather than on the state.

8. Interestingly, at the time that the investiture controversy made the church-state issue so volatile in Europe, the Jewish communities represented, for the most part, an island of calm within the general storm. Religious and lay leadership generally coexisted harmoniously because of the "foreign power" without and the universally accepted hegemony of religious law within.

9. Rabbi Kook, the most influential of religious Zionism's theoreticians, is clearly an exception to the rule in that his approach, although speculative, is profoundly organic. Yehuda Halevi and the Maharal (Rabbi Yehuda Loew of Prague) are exceptions as well, but it was the "individualist tendency" expressed by Sa'adia and Maimonides that predominated in the philosophical literature.

10. Spinoza notes that the limitation on a regime by religio-political law is effective only insofar as the authority to interpret this law is not in the hands of the regime itself, *Tractatus Theologico-Politicus*, paragraphs 207–208.

11. See Ervin Rosental, "Political Philosophy in Judaism and Islam," *Judaism* (1968): 430–39; and Shlomo D. Gotein, "The Attitude to the State in Judaism and Islam," *Tarbitz* (Hebrew) (1948): 153–58.

12. An independent religious authority (the Rabbis) empowered to interpret a body of authoritative religio-political law makes this religious authority a partner in the legislative process alongside the "secular" government. This is far closer to "separation of powers" or "checks and balances" than to "two swords." In this sense, one noted scholar characterizes the Jewish regime as a "diarchy." Menachem Elon, "The Position of the Pharisees on the Roman Regime and the Herodian dynasty," *Studies in the History of Israel* (Hebrew), vol. 1 (Tel Aviv, 1967), p. 31.

13. For a treatment of the place of "natural law" in the Jewish political tradition see E. Aurbach, *The Sages* (Jerusalem: Magnes Press, 1975). See also Marvin Fox, "Maimonides and Aquinas on Natural Law," *Dinei Israel*, vol. 3 (Tel Aviv University Faculty of Law, 1972), pp. v–xxvi; Leo Strauss, "The Law of Reason in the Kuzari," *Persecution and the Art of Writing* (Glencoe, 1952), pp. 95–141; Ralph Lerner, "Natural Law in Albo's Book of Roots," in *Ancients and Moderns*, ed. Joseph Cropsey (New York, 1964).

14. For the *Neturei Karta*, see Norman Lamm, "The Ideology of the Neturei Karta—According to the Satmarer Version," *Tradition*, 13, no. 1 (1971): 38–53.

15. The dictum is limited to a duly constituted, "legitimate" authority acting legally and in accordance with "natural justice." Some sources would further limit its applicability to acts done for the "public good." Most actions that intrude upon Jewish religious practice are likewise excluded. Interestingly, the dictum, according to many authorities, applies only to foreign rule and not to the sovereign Jewish state. See Shiloh, *Dina de Malchuta Dina*, especially pp. 201–53. While these criteria are obviously vague, they indicate that the duty of political obedience is far from absolute—as it is in Islam and with many Christian thinkers.

16. Martin Buber is the major contemporary spokesman for this position. See his *Kingship of God* (New York, 1967), *The Prophetic Faith* (New York, 1960) and

*Moses: The Revelation and the Covenant* (New York, 1958). Buber's biblical interpretations, which are at one with his political philosophy, de-emphasize the role of the monarchy and the centralized rule of institutionalized theocracy. His position is anarcho-theocratic. Yehezkel Kaufman, one of Buber's staunchest critics, contends that following the period of the Judges the anarcho-theocratic model was rejected and replaced by the ideal of a national monarchy. Y. Kaufman, *History of the Faith of Israel* (Hebrew), vols. 1–3 (Jerusalem, 1960), p. 686–708.

17. Josephus writes that the "Zealots" who led the revolt against Rome believed it was forbidden to subjugate oneself to human rule because God himself was the only true Lord. *Jewish Antiquities*, trans. Louis H. Feldman (Cambridge, 1985), Book xviii, pp. 21–23. Don Isaac Abravanel is another figure in this tradition. See his commentary to Genesis 11, Deuteronomy 15 and Samuel 1, 8 as well as D. Netanyahu, *Don Isaac Abravanel: Statesman and Philosopher* (Philadelphia, 1972), pp. 150–95.

18. As has been convincingly argued, "Jewish liberalism" stresses only one of the many currents in Jewish political thoughts. This liberalism is, therefore, to be seen in a sociological rather than religious-intellectual light. Were it otherwise, those closest to the tradition would be the most liberal—which is clearly not the case. See Charles S. Liebman, *The Ambivalent American Jew* (Philadelphia, 1973), and Ben Halpern, "The Jewish Liberal," *Midstream* (December 1970): 32–49.

19. While the law remains sacrosanct and immutable this does not preclude citizen participation in legislation, political appointment, and public policy. See Daniel J. Elazar, *Israel: From Ideological to Territorial Democracy* (New York, 1971), p. 12.

20. Salo Baron writes: "Jewish history has increasingly become a rare combination of national and universal religion," *Social and Religious History of the Jews* (Philadelphia, 1952), vol. 1, p. 31. Buber too characterizes the prophetic religion as "national universalism"; *The Way of Scripture* (Hebrew) (Jerusalem, 1964), p. 88.

21. Daniel J. Elazar is the main spokesman for the covenant theory. See D. Elazar, chapter 1 of this volume.

22. The term is used by Gerald Blidstein in this volume.

23. See Avraham Even-Shoshan, *Hamilon Hachadash* vol. 2 (Jerusalem: Kiryat Sefer, 1992), p. 769.

24. The opposition of religious leaders during the Second Temple period to many of the Hasmonean and Herodian leaders is a prime example. See Gedaliah Allon, "Did the Nation and its Sages Forget the Hasmoneans?" *Studies in the History of Israel* (Hebrew), vol. 1, pp. 15–25 and "The Position of the Pharisees on the Roman Regime and the Herodian Dynasty," ibid., pp. 26–47.

25. Parenthetically, this undermines to some degree the prevalent assumption in the sociology of religion that religious universalism is the key to a critical and independent stance towards government. See Milton Yinger, *Religion, Society and the Individual* (New York: Macmillan, 1963), p. 433. Moreover, the national element in Judaism encouraged resistance to foreign regimes in a way that universal religions could not.

26. For a fuller discussion, see Alan Greilsammer, Eliezer Don-Yehiya and Bernard Susser, "Religion, Nationalisme et Etat dans le Judaisme," *International Political Science Association Papers* 7, no. 1, p. 3 (1973).

27. Roland de Vaux, *Ancient Israel*, 2 vols. (New York: McGraw Hill, 1965); "The state," De Vaux writes, was "subordinate and secondary and Israel, during the longer part of its history, did without it" (p. 110). De Vaux's position is neverthe-

less moderate and qualified in its stress on the "apolitical" nature of the Jewish tradition. See ibid., esp. pp. 98–99.

28. Salo Baron is also a moderate of the "apolitical" school. "The Israelitic prophets and priests may . . . .be designated the first exponents of a religious and cultural nationalism . . . .in which political aspirations were considered secondary." *Modern Nationalism and Religion* (Philadelphia, 1960), pp. 213–17. Elsewhere Baron writes that Jewish history is the record of "the emancipation from state and territory." *A Social and Religious History of the Jews,* vol. 1, pp. 16–25.

29. In regard to the period following the destruction of the First Temple, Moore writes:

> Fidelity to their religion and to the authority of the interpreters of the law had completely displaced political loyalty and the sense of civic duty; the principle that Paul lays down in *Romans* 13 ["Let every soul be in subjection to the superior authorities, for there is no authority except by God."] expresses the general attitude of the Jewish teachers. (*Judaism* [Cambridge, 1966], pp. 112–13)

30. A more extreme position claiming that Judaism is not only indifferent to statist ideas but is consciously set against them is expressed by Hermann Cohen. Judaism, he claims, fulfills its mission precisely by renouncing the statist framework. See, for example, *Religion der Vernunft* (Frankfurt a.m., 1929), pp. 229, 296–97, 421–22, as well as his "An Argument against Zionism: A Reply to Dr. Martin Buber's Open Letter to Hermann Cohen," in *Reason and Hope: Selections from the Jewish Writings of Hermann Cohen* (New York, 1971), pp. 164–70.

31. Kaufman sees the national monarchy as the ideal of the Jewish tradition. Even if it was forced at times to lead a *sub rosa* existence it never disappears and is responsible for the revolts against the Greeks and Romans and, after their failure, for the messianic idea. *History of the Faith of Israel* (Hebrew), vols. 1–3, pp. 688–94.

32. See Allon's "Did the Nation and its Sages Forget the Hasmoneans?" The teaching of the Pharisees, he argues, is very political; "They wished not to denigrate the state only to reform it" (p. 16).

33. For example, the Jewish historian Dubnow, who belongs to the "apolitical" camp, was quite unenthusiastic about Zionism. In contrast to Allon (fn. 32) he presents the Pharisees as "Theo-democrats" who opposed the Hasmonean tendency to make of Judea a monarchic military state, *History of the Jews*, vol. 1 (New York, 1967), p. 588ff. Hermann Cohen for his part viewed Zionism as a failure of nerve, "a retrograde step" in the development of Judaism. See his "Argument Against Zionism." Allon and Kaufman, on the other hand, are sympathetic to Zionism.

34. A contemporary example of unqualified assertions can be found in Gershon Weiler's argument that there is an irresolvable antagonism between the Jewish religion and the very notion of a "Jewish" state. See *Jewish Theocracy* (Tel Aviv, 1976), p. 9 (Hebrew).

35. One of the most dramatic signs of the weakening of the "political tendency" after the Bar Kochba revolt is the talmudic "prohibition" against taking political action to restore Jewish independence (Babylonian Talmud, Ketubot 111), a prohibition taken very seriously by the ultra-Orthodox Neturei Karta in their opposition to Zionism.

36. Simon Dubnow is the major theoretician of diaspora nationalism. See esp. his *Nationalism and History* (Cleveland, 1962) and Koppel S. Pinson's introduction:

"Dubnow as a Political Philosopher." The Socialist Jewish "Bund" is yet another and quite different version of this position.

37. The Neturei Karta represents the extreme right-wing of this position while the Agudat Yisrael covers a spectrum of opinions from one quite close to the Neturei Karta to a more moderate position such as that of the "neo-Orthodox" disciples of Shimshon R. Hirsh. See Isaac Breuer, *Concepts of Judaism* (Jerusalm: Israel Universities Press, 1974), and Moshe Samet, "Ultra-Orthodoxy in Modern Times," *Mahalachim* (Hebrew), no. I, p. 30.

38. The various Zionist positions are thoroughly treated in Ben Halpern's *The Idea of Jewish State* (Cambridge, 1961).

39. See Robert N. Bellah, "Civil Religion in America," in *Religion in America*, ed. William G. McLoughlin and Robert N. Bellah (Boston, 1968), pp. 3–23. For an application of this concept to the Israeli reality see Charles S. Liebman, "Religion and Political Integration," *The Jewish Journal of Sociology* (June 1975).

40. See Yonathan Ratosh, "The New Hebrew Nation," in *Unease in Zion*, ed. Ehud Ben Ezer (Jerusalem, 1974), pp. 201–34, Simon N. Herman, *Israelis and Jews* (New York, 1970), and Baruch Kurzweil, "The Nature and Origins of the Young Hebrew (Canaanite) Movement," in *Our New Literature: Continuation or Revolution* (Hebrew) (Jerusalem, 1965), pp. 270–300.

41. One interesting instance is Shlomo Avineri's contention that Israeli democracy rests upon the tradition of Jewish communal organization. See his "Israel as a Democratic State," *Monthly Review* (Hebrew), no. 5 (May 1973): 25–37.

# 5

# The Jewish People as the Classic Diaspora: A Political Analysis

*Daniel J. Elazar*

There is little doubt that the Jewish people represent the classic diaspora phenomenon of all time. Indeed, it seems that the term diaspora itself originated to describe the Jewish condition.[1] The Jewish diaspora has existed for at least 2,600 years and, if certain local traditions are accurate, perhaps even longer. It has existed alongside a functioning Jewish state and, for almost precisely 2,000 years, without any state recognized as politically independent. Moreover, for 1,500 years the Jewish people existed without an effective political center in their national territory, that is to say, exclusively as a diaspora community, so much so that the institutions of the Jewish community in Eretz Israel were themselves modeled after those of the diaspora and the Jews functioned as a diaspora community within their own land.[2] Nevertheless, the Jewish people not only preserved their integrity as an ethno-religious community, but continued to function as a polity throughout their long history through the various conditions of state and diaspora.

## Approaching the Jewish Diaspora

Most analyses of diaspora phenomena focus on the diaspora group as a sociological category, whether it is considered an ethnic group, a religious group, or both. Political analyses of this sociological phenomenon will go a step further to examine the impact of this sociological category on the host societies in which the diaspora group finds itself. These are certainly important dimensions of the diaspora experience for Jews as well as for every other group. Jewish self-preservation through religious and cultural differentiation and endogamy are without doubt worthy of examination from a sociological perspective. For example, the way in which the Jews as a diaspora community created a way of life of their own, involving a calendar of daily specificity which established a separate rhythm of Jewish life, setting them apart from their neighbors, is worthy of the closest study. In a parallel way, it is possible to study the nature of Jewish exclusion from Christian and Muslim societies through a combination of anti-Jewish attitudes and measures on the one hand, and the mutually acceptable principle that the Jews were a nation in exile and hence deserving of corporate autonomy, on the other.

A focus on either of these, however, would be essentially historical, since both have undergone great changes in the modern epoch and to the extent that they survive at all, survive only as remnants in the postmodern epoch. Thus, while *halakhah* (Jewish law) still specifies a completely separate rhythm of life for Jews, no more than 5 percent of Jews in the diaspora today live so fully in accordance with that rhythm that they separate themselves from the society around them, and perhaps another 10 percent live sufficiently according to that rhythm to be considered fully part of it. Other Jews are touched by that rhythm to varying degrees depending on the extent of their connection to Jewish life. In every case it is a voluntary matter since with the rise of the modern nation-state, the notion of the Jews as a separate nation in exile was abandoned, first by the state builders and then by most diaspora Jews as they accepted the terms of emancipation.[3]

Similarly, the anti-Jewish attitudes of Christians and Muslims that developed in an age when religion was at the center of life were transformed into modern anti-Semitism.[4] The latter remains a factor in shaping the Jewish diaspora, certainly one that is high in the consciousness of Jews everywhere. It substantially diminished as an active force in the aftermath of the Holocaust and is only now beginning to reappear in certain circles as a legitimate form of expression.

It would be more useful to examine the role of the Jews as an ethno-religious community within the societies of which they are a part. In most of these societies they play the role of a catalytic minority, making a contribution far in excess of their percentage of the total population, in a variety of fields, especially those at the cutting edge of social activity.[5]

One marked characteristic of the Jews as a group in their relationship with the rest of the world is their strong tendency to gravitate to the center of whatever universal communications network exists at any particular time and place. According to the best opinion of the historians of the ancient world the first Jews, symbolized by Abraham, Isaac, and Jacob, were already involved as nomads in the trading patterns of the Fertile Crescent. Their settlement in Canaan put them at the very center of that network with its two anchors in Egypt and Mesopotamia.[6] Subsequent generations of Jews have continued that tradition. Thus, Jews have always gravitated to the capital cities of the world, and have been able to make their influence, as individuals and as a group, felt disproportionately. Not only that, Jews have always been involved in communication-related enterprises; whether communicating religious ideas, as in their earliest history—ultimately to half of mankind—or in radio, motion pictures, and television in the twentieth century, communicating new life-styles worldwide.

This phenomenon has left the Jews exposed as well as influential, and Jews have paid the price for that exposure. In other words, Jews have played a very dangerous game as a small group of extraordinary importance and centrality in world affairs. As such, they have generated both strong positive and negative images and expectations, which have led to periodic efforts to cultivate them and equally frequent attacks upon them—outbreaks of persecution which have at the very least culminated in expulsion and at the worst in massacres and the Holocaust.

As a result of these pushes and pulls, the Jewish diaspora is different from other diasporas except, perhaps, the Gypsies, because it has been a diaspora in constant movement.

The conventional view of Jewish history is that of shifting centers of Jewish life, so that the Jews themselves have the self-image of a people on the move. These constant migrations were, on the one hand, disrupting, but, on the other, they offered the Jews as a group opportunities to renew life and to adapt to new conditions. In other words, they served the same purpose as Frederick Jackson Turner and his school have suggested that the land frontier served in the history of the United States—enabling life repeatedly to begin anew, willy-nilly if not by choice (and it was a mixture of both, since Jews often chose to migrate to new areas and were not simply forced to do so), which offered new opportunities for adaptation and change.[7]

At the same time, the constant migrations generated a religious culture based upon time rather than space, upon the shared expressions of a common temporal rhythm rather than rootedness in a common land.[8] Every civilization must somehow combine the spatial and the temporal; it must be located geohistorically. Particularly in premodern times, most emphasized the spatial over the temporal, existing and functioning because of deep-rootedness to a particular land and relatively unaware of the changes wrought by time. The accelerated pace of change since the opening of the modern epoch, and even somewhat before, has made people aware of time and its passage in ways that did not obtain earlier.[9] For most, however, the emphasis on space over time has remained, transformed by the rise of the modern state with its emphasis on territoriality and sovereignty within particular territories as the guiding principle in the organization of civilization.

The Jews remained the anomaly in all this. Not having a functioning territorial state of their own and not even being concentrated in a particular territory, the Jews emphasized the temporal and organized time in the service of Jewish survival and self-expression. *Halakhah* (literally, the way) emphasizes the organization of time, the rhythm of its passage, and the obligations of Jews to sanctify those rhythms—in daily prayers and study, the weekly Sabbath, and through holy days, festivals, and celebrations at representative seasons.

On the other hand, the Jews were not unconcerned about space— that would have made them unidimensional. The Land of Israel remained a vitally important space for them, one to which they expected to be restored at the right time and in which they sought to maintain organized Jewish life at all times, through regular reinforcements from the diaspora even when things were at their worst.[10] Ultimately, modern Jews took matters into their own hands rather than wait for the restoration only in messianic times. Through the Zionist movement they reestablished first an autonomous Jewish community and then a Jewish state in the Land.[11]

Despite the success of Zionism, for two-thirds of world Jewry the State of Israel still remains "over there." They are devoted to it, but do not seek to make it the state of their citizenship or residence. So, just as moderns transformed the premodern commitment to space over time into a more modern commitment through the modern state system so did modern Jews or, more accurately, postmodern Jews, transform the particular Jewish relationship between time and space formed in premodern times into a more contemporary expression of the same.

This new relationship is at the heart of the new forms of Jewish diaspora political expression vis-à-vis the external world. Working on behalf of Israel has become a principal expression of Jewishness in the postmodern epoch whose secular character has served to diminish further the religious dimension of Jewish identification.[12] The existence of Israel has stimulated a sense of political efficacy among diaspora Jews as well as among those in the Jewish state, which not only manifests itself in Jewish lobbies for Israel but also in Jewish political self-assertion in other matters which Jews perceive as affecting the Jewish people as a group.

The definition of what Jews see as affecting them as a group can also be examined extensively. In the latter half of the modern epoch, Jewish self-interest came to be considered almost totally coincident with liberalism and even left-liberalism, since the liberals and the left were the principal advocates of Jewish emancipation while the conservatives and the right, in their support for the *ancien regime*, implicitly if not explicitly denied Jews full entry into the larger society.[13] Certainly by the latter half of the nineteenth century the vast majority of all Jews, traditional or modern, accepted the liberal outlook if only because they had no other choice. This convergence of interest was so great that Jews came to believe that it had always been so, whereas, in fact, in premodern times the interests of diaspora Jews converged at least as frequently—and usually more—with the conservatives and guardians of the *status quo* as with those seeking change, often at Jewish expense.

This overwhelming Jewish identification with liberalism had a latent functional utility in providing a unifying ideology for Jews at a time when traditional Jewish society was breaking down and Jews were losing the traditional bonds which had united them. The reestablishment of the Jewish state and the shifting goals of left-liberalism have led to the gradual breakdown of that automatic convergence, at the same time as the Jews found another rallying point around which to coalesce. Today, faithfulness to liberalism is no longer a requisite for the maintenance of common Jewish ties in the diaspora. Israel now serves that purpose, even for those who may be critical of the policies of a particular Israeli government.

## Viewing the Jewish People as a Polity

These lines of analysis can be pursued and deserve to be. The remainder of this chapter, however, will focus upon the Jewish people as a polity, especially as seen from the inside.

The suggestion that it is possible to talk about a world Jewish polity is based upon a combination of factors. In part, it rests upon the persistence of the sense of common fate among Jews all over the world, the sense of which was reactivated as a result of the events of this century. This sense has led to concrete efforts to work together to influence the shape of that fate wherever Jews have settled, particularly whenever they have required the assistance of their brethren. This, in turn, has led to the development of institutionalized frameworks for cooperation in a variety of contexts, in our times increasingly revolving around the State of Israel for self-evident reasons.

Finally, the entire effort has acquired a certain legitimacy in the eyes of Jews and non-Jews alike as a result of the emerging redefinition of what constitutes the proper context for political linkage and action, namely, the recognition—in the Western world, at least—that there are other forms of political relationship than those embraced within the nation-state, that polity is a far more complex condition than statehood, and that it can involve multiple relationships, not all of which are territorially based. In many respects, this represents a rediscovery of what had been an accepted phenomenon in the Western world until the modern era.

In short, we are beginning to recognize that all polities are not states. The Greeks, as usual, had a word for it. The Hellenistic world coined the term *politeuma* to describe phenomena such as the worldwide Jewish polity of that age in which Jews simultaneously maintained strong political links, including citizenship, with their respective territorial polities, the Hellenistic cities, and with one another across lands and seas.

## A Historical Survey

Jewish tradition has it that the Jews were born as a diaspora people, although a central aspect of their birth was identification with the land which became known to them as Eretz Israel—the Land of Israel. According to the Bible, the first Jew was Abraham, son of Terah, who was born in Ur of the Chaldeans, located in southern Mesopotamia near the Persian Gulf, and migrated with his family to Haran, now in northern Syria. On God's instructions, Abraham migrated to the land of Canaan (now Israel), which he subsequently left briefly because of a famine, but to which he soon returned.

Of Abraham's immediate descendants, only his son Isaac never left Canaan. His grandson Jacob (renamed Israel) sojourned for 20 years in Aram (now Syria) as a young man, returned to the land, and then spent his final days in Egypt. Abraham's great-grandson, Joseph, was forcibly taken to Egypt but remained there, later bringing his whole family which expanded from an extended family into a league of tribes while in Egypt.

The B'nai Israel (Children of Israel or Jacob) left Egypt as a people in a dramatic exodus led by a charismatic figure, Moses. In the course of the immediate exodus, Moses, as God's spokesman, established the basis for citizenship, promulgated a common law for the tribes immediately following the passage through the waters, and organized a full-blown polity at the foot of Sinai within seven weeks, through a national covenant and the introduction of a more regularized judicial structure and political organization.[14] Whether the traditional account is historically accurate is far less important than what that account teaches us about the origins of the Jewish people and how it has shaped the Jews' self-perception over at least three and perhaps closer to four millennia. As a people who perceives itself to have been born in exile, as it were, diaspora is not an abnormal condition even if it is not a desired one. The people's political, social, and religious institutions were, from the first, organized so that they were portable and did not need to be attached to the national soil in order to function.

No doubt as a consequence of these experiences, the basic form of Jewish organization was designed to accommodate migration as well as concentration in a national state. Since the beginning of political science, all political theory has converged on one or another of three basic forms of political founding, organization, and development: hierarchical, organic, and covenantal.[15] Hierarchical forms, which usually are the result of some initial conquest leading to the establishment of a political order, require a high concentration of power within a power pyramid, a more or less orderly structure, with a clear chain of command. Hierarchical forms are particularly useful for the governance of peoples concentrated within a single structure and clearly subject to the authority of those who dominate it. This kind of government went against the grain of Jewish political culture from earliest times, even when the Jews were concentrated in one land. Once they were scattered, and without any state whatsoever, this form of political organization was utterly impractical.

The organic form presumes a gradual and continuous development of political institutions serving a population rooted in one place into a political system which can continue to function as long as the population is so rooted, but which once detached no longer has the wherewithal to survive. Obviously for the Jews this was equally impractical.

The covenantal form of political organization emerges out of agreements among equals, or at least equals for the purposes of the agreement, to form partnerships for purposes of political organization. It does not presuppose a territory, a clear chain of command, or organic development in a particular place. On the contrary, it is flexible in form, it can be territorial or aterritorial as the case may be, and it is capable of binding people who cannot be bound by force or by custom because they are not bound to a particular territory.

The Jewish people opted for the covenantal form no later than the exodus from Egypt and so organized themselves during their formative generation in the desert. Granted, the tribes themselves had an organic dimension in the sense that the members of each claimed to be descended from a common ancestor. In that sense, the Jewish people have always tried to combine kinship and consent, the organic with the covenantal dimension, to secure its unity.[16] As a result, the Jews have been able to function as an ethnic group based upon primordial ties of kinship, a religious group based upon acceptance of the responsibilities of the Jewish religion, and a polity which rests upon the combination of both kinship and consent.

Over the centuries the Jews have refined this form of polity building. After the founding covenant at Sinai, the Israelite tribes renewed that covenant in the plains of Moab just before entering the land and then renewed it again at Shekhem under Joshua at the time of the conquest of Canaan.[17] When Israel changed its regime to add a king to the tribal federation, the first strictly national-political covenant was made between the tribes and David.[18] Much later, after David's kingdom had been divided and the northern kingdom conquered by Assyria, the regime was reconstituted under King Hezekiah through another covenant.[19] When the exiles returned from Babylonia after the first diaspora, they covenanted once again to reestablish the state of Judea within the framework of the Persian Empire.[20] Finally, in the last reconstitution of the Jewish polity within the Land of Israel until our own times, Simon the Hasmonean reconstituted an independent Jewish state through a covenant with the representatives of the people and the other institutions of the community.[21]

Subsequent to the exile, when it was no longer possible to use covenants in state building, they were transformed into instruments for community building with any ten men able to constitute themselves as a community and as a court of law within the context of the Torah through an appropriate covenant.[22] Finally, in our own times the reestablishment of the State of Israel rested on a series of covenants, culminating in the Declaration of Independence, referred to in Hebrew as the "Scroll of Independence," which was accepted, witnessed, and signed by a wall-to-wall coalition of the Jewish community in Eretz Israel at the time as at least a quasi-covenantal document, and has been so treated by the courts.[23]

Beyond the fact of communal survival, consent has remained the essential basis for the shaping of the Jewish polity. Jews in different localities consented (and consent) together to form congregations and communities—the terms are often used synonymously.[24] They did (and do) this formally through articles of agreement, charters, covenants, and constitutions. The traditional Sephardi term for such articles of congregational-communal agreement, *askamot* (articles of agreement), conveys this meaning exactly. The local communities were (and are) then bound by further consensual arrangements, ranging from formal federations to the tacit recognition of a particular *halakhic* authority, *shtadlan*, or supralocal body as authoritative.[25] When conditions were propitious, the *de facto* confederation of Jewish communities extended to wherever Jews lived. When this level of political existence was impossible, the binding force of Jewish law served to keep the federal bonds from being severed.

Thus, over the course of many centuries a very distinctive kind of polity has developed as the organized expression of Jewish communal life. While it has undergone many permutations and adaptations, an unbroken thread of institutions and ideas has run through the entire course of Jewish political life to give the Jewish people meaningful continuity.

It is important to emphasize this covenantal device, because of the way in which it made possible organized Jewish life in the diaspora beyond the merely religious sphere. Covenanting was only one of a range of complementary devices developed by the Jewish people to maintain their collective integrity even in the diaspora, with or without a center in the Land of Israel. In premodern times, when the Jewish community was all-embracing, whether in the state or the diaspora, these devices formed a framework within which all or virtually all Jews functioned. After the autonomous Jewish community had given way to the integration of individual Jews into the states in which they lived, this framework had to be readapted to a voluntaristic situation in which it provided a core, or magnet, around which those Jews who wished to could coalesce—rather than a framework embracing Jews whether they wanted to be included or not.[26] But the basic instruments have survived the transition and continue to offer the opportunity to do so under these new circumstances.

In sum, the Jewish people have the distinction of being the longest-lasting and most widespread "organization" in the history of the world. Its closest rival to that title is the Catholic church. Curiously—and perhaps significantly—the two are organized on radically opposed principles. The Catholic church is built on hierarchical principles from first to last and gains its survival power by their careful and intelligent manipulation.[27] The Jewish people is organized on covenantal or federal (from the Latin *foedus,* i.e., covenant) principles from first to last and enhances its survival power by applying them almost instinctively in changing situations. The contrasting characteristics of these two modes of organization are intrinsically worthy of political and social investigation. So, too, is the role of the Jewish polity in the development and extension of federal principles, institutions, and processes.[28]

## Heterogeneity of the Jewish Diaspora

Sometime in the thirteenth century B.C.E. the Israelite tribes crossed the Jordan into Canaan and began an unbroken period in what was renamed Eretz Israel. For seven and a half centuries the Jews remained concentrated in their land under independent governments of their own. This is the classic period of Jewish history as described in the Bible. During that period there may have been temporary settlements of Jews outside of the country and there are traditions of permanent Jewish settlements in such places as Yemen, although there is no corroborative evidence of this. But, in fact, 99 percent of the Jewish people were located in the Land of Israel.

In 721–22 B.C.E. the northern kingdom, comprising ten of the twelve original tribes, was conquered by Assyria and a major if undetermined portion of its population exiled to other parts of the Assyrian Empire, apparently in northern Mesopotamia. Popular legend has it that these exiles disappeared by assimilating into the local populations but there are traditions among the Jews of northern Iraq, Iran, and Afghanistan that they are descended from those exiles. Some historians hypothesize that at least a segment later merged with the subsequent infusions of the Jews from Judea who were exiled from their country after the conquest of the southern kingdom by the neo-Babylonians in the first decades of the sixth century B.C.E.[29]

Whether this was the first diaspora or not, it is clear that the recognized Jewish diaspora begins with the Babylonian captivity. It was then that organized communities of Jewish exiles were established in Babylonia and Egypt. They quickly developed institutions to accommodate their corporate needs in the diaspora, including the *bet knesset* which has come to be known to us in its Greek translation as the synagogue and which, in fact, means house of assembly, a kind of town hall, where Jews could undertake all their public functions, especially governance, study, and worship. Indeed the Hebrew term *knesset* (assembly) comes from the Aramaic *kanishta* which in turn is a translation of *edah*, the original Hebrew term describing the Jewish polity, the assembly or congregation of the entire people. Hence, the *bet knesset* was a miniature version of that larger assembly—one that could be established anywhere.[30] Thus, the framework established over 2,500 years ago has remained the basic framework for diaspora Jewish organization ever since.

It should be noted that the *bet knesset* is a product of the Babylonian exile; Jews who left Eretz Israel for Egypt tried to develop another framework around a temple constructed as a surrogate for that in Jerusalem, a system which required territorial permanence and did not gain acceptance outside of Egypt.[31] Even there it was replaced by the Babylonian system some 400 years later, precisely because of the portability of the *bet knesset* and the possibility of establishing synagogues wherever ten Jewish men gathered.

Seventy years after the destruction of Jerusalem in 537 B.C.E., Cyrus the Great conquered the neo-Babylonian Empire and, following his policy of the conciliation of minority peoples through the granting of cultural autonomy, allowed the Jews to return to Judea to rebuild their Temple. In fact, only a relatively small number of Jews chose to do so and while they and subsequent migrations, culminating in the great reconstitution of Ezra and Nehemiah approximately a century later, did succeed in reestablishing Eretz Israel as the center of Jewish life, a large diaspora community remained in Babylonia and, indeed, under Persian rule, spread throughout the Persian Empire. It was paralleled by a somewhat smaller but still significant diaspora in Egypt which spread into other parts of northern Africa, Cyprus, and Asia Minor.

For the next millennium the Jewish people were organized in a point-counterpoint arrangement. The Jewish concentration in the Land claimed and usually exercised hegemony within the Jewish polity, but with a substantial population, perhaps consistently a majority, scattered in diaspora communities throughout the civilized world at that time. Until its destruction in 70 C.E., the Temple in Jerusalem served as the focal point for both, with the Temple tax uniting Jews in the land and outside of it.

The principal institutions of the *edah*—the Jewish people as a whole—were located on the Temple Mount. New institutional arrangements were developed to provide representation for diaspora Jewry in those institutions, the first of which was known as the *Anshei Knesset Hagedolah* (men of the great assembly), which later gave way to a successor institution, the Sanhedrin, which is a corruption of the Hebrew corruption of the Greek term for assembly. But given the problems of transportation and communication in that period, there were difficulties in providing diaspora Jews continuous access and representation in those common institutions.[32]

In the diaspora itself two patterns developed, each a response to the particular host civilization in which Jews found themselves. In most of western Asia, where the Persians and their successors ruled, the Jews tended to be concentrated in particular areas and could organize their public life on a quasi-territorial basis, with regional as well as local institutions. Out of this evolved the "Babylonian" Jewish community, which was concentrated in what is today the heartland of Mesopotamia. By the second century C.E. it had an extensive political structure headed by a *resh galuta* (exilarch) whose powers were those of a protected king—for Jews a constitutional monarch who was recognized as being a descendant of the House of David. The *resh galuta* shared his powers with two great *yeshivot* (another Hebrew term for assembly) which had custody of the teaching and interpretation of the Torah. Together these institutions governed the collectivity of local Jewish communities within the empire.[33] This framework persisted until the eleventh century, even after the seventh-century Arab conquest which transformed the language, culture, and religion of western Asia. Until the fifth century C.E., it was at least formally subordinate to the equivalent polity in Eretz Israel which had a similar structure, but after the elimination of that polity the *resh galuta* and the *yeshivot* extended their control over virtually the entire Jewish world.

This was facilitated by the Arab conquests of the seventh and eighth centuries that brought over 95 percent of all Jews under the rule of the Muslim caliphate, which empowered the *resh galuta* and the *yeshivot* to represent the Jewish community as their predecessors had. It was only with the breakup of the original Muslim empire and the development of independent successor states that the Jews lost this common, well-nigh worldwide diaspora structure.[34]

Meanwhile, in the Mediterranean world, where Hellenistic civilization held sway and first the Greek and then the Roman empires provided a common political structure, the Jews were concentrated in cities. (The exception here was Egypt, which also had a wider territorial concentration for several centuries). There they formed a part of the *polis* organization developed for each city as part of its Hellenization after the Alexandrian conquests of the fourth century B.C.E.

It was in those cities that Jews formed autonomous communities within each *polis*, for which the Greek term *politeuma* was invented. Each of the *politeumata* represented a separate structure with connections to Jerusalem but with no formal linkages between one another. Thus, the Jewish communities in the Hellenistic and Roman worlds were far more fragmented. The institutions within each *politeuma* were based on Jewish models influenced by Greek practices and often bearing Greek names, but each was autonomous even when the Jews had citizenship within the *polis* itself.[35] Most of these *politeumata* were destroyed during the uprising of the Hellenistic diaspora against the Romans in the years 115–117 C.E. The communities reconstituted subsequent to that event had more limited rights. It was only after the Arab conquest that regional organizations of communities were established in those countries linked to the *resh galuta* and *yeshivot* in Babylonia, which was also the seat of the caliphate.

Both forms of diaspora organization were linked to Jerusalem when an independent Jewish state was reborn in the middle of the second century B.C.E. That state survived for less than a century, then went through a period of upheavals for the next 200 years until the failure of the Bar Kokhba rebellion (132–135 C.E.) led the Jews to abandon major efforts to rebel against Rome and rather reconstitute themselves along the model of the diaspora communities within their own land. The *nesiut* (patriarchate) and Sanhedrin which formed the new structure of the community of Eretz Israel also functioned as *prima inter parus* in the governance and religious leadership of the Jewish people, until those institutions were abolished in the middle of the fifth century, after which Jewish communal organization in Eretz Israel became even more diaspora-like in character, undergoing changes under different rulers from then until the reestablishment of the Jewish state in 1948 some 1,500 years later.[36]

Thus, the diaspora became the moving force in Jewish life. For 600 years the Babylonian center predominated. In the eleventh century there was increased Jewish migration to both southern and northern Europe which led to the transfer of power to the Jewish centers in Spain and, to a lesser extent, northern France and the Rhineland. The Iberian Peninsula and west central Europe remained the centers of Jewish life until the fifteenth century, when expulsions on the one hand and attractive offers of refuge on the other led the Jews from both centers to move back eastward: Iberian Jewry forming new concentrations in the Ottoman Empire, particularly in the Balkans, and central European Jewry concentrating in Poland. These two regions remained the principal centers of Jewish life until the nineteenth century.[37]

At first, Spanish Jewry—the Sephardim—followed the Babylonian pattern of regional organization, with local communities subordinate to the regional leadership. Under Christian rule, the local communities rose to predominance and the regional organization was limited to confederal arrangements. That pattern was later preserved in the Ottoman Empire where every congregation was autonomous and even within the same city congregations were often no more than confederated. The Jews of west central Europe—the Ashkenazim—developed local autonomy from the first, with loose leagues or confederations of communities providing whatever unification there was. But once they moved eastward to Poland they formed regional structures culminating in the *Vaad Arba Aratzot* (Council of the Four Lands), a fully articulated federation of the Jewish communities of Poland, and its parallels in Lithuania, Bohemia, and Moravia.

Worldwide, the Jewish people lost any common political structure after the middle of the eleventh century but remained tied together by a common constitutional-legal system (the *halakhah*), which was kept dynamic by a system of rabbinic decision making that was communicated to Jews wherever they happened to be through an elaborate network of *responsa*—formal written questions posed to leading Jewish legal authorities which produced formal written responses that came to constitute a body of case law. This was possible because 1,500 years earlier, at the time of Ezra and Nehemiah, the Jews had developed a legal system parallel to their political structure which translated the original constitutional materials of the Torah into an elaborate edifice designed to enable every Jew to conduct his entire life within the framework of Jewish law, no matter where he happened to reside.[38]

The legal system that emerged became, in effect, a portable state. The *halakhah's* avowed purpose was to transform each individual Jew into a person concerned with holiness. Hence it was not designed with a political purpose in the usual sense; yet this very concern for individual and collective holiness in a larger sense became a political end which served to provide a basis for the unity of Jewry, even in exile, as long as there was a general commitment to this end or at the very least to living under Jewish law as distinct from any other law.

While it is clear that not every Jew had the same commitment to holiness as an ultimate end, or to the particular path to holiness developed by the *halakhah*, in the centuries immediately following the destruction of the Temple this legal system gained normative status among Jews so that even those who were not highly motivated by its ultimate goals but who wanted to stay within the framework of the Jewish community felt the necessity to conform. Because of its attention to minute detail, every aspect of life, public and private, civil and criminal, religious and "secular" (a category which did not exist within the Jewish vocabulary), the *halakhah* was able to become all-embracing. The political structures developed by the Jews to conduct their public affairs were authorized by the *halakhah* and rooted in it, and a major task of Jewish communities was to enforce *halakhic* regulations.

The opening of the modern epoch in the middle of the seventeenth century slowly eroded this comprehensive framework, in waves rolling from west to east. Jewish autonomy was the first casualty in western Europe as the new nation-states dismantled medieval corporatism, a system that had protected Jewish communal separatism. At first, Jews became people without civic status in the new states and without the possibility of maintaining their own states within the state. This led them to demand emancipation and citizenship as individuals, which they ultimately gained after a struggle sometimes taking two centuries.[39] Finally, in the nineteenth century, the elimination of Jewish autonomy and then emancipation moved eastward to engulf the major concentrations of Jews in eastern Europe and the eastern Mediterranean, although it was not until the twentieth century that emancipation was completed in either region.[40]

While these changes were taking shape, a two-pronged demographic shift of great importance began. In the first place, the live birth and survival rate among Jews rose rapidly, causing the number of Jews in the world to soar. In the second, the Jews began to migrate at an accelerating pace to the lands on the Western world's great frontier: the Western hemisphere, southern Africa, and Australia in particular, but also in smaller numbers to East Asia, thus initiating a shift in the balance of Jewish settlement in the world.[41]

Medieval corporatism never gained a foothold in the New World and the Jews who migrated to those lands entered into their host societies as individuals.[42] Hence, all Jewish life was voluntary in character from the first.

While the majority of Jews readily abandoned communal separatism for the advantages of modern society, only a minority were ready to give up fully their Jewish ties in return. Most wanted to find some way to remain within the Jewish fold even while participating as individuals in the civil societies in which they found themselves or to which they migrated. Hence, they were faced with the task of adapting Jewish institutions to a new kind of diaspora existence.

Once again the great flexibility of covenantal institutions proved itself. The Jews transformed their *kehillot* (communities) into voluntary structures. In the Western world, where pluralism was tolerated principally in the religious sphere, the Jews transformed the *bet knesset* into the synagogue as we know it, whose manifest purposes were avowedly religious and whose central functions revolved around public worship, but which was able to embrace within it the various ethnic, social, educational, and welfare functions which the Jewish community sought to preserve, principally on a supplementary basis.

In eastern Europe, where modernization frequently meant secularization, new forms of Jewish association developed, primarily cultural and political, utilizing similar principles and, with the exception of the public worship dimension which was absent from them, devoted to the same ethnic, social, educational, and welfare purposes, only on a more extensive basis because Jews remained nationally separate in that part of the world. By and large, Jews in the Arab world followed the Western pattern when they began to modernize, but within a framework in which their separate ethnic identity was clearly recognized by one and all, and in which they preserved a certain legal authority over the community members by virtue of their continued control of personal status laws involving marriage, divorce, and inheritance.[43]

Nevertheless, the new voluntarism did make it very difficult, if not impossible, to provide a comprehensive framework for the maintenance of Jewish culture and civilization. It rapidly became clear that the open society would lead to the assimilation of many of the most talented members of the Jewish community who saw greater opportunities outside of the Jewish fold. It was in response to this as well as to anti-Semitism that the Jewish national movement developed, which made as its goal the restoration of Jewish statehood in Eretz Israel. This movement, known as Zionism, was initially organized on the same covenantal principles as every other such Jewish endeavor, developing first through local societies and then, in a massive leap forward represented by the First Zionist Congress in 1897, through the World Zionist Organization established at that congress. In 50 years the WZO succeeded in bringing about the establishment of a Jewish state.[44]

Zionism from the first embodied two conflicting goals. There were those who were Zionists because, while they wanted the Jewish people to survive, they wanted them to become normalized like other nations. They believed that if the Jewish people or some substantial segment of them were to return to their own land, they could live like the French, the Italians, the Czechs, the Poles, etc. The other trend in the Zionist movement regarded Zionism as a means of restoring the vitality of Jewish civilization, which would retain its uniqueness but be better able to survive under modern conditions by being rooted in a land and state where Jews formed a majority.

The first approach more or less negated the continued existence of a diaspora once a Jewish state was established. According to it, those Jews who wanted to remain Jews would settle in the state where they would live increasingly normalized lives, interacting with the rest of the world as nationals of any state interact with nationals of any other. The rest of the Jews would assimilate as individuals into their countries of residence, no longer needing to preserve their Jewishness. Many of those who embraced the second view also wished to negate the diaspora in the sense that they wanted all Jews to settle in Israel. But they did not see diaspora existence as impossible per se. Rather, the Jewish state could become the focal point of the renewed Jewish people, whether living in the state or in the diaspora.[45]

Reality forced the issue. The state was established; even after an initial mass migration of Jews from Europe, North Africa, and Western Asia, only about 20 percent of the Jewish people were concentrated within it (the figure is now one-third). Moreover, despite assimilatory tendencies, the great bulk of the Jews outside the state showed every inclination of wanting to remain Jews. Consequently, a new interplay between state and diaspora began to emerge. In this, the second generation since the establishment of the state, it is still evolving.[46]

## The Contemporary Situation

World War II marked the culmination of all the trends and tendencies of the modern era and the end of the era itself for all mankind. (The dates 1945–1948 encompass the benchmark of the transition from the modern to the postmodern era.) For the Jewish people, the Holocaust and the establishment of the State of Israel provided the decisive events that marked the crossing into the postmodern world. In the process, the focus of Jewish life shifted and virtually every organized Jewish community was reconstituted in some way.

Central to the reconstitution was the reestablishment of a Jewish commonwealth in Israel. The restoration of a politically independent Jewish state created a new focus of Jewish energy and concern precisely at the moment when the older foci had almost ceased to attract a majority of Jews. As the 1967 and subsequent crises demonstrated decisively, Israel was not simply another Jewish community in the constellation but the center of the world for Jews.

The Jewry that greeted the new state was no longer an expanding one that was gaining population even in the face of the attrition of intermarriage and assimilation. On the contrary, it was a decimated one (even worse, for decimated means the loss of one in ten, whereas the Jews lost one in three), a Jewry whose very physical survival had been in grave jeopardy and whose rate of loss from defections came close to equaling its birthrate. Moreover, the traditional strongholds of Jewish communal life in Europe (which were also areas with a high Jewish reproduction rate) were those that had been wiped out.

At the end of the 1940s, the centers of Jewish life had shifted decisively away from Europe to Israel and North America. By then, continental Europe as a whole ranked behind Latin America, North Africa, and Great Britain as a force in Jewish life. In fact, its Jews were almost entirely dependent upon financial and technical assistance from the United States and Israel. Except for those in the Muslim countries that were soon virtually to disappear, the major functioning Jewish communities had all become sufficiently large to be significant factors on the Jewish scene only within the previous two generations. Indeed, the shapers of those communities were still alive, and in many cases were still the actual community leaders. The Jewish world had been thrown back willy-nilly to a pioneering stage.

This new epoch is still in its early years, into its second generation; hence, its character is still in its formative stages. Nevertheless, with the establishment of the State of Israel in 1948 the Jewish polity began a constitutional change of revolutionary proportions, inaugurating a new epoch in Jewish constitutional history. For the first time in almost two millennia, the majority of the Jewish people were presented with the opportunity to attain citizenship in their own state. Indeed, Israel's very first law (*Hok Hashevut*—the Law of Return) specified that citizenship would be granted to any Jew-qua-Jew wishing to live within the country. In fact, the Law of Return is more complex than that. In an effort to show the Nazis that the Jewish people survived after all, the Knesset adopted many of the standards included in the Nuremburg laws for defining who is a Jew . At the same time, to accommodate Jewish tradition, the law provides for non-Jews to be converted to Judaism, presumably in a *halakhic* manner, although that is not exactly specified in the law, in order to qualify. Finally, the Israel Supreme Court has held (the Brother Daniel case is the leading decision) that a person will not be recognized as a Jew if he has converted or embraced another religion, although that is equivocal from a *halakhic* point of view. Jewish sensibilities, including the sensibilities of traditional Jews, have always accepted that limitation.

The reestablishment of a Jewish state has restored a sense of political involvement among Jews and shaped a new institutional framework within which the business of the Jewish people is conducted.

The virtual disappearance of the remaining legal or even social or cultural barriers to individual free choice in all but a handful of countries has made free association the dominant characteristic of Jewish life in the postmodern era. Consequently, the first task of each Jewish community has been to learn to deal with the particular local manifestation of this freedom.

The new voluntarism extends itself into the internal life of the Jewish community as well, generating pluralism even in previously free but relatively homogeneous community structures. This pluralism is increased by the breakdown of the traditional reasons for being Jewish and the rise of new incentives for Jewish association. At the same time, the possibilities for organizing a pluralistic Jewish community have also been enhanced by these new incentives. What has emerged is a matrix of institutions and individuals linked through a unique communications network, a set of interacting institutions which, while preserving their own structural integrity and filling their own functional roles, are informed by shared patterns of culture, activated by a shared system of organization, and governed by shared leadership cadres.

The character of the matrix which has emerged and its communications network varies from community to community. In some communities, the network is connected through a common center which serves as the major (but rarely, if ever, the exclusive) channel for communication. In others, the network forms a matrix without any center, with the lines of communication crisscrossing in all directions. In all cases, the boundaries of the community are revealed only when the pattern of the network is uncovered and this in turn happens only when both of its components are revealed—namely, its institutions and organizations with their respective roles and the way in which communications are passed between them.

The pattern itself is inevitably a dynamic one. That is to say, there is rarely a fixed division of authority and influence but, rather, one that varies from time to time and usually from issue to issue, with different elements in the matrix taking on different "loads" at different times and relative to different issues. Since the community is a voluntary one, persuasion rather than compulsion, influence rather than power, are the only tools available for making and executing policies. This, too, works to strengthen its character as a communications network since the character, quality, and relevance of what is communicated and the way in which it is communicated frequently determine the extent of the authority and influence of the parties.

The structure of the contemporary Jewish polity is that of a network of single and multipurpose functional authorities, no single one of which encompasses the entire gamut of Jewish political interests, although several have attempted to do so in specific areas:

1. "National institutions"—for example, Jewish Agency, World Zionist Organization, Jewish National Fund.
2. Multicountry associations—for example, ORT, World Jewish Congress.
3. Educational institutions defined as under the auspices of the entire Jewish people—for example, the universities in Israel.
4. Organizations under more specific local sponsorship whose defined sphere of activity is multicountry—for example, the Joint Distribution Committee.

Another way of grouping the multicountry associations is by their principal goals. Table 5.1 lists the broad categories, with prominent examples for each.

The political associations listed here as "general" are those concerned with the status of the Jewish people as a whole; in this they are both outer-directed to the non-Jewish world and inner-directed to the Jewish community. Although defacto the Israeli government can largely preempt political activity on the world scene if it chooses (other Jewish bodies normally acquiesce if Israel wants to do so), it has not explicitly claimed to act as the diplomatic agent for the Jewish people

### TABLE 5.1

| Principal Goal Characteristics | Organization |
| --- | --- |
| Political—general purpose | World Zionist Organization (WZO)<br>World Jewish Congress (WJC) |
| Political—special purpose | World Conference of Soviet Jewry |
| Distributive | Conference on Jewish Material Claims<br>Against Germany<br>Memorial Foundation for Jewish<br>Culture |
| Services—operational | World ORT Union |
| Services—coordinating | European Council of Jewish<br>Communities |
| Religious | World Union for Progressive Judaism<br>World Council of Synagogues<br>Agudat Israel World Organization |
| Association—fraternal | B'nai B'rith International Council |
| Association—special interest | World Sephardi Federation<br>World Union of Jewish Students |

beyond its borders. This leaves some room for diplomatic activity by the Jewish nongovernmental organizations, especially where Israel is not represented or is particularly limited in its access.[47]

## Jewish Communities in the New Epoch

Jews are known to reside in 135 countries, 97 of which have been permanent organized communities.[48] At least three and perhaps as many as twelve others are remnant communities where a handful of Jews have custody of the few institutions that have survived in the wake of the emigration of the majority of the Jewish population. Fourteen more are transient communities where American or Israeli Jews temporarily stationed in some Asian or African country create such basic Jewish institutions (e.g., religious services, schools) as they need. Only twenty-one countries with known Jewish residents have no organized Jewish life. Some 94 percent of all Jews reside in ten countries. In 1993, the largest communities were:

| 1.  | United States  | 5.6 million |
|-----|----------------|-------------|
| 2.  | Israel         | 4.2 million |
| 3   | France         | 530,000     |
| 4.  | Russia         | 415,000     |
| 5.  | Canada         | 365,000     |
| 6.  | Ukraine        | 276,000     |
| 7   | United Kingdom | 298,000     |
| 8.  | Argentina      | 211,000     |
| 9.  | Brazil         | 100,000     |
| 10. | South Africa   | 100,000     |
| 11. | Australia      | 90,000      |

In the late 1940s and the 1950s the reconstruction and the reconstitution of existing communities, and the founding of new ones, were the order of the day throughout the Jewish world. The Jewish communities of continental Europe all underwent periods of reconstruction or reconstitution in the wake of wartime losses, changes in the formal status of religious communities in their host countries, emigration to Israel, internal European migrations, and the introduction of new, especially communist regimes. Those communities in Muslim countries were transformed in response to the convergence of two factors: the establishment of Israel and the anticolonial revolutions in Asia and Africa. The greater portion of the Jewish population in those countries was transferred to Israel, and organized Jewish life, beyond the maintenance of local congregations, virtually came to an end in all of these countries except Iran, Morocco, and Tunisia.

English-speaking Jewry and, to a somewhat lesser extent, Jews of Latin America were faced with the more complex task of adapting their organizational structures to three new purposes: to assume the responsibility passed to them as a result of the destruction of European Jewry, to play a major role in supporting Israel, and to accommodate the internal changes of communities still in the process of acculturation. Many of the transient Jewish communities in Asia and Africa were actually founded or shaped in this period, while others, consisting in the main of transient merchants or refugees, were abandoned.

The collapse of the U.S.S.R. and its Communist empire, which had the last major concentration of Jews in Europe, led to another spurt of community-building in the years immediately after 1989. Demonstrating the Jewish talent for self-organization, organized Jewish communities rapidly appeared throughout the former Soviet Union, first local communities, then countrywide. While many of those who led in the establishment of these communities later emigrated to Israel, the communities have continued to exist. Thus, after seventy years of being denied the right to organize as Jews, with very few exceptions, every significant Jewish population concentration once again had an organized community.

At first, the pattern of Jewish communal organization followed that of the modern epoch with some modifications, but as the postmodern epoch leaves its own imprint, the differences in status and structure are diminishing. A common pattern of organizations is emerging, consisting of certain basic elements, including:

1. *Government-like institutions*, whether umbrella organizations or separate institutions serving discrete functions, that play roles and provide services at all levels (countrywide, local, and, where used, intermediate), which, under other conditions, would be played, provided, or controlled, whether predominantly or exclusively, by governmental authorities (for instance, services such as external relations, defense, education, social welfare, and public, that is, communal, finance), specifically:
   * a more or less comprehensive fundraising and social planning body;
   * a representative body for external relations;
   * a Jewish education service agency;
   * a vehicle or vehicles for assisting Israel and other Jewish communities;
   * various health and welfare institutions.

2. *Local institutions and organizations* that provide a means for attracting people to Jewish life on the basis of their most immediate and personal interests and needs, specifically:
   * congregations organized into one or more synagogue unions, federations, or confederations;
   * local cultural and recreational centers, often federated or confederated with one another.

3. General purpose mass-based organizations, operating countrywide at all levels, that function to: (a) articulate community val-

ues, attitudes, and policies; (b) provide the energy and motive force for crystallizing the communal consensus that grows out of those values, attitudes, and policies; and (c) maintain institutionalized channels of communication between the community's leaders and "actives" ("cosmopolitans") and the broad base of the affiliated Jewish population ("locals") for dealing with the problems facing the community, specifically:
  • a Zionist federation and its constituent organizations;
  • fraternal organizations.

4. *Special interest organizations* which, by serving specialized interests in the community on all planes, function to mobilize concern and support for the various programs conducted by the community and to apply pressure for their expansion, modification, and improvement.

## The United States

The United States, with over half of all the Jews in the diaspora, stands in a class by itself. The situation of a very large, fully modern society, established from the first on individualistic principles, pluralistic in the full sense of the word, settled by several significantly different waves of very adventurous Jewish immigrants who shared a common commitment in seeking new lives as individuals, was not conducive to the development of sufficient homogeneity to permit the formation of a neat communal structure.[49]

The organized American Jewish community is entirely built upon an *associational base*. That is to say, not only is there no inescapable compulsion, external or internal, to affiliate with organized Jewry, but all connections with organized Jewish life are based on voluntary association with some particular organization or institution, whether in the form of synagogue membership, contribution to the local Jewish Welfare Fund (which is considered to be an act of joining as well as contributing), or affiliation with a B'nai B'rith lodge or Hadassah chapter. Indeed, the usual pattern for affiliated Jews is one of multiple association with memberships in different kinds of associations that reinforce one another and create an interlocking network of Jewish ties that bind the individual more firmly to the community. Without the associational base, there would be no organized Jewish community at all; with it, the Jewish community attains social, and even a certain legal, status that enables it to fit well into the larger society of which it is a part.

The associational basis of American Jewish life is manifested in *a wide variety of local and countrywide organizations designed to suit every Jewish taste.* While these organizations may be confined to specific localities or may reflect specific interests, classes, or types on a strictly supralocal basis, the most successful ones develop both countrywide and local facets. It is no accident that B'nai B'rith, a countrywide (even worldwide) federation of multistate districts and local lodges, and Hadassah, a countrywide organization that emphasizes the role of its local chapters (which are further divided almost into neighborhood groups), are the two most successful mass Jewish organizations in the United States. The key to their success is that they provide both an overall purpose attuned to the highest aims of Jewish life as well as local attachment based on the immediate social needs of the individual Jew in such a way as to allow people to be members for either reason. Sooner or later, all large countrywide Jewish organizations have found that their survival is contingent upon developing some sort of serious local dimension to accommodate the very powerful combination of American and Jewish penchant for organizational arrangements on federal principles.

While certain of its organizations sometimes succeeded in developing from the top down, *the institutions of the American Jewish community are essentially local* and, at most, loosely federated with one another for very limited purposes. The three great synagogue movements, for example, are essentially confederations of highly independent local congregations, linked by relatively vague persuasional ties and a need for certain technical services. The confederations function to provide the requisite emotional reinforcement of those ties and the services desired by their member units. As in the case of the other countrywide organizations, they combine countrywide identification with essentially local attachments. With the exception of a few institutions of higher education (and, once upon a time, a few specialized hospitals, now nonsectarian), all Jewish social, welfare, and educational institutions are local in name and, in fact, some loosely confederated on a supralocal basis.

The demands placed upon the American Jewish community beginning in the late 1930s led to a growing recognition of the need to reconstitute the community's organizational structure at least to the extent of rationalizing the major interinstitutional relationships and generally tightening the matrix. These efforts at reconstitution received added impetus from the changes in American society as a whole (and the Jews' position in it) after 1945. They signaled the abandonment of earlier chimerical efforts to create a more orthodox organizational structure in imitation of foreign patterns which, given the character of American society as a whole, would have been quite out of place.

What has emerged to unite all these highly independent associations is a number of *overlapping local and supralocal federations* designed for different purposes. The most powerful among them are the local federations of Jewish agencies and their countrywide confederation, the Council of Jewish Federations (CJF), which have become the framing institutions of American Jewry and its local communities. They are the only ones able to claim near-universal membership and all-embracing purposes, though not even the CJF has the formal status of an overall countrywide umbrella organization. Other federal arrangements tend to be limited to single functions and their general organizations rarely have more than a consultative role or power of accreditation.

This *unity on a confederative basis*, which characterizes American Jewry, is very different from unity on a hierarchical one; what emerges is not a single pyramidal structure, nor even one in which the "bottom" rules the "top" (as in the case of most of the communities with representative boards), but a matrix consisting of many institutions and organizations tied together by a crisscrossing of memberships, shared purposes, and common interests, whose roles and powers vary according to situation and issue.

### Jewries of the British Commonwealth

While there are variations among them, characteristic of all of the Jewish communities whose origin is in the British Commonwealth is an ambivalence in defining their Jewishness. On the one hand, there is the sense on the part of both the community and the larger society of which it is a part that Jewish attachment is a form of "religious affiliation" and that every individual has free choice in the matter. On the other, there is an equally strong feeling that somehow Jews stand apart from the majority "Anglo-Saxon" population and can never bridge that gap. Regardless of the intensity of their Jewish attachments, the overwhelming majority of Jews in these countries have culturally assimilated into the wider society's way of life. Thus, the associational aspects of Jewish affiliation are far more important than the organic ones, however real the latter may be, and the community structure is built around associational premises from top to bottom.[50]

The communities themselves have no special status in public law. At most, there is an umbrella organization which is formally or tacitly accepted as the "address" of the Jewish community for certain limited purposes, and subsidiary institutions which are occasionally accorded government support (along with similar non-Jewish institutions) for specific functions. Nor do the communities have any strong tradition of communal self-government to call upon. All are entirely products of the modern era, hence their founders were either post-emancipation Jews or Jews seeking the benefits of emancipation and desirous of throwing off the burdens of an all-encompassing corporate Jewish life.

The larger communities in this category, at least, were created by successive waves of immigration, the greatest of which arrived in the past 100 years; hence, the history of their present communal patterns does not go back more than three or four generations, if that. Most of their present leaders are sons of immigrants, if not immigrants themselves.

### Boards of Deputies

Eleven of these communities have representative boards, usually called "Boards of Deputies," as their principal spokesmen. These representative boards in most cases formally embrace virtually all the other Jewish institutions and organizations in the community. Those other organizations, however, while nominally associated with the Board are, for all practical purposes, independent of and even equal to it in stature and influence. Fundraising, religious life, and social services tend to be under other auspices. The Board tends to be pushed in the direction of becoming the ambassador of the Jewish community to the outside world rather than its governing body. This tendency has been accelerated since World War II by the "coming of age" of the last great wave of immigrants and the consequent diminution of the monolithic character of most of the communities. The increase in competing interests, the decline in religious interest, and the growth of assimilatory tendencies have all contributed to this change.

Communities with representative boards are also constructed on federal lines. At the very least, the Boards become federations of institutions and organizations. In federal or quasi-federal countries, they become territorial federations as well.

## Latin America

The Eastern European Jews who migrated to Latin America in the twentieth century established replicas of the European *kehillah*, without official status but tacitly recognized by Jews and non-Jews alike as the organized Jewish community. The central institutions of these communities have a distinct public character but no special recognition in public law. Founded in the main by secularists, these communities were built in the mold of secular diaspora nationalism as it developed in Eastern Europe and emphasize the secular side of Jewish life. Since they function in an environment that provides neither the cultural nor the legal framework for a European-model *kehillah*, they must rely on the voluntary attachment of their members. The Latin American communities were relatively successful in maintaining this corporate pattern until recently because the great social and cultural gap between Jews and their neighbors aided in giving the Jews the self-image of a special and distinct group, but it has become increasingly difficult to maintain this as the gap disappears.

Ashkenazim and Sephardim organized their separate communities, in some cases by country or city of origin. Just as Jewish immigrants did not assimilate into their host countries, so, too, they did not assimilate among themselves. In the course of time, these communities loosely confederated with one another to deal with common problems that emerged in their relations with their external environment, essentially problems of immigration, anti-Semitism, and Israel. At the same time, each country-of-origin community retains substantial, if not complete, autonomy in internal matters and control over its own institutions.

In three of the larger Latin American countries (Argentina, Brazil, and Colombia) the indigenous federal or quasi-federal structure of the countries themselves influenced the Jews to create countrywide confederations based on territorial divisions (officially uniting state or provincial communities which are, in fact, local communities concentrated in the state or provincial capitals). In the other countries, the local community containing the overwhelming majority of the Jewish population itself became the countrywide unit, usually by designating its federation as the "council of communities." The community councils of the six Central American countries (total Jewish population 7,800) have organized the Federation of Central American Jewish Communities to pool resources and provide common services.

None of these tacitly recognized communal structures has been in existence for more than three generations, and the communities themselves originated no more than four generations ago. Most of the smaller ones are just now entering their third generation, since they were created by the refugees of the 1930s and 1940s. Consequently, many, if not most, are still in the process of developing an appropriate and accepted communal character.

The great postwar adjustment that has faced the Latin American communities centers on the emergence of a native-born majority. This new generation has far less attachment to the "old country" way of life with its emphasis on ideological and country-of-origin ties, hence the whole community structure is less relevant to them.

Moreover, most of the 625,000 Jews living in Latin America are located in unstable environments that do not necessarily encourage pluralism. Many of them are already beginning to assimilate into their countries, or at least into the local radical movements, in familiar Jewish ways. For an increasing number of Jews, the *deportivo*, or Jewish community recreation center, often seems the most relevant form of Jewish association and the building block for Jewish organizational life. The rise of these new institutions may foreshadow a new communal structure, based on local territorial divisions, that is emerging in these communities, with its accompanying substructure of associational activities whose participants are drawn in on the basis of common interest rather than of common descent.[51]

## Europe

In the wake of the destruction in World War II and subsequent communal reconstruction, the Jews in this region have developed new forms of communal association while at the same time retaining the formal structures of governance of the previous epoch. This is most obvious in the case of those communities which in the modern epoch had exhibited either the characteristics of a *Kultusgemeinde* (comprehensive state-recognized communal structure) or a *consistoire* (state-recognized or semi-official religious structure).

*Kehillot,* or state-recognized communal structures, were to be found in Central Europe, or areas influenced by Central European culture, before World War I. In recent years these communities have, by and large, lost their power to compel all Jews to be members and must now build their membership on a consensual basis. This usually means that all known Jews are automatically listed on the community's rolls but have the right to opt out if they choose to do so.

Structurally, the *kehillah* communities remain all-embracing. All legitimate institutions or organizations function within their overall framework, except where the state has allowed secessionist groups to exist. As countrywide communities, they are generally organized along conventional federal lines with either "national" and "local," or "national," "provincial," and "local," bodies, each chosen through formal elections and linked constitutionally to one another with a relatively clear division of power. In some cases, authority remains in the local community, perhaps with some loose confederal relationships uniting the various localities. The greatest source of strength of the state-recognized communities lies in their power to tax or to receive automatically a portion of their members' regular taxes from the authorities.

The state-recognized community, once the basis of Jewish life, is losing ground in size and importance in the Jewish world at the same time as it is losing its compulsory character. Most are declining communities, decimated by war, emigration, and assimilation. Moreover, an increasing number of Jews within those communities may be opting out of community membership (and the taxes that go with it). In 1980, 150,000 Jews lived in such communities.[52]

Despite its importance during the nineteenth century, only a remnant of the *consistoire* pattern still exists in France. Somewhat more faithful models are to be found in those countries within the orbit of French culture in Europe and Africa. In some, the *consistoire* has a certain legal status as a religious body and its officials are usually supported by government funds, but affiliation with it is entirely voluntary. It is distinguished by its emphasis on the exclusively religious nature of Judaism and its centralized character.

The *consistoire* is a casualty of the growing pluralism within the Jewish community. The refugees from Eastern Europe and, later, North Africa, who became major, if not the dominant, forces in many of the *consistoire* communities after World War II rejected its exclusively

sacerdotal emphasis, while the growth of secularism made Jewish identification via a state-recognized religious structure increasingly incon-
gruous. The new ultra-Orthodox congregations created by certain of
the refugees rejected the laxity of the official "orthodoxy" of the
*consistoire*, and the tasks of communal reconstruction in the aftermath
of the war proved too much for the consistorial bodies to handle alone.
Above all, the rise of Israel generated demands for mobilization of
diaspora resources that went beyond the capabilities of the *consistoire*
structure, necessitating more appropriate organizational arrangements.
In a broader sense, the times themselves conspired against the old
system, as committed Jews the world over rediscovered the national-
political aspects of Jewish existence.

New, entirely voluntary organizations began to emerge with a civil
orientation to reach those elements that were otherwise not part of the
official community. In the process, they began to assume the functions
of umbrella organizations to the extent that their local situation encouraged such organizations within the context of an emerging pluralism in Jewish communal life. Consistorial bodies survive, but without
the centrality they once had in Jewish life.[53]

## The Former Eastern Bloc

The communities located in the formerly Communist countries of
Eastern Europe are basically remnant communities, most of whose
earlier residents either died in the Holocaust or emigrated to Israel.
Under Communist rule they were subjugated in the way that all potential rivals for the citizens' interests are curbed in totalitarian societies.
Since the collapse of Communist rule, they have been revived, usually
in the form they had acquiesced before World War II. The communities in Czechoslovakia, Hungary, and Rumania actually have a formal
status similar to that of their sister communities in other continental
European countries and function through state-recognized communal
or religious structures. The communities of Bulgaria and Poland are
organized under what were originally Communist-imposed structures.

## The Former Soviet Union

Soviet Jewry, subjugated after World War I, lost the last remnants
of its organized communal life in the Stalin purges that came in the

aftermath of World War II. As glasnost and perestroika spread in the U.S.S.R. of the 1980s, Jews in local communities across the Soviet Union began raising their heads to establish free Jewish universities, cultural circles, or theater groups as nuclei of new community organizations. In 1989 these were expanded to include the normal institutions of an organized Jewish community and by 1991 the phenomenon had spread throughout the by-then dying U.S.S.R.[54] While the U.S.S.R. existed, there was a national body that claimed to speak for all Soviet Jews that had been established by a convention of representatives from all the local communities. Now that the U.S.S.R. has broken apart, similar or appropriate organizations were established in the newly independent republics.

## The Muslim World

The communities located in the Islamic countries of the Middle East are the remnants of what were, until the rise of Israel, flourishing traditional *kehillot*. Their present state of subjugation or dissolution dates from their host countries' attainment of independence or from the establishment of Israel, and therefore reflects another kind of postwar reconstitution. The character of the subjugation varies from virtually complete suppression of all communal and private Jewish activities (Iraq) to government appointment of pliable leadership to manage the community's limited affairs (Tunisia). Only Morocco and Turkey have allowed their Jewish communities to continue to function with a minimum of disturbance, albeit under close government supervision.

In every case, the Jews' situation has deteriorated after each Israeli victory and the number of Jews remaining in the communities has decreased. Since emigration from the larger ones is not impossible, it seems clear that they, too, are fated to disappear or to become no more than very small remnant communities in the near future. In the meantime, communal life continues as much as possible. This usually means some form of religious life, increasingly limited opportunities to provide children with a Jewish education, and a few limited social services.[55] Iran, the last major concentration of Jews in the Muslim world, watched its Jewish community flee after the fall of the Shah who had been the Jews' protector, and the establishment of the Islamic republic. In Morocco, where the king continues to protect the Jews, the exodus has been more gradual. Each of those communities today has approximately 13,000 Jews. In Morocco, the future looks promising as a result of the Israel-Arab peace process, while in Iran it seems quite gloomy. Today Turkish Jewry remains the largest Jewish community in the Muslim world. While the Jews in Turkey are essentially free and protected, they are also closely supervised by the government, which does so with a velvet rather than an iron hand.

## Considerations

What can be learned about diaspora existence from the Jewish experience which is new and unique? Four points can be made in particular.

1. Long-term diasporas seem to be an Asian phenomenon, in that the peoples who seem to be able to produce and sustain diasporas are overwhelmingly Asian or emerged from Asia. European émigrés to new territories break off into fragments of their original cultures, as Louis Hartz has pointed out in *The Founding of New Societies*, and then become separate peoples in their own right.[56] Traditional African cultures remained tribal, even in the case of the great tribal empires, and handled migration within Africa through the breakoff of families or clans and their reconstitution as new tribes. Africans who migrated outside of Africa did so on a forced basis as slaves and hence were given no chance to establish a diaspora. Although in recent times there has been some effort to impose a diaspora-style context on American Blacks, it has not succeeded. It seems that the nature of peoplehood in Asia and its relationship to statehood—whereby peoples are far more enduring than states—is an essential condition for the creation of diasporas. The Jews are a prime example of an Asian people who carried their diaspora first into North Africa, then Europe, and then into the New World, but they never lost this Asian dimension of their being.

2. A second point is that the Jewish experience is the quintessential example of how diasporas can be state initiators. The history of the reestablishment of the State of Israel may be the classic of its kind, but it is not the only such example. It was the Norwegian diaspora in the United States which initiated the separation of

Norway from Sweden, which led to Norwegian independence in 1905, and the Czech diaspora which initiated the establishment of Czechoslovakia after World War I. At any given time there may be a number of diasporas that are actively trying to establish states, such as the Armenians, for example. This is an important dimension in the reciprocal state-diaspora relationship.[57]

3. A third point is that the nature of interflows between state and diaspora and segments of the diaspora needs to be more fully examined. This chapter has suggested some of those interflows in the contemporary Jewish world. Elsewhere, I have mapped the shifting nature of such flows and the different institutional frameworks for them in different epochs of Jewish history.[58] One would expect that this would be useful to do in connection with other diasporas as well.

What has been characteristic of the Jews is that at times they have had highly visible frameworks for such interflows. We have already noted how, in the days of the Second Temple, Jews throughout the world made pilgrimage and paid an annual Temple tax as well as accepted the authority of the Sanhedrin, which sat in the Temple. Several hundred years later, the *resh galuta* and *yeshivot* in Babylonia exercised authority over 97 percent of the Jews of the world who happened to be within the Arab caliphate. At other times, the institutional structure was articulated but not quite as apparent to most Jews, even if they were influenced by it. That is the condition today regarding the various authorities which link Israel and the diaspora and the various diaspora communities with one another. What is becoming clear to those involved is that the reconstituted Jewish Agency for Israel and its constituent organizations are beginning to play a similar role on a voluntary basis.

4. There were situations in which external conditions prevented any visible institutional framework other than the institutions of local decision making, whereby *halakhic* authorities from all parts of the Jewish world were in correspondence with one another and turned to one another for decisions binding on the entire Jewish people. The communications among these authorities helped maintain the formal constitutional structure of the Jewish

people, which helped keep the Jewish constitutional framework intact even when Jews had no political institutions to unite them. This formal legal framework was supplemented by the continuing movement of travelers and migrants among most, if not all, of the communities of the Jewish world at any given time, which served to preserve the ethnic as well as the constitutional ties uniting the Jewish people.

5. Finally, any proper study of diasporas should consider the role of technology in making possible the maintenance of links between diaspora and state or one diaspora community and another. At the beginning of the Jewish diaspora, 2,500 years ago or more, it is very likely that Jews who spread beyond the limits of ongoing communication with their brethren (such as the Jews who settled in China), given the technologies of the time, disappeared as Jews. No doubt, the fact that first the Persians and then the Romans emphasized road building to facilitate communication among the far-flung reaches of their respective empires had a vital impact on the Jews' efforts in maintaining their links.

Later, in medieval times, the relative ease of water communication in the Mediterranean world held the Jewish communities of the Mediterranean Basin together while Jews who moved north of the Alps, though not out of communication with the rest of the Jewish world, developed a subculture of their own. The two subcultures persist to this day in the form of Sephardim and Ashkenazim.

In our own times, it is clear that the possibility of reviving common institutions for the Jewish people has been strengthened by the availability of such instruments as the telephone and the jet plane. Certainly, technology has served to heighten diaspora consciousness among other peoples. It would be worth investigating whether this has also helped foster links between other groups in the way it has with the Jews.

Because of the rapid changes in transportation and communications technology, the increased mobility of individuals across state lines, and the greater interdependence of states throughout the world, it may be that diaspora and the state-diaspora relation as they were known in the past will themselves undergo a sea change. While diasporas will continue to grow as they have since the end of World War II, there will also be a situation in which significant populations will not be identifiable as living either in their state or in its diaspora. That is to say, they will live in both places, spending part of the year in one and part in the other, or traveling back and forth with great frequency. Maintaining their homes in one and their business interests in the other will be a common feature. Thus, the whole idea of what is a diaspora will have to shift to accommodate new trends.

## Notes

1. According to the *Oxford English Dictionary*, the term diaspora originates from the *Septuagint*, Deuteronomy 28:25, "thou shalt be a diaspora in all kingdoms of the earth" (1897 ed., p. 321).
2. See S. W . Baron, *A Social and Religious History of the Jews* (New York: Columbia University Press, 1973); Yehezkel Kaufman, *Gola V'Nechar* (Diaspora and Exile) (Tel Aviv: Dvir, 1958); Raphael Patai, *The Tents of Jacob: The Diaspora Yesterday and Today* (Englewood Cliffs, N.J.: Prentice-Hall, 1971); A. Tartakower, *Hahevra Hayehudit* (Jewish Society) (Tel Aviv: Dvir, 1959).
3. See Daniel J. Elazar, *Community and Polity: The Organizational Dynamics of American Jewry* (Philadelphia: Jewish Publication Society of America, 1976), pp. 70–77, and *People and Polity: The Organizational Dynamics of Post-Modern Jewry* (Detroit: Wayne State University Press, 1989).
4. Cf. James William Parkes, *The Conflict of the Church and the Synagogue* (New York: Atheneum, 1969), and *The Jew and His Neighbour* (London: Student Christian Movement, 1930).
5. See S. W. Baron, *A Social and Religious History of the Jews*, esp. vol. 12; W. P. Zener, *Jewish Retainers as Power Brokers in Traditional Societies*, paper presented at the 74th meeting of the American Anthropological Association, San Francisco, December 4, 1975.
6. See W. F. Albright, *The Biblical Period from Abraham to Ezra* (New York: Harper and Row, 1963); J. Bright, *A History of Israel*, 3rd ed. (Philadelphia: Westminster Press, 1981); Harry M. Orlinsky, *Ancient Israel*, 2nd ed. (Ithaca: Cornell University Press, 1967).
7. See F. J. Burner, *The Frontier in American History* (New York: Holt, 1920); R. A. Billington, *Westward Expansion: A History of the American Frontier* (New York: Macmillan, 1949); W. P. Webb, *The Great Frontier* (London: Secker and Warburg, 1953).
8. See A. J. Heschel, *Israel: An Echo of Eternity* (New York: Farrar, Strauss and Giroux, 1969).
9. See Daniel J. Elazar, *Cities of the Prairie* (New York: Basic Books, 1970), pp. 7–10; J. Goody, "Time" in *International Encyclopedia of the Social Sciences*, vol. 16, p. 30, et. seq., esp. pp. 39–41.
10. See Isidore Epstein, *Judaism: A Historical Presentation* (England: Penguin, Middlesex, 1974); B. Halpern, *The Idea of a Jewish State*, 2nd ed. (Cambridge, Mass.: Harvard University Press, 1969); J. W. Parkes, *A History of Palestine from 135 A.D. to Modern Times* (New York: Oxford University Press, 1949).
11. See W. A. Laqueur, *A History of Zionism* (New York: Shocken Books, 1976); D. Vital, *The Origins of Zionism* (Oxford: Clarendon Press, 1975).

12. See Steven M. Cohen, *American Modernity and Jewish Identity* (New York: Tavistock, 1983), Daniel J. Elazar, "Renewable Identity", *Midstream* (January 1981); Peter Y. Medding, "Toward a General Theory of Jewish Political Interests and Behaviour in the Contemporary World," in *Kinship and Consent: The Jewish Political Tradition and Its Contemporary Uses*, ed. Daniel J. Elazar (Ramat Gan, Israel: Turtledove, 1981).

13. See L. H. Fuchs, *The Political Behaviour of American Jews*, (Glencoe, Ill.: Free Press, 1956); M. Himmelfarb, *The Jewish of Modernity* (New York: Basic Books, 1973); Stephen Isaacs, *Jews and American Politics* (New York: Doubleday, 1974); Charles S. Liebman, *The Ambivalent American Jew* (Philadelphia: Jewish Publication Society of America, 1973); P. Y. Medding, "Patterns of Political Organization and Leadership in Contemporary Jewish Communities," in *Kinship and Consent*, ed. Daniel J. Elazar; M. Sklare, *The Jew in American Society* (New York: Behrman House, 1974); J. Weyl, *The Jew in American Politics* (New Rochelle: Arlington House, 1968).

14. See W. F. Albright, *The Biblical Period from Abraham to Ezra*; Daniel J. Elazar and Stuart A. Cohen, *The Jewish Polity* (Bloomington: Indiana University Press, 1984).

15. I have elaborated this thesis more fully in "Covenant and Freedom in the Jewish Political Tradition," *Annual Sol Feinstone Lecture*, Gratz College, March 15, 1981.

16. See Daniel J. Elazar, "Covenant as the Basis of the Jewish Political Tradition," *Jewish Journal of Sociology*, no. 20 (June 1978): 5–37; G. Freeman, "Rabbinic Conceptions of Covenant," in *Kinship and Consent*, ed. Daniel J. Elazar; D. R. Hiller, *Covenant: The History of a Biblical Idea* (Baltimore: John Hopkins, 1969).

17. Deuteronomy 34:1–4; Josh. 24:1–25.

18. II Samuel 5:1.

19. II Kings 18.

20. Ezra 1:2; Nehemia 8:1–8.

21. I Maccabees 8:1–9.

22. Cf. G. Blidstein, "Individual and Community in the Middle Ages," and M. Elon, "On Power and Authority: Halachic Stance of the Traditional Community and Its Contemporary Implications," both in *Kinship and Consent*, ed. Daniel J. Elazar; M. Elon, ed., *The Principles of Jewish Law* (Jerusalem: Institute for Research in Jewish Law Publications, 1975).

23. Cf. Y. Aricha *Megilat Haazmaut—Chazon Vemetsiut* (Declaration of Independence—Vison and Reality), Faculty of Political Science, Bar Ilan University (unpublished); H. M. Kallen, *Utopians at Bay* (New York: Theodor Herzl Foundation, 1958); Amnon Rubinstein Hamishpat Hakonstituzioni shel Medinat Yisrael (The Constitutional Law of the State of Israel) (Jerusalem: Shocken Books, 1979).

24. Leo Baeck discusses this phenomenon in *This People Israel* (Philadelphia, 1965). See also Daniel J. Elazar, "The Quest for Community: Selections from the Literature of Jewish Public Affairs, 1965–1966," *American Jewish Yearbook*, vol. 68 (New York and Philadelphia: American Jewish Committee and Jewish Publications Society, 1967).

25. See, for example, C. Finkelstein, *Jewish Self-Government in the Middle Ages*, 2nd ed. (New York: Feldheim, 1964); and H. H. Ben-Sasson, *Perakim Betoldot Hayehudim Beyamei Habaynayim* (chapters in the history of Jewish in the Middle Ages) (Tel Aviv, 1969).

26. See Daniel J. Elazar, *Community and Polity*; M. Himmelfarb, *The Jews of Moder-*

*nity*; C. S. Liebman, *The Ambivalent American Jew*; H. M. Sachar, *The Course of Modern Jewish History* (New York: Dell Publishing Co., 1958).

27. See, for example, E. Samuel, "The Administrator of the Catholic Church," in *Public Administration in Israel and Abroad, 1966* (Jerusalem, 1967), one of the few such studies available.

28. A few historians and social scientists have taken note of the covenant community as a distinct sociopolitical phenomenon from this perspective. Margaret Mead, for example, suggests that the Jewish polity and other covenant communities deserve special exploration; see her "Introduction" to M. Zborowski and E. Herzog, *Life is with People* (New York, 1952). For an eloquent evocation of the spirit and character of the covenant community, see Page Smith, *As a City Upon a Hill* (New York, 1967).

29. See A. Malamat, "Assyrian Exile," in *Encyclopedia Judaica*, vol. 6, p. 1034; I. Ephal, "Israel: Fall and Exile," in *The World History of the Jewish People*, vol. 4, ed. A. Malamat and I. Ephal (Jerusalem: Massada Press, 1979), chapter 8; H. H. Ben-Sasson, ed., *A History of the Jewish People* (London: Weidenfield and Nicolson), chapter 9.

30. See L. Baeck, *This People Israel: The Meaning of Jewish Existence* (Philadelphia: Jewish Publication Society, 1965), S. W. Baron, *The Jewish Community: Its History and Structure to the American Revolution* (Westport, Conn.: Greenwood, 1972); Isaac Levy, *The Synagogue: Its History and Function* (London: Valentine Mitchell, 1963).

31. See B. Porten, *Archives from Elephantine* (Berkeley: University of California Press, 1960), chapter 4.

32. See S. Hoenig, *The Great Sanhedrin* (Philadelphia: Dropsie College, 1953); H. Mantel, *Studies in the History of the Great Sanhedrin* (Cambridge, Mass.: Harvard University Press, 1961).

33. See M. Baer, *Rashut Hagolah B'Bavel Bimei HaMishna VhaTalmud* (Leadership and Authority in the Times of the Mishna and the Talmud) (Tel Aviv, 1967); J. Neusner, *There We Sat Down: Talmudic Judaism in the Making* (New York, Ktav, 1978).

34. See Daniel J. Elazar and Stuart A. Cohen, *The Jewish Polity*.

35. See S. W. Baron, *The Jewish Community*.

36. See C. Albeck, "Hasanhedrin U'Nesieiha" (The Sanhedrin and Its President) *Zion* 8 (1963), pp. 165–78; S. L. Albeck, *Batei Hadin Bimei HaTalmud* (Courts of the Talmudic Period); G. Along, *The Jewish in Their Land in the Talmudic Age (70–640 c.e.)*, vol. 1, trans. and ed. G. Levi, (Jerusalem, 1980); M. Avi-Yonah, *The Jewish of Palestine: A Political History from the Bar Kochba War to the Arab Conquest* (Oxford, 1976); A. I. Baumgarten, "The Akiban Opposition," *Hebrew Union College Annual* 50 (1974): 179–97; E. Goldenberg, "Darko Shel Yehuda Hanasi," (In the Arrangement of the Mishna) *Tarbitz* 28 (1959): 260–69.

37. S. W. Baron, *A Social and Religious History of the Jews*, vol. 10, chapter 45, and vol. 16; M. Elon, ed., *Principles of Jewish Law*.

38. See S. Assaf, *Tekufat Hagaonim Vesifruta* (The Period of the Sages and Its Literature) (Jerusalem: Mosad Harav Kook, 1955); Boaz Cohen, *Law and Ethics in the Light of the Jewish Tradition* (New York: Ktav, 1947), and *Law and Tradition in Judaism* (New York: Katav, 1969); M. Elon, ed., *The Principles of Jewish Law*; S. B. Freehof, *The Responsa Literature* (New York: Ktav, 1973); L. Ginsberg, *On Jewish Law and Lore* (New York: Atheneum, 1970); C. H. Tchernowitz, *Toledoth Hahalacha* (The History of Halacha) (New York: Vaad Hayovel, 1953).

39. See S. W. Baron, *A Social and Religious History of the Jews*; H. M. Sacha, *The Course of Modern Jewish History.*
40. See H. P. Friedenrich, *The Jews of Yugoslavia* (Philadelphia: Jewish Publications Society of America, 1979); J. Datz, *Tradition and Crisis* (Cambridge, Mass.: Harvard, 1974) and *Out of the Ghetto* (Cambridge: Harvard, 1976); N. Katzburg, *Hungary and the Jews* (Ramat Gan, Israel, 1981); J. Levitats, *The Jewish Community in Russia, 1772–1844*, (New York, 1943); E. Mendelsohn, *The Jews of East Central Europe between the World Wars*, (Bloomington, Ind., 1983); B. D. Weinreib, *The Jewish of Poland* (Philadelphia, 1972) M. Wilenski, *Hasidim Umitnagdim* (Jerusalem, 1970).
41. See A. Altman, *Moses Mendelsohn: A Biographical Study*; S. W. Baron, *A Social and Religious History of the Jews*, vol. 15; S. Ettinger, "The Modern Age," in *A History of the Jewish People*, part 3, ed. H. H. Ben-Sasson (Cambridge, Mass., 1976); A. Hertzberg, *The French Enlightenment and the Jews*, (New York, 1968) J. Reinharz, *Fatherland of Promised Land: The Dilemma of the German Jews, 1893–1914* (Ann Arbor, 1975); C. Roth, *History of the Jews in England*, 3rd ed. (Oxford, 1964).
42. See Daniel J. Elazar, *Community and Polity* and *People and Polity*; with P. Medding, *Jewish Communities in Frontier Societies* (London and New York: Holmes and Meir, 1983.
43. See Daniel J. Elazar, "The Reconstitution of Jewish Communities in the Post-War Period," *Jewish Journal of Sociology* 11, no. 2 (December, 1969).
44. See W. A. Laqueur, *A History of Zionism*; D. Vital, *The Origins of Zionism.*
45. See A. Herzberg, *The Zionist Idea* (Westport, Conn.: Greenwood, 1975).
46. See the series *HaChug L'Yediyat Am Yisrael B'Tfutzot B'Beit Nasi Hamedina* (Study Circle on World Jewry in the Home of the President of Israel), Shagar Library, Institute of Contemporary Jewry, Hebrew University of Jerusalem, especially B. Halpern and I. Kolatt, "Amadot Mishtanot B'Yehesai Medinat Yisrael VeHatefutsot" (Changing Relations Between Israel and the Diaspora), Third Series, No. 607 (1970–1971); E. Schweid, "HaKarat HaAm HaYehudi B'Hinuch B'Yisrael" (Identification with the Jewish People in Israeli Education) Sixth Series, No. 6 (1972–1973); N. Rotenreich, Z. Abromov, and Y. Bauer, "Achrayuta Shel Medinat Yisrael Latfutzot" (Israel's Responsibility to the Diaspora) Ninth Series, No. 7 (1977–1978).
47. Cf. Daniel J. Elazar and A . M. Dortort, eds., *Understanding the Jewish Agency: A Handbook* (Jerusalem: Jerusalem Center for Public Affairs, 1984); E. Stock, "Jewish Multi-Country Association" in *American Jewish Yearbook 1994* (New York: American Jewish Committee, 1994).
48. See Daniel J. Elazar, "The Reconstitution of Jewish Communities in the Post-War Period," *Jewish Journal of Sociology*; Daniel J. Elazar and Stuart A. Cohen, *The Jewish Polity.*
49. See L. Hartz, *The Founding of New Societies: Studies in the History of the United States, Latin America, South Africa, Canada, and Australia* (New York: Harcourt, Bruce & World, 1964).
50. See Daniel J. Elazar, *People and Polity: The Organizational Dynamics of World Jewry* (Detroit: Wayne State University Press, 1989), chapter 11.
51. Ibid., chapter 13.
52. Ibid., chapter 15.
53. Ibid., chapter 14.
54. See Zvi Gittelman, "Former Soviet Union," *American Jewish Yearbook 1994*, pp.

337–345; Betsy Gidwitz, "Post-Soviet Jewry at Mid-Decade," parts 1 and 2, Jerusalem Letter No. 309, February 15, 1995, and No. 310, March 1, 1995; Irwin Cotler, "Revolutionary Times in the Soviet Union" in *Jerusalem Letter/Viewpoints*, no. 93 (October 2, 1989).

55. See George E. Gruen, "Jewish in the Middle East and North Africa," *American Jewish Yearbook 1994* (New York: American Jewish Committee, 1994).

56. Hartz, *The Founding of the New Societies.*

57. See B. Azkin, *State and Nation* (London: Hutchinson University Library, 1964).

58. See Daniel J. Elazar and Stuart A. Cohen, *The Jewish Polity: Jewish Political Organization from Biblical Times to the Present* (Bloomington: Indiana University Press, 1985).

# 6

# The Attitude Towards the State in Modern Jewish Thought Before Zionism

*Eliezer Schweid*

Those who study the history of the Jewish people generally assume that the transition from the political order of the Middle Ages to that of modern times and the expansion of the role of the modern state, which is characterized by state centralization and its sovereignty over all areas (including religious institutions), are primarily what distinguish the modern era. Hence, it is not surprising that the proper role of the state and its influence on society and culture have represented a central problem for modern Jewish thought from its inception.

Four primary questions were raised: (1) What is the vision of the state in the Bible and the traditional Jewish sources? (2) What are the implications of this vision for the views and ways of life of modern Jews? (3) What kind of attitude toward the modern state is made obligatory by the traditional Jewish vision of the state? (4) What are the changes which need to and can be made in the traditional vision of the state and in the Jewish way of life, or, perhaps, in the modern understanding of the state, to adjust the Jewish people to this new reality without causing them to lose their separate identity? In the following discussion, I will try to briefly present what appear to me to be the typical approaches to these questions.

Every discussion of modern Jewish political thought must begin by responding to Spinoza. Although Spinoza cannot be considered a particularly Jewish thinker, still, in his break with Judaism, he made obvious the challenge to which almost all of those who followed him responded. We should also recall that Spinoza's break with Judaism took place against the background of a new political reality while struggling to realize a new political idea. Spinoza discovered that it was possible to live as a private citizen within a state without belonging to the Jewish community and without changing one's religion. This phenomenon in itself depicts the modern political reality. Spinoza's attempt to formulate the role of a political order in which state sovereignty stands above the religions within the state and demands freedom of thought for the individual also influenced his studies of the history and character of the Jewish state, and led him to portray Judaism as a basically political phenomenon, in some respects a positive one, but in the final analysis, completely anachronistic. Spinoza portrayed the Judaism of his time, with its medieval theology and communal way of life, as a total distortion of the idea depicted in the Bible, and totally irrelevant to modern times.

The Jewish political vision embodied in the Bible, as Spinoza saw it, was a theocracy characterized by the absolute identity of state and religion. God was considered the Sovereign of the Jewish state. Although this was a political fiction—in actuality all theocracies are ruled by men—for Spinoza, the Jewish theocracy nevertheless had practical significance in that Moses and the prophets who succeeded him believed that they were carrying out God's will. The practical significance of the theocratic political order lay in the fact that sovereignty was never completely deposited in the hands of any human authority, but was divided among the military leaders, the elders of the community, the priests, and the prophets. All were interdependent. No one group had ultimate power since succession within these groups, with the exception of the priests, was not based on heredity (and, according to Spinoza, it was this exception that initiated the destruction of the Jewish state). According to the Bible, no political institution had sovereignty over the people, nor did the people have sovereign powers to elect their representatives; in this sense, it can truly be argued that God Himself was the leader who chose his representatives from among the people. In addition, ritual legislation was an integral part of the political order. It contributed to the unity of the people, to its complete loyalty to its state, and to the cultivation of sense of importance and a feeling of superiority over the neighboring peoples. All of this explains the success of the Jewish theocratic state. Moreover, Spinoza saw such a political arrangement, in which there was an equal balance between the various ruling authorities, as ideal for a people who had emerged from slavery. This was the only type of "democracy" that was appropriate for a people not yet prepared for true democracy. However, over the course of time, it was impossible to prevent the process of disintegration as each of the ruling authorities became entrenched and began to seek complete sovereignty, thus leading to the destruction of the Jewish state from within.

The analysis of the essence and the fate of theocracy was important to Spinoza in order to draw conclusions of practical significance for his own time. He sought to show that his view of the proper relationship between religion and state paralleled that of the Bible. (According to Spinoza, the Bible does not sanction the interference of religion in political matters, but rather sees religion as the political order itself. On the contrary, interfering with the state's legitimate sovereignty is self-destructive.) Therefore, his basic criticism is leveled not against the idea of theocracy but against the results of the degeneration of theocracy, even though he believed the degeneration to be caused by an essential flaw in theocracy itself. Thus, Spinoza's basic criticism of Judaism was directed against Maimonides who represented for him Rabbinic Judaism. In order to respond to our second question—the implications of the biblical vision of the state for us toady—we must explore Spinoza's stand on this matter.

As we have seen, Spinoza did not oppose the theocratic idea as it was realized in the Bible. He believed it to be an excellent solution for the people of Israel in their particular historical circumstance. Hence, he never dismissed the possibility of the renewal of the Jewish state. The Jewish people, oppressed, persecuted, but able to preserve its separate identity among the nations of the world, could presumably establish a state based on its own laws. However, in Spinoza's opinion, from the perspective of good political theory, Jewish law (*halakhah*) has no authority in the political reality of the diaspora, and is not binding on the Jewish community. The Jews living in a particular state are bound by the laws of that state, and the separate laws of the Jewish community have no validity. Rabbinic Judaism opposed this view, maintaining that the laws of the Torah carry full authority and that the religious institutions have the right to enforce them. Maimonides' position, which Spinoza viewed as that of Rabbinic Judaism, was in his opinion analogous to that of the Catholic church. Maimonides believed that the Torah leads to spiritual fulfillment—a goal superior to that of the state which seeks only mundane fulfillment. Hence, the community may use political means to enforce observance of the Torah. For Spinoza, this was a total perversion which exposed the community to two primary dangers: (a) the pretence of ordering beliefs, limiting the individual's freedom of thought; and (b) the intervention of the religious establishment in the political arena, possibly endangering the public order. Clearly, the first danger is more plausible in a criticism of the Jewish community, whereas the second danger is reflected in the actions of the Catholic church, and Spinoza's attack on Maimonides in this matter was no more than an indirect attack on Catholicism. Still, for Spinoza, the answers to the last two questions posed at the outset of this analysis are that the Rabbinic approach, especially as defined by Maimonides, stands in opposition to the modern political idea which he fought to realize. There could be no compromise between them, and the simple solution was the abolition of the authority of the Jewish community over the individual Jews. Should the Jews succeed in establishing their own state in which they would live according to the laws of the Torah, this would certainly be acceptable, but until then no institution has the authority to demand observance of religious laws and certainly not acceptance of principles of faith. Furthermore, for Spinoza, the *halakhah* was anachronistic. These laws had no utilitarian benefit and no justification within the context of the modern political reality. In his opinion, the "salvation" of Judaism lay in its complete abolition. He acted accordingly, and in his personal life symbolized the position of those who sought their "salvation" by dissociating themselves from the Jewish community and by assimilating as private citizens within the state.

Moses Mendelssohn, one of the fathers of modern Jewish thought, was also the first to respond seriously to Spinoza's challenge. If Spinoza presented the general political interest from the general political point of view, Mendelssohn sought to present Jewish interests, as well as what he saw to be the essence of Judaism. He did this using concepts similar to Spinoza's, concepts that were common to modern political thinkers. The Jewish interest which Mendelssohn sought to present was that of equal rights for Jews within the modern state. Thus, in his book,

*Jerusalem*, Mendelssohn is not concerned with the essence of the ideal state, nor with the individual's freedom of thought, and even the interrelationship of state and religion is not of primary importance for him. What is primary is the need to establish the equality of the various religions within the sovereign state in order to abolish political discrimination stemming from religious affiliation. Although Mendelssohn agreed with Spinoza on the question of individual freedom of thought, he sought—on the basis of this principle—to develop a theory of tolerance that would grant the Jews a political status equal to that of the Christians. Mendelssohn believed that, unlike Christianity, what was basic to Judaism was its attitude of tolerance, which he saw as the proper relationship between state and religion. Mendelssohn distinguished two components of all religions: that based on universal reason, and the historical component. The first component is common to all religions since reason is intrinsic to man. Reason gives rise to the belief in a Creator of the universe whose benevolent direction governs it. The second component distinguishes the religions from one another. It comprises the historical events of a particular religion's foundation and development, plus its special forms of worship and ways of life. In other words, every religion contains within it both universal and particular elements. It should be noted that Mendelssohn did not believe in a "religion based on reason" existing separate from the various historical religions. A religion based on reason is the first component of every religion, but it cannot exist by itself; without a historical foundation, religion cannot propagate a way of life. The task of religion is to educate people toward moral and spiritual wholeness. The fact that all religions share the common element of reason also serves, according to Mendelssohn, as the basis for tolerance. On the basis of this shared foundation, which is fundamental to all religions, each person can respect the unique historical character of other religions. How? By clearly recognizing the historical component of every religion, including his own. The rational component of religion possesses universal evidence, whereas the historical component is *ipso facto* subjective and particular. A person is convinced of that which is particular to his own religion because he is so educated. His beliefs stem from the trust he places in his parents and teachers. Precisely for that reason, however, he must understand that a person who holds other religious beliefs is equally convinced of the validity of the traditions of that religion, though these may seem strange to the uninitiated. In other words, although each person has sufficient basis for clinging to his historical background and to the ways of life particular to his religion, he does not have sufficient basis to be able to win over to his religion a person raised in another tradition, or to cast doubt on the other's tradition. He must respect each religion as truth for those who are educated in it, just as he respects his own beliefs as truth for himself. Of course, this concept of tolerance is not unlimited. Religions are worthy of favorable judgment only when they contain a rational component. Any religion which denies rational religious principles does not deserve the tolerance of others. Mendelssohn believed that the government could and must adopt an intolerant attitude toward atheistic ideas. In fact, he maintained that the state must oppose atheism since faith, or rational religion, is the basis of the moral order. In practice, however, the state should be lenient towards atheists, although in principle it has both the right and the duty to restrain them. Mendelssohn's entire discussion was motivated by his desire to alter the status of the Jews. Since the Jewish religion has a rational component and educates its adherents to a moral way of life and to responsible citizenship, the state must accord the Jews equal political standing within it, and not discriminate between them and its Christian citizens.

Mendelssohn presented the above view of tolerance as constituting the basic approach of Judaism. Unlike Spinoza, however, he found this tolerance present in the ancient Jewish state. It is true that the ancient Jewish state chose God as its sovereign. For Mendelssohn, this was not a prophetic fiction but a concrete historical fact. God made a covenant with His people. He led the people as its sovereign until they demanded a king like other nations. Since we are dealing here with the true kingdom of God—a phenomenon which is undoubtedly singular in occurrence and character—certain conditions which would have been prohibited in a polity ruled by mere mortals were permissible and even necessary here. It is understandable that when God Himself is the sovereign, all religious laws will be state laws and there will be political justification for state enforcement of those religious laws. Under such circumstances, whoever rejects the religious law in fact challenges the sovereign's authority. But God, as a ruler, could be relied upon in a way not applicable to a mortal king. For Him, rule was not an end in itself but an educative means to further the nation's spiritual fulfillment, bringing it to true moral perfection, and hence God's leadership was purely educational in nature.

In the ancient Jewish state, in the event of the violation of a commandment, punishment was inflicted in full only when this was deemed necessary in order to achieve definite educative goals. In fact, a considerable degree of tolerance and leniency generally prevailed. Spinoza thus erred in his description of the commandments as political measures designed to unite the people against its enemies. Their purpose, rather, was both moral and religious. In Mendelssohn's opinion, the commandments of the Torah aimed to create a way of life which would prevent degeneration into idolatry. They served as daily symbols and actions which recalled the rational truths fundamental to the establishment of a moral society. This was the mission of the Jewish state, and its uniqueness. Mendelssohn's answer to our first question is clear: the ancient Jewish state was a utopia which was realized within its historical context.

But what are the implications of all this for the Jews in modern times? Here we come to an interesting shift: it seems that by idealizing the Jewish state, Mendelssohn tried to show that the Jewish view really embodies Spinoza's view of the proper relationship between state and religion, and that Judaism, unlike Christianity, is especially relevant to the modern state. His reasoning is simple: enforcement of religious law was justified only when God Himself was the actual sovereign. As soon as this situation changed, the Jewish view demanded a clear separation between the various realms, the rulers on one hand, the priests and prophets as educators on the other. And this was certainly true after the destruction of the Jewish state, when the Jews came to live under the protection of Gentile states. This, then, is Mendelssohn's answer to the second question: What are the implications of the vision of the ancient Jewish state for present day Jews? It could be said that what Spinoza saw as a requirement for the future, Mendelssohn presented as already existing: the commandments of the Torah relating to the Jewish religion's unique historical position have no obligatory validity from an institutional point of view in the diaspora. This is not to say that Mendelssohn agreed with Spinoza in everything. Mendelssohn differed with him in his belief that the kingdom of God in the past was a reality not a prophetic fiction, as well as in his belief that the laws of the Torah were legislated by God and not man. The laws of God demand compliance forever, or until God Himself changes them. Unlike Spinoza, therefore, Mendelssohn believed that all Jews were obliged to perform the commandments of the Torah. But these laws were moral obligations of the individual Jew to his Creator, and no political institution of man has the power to force compliance with these obligations. Therefore, Mendelssohn called for the abolishment of the excommunicative authority of the Jewish community. For him, this was the necessary conclusion to be drawn from the principle on which he based his demand for equal rights for the Jews. Religion must educate through instruction and persuasion. It does not have the right to coerce. This was, for Mendelssohn, the true Jewish view, although he was well aware of the fact that most of the Jewish leaders of his generation did not agree with him.

Mendelssohn's answer to the third question is fairly simple. Judaism endorses the principle of the sovereign state, and it requires that the state apply this same principle to the Jewish people. At first glance, it appears that the fourth question is never raised. Judaism, from the outset, meets the conditions of the state, and the state is finally being asked to recognize this. But Mendelssohn knew, of course, that this was too simplistic a presentation—not only because the leaders of the Jewish community would not be prepared, *post factum*, to give up their excommunicative powers, nor to accept the social organization of the Jews and the fulfillment of the *mitzvot* (commandments) as voluntary, with each Jew acting according to his own conscience, but also because a Jew who recognized his moral obligation to observe the *mitzvot* was liable to encounter conflicts of interest in the course of his integration into the political life of the state where he sought to be a full citizen. How should he respond in cases where there was a contradiction between the law of the state and the *mitzvot* of the Torah? Mendelssohn himself encountered this problem when the state sought to require the Jews to comply with the general burial law, although this law was contrary to the accepted *halakhah*. Mendelssohn reacted by arguing that the law of the state was actually identical to the original *halakhah* and should be adopted. But the fundamental problem was not yet solved, and certainly not the problem of coexistence of alternative life styles. Mendelssohn felt the difficulty keenly. He called upon the non-Jewish society to be understanding. But in so doing he only admitted that his solution was not sufficient. Something fundamental had to be changed in the life-style of Torah observance, or in the state's laws, or in both, in order for the Jews who remained faithful to their religion to live in the modern state as equal citizens.

Mendelssohn thus attempted to find an ideal balance between the sovereign state and Judaism as each existed at the time. However, towards the end of his life, it became clear that it was impossible to maintain such a balance, and in the generation following Mendelssohn, four alternatives (aside from that chosen by Orthodoxy—to continue in their traditional ways despite the complete change in the existing reality) emerged. These can be grouped as two paired sets: to give up entirely the features which distinguish Judaism in order that the Jews might integrate into the nation-state, either as it existed then or as it should develop in the future; to maintain the separate Jewish framework and to find a way to achieve a compromise with the state—again, either as it had already developed or as it should develop in the future. Examples will be given below to illustrate these alternatives.

The first alternative—that of giving up a separate existence in order to gain citizenship and integrate into the society as it existed, was expressed in two related philosophies which complement one another: those of Solomon Maimon and Saul Ascher. According to Solomon Maimon, Judaism in the past was indeed a political religion, that is, a religion which influenced the society through political institutions. But, unlike Spinoza, Maimon believed that, despite this, political interests were far from representing the essential principle of Judaism. On the contrary, Judaism was distinguished from other classical political religions in the pagan world in that, for Judaism, the regime was not an end in itself. In Judaism there was never a hierarchy claiming to be based on the knowledge of the "secrets" which served as a means for maintaining absolute rule over the people. Religious truths were the province of the entire nation and the goal of Judaism was the spiritual and moral education of the people. On the other hand, Solomon Maimon disagreed with Mendelssohn's assumption that the Torah distinguishes in principle between state and religion, and that this distinction was actually put into effect with the establishment of the kingship in Israel at the end of Samuel's lifetime. Even in the diaspora, the religion of Israel continued to exist as a clear political framework— that is to say, the *halakhah* and the community's institutions based on the *halakhah* created a kind of portable political entity. The Jews carried their separate "state" with them even when living among different peoples and in foreign countries. Moreover, Solomon Maimon did not question the right of the Jews to maintain their separate "state." But, if they did so, they were to be consistent, and understand that they could not at the same time be citizens of their own state and citizens of the nation in which they lived. In other words, the enlightened Jew who sought emancipation faced a choice: he could cut himself off completely from Judaism, ceasing to avail himself of the Jewish communal institutions, rejecting the *halakhah*, not accepting any responsibility for the community, and becoming a private citizen like any other in the sovereign state; or he could take upon himself all the obligations stemming from his membership in the Jewish community, enjoying the privileges of its members, and waiving his citizenship in the sovereign state.

Solomon Maimon chose the first alternative. He argued that the Jewish community's institutions did not obligate him since he had renounced all his rights as a member of that community and considered himself a German citizen. Saul Ascher built a similar theoretical model but, unlike Maimon who presented the problem from the point of view of the individual, Ascher presented the problem from the point of view of the community, for he realized that the problem of the individual would not be solved until a satisfactory solution were found to the problem of the Jewish community as a whole. Saul Ascher, too, believed that Judaism had been a "political religion," even in ancient times. He added an important distinction between a religion which functions in the state "regulatively" and between a religion which functions "constitutively." The pagan religions set up the political framework and functioned within it. They directed the laws and actions of the state from a center of current, constantly renewed authority and hence were "regulative." The Jewish religion did, indeed, undergo an initial "regulative" period. The prophets guided the life of the Jews through the constantly renewed word of God, but this period was relatively short. As a religion of revelation, Judaism tended to become a constitutive religion, requiring the state to submit to laws given at a specific time by an absolute authority. One can easily assume that Ascher viewed this limitation of the state's sovereignty as a negative, stultifying phenomenon, but he, too, did not consider political rule to be an important principle for Judaism as a belief, a philosophy, and a way of life. What is primary for Judaism is the eternal truth of ethical monotheism. This principle was revealed in prophecy, not in a rational manner but rather in a form of imagery which was open to intellectual illumination. Hence, Judaism, even in its *halakhic* patterns, worked towards the moral education of the people and not towards political rule. Like Solomon Maimon, Saul Ascher believed that the political aspect of Judaism was preserved in the diaspora in its *halakhic* patterns. However, Ascher's sensitivity to the historical perspective (a sensitivity that is lacking in the writings of both Mendelssohn and Maimon) made him realize that the existence of "state" within a state could not continue very long. Subjectively this was impossible, since more and more Jews sought to acquire citizenship in a sovereign state. These individuals found their way barred, for as long as the Jewish community, as a community, remained separate and alien, the state and its society would refuse to accept them, and those who wished to become citizens of the state would use every means within their power to change the status of the Jewish community. Objectively, this was equally impossible, since the isolation of the Jews was an intolerable political anachronism from the point of view of the sovereign state. Hence, Ascher did not present the individual Jew as faced with several alternatives, but rather suggested a gradual process whereby Judaism as a "political religion" would be abolished, that is, the *halakhah* would be abolished, leaving only the eternal essence of faith along with several ritual commandments which would give symbolic expression to that faith. In other words, Judaism would be broken down into its constituent parts, being totally absorbed by the sovereign state on the one hand, and by faith, viewed as a "rational religion," on the other.

The second alternative—namely, to renounce a separate existence in order to become integrated into the state as it would develop according to a vision seen as Jewish in origin and in essence—was expressed in the teachings of Samuel Hirsch (in his German period). We should begin with Hirsch's sharp criticism of the European state as its existed in his time. Hegel's enthusiasm for the "state of law" was as foreign to Hirsch as it was to Marx. Indeed, the dialectic parallel between Hirsch and Marx on this question is most instructive. Hirsch, too, believed that formal equality before the law was not enough. The idea of freedom and justice must be realized in the relationships between the individual and the society, and in the relationship between individuals. Thus, just as a state based on law does not realize the idea of freedom, neither does it realize the idea of the emancipation of the Jews. In this, too, Hirsch was not content with a formal legal act. Emancipation must be realized as a way of life, as a network of relationships between people, or else it should not be realized at all. Hence, we must fight against the existing state, and the vision that Hirsch held up as a model for those longing for freedom was that of the "Christian state," which he believed was Judaism in its ideal form. This position undoubtedly seems strange and perplexing to the Jews of today. It should be noted that Hirsch viewed Jesus, the founder of Christianity, as a complete Jew, who succeeded in fully realizing the spiritual-ethical ideal of Judaism, translating it into a way of life. Thus, he symbolized the highest Jewish object—the personal realization of the religious-moral ideal in daily life. But historical Christianity did not follow in the path of its founder. In order to influence pagan peoples, Christianity adopted elements that were clearly pagan, one of which is reflected in the attempt of the Church to place itself above the secular state. The pagan deviation of Christianity was historically inevitable, but the dialectic historical process would in the end return Christianity to its Jewish sources. Indeed, it is in light of this return to the Jewish sources that we should understand Hirsch's proposal to identify Judaism with the vision of the "Christian state." Christianity would no longer be the church of an unworldly kingdom. It would no longer operate within and above the state, but rather as a state itself, and its goal would be to create a moral way of life, embracing the smallest details of interpersonal relations. This means, in fact, the abolishment of the church. The state would replace the church and would serve in the true spirit of religion in all areas under its jurisdiction.

How did Hirsch believe that the Christian state would, in fact, operate? Unfortunately he is not clear on this point. It is clear, though, that Hirsch believed that idealism would guide both its leaders and its citizens, and that the Jews would therefore be able to find their place within it. Their loyalty to the Christian state—the realization of the Jewish ideal—would be equivalent to their loyalty to Judaism. Nevertheless, it should be emphasized that Hirsch viewed this as a long process. Christianity of his time, including Protestantism, was, in his view, still imbued with paganism. The same was true of the secular state. And as long as paganism reigned in their thought and their way of life, the Jews could not abandon their separatism; nor could they give up anything that was essential to Judaism for the sake of equal civil rights, even under political pressure, for the state cannot demand of anyone that they yield on fundamental matters. Emancipation would come when the Christian society would be ready to accept Judaism, and not just the Jew who renounces his Judaism. Changes in Judaism, even far- reaching changes, were indeed necessary—not those dictated by the desire to resemble others and to live in peace, but rather changes that would be congruent with the fundamental principles of Judaism and with its duty to strive towards the realization of its ideas within society as a whole. Hence, the modern state would have to undergo a process of radical change leading towards a realization of the Jewish social and moral vision in order that the Jewish people might be integrated into it.

The third alternative, as stated above, was for the Jewish people to retain its uniqueness as a national unit while arriving at some compromise with the state. This alternative was expressed in several ways, and the differences between them are both fundamental and worthy of note. Three such views are: the national-spiritual position adopted by Rabbi Nahman Krochmal, the neo-Orthodox position adopted by Rabbi S. R. Hirsch, and the positive-historical position adopted by Heinrich Graetz.

The state occupies an important place in the historio-sophical outlook of Nahman Krochmal. The central period in the history of every nation, the period of "strength and building," is also the period of its political consolidation within a strong central institutional framework, possessing both internal and external strength. This is the historical pattern of every nation including the people of Israel. The period of "strength and building" in its first cycle (which extended from the time of the patriarchs until the Babylonian exile) was the kingdom of David and Solomon. The corresponding period in the second cycle, which lasted until the end of the Bar Kochba rebellion, was that of Alexander Yannai and Salome Alexandra. The decline of each of these historical cycles began with political dissension, and it is significant that, for Krochmal, the events which marked their conclusion were not the destructions of the First and Second Temples, but the murder of Gedaliah Ben Ahikam and the suppression of the Bar Kochba rebellion, in other words, the loss of the last shred of political independence. A nation can be said to come into being when it creates the foundations of custom, law, and justice—these are the means by which a society is born. The nation reaches its apex when it forges a solid, unifying political framework, and it begins to decline when this unifying political framework disintegrates. It appears, then, that Krochmal also saw the building of the temple from a political perspective. It symbolized the national-political unity of the Jewish people and served as an important means to ensure its continuation. In this context, it should be mentioned that, in his discussions of the First and Second Temples, Krochmal does not point to any singularity distinguishing the Jewish kingdom from any other. The spiritual creativity of the people during the time of David and Solomon and under Hasmonean rule did, indeed, have a special quality, but the kingdom, as a political framework, was not different from others of its time, and Krochmal therefore did not hesitate to fix a second period of "strength and building" during the time of Alexander Yannai, although the sages of his time strongly disagreed with his ways. Thus, curiously, the apex of the Jewish people's spiritual accomplishment was reached not in the time of Moses, the Judges, and Samuel during the first cycle, and not in the time of Ezra and the Great Assembly during the second cycle, but under David and Solomon, Alexander Yannai and Salome, powerful monarchs who acted in ways not unlike the kings of the nations around them. If there was something unique in the political life of the Jewish people, according to Krochmal, it lay, from a historical perspective, in the fact that its external framework gradually weakened, or retreated, allowing more and more room for internal social organization. During the First Temple period, the Jewish people enjoyed full political independence; at the time of the Second Temple, even in its heyday, it was politically dependent to some extent on foreign rule. But the gradual weakening of the political framework is most noticeable in the third cycle, when the Jewish people had only limited autonomy under powers far stronger than it, and if the Jews possessed any political power, it was based on their actions as individuals in the courts of foreign rulers. But, precisely during the third cycle, it became apparent that the decline of the political framework was accompanied by the growth of an internal *halakhic* framework, which allowed the Jewish people to preserve its unity, to protect itself against pagan influence while absorbing the best of the surrounding cultures and, finally, to influence those cultures. Thus, the process which was, to all appearances, a decline, was really a process of internal growth. This revealed the supra-political content of the patterns of life, which, being only superficially political, could be adapted to different external political frameworks.

If we extend this line of thought from the third to the fourth historical cycle, which, according to Krochmal, began after the collapse of the Sabbatian messianic movement, we can understand Krochmal's view of the relationship of the Jews to the political reality of his day. It is clear that Krochmal did not envision the renewal of an independent Jewish kingdom. But it is equally clear that he did not want the Jewish people to give up its uniqueness as a people who could exist within any political framework. If one examines the matter carefully, it becomes clear that the gradual weakening of the independent political framework was not interpreted, even in the third cycle, as a process of renunciation. Actually, Krochmal described a balance, albeit a strained and unstable balance, between the internal *halakhic* framework and that borrowed from other nations. During the Middle Ages, the internal *halakhic* framework had to be inflexible both inwardly and outwardly, because the borrowed political framework could not protect the Jewish community from harmful influences and from the animosity of the surrounding gentile society. In modern times, the internal *halakhic* framework could be much more flexible because the framework borrowed from the outside world would be more stable. This assessment was based on the belief that the process of emancipation was an expression of a real change in the attitude of the European nations to the Jewish people, to which their spiritual affinity and the spirit of national-political freedom contributed. The Jews would be allowed to exist as a people within the countries in which they lived and they, in turn, would create a suitable *halakhic* framework within which cultural creativity, in the widest sense, would thrive: custom, law and morality, art, religion, science, and philosophy. These are, of course, only general statements. Krochmal did not specify just how his hopes for the modern period would be realized; he merely indicated the general direction.

There is a significant parallel between Rabbi S.R. Hirsch's neo-Orthodox view and that of the Reform movement in their assessment of both the Jewish state in the past and the modern European state. What is common to them is their assumption that a separate political-national framework is not essential to Judaism. Not only can Judaism exist without it; it is not necessary for a complete Jewish existence. Nevertheless, both philosophies also agree that a national state is a positive thing, for without it socio-cultural creativity is unlikely. That is to say, in the last analysis, Judaism, too, requires a political framework, but not necessarily a political framework of its own. Hence, they conclude that the Jew must accept the rights and obligations of the nation in which he lives. He must identify himself with the national interests of the host country, perhaps even seeing himself, from a national-political point of view, as an integral part of that country. It is indeed true that Hirsch, unlike the Reformers, did not abandon the national-traditional belief in the coming of the Messiah; moreover, he refers to the Jews as both a people and a nation. However, he saw the messianic hope as a vital dimension of the current experience of the Jews in the diaspora, such hope being renewed in the yearly cycle of Sabbaths and holidays, and not as a basis for Jewish political activity: the Jew hopes and prays, and God will fulfill his promise when He sees fit. These hopes and prayers are part of the nationalistic feeling present in the heart of every Jew, but they do not in any way interfere with his loyalty to his country. As long as he lives in that country, it is his national homeland, and his loyalty to it is no less than that of any other ardent patriot. We can now understand the concepts "people" and "nation" as Hirsch applied them to the Jews. S. R. Hirsch limited the national life of the Jewish people to the community, which served as a framework for a way of life based on the *mitzvot* of the Torah. The community sought recognition from the state as an independent body for this end alone: to order the lives of those members who wished to live according to the Torah. The Jewish people is not a natural people, and its nationalism, although he accepts it, is not a proper goal. Its nationalism is the basis, the means for achieving a life based on the Torah, and hence the Jew does not require any separate national framework. On the contrary, such national activity would hinder the Jew's mission among the nations. The result, then, is a dual way of life. The Jew lives in his community according to the Torah—representing the eternal aspect of his life—while, as a man, he lives in a non-Jewish state as a citizen in the fullest sense of the word—representing the relative and provisional aspect of his life. Of course, his loyalty to the Torah is absolute, whereas his loyalty to the state is relative. But Hirsch believed that the correct delimitation of both spheres could create a harmonious relationship between them, and that there was no contradiction between living according to the Torah and mitzvot on the one hand, and being a loyal citizen in a non-Jewish state based on humanistic social morality on the other.

The positivistic historical view of Rabbi Zechariah Frankel does not represent an original position on this question. Frankel's positive attitude towards the Jews' existence as a people, not only based on the Torah but as a source for renewed Torah creativity, did not bring with it a desire for a separate political existence. Apparently he does not differ significantly with Hirsch on this point. However, the philosophy of his friend and disciple, Heinrich Graetz, reveals an interesting shift, noteworthy in and of itself. Graetz believed that Jewish history embodies two complementary ideas, the "idea of God" and the "national idea." The "idea of God" refers to ethical monotheism, and the "national idea" to the national fulfillment of the people of Israel within its own political framework. As noted at the outset, these ideas complement one another. The "national idea" allows for the realization of the "idea of God," while the "idea of God," expressed in the moral life of the people, is one of the most important ingredients of the national, political fulfillment of the people. Therefore, neither of these ideas can be abandoned in favor of the other. Only together can they achieve wholeness. However, Graetz points out, these two ideas were not realized equally in the various eras of Jewish history. At times one was dominant, and at times the other. At first, the Jewish people devoted their efforts towards realizing the national idea, that being the consolidation of a separate political framework. The idea of God was, indeed, not forgotten, but was viewed as a means for national unification. Afterwards, during the period of exile, the opposite occurred. The Jewish people devoted themselves directly to the realization of the idea of God, while the national idea was viewed as a means. This approach allowed Graetz to view the Galut in a positive light. The Jews benefited from the exile in their spiritual development. They had to be freed from national-political responsibilities in order to devote themselves to the spiritual ideal. But this approach does not view the Galut, even in its agreeable and receptive form (and Graetz did not put much trust in this reception), as a final situation, let alone an ideal situation. The exile was a transition period, and its one-dimensional nature was a fundamental flaw. The period of exile must be followed by a period in which Jewish national-political independence would be renewed, based on a life-style of Torah. Only in its own state would the Jewish people be able to find the proper balance between the idea of God and the national idea. It appears that Graetz did not see the uniqueness of the Jewish people in the "idea of God" as such, but rather in the combination of this idea with the national idea, in the synthesis between a moral, spiritual way of life and a national way of life. Thus, only in an independent state of their own would the Jews find their place among the nations of the world and be able to carry out their mission. Nevertheless, despite Graetz's positive view of Hess'

*Rome and Jerusalem,* and of the "Hibbat Zion" movement, he did not have a concrete vision of the Jewish state and did not foresee its establishment. For him, it was a distant dream, which was not to be realized in the near future. In retrospect, his dream helped him to understand the present, and to bring some order into the complex relations between the Jewish people and its host countries.

The fourth alternative, that of the Jewish people's continued separate existence in a new national framework—an alternative based on a negative view of the modern nation-state—had few spokesmen among the Jewish thinkers of the nineteenth century. The dominant Jewish approach was a conformist one, which accepted the state as it was while expressing the desire to change its relationship towards the Jews and Judaism. A nonconformist approach to the state, to the extent that such an approach emerged, was adopted by those Jews who wished to assimilate completely, most of whom had already decided to cut themselves off entirely from their people and found that there was no place for them among those loyal to the existing socio-political order, but only among those striving towards a utopian future. For them, to join the forces fighting to change the existing order was the true consummation of emancipation. A state that would reject earlier injustices would accept individuals of Jewish origin as citizens having equal rights and obligations. We can, nevertheless, point to at least one important thinker, unusual in several respects, who spoke of the possibility of changing the existing political order in order to ensure the continued separate existence of the Jewish people as a people. This man is Solomon Ludwig Steinheim. It is worthwhile to dwell on his views, not only because they are interesting and original, but because they bear a clear similarity to an important trend in twentieth-century Jewish thought, especially Zionist thought.

Like S. R. Hirsch, Steinheim saw the state in general, and the secular state in particular, as a purely pagan creation. A state is a mechanical structure of rule. It operates through a set of laws forced upon the society by those in power, who boast of a superhuman authority. Thus, the state denies the fact that man is a free, responsible agent. Instead it adopts the pagan view that man is subject to nature and to fate, as well as to the laws of the state; indeed, tyranny and subjection are, for him, the essence of the state. Steinheim did not exclude from this general rule the ancient democratic state of Greece, for, being based on slavery, the freedom of the minority was, in fact, the tyranny of the rulers. Neither did he exclude the modern state, despite the fact that it is based on laws which recognize the equality of all citizens before the law. Its paganism is revealed in two phenomena which are fundamental to it: the oppression of smaller nations by larger ones, creating superpowers that threaten one another; and the destruction of the organic social cells of all peoples—the family and community cells—creating in their place an anonymous mass of individuals under the direct control of the government. In this sense, therefore, the modern sovereign state is an essentially pagan phenomenon.

In place of the pagan state, Judaism proposes the idea of theocracy. What is theocracy, according to Steinheim? It can be defined as an apolitical fellowship or union which, unlike Spinoza's view of theocracy as a religious version of a democratic state, is a social way of life without the framework of a state, that is, without an institutionalized regime. In a theocracy there is no hierarchy, neither of priests nor of statesmen. The leadership emerges naturally from the direct social relationships—the family, the extended family, and the tribe. It is anchored in the simple trust that individuals place in the heads of the families and the prophets, and not in an aggregate of ruling forces. The golden age of theocracy, according to Steinheim, was the era of wandering in the desert and the time of the Judges. Of course, when the people of Israel settled in Canaan, they had to compromise with the pagan idea of kingship, but the prophets kept the spark of theocracy alive. In the diaspora, the Jews succeeded in surviving as a nation without a hierarchy by virtue of the spiritual authority of the sages. The apolitical fellowship found its most intensive expression in the family and the community. Indeed, the Jewish people succeeded, more than any other nation, in preserving its uniqueness as a nation despite its dispersion among the nations, and even the modern state could not destroy it. Despite the disintegrative processes of the modern era (which Steinheim did not ignore), Jewish peoplehood remains as strong as ever. It finds its expression today in the unusual intensity of Jewish family life, which puts its stamp on the lives of every individual, even those who have strayed from the fold. Therefore, Steinheim did not fear the trend toward alienation so evident in the younger generation. He viewed it as a temporary, passing trend, as a reaction to a severe crisis, which would soon be followed by their reintegration. Against this background, Steinheim viewed the traditional rabbinic leadership and its *halakhic* creativity favorably. He did, in fact, see in them excessive authoritarian tendencies, especially in the last generations (as a reaction to the crisis), and he believed that it was necessary to purge the *halakhah* of the chaff which it had collected, but he justified what he considered to be its internal goal: to educate the people, towards an internalization of the moral principles of the Torah, and to prepare them for a higher realization of the theocratic idea. Therefore, Steinheim, like the leaders of the Reform on the one hand and Hirsch on the other, was opposed to a national-political definition of Judaism. The difference between them, however, lay in the fact that Steinheim was opposed to the national-political definition of all peoples and, as a result, took a strong, positive view of Jewish existence. But even this statement must be qualified. The Jewish people, according to Steinheim, is not a natural people. A natural people lives in its own country, speaks its own language, and creates a culture which grows out of the way of life in a particular land and the nuances of a particular language. This was not true of the Jewish people, which existed without a land and without a spoken language. Its culture was nurtured by the Torah alone. In all other respects, the Jews participated willingly in the culture of the peoples among whom they lived, and so it should be. But it is precisely their uniqueness as a nation that accounts for their vitality. The people of Israel will be able to live freely and develop its culture, based on the Torah, while at the same time participating in the natural culture of the their hosts when the pagan state is replaced by a mature theocracy.

With Steinheim's utopia, we conclude the discussion of modern Jewish thought within the scope of this chapter. The thinkers who followed were nationalist thinkers who wished to renew the political independence of the Jewish people. This is a field that must be considered separately. But, now that we have concluded the subject under consideration, the following question arises: are the views discussed above meaningful today? The answer to this question should be: yes. However, rather than presenting my conclusions in full, I will simply open the discussion with several comments.

If we accept the assumption that a knowledge of the past is the starting point for dealing with problems of the present, the views discussed above are important from two perspectives: The first is that of our recent past, in which are to be found the forces that shape the present. The views we have discussed came to grips with these same forces, and the movements that grew out of them are still active today.

The second is that of our ancient past, to which these views refer in order to formulate the criteria for the identity and continuity of Jewish existence. The first aspect will be dealt with below, while the second will serve as a point of departure for us as well.

Contemporary Jewish thought, which is concerned with the life of the Jewish state, as it exists and as it is being formed, devoted surprisingly little effort, on the theoretical level, to the question of what is the essence of the Jewish state. The Jewish state, in and of itself, was a longed-for goal, and it is still portrayed as such. But what is the Jewish ideal of the state? In what ways has this ideal been expressed in the state's laws and practices? Practical answers to this question, based on the necessities of life, have been offered but no comprehensive theoretical examination based on an interpretation of the sources in light of the present reality has been carried out. It is for this reason that I believe the contribution of the thinkers discussed above to be important, first because they were aware of this obligation, and second because their statements are important in themselves. The different interpretations of the essence of theocracy and the investigations into the meaning of tolerance are the beginnings of a discussion that must be continued and expanded. Furthermore, we have not yet tested the validity of the social and political ideals which these thinkers raised. A generation that tends to be highly critical of the functioning of the state might perhaps gain valuable insight from the critical thought of prior generations, which was anchored in a moral-religious worldview and closely related to the traditional Jewish sources.

Let us return now to the first perspective. Spinoza argued that Rabbinic Judaism, whose views and ways of life were formed during the Middle Ages, cannot be integrated into the centralized sovereign state because it is founded on an antithetical principle. This argument was later endorsed by those thinkers who sought to criticize it. The various alternatives that were proposed in order to preserve, if only in part, the framework of a separate Jewish existence all came up against a certain unyielding "snag." The above analysis revealed three points of tension. The first is Spinoza's doctrine that the authority of religious institutions cannot coexist with the sovereign authority of the state because the religious institutions legislate and pass judgment in areas within the jurisdiction of the state. The inference that Spinoza drew from this was a negative view of the religious institutions, whereas Mendelssohn, who sought to prove that Jewish religious institutions could retreat to a voluntary framework, discovered another point of tension—two different ways of life which cannot be reconciled with one another, or exist side by side, without creating a dangerous conflict—a tension that remains even if he is correct in his assumption that these life-styles are not based on conflicting moral or political principles. The very fact that they are different, that they represent different alternatives, is in itself an obstacle, and this obstacle is felt most keenly in the modern state which considers the unity of law and the uniformity of life-styles to be of vital importance. Mendelssohn's idea of tolerance was a supreme effort to resolve the problem and, as such, remains an important conceptual foundation to this day, but he himself recognized that his philosophy required the Jew seeking emancipation to take upon himself a particularly heavy burden in face of the reservations of those around him. Out of this there emerges the third point of tension: a way of life based on the Torah requires a more complete societal infrastructure and a more cohesive communal organization than that which the tolerant attitude towards religion, based on the Christian model, could allow. Moreover, a way of life based on the Torah demands an intimate identification on the part of the individual with his community as opposed to the individualism which the state facilitates and promotes in its comprehensive framework.

The various perceptions of the theocratic idea and its effect on Jewish life in the diaspora alternately emphasize these different points of tension. Nevertheless, it seems that Spinoza's argument, in its simplicity and its unyielding one-dimensionality, is both hasty and erroneous. Alongside the areas of tension that have been discussed, those thinkers who came to grips with the problem succeeded in identifying moral, social and political principles which allowed the unique Jewish community to continue to exist within the framework of the modern European state. Or, to be more exact, these thinkers proved that a dynamic and flexible approach to *halakhah* and its institutions on the one hand, and to the state on the other, could bring them closer together. Moreover, this convergence grows out of both the principles of Judaism and the principles of the state. That is to say, tension exists, but there is also room for modification which could create a basis for consensus, even if this consensus requires occasional reevaluation. However, what is common to these thinkers is the desire for a unidimensional solution. This desire was expressed in both the extremist positions and in the compromises: the total abolishment of the authority of the Jewish community, accepting the authority of the state in all areas, or the questioning of the legitimacy of the sovereign state on the one hand; and, on the other, the intermediary positions—the hard and fast division between the jurisdictions of the state and the religious institutions, the organization of the Jews according to the model of the Church, with the Jews as citizens following "the religion of Moses," or even the "Judaisation" of the entire state, as Samuel Hirsch suggested. It seems that the utopianism that characterizes all these approaches stems from the search for a unidimensional solution, a solution that would solve the problems according to a simple and convenient formula. There is an important lesson to be learned from this. It is no overstatement to say that the points of tension mentioned here reappeared, albeit in different form, between "religion" and political institutions in the State of Israel. The fact that this is a modern Jewish state, whose internal network of relationships depends on Jewish institutions, increases the tension while raising hopes of an original solution. But a prerequisite for finding such a solution is the awareness that it cannot be absolute or simple, and, moreover, that absolute, simple solutions are not desirable. The tension between a vision of the state based on a religious-Torah worldview and any existing state, not only with regard to the demand for purity of action but also with regard to the perception of its structure and purpose, is a phenomenon that is both inevitable and inherently positive. It is positive both from the point of view of the state, whose claim to absolute sovereignty is understandable but dangerous to the society as such and to the individuals within it, and from the point of view of the Torah and the way of life it seeks to create. For both these outlooks, criticism is needed in order to curb and to balance them, and the desired solution is one that will allow for differences in theory and practice while recognizing the common responsibility towards the people and its heritage.

# III

# Institutional Dynamics

# Introduction: The Epochs Explored

The first two epochs, which are by far the most obscure, reflect the biblical traditions of the Patriarchs and the Egyptian bondage. The first (roughly the nineteenth-sixteenth centuries B.C.E.) begins with the covenant with Abraham which marks the first emergence of the Jews as a distinctive entity and culminates with the descent of Jacob's family into Egypt. Under this original covenant, it might be said that the family which later became the Jewish people first began to function as Jews. The operative elements of the constitution were probably an unwritten set of tribal traditions rather than a written code. This does not lessen its importance as a fundamental organic law which could be, and was, applied and developed as the basis of Jewish life until the time of Moses and the Exodus. The second (roughly the sixteenth-thirteenth centuries B.C.E.) embraces the generations of slavery in Egypt where the descendants of Jacob retained their identity and traditional tribal organization.

The third epoch (c. 1280–1000 B.C.E.) marks the emergence of the Jewish people in its first "national" stage, as an *edah*—a tribal confederacy—and as a religious civilization based on a fundamental organic law, or constitution, the original Mosaic Torah (*Torat Moshe*) that was promulgated at Sinai after the covenant there. Under *Torat Moshe*, the Jewish people conquered Canaan, became conscious of a basic common identity and destiny, and embarked on the road toward national unity under the monotheistic Jewish religious civilization with all that it entailed.

The fourth epoch (1000–722 B.C.E.) begins with the emergence of the first major revision of the Mosaic constitution, the establishment of a federal state under a constitutional monarchy at the time of David. The constitutional form used in this period was the covenant between the people through their tribes and the king before God. Apparently, each new ascendant to the throne had to bind himself to maintain that covenant, which was designed, among other things, to protect the Torah as constitution and the traditional liberties of the tribes.

The division of the kingdom after the death of Solomon changed the framework of the monarchic covenant but did not change its basic constitutional form, particularly since both David and Solomon actually reigned over two separate entities, Judah and Israel. The monarchic constitution continued as a dual one, as it were, existing as the organic law of two related kingdoms, with each developing its own operational variants (e.g., dynastic consistency in Judah). The Bible itself provides illustrations of how the common heritage of the Jewish people was maintained in the twin kingdoms.

The real end of the fourth epoch came with the destruction of the northern kingdom and the formal end of the tribal confederacy. In the southern kingdom, the Davidic dynasty was completely entrenched in a unitary state, whose boundaries were extended by Hezekiah and his successors to include significant portions of Israel. Hezekiah himself acted to reunify the people through a renewal of the *Pesah* (Passover) observance in Jerusalem, a covenantal act. The consolidation of the monarchy and the centralization of political power coincided with the rise of the prophetic tradition in its second form, as a counterweight to king, court, and temple. It was this somewhat revised prophetic tradition which was used by the prophets to review and modify the revised organic law, establishing the fifth epoch (721–440 B.C.E.) as the period in which the Prophetic Torah took form.

The climactic event of the fifth epoch was the Josianic Reform. This important event followed on the heels of a period in which the old constitution had been persistently violated and even abandoned by the power holders in Judah. It involved a recovenanting between the king, the people, and God under the auspices of the high priest. When the opportunity came for the restoration of the fundamental law, its restorers were able to capitalize on the chaotic situation to revise the constitution so as to include the body of prophetic doctrine that had been progressively developed under the Prophetic Torah. The account of this constitutional reform is embodied in the biblical discussion of the rediscovery of the Book of Deuteronomy. It was this Deuteronomic constitution, as interpreted by the later prophets, which formed the basis for the maintenance of Jewish national existence during the transition from a rooted nation in Judea to an exiled people in Babylonia and back to a new form of nationhood in Judea again. Constitutionally, then, the destruction of the Temple did not mark the end of the epoch. Rather, it enabled the prophets to establish their constitution more firmly without the heavy counterweights of an enthroned king and a temple. The offices of king and high priest continued to exist in exile but lost most of their real power.

It was only with the restoration of the national home in Judea under Persian rule that conditions became sufficiently different from those of the previous epoch to require another constitutional revision, particularly once it became clear that the monarchy would not be restored. Ezra and Nehemiah introduced a fourth revision of the fundamental law as embodied in the Torah and in doing so formally brought the Jewish people into a sixth historical epoch (440–145 B.C.E.). Its founding act was the *Sukkot* (Tabernacles) covenant described in the Bible. The body of interpretations that had developed around the Deuteronomic Constitution to enable it to meet the new national needs was incorporated into the new framework, which was further developed through the *takkanot* (ordinances) of Ezra, the *soferim* (literally "scribes"), and the *Knesset ha-Gedolah* (Great Assembly). Under the Ezra Torah, new approaches and interpretations were developed to make possible the preservation of the greatest degree of Jewish autonomy feasible under foreign imperial rule.

This constitution and its practical application were sufficient until the Seleucid oppressions that led to the Hasmonean Revolt. That event was, in great part, the result of a constitutional crisis stemming from the attempt by the Seleucids and the Hellenizing Jews to substitute the constitution of a Greek polis for traditional Jewish organic law. In the process of overthrowing Seleucid domination and reestablishing an independent Jewish commonwealth, the sixth modification of the Jewish constitution emerged, established by Simon the *Nasi* by covenant with the people as described in 1 Maccabees, marking the beginning of the seventh epoch in Jewish history (145 B.C.E.-140 C.E.). This was the era of the Hasmoneans and the *tannaim*. It was marked by Hasmonean political control so long as Jewish independence continued and the rise of the several Tannaitic parties (the Hasidim, the Pharisees, etc.) to a position of power in national life and particularly in regard to the constitutional process. By the time the monarchs of the Hasmonean dynasty ceased to reign (some time after they had ceased to rule), Jewish organic law was well concentrated in the hands of the *tannaim* (literally "masters of teaching"), particularly as they were constituted in the judicial-legislative body know as the *Sanhedrin*. The political upheavals of the epoch led to various regime changes during its course and had far-reaching constitutional implications for the Jewish people. Nevertheless, they were tied together by a coherent and continuous constitutional superstructure throughout.

In this respect, the destruction of the Second Temple may have been the climactic event of the epoch, but was not, in itself, a constitutional change. It provides a good example of how, within the general framework of every epoch, there occur historical events of the highest significance. It is only when such events and the developments surrounding them significantly alter the framework itself that constitutional revision becomes necessary and a new period can be said to replace the old one. Events such as the destruction of the Temple must be understood in that context, even if that reduces their dramatic quality somewhat.

The seventh epoch lasted until the Bar Kokhba revolt put an end to the possibility of a Jewish state, even within the framework of the Roman Empire. At that time, the interpretations of the *tannaim* were put into a systematic framework by R. Akiva which became the basis of the *Mishnah*, which was added to the corpus of Jewish constitutional law early in the eighth epoch (140–429 C.E.). The new epoch under the Mishnaic constitution featured rule by the *Nesi'im* (mistranslated Patriarchs) and the Sanhedrin. During this epoch, the Jewish community in Eretz Israel came under Byzantine control and began to decline. The Mishnaic constitution served as the basis, which eased the transfer of the center of Jewish life and authority to Babylonia and whose interpretations in the process led to the compilation of the Gemara.

The abolition of the office of *Nasi* marked the end of the eighth epoch, while the compilation of the Gemara (c. 500 C.E.) ushered in the ninth (429–748 C.E.). During the more than three hundred years of this epoch, the definitive text of the Talmud was completed and was applied in a new way, to a diaspora-centered Jewish national life. The completion of the Talmud marked the last all-embracing textual change in the constitutional documents. Subsequent epochs are marked by the development of codes based on the Talmud that included progressively less in the way of basic constitutional modifications.

The first of these periodic codal revisions was embodied in the two codes compiled in the middle of the eighth century in Babylonia, the *Halakhot Pesukot* and the *Halakhot Gedolot*. These two codes have been overlooked as constitutional documents. Despite their modest character as codes, they mark an epochal change in the character of constitutional revision, initiating a thousand years of codes. With them, the period of debate over fundamentals seems to have ended. As the national homeland became more a memory of the past and a hope for the future only, the Jewish constitutionalists felt the need for definitive statements, not permissive discussions. They represent the first constitutional revisions based entirely on a diaspora-centered Jewry, encompassing the interpretations of the early talmudic period and preparing the way for the epoch of the *Geonim* and *Yeshivot* (c. 748–1030 C.E.). Hence, for the first time, the laws concerning Eretz Israel are omitted while the 613 commandments first appear in that form.

European Jewry, which inherited the mantle of leadership from the Babylonian community, was the source of the next major constitutional revision, which came in the middle of the eleventh century. The first landmark of this revision, which also marked the beginnings of the middle talmudic period, was the *Sefer ha-Halakhot* of R. Isaac Alfasi, the first comprehensive codification of Jewish law. The epoch's high point was marked by the *Mishneh Torah* of Maimonides and the controversy surrounding it. This eleventh epoch lasted from 1038 to 1348 C.E.

This epoch brought with it the development of the *kehillah* and a set of constitutional devices used throughout European Jewry to provide a basis for Jewish self-government in the absence of overarching national or even regional political institutions. One of the principal constitutional devices to emerge was the rabbinical responsum as a vehicle for constitutional interpretation. Both were authentically Jewish responses to the new conditions of the High Middle Ages in which the Jews found themselves. In principle, each new *kehillah* was organized as a partnership with the authority of a *bet din* (court authorized to enact ordinances) on the basis of a local covenant which followed a standard *halakhic* mold.

The twelfth epoch (1348–1648 C.E.) began with the communal re-constitutions required in the aftermath of the dislocations generated by the Black Death (1348). The principal documentary expressions of the new constitutional epoch were the *Arba'ah Turim*, which established the organization used in all subsequent codifications, including the *Shulhan Arukh*, and the codification of communal ordinances in Spain which brought together the basic constitutional framework for Jewish self-government. The Iberian expulsions represented its climactive events. They actually infused new life into Sephardic Jewry, which created its own diaspora including the centers in Safed, Salonika, and Constantinople. By the late seventeenth century, however, the real decline did set in. From that point on, the leadership of world Jewry began to pass to the Ashkenazim.

The culminating events of the epoch revolved around the Sabbatean movement, which brought an end to medieval forms of messianism, on one hand, and opened up new avenues for the succor of individual Jews in new lands, on the other. This transition was marked by another constitutional revision, the last to take place fully within the traditional *halakhic* framework. It signified the beginning of the thirteenth epoch in Jewish history (1648–1948 C.E.), parallel to the modern epoch in world history. Though it is common to date modern Jewish history from the middle of the eighteenth century, a closer examination of the history of recent centuries strongly indicates that a more accurate reckoning will place the change in the middle of the seventeenth century, when the Jews began to enter western society. Its culmination is to be found in the Holocaust and the rise of Israel.

The completion of the *Shulhan Arukh* by R. Joseph Caro and the *Mapah*, its Ashkenazic modification, by R. Moses Isserles in the latter quarter of the sixteenth century provided the code for the new epoch, for those who remained within the fold of tradition. These twin documents also marked the culmination of significant constitutional revision in the *halakhic* pattern since they virtually abolished the amending process. This closed pattern was reflected in the period it served, both in the normative Judaism of the era and its challengers. One result of this was that, parallel to the continued life of the majority of Jews, Sephardim and Ashkenazim alike, within the framework of *halakhah*, there emerged a growing share of world Jewry who lived outside the framework of *halakhah* and who had to be bound to the Jewish community, if at all, by different constitutional devices and forms. Emancipation, the climactic event of this period, provided the new direction for more and more Jews. Moreover, the emancipated Jews increasingly dominated the cutting edge of Jewish life.

The rise of modern Zionism provided the basis and the actions necessary for the task. In bringing together the various currents of the nineteenth century and providing a means for reconstitution of the Jewish people in a meaningfully Jewish way to meet the challenges of the modern age, the Zionist movement initiated a constitutional revolution that is still under way. The establishment of the State of Israel marked the initiation of a new constitutional and historical epoch in Jewish life, parallel to the postmodern epoch in world history which began at the same time. For the first time since the collapse of the Second Commonwealth, the basis for inclusion in the Jewish body politic was something other than *halakhah*; in this case it became Jewish peoplehood.

It is not yet clear what kind of constitution will emerge from the revolution, but it is likely to take the form of a new covenant of peoplehood. It is not likely to turn on a single constituting event or written document. Rather it is developing through a series of pacts and procedures which are already becoming identifiable and are governing expression through a developing institutional framework. The results produced by the application of this new constitution already are visible in Israel and the world Jewish community. Today we are living in the early stages of the fourteenth epoch of Jewish history, a period that shows every sign of being one of great constitutional and historical change. Nevertheless, revolutionary as it may be, it involves a revision, not an abandonment, of the old constitution.

# 7

# The Transition from Tribal Republic to Monarchy in Ancient Israel and Its Impression on Jewish Political History

*Moshe Weinfeld*

During the period of the Judges the political system was essentially based on a voluntary federation with a "democratic character" unlike the monarchic regime which generally dictated from above. This essential difference between the period of the Judges and the period of the monarchy left its mark on practically all the religious and social institutions of the Jewish people.

First and foremost were the development of two phenomena: (1) the creation of an established religious center (the Temple of Solomon), and (2) the establishment of a permanent dynasty. These two innovations in a sense broke with the former "holy" frameworks, "the chosen House" and "chosen Dynasty," concepts that began to crystalize during the days of the unified kingdom and that contradicted the tradition of Israel which prevailed after exodus from Egypt and during the period of the Judges. But after they became rooted in the people they took on a religious legitimacy, and became a cornerstone in the religion of Israel, even taking on a higher universal dimension which served as signpost to other great monotheistic religions.

The primary concern here will be the transition from a nomadic

Tabernacle to a permanent Temple and from a charismatic leadership of a spontaneous character to an established dynasty. But first we must devote a few words to general changes which began to occur in the organization of the national institutions when the monarchy arose.

## The "Edah" and Its Organization

In order to fully comprehend the term *edah* one must point out that this term, which referred to the tribal organization in the desert and during the time of the Judges, appears in historical literature of Scripture for the last time in connection with the Kingdom of Jeroboam (I Kings 12:20). This may indicate that with the establishment of the kingdoms of the north and the south, this body gave way to the institution of the monarchy. To ascertain the nature and function of the *edah* and its authorities we must refer primarily to Joshua 22:9ff and to Judges 20–21. Here we find the *edah* and its *nesiim* (literally "those raised up") deciding: (a) matters of war against noncomplying tribes (Joshua 22:12, Judges 20:1–2, 9, etc.); (b) excommunication of tribes not carrying out the decisions of the *edah* (Judges 21:1, 18); (c) extermination of people who did not participate in the war of the *edah* (21:10); (d) calling for peace (21:13); and (e) making covenants with foreigners (Joshua 9:18–21).

Even when a national leader (a judge) appears in this era, his primary activity is in the sphere of war and not in carrying out national civil policy whether foreign or internal. Even after a victory, he does not set up a permanent religious or secular center and he certainly does not bequeath his position to his children. Furthermore, the position of the judge is established by the *edah* and its elders (Judges 8:22, 11:8, etc.; I Samuel 8:4, etc.) and it is they who decide national, religious, and social matters such as those mentioned in Judges 20–21, and foreign policy such as that mentioned in Joshua 9 (the covenant with the Gibeones).

True, the king too would consult the elders of the nation (see I Kings 20:7), but he alone was ultimately responsible for conduct of the regime's affairs. It is not by chance that evil done in the eyes of God during the monarchy was attributed to the king himself, whereas evil done during the time of the Judges was attributed to the entire people of Israel. The king had the power to do away with foreign worship, to remove *bamot* (idolatrous altars) and to prevent oppression of widows and orphans. Hence, he was ultimately responsible for the religious-social condition of the people during the monarchic period. Contrarily, during the time of the Judges, the *edah* of the children of Israel was that body which could eradicate evil from the midst of the people (cf. Judges 20:13), and the responsibility for what was done rested on it alone.

At the head of the *edah* stood the *nesiim* of whom we no longer hear during the period of the monarchy. Hence, instead of the cursing of God and the *nasi* (which we find in Exodus 22:27), we hear in the period of the monarchy of the cursing of God and the king (I Kings 21:10, Isaiah 8:21).

## Army and War

This important, vital institution during the time of the Judges comes under the authority of the *edah*. Most of the time, however, the Judges led the people in war, but they were only messengers of the *edah*. The organization and the draft were made by the *edah* and mainly by *ish yisrael* (Judges 7:23, 20:10, etc.), as a body which represented the tribes of Israel and which appeared primarily in a military connection (Judges 20:11, II Samuel 17:14, 24, etc.). *Ish Yisrael*, "the men of Israel," appeared in the war of Absalom and David when according to Tadmor, Absalom attempted to revive the patriarchical institution and to have it face David's mercenary army. In this connection one should mention that just as the *edah* disappears from historical literature after the splitting of the kingdom, so we hear nothing of *Ish Yisrael* after the days of Solomon.

During monarchic rule the army and its organization was under the king's exclusive jurisdiction. Although the military organization was still run on the basis of the tribal framework, the king kept permanent military units, including foreign mercenaries, which served as the major striking force acting quickly and effectively (II Samuel 20:5, etc.). The change that occurred in this area with the rise of the monarchy is well expressed in the king's law in I Samuel 8:11–12. "He will take your sons, and appoint them unto him, for his chariots, and to be his horsemen; and they shall run before his chariots . . . .he will appoint captains of thousands, and captains of fifties."

The creation of a nucleus of a standing army is described already during the days of Saul, "and when Saul saw any mighty men, or any

valiant man, he took him unto him" (I Samuel 14:52; see also 13:2).
And during the time of David, we bear witness to an institution referred to as "the strongmen of David" and likewise "the servants of
David," who stand opposing the national army organized by Absalom,
which was referred to as *Ish Yisrael*, "all the men of Israel," (II Samuel
17:14, 21) and the people of Israel (ibid., 18:7). It is hardly necessary
to remind the reader that the hired troops such as the Cherethites and
Pelethites began to act during the days of David (see II Samuel 15:18).

If during the time of the Judges and Saul, the army was viewed as
"the people of God" (Judges 5:11, II Samuel 1:12), or the community
of the people of God (Judges 20:2), in David's time and afterwards,
the army little by little turned into David's army: "David's men" (II
Samuel 5:6), David's servants (II Samuel 11:11, 20:6, etc.), in other
words, the king's army.

### *"Cherem"*—Ban

The wars of the *edah* were considered God's wars, or holy wars, by
traditional standards. The enemy, who was God's enemy (see Judges
5:31), had to be destroyed according to God's commandments and
without compromises. So we read in the book of Joshua about the total
destruction of Jericho, "And they utterly destroyed all that was in the
city, both man and woman, both young and old, and ox and sheep, and
ass, with the edge of the sword" (Joshua 6:21). A similar situation is
found in Samuel's admonition to Saul concerning the destruction of
Amalek: "And utterly destroy all that they have, and spare them not;
but slay both man and woman, infant and suckling, ox and sheep,
camel and ass" (Samuel 15:3).

Saul himself carried out such destruction on Nob, the city of the
priests. As it states, "And Nob the city of the priests smote he with the
edge of the sword, both men and women, children and sucklings, and
oxes and asses and sheep, with the edge of the sword" (I Samuel
22:19). A similar *"cherem"* was carried out against the tribe of Benjamin in the matter of the "concubine of Gibeah" where it is recounted
that the men of Israel killed the tribe of Benjamin "and smote them
with the edge of the sword, both the entire city and the cattle, and all
that they found; moreover all the cities which they found they set on
fire" (Judges 10:48). This type of destruction carried out against the
Israelite population reminds one of the "banished city" in Deuteronomy
13 whose inhabitants and cattle were to be smitten by the sword and

burnt, and whose entire spoils belonged to God (verses 16–17), and so too in Judges 20 we hear that the men of Israel smote the city of Givat Binyamin by the sword and that "the whole of the city went up in smoke to heaven" (verse 40).

A different type of destruction is mentioned in the Torah involving the killing of "all males and all females that had known man by lying with him" (Numbers 31:17). This type of destruction the *edah* carried out against the men of Jabesh-Gilead who did not participate with the Israelites in joint activity (Judges 21:11).

Similar procedures are attested to in the Greek twelve tribe federations (Amphictyonnies, which in many ways bear similarities to the federation of the tribes of Israel). There, too, we find that if one of the tribes violates the sacred treaty, the other tribes destroy it with its cities (Aeschines II, 115). Elsewhere it says that one should fight the enemy, enslave the population, and sanctify the land of the gods; the land was not to be worked or ploughed (Aeschines III, 108f).

From the time of David and Solomon onward we hear no more of this type of destruction. The prophets rebuke the kings for not carrying out the destruction in its entirety (I Samuel 15, I Kings 20:42), but here the kings act according to political considerations and are no longer strict in carrying out the commandment of the "*cherem*." Scripture clearly states that the remnants of the Canaanites who were not destroyed by the Israelites were made "a levy of bondservants" (I Kings 9:21).

## Curse and Oath as Legal Sanction

The *edah* and its leaders would make use of sacral sanctions in order to prevent transgressions. They did this by a general pronouncement of a curse which was somewhat excommunicative (see below) upon anyone who would sin or attack holy standards. Hence, we hear after the conquest of Jericho that Joshua proclaimed: "Cursed be the man before God who will arise and build this city" (Joshua 6:26). The men of Israel in Mitzpeh make the people swear that "cursed" will be those who will give their daughters to the "tribe of Benjamin" (Judges 21:1, cf. verse 18). The last time we hear of a similar curse involves Saul who, in his war against the Philistines, proclaimed: "Cursed be the man that eateth any food until it be evening, and I be avenged on mine enemies" (I Samuel 14:24).

In this matter, too, we find comparisons with the Greek tribal federation. The Greek amphictyonies destroyed the city which violated the sacred oath and pronounced a curse upon all who would rebuild it (Aeschines III, 108f). Similarly, we find concerning the captured Lacedemonians during war that they were not to return to their homes until the enemy was destroyed (Strabo 279C). This is reminiscent of Saul's curse above, as is the commitment made by the tribes of Israel concerning the war in Gibea, "We will not any of us go to his tent, neither will we any of us return unto his house" (Judges 20:8).

The "cursed" is similar to one who has been separated from the community (Judges 5:23) and even the Talmudic Rabbis testify (Shavuoth 36a) that the cursed is as one excommunicated. Hence, in this way we can understand the "cursed" found in Deuteronomy 27 in the ceremony of Mt. Gerizim and Mr. Ebal. What is special about the curses in Deuteronomy 27 is that they are tied to sins done privately, which the community cannot punish. The *edah* felt that it would be punished for the existence of sinners in its midst (compare to the case of Achan) and it could purify itself only by expelling the sinners from the *edah* by means of a curse which was sounded in a binding ceremony. It is not by chance that this ceremony took place in Shechem, the city sanctified from the time of the patriarchs and in which Joshua made a covenant with the people of Israel before God (Joshua 24).

It is quite possible, even after the reigns of David and Solomon, that the practice of excommunication by curse continued. However, it appears that the transfer of authority to the king in political matters caused a decline in the use of sacral sanctions which originated in the pronouncement of the *edah* and its leaders.

## Spiritual Leadership During War

When the *edah* functioned it was customary during time of war for the army to be accompanied by the Ark of the Covenant and the holy vessels (Numbers 10:35–36, 31–6; Joshua 6; Judges 20:27; I Samuel 3–5). The last time one hears of the ark at the battlefield site is during the war between David and the Amonites (II Samuel 11:11) and henceforth nothing is mentioned about the ark and the holy vessels in war. It appears that in this area, too, a change took place during the days of the monarchy: war was secularized.

## The Use of Prophetic Means

Until the end of the time of David's reign, oracles were sought of God via the *Urim VeTumim*. Afterwards the people depended on prophetic intuition alone and we no longer hear of mechanical mantic prophecy. Moreover, the prophets during the era of the monarchy acted primarily within the king's court and some even refer to these prophets as the "court prophets."

Apparently with the founding of the monarchy the political, religious, and social institutions, which grew out of the ancient *edah*, were destroyed. The *edah* and its *nesiim* ceased to be prime movers in the military organization. The institution of the *cherem* began to disappear. We no longer hear of the practice of cursing and excommunication. And the feeling for the holy vessels, the ark, and the *Urim VeTumim* was considerably weakened. By way of summary, one can say that with the establishment of the monarchy in Israel, the regime passed from God's *edah* and God's community to the hands of the king alone, and hence the Kingdom of God, so to speak, gave way to the kingdom of man (see below). Thus, as hinted above, the setting up of the dynasty and the construction of a permanent Temple caused a revolution in the life of Israel and in its religious observance. The ancient view held that God's spirit may rest on everyone at any time and that the Divine Presence may be revealed at any place. Now with the founding of the monarchy and the establishment of a temple, there was a specific place for revelation and a permanent family from which the leaders were to arise. Let us describe the nature of this revolution.

## The Transition: The Chosen Dynasty and Chosen City

Opposition to a monarchy of flesh and blood was first given expression by Gideon in his words to the nation: "I will not rule over you, neither shall my son rule over you; the Lord shall rule over you." In mentioning himself and his son, Gideon intended to completely remove the possibility of establishing a monarchic dynasty in Israel. Thus, in the following chapter we hear of the complete failure of Gideon's son's (Abimelech) attempt to reign as king over Israel, and the historiographer even refrains from referring to his position as monarchical. Thus, it states, "And Abimelech was *prince* over Israel three years" (Judges 9:22). Even Jotam's parable opposing Abimelech's king-ship is somewhat of an anti-monarchic polemic. It is true the point is directed toward Abimelech, the thorn bush, and not against monarchy itself. Nevertheless, it should be noted that the fact that the fruit-bearing trees refuse to accept for themselves a monarchic role bears witness to a deprecating attitude toward monarchy which is presented as a useless institution. The monarchy was something nonproductive. Samuel presents this view in an even more extreme manner (I Samuel 12:17) "and ye shall know and see that your wickedness is great, which ye have done in the sight of the Lord in asking you a king." And the people agreed, "Pray for thy servants unto the Lord thy God, that we die not; for we have added unto all our sins this evil, to ask us a king" (ibid., 19). The request for a king was viewed as an open rebellion against God, and an ungrateful act. God the King of Israel would send from time to time men who would rescue the people from their enemies (I Samuel 10:18–19, 12:10–11), but the children of Is-rael forgot the kindness done them by God and when Nachash the king of Ammon threatened them, they emphatically demanded a king despite the fact that their true king was the God of Israel: "Ye said unto me: Nay, but a king shall reign over us; when the Lord your God was your king" (I Samuel 12:12, 10:19). Moreover, in requesting a king, the people of Israel deny their uniqueness, wanting to be like all the other nations by having a king who will rule over them like all other nations (I Samuel 8:5). This is also reflected in the beginning of the law concerning the king in the book of Deuteronomy. "I will set a king over me like all the nations that are round about me" (Deuteronomy 17:14).

The critics of the Wellhausen school negated the validity of that evidence and treated it as material serving a theocratic purpose at the time of the destruction of the Temple. According to Wellhausen, dis-enchantment with the monarchy during the time of the destruction was the source of the ideological view of a monarchy as sinful. Another opinion viewed the period of the destruction of Samaria as the source for this ideology, backed up by Hosea's prophecy which occurred during the destruction of Samaria. Opposing this view were Martin Buber and Yehezkel Kaufman, each in his own way. They attempted to show that the struggle against the monarchy was not a later devel-opment, but rather it was a struggle anchored in an ancient period, from the very initiation of the monarchy. Many commentaries and critics in recent times have come to a similar conclusion and Wellhausen's opinion that the antimonarchic tales are from the time of the destruction of Jerusalem has few supporters.

The monarchy in Israel was a radical innovation which required religious legitimization, and the dynasty especially required a religious justification which is found in the Scripture in Nathan's prophecy to David (II Samuel 7). In this prophecy, God promises David an everlasting dynasty. This promise is built on the same format as the covenant between God and Abraham concerning the granting of the Land of Israel. The covenant of Abraham consists of two promises: seed and land. Abraham's *seed* will inherit the *land* forever. The covenant with David is similar: David's seed will inherit the monarchy forever. In both cases the covenant is made without conditions in the manner of known covenants in the ancient East. In these covenants there is a promise of land and dynasty to Israel, to the servants of God. Abraham the servant of God is given the promise of land, and David, the servant of God, is given the promise of dynasty. Israel, chosen from all the nations, will inherit the promised land forever, and so will David, chosen of all of Israel, receive the dynasty forever. The principle of charismatic leadership by which God puts his spirit each time on a different person does not exist anymore. Henceforth God's covenant commitment (*hesed*) is given to David, to accompany him and his descendants forever.

And now let us go on to the second revolutionary innovation—the Temple.

## The Temple

While the idea of a permanent dynasty received legitimization during the days of David himself, the idea of a temple received approval only in the days of Solomon. Apparently it was difficult for one generation to accept two innovations at one time. Let us investigate the innovation of choosing Jerusalem and its significance.

During the wandering in the desert and during the time of the Judges, there was no permanent place for God's Tabernacle. The tent of assembly and the ark of the covenant, which symbolized God's presence, were constantly found in different locations. Thus, in Judges 19:21 and 20:1 we hear of the people congregating before God in Mitzpeh. Further on we read that the people went up to Bet El "for the ark of the covenant of God was there in those days" (verse 27; cf. verse 18 and 21:1). At the end, we hear of a holiday to God in Shiloh (21:19) where the tent of assembly and the ark were (Joshua 18:1; I Samuel 1:1, etc.). In Joshua 8:33, we find the ark in Shechem, between Mt. Gerizim and Mt. Ebal.

The fact of the mobility of God's house was given pointed expression in God's words to Nathan as a reaction to David's desire to build a house of cedar wood for God's ark. "Shalt thou build Me a house for Me to dwell in? For I have not dwelt in a house since the day that I brought up the children of Israel every day even to this day, but have walked in a tent and in a tabernacle." (In a parallel version in I Chronicles 17:5, "from tent to tent and from one tabernacle [to another].") "In all places wherein I have walked among all Israel, spoke I a word with any of the judges of Israel who I commanded to feed My people saying: Why have ye not built Me a house of cedar?" (II Samuel 7:4–7).

God thus walks in the midst of the children of Israel and does not want to establish himself a permanent dwelling within any one of the tribes. Perhaps this can be understood as an attempt to avoid discrimination so that the tribe in which the tent of God was found would not view itself as preferred. There probably was some program for the tribes in this matter. The principle was nevertheless clear: just as God does not let his spirit dwell in any particular family or household, so does He not dwell permanently in the inheritance of any particular tribe.

In His answer to David, God on the one hand says that He does not want a House, but on the other hand, he promises David a dynastic House. God relinquishes His House but does want to establish David's house and David's dynasty. Only in Solomon's time does the principle of a permanent dwelling for God materialize and the argument given for it is that in his days peace and inheritance were attained, and hence God comes to his rest. The idea is given full expression in Psalms 132: "For the Lord hath chosen Zion: He hath desired it for His habitation: This is My resting-place for ever: Here will I dwell: for I have desired it. . . . .There will I make a horn to shoot up unto David. There have I ordered a lamp for Mine anointed." Here the idea of the House of David and the Temple are intertwined, a closed circle.

In truth, both of these ideas were born out of changing political historical circumstances. In order to establish a monarchy "like all the other nations" it was necessary to create a dynasty, on the one hand, and a Temple, on the other. In the words of Amos: "for it is the king's sanctuary, and it is royal house" (7:13). The sanctuary is the "House of Cedars" and the use of cedar trees for building holy edifices is known to us from the third millennium B.C.E.

Concerning Jerusalem and the House of David, one has to take into consideration another aspect. Jerusalem is called "the City of David" since David and his men conquered it (II Samuel 5:6). One may refer to II Samuel 12:28 where Joab requests of David to take Rabbah of the children of Ammon for otherwise Joab would do so and it would be called after his name. Hence, this conquest was somewhat of a private operation (David and Solomon were given a free hand in the development of institutions by introducing change in the tradition). Zion and Jerusalem were viewed as David's inheritance, and not for nothing do we hear of the northern rebellious tribes saying: "We have no portion in David, neither have we inheritance in the son of Jesse; every man to his tents, O Israel" (II Sam. 20:1; cf. I Kings 12:16). The tribes felt no attachment to the Jebusite city and were not prepared to accept the authority of Zion and the House of David.

The revolutionary innovations introduced during the reigns of David and Solomon, in the course of time, became acceptable religious ideals which through the prophets became fundamentals in Jewish and Christian eschatology. From the strong emerged the sweet: the election of a king like all the other nations gave birth to the idea of a light to the nations, and the temple and king's palace that were erected after a severe struggle became a house of worship for all peoples, a world center for peace. Let us follow briefly the development of the idea of election of Jerusalem and the House of David, and let us see how ideas and aspirations which were born out of a political background became moving factors in the development of higher religious-moral-universal ideas.

## Jerusalem as Center of the World

Already in Mesopotamia from the third millennium B.C.E. we hear of a world center to which nations from all over the world converged and come to worship the great god in that central sanctuary while bringing their sacrifices. This central sanctuary served as a high court for god who dwelt there (something which is reminiscent of Isaiah

2:1–4). The idea continued in Mesopotamia and we find it in the days of the neo-Babylonian kings in the sixth century B.C.E.

The first center to which these ideas were passed was in the Sumerian city Nippur. Babylonia, which arose afterwards and which viewed itself as taking the place of Nippur, took over this ideology for itself.

The cities of Nippur and Babylon were each considered centers for heaven and the earth (Sumerian *dur-on-ki* = the bond of heaven and earth and in Babylonian *markas same u erseti*) or the center of the land (*markas mati*), and in Hebrew this is expressed by "Tabur Haaretz"—navel of the earth. These concepts are found in Scripture with reference to Shechem (Judges 9:37) and Jerusalem and Israel (Ezekiel 38:12), two important centers, one in the north and the other in the south. It appears that Beit El, which was the king's palace in the north (Amos 7), also was viewed as the world center. This was the place where the ladder stood whose top reached the heavens and upon which the angels of the Lord ascended and descended. Jacob in fact called it "the gateway of heaven." The Babylonian references to the temple belong to this same ideological framework: The Babylonian Temple is referred to as "esagila," meaning the foundation house whose top is elevated, and "etemenanki," meaning the foundation house of the heaven and earth. A hint of this view in Israel can be found in Psalms 78: "And He built His sanctuary like the heights, like the earth which he hath founded forever" (verse 69), next to which we find "He chose David also His servant."

All this explains the capital sanctuary in Mesopotamia and in Israel as the highest place in the world. The sanctuary of Nippur is called the great mountain (Kurgal) and the sanctuary of the Canaanite Baal is called "the sanctuary in the mountain of his inheritance," which is the northern mountain, a high mountain in Northern Syria, Jebel Akra (Mt. Cassius).

Ezekiel sees in his vision the sanctuary on a "very high mountain" (40:2) and in the songs of Zion the Temple Mount is called "Mount Zion, the uttermost parts of the north" (Psalms 48:3). Hence, when Isaiah speaks of the "Mountain of God's temple at the head of the mountains, the highest of the hills," he uses a conventional formula accepted in the ancient east concerning sanctuary capitals.

The court ideology that we have described finds literary expression in Sumerian hymns which have been preserved from the second millennium B.C.E. and also pervaded the royal court in Assyria, Egypt, and Israel.

The outstanding characteristics of this ideology are:

1. All the nations bring to the capital city and its king a tribute and gifts in abundance.
2. The leader of the capital, that is, its king, rules the world, and the nations submit to him.
3. His reign extends to the corners of the earth: "From the upper seas to the lower seas."
4. The king rules in justice and righteousness.

When we investigate the king's songs in Psalms we see these same characteristics and the same ideology:

1. To Jerusalem and the reigning son of David, the kings of Tarshish and the kings of Sheba bring gifts (72:10). To the Temple in Jerusalem kings bring gifts (68:30). This same view is very obvious in the prophecy of the return of Zion when the sanctuary was in a process of building and reconstruction. "Because the abundance of the sea shall be turned unto thee, the wealth of the nations shall come unto thee. . . . .They shall bring gold and frankincense, and shall proclaim the praises of the Lord. All the flocks of Kedar shall be gathered together unto thee, the rams of Nebaioth shall minister unto thee" (Isaiah 60:5ff). And in Haggai 2:7 it states, "and I will shake all nations, and the choicest things of all nations shall come, and I will fill this house with glory saith the Lord of hosts" (cf. also to Isaiah 18:7).
2. The ideal king vanquishes his enemies. "Let them that dwell in the wilderness bow before him; and his enemies lick the dust." "Yea all kings shall prostrate themselves before him. All nations shall serve him" (Psalms 72:11). "Thou shalt break them with a rod of iron" (Psalms 2:9) (see 110:2, 45:9, 18:39, 48). Similarly we read in the songs of the Sumerian king: "His rod will vanquish the rebellious land, and will rule them in strength."
3. The reign of Jerusalem according to these songs will extend "from sea to sea, And from the River unto the ends of the earth" (72:18), "on the sea" and "on the rivers" (89:26) "to the sea . . . .and to the river" (chapter 11). This view is also found in prophetic songs (Micha 7:11–12, Zechariah 9:10, "And his dominion shall be from sea to sea, And from the River to the ends

of the earth").

4. The king will rule with justice and righteousness, "That he may judge Thy people with righteousness, and thy poor with justice." "May he judge the poor of the people, And save the children of the needy, And crush the oppressor" (Psalms 72:2–4; cf. Psalms 45:7–8).

## Court Ideology Turned into Prophetic Utopia

These ideas, which reflect a clear political ideology, the basis for the reign of a great king and his limitless expansion, took on tremendous spiritual significance through the prophets, each prophet developing them in his unique way.

### Tribute of Nations

Nations will come to Jerusalem not necessarily to bring gifts but to accept the dominion of the God of Israel while rejecting their idolatry "Unto Thee shall the nations come from the ends of the earth, and shall say: 'Our fathers have inherited nought but lies, vanity and things wherein there is no profit'" (Jeremiah 16:10). The comforting prophet does not reject the idea of gift bringing to Jerusalem when Jerusalem is in need of it (cf. 60:5ff) and even extends the idea and sees the nations bringing as gifts to Jerusalem her sons who were in captivity (39:22, 60:9, 10, 20). He describes a caravan of foreigners coming from Egypt and Ethiopia passing Jerusalem and expressing their faith in the God of Israel. They bow and pray, "Surely God is in thee, and there is none else" (Isaiah 45:14). The prophet sees the nations walking in the light of Zion, and kings in its brightness (Isaiah 60:1–3).

In fact this is the prophet who coined the term "light of the nations" (Isaiah 42:6, 49:6), concerning the mission of Israel. And it is interesting that this expression is also found in the ideology of the Babylonian kings: the King is "the light of the universe." But there it serves to glorify the greatness of the king whereas in the second Isaiah's prophecy it has a religious-spiritual-idealistic significance.

Jeremiah introduced a unique nuance in the idea of the nations coming to Jerusalem. In his special way, built on changing values, he says that the ancient national symbol "the ark of the covenant," which was considered a sort of "throne of God," will no longer exist. Jerusalem in its entirety will be called "the throne of God" and in the future the nations will gather there in order to mend their ways (Jeremiah 3:16–17). In other words, instead of national pilgrimages to the site of the "ark of the covenant" there will be international pilgrimages not connected with temple worship but with internal spiritual purification.

## The Ruling King

Isaiah the son of Amoz is the one who created a metamorphosis of this idea. In conventional ideology the king rules his enemies ("Thou shalt break them with a rod of iron; Thou shalt dash them in pieces like a potter's vessel" [Psalms 2:9]); "The rod of thy strength the Lord will send out of Zion: Rule thou in the midst of thine enemies" (ibid., 110:2). Isaiah on the other hand describes the ideal king as striking not with a rod of iron but with "the rod of his mouth and with the breath of his lips" (11:4). As a result of his actions in the spirit of the Lord, in faith and justice, not only will enemies among men be liquidated but even enemies among the animals (ibid., verses 6ff). A similar portrait is drawn in the song about God's servant in Isaiah 42:1ff. God gives his spirit to his servant who dispenses justice to the nations.

> He shall not cry, nor lift up, nor cause his voice to be heard in the street. A bruised reed shall he not break, and the dimly burning wick shall he not quench; He shall make the right to go forth according to the truth. He shall not fail nor be crushed, till he have set the right in the earth, And the isles shall wait for his teaching.

## Peace on Earth

According to Isaiah not the physical rule of Jerusalem will extend but the spiritual one. The nations will come to the Temple Mount as pilgrims and will seek to learn God's ways and His paths, for out of Zion shall go forth the law and the word of the Lord from Jerusalem (Isaiah 2:2–4). As a result of accepting the reign of the God of Israel: "They shall beat their swords into plowshares, and their spears into pruning hooks. . . . .Neither shall they learn war any more." To understand the uniqueness of this portrayal we must compare it to the portrayal of peace drawn in the conventional ideology, and especially in the Songs of Zion. Psalms 46 speaks of Zion where "God shall help her, at the approach of morning." God lets His voice be heard and the nations and kingdoms (apparently those who come up to Zion) totter. God fights wars, breaks bows and spears, burns chariots in fire. The song ends with the trusting proclamation that "the Lord of hosts is with us; The God of Jacob is our high tower." Beforehand it talks of God "who hath made desolations in the earth" (verse 9). At any rate it talks of God who destroys the weapons of the nations, not as in Isaiah where they destroy their own weapons. In chapter 76 complete peace is also attained as a result of the destruction of bow, shield, and sword by God. At the end of the song, however, we hear of the bringing of "presents unto Him that is to be feared"—this apparently in connection with Aram and Hamath with whom they fought. Other prophets also depict peace following the submission of the enemy: so, for example, in Zechariah 9:10, "And I will cut off the chariot from Ephraim, and the horse from Jerusalem, And the battle bow shall be cut off, And he shall speak peace unto the nations; And his dominion shall be from sea to sea, and from the River to the ends of the earth." The king thus speaks peace to the nations, he determines the conditions of peace through his reign "from sea to sea," the ideal span as is known to us from the kings' courts of the ancient east. Micah, too, a contemporary of Isaiah, speaks of peace which will come when the land of Assyria will be wasted by the sword (see 5:4).

We must therefore realize that the ideal picture of peace between the nations who accept it voluntarily, and the ideal king who rules in peace by the words of his mouth, is characteristic of Isaiah and is not of the other classical prophets.

## Justice and Righteousness

Here, too, the prophet draws from the store of conventional concepts. Isaiah describes going up to the High Court where justice is meted out unequivocally. The nations flock to Jerusalem from whence comes the "word" and the "Torah." "For out of Zion shall go forth the law and the word of the Lord from Jerusalem." In order to understand the significance of "law" and "word" we should refer to the court that will be chosen as put forth in Deuteronomy 17. The judge who cannot make a decision in a case is to go to the chosen place and act according to the "word" and the "law" which is instructed to him. In Isaiah 2 we also hear of "nations" who "go up" from all over the world to accept arbitration between the nations. Following these arbitrations, international wars will come to an end. Elsewhere the prophet describes God preparing a feast for all the nations on this mountain and ending with God's swallowing up "death for ever" and wiping away "tears from all faces" (25:6–8). And then it will be said, "Lo this is our God, For whom we waited, that He might save us; This is the Lord, for whom we waited, We will be glad and rejoice in this salvation."

## The King Acts in Justice and Righteousness

This ideal was also accepted in the kings' courts of the ancient East and its basis lay in social reforms which were common in the courts of the Babylonian kings. From Babylonia we learned that the economic-social reforms (misarum) were done by the king close to his coronation, and it is understandable that the king thus gained the trust of the people. The psalm to Solomon in Psalms 72 was apparently said when he took authority (compare with the "king's son" in verse 1). It begins: "Give the king thy judgments, O God, and thy righteousness unto the king's son." In prose we would say, "give Justice and Righteousness to the King's son," that is, give him the capacity to do justice and righteousness. Compare to I Kings 10:9 (concerning Solomon) "therefore He made thee king, to do justice and righteousness"). According to 11 Samuel 8:15, "David established justice and righteousness for all his people."

David's actions—and perhaps even those of several who came after him—became an ideal for the prophets. They envision ideal kings who will sit "on David's throne" who will base their reign on justice and righteousness forever (Isaiah 9:6, cf. 15:5). And in the words of Jeremiah, "Behold the days come . . . .That I will raise unto David a righteous shoot, And he shall execute justice and righteousness in the land" (23:5).

Moreover, David is the stereotype of the king who does justice and righteousness, not only by national standards but by international standards. Isaiah describes the shoot which shall come forth out of the stock of Jesse, who shall judge the poor in righteousness and shall destroy the wicked (11:1ff).

## Summary

As a result of historical circumstances, the establishment of the monarchy and of the Temple in Jerusalem, which in their time were considered a sin, led to the creation of institutions with strong religious values which changed the face of Israel's history and brought about the universal, lofty prophetic visions.

# 8

# The Kehillah

*Daniel J. Elazar*

## The Kehillah as an Institution

The *kehillah* (literally, community—parallel term: *kahal*) is the distinctive Jewish form of local organization and government. As such, it is parallel to the *edah* (literally, congregation), the Jewish people as a whole in its political constitution.[1] The origins of the *kehillah* go back to the period of the Second Commonwealth and the emergence of the *bet knesset* (literally, house of assembly) as an all-purpose unit of local organization.[2] The *kehillah* assumed the forms by which it was best known in Europe in the eleventh century and flourished for nearly a millennium until the twentieth century. The classic *kehillah* in its various forms was essentially a product of European Jewry, both Sephardic and Ashkenazic, and flourished during the periods when European Jewry was ascendant.[3] In the larger sense, however, the *kehillah* is a continuing phenomenon of Jewish corporate existence—portable (Leo Baeck referred to it as the Jewish vehicle for colonization that could be implanted anywhere), adaptable, easily constituted or reconstituted, and capable of serving a wide variety of purposes.[4] For many centuries it was the sole custodian of Jewish political autonomy and manifestation of the Jewish political tradition.

What has characterized the Jewish people since its very beginnings is that it has persisted to maintain its character as a body politic whether or not it has had a state.[5] The kehillah as the local unit of that body politic was invariably important, although its precise role at any given time depended on the overall political structure of the people as a whole. The Jewish *edah* has always been, by its very nature, one with a strong religious dimension. The formal term for the *kehillah—kehillah kedoshah* or *kahal kadosh* (holy community)—reflects this combined sense of political self-definition and religious aspiration. This religious dimension is not simply a matter of public enforcement of religious law, although that is a part of it, but the idea that the very existence of the community is predicated on the striving to become a holy commonwealth. It is for this reason that Judaism never became embodied in a church but rather in a community.

The Jewish people is a product of both kinship and consent—a family of tribes reshaped by virtue of its covenant with God and is formed into an *edah,* a body politic based on consent. The term itself refers to an assembly that meets regularly. Weinfeld has argued that the term *edah* actually described the Israelite regime prior to the introduction of the monarchy.[6] From the first, it became the Hebrew equivalent of "commonwealth" or "republic," in the original sense of *res publica* (a public thing) rather than the private preserve of any person or group, with strong democratic overtones.

The Jewish people has persisted as an *edah* ever since. Precisely because the *kehillah* is the local manifestation of the *edah,* the pattern of its development throughout the ages has followed closely the pattern of constitutional development of the *edah* as a whole. At the beginning of each epoch, the Jewish people as a whole underwent a reconstitution which gave them an altered constitutional-legal framework and, at the same time or shortly thereafter, a different set of political and communal constitutions to govern both the *edah* and its various subdivisions, including the *kehillot,* which then were dominant until the beginning of the next reconstitution. Each epoch covers some nine generations, a pattern that has held with extraordinary consistency at least since the Exodus.[7]

The character, structure, functions, and role of the *kehillah* in each epoch has depended upon the overall constitutional character of the *edah* as a whole. So, for example, during the golden age of the *kehillah,* the comprehensive institutions of the *edah* were at their lowest ebb, not only allowing the *kehillah* to take up the slack, but requiring it to assume tasks and responsibilities far greater than any entrusted to it in other constitutional epochs, when the *edah* as a whole had a king or Sanhedrin, a *nasi* (patriarch), a *rosh galut* (exilarch), or a *gaon* to direct its affairs.[8]

Several other characteristics of the *edah* are worthy of note in attempting to understand the role of the *kehillah*. One is that, since the first epochs of Jewish history, the Jewish people as a whole has rarely lived under any single overarching authority of its own that has encompassed all Jews. At the same time, the lack of an overarching political authority has not meant that the Jewish people has been simply fragmented. Rather, the *edah* has been maintained through a complex but systematic communications network rooted in a common law and constitution. If there was no overarching authority within any particular period, a rather clear-cut matrix of authoritative relationships existed, linking whatever political institutions had developed for governance of the *edah* and its *kehillot* at that particular time.

It is not improper to refer to the relationships within the matrix as federal ones and to the Jewish polity as basically federal in character. This federal character manifests itself in two ways. The word federal is simply an adaptation of *foedus,* the Latin word for *brith.* The Jewish *edah* was established, according to tradition, through a *brith* between the Jewish people and God; its political institutions, once the people was settled in its land, were defined by subsidiary covenants, renewed with every constitutional change. Ultimately every *kehillah* was legitimized, often through a covenant of its own, as an organized expression of the great covenant.[9] Especially during the golden age of the *kehillah,* the people in each locality came together to covenant among themselves to establish their local institutions. Sometimes the links between *kehillot* or other units of the *edah* were formal, often through specific covenants, but even when they were not, an implicit covenant existed between them to make the links legitimate.

It was because of these federal relationships that the *kehillah* could become a powerful instrumentality, since, for most of Jewish history, there has been no authoritative hierarchy of institutions. Since the division of powers has been on the basis of the size of the arena to be served, it has been possible for the smallest arenas, that is, the *kehillot,* to assert themselves authoritatively when necessary. At times, the small arenas have been integral parts of larger ones, as in the days of the *gaonim* when central authority existed at least on paper over a large segment of Jewry. At other times, the local arenas have functioned as fully authoritative units without any overarching body, as in medieval western Europe. At other times, the local arenas have themselves joined together to constitute a common larger arena under their joint control as in the case of Poland in the days of the Council of the Four Lands. Whatever the prevailing power arrangement, each arena was as fully legitimate as any other, drawing its authority directly from the same constitutional sources.

Another characteristic of the *kehillot* is that they have always been basically republican in character, like the *edah* itself. This republicanism manifests itself in two ways. In the first place, *the kehillah,* like the *edah,* is republican. It has always been considered to be the property of its citizenry and not the private preserve of any one person, family, or group.

Under Jewish law as it developed early in the development of the European *kehillot,* a *kehillah* was considered to be either a limited purpose partnership or a covenanted community.[10] If a partnership, then all partners had an equal share in every aspect of its activities which were in turn limited to the terms of the partnership and which required the consent of every partner to be altered. If a covenanted community, then the members were conceived to have created a new union in which they all had an undiluted share, but which had an existence of its own in addition to being an association of partners. Both of these were republican forms.

The *kehillot* have been republican in a more immediately practical way as well in the sense that they generally have been governed through republican forms. In small communities and in some larger ones at particular periods of time, they were democratic republics. In more of the larger communities throughout most of Jewish history, they were aristocratic or oligarchic republics in the sense that they were ruled by more limited groups of notables acting as trustees (aristocracy), under degenerated circumstances, exercising power primarily to safeguard their own interests (oligarchy). In rare cases, a single individual (the proverbial *gvir* or powerful one) dominated a particular community. This commitment to republican procedures as well has been an important dimension of the *kehillah* as a political entity.

## The Antecedents of the Kehillah

*The Earliest Periods and the First Commonwealth*

The first governmental institutions of the *edah* were based on family and tribe. After the emergence of fully articulated tribes and the tribal confederacy, the *bet av,* or extended family, was the functional equivalent of the local arena, but it was not a *kehillah* or even a proto-*kehillah* in any real sense because it was based entirely on kinship and had no separately articulated political institutions. Once the Israelites settled in Eretz Israel, however, proto-*kehillah* did come into existence. While the biblical accounts are fragmentary, scholars have generally concluded that during the biblical period every "city" (which was not an urban settlement but more like the New England town which combined urban and rural settlement and pursuits within a single jurisdiction) had its own local institutions, that is, elders who assembled at the gates of the city to serve as a local council and court as well as various officers and functionaries to handle local government tasks which ranged from regulation of markets to defense.[11]

As long as the tribes existed as organized political entities, the towns were directly linked to them and there is every indication that the tribal assemblies consisted of town elders (it may be that the same people were eligible for both roles because of their family positions). This arrangement is particularly marked in the southern kingdom which, for all intents and purposes, consisted of one tribe. The Bible suggests that when the king assembled the elders of Judah he was calling together the town leaders.[12]

While the Babylonian exile brought about some dramatic changes in the social and political life of the Jewish people, it brought fewer immediate constitutional changes than is commonly believed. Even the establishment of a permanent diaspora antedated it (although belonging to the same constitutional period),[13] but the Babylonian diaspora was the first to acquire a political framework and a certain legitimacy as a result. Part of the legitimacy of the Babylonian exile stemmed from the fact that the Judaean royal court was reestablished there virtually intact.[14] Moreover, the Jews were settled as a group in a contiguous and separate area, as part of the colonization plans of the neo-Babylonian empire so that they were able to establish all-Jewish townships to which they transplanted much the same form of government as had existed in the land of Israel. Unfortunately, too little is known of those centuries to draw any clear picture of their local institutions although it is assumed that the *bet knesset* (house of assembly or synagogue) was developed as a major local institution at that time.[15] Meanwhile the Jews who fled to Egypt after the destruction also established colonies of their own where they recreated the institutions with which they were familiar, including a Temple at Elephantine.[16]

## *Reconstitution Under the Second Commonwealth*

The real change in Jewish political institutions came after the restoration and the rebuilding of the Temple, the time of Ezra and Nehemiah. It was not until the failure of Zerrubavel to reestablish the monarchy in Eretz Israel two generations later that the Jews even began to seek alternate forms of authority. That search ultimately culminated in the constitution promulgated by Ezra at the time of the Succoth covenant in 340 B.C.E.

The major innovation in local government under the revised constitution was the *bet haknesset* which apparently came to serve as the focal point of the local community. In keeping with the Jewish thrust toward linking holiness and community, or, in modern terms, the theological and political dimensions of life, the *bet haknesset* served both functions. It was at one and the same time a place for carrying out the public ceremonials of the Jewish way of life and the seat of the local assembly and the institutions of local government. While the latter is generally acknowledged, its full implications are not always understood by moderns who have come to see the *bet haknesset* in a more purely religious context.[17]

This role of the *bet haknesset* was probably particularly strong in the smaller communities where a single one could serve the entire population. Other arrangements would doubtless have obtained in the larger cities so that as the Jews became urbanized during the latter part of this constitutional period, they were probably faced with the necessity of developing more complex local institutions. The institution of *tuvei ha'ir* apparently dates from this period. The *tuvei ha'ir,* variously three, five, seven, or nine in number, formed a local council that handled matters of governance. Unfortunately our records are too sparse to enable us to know much about specific developments.[18]

*From the Hasmoneans to the Patriarchs*

The Hasmonean revolt inaugurated a new constitutional period for Jews in the land of Israel while at approximately the same time the *politeuma* emerged as a serious institution in the Hellenistic diaspora (see below). The Hasmonean rulers established a strong national authority, which persisted even after the Hasmoneans themselves lost their power, first to the Herodians and then to direct Roman rule. But the changing boundaries of their state meant that even when it was strong, many Jews continued to live in local communities in the land of Israel not under the authority of any Jewish general government. Moreover, the party struggles of that period manifested themselves locally as much as nationally, with sectarians building colonies of their own and existing communities choosing Saducean or Pharisaic ways. Thus, the Hasmonean period apparently saw the strengthening of local as well as national institutions. As the latter passed into the hands of aliens, the former became even more important for the preservation of Jewish political and religious life.[19]

These local governments were of two kinds. On one hand, there were the traditional local governments, structured along lines indigenous to the Jewish political tradition. On the other, there were those municipalities that had acquired the form of a Greek *polis*. Thus, Tiberias and Sepphoris, while containing overwhelming Jewish majorities for most of this period, had at some stage acquired Hellenistic constitutions. They continued to be governed by Jews utilizing Greek forms. Unlike most of the *kehillot* in the diaspora, these communities, whatever their form, consisted of whole territories in which the total population or the overwhelming majority was Jewish. Hence, their pattern of governance was different from those in the diaspora where Jews represented a minority, even if a territorially compact one, within some larger municipal unit. Although the number of *kehillot* declined more or less steadily from the first century C.E. onward, these *kehillot* shared the burden of responsibility for Jewish self-government throughout the period of the patriarchate and then continued to exist after the more comprehensive office was discontinued in 425 C.E. Jewish local self-government of this kind did not disappear from the country for many centuries.[20]

*Diaspora and Politeuma*

After the conquest of the Middle East by Alexander in the fourth century B.C.E., Hellenistic influences began to have their impact on Jewish local institutions. Moreover, the growth of the Jewish diaspora outside of Babylonia meant that new institutions had to be created to deal with radically different circumstances. The diaspora Jews of the Hellenistic world did not settle in rural areas where they could form the majority if not the total population, but rather in the big cities where they represented minorities of greater or lesser size. Moreover, the cities themselves were city-states, autonomous bodies within relatively amorphous empires, based upon the principle that the *polis,* or city-state, would be the fundamental building block of the political order.[21]

In a sense, it was out of this experience that the first true *kehillot* emerged, that is to say, communities based upon essentially voluntary adherence outside of the territorial boundaries of an all-embracing Jewish autonomous entity whether state or province, directly dependent for their existence upon the policies of non-Jewish rulers of the territory in which they were located. At first these urban-dwelling diaspora Jews simply transplanted the *bet knesset* to the urban setting where it was even better suited in many ways to serve as a focal point. Located in the midst of what would be a Jewish neighborhood (even under diaspora circumstances some kind of territorial base was needed to provide for communal cohesion and the efficient conduct of religious and communal activities), it was the ideal focal point for an unbounded population.

As long as the Jewish populations in the Hellenistic cities remained relatively small, one *bet knesset* could serve as the focus for each community, perhaps growing to inordinate size (e.g., the legendary synagogue of Alexandria) in the process. Sooner or later, however, in the biggest cities the Jewish population grew too large to be accommodated even in the most massive synagogue. Moreover, Jews began to migrate from diaspora community to diaspora community bringing with them different nuances of ritual behavior and religious association based on their own variations in Jewish law and custom, which they wished to preserve through their own institutions. In this way, multiple synagogue communities emerged in the same city. The Jews themselves might have been content with this state of affairs, but it did not serve the purposes of the non-Jewish rulers who, for the most part, wished the Jewish minority to be under some coherent structure so that it could be properly managed in the interests of the larger *polis* or empire. As a result, the *politeuma* was created, a polity within a polity.

The *politeuma* was a Hellenistic device to accommodate the existence of ethno-religious minorities within the Mediterranean world. While other groups were organized into *politeumata* as well as the Jews, as seems to be inevitably the case, the framework seemed even more suited for the Jews with their strong drives for autonomous existence than for any other group. While the *politeuma* as a type was well-nigh universal throughout the Hellenistic world, it was structured in a variety of ways. In Alexandria, power was vested in the hands of an ethnarch and a *gerousia* (council of elders). Others were led by councils of nine, seven, five, or three archons. In Rome, the *batei knesset* remained the bases for communal organization, with the overarching structure ranging from weak to nonexistent.[22] These two basic forms of local organization, the one with the *bet knesset* as center and the other with a number of *batei knesset* functioning within an overarching communal organization, carried over into later periods and continued to be the two principal structural variants among *kehillot*. So, too, were the institutional arrangements for governance developed at the time of the *politeuma* carried over into later periods, perhaps as a result of direct influence and perhaps because there are relatively few forms to choose from in matters of local government under any system.

## The Babylonian Experience

In the Babylonia of the *Amoraim,* no *politeuma* developed. In the first place, it lay outside of the Hellenistic world. More importantly, the character of Jewish settlement was such that an overarching countrywide authority continued to exist throughout the period and much beyond it, headed by the Exilarch. Babylonian local communities were just that. They were not autonomous bastions of Jewish control, but subordinate to the overarching leadership.[23]

As the *yeshivot* developed, however, they mounted a challenge against the Exilarch for power in the countrywide community, one that ultimately led to a compromise between the two forces, creating something of a separation-of-powers system, though not always clearly defined.[24]

The struggle between the two forces, which was additionally complicated by the fact that there were two major *yeshivot,* each of which
produced its own *halachic* leaders and had its own constituency, enabled the *kehillot* to gain a fair measure of autonomy even within a
system that was at least nominally quite centralized. While the evidence
is fragmentary, there is little doubt that *kehillot* were able to utilize the
opportunities presented them and choose between the different factors
in the political struggle to gain support for local aims and interests on
the part of one countrywide political power or another. The Talmud has
some suggestive passages attesting to the results. So, for example, while
the power to appoint local judges was vested in the countrywide authorities, provision was made in the *halachah* for the local communities
to veto the choices that they opposed.[25]

This pattern persisted even after the Muslim conquest of the Near
East through the period of the *gaonim* and the *neggidim,* although with
much diminished force after the middle of the fourteenth century.[26] It
was only eliminated under the Mamaluks and the Ottomans when the
old institutions were formally abolished, though by that time the Jews
themselves had moved beyond the earlier framework.

### The Emergence of the Classical *Kehillah*

It was only with the gradual shift of the Jewish population to Europe that significant changes took place in the form of *kehillah* organization. Mediterranean Europe was the transition zone. In Muslim Spain,
at first efforts were made to continue the pattern of centralized authority developed in Babylonia, albeit in a decentralized fashion. But Spain
was too far away from the major centers of Arab power and, for that
matter, the major centers of Jewish power within the new Muslim
empire and it soon began to develop its own pattern based upon much
greater local autonomy.[27] The Jewish communities of Christian Europe had never really known centralized authority from their beginnings in Greece and Italy. As the patterns established in those countries spread northwestward, even the symbolic overarching authorities
disappeared. Increasingly all segments of European Jewry came to
live in *kehillot* which were autonomous within the common framework of the *halachah* and which assumed full powers of internal legislation and governance. This was the classical *kehillah.*[28]

One of the primary characteristics of this classical *kehillah* during the

first epoch and a half of its existence (some 450 years) was its comprehensiveness; that it to say, all the Jews in a particular locality would be
members of the same *kahal*. In the many small localities of this period,
which were the predominant form of Jewish settlement, the *kahal*
consisted of a single congregation using a single synagogue, with all
adult members functioning as the general meeting. In the few larger
communities where there was more than one *bet knesset,* all were part of
the same overarching communal structure. By and large, this was
because the communities were or rapidly became homogeneous. During
the epoch stretching from the middle of the eleventh to the middle of the
fourteenth centuries when homogeneity was the rule, it was frequently
enforced through the use of the *herem hayishuv,* which prevented Jews
from outside the community from settling within it.

The wave of migrations that began after 1492 ended this homogeneity, with Jews from various parts of the Jewish world coming together in new localities to create new communities. There, they sought
to preserve customary differences that had developed in their respective lands of nativity, thus leading to heterogeneous communities, some
of which were able to create overarching structures and many of which
were not. During these years, Jews tended to settle in larger numbers
in a particular locality where each country-of-origin community would
establish its own *kahal* and ancillary institutions.[29]

The style of Jewish self-government in Spain until the middle of the
eleventh century more or less followed that of the Muslim East, with
strong central authorities on a countrywide basis. The decline and
demise of the Umayyad dynasty and the invasion of the Almoravids
marked the end of the golden age of the Jews in Muslim Spain, the
breakup of the Arab caliphate and with it the Jewish community. At
the same period, the Christian reconquest gained momentum and by
the end of the century a substantial part of the peninsula was again in
Christian hands. Moreover, there was every incentive for the Jews to
flee from the Muslim areas now ruled by fanatics from North Africa
and to establish communities in Christian Spain. These communities
were already classic *kehillot.* As their name, *aljama* (Arabic for *edah*
or *kahal*) reveals, the form of these *kehillot* dated back to Muslim
times. What was changed were their powers. Each became an independent political entity directly linked to the throne of the kingdom in
which it was located, paying its taxes to the royal treasury and maintaining full administrative and judicial autonomy.[30]

To the extent that generalizations can be made, the political life in
those communities followed a course from direct democracy to oligarchic domination by a few families, to a more representative oligarchy.
When the communities were small and economic differences among
the members not great, all adult males were more or less equal. As
some Jews grew wealthy and, perhaps more important, became figures
in the public affairs of the kingdoms in which they were located, they
gained control of the communities and often managed them in an
oligarchic manner. This led in turn to a democratic reaction in the
thirteenth century which led to a transformation of the oligarchic rule
into one of a more representative character.

As the reconquest spread, so did Jewish communities, either as a
result of conquest of existing communities or through Jewish colonization following the Christian armies. Wherever a Jewish community
appeared, an *aljama* was established with all the rights and privileges
thereof, often as the equal of Christian and Muslim local government
bodies on the same municipal site. The powers of these *aljamas* varied
by kingdom and period, but were generally substantial, including civil
and often criminal jurisdiction as well as the standard municipal functions. Formulas developed for the founding of these communities and
their various institutions, as reflected in the *Sefer HaShtarot* of R.
Yehudah a Barceloni, whereby the founders could covenant among
themselves to establish their collective authority to function as a *bet
din,* enact *takkanot,* levy taxes, and deliver judgments.

For the first half of this period, from the middle of the eleventh to
the beginning of the thirteenth century, the record of the Jewish communities was one of general growth and prosperity. Beginning early in
the thirteenth century, however, anti-Jewish feeling made its appearance and a Christian reaction grew until, by the end of the period, the
Jews were already in a precarious position. The decimations brought
about by the Black Death in 1348 opened the door to both increased
Christian persecution on one hand, particularly in Aragon, but a generation later in Castile as well, and to a reorganization of the *kehillot*
on the other. In 1354 an effort was made by the communal leaders of
Aragon to establish a kingdom-wide confederation of communities to
defend Jewish rights, the first in a number of efforts to create such
confederations that were to persist with periodic success until the exile
of the Jews from Spain.[31] Perhaps the most notable phenomenon of
the last century of Spanish Jewry was the reorganization of Castilian

Jewry along federal lines in 1432. Under the *takkanot* adopted at a convention of representatives in Valadollid that year—in effect, a constitution for Castilian Jewry, new regulations on taxation and education, the election of judges, and relations between the communities and the Rab de la Corte of all of Castile were adopted. This restructuring was necessitated by the plight of the communities in Castile at that time but it also revealed that they still had sufficient vitality to undertake a major internal reconstitution in order to overcome their difficulties.[32] The *takkanot* of Valadollid were to serve as the basis for many of the communities of the subsequent Sephardic diaspora.

## Northern Europe

If the development of the *kehillah* in Spain was, to some extent, an evolution out of the pattern of Jewish self-government in the Muslim world, the Jews of Christian Europe had to develop their institutions more consciously, without recourse to easily obtained precedent. While all local Jewish communities emerged as a result of concrete founding acts, the Spanish communities inherited formulae to use for constituting themselves into *kehillot,* while those of Western Europe, in effect, had to invent appropriate formulae, searching the Talmudic sources directly for principles and precedents to guide them. Synods of scholars designed to consider questions of communal concern so as to provide guidance for local communities in their enactment of *takkanot* became fairly widespread in Western Europe during this period. It was in the process of developing a constitutional basis for the *kehillot* that some of the greatest debates in Jewish political history occurred: regarding *hefker bet din,* majority rule and the rights of the individual, *herem hayishuv* and the exclusion of Jews from particular communities, the rights of minorities, who shall vote, and the fundamental questions of who constitutes a community and how. These questions are all reflected in the responsa of the period. While as usual in the case of such discussions, no single position was unanimously adopted, it was generally agreed that Jewish communities were constituted by all adult males within their boundaries at the time of their constitution, that because they were bound by the covenant at Sinai as Jews they did not have to recovenant every year as did the non-Jews but that the community could maintain its existence once the basic *takkanot* had been adopted, that a *kehillah* could restrict entry of other Jews for purposes of *settlement,* that a majority could decide on most issues although some basic ones required unanimity, and that individuals and minorities did have certain basic rights even within the framework of majority rule.[33]

The political theories developed through the synods and the responsa passed back and forth between the communities and the leading rabbinical scholars of the day, to create a common political climate and constitutional tradition. At the same time, every community was virtually an independent republic for all intents and purposes. Occasionally, federations of communities were established within particular geographic regions, but their importance was limited and they were invariably confederations or leagues rather than unions of *kehillot* in this period.[34]

The organization of these communities was based upon a relatively high degree of internal discipline. The *herem hayishuv* was one example of the tight control exercised by the community through its leaders over membership. All communities could exercise discipline over recalcitrant members in certain respects and, in some cases, could expel them.

*Communal governance.* Since the communities continued the Jewish political tradition of aristocratic republicanism, the danger of lapsing into oligarchic rule was always present. Nevertheless, democratic ways were surprisingly widespread, particularly considering the era, and constantly being revived. The natural leaders of the community were drawn from the learned, the wealthy, and the well-born.[35] Learning was inevitably a source of communal leadership, since even in the most democratic communities rabbinical authority was needed to sustain communal decisions. In some cases this merely involved appeals to rabbinical authority when a communal decision was challenged, and then the acceptance of the rabbinical judgment with the authority functioning as a constitutional court. In a few cases positive rabbinical assent to *takkanot* and other major communal decisions was required before they could be considered enforceable. The role of the rabbi in exercising constitutional judgment was a reflection of the manner in which every *kehillah* was considered to be responsible in two directions—to the people who constituted it on one hand and to God through the Torah on the other. This, indeed, is the classic formulation of the lines of responsibility in the *edah.* Thus, the *kehillah,* like other Jewish political institutions, was maintained as an instrument of the Jewish people and the Divine purpose, both rather than a reified entity in its own right, a fact of great importance in the transmission of the Jewish political culture to later generations.

The tendency of the wealthy to attain power in the communities was principally a function of the problem of external taxation. The community as a unit usually served as the tax gatherer for the non-Jewish ruler. The ruler would levy taxes on the community as a collectivity and then rely upon the community to apportion them however it pleased among its members. Thus, the wealthy had a special stake in gaining and maintaining control over those communal institutions which determined that apportionment and, of course, the additional taxation levied for the internal purposes of the community itself.

As is the case in every such situation, the wealthy were also best able to pursue their interests. Being wealthy, their money was needed to ease the burden on the other members of the community. Moreover, their wealth was usually gained because of their favored positions in the non-Jewish world, so that frequently they could appeal outside of the community to gain some exemption from the tax burden, or at least a reduction in the pressures upon them to the detriment of the rest of the community, and it was in the interests of the community to prevent or minimize this. Finally, since they were wealthy, they also had the leisure time to function as community leaders and could afford the costs that were frequently involved in doing so, something that people of average income or the poor could not do since they were preoccupied with economic survival and had no surplus of either time or money to contribute to community affairs. Thus, power gravitated toward the wealthy as a matter of course.

Under the right circumstances, the wealthy along with the well-born and the learned would serve as trustees for the whole community, that is, fulfill the demands of aristocratic republicanism. But, where the wealthy were primarily interested in protecting their own interests, matters rapidly degenerated into oligarchy. The history of Jewish communal life can be viewed, in part, as a continuing struggle between democratic and oligarchic trends. The fact that there were strong democratic trends, however, testifies to its truly republican character.

The well-born were frequently wealthy and, if not, often produced the scholars who became the rabbinical leadership. While Jewish society was never feudalized and the hierarchy of rank common to Christian Europe barely found an echo within Jewish circles, class divisions did appear in no small measure as a result of the influence of the outside world. Thus, certain families gained status by virtue of their services to gentile rulers and were able to translate that status into equivalent positions within the Jewish community. Spain, in particular, produced a number of patrician families which persisted over the generations as a gentry, if not a nobility, and which functioned on the basis of *noblesse oblige* as well as to protect their interests in positions of community leadership.

In both theory and practice, leaders of the community were elected, but the elections were not necessarily direct ones. Even a rabbi had to be elected to his position by the community, perhaps by the council rather than by the whole membership.[36] Rabbinical responsa record more than one controversy in which a rabbi's election was challenged or revoked and in which other rabbinical authorities had to determine what his status was.

In the most democratic communities, usually the smaller ones, direct elections were the rule, frequently for one-year terms. As communities got larger or became more oligarchic, longer terms were introduced and elections were frequently relegated to *borerim* who served as an electoral college chosen either by the communal membership or by lot to choose the communal leaders. The rules regarding eligibility and mode of election of *borerim* represent a substantial part of the literature on *kehillah* governance from the Middle Ages.

In the very smallest communities where all adult males met regularly in the synagogue and so could act as a common council to deal with any matter on very short notice (daily, if necessary), a single officer appointed to handle the administration of communal affairs was often sufficient. As communities became larger, the general meeting inevitably became less efficient and it was necessary to elect councils of elders known variously as *rashum, parnasim, tovim, neemanim,* or *gabbayim* (or occasionally some other term). The administrative systems of these communities developed apace with special committees and authorities to undertake specific tasks such as *gabei hamas, berurei aveira, shamashim, shochetim, sofrim* and the like. In general, it can be said that the principle of community organization was to divide powers among a number of different authorities connected to the *kehillah* through various channels.

Often, a rudimentary tripanite separation of powers existed with a rabbi serving as *dayan* representing the judicial power, a council representing the legislative power, and various administrative officials assigned to different tasks, perhaps under an overall head, perhaps not, representing the executive power. The division was rarely quite that clear-cut since each of the three groups tended to have some powers generally associated with the tasks of one or both of the others. In some cases, these were overlapping functions. So, for example, the *takkanot* of the council might require the assent of the rabbi because of the obligations of every *kehillah* to conduct its affairs in accordance with the laws of the Torah (a situation not dissimilar from certain contemporary separation-of-power systems whereby the enactments of the legislative body must pass constitutional review before they are in force). In other cases, the functions were divided so that every body or agent exercised a limited share of all three powers in some way, in the manner of modern governmental functional authorities *(reshuyot)*. In many communities the practice was to entrust general executive authority to a different *parnas* every month on a rotating basis.

Foreign affairs of the *kehillah* were handled first by the officers of the community, or informally by some prominent member of the community who had the ear of the local ruler. In later years the office of *shtadlan* was developed. The term first appears as *mishtadlim* in Spain in the latter half of the first era of the *kehillot,* namely, in the thirteenth and fourteenth centuries. The conference of the communities of Catalonia and Valencia, which met in Barcelona in December 1354, defined *shtadlanut* explicitly in their appeal to the King of Aragon to prevent mob violence against Jews.[37] The major function of the *shtadlan* was to protect Jewish rights. The institution reached its highest development in the later medieval period in central Europe when the *shtadlan* became a paid professional employed by the community to undertake the difficult diplomatic role of *shtadlanut*.[38]

*Communal functions.*[39] The functions of the *kehillah* were comprehensive since it was virtually a Jewish city-state that offered religious, educational, and social welfare services to its members, and handled legislative, judicial, administrative, and financial tasks. Every community, no matter how small, had to provide at least one *bet knesset* (synagogue), a cemetery, a *mikvah* (ritual bath), facilities for *shechitah* and supplying kosher foods, and provisions for supplying other ritual needs. The smallest communities had only one of each of these facilities. As communities grew larger, the number of *batei knesset* invariably multiplied as Jews sought to worship in the company of those with whom they were most intimately associated.

Educational arrangements generally remained the responsibility of each Jewish family, but supervision of schools and the provision of education for the children of the poor was a communal responsibility, either handled directly by an institution of the *kehillah* or through an association established for that purpose under the *kehillah's* auspices. *Kehillot* often raised funds for educational purposes, set the number of students allowed per teacher, controlled competition among teachers, and otherwise regularized the systems of instruction. Construction of schools was confined primarily to those for poor children or *batei midrash* for adult study and higher learning.

Social welfare was more often handled directly by the community, although there, too, special associations were at times created under its auspices. Welfare services included assistance to the sick, provision for widows and orphans, and funds for the ransoming of captives resulting from war, piracy, or actions on the part of local rulers. Funds were also collected locally on a sporadic basis for the relief of other communities in times of disaster and, somewhat more regularly, for the support of the surviving Jewish settlements in Eretz Israel. The communities provided the very poor with shelter, clothing, food, and occasionally money. Itinerant beggars had a claim on the community treasury, usually to assist them to move on, and special officials were appointed to deal with them.

The *kehillot* were extensively involved in the regulation of morals, with communities engaged in constant struggles with regard to such matters as gambling, the maintenance of proper standards of family life, costume and dress, mixed dancing, sexual morality, and card playing. It was through the *kehillot* that the Ashkenazic rabbinate won the fight against polygamy in Christian Europe during this period.

A major function of the *kehillah* authorities was to regulate commerce. Each *kehillah* took stringent steps to control prices, regulate markets, prevent undue competition (often very narrowly defined), maintain honest weights and measures, control rents, and the like. The concept of *hazakah* was applied widely in this regard to protect the spheres of local artisans, merchants, and even teachers.

The criminal and civil jurisdiction of the *kehillot* represented a very important source of their power. During most of this period, the *kehillot* were granted extensive powers in criminal as well as civil law by the gentile rulers, particularly in Spain, where the tripartite division of Muslim, Christian, and Jewish authorities prevailed.[40] Since the communities themselves were basically autonomous, their powers were well-nigh absolute. In France, communal judicial autonomy was supported by the *herem bet din,* established from the twelfth century onward. Decisions of communities could be appealed to authorities beyond their jurisdiction, but only when the community authorities allowed such appeals. This led to the development of elaborate court systems under *dayanim,* with carefully developed proceedings. The *herem* (excommunication) was a heavily used device for many offenses, fines were extensively used as in traditional Jewish jurisprudence, and some communities even had the right to impose capital punishment. Corporal punishment was frequently imposed, and imprisonment was also an option.

In the realm of taxation, the *kehillah* imposed all varieties of taxes known to man at the time, both direct and indirect, import and export duties, and tolls. Taxes were frequently levied on Jews by the gentile rulers to exempt them from military service (a matter over which they had no choice) or from forced labor. The control over tax exemptions was a major power adhering to the community leadership, one that helped promote oligarchy as the wealthy sought office so as to favor their own interests. At the same time, democratic responses frequently prevented excesses in that direction.

## The Classical Kehillah in Its Second Epoch

*Eastern Europe*

If the period from the middle of the eleventh to the middle of the fourteenth century brought the flourishing of the classical *kehillah* of Ashkenazi Jewry in Western Europe, the following period brought the flourishing of the classical models of Jewish communal life in Eastern Europe. The Western European communities were periodically destroyed, first by the Crusades, then by the Black Death, and from time to time by expulsion, forcing Ashkenazi Jewry to migrate eastward to greater Poland where they were encouraged to settle by ambitious rulers seeking to build states that could compete with the West. The first settlers transplanted the *kehillah* institutions with which they were familiar to the Eastern European scene. Perhaps because they were functioning within a large, consolidated domain, however, they did not long repeat the pattern of *kehillah* autonomy common in the fragmented Holy Roman Empire, with its feudal base and virtually independent principalities, duchies, and counties scattered throughout its putative realm.

In the sixteenth century, in both Poland and the Grand Duchy of Lithuania which was linked with the Polish crown, countrywide councils were established linking the *kehillot* in each. In Poland the well-known *Vaad Arba Aratzot* linking the four Jewish provinces of that country emerged as the most comprehensive communal structure the Jewish people was to know between the decline of the gaonate and the modern era.[41] Parallel to it in Lithuania was *Vaad Medinat Lita.*[42] Both grew out of what had originally been ad hoc assemblies of local communities that had become more closely associated in their respective provinces and were designed to answer the need for the regular links among the various Jewries. In no small measure the councils arose to offset a Polish government effort to establish a centralized Jewish leadership outside the purview of the *kehillot.* Thus, beginning in about 1519, the Jews began to convene councils at the great fairs held annually, with the *Vaad Arba Aratzot* meeting at the Lublin fair. The *Vaad* involved both voluntary and rabbinical leadership. It was soon endowed with the status of a *bet din,* the key to gaining halachically recognized political authority under the political principles developed in the earlier period. Lithuanian Jewry organized in the 1530s and its administration was centralized beginning in the 1560s.

It should be noted that at no point did the individual *kehillot* surrender their autonomy. They remained the repositories of all powers of self-government, delegating those powers to the provincial and countrywide councils. Thus, the system was truly federal in character. The council itself consisted of two bodies, one the assembly of the *rashei hamedinot* and the other the assembly of *dayanei ha'aratzot.* The first consisted of the voluntary leaders and the second of the rabbinical leadership. At times, the largest communities, the so-called *kehillot rashiot,* were directly represented in the *Vaad Arba Aratzot.* Thus, in 1717, the *Vaad* was comprised of eighteen entities, nine of which were *kehillot* represented directly and nine provinces.

The council maintained five executive offices: the *parnas,* who presided and was selected from among the *rashei hamedinot;* the *neeman,* chosen from either body, who was salaried and functioned as treasurer and chief secretary; the *shtadlan,* also salaried, with a salary commensurate to the risks involved; a *kotev,* who served as clerk for the council and who had a number of assistants; and the *shamaim,* or assessors. The assembly of the *dayonei ha'aratzot* was headed by an *av bet din.* In its heyday, the council met semi-annually at the fairs of Lublin and Yaraslav. The Lithuanian council met less regularly. Election to the council was through limited franchise. Smaller communities did not participate at all and in the larger communities only a small percentage of the householders were entitled to vote.

By and large, the council had powers over external relations only, although it could formulate certain kinds of legislation for the communities. When it did seek to intervene into the internal affairs of the communities, it frequently met opposition. Its major powers flowed from the fact that the taxes paid to the Polish government were levied through it, whose responsibility it was to apportion them among the communities. The council also exercised judicial jurisdiction over certain offenses against Jewish law. The council's biggest success in internal affairs was in the regulation of economic activities, both to protect Jewish businessmen and to maintain proper moral standards in the conduct of business affairs. The council also involved itself in efforts to supervise education and to lay down common standards in the field of social welfare and fund-raising for Eretz Israel, but apparently with somewhat less success.

The council was abolished in 1764 because of Polish discontent over the level of taxation being imposed on the Jewish community. The provincial councils continued to exist, but met irregularly as Poland itself was partitioned shortly thereafter.

### The Ottoman Empire

If the Council of the Four Lands represented the high point of Jewish unity on the eve of the modern era, the situation in the Ottoman Empire represented the high point of Jewish fragmentation, even though Jews living within the framework of a single empire had several opportunities to create common institutions. It was there that the practice of multiple *kehillot* within the same city, reflecting the differences in country-of-origin of refugees to the Ottoman Empire, became most pronounced. Salonika was the prime example of an extremely fragmented community until the later stages of the empire.[43]

At first, the Ottoman rulers tried to continue the already established Middle Eastern pattern of a single leader for the Jewish millet, at least for certain purposes.[44] There is some question as to whether even before the arrival of the Sephardic exiles the rabbis appointed to this position were able to exercise authority much beyond Constantinople. Since they were drawn from the Romaniot or old Greek Jewish community, they were challenged even within that city by the Italian and Ashkenazi communities which considered themselves independent, if not superior. When the Sephardic exiles arrived they were not even willing to create a common Sephardic communal structure, much less accept dictation from Jews of the East whom they believed to be inferior in learning and in their customs.

Bowing to the pressure of the newly arrived Sephardim, the Ottoman sultan allowed the position of chief *dayan* to lapse after the death of the second incumbent. From then on, every new group of settlers in the Ottoman Empire created its own *kahal* wherever it settled. Since the Ottoman Empire was a chief haven for Jewish refugees from the fifteenth through the seventeenth centuries, the number of different communities was magnified. Sixteenth-century Istanbul had some forty different congregational communities. Even Safed in that century had twelve different ones. Salonika, the Jerusalem of the Sephardic diaspora, was even more fragmented, since so many Jews settled there that factionalism divided even the country-of-origin communities. In effect, each congregation was the equivalent of a town in and of itself, with as many of the requisite institutions as it could muster. Unity among the congregations was achieved only in the face of grave common problems, as when some external danger faced the entire community, or in the case of raising funds to redeem captives or support Jewish settlements in Eretz Israel.

It was only in the nineteenth century, when the empire reorganized all the millets, that a common authority was established for Ottoman Jewry in Constantinople in the person of the *haham bashi* (whose powers were never as extensive in fact as they were on paper) and that the various congregations were brought under common local umbrella bodies. The reverse arrangement prevailed in Jerusalem. There, upon the growth of Jewish settlement in the sixteenth and seventeenth centuries, the *Vaad haEdah haSepharadit beYerushalayaim* did come to exercise control over the entire community, absorbing those Ashkenazim who came to settle in the holy city. The *Vaad haedah* was organized as a typical *kehillah,* based at least in part on the model of the Valadollid *takkanot,* with a council of *baalei batim* and a chief rabbi, the *Rishon le Zion,* sharing power and services administered through a wide variety of authorities. It was only in the late nineteenth century, with the migration of large numbers of non-Sephardic Jews who insisted upon their own communities, that fragmentation was introduced. The Turks ultimately agreed to free various groups from the rule of the *Vaad haedah,* primarily because of the pressure from the European governments whose nationals they were. In effect, the Jewish community underwent the same problem of fragmentation as a result of the capitulations that the Ottoman Empire underwent as a whole.[45]

The pattern in Ottoman-ruled North Africa was somewhat different in form, but essentially the same in substance.[46] There, the title *naggid* persisted, but the number of *neggidim* multiplied. It seems that these *neggidim* were chosen by the local rulers to whom they were responsible, with the assent of the Jews over whom they exercised authority. In fact, the office frequently became hereditary. In effect, the *naggid* became the head of the *kehillah,* ruling along with a council that usually consisted of seven *tuvei ha'ir* and the local rabbinical court. This tripartite division was held more closely responsible to the entire community than was the case in much of Europe during the same period. After the sixteenth century, any *takkanot* enacted by the *tuvei ha'ir* with the *naggid* required the consent of the local *bet din* and the entire community. The system of *shtadlanim* prevailed as well, although at least in Algeria the *shtadlan* was known by the Arabic name of *mukkadim.* In the course of time, the *shtadlan* gradually acquired the power of *naggid* because of his position in court.

## The Transition to Modernity

With the rise of the modern nation-state and the decline of feudalism, the structuring of society along corporate lines became increasingly obsolete. Individual Jews were ultimately beneficiaries of the change, since they now could be admitted as individual citizens to the bodies politic in which they found themselves without renouncing their Jewish ties (although many did). As a collectivity, however, the Jewish community suffered a severe blow, since in country after country it had to surrender its autonomy, transfer most if not all of its civil functions to the state authorities and reconstitute itself as a voluntary association limited principally to the provision of obviously religious services in the western sense of the term. The transformation was every bit as revolutionary as the sixth century B.C.E. transformation from a self-contained *edah* in its own land to a people divided among several diasporas.

## Portuguese Communities in Western Europe

The Marranos fleeing from Spain and Portugal to countries in which they could openly return to Judaism were the first to create communities in the modern vein.[47] While in many cases they still sought the same corporate rights and privileges common in previous centuries, their own extensive involvement in the economic life of the countries in which they settled, quasi-legal status as semi-Jews-semi-Christians, and expectations of freedom of movement that had resulted from their long existence as parts of the larger society in their countries of origin limited the degree to which they sought self-contained communal status. Moreover, the countries in which they settled were those that were in the forefront of modernization—the Netherlands, the Baltic city-states of Germany, England, Denmark, Bordeaux in France—and could no longer accept the kind of state-within-a-state arrangements which the medieval world found so congenial. Thus, these communities were organized from the first as extended religious associations, whose members were not quite equal citizens alongside their non-Jewish brethren, but were not excluded from the authority of the body politic either. In some respects, the institutions of these communities were more coherently organized (in the western sense) than their predecessor. Thus, the Jewish community of Amsterdam created a Talmud Torah that was a model of its kind, far ahead of the common forms of Jewish schooling of the age. By and large, these were small communities built around single congregations.

## Central Europe

Other migrations within the interior of Europe also led to the development of new forms of communal organization. As Prussia rose to prominence, Jews began to settle within its borders, where few had resided before. As they established new communities, they had to conform to the demands of Prussian statism, which meant that their *kehillot* were either organized under state control from the first or came under such control in the early years of the modern era, leading to the end of autonomous Jewish corporate existence in the eighteenth century. The *Landjudenschaft* was the major new communal institution to emerge in the transition period. In the Germanies, the *Landjudenschaft* was the first association of individuals to transcend the local community, being organized on a regional or *Land* basis through an assembly of all the heads of families in the *Land*. In Bohemia, Moravia, and Alsace, the *Landtaggen* (land assemblies) were comprised of delegates from the communities in a more traditional confederal arrangement. While the beginning of the *Landjudenschaft* can be traced back to the sixteenth century, it was only in the seventeenth that the institution acquired its full form and became the dominant one in Central Europe. Thus, of the first ten established, one was founded in 1616 (Hesse Kassel) and all the rest between 1649 and 1678.[48]

The *Landjudenschaft* of Bohemian Jewry was created in the 1650s after the end of the Thirty Years War. Its constitution was adopted in 1659. It came into existence as a result of a revolt against the domination of Bohemian Jewry by the Prague Jewish community. The smaller *kehillot* in the provinces forced the creation of a federation in which they had substantial power.

Ultimate authority in the *Landjudenschaft* rested with the assembly of all heads of families within each or representatives of the various communities who met every three to five years, depending on the particular *Land,* to fix the taxation pattern, to enact *takkanot* and elect the *abad hamedinah* (*abad = av bet din,* or chief justice), the *dayanei hamedinah* (judges) and the *baalei batim* (householders) who constituted the executive committee (small council), *oberparnas* (chief executive), *parnasei medinah* (executive officers), *tovim* (councilmen), and *ikurim* (inspectors). Other officials chosen by this plenary body included the chief treasurer, the tax collectors, accountants, scribe, and the *shamash*. By accepted practice, the *oberparnas* was also the *shtadlan*. In certain cases, the position remained in the same family for generations. While there was at least a formal separation of powers between the rabbinical and other communal institutions, since many of the rabbis also came from rabbinical families and were drawn from the same elites as the *parnasim,* there was a fair amount of intermixing of functions in practice.

As the German states modernized by extending their authority into all spheres of society within their boundaries, they also took an unprecedented interest in Jewish communal organization. In the eighteenth century they centralized payment of taxes and compelled the leaders of the *landjudenschaften* to utilize government to coerce recalcitrant taxpayers. This was the opening wedge in the expansion of government control which ultimately led to the transfer of many of the functions of the *Landjuderschaft* to the new state bureaucracies and then the establishment of commissions for Jewish affairs in numerous states to centralize activities further. The commissioners began to attend *Landtag* meetings, then became the chairmen of the meetings, and exercised control within the *Landjudenschaft* itself. The scope of the rabbinical courts was restricted and increasingly Jews were required to bring their litigation before state courts with Jewish jurisdiction ultimately restricted to religious matters. With the coming of emancipation, the *Landjudenschaft* was abolished or, as was the case in Bohemia, so stripped of its powers that it remained in existence only as a shell.

*France*

In France, England, and the United States there was no need to transform medieval institutions since none existed. French Jewry, outside of Alsace, was not formally recognized before the French Revolution, although local arrangements had been developed to allow Jewish institutions to function in those places where Jews were tolerated.[49] The Revolution brought emancipation in stages, culminating with Napoleon's convening of his Sanhedrin in 1807 through which the Jews formally abjured their separate national status and pledged themselves to be citizens of France in every respect. In return, Napoleon established the consistorial system whereby the Jews were organized for religious purposes in a centralized congregational structure paralleling that of the new centralized state which Napoleon was in the process of erecting.[50] This consistorial pattern, under which the Jewish community was confined almost entirely to synagogual activities and was under the formal direction of a chief rabbi and subsidiary rabbinical leaders who served with government support, persisted unchanged until 1905 when the Third Republic ended state subsidization of religious bodies, after which it continued to dominate French Jewry on a voluntary basis until after World War II. It still remains one of the pillars of the French Jewish community.

## England

In England, early in the eighteenth century, the Sephardim were joined by an Ashkenazi migration that had come through northwestern Europe. At first the Ashkenazim joined the Sephardi congregation, but as they became sufficiently numerous, they developed their own synagogues where they could express themselves in familiar idiom. At no point did either the Sephardim or the Ashkenazim seek to erect corporate communal structures in England. Rather, they were more than content with their privileges in English society and confined their Jewish activities to synagogual affairs.

Only after a wave of anti-Semitism in the mid-eighteenth century did they come together to organize a Board of Deputies (1760) which brought together the various elements of Anglo-Jewry to provide for coordinated representation to the authorities to protect Jewish interests.[51] The Board of Deputies gradually developed into a congregationally based, more or less representative body for English Jewry, but confined its role to representational activities. In internal affairs the Jews created voluntary associations of one kind or another to provide religious, educational, and welfare services as people felt the need to do so. In the late nineteenth century, even the representational function of the Board of Deputies was partially superseded by the Anglo-Jewish Association, an elite group which functioned as the major power in the community for about a generation until World War I. Then the nascent Zionist movement captured British Jewry and restored the role of the Board, whose base was correspondingly expanded.

## The United States

American Jews were the most emancipated of all from the very first, suffering almost no discrimination by virtue of their Jewishness (in some cases they were excluded from citizenship and office because they did not belong to the dominant religion of a particular colony, but in a manner no different than others not of that religious sect). Moreover, those who came to the New World, while often seeking to preserve their Jewish ties, were far more individualistic in their orientations and desirous of getting ahead on an individual basis than many of their more conservative brethren in Europe. Hence, they were content to organize congregations where they could maintain their religious practices, perhaps provide some education for their children, and supply a modicum of relief for their poor in a period in which government did little if anything in those fields. Moreover, the small number of Jews prevented the development of any elaborately articulated set of institutions in British North America, or the new United States, until well into the middle of the nineteenth century.[52]

Thus, congregational communities were established at various points where sufficient concentrations of Jews settled. Individual Jews living outside of those communities frequently affiliated with them so as to maintain some attachment. The congregations themselves at first tried to enforce religious standards, but found that to be impossible on the free-flowing American scene and soon gave up the effort. Until the 1820s, with one exception, there was only one congregation per locality, to which everyone who wished to remain a member of the Jewish community belonged, no matter what their country of origin. It was not until the 1840s that permanent noncongregational associations emerged (Bnai Brith was the first) parallel to the synagogues. Like the congregations themselves, all were entirely voluntary, government taking no interest whatsoever in whether or not Jews organized for whatever purposes they chose. This pattern of small voluntary bodies—religious, social, or fraternal—spread rapidly as the Jewish population grew in size and scattered across the countryside. By the late nineteenth century, large Jewish communities of thousands, tens of thousands, and, at least in the case of New York, over a hundred thousand had formed, each of which represented a congeries of synagogues, welfare institutions, schools, and social clubs with no overall organization or direction and often with few even informal links among them.[53]

### The Kehillah and the Emancipation

Meanwhile, in the areas of Jewish concentration in Europe, the Jewish communities had to be transformed with the Jews in place, as it were. By and large, the Jews were quite ready for the transformation to take place. Not only did they seek emancipation as individuals in order to enjoy the benefits of modernity, but the *kehillot* had all too often degenerated into the worst kinds of oligarchies whereby the wealthy and the scholarly protected their own interests, particularly in matters of taxation, and transferred the burdens to the poor. Internal quarrels were the order of the day and communal debts were mounting. In Eastern Europe, the fight between Hassidim and Mitnagdim further aggravated the situation, since the battle that swept the region was reenacted in *kehillah* after *kehillah,* with all the bitterness that an ideological fight of the first order can generate.

Finally, migration was transforming the face of Jewish Europe. Jews were moving westward, leaving old communities depleted, both in sheer size and in talent, and then in the nineteenth century urbanization transferred Jews from small towns to big cities where they had to reorganize their lives as Jews on a new urban basis without the intimacy that the small town afforded. More sophisticated and impersonal institutions were required and in every community there was a question as to whether or not the particular Jews who settled there had the talent and resources to meet the new challenge.

*Ashkenazic Jewry*

In Western Europe it seemed that for awhile the consistorial pattern developed by Napoleon would become the norm, but in the reaction to French imperialism which followed the fall of Napoleon, some combination of consistorial techniques with other patterns were developed in every country except Belgium, which held more tenaciously to the Napoleonic system than did France itself.[54] What characterized the various systems was that each was designed to be comprehensive, was based upon the congregation or synagogue as the principal local unit, was dominated by rabbinical leadership by governmental design (emphasizing the religious as distinct from the national character of the Jewish community), and was state-recognized. For much of the nineteenth century, membership in the Jewish community was compulsory for Jews who had not converted, but the wave of liberalism at the end of the century tended to eliminate this compulsory dimension. (Significantly, it was restored in Fascist Italy in 1931). In most cases, Sephardi and Ashkenazi divisions were preserved, but within the same overarching body. In highly centralized states, the Jewish communities were highly centralized in their formal structure, although in fact the Jews maintained much more local control than that to which they were formally entitled. In countries like Germany, Switzerland, Austria, and the Netherlands where federalism or decentralization was the norm, the communal structures tended to reflect federal or constitutionally decentralized arrangements.

As befits the kind of political culture prevalent in Central Europe, the Jewish communities in Germany, Austria-Hungary, and the German cultural orbit remained the most highly organized and comprehensive of all, albeit in a modern form. A single state-recognized community was constituted in each locality in which membership was compulsory and all members were obliged to pay the internal taxes. It was not until the later nineteenth century that the possibility of resigning from the Jewish community without conversion was instituted. These local communities were either united or federated on a territorial basis and after the unification of Germany a countrywide body was established. Government control in the Germanies remained relatively direct until the inauguration of the Weimar Republic, whose 1919 constitution provided for full Jewish communal autonomy but specified that communal procedures had to be democratic including the enfranchisement of women and elections by proportional representation.[55]

During the mid-nineteenth century the local communities were taken over by Reform Jews with increasing frequency, leading the Orthodox Jews to seek the right to secede to form their own separate communal institutions within the same locality. At first this was resisted by the government as much as by the Jewish communities, but in the end the Orthodox had their way and separate bodies were established, sometimes fully autonomous, sometimes nominally subsidiary to the overarching local community. While the situation in the Austro-Hungarian Empire paralleled that of the Germanies in its general outline, the wide variations in local governing systems within the Empire were also reflected in the specifics of Jewish communal organization. The Jews of Bohemia and Moravia preserved more autonomy than those of any other part of Central Europe, with the fifty-two autonomous communities of Moravia maintaining separate municipal administrations and police until 1890 when the Empire enacted a single uniform law for organizing its Jews. That law essentially adopted the German model and applied it to Austrian conditions. In Hungary, on the other hand, the struggle between liberal and Orthodox factions was even more intense than in Germany, leading finally to a government-approved division of the local community unions into three separate sections—liberal, Orthodox, and status quo (those who were not involved in the struggle)—the situation which prevailed after 1871.

In Eastern Europe, the Russian government abolished the *kahal* in 1844, but while it no longer existed officially, it continued to function covertly and held on tenaciously throughout the vicissitudes of the nineteenth century.[56] The Russians alone of the major European powers did not allow the Jews to create more than local institutions, deliberately preventing their combination on a regional or countrywide basis. Indeed, since the Russian policy was to destroy Jewish life in its entirety, Jewish communal organization was a special target, in recognition of its importance for the maintenance of Judaism.

After the abolition of the *kahal,* formal responsibility for Jewish communities in Russia was handed over to the police and to the non-Jewish local governments. The local *kehillot* still retained the onerous burdens of tax collecting for the state and recruitment for the army, which further discredited them in the eyes of the average Jew. As early as 1835, the government began to appoint local rabbis to handle the formal rabbinical functions, such as registration of births, deaths, and marriages. Thus, the nineteenth century was one of continued decline of the *kehillot* which the Jews fought tenaciously. In the *shtetl,* another phenomenon emerged. The educational, social, and religious functions of the *kehillot* were fragmented among many different associations *(hevrot)* which become highly privatized in contradistinction to the historical pattern of Jewish self-government.

World War I and the Russian Revolution brought about far-reaching changes. For a brief moment in the early days of the Revolution, Russian Jewry was able to establish a federation of democratically elected local communities. The Bolsheviks abolished this structure, replaced it briefly with a Jewish commissariat, and then reverted to the Czarist position of preventing any countrywide or regional Jewish organizations. Under Soviet rule, with the exception of the Jewish colonies that flourished in the Crimea in the 1920s and 1930s and the brief experiment in Birobidjan, Jewish communal life has been confined to a consistently declining number of synagogues limited to conducting religious services and always under tremendous pressure. In effect, there is no Jewish communal government in Russia, nor has there been since the early 1920s.

The other Eastern European countries managed to preserve some of their older patterns of Jewish communal organization, depending on how tight the Russian embrace was. Congress Poland, for example, replaced the traditional *kahal* with something like a *consistoire* in 1822, attempting to limit the functions of the community to religion and social welfare and placing its governance in the hands of a rabbi, an assistant rabbi, and elders. Needless to say, the Jews tried to maintain their own structures despite these formal changes.[57]

World War I also brought great changes in two ways: the restoration of the independence of Poland and the Baltic states was accompanied by formal guarantees of minority cultural rights for Jews and others. While these rights were honored far more in the breach than in reality, the Jews did gain some opportunities for providing education in Hebrew and Yiddish for those of them who wished it (not necessarily the majority). Jewish communal organizations were regularized by law, following the German pattern more than the French, and Jews were represented as a community in the general parliaments of their respective countries.[58]

Nevertheless, the whole history of the Eastern European Jewries in the interwar period is one of decline, reflecting the ambivalence of the host governments, who on one hand were trying hard to consolidate their states on the basis of modern nationalism which saw every citizen as standing in equal relationship to every other without communal differences, and on the other hand did not wish to absorb the Jews on the basis of equality. The Jews kept their internal organizations, developed a flourishing politics as a result of the competition between Zionist and non-Zionist, Orthodox and socialist parties, and tried to maintain a full range of education and cultural institutions, but always under great pressure to both conform and remain apart. All this, of course, ended with the coming of World War II and the destruction of Eastern European Jewry.

Rumania, which was a persistent resistor of emancipation in the nineteenth century, actually transformed membership in the *kehillot* from voluntary to compulsory in 1928, although it allowed the Sephardim and the Orthodox in regions that had formerly been Hungarian to affiliate with their own *kehillot* instead. The *kehillot* were organized in the consistorial pattern and the chief rabbi represented the Jews in the Rumanian senate.[59]

*Sephardic Jewry*

The revolutionary conditions that prevailed in the Balkan states, particularly after the Balkan wars and World War I, led to the alteration of Jewish communal life there as well. As long as the Balkans were under Ottoman rule, the late medieval patterns of Jewish communal organization persisted, slightly modified by nineteenth-century reforms. As the Balkan countries became independent, however, they had to make their own arrangements, most of which reflected their strong sense of nationalism and their reluctance to allow communal autonomy of any kind. Bulgaria opted for the consistorial pattern in 1878, but with the Jews preserving more of a communal basis for their internal life because of the greater sympathy of the Bulgarian authorities for their national aspirations.[60] Thus, after 1878, Bulgarian Jewry had a countrywide congress, an executive, and a chief rabbinate presiding over the rabbinical courts, while every local *kehillah* had its own council and religious court. Greece, on one hand, tried to discourage Jewish separatism, but on the other, provided government support for Jewish institutions and encouraged democratically elected bodies for local Jewish communities.

Each of the Yugoslav national states or regions developed its own variations of the same pattern that generally prevailed in Greece, with emphasis again on restricting Jewish activities to the religious-educational sphere.[61] This was also the case in Turkey after the Ataturk revolution. While the Turks had been required by the Treaty of Lausanne to grant the Jews and other minorities rights in 1923, they formally denounced that clause. Since then the Jewish community has been formally restricted to purely religious matters, although the *haham bashi* remains the honored head of the community in terms of his formal position in the Turkish hierarchy.[62]

The Jewries of North Africa also underwent substantial changes in the modern era.[63] Algeria was annexed by France in 1930 and the consistorial system was applied to its Jews on a gradual basis beginning in 1845. In 1867 the authority of the Consistoire Central in Paris was extended to the three Algerian *consistoires* in the north, leaving only the Jews in semi-pacified southern Algeria with their traditional institutions. In 1870 the bulk of Algerian Jewry was granted French citizenship and in the twentieth century, the French pattern was deepened, including the patterns of assimilation common to French Jewry.

Since neither Morocco nor Tunisia became part of metropolitan France in the manner of Algeria, in both the Jewish communities preserved modified versions of their traditional institutions, although French influence was felt in shaping the modifications. Thus, the role of the rabbinate was enhanced in both communities and emphasis was placed on their directly religious activities. At the same time, the powers of the communal authorities in both remained more substantial than in any other countries that came under western rule in the modern era.

### The New Worlds

In the nineteenth century, Jewish communities arose in the new worlds of the Americas, southern Africa, and Australasia.[64] Latin America had, indeed, seen the establishment of secret communities of Crypto-Jews in the sixteenth and seventeenth centuries, but these were all wiped out by the Inquisition, assimilation, or emigration. Only in the Caribbean area and the Dutch possessions on the northeast coast of South America were permanent communities of ex-Marranos established, basically individual congregations following the pattern of comprehensiveness of the Amsterdam *kehillah.*

It was not until the latter half of the nineteenth century that permanent Jewish settlements were established in Latin America proper. At that time, congregations were established by Central European Jews who for the most part rapidly assimilated. They were followed by Sephardim from the Near East who established communities following their traditional congregational models, which continue to be among the most comprehensive congregations on the continent.

In the last years of the nineteenth century and the first generation of the twentieth, Eastern European Jews came in substantial numbers to Argentina, Brazil, Mexico, and Uruguay and in lesser numbers to the other Latin American countries where they established communities based upon the models then coming into vogue in Eastern Europe, namely, religio-cultural communities based upon ethnicity rather than religious commitment, emphasizing Yiddish language and culture and the trappings of diaspora nationalism. The Ashkenazi communities were governed by community councils of one sort or another, which were themselves federations of country-of-origin associations, perhaps confederated countrywide as well. Partisan elections became the norm, with party politics of the most intense kind among those few at all interested in communal life. All the major Zionist parties would be represented plus the socialist and occasionally the religious parties as well in the manner of Eastern Europe between the wars. The Sephardim were almost entirely excluded from the communal structures of the Ashkenazi majorities. These community federations established a wide range of services, even though they were of entirely voluntary character, particularly during the interwar years when underdeveloped Latin America could not provide the educational and social services to which the Jews were accustomed. Jewish banks, cooperatives, schools, welfare institutions, and the like all flourished under the encouragement of a highly nationalistic immigrant generation. These services persisted until near the end of the post World War II generation but are now in decline as the immigrant generations pass from the scene.[65]

South African Jewry also had its origins in the establishment of individual congregations, in this case by Jews coming from England, and its primary development after a massive wave of immigration from Eastern Europe, in its case from Lithuania. The Litvaks soon overwhelmed the English Jews and established a comprehensive network of institutions which became the principal institutions of the South African Jewish community. The South African Jewish Board of Deputies was an offshoot of the British Board, but from the first was more comprehensive in scope, even though it did not attempt to be all-embracing in control of functions. It has consistently striven to be representative of the entire community. The community accepted the authority of the chief rabbi of the British Empire, although, given its modern character, that authority hardly carried the weight of a chief rabbi in previous ages.

The Litvaks were intensely Zionist and the Zionist Federation became the great political force in the community. For a while it tried to compete with the Board of Deputies and then more or less accepted its role as the animator of the Board rather than its competitor. Congregations remain important Jewish instrumentalities.[66]

Australian Jewry had its origins in the earliest days of Australian settlement, but did not develop as a community beyond the congregational plane until the twentieth century. Most of its Jews came after World War II. They inherited a Board of Deputies patterned on the South African model and expanded it along lines more suitable to Australian society. Thus, each state has its own board of deputies, joined together by the Executive Council of Australian Jewry in a confederal arrangement. Elections to the boards are often strongly contested, although by a very small percentage of the Jewish population. Common to these English-speaking communities is a pattern already visible in England whereby the overarching body exists primarily to represent Jews in external affairs while each functional area has its own comprehensive authority, not necessarily linked with any of the others in more than nominal ways, if that.

The nineteenth century saw the emergence of American Jewry as a major force on the world Jewish scene and the twentieth brought it to the status of the largest Jewish community in the world, perhaps in all of Jewish history, certainly the largest ever to exist under any common organization. By the second generation of the nineteenth century, when some 300,000 Jews lived in the United States, American Jewry was organized principally on a congregational basis, with the congregations united in a common Union of American Hebrew Congregations. Parallel to the congregations was the International Order of Bnai Brith with its local lodges and local Hebrew charities, not connected with one another except within each locality. With a few exceptions, schools were essentially private enterprises, as was the management of kashrut. The congregational union was not quite all-embracing because of its Reform tendencies, which made traditional congregations, even those that had originally helped in its creation, abstain from further association with it. While a board of deputies was established in 1859, its role was far more limited than its British counterpart and it never became the overarching body of American Jewry. (It was later merged into the UAHC.) After the mass migration began in the late 1870s and the early 1880s, the fragmentation of American Jewish life grew even greater. By World War I, there were three major synagogue bodies plus hundreds of unaffiliated synagogues, several networks of fraternal lodges on the order of Bnai Brith, and myriad benevolent, social welfare, and educational institutions under communal, private, and semi-public auspices. Moreover, two major efforts to bring some order to the community had failed: the effort to establish an American chief rabbinate in the 1890s and the attempt to establish a *Kehillah* in New York on the eve of World War I. Both foundered on the American commitment to free enterprise and voluntarism. No one had to obey a chief rabbi if he did not want to and sufficient numbers of rabbis were "in business for themselves" and saw no reason to have their opportunities restricted by a self-appointed chief. The *Kehillah* tried to develop revenue sources by regulating shechita. It was threatened with an anti-trust suit under the laws of the State of New York and had to abandon the idea, thereby leaving its organization without a steady source of funds or control.[67]

At the same time, however, the already established Jews were creating the local federation, which was to become the key to Jewish communal unity in the United States. Between 1891 and World War I, some seventeen cities had created federations of social welfare organizations, in some cases including educational institutions as well, for purposes of joint fund-raising. During the generation following the war, this federated approach to philanthropy spread throughout Jewish America and every Jewish community of any size established its own federation. In addition, a countrywide Council of Jewish Federations and Welfare Funds was organized as a forum for exchanging information.[68]

At first, the federations remained very much attuned to local needs, particularly in the health and welfare fields. Only an occasional federation added Jewish education to its list of concerns. Fund-raising for overseas and Zionist work was handled separately. Then the rise of Hitler required a far greater financial effort on the part of American Jewry and the United Jewish Appeal was created to coordinate the fund-raising for European relief through the American Jewish Joint Distribution Committee (established in 1914 as the first countrywide body to link all the elements of American Jewry for a common effort) and the United Palestine Appeal. It was almost immediately decided that the UJA funds hence would be raised through local instrumentalities, which usually turned out to be the local federations, so that between 1938 and 1940 the federation movement gained an additional impetus. By the end of World War II, it was clear that the federations were the locus of fund-raising in the community. It remained for the postwar generation to transform them also into the community planning agencies and an American continuation of the *kehillah*. Significantly, in the United States as in most of the Jewish world, voluntarism brought with it a return to federal forms of organization.

On the countrywide plane, the developments of the first generation of the twentieth century were more competitive than cooperative. By the end of World War I, three major community relations organizations were functioning on the American scene—the American Jewish

Committee, established in 1906 as the arm of the American Jewish elite to undertake quiet representational activity in the manner of the *shtadlanim,* the Anti-Defamation League of Bnai Brith, dedicated to combatting anti-Semitism in local communities as well as country-wide by more open means, and finally the American Jewish Congress, which combined a strong social action program with community relations goals. In addition, local communities developed community relations councils in the years following World War I under the auspices of the federation leadership, if not the federations themselves. It was only in the 1940s, under pressure from the federations, that some measure of coordination among these groups was introduced.

The synagogue groups also continued to go their own way, although there the competition was less severe and the overlapping not particularly noticeable since each synagogue movement was involved with its own congregation, which represented a particular ideological orientation. A Synagogue Council of America was established in the 1920s to coordinate the religious interests of American Jewry but did not become an effective force. Since each congregation was a private institution under American law and practice, the synagogues remained unconnected with other communal institutions.

Jewish education was essentially a local matter and had no real countrywide voice, although the National Council for Jewish Education, the association of professional Jewish educators, did acquire importance in professional circles in that period. Order was introduced into the chaos of *hadarim* that existed until World War I, and standards were raised first through the Talmudei Torah under communal or quasi-communal sponsorship and then through congregational schools. Day schools hardly existed.

In sum, the American Jewish community acquired some semblance of organization locally, although the division between the federation world on one side, the congregations on the other, and the Zionist groupings, primarily rooted in the Eastern European immigrant generation, meant that no overall *kehillah* emerged. Countrywide, it was truly every organization for itself. It was not until after World War II that this situation was transformed and the federation movement became the powerful force that it now is and introduced a certain amount of structure into American Jewish life.

## Conclusion

In the last analysis, what is especially significant about the *kehillah* as it has expressed itself over time, is not so much the variety of forms it has taken, but the degree to which certain patterns have persisted: the fact that *kehillah* have remained republican in their character under such a variety of circumstances; the fact that within the context of republicanism, leadership has been so frequently aristocratic or oligarchic; the fact that the *kehillot* have so often been organized on federal principles, both internally and in their relationships to one another or to the *edah* as a whole—all testify to the existence of a Jewish political tradition that has found concrete institutional and procedural expression on the local plane through the generations, regardless of location in time or space.

## Notes

1. The term *edah* is the Hebrew equivalent of commonwealth, a meaning that attended to congregation before that term came to be applied almost exclusively to a religious body. Cf. Robert Gordis, "Democratic Origins in Ancient Israel," in *Alexander Marx Jubilee Volume* (New York: Jewish Theological Seminary of America, 1950); and Moshe Weinfeld, "Congregation" in *Encyclopedia Judaica* (hereafter EJ), 5:893–96.
2. Salo W. Baron, *The Jewish Community* (Philadelphia: Jewish Publication Society, 1942), vol. 1, chap. 3, "Synagogue."
3. Baron, *Jewish Community.*
4. Leo Baeck, *This People Israel* (Philadelphia: Jewish Publication Society, 1965).
5. Daniel J. Elazar and Stuart A. Cohen, *The Jewish Polity* (Bloomington: Indiana University Press, 1984).
6. Moshe Weinfeld, "From God's Edah to the Chosen Dynasty: The Transition from the Tribal Federation to the Monarchy," chapter 7 in this volume, and M. Buber, "Shmuel veHishtalshelut haReshuyot beYisrael" ["Samuel and the Evolution of the Authorities in Israel"] *Zion* 4, no. 1 (1939): 1–29.
7. For an overall picture of the progression of constitutional epochs, see Daniel J. Elazar, *The Constitutional Periodization of Jewish History, A Second Look* (Jerusalem: Center for Jewish Community Studies, 1978).
8. The institutional arrangements in the various epochs are delineated in Daniel J. Elazar and Stuart Cohen, *Gazetteer of Jewish Political Organization* (Jerusalem: Center for Jewish Community Studies, 1981), experimental edition.
9. For formulary examples of such covenants, see R. Judah HaBarceloni, *Sefer Ha-Shtaroth* ["The Book of Deeds"] (Jerusalem, 1967), pp. 131–38. For a specific example, see the Covenant of the Jewish Communities of Aragon (1354) published in Louis Finkelstein, *Jewish Self-Government in the Middle Ages* (New York: Philipp Feldheim, Inc., 1964), 2nd printing, pp. 328–47.

10. For a full discussion of this point, see Menachem Elon, "Authority and Power in the Jewish Community," in Elazar, *Kinship and Consent,* and H. Ben-Sasson, "HaMaase veHaMegamot shel haHanhaga haAtzmit beYemei haBeinayim" ["Practice and Trends of Self-Administration in tho Middle Ages"] in *Perakim beToldot haYehudim beYemei Habeinayim* ["Chapters in the History of the Jews in the Middle Ages"] (Tel-Aviv: Am Oved, 1969).

11. E. A. Speiser, "'Coming' and 'Going' at the 'City Gate'," in J. J. Finkelstein, ed., *Oriental and Biblical Studies: The Collected Writings of E. A. Speiser* (Philadelphia, University of Pennsylvania Press, 1967).

12. E.g., Jeremiah 26:17, II Kings 23:I.

13. Cf. Avraham Malamat, "Exile, Assyrian" in *EJ* 6:1034–36.

14. Hayim Tadmor, "The Babylonian Exile and the Restoration," in H. H. Ben- Sasson, *A History of the Jewish People* (Cambridge, Mass.: Harvard University Press, 1976), pp. 162–64.

15. Ezekiel 8:6, 14:1, 20:1; Babylonian Talmud Megillah 29a; Baron, *Jewish Community,* vol. 1, pp. 55–74.

16. Bezalel Porten, *Archives from Elephantine: The Life of an Ancient Jewish Military Colony* (Berkeley: University of California Press, 1968).

17. Baron, *Jewish Community,* 1.

18. Ibid.

19. Victor Tcherikover, *Hellenistic Civilization and the Jews* (Philadelphia and Jerusalem: Jewish Publication Society and Magnes Press, 1959), part 1, and Solomon Zeitlin, *The Rise and Fall of the Judean State* (Philadelphia: Jewish Publication Society, 1962), vol. 1.

20. M. Avi-Yonah, *The Jews of Palestine, A Political History from the Bar Kokhba War to the Arab Conquest* (New York: Schocken Books, 1976); S. Safrai, "Hair haYehudit beEretz Israel baTekufat haMishnah vehaTalmud" ["The Jewish City in Eretz Israel in the Period of the Mishnah and the Talmud"], in *Hair vehaKehillah* ["City and Community"] (Israeli Historical Society, 1968), pp. 227–36.

21. Baron, *Jewish Community,* vol. 1, chap. 4; Tcherikover, *Hellenistic Civilization,* part II.

22. Baron, *Jewish Community,* vol. 1, chap. 4.

23. Moshe Baer, *The Babylonian Exilarchate in the Arsacid and Sassanian Periods* (Hebrew) (Tel-Aviv: Dvir, 1970); Jacob Neusner, *A History of the Jews in Babylonia* (Leiden: E.J. Brill, 1965–1970), 5 vols.

24. Jacob Neusner, *There We Sat Down* (Nashville and New York: Abingdon Press, 1972), and "Rabbi and Community in Third Century Babylonia," *Religious in Antiquity. Essays in Memory of Erwin Ramsdell Goodenough,* ed. Jacob Neusner (Leiden, 1968), pp. 438–59.

25. Chaim Kalchheim, *Sugiyot beSidrei haHayyim haTziburiim beHalakhah uva-Masoret hayehudit* ["Studies in Patterns of Communal Life in Halakhah and the Jewish Tradition"], Sourcebook (Ramat-Gan: Bar-Ilan Institute of Local Government, 1978); M. Piron, "Hanhagat Ir beHashkafat Hazal" ["City Administration in the Rabbinic View"] *Mahanayim,* 128–30 (July 1972): 28–33.

26. S. D. Goitein, *A Mediterranean Society* (Berkeley and Los Angeles: University of California Press, 1971), vol. 2, "The Community"; and "Political Conflict and the Use of Power in tho World of the Geniza," in Elazar, *Kinship and Consent;* Y. Ashtor, "Kavim leDemuta shel haKehillah hayehudit beMitzraim beyemei haBeinayim" ["On the Character of the Jewish Community in Egypt in the Middle Ages"], *Zion,* 30:1–2, 3–4 (1965): 61–78, 128–57.

27. Yitzhak Baer, "HaYesodot vehaHathalot shel Irgun haKehillah haYehudit beYemei haBeinayim" ["The Foundations and the Beginnings of the Organization of the Jewish Community in the Middle Ages"], *Zion* 15 (1950): 1–41. Sh. Albeck, "Yesodot Mishtar haKehillot beSefarad ad Ha'ra'm'ah (1180–1244)" ["The Governmental Foundations of the Communities in Spain until the Ra'm'ah (1180–1244"], *Zion* 25, no. 2 (1960): 85–21. M. Elon, "LeMahutan shel Takkanot haKahal baMishpat haIvri" ["On the Nature of the Communal Regulations in Jewish Law"] *Mehkarei Mishpat leZekher Avraham Rosenthal* [Studies in Law in Memory of Abraham Rosenthal"] (Jerusalem, 1964), pp. 1–54.
28. Irving A. Agus, *Urban Civilization in Pre-Crusade Europe* (New York: Yeshiva University Press, 1968), 2 vols.; "Democracy in the Communities of the Early Middle Ages," *Jewish Quarterly Review,* N.S., 43 (1952/53): 153–76; and *The Heroic Age of Franco-German Jewry. The Jews of Germany and France of the Tenth and Eleventh Centuries, The Pioneers and Builders of Town-Life, Town-Government and Institutions* (New York, 1969), pp. 158–276 (Community Organization).
29. Israel M. Goldman, *The Life and Times of Rabbi David Ibn Abi Zimra* (New York: Jewish Theological Seminary, 1979), esp. chaps. 6 and 14; David A. Recannati, *The Memory of Saloniki* (Hebrew—Tel-Aviv: Committee to Publish the Book of the Saloniki Community, 1972), vol. 1; *Saloniki, Mother City in Israel* (Hebrew—Jerusalem and Tel-Aviv: Institute for the Study of Saloniki Jewry, 1967); Shlomo Simonsohn, *History of the Jews in the Duchy of Mantua* (Hebrew—Jerusalem: Kiryat Sefer, 1963), 2 vols.; Cecil Roth, *History of the Jews in Venice* (Philadelphia: Jewish Publication Society, 1930); Sh. Simonsohn, "HaGhetto beItalia uMishtaro" ["The Ghetto in Italy and Its Government"], *Sefer haYovel leYitzhak Baer* ["Yitzhak Baer Jubilee Volume"] (Israeli Historical Society, 1961), pp. 270–86; and "HaKehillah haYehudit beItalia vehaCorporatzia haNotzrit" ["The Jewish Community in Italy and the Christian Corporation"], *Dat veHevra* ["Religion and Society"] (Israeli Historical Society, 1965), pp. 81–102.
30. Yitzhak Baer, *A History of the Jews in Christian Spain* (Philadelphia: Jewish Publication Society, 1961 and 1966), 2 vols.
31. Ibid., vol. 2; Finkelstein, *Jewish Self-Government in the Middle Ages.*
32. Baer, *A History of the Jews,* esp. vol. 2, pp. 261–70; Finkelstein, *Jewish Self-Government,* pp. 348–75; Baron, *Jewish Community,* vol. 1, chap. 7.
33. Agus, *Urban Civilization;* Elon, chapter 10 in this volume; Gerald Blidstein, *Notes on Hefker Bet Din in Talmudic and Medieval Law* (Jerusalem: Center for Jewish Community Studies, 1975); and "Individual and Community in the Middle Ages: Halachic Theory," chapter 11 in this volume.
34. Finkelstein, *Jewish Self-Government.*
35. Haim Hillel Ben-Sasson, "HaHanhaga haAtzmit shel haYehudim" [:The Self-Administration of the Jews"], *Perakim beToldot,* pp. 84–128; Baron, *Jewish Community,* vol. 2; D. Cohen, "HaVaad haKatan shel Bnei Medinat Aschenbach" ["The Small Council of the Aschenbach Polity"], *Sefer haYovel leYitzhak Baer,* pp. 351–75.
36. Baron. *Jewish Community ,* vol. 2.
37. Finkelstein, *Jewish Self-Government.*
38. Selma Stern, *Josel of Rosheim* (Philadelphia: Jewish Publication Society, 1965).
39. For a good summary of the legislation dealing with these phenomena, see Menahem Elon, "Takkanot," in *EJ* 15:712–28 and Isaac Levitats, "Takkanot Ha-kahal," in *EJ* 15:728–37. For full treatment, see Menachem Elon, *HaMishpat HaIvri* (Jerusalem Magnes Press, 1978), and Baron, *Jewish Community,* vol. 2.

40. Baer, *Jews in Christian Spain.*

41. Simon M. Dubnow, *History of the Jews of Russia and Poland* (New York: Ktav Publishers, 1975), vol. 1; Bernard D. Weinryb, *The Jews of Poland* (Philadelphia: Jewish Publication Society, 1973); Israel Halpern, *Eastern European Jewry* (Hebrew—Jerusalem: Magnes Press, 1968), esp. part 1; Haim Hillel Ben-Sasson, *Thought and Leadership* (Hebrew—Jerusalem: Mossad Bialik, 1959). Y. Halpern, "Mivne haVaadim b'Eropa haMizrahit vehaMercazit baMea ha17 veha18" ["The Structure of the Councils in Eastern and Central Europe in the 17th and 18th Century"], Proceedings of the World Conference of Jewish Studies, vol. 1 (Jerusalem, 1972), pp. 439–45; and "Reshito shel Vaad Medinat Lita veYahaso el Vaad Arba Aratzot" ["The Beginning of tho Council of Lithuania and Its Relationship with the Council of the Four Lands"], *Zion* 3, no. 1 (1938): 51–57. S. Ettinger, "Irguno shel haTzibbur haYehudi. HaYishuv ha-Yehudi beUkraina min haIhud haLublini ad leGzerot Tah" ["The Organization of the Jewish Community. Jewish Settlement in the Ukraine from the Lublin Union until the Decrees of 1648"] (Ph.D dissertation, Hebrew University of Jerusalem, 1957), pp. 59–121; and "HaHanhaga haHasidit beitzuva" ["The Shaping of the Hasidic Leadership"], *Dat veHevra,* pp. 121–34.

42. Weinryb, *The Jews of Poland;* Halpern, "Mivne."

43. See endnote 29.

44. Leah Bornstein, *The Structure, Organization and Spiritual Life of the Sephardic Communities in the Ottoman Empire during the 16th-18th Centuries* (unpublished manuscript); M. A. Goldblatt, *Jewish Life in Turkey in the XVIth Century as Reflected in the Legal Writings of Samuel De Medina* (New York, 1952); A. Namdar, *Hakikat Takkanot hakahal al pi Hokhmei Saloniki bamea ha16* ["The Legislation of Communal Regulations According to the Rabbis of Saloniki in the 16th Century"] (Master's thesis, Hebrew University of Jerusalem, 1973).

45. Abraham Elmaliah, *The Rishonim LeZion* (Hebrew—Jerusalem: Reuben Mass, 1970); Ben Zion Gath, *The Jewish Settlement in Eretz Israel, 1840–1881* (Hebrew—Jerusalem: Ben Zvi Institute, 1974).

46. Andre N. Chauraqui, *Between East and West, A History of the Jews of North Africa* (Philadelphia: Jewish Publication Society, 1968); H. Z. Hirschberg, *A History of the Jews in North Africa* (Hebrew—Jerusalem: Mossad Bialik, 1965).

47. Cecil Roth, *A Life of Manasseh ben Israel* (Philadelphia: Jewish Publication Society, 1945), *The House of Nasi: Dona Gracia* (Philadelphia: Jewish Publication Society, 1947), and *The Duke of Naxos* (Philadelphia: Jewish Publication Society, 1948); Arthur Hertzberg, *The French Enlightenment and the Jews* (New York: Columbia University Press, 1968).

48. Eric Zimmer, *Harmony and Discord* (New York: Yeshiva University Press, 1970).

49. Hertzberg, *The French Enlightenment.* S. Posener "The Social Life of the Jewish Communities in France in the 18th Century, the Organization and the Administration of the Communities," *Jewish Social Studies* 7 (1945): 213–24.

50. Phyllis Cohen Albert, *The Modernization of French Jewry Consistory and Community in the Nineteenth Century* (Hanover, N.H.: Brandeis University Press, 1977).

51. Maurice Freedman, ed., *A Minority in Britain* (London: Vallentine, Mitchell, 1955); Cecil Roth, *Essays and Portraits in Anglo-Jewish History* (Philadelphia: Jewish Publication Society, 1962); Todd M. Endelman, *The Jews of Georgian England 1714-1830* (Philadelphia: Jewish Publication Society, 1979); J. Parkes, "The Synagogue Structure of Anglo-Jewry," in M. Freeman, ed. *A Minority in Britain* (London, 1966), pp. 16–31.

52. Jacob R. Marcus, *Early American Jewry* (Philadelphia: Jewish Publication Society, 1953), 2 vols.; Lee M. Friedman, *Jewish Pioneers in America* (New York: Behrman, 1938) and *Pilgrims in a New Land* (Philadelphia: Jewish Publication Society, 1948).

53. Daniel J. Elazar, *Community and Polity: The Organizational Dynamics of American Jewry* (Philadelphia: Jewish Publication Society, 1976); and "The Institutional Life of American Jewry," *Midstream* (June 1971).

54. Daniel J. Elazar, "The Reconstitution of Jewish Communities in the Postwar Period," *Jewish Journal of Sociology* (December 1969).

55. Jacob Katz, *Tradition and Crisis: Jewish Society at the End of the Middle Ages* (New York: Free Press, 1961) and *Out of the Ghetto: The Social Background of Jewish Emancipation* (Cambridge, Mass.: Harvard University Press, 1973); Michael A. Meyer, *The Origins of the Modern Jew* (Detroit: Wayne State University Press, 1967); Josef Trenkel, ed., *The Jews of Austria* (London: Vallentine, Mitchell, 1967); Society for the History of Czechoslovak Jewry, eds., *The Jews of Czechoslovakia* (Philadelphia: Jewish Publication Society, 1968 and 1971), 2 vols.; K. Eilhelm, "The Jewish Community in the Post-Emancipation Period," *Leo Baeck Institute Year Book* 11 (1957): 47–75; A. Kober, "Jewish Communities in Germany from the Age of Enlightenment to Their Destruction by the Nazis," *Jewish Social Studies* 9 (1947): 195–238; I. Eisenberg, "Am Yehudei Austria" ["The Jewish People of Austria"], *Gesher* 12 (1966): 62–66; Y. Ben David, "HaHathalot shel Hevra Yehudit Modernit beHungaria be-Reshit haMea ha19" ["The Beginnings of a Modern Jewish Society in Hungary, in the Early 19th Century"], *Zion* 17 (1952): 101–28.

56. Simon M. Dubnow, *History of the Jews in Russia and Poland,* vol. 2; B. Eliav, M. Buba, A. Kremer, eds., *Perakim betoldot Yahadut Latvia; 1651–1918* ["Chapters in the History of Latvian Jewry; 1651–1918"] (Tel Aviv, 1965); R. Mahler, *Divrei Yemei Israel, Dorot Aharonim* ["History of Israel, the Last Generations"], vol. 1, book 3 (Merhavia, 1955), vol. 2, book 1 (1961); M. Nadav, "Toldot Kehillot Pinsk (1506–1880)" ["History of the Pinsk Community (1506–1880)"], *Sefer Pinsk,* part 1 (Tel-Aviv, 1973), pp. 28–31, 77–97, 99–102, 136–147; Jacob Frumkin et al., eds., *Russian Jewry 1917–1967* (New York: Thomas Yoseloff, 1969).

57. Mahler, *Divrei*; M. Balaban, "Ma'amadam haHuki shel haYehudim veIrgunam" ["The Legal Status and Organization of the Jews"], *Bet Israel bePolin* ["The House of Israel in Poland"], part 1 (Jerusalem, 1948), pp. 44–65; William M. Glicksman, *A Kehillah in Poland During the Interwar Years* (Philadelphia: M.E. Kulish Folkschool, 1969); Bernard Juhapoll, *The Politics of Futility* (Ithaca, N.Y.: Cornell University Press, 1967).

58. Jacob Robinson , *Were the Minority Treaties a Failure?* (New York: Institute of Jewish Affairs, 1943); William M. Glicksman, *A Kehillah in Poland.*

59. Michael Landau, *Ishim u'Zmanim* ["Portraits and Times"] (Ramat Gan; Massada, 1975) and *Maavak Hayai* ["My Life and Struggles"] (Ramat-Gan: Massada, 1970).

60. Haim Kishals, *Korot Yehudei Bulgaria* ["History of the Jews of Bulgaria"] (Tel-Aviv: Davar and Meitav, 1972–3), 5 vols.

61. Yakir Eventov, *Toldot Yehudei Yugoslavia* ["A History of Yugoslav Jews"] (Tel-Aviv: Hitahdut Olei Yugoslavia, 1971).

62. Clarence R. Johnson, *Constantinople Today* (New York: Macmillan, 1922), esp. pp. 153–56.

63. H. Z. Hirschberg, "HaRova haYehudi bar haMuslemit" ["The Jewish Quarter in the Moslem City"], *Gesher* 13 (1967): pp. 53–59; J. Landau, *HaYehudim be*

*Mitzraim baMea ha19* ["The Jews in Egypt in the 19th Century"] (Jerusalem, 1967).

64. Daniel J. Elazar with Peter Medding, *Three Jewries on the Great Frontier* (New York: Holmes and Meier, forthcoming).

65. H. Avni, *Yahadut Argentina; Ma'amada haHevrati veDmuta haIrgunit* ["Argentinian Jewry: Its Social Status and Organizational Character"] (Jerusalem, 1972).

66. Gustav Saron and Louis Hotz, *The Jews in South Africa, A History* (Capetown: Oxford University Press, 1955); S. A. Aschheim, "HaIrgun haKehillati shel Yehudei Drom Africa" ["The Communal Organization of South African Jewry"], *Tefutsot Israel* (March-April, 1972): 63–106.

67. Arthur Goren, *New York Jews and the Quest for Community* (New York: Columbia University Press, 1970).

68. Harry L. Lurie, *A Heritage Affirmed* (Philadelphia: Jewish Publication Society, 1961); Elazar, *Community and Polity;* M. J. Karpf, *Jewish Community Organization in the United States. An Outline of Types of Organization, Activities and Problems* (New York, 1938).

# 9

# Political Conflict and the Use of Power in the World of the Geniza

*Shlomo Dov Goitein*

While searching Jewish tradition for a "usable past" relevant to our own time we could not make a better choice than the 300 years between Saadya Gaon (d. Baghdad, 942) and the Nagid Abraham, the son and successor of Moses Maimonides (d. Old Cairo, 1237). That period was:

- *Authoritative*: Every aspect of what we regard today as Judaism—the synagogue service and the Siddur, law and ritual, theology and ethics, the text of the Bible, the grammar and vocabulary of the Hebrew language,—was consolidated, formulated, and canonized during that age;
- *Exemplary*: Classical Islam, especially during the Fatimid period (969–1170), with which we are mainly concerned here, left a large measure of legal and communal autonomy to the religious minorities, and Jewish life was professedly based on the Torah and the Talmud. Many of the ancient institutions, such as the Sanhedrin (then mostly referred to by its Hebrew term *Yeshiva*), represented by the yeshivas of Baghdad and Jerusalem, still were operative, so that Jewish communal life was genuinely Jewish;

- *Well attested*: The treasure trove of the Cairo Geniza with its thousands of letters and documents enables us to know Jewish life not only as it should have been (and was expressed in our literary sources), but as it actually was;
- *Both similar and dissimilar to present-day Judaism in the diaspora (and partly also in Israel) in significant ways:* Revenue of the community was based on free contributions. Office was basically honorary. The difference was that Jews (and Christians) formed "nations" by themselves and were not ordinary citizens. This made it easier to lead a Jewish life, but more difficult to live as an ordinary human being.

This Geniza period, however, was an *age of transition*. It started out with ecumenical organizations, the yeshivas of Baghdad and Jerusalem, and local corporations like the religious democracies of late antiquity, but ended in complete diaspora, independent territorial and local units and Islam-like autocratic rule within the community as of the late Middle Ages. By then the Jews of the East had become assimilated in their organizational life to Islam, with the *Dayyan* becoming more or less like the qadi.

The Jewish *kahal* was a unique creation. Islamic society was amorphous, governed by a local judge, a governor, a general, or police commandant, subordinate to a caliph or sultan; they did not have anything like the *kehilla*. The Christian communities were a bit more like *Kehillot*, but within them the clergy was so much in command that, again, they were not what the Jewish *kehilla* was to Jews, where laymen were in charge of the finances and the social services. Since the *kehilla* lived according to the Talmud and based its public life on the laws of the Torah, it realized the idea of an intrinsically Jewish community.

During the first half of this period, the ecumenical Jewish institutions, namely, the *yeshivot*, were still functioning. A *yeshiva* was not an institution for education; no student was ever admitted to a *yeshiva*. *Yeshiva* is either the Hebrew translation or the Hebrew original of the Greek word *Sanhedrin*. *Sanhedrin* means sitting together, and *yeshiva* designated the place where the leading religious scholars sat together and decided actual or theoretical questions of *halakhah*. A *yeshiva* was a combination of an academy, a parliament, and a high court. It was headed by a *gaon*, or *rosh yeshiva*, who was assisted by an *Av Beit Din*, or head of the supreme court.

In those days there existed not one, but three *yeshivot*. One was the *"Yeshivat Gaon Yaacov"* of Jerusalem, and the other two, the *yeshivot* of Sura and Pumpedita, both of which (at that time) had their seats in Baghdad. The three divided the Jewish world among themselves.

As a result, in Fustat, the old capital of Egypt, where the Geniza was found, there existed parallel congregations under different authorities. There was a *Kenesset Yerushalmiyim,* a congregation of Jerusalemites—not necessarily people who had come from Palestine, although many actually did, but people who were under the *reshut* (authority) of the Gaon of Jerusalem. There was also a *Kenesset Bavliyim*—Jews who were under the *reshut* of one of the *yeshivot* of Babylonia.

As a rule, in every large city there were three *kehillot,* one of the Yerushalmiyim, one of the Bavliyim, and a third of the Kara'im (Karaites). Each *Kehilla* formed a separate unit, but there were many forms of cooperation, not only between the two Rabbanite communities but with the Karaites as well.

Jewish communal life in the Gaonic period bore a certain similarity to that of our own time. Membership in the Jewish community was voluntary. Everyone contributed in accordance with his means and wishes—of course, under the kind of social pressure as exercised today by any Jewish country club in America. Leadership was also voluntary, and holding office an honor. I would even suggest that the ecumenical developments that we have in our own time represent a counterpart to the Gaonic period. While we do not have *yeshivot* of the type existent in those days, we do have central Jewish organizations once again, from the Zionist Organization and the World Jewish Congress to Hadassah, Wizo, Pioneer and Mizrachi Women, the organizations of the Conservative, Orthodox, and Reform movements, and similar public bodies. Thus, instead of three *yeshivot* a number of ecumenical organizations hold the Jewish people together.

Before characterizing the Jewish community in Geniza times as a "religious democracy," I hesitated very much. I use the word "religious" in its Latin sense of "binding." It was a democracy bound by divine law. This means that there were certain tenets, injunctions, and practices that could not be questioned because they were laid down in the Torah or the Talmud. That democracy had no "law makers," only authorized interpreters of a law that was freely recognized by everyone.

The nature of the Jewish community is defined in a famous *teshuva,* or responsum, of Shmuel be Hofni, one of the great *geonim* of Baghdad, in which he writes: "In all decisions on public life, the last word is with the spiritual leader, the *gaon,* who consults the *yeshiva.*" The *yeshiva* was really consulted. In the month before Pesach (Passover) and that before Succot (Feast of Tabernacles) the members of the *yeshiva* assembled for study and discussion, and the mail that went out from Baghdad after Pesach brought the *teshuvot* to the *kehillot.* Shmuel ben Hofni adds, however, in the responsum just mentioned: "Should the community live in a place in which it has no direct connection with the *rosh hayeshiva,* it is free to make all decisions according to its own wisdom." All this shows that the gaon, as the ultimate authority interpreting the word of God, was called upon to issue final decisions in all matters sacred and secular, but he had to consult his fellow interpreters, and, in absence of communication with the *yeshiva,* "the word of the people was like the word of God."

The medieval communities were astoundingly small. Rome, which was a city of a million or more at the time of Augustus, had a population of only 35,000 in the twelfth century. The Jewish community of Fustat, according to my estimate, had somewhere between 3,000 and 4,000 souls, including women and children, divided among three congregations. In the last analysis each congregation was likely to have some 200 or 300 heads of family; thus, each formed a very small community. Hence, the common people could take part in decision making. Every man could make himself heard, and, as the Geniza shows, did so.

The community was called in Arabic *jamaia,* in Hebrew *kahal,* but more regularly Israel. For example, a protest against a man who had leased to a Muslim a house opposite the staircase leading up to the women's compartment in the synagogue (written in Arabic) opens with the words: "You, the community of Israel."

Life in the congregation was very active. Besides sabbaths and holidays one came to synagogue regularly on Monday and Thursday mornings, when the Torah was read, on the New Moon day *Rosh Hodesh,* and on fasts. The courts say on Monday and Thursday mornings, when everyone was present. The congregation was by no means an oligarchic organization.

The pluralism of congregations was not like the situation in Salonika or Istanbul in the fifteenth century, where numerous different congregations of variegated origins existed side by side. In the Geniza period they were very strict about not permitting more than one congregation per *reshut,* or Gaonic authority, for otherwise they could not maintain the social services. On Yom Kippur everyone pledged how much he would give every week for the coming year. Every Tuesday and Friday there were distributions of bread. The poor were also provided with clothing, money, and so forth. All this had to be financed, and community revenues were based to a large extent on pledges made during services. Consequently, prayer assemblies in private homes, as a rule, were not tolerated. As the Geniza records show, the communal chest (expenditure for social services, employees, maintenance of buildings, and pious foundations) was shared by the Rabbanite congregations in common.

There were other opportunities for cooperation between the congregations. When a local or itinerant preacher read a *derash* in a synagogue, members of the other synagogue were customarily invited. In times of emergency—for instance, *pidyon shevuyim,* the ransom of captives which was a very expensive matter—all the Jews in a town, including the Karaites, cooperated. Contrary to the modern practice of holding fund-raising dinners, they raised funds by proclaiming fasts. A fast was proclaimed, stores were closed, and everyone had to attend the public prayer. Karaites and Rabbanites would fast together; everyone came to hear the reading of the Torah, and made his pledge.

## Power in a Religious Democracy

*Learned Lay Leadership*

As said before, the community lived or tried to live according to the laws of the Torah, as developed in the Talmud, and adapted to the then prevailing conditions by the Gaonim. Communal leadership could be held only by persons who were versed, to some degree, in the sources of religion. The nonrabbinical leaders were the religiously learned merchants, bankers, physicians, and so forth; thus, power was partly derived from conformity with the spiritual ideals of the community.

The business of the community was conducted by the *zekenim,* the elders. In order to be an elder, one did not need to be old. Many Geniza documents refer to *hazaken ha-bachur*—the elder who is a young man.

There were no formal elections. The "elders" acted as a body of representatives. This body was either formally constituted by a communal statute adopted by the *kahal* and confirmed by the *Gaon,* the Head of the Yeshiva-Sanhedrin, or came into being otherwise.

Everyone present in the synagogue was free to oppose a nomination or a proposal. The finances of the community were administered by the lay leadership and they also assisted the spiritual leader—then called *dayyan,* judge (not rabbi)—as members of his *beit din.* A good example of the working of a medieval religious democracy is provided by the *takkana*—or resolution, statute—of al-Mahalla, an Egyptian provincial town, which deals with the problem of simony, or the buying of office. In the dangerous period between the end of Fatimid caliphate and the beginning of Ayyubid rule, approximately the time when Maimonides came to Fustat, a particular person obtained the official leadership of the Jewish community from the new rulers. He was called by his adversaries, Zuta, Mr. Small. Like a Muslim potentate he tried to sell the office of *dayyan,* or Jewish judge. Among others, he sold the office of *dayyan* in al-Mahalla. But the community refused to accept as judge a man appointed in this way, relying on a decision by Maimonides, who ruled that sale of public office was forbidden by the Torah. "When the appointee comes, we shall leave the synagogue, we shall not pray at a service over which he presides. We solely recognize the incumbent judge." The signatures attached to the document were a proof that it represented the community at large.

Regarding the question of majority versus minority, Maimonides held that a *takkana* proposed by the elders was binding only on those who were present in the synagogue, and who expressed their agreement, either by actually signing it, or by being present and not objecting. There are letters, however, signed by many people sent to a *gaon* or a *nagid* saying: "We are the *zekenim.* The others are boys," meaning people who don't count.

A man became a leader through some combination of learning, social standing, and political connections. He had to be a man who came from a good family with at least a minimum of economic resources in order to be free to dedicate some time to public service. The very rich Jews were outside the community and did not normally become heads of congregations. Often a son followed in his father's footsteps—a *parnas* was the son of a *parnas. Parnas* was not a high office in the world of the Geniza. It can be translated as "social service officer"—for example, the persons who collected the rents of the house that belonged to the community and distributed the proceeds among the poor were called *parnasim.*

Laymen were appointed to be members of courts, or associate judges. Under Jewish law, in all civil cases there have to be at least three judges: one professional *dayyan,* and at least two associates. In fact, in most cases there were more than two, often three, four, or five. Maimonides says that nine or ten associates are desirable, and there are cases with nine or ten actually signing a court record. This jury-like aspect of the Jewish court constituted its strength. The people who sat on it were themselves businessmen, operators of workshops, bankers, and so on, people engaged in economic activities. In the *shimmushim,* the court records of the Geniza, on one page a man appears as a judge, and on the next as a party.

Another vital aspect of the Jewish *kehilla* was that most of the services which today we receive from the federal government, the state, or the municipality had then to be provided by the community. The community had to take care of its poor, orphans, widows, sick and old people, and to provide education for orphans and poor children.

Finally, the *zekenim,* together with the spiritual leader, had to watch over the religious observations and moral conduct of the community, which task made them responsible both toward the Moslem government and the highest Jewish authorities. The missives of the heads of the *yeshivot* were read out in the synagogue, publicly discussed, and, after consultation with *zekenim,* answered by the *dayyan.*

## Spiritual Leadership

The second, but ideally first, power in the community was the spiritual leader, on the *ecumenical level* the *gaon,* who was the highest authority for all decisions on religious and public affairs, as well as for the confirmation of local spiritual and lay leaders. The *local* spiritual leader at that time was either a *dayyan,* since he was largely occupied with legal matters, or a *haver,* that is, member of the Yeshiva-Sanhedrin, if he was learned enough to earn that title.

Alongside the *gaons,* the institutional spiritual leaders, there were independent religious authorities such as Rabbenu Hananel and Rabbenu Nissim in Tunisia, and Shemarya, his son Elhanan, and later Judah b. Joseph ha-Kohen in Egypt, all in the eleventh century, or Maimonides at the end of the twelfth century.

The independent religious authority was referred to as *ha-rav,* or, preferably, *ha-rav ha-gadol.* This was the way in which Maimonides was addressed by his contemporaries. In Islamic nomenclature, this term corresponds to *grand mufti.* Although he wrote hundreds of *teshuvot,* Maimonides, unlike his son, the Nagid Abraham, was not formally a judge, but a jurisconsult, a respondent. (In addition, as we shall see, he was, but only for two short periods, *rayyis al-yahud,* official head of the Jewish community in the Ayyubid empire).

Here we must not overlook the contrast between the contemporary Jewish world and the world of the Geniza. In our world we have a dichotomy between what I would call professional Jews and lay Jews—the professional Jews, meaning the rabbis and all others who are engaged in the spiritual and educational activities of the Jewish community—professors, teachers, writers—and the laymen who provide the means and organization for such activities, but who mostly are not very well versed in Jewish things. In the High Middle Ages this dichotomy between the lay and spiritual spheres did not exist, or at least was not so much pronounced.

Various reasons accounted for this. First of all, everyone received a certain amount of Jewish education in school. There was no other formal education for boys. Second, regular study of the Torah was regarded as the duty of a Jewish person, so everyone did a little bit in this way. Finally, both Jewish and general knowledge were so much simpler and so much more restricted that even a busy man could acquire a certain degree of learnedness when he dedicated part of his time to this aim.

There was, therefore, a constant movement back and forth between the "lay" world and the "spiritual" world. To give a famous example from the Geniza, Nahray ben Nissim was a great merchant and banker, to whom hundreds of business letters were addressed during the fifties and sixties of the eleventh century. But in the seventies and eighties he was a *gedol ha-yeshiva,* "the most prominent member of the Yeshiva." He continued to do business, but received also emoluments from the community as its spiritual leader.

Those who have read the Responsa of Maimonides know that there was a great *dayyan* of Cairo, Yitzhak ben Sasson, whom Maimonides regarded as his peer, and Sasson's son, Menahem ben Yitzhak, occupied a similar position in the time of Abraham Hanagid, Maimonides' son. The Sassons came from an old family of judges, but were also successful and munificent merchants.

The spiritual heads of the communities received small salaries from their respective communities, only to cover *battala* (the time when they could not work because they were engaged in the study of Torah). *Dayyanim* were not permitted to be salaried in their capacity as judges. They, too, lived from *s'char battala*. This was normally a very modest salary, so in addition they earned money by writing legal documents, receiving fees from the parties involved, or being active in business or a similar profitable occupation.

## The Office of *Nagid* in Egypt

Since we are dealing here with political conflict and the use of power, special attention must be paid to the office of *Nagid,* especially in Egypt, which was a combination of communal and spiritual leadership backed by the government. This office did not come into being in opposition to the leadership of the Exilarch, the *Resh Galuta,* or the yeshivas, nor was it created by the Muslim rulers, as had been previously assumed. It developed under the very special circumstances, as I tried to show in the second volume of my book *A Mediterranean Society,* subtitled *The Community.*

Originally, the word *Nagid* did not designate an office, but was an honorific title bestowed by a Babylonian yeshiva on a very meritorious benefactor. Later it was granted by Hay Gaon to the (temporal) leader of the Tunisian Jewish community and subsequently to Shmuel ha-Nagid of Spain. However, only in Egypt this honorific title gradually became identified with an office of a special character, which developed in that country. It all began in the last third of the eleventh century, at a time when the Gaon of Jerusalem, the official head of the Jews of the Fatimid empire, had to leave the Holy City in the wake of its conquest by the Seljuks (around 1072) and to take his seat in Tyre, and when the Palestinian yeshiva in general lost its coherence and continuity owning to Muslim internecine warfare in the country. A new central authority had to be created. It was a lucky coincidence that in those critical days two brothers, Judah and Mevorakh, the sons of Saadya ha-Rofe, were both learned, bearing honorific titles bestowed on them by the yeshivas of both Babylonia and Palestine and as court physicians, were also in intimate contact with the government. Judah was the first to bear the title *Nagid*. He was succeeded by his brother Mevorahk, the real founder of the new dignity. As from hi time on, it was the *Nagid,* or head of the Jews of Egypt who appointed or confirmed in their appointment the chief judges and all the other officials of the Jewish community. Legal documents were now issued in the name of the *Nagid,* not in the name of the head of the Jerusalem yeshiva, and matters of communal or religious concern were subject to the *Nagid's* ultimate approval. This office developed slowly. By the time of Abraham ha-Nagid, it became hereditary in the Maimonides' family, an unhealthy development, influenced by the example of similar practices in Muslim society.

## The Third Power

Besides its spiritual and law leaders, the Jewish community was in need of other powers for its safety and welfare. Real power rests with the guns, the government with the military and police behind it. The *Gaonim* and local judges needed governmental confirmation, and in cases of internal conflict the last word lay with the government, and, consequently, with Jews who had close access to it. As a rule, these were men who were not active as leaders within the community, but people who were connected with the government, and whose help was sought. This, too, was not a specifically Jewish phenomenon but, rather, the system of law under Islam. A community could secure its rights only if it had someone connected with the government who was influential there and who could apply pressure on its behalf. However, the Nagids Judah and Mevorakh and later Samuel b. Hananya and Netanel ha-Levi Gaon were both communal leaders and, as court physicians, influential with government.

## Conflict in a Religious Democracy

The Geniza documents regularly refer to "conflict" and "peace" by using the Hebrew words *mahloket* and *shalom,* although the texts containing them are mostly in Arabic. This detail of terminology seems to indicate that conflict within the Jewish community with its specific corporate character had no exact counterpart in the amorphous, autocratically ruled Muslim environment.

Another Hebrew term constantly mentioned in this context is *reshut,* authority. The great question was always whether a congregation or an individual recognized, or was under the jurisdiction of, Jerusalem or

Baghdad, or which of the two *yeshivot* of Baghdad, and, from the end of the eleventh century, which *Nagid* in Egypt.

*Reshut* had to be indicated before every *drashah*—that is, no one had the right to give a sermon or lecture in a synagogue before indicating under whose *reshut* he was. Every marriage contract opened with an indication of the authority under whose *reshut* it was made, so that in case of disagreement the proper official could be approached. In the synagogue every Saturday and holiday a special prayer was recited for the *reshut* under which the congregation functioned. Similarly, the grace said at a festive meal opens with the words *"Birshut maranan rabbanan v'rabbotay"*—"with the permission of our masters and lords and my lords"; *rabbotay,* "my lords," refers to the people present, while *maranan v-rabanan* refers to the authorities recognized by the members of the assembled company. The question of whose *reshut* was to be acknowledged was one of the great causes of conflict in the community. So much so that at the time of Rabbenu Abraham Maimonides, a *takkana* was made prohibiting the mention of *reshut* in public or private for the duration of thirty years.

## The Prerogatives of Eretz Israel

A person or congregation under the *reshut* of Eretz Israel had to accept unflinchingly the ruling of the Jerusalem Yeshiva. The question was whether the native aristocracy of Eretz Israel as such had religious and communal prerogatives. Such a claim was made by the Gaon Nathan b. Abraham against his rival, the incumbent Gaon Solomon b. Judah, a native of Fez, Morocco, and by Evyathar b. Elijah Gaon against David, the son of the Babylonian Nasi and Gaon Daniel b. Azaryah. These claims did not carry much weight. Solomon b. Judah was generally recognized, and David b. Daniel was replaced by the Egyptian Nagid Mevorakh. However, the famous conflict over the calendar of the years 922 (which had its parallels in the Eastern churches) proved that the claims of precedence for the Jerusalem Yeshiva had deep roots. This did not hinder Solomon b. Judah, *Gaon* of Jerusalem, from sending his son to Baghdad to study with the great Hay Gaon (d. 1038).

## Inner Jewish Migration

There were other great issues contributing to unrest and conflict in the communities. One of these was the migration of Jews from east to west in this period. The most decisive event of post-Talmudic Jewish history was the devastation, in the ninth and tenth centuries, of Iraq and western Iran, once the main seat of the Jewish population and the heart of the Islamic empire. The rich and well-educated Jews of that region migrated westward and imposed their laws and ways of life (the Babylonian Talmud) on the rest of the Jewish world. "Babylonian" congregations sprang up not only in Syria and Egypt, but in Eretz Israel itself.

By the eleventh century this process was almost completed. As the Geniza texts show, even the "Palestinian" congregations had accepted specialties of Eretz Israel. The spiritual amalgamation was successfully completed. But a certain tension between "Babylonians" and "Palestinians" prevailed throughout this period.

## Karaites and Rabbanites

Another source of conflict was the struggle between the Karaites and Rabbanites. Today the Karaites have no great significance any more, but in those days they were the best educated and richest Jews: they knew most about language, about philosophy and theology, and they were closest to the government; in short, they were a very strong element. In this respect there was a great difference between Egypt and Eretz Israel. In Eretz Israel, the conflict between Karaites and Rabbanites was fierce and bitter. Most of the Rabbanites there were poor, and many of them had no occupations, devoting themselves to prayer and study. Therefore they had time to spare for communal strife. In Egypt, where the socioeconomic antagonism was less felt and everyone did business the relations were more peaceful. The leaders of both groups mostly were opposed to such squabbles.

We have numerous marriage contracts that bear witness to "mixed marriages" between Karaites and Rabbanites in Egypt, and these are really shining examples of tolerance and consideration. For example, intimate relations between husband and wife on Sabbaths and holidays are anathema according to the Karaites, but were Rabbanite custom. Or, the Karaites do not permit any light on Sabbath—so the Rabbanite husband might sit with light and the wife in darkness. However, the marriage contracts stipulate that the two parties were obliged to be considerate of each other.

It must be noted that a marriage contract in those days was a very effective legal document; it had no similarity at all to contemporary marriage contracts. It fixed exactly the rights of the two partners in respect. Simply by reading the document it was immediately apparent who was the stronger partner. Family was the determining factor. If the woman's family was the stronger, she could even stipulate that her husband was not permitted to leave town except with her permission or on her command, and so on. Normally the Karaite girls were rich and the Rabbanite boys were not. What is decisive is that not only do we have numerous actual contracts of mixed marriages, even between a *nasi* and *rosh yeshiva* and a Karaite woman, but formularies, too, have been preserved which show that such family connections were nothing exceptional.

There were shining examples of joint appeals of Rabbanites and Karaites, as well as of mutual help (especially on the side of the Karaites). What religious fanaticism, on the one hand, and reason and responsibility on the other can do may be learned from the Geniza texts on the relations between Karaites and Rabbanites.

## Personalities

The most common reason for conflict in the Geniza world, as everywhere, was conflict between personalities—various people who sought office, or who wanted to dislodge someone else from office, whether an incumbent man or an entrenched family. Maimonides is a case in point. He came to Egypt in 1168, already possessing great authority, because he had written his *Perush HaMishnah*. In 1171 he was appointed *Rosh Hayehudim*. Why? Because at that time Saladin had put an end to the Fatimid empire, and the old and illustrious family of Natanel Halevi, which had held high office before, preferred to step down because they were connected with the dethroned caliphs. But in 1176, five years later, the Levi family became powerful again and Maimonides was ousted in turn. He remained out of office for twenty years and only returned to the position at the end of his life, approximately in 1196. During those twenty years in which he was out of office, he had time to write the *Mishneh Torah* and the *Guide of the Perplexed*.

Abraham HaNagid, the son of Maimonides, on the other hand, was elected head of the Jews of Egypt only a few years after his father's death, when he was still very young, and remained in office from then until the end of his life. He was also the Chief Dayyan. The Geniza has preserved many decisions of his, which indicates that his communal activities must have been detrimental to his scholarly work. No complete copy of his great "Guide for the Servants of God" has come down to us, and his attempts at a pietistic reform of Jewish religious life came to nil.

## Religious Ritual and Public Funds as Objects of Contention

The most common accusation against a rival religious head was that his *shehita* was unreliable. The charge commonly made against Muslim judges, that they "eat the money of orphans and widows" and lay their hands on the pious foundations, was rare among the Jewish communities. But even such *Hassidim* as Solomon b. Judah Gaon and Moses Maimonides did not escape such accusation, which were regarded, however, as ridiculous.

## "Men With Titles"

Everyone in the community who had acquired merit by public service, munificence, or learning, tried to have such merit publicly acknowledged by a title conferred on him by a Rosh Yeshiva, an exilarch, a *Nagid,* or by the acclamation of the *Kahal.* Many were accumulating titles. The Nagid Mevorakh b. Saadya had fourteen by the end of his life. When a man was called to the Torah, he was blessed with all the titles he possessed, and woe to the cantor who forgot one. This striving after titles proves how everyone was eager that his proper position within the community should be publicly recognized.

## The Vitality of Jewish Communal Life

The popularity of titles and the many aspects of communal strife apparent in the Geniza were signs of vitality. They showed that the personalities concerned sought and often found outlets for their abilities *within* the community. The election of the Rosh Yeshiva of Baghdad or Jerusalem concerned not only the *bene-geonim,* the families of gaonic parentage, and the leading Jewish laymen of Iraq or Palestine, but also the communities abroad. After the death of the Palestinian Gaon David b. Azarya (ca. 1063) we read in a letter:

> My cousin (Nahray b. Nissim, "the prominent member of the Yeshiva," living in Egypt) makes propaganda for Yehuda b. Yosef ha-Kohen (the *Rav Gadol* or "grand mufti" of the Jews of that country) to be chosen as *Rosh Yeshiva*. He (Nahray) has already collected money for that purpose; he visits important personalities and has attracted supporters.

This sounds rather familiar to us. In the Geniza society of the eleventh century we are justified to speak of a religious democracy, because public life was intensely religious and everyone strove to obtain some of the honors that it bestowed.

# 10

# On Power and Authority: The *Halakhic* Stance of the Traditional Community and Its Contemporary Implications

*Menachem Elon*

On the face of it, a discussion of the Jewish political tradition should focus on such examples as the history of the kingdoms of David and Solomon, the Hasmonean period, or at least the days of the *Nesiim* (Patriarchs) in Israel, or the *Roshei Golah* (Exilarchs) in Babylonia. Indeed, one might ask, what does the Jewish community of the Middle Ages—a period when Israel had no King or *Nasi*, a period repudiated by the architects of modern Jewish attitudes—have to do with our political tradition? But the concept on which this perplexity is founded—a concept that is deeply rooted and commonly accepted by many—is both erroneous and misleading. On the contrary, Jewish internal rule, as embodied by the *Kehillah,* the characteristics of such Jewish autonomy, the problems encountered, and the tremendous creative vitality revealed in the establishment of the framework and content of this autonomy—all these are of special, far-reaching significance today.

## The Autonomy of the Jewish Community (*Kehillah*)

When we speak of the *kehillah* as an autonomous body that fulfilled internal political functions in all areas of communal life—legal, social, and economic—and which imposed its rules and regulations upon its members, we are speaking of the *kehillah* as it began to emerge in the middle of the tenth century, continuing until the period of the emancipation at the end of the eighteenth century. Indeed, Yitzhak Baer has already pointed out that "the foundations of the *kehillah,* which remained in existence until the Enlightenment, were laid mainly in the first generations of the Second Temple period,"[1] and it is to this early period that we must ascribe several Tannaic sources that discuss the laws governing *bnei ha'ir* (the citizens, literally "the children of the city") and *anshei ha'ir* ("the people of the city").[2] But, for this long period of history, there remain no records of the special autonomous powers of the community in the sphere of local and judicial rule.

Towards the end of the Gaonic period, a basic change occurred in Jewish life, giving rise to a change in the status and role of the *kehillah*. Until then, there had generally been one center with spiritual hegemony over the scattered Jewish communities. This center had originally been Eretz Israel; later it was Babylonia. In the tenth century, a fundamental change took place in this situation. As a result of various external and internal factors, the Babylonian center declined and, with its decline, the hegemony of a single Jewish center ceased to exist. A series of centers arose, functioning alongside one another, none of which was recognized to have spiritual hegemony over the others. In addition to the centers in Babylonia, North Africa, and Italy, in the course of time other centers arose in Germany, Spain, France, Eretz Israel, Turkey, the Balkan countries, Poland, Lithuania, and elsewhere. Although there were occasionally great spiritual leaders whose authority was recognized by the various communities, as a rule, each center was autonomous in most matters of law and justice, and looked for guidance to its own halakhic scholars. There was no center that issued decisions binding on all the communities of the diaspora.

This great historic change led to a modification in the character and status of the *kehillah*. The scope of the *kehillah's* jurisdiction and control was extended to cover the entire range of its members' activity, shaping their social life and spiritual image. It enjoyed a large measure of autonomy: it had its own internal governing bodies, on which both elected and appointed representatives served; it fulfilled the educational and social needs of its members; it had its own courts with the authority to deal with civil, administrative, and, to a certain extent, even criminal cases; it levied and collected taxes in order to pay the tax imposed on the community by the non-Jewish rulers, as well as to finance communal services. Often a federation of several *kehillot* would perform a large number of these functions, including the maintenance of governing bodies and the collection of taxes.

In order to exercise this autonomy, two prerequisites—one external and one internal—had to be met. The external factor was the opportunity granted to a group of people living as a minority under foreign rule to exercise autonomy, and the *readiness* of the foreign regime to grant this autonomy. As this is not the major concern of our discussion,[3] let us note briefly that both opportunity and readiness existed. The reason for this was rooted in the political-legal understanding of the concepts of government and jurisdiction which prevailed until the eighteenth century as well as in the fiscal and social relationships existing between the regime and the various classes—including aliens—living within its jurisdiction. The state was not interested in centralization. It was a corporate state made up of various autonomous bodies—the aristocracy, the burghers, the guilds, and so forth—which often vied with one another or with the central authority. At times, the Jewish community served as a point of controversy between the various groups and the central regime. The judicial system was based on personal-group identification, and the state recognized the legal systems of the various groups living within it. In this political-legal environment, a legally autonomous Jewish entity was able to exist. The willingness of the central regime to grant the Jews such autonomy stemmed from various considerations: a certain degree of tolerance towards other religions, varying according to time and place; religious and ideological considerations; and, finally and most importantly, fiscal considerations. The government felt that it was both its duty and its "right" to levy heavy taxes on the Jews—"tolerance money"—for the privilege of being allowed to live on its land. In order to collect these taxes, the government found it more convenient to demand the entire tax from the Jewish community as a whole. For this purpose, the community was allowed to exist as a cohesive, autonomous unit with leaders responsible for delivering the taxes collected by each communal organization from its members.

The second factor accounting for the existence of Jewish autonomy—and, in the last analysis, the primary factor—was the desire of the Jews themselves to maintain their own internal authority. They had the necessary intellectual capacity and practical ability to create the framework and organs for their self-government, both of which were suited to the prevailing historio-social conditions in the diaspora.

## The Authority of Communal Government—Legal Problems

It is clear that internal Jewish rule during this period did not mean the rule of the individual—as embodied by a king, *nasi,* or *rosh golah*—but rather communal rule, either in the early, simple meaning of rule by the entire community or by representatives chosen or appointed to represent the community and constituting its political system. Of course, since this was a society whose members and leaders both recognized the Torah and the *halakhah* (Jewish law) as the supreme authority, Communal government, in the form of the *kehillah,* had to be based on *halakhah*. This brings us to the following question: what was the place of such communal rule in the world of *halakhah*?

Let us clarify the problem. A basic component of the concept of government is the principle of authority, the power of government to compel the individual to obey the law; hence government is classified under public as opposed to private law. The commonly accepted definition of these two branches of law, applicable to Jewish law as well, is worth noting here. Public law includes "a large number of norms issued by public institutions intended to be binding upon the individual. . . . .This power to compel is what constitutes the *authoritative* character of these norms; the sum total of the authoritative norms of the state is known as the *public law* of that state."[4] On the other hand, where the norms of the private law are concerned, we find that: "What is common to these norms or transactions is the lack of compulsive power over the individual without his consent; that is to say, they lack an authoritative quality. This set of norms or transactions is called *private law*.[5]

This principle—the right to compel someone to act in a certain way without his consent—is also found in Jewish public law, in the authority of the king, and later of the *nasi* or the *rosh golah* who, from a historical and halakhic point of view, were regarded as continuations of the monarchy and its authority. But the community, or its representatives, did not, at that time, possess this authoritative power. In fact, according to the *halakhah,* the community—or the *kehillah*—had no such power. According to the Talmud, ten, twenty or even a hundred Jews living in a community are considered partners and the laws of partnership—or private law in general—does not provide for compulsion; rather, any decision requires the consent of each and every individual. To quote Rabbi Asher ben Jehiel (Rosh), "One individual restricts the actions of another, and the individual restricts the actions of the majority."[6]

Because of this, the scholars and communal leaders were faced with a basic problem: can a community, or its representatives, exercise authority without possessing compulsive power over the individual; that is to say, is the decision of the majority binding upon the minority, and is such a decision enforceable. Although the Torah states, "By a majority you are to decide," this rule was interpreted by the scholars of the Talmud as referring to halakhic decisions or legal judgments which must, according to law, be made by the majority, or regarding the majority as a legal presumption (*Praesumptio Juris*), but not to the right of a majority of the community to impose its will on the minority. (It should be noted here that, during the twelfth century, the prevailing legal view in Europe—unlike that of Roman law—was that decisions of the public were valid only if they were taken unanimously. In controversies between the majority and a minority, the majority had to win the consent of the minority through negotiation or by force. Thus, according to a few halakhic scholars, the foremost of them Rabbenu Tam, the decision of the majority was not binding upon the minority. But this solution was unacceptable to the majority of halakhic scholars, for it did not provide a basis for the establishment and maintenance of orderly communal government.)[7]

This problem was only one among many. The social, economic, and commercial life of the Jews, different in every country of their dispersion, and the relations of each Jewish community with the non-Jewish environment and the general government, created many new problems in the areas of civil and criminal law. Other problems arose as a result of the new character of the *kehillah,* its representative and elective bodies: what should be the network of relations between the individual citizen and the community, between the communal government and its employees? How should the communal institutions be organized and legally administered? How were elections and appointments to communal institutions and other public positions to be carried out? How were taxes to be levied and collected? In addition to these questions, the scholars were faced with a long list of other problems related to the legal aspects of the economic and fiscal relations of the *kehillah*. Some of these were solved through the accepted methods of the *halakhah*: rabbinical decisions and ordinances (*takkanot*), custom, and so forth. But these methods did not always meet the dynamic needs of the community, and a significant number of them called for new *takkanot* to be enacted by the *kehillah* and its representatives, or by the federations of *kehillot* and statewide councils. This phenomenon of communal ordinances (*takkanot ha-kahal*) was an innovation stemming directly from the new reality—the authority of the *kehillah*. Indeed, as we have noted, even in the days of the Tannaim, the community had established a system of weights and measures, wages, and so forth, but this activity was marginal and most major decisions stemmed from the central halakhic authority. In the Middle Ages, however, the legislative activity of the *kehillah* was extended to many areas of Jewish law, both civil and public, and, to a certain extent, even criminal.

These far-reaching changes in the scope of communal legislation raised many fundamental legal questions that could not be answered by the existing *halakhah*. Thus, for example, we find no discussion in the Talmud on the source of the community's authority to issue *takkanot,* and hence the degree and scope of this authority were not clear. This was true of many fundamental questions concerning legislative procedures and the scope of their application. For example, do decisions on communal *takkanot* have to be made by the entire community with all members present, or can they be made by their representatives?

Similarly, with the question already raised: is a decision passed by the majority binding upon a dissenting minority? Finally, are decisions binding on a person who was outside the community or who was not yet born at the time the decision was taken, and if so, to what extent? These questions and their solutions are, by their very nature, in the realm of public law, but the Talmud does not deal with these problems and they cannot be solved through analogies to private law (for example, laws of partnership). The solution required by public law is in opposition to the very essence of private law, which, by definition, cannot be binding upon an individual without his consent.[8]

## The Authority of Communal Government

### A Solution Based on Jewish Law

The solution that the halakhic scholars found in order to grant authority to the new political reality of the *kehillah* was both simple and revolutionary: simple in its conclusion that the community, when acting as a community, is subject to the regulations of Jewish public law, and all that this implies; revolutionary in the extensive use made by the scholars of those days of the accepted methods of creation in the world of *halakhah-midrash* (interpretation), *takkanah* (ordinance), *minhag* (custom), and *ma'aseh* (case and precedent). The basis of all these methods was a bold and far-reaching use of the creative source of legal logic (*sevarah*), that is, the reasoning and logic of the scholars, based on a penetrating insight of the halakhic world against the background of the practical realities of daily life.[9] Different rabbis cite various Talmudic sources to prove that the rules concerning public law differ from those concerning the individual,[10] but this was no more than an attempt to find some support for their decision. From all these sources we can conclude only that the Talmud viewed public and private acts differently (for example, the laws governing vows made with public consent), but this distinction had no further legal significance.[11] Certain scholars found a solution to some of the problems cited above, such as the right of the majority to impose its will and decisions on the minority, through expansive interpretation. Thus, they extended the meaning of the precept that the residents of a city can compel their fellow townsmen to build a synagogue or to purchase a Torah scroll[12] to mean provision for all the needs of the community.[13] Similarly, the scope of "By a majority you are to decide" was extended to include not only legal decisions and judgments, but also "matters which concern the public."[14] Others solved this problem by referring to the *midrash aggadah,* which relates that "The tribes decided (by threat of ban) amongst themselves that they would not reveal the sale of Joseph, and when Reuben, who had been absent, returned and said, 'The boy is gone! Now, what am I to do?,' the brothers told him what they had done and he was silent."[15] But even these solutions did not solve all the problems that arose in the governing of the community.

A general solution to these problems was found in the decision of the halakhic scholars to consider the community, from a legal point of view, as equivalent to those bodies included within the scope of Jewish public law, such as the King or *Nasi* and, most importantly, the Court, or even the High Court. "In each community, the individuals are subject to the authority of the majority and they must act according to the majority in all matters. They are to their fellow townsmen as Israel is to the High Court or to the King."[16] "No one can exclude himself from the enactments of the community and its ordinances; because the individuals are subservient to the community, and just as all the communities are subservient to the High Court or to the *Nasi,* so is each and every individual subservient to the community in his city."[17] "For the power of the community over the individuals is like the power of the *Nasi* over all of Israel."[18] Thus, the parallel can be stated as follows: the relation of every community to the individuals comprising it is like that of the King, the *Nasi,* or the High Court to Israel as a whole.

The parallel between the townspeople and the *Nasi* is vaguely alluded to in the Mishnah: "He who is banned from his city, is banned from all other cities; he who is banned from the presence of the Nasi, is banned from the presence of all Israel."[19] The parallel between the *kehillah* and the court, however, is both revolutionary and far-reaching, appearing for the first time in the tenth century, with no precedent in Talmudic *halakhah* or *aggadah.* Furthermore, the rabbis did more than draw a parallel between them—they affirmed, in fact, that the community functions as a court, with each and every member a judge. To quote Rabbi Elijah Mizrahi, one of the great scholars of Turkey in the second half of the fifteenth and early sixteenth centuries:

> The community as a whole is like a court in these [communal] matters. They are like judges to assemble in court and are not free to leave although there are differences of opinion between them: pure or impure; innocent or guilty; rather, they must be counted and must follow the majority decision, as it is written in our holy Torah: "By a majority you are to decide"; and he who opposes the majority is considered a sinner. It makes no difference whether the majority be wealthy or poor, wise men or ordinary people, because the entire community is considered a court in matters concerning its members.[20]

As previously noted, no basis for such a parallel between the authority and status of the *kehillah* and those of the court was to be found in the *halakhah* of the Talmud. The scholars of the post-Talmudic period simply stated that the authority of the community, or of the majority, was comparable to that of the court, but they did not give any legal-halakhic argument to support this far-reaching conclusion. At a later period, the halakhic scholars did cite arguments in support of this parallel, two of which are given here.

Rabbi Elijah Mizrahi, quoted above, based his argument on the fact that the power and authority of the court and the communal leaders are both derived from the same source—the community as a whole. He stated:[21]

> For the power which was granted to the High Court in Jerusalem and to every court in every generation—as our sages interpreted the passage (from Deuteronomy), and appear before the heretical priests, etc., whether he be Jephthat or Samuel, although one cannot be compared with the other—was granted because the decrees, ordinances and customs of the High Court in every generation were and are recognized by all members of that generation, and for this reason the High Court was granted greater power than the other courts of that generation to issue decrees and ordinances and to establish customs. And although it was not explicitly chosen and no specific conditions were agreed upon, it is well-known that all its decisions were recognized by everyone as conclusive; and although someone may object, it is as if he explicitly gave his consent and then changed his mind. Therefore, wherever this principle applies, the authority in question has the power which was granted to the High Court in Jerusalem without reservation. This also applies to the leaders of the city, for all the townspeople recognize their authority in matters related to the improvement of communal life, and they, the townspeople, all rely on them. Thus, it is as if the leaders were explicitly chosen, and all their decisions stand. And although some may object to their decrees and ordinances, it is as if they explicitly gave their consent and then changed their minds.[22]

The argument put forward by one of the great contemporary halakhic scholars, Rabbi Avraham Yeshayahu Karelitz, the *"Hazon Ish,"* is interesting. He stated: "This may have been a *takkanah* of the sages, designed to grant the townsmen the authority of a court."[23] That is to say, this was a special *takkanah* of the halakhic scholars, the purpose of which was to grant the communal leaders the status and authority of a court,[24] in order to establish Jewish autonomous rule.

If the question is asked: why was it not sufficient to compare the status of the community to that of the King or *Nasi*—a logical comparison, for the rule of the *Kehillah* was a continuation of the internal rule exercised after that of the King and the *Nasi*?[25] Why did they find it necessary to compare its status to that of the court? The answer is simple: Drawing a parallel to the King or *Nasi* was not sufficient to solve all the problems with which the halakhic scholars were faced. For example, the *takkanot* of a community would often be in conflict with a particular ruling of the *halakhah*. One such case was the *takkanah* allowing witnesses to testify, and judges to sit in judgment, in cases involving their own families or personal considerations, when the case involved communal matters, such as taxation, charitable trusts, and so forth. The reasoning was that otherwise there would not be a single witness who could testify, or judge who could sit, in matters concerning his own community. This was true of many *takkanot* in various civil matters and in criminal law which prescribed punishments for criminal acts which, while harmful to the community, could not be punished under halakhic law. This community authority was based on the Talmudic principle which granted the sages the authority to issue *takkanot,* even when they were in opposition to established halakhah—in civil matters, by virtue of the principle that the court has the power to revoke private ownership (*hefker bet din hefker*); and in criminal cases, by virtue of the principle that the court may mete out punishments not prescribed by law. Thus, because of the parallel between the community and the court, it was established that the community, like the court, has the power to revoke private ownership and to inflict punishments not specified by law.[26]

To cite another example: Jewish law generally requires a *qinyan* (an act whereby a person voluntarily obtains proprietary or contractual rights) to make a legal transaction valid. This formal requirement hampered legal relationships between the community as a public authority, with its network of affairs, and anyone needing to negotiate with it. Thus, beginning in the twelfth and thirteenth centuries, we find a new legal principle that any legal transaction by the community is valid even without a *qinyan*. And, after a short time, it became an accepted custom and rule that "All public matters are valid even without a *qinyan* and the laws of *qinyan* are not applicable in these cases."[27] Here, too, there is no basis in Talmudic law for exempting the community from the *qinyan*. This innovation was based on the parallel between the community and the court, the actions of which are valid without a *qinyan*.[28] Using this same principle, other far-reaching allowances were made for the community, such as the right to purchase and sell articles that did not yet exist; in addition, it was decided that the defect of *asmakhta* does not apply to the conduct of transactions made by the community.[29]

## Basic Principles in Administrative Law
## and Public-Private Relations

The authority of the Jewish communal government—the *kehillah*—was founded on several basic principles set down by the halakhic scholars, which endowed the *kehillah* with great power. This power did not depend upon physical forces but, on the contrary, on spiritual strength, resulting in fact from the limitation and supervision of such physical forces. It is difficult to say which was more important—the granting of physical power or its limitation—but it is clear that only both these factors together can create a governing authority with practical and spiritual stability.

In the public life of the Jews in the *kehillah,* as in every community, there were social tensions between the various classes which often brought them into sharp conflict. There were also cases of criminal offenses against property, morality, and family life; there were forgeries, assaults, and sometimes, though quite rarely, even murders. These pathological phenomena, though relatively few in number, can also be found in the responsa literature, which reveals how the *halakhah* succeeded in dealing with them, either by means of existing laws or new rulings. At times, the actions of the community leadership were called into question, whether in the form of simple offenses on the part of a communal leader, or of questions of a socio-constitutional nature. These required the intervention of halakhic scholars in order to protect the basic rights of the minority and the weak, to establish norms for relations between the different classes in the community, and so on. This complex of problems resulted in the creation of many new fundamental principles in Jewish public law. Some examples follow.

### "Clean Hands" as a Condition for Public Office

Certain problems were solved by virtue of the principle that drew a parallel between the community and the court. In a particular case, a man made a false statement in declaring his taxes; he was fined by the appropriate authority, and then an agreement was reached with the *kehillah* as to the sum he was to pay in tax. After a while, this same man sought to be appointed as a leader of the community. Rabbi Israel Isserlein—a scholar living in Germany in the fifteenth century—was asked[30] whether "this man could sit with the elders of the community for the purpose of tending to the public good . . . .and of supervising public and private matters," since it was clear that he had previously sworn falsely. Rabbi Israel answered that he could not serve as a leader of the community, having sworn falsely out of lust for money; because of this act, he was comparable to a thief or robber and was therefore disqualified from being a judge—and "the elders of the community, when supervising public and private affairs, act in the place of a court." This principle served as a guideline for determining who was qualified for public service, and was accepted as *halakhah*: "The elders of the community, who are appointed to deal with public or private matters, are viewed as judges, and he who is disqualified from judging because of wrong-doing cannot be appointed to sit among them."[31]

## A Community Cannot Claim: "We Were Wrong"

This same principle of the existence of a parallel between the community and the court implies that the community cannot argue that it did not seriously consider a certain matter, or that it misunderstood it and had arrived at an erroneous decision. Rabbi Solomon ben Simeon Duran (Rashbash), son of the author of the Tashbetz and, during the fifteenth century, spiritual leader of the Jewish community in North Africa, stated: "Observe how this is done in all the holy communities; a decision is never rescinded. . . . .For it is a disgrace for a community to say: 'We were mistaken'. . . . .The power of the community is like the power of the court, and if we invalidate a sale made by the community, what is the power of the court?"[32]

## Principles of Justice and Equity

Restrictions on the arbitrary authority of the communal leaders can be found in the control that the halakhic scholars maintained over the content of communal *takkanot*. As stated above, a communal *takkanah* could contradict the content of a specific ruling or *halakhah,* and the rabbis generally accepted this. But communal *takkanot* could not contradict essential principles that were basic to the framework of Jewish law—for example: equality before the law, protecting the rights of the minority or the weak, improving the social order, and so forth. Thus, a framework of general principles of justice and equity was crested in Jewish law.

## Controlling the Management of Public Affairs

In a certain community there was a functionary whose duty it was "to strive to eradicate crime and punish transgressors"—in modern terms, a kind of state or city comptroller. One day, by a *takkanah* issued by the majority, it was decided to discontinue this position. The minority turned to Rabbi Solomon ben Aderet (Rashba)—the halakhic authority of Spanish Jewry in the late thirteenth century—and asked him whether such a *takkanah* was valid, since it would lead to an increase in immoral behavior. He replied unequivocally that such a decision was indeed null and void. "And although it was implemented by the people responsible for most of the community's needs, laws are made by them to maintain order and not to disturb it, and they cannot violate the lines on which the Torah is based."[33] Rashba added that one comptroller may be replaced by another if he is considered to be better, but a decision discontinuing the function as such cannot improve a situation but only aggravate it and hence is void.

## Restrictions on the Power to Levy Taxes: The Case of a Person Who is Unable to Pay

In a question addressed to three scholars in Mainz early in the thirteenth century, we read of a *takkanah* enacted in a community obligating every person to pay a minimal tax. One man refused, arguing that he was poor and could not afford the tax, and so he was willing to swear. The community representative (referred to as the "*apotropa*"), on the other hand, argued that the community had decided

> not to allow anyone to swear; rather they would be required to pay a certain amount according to the sum paid the previous year. . . . .It was not in the public interest for the members of the community to take an oath. . . . .The community can take action in order to meet the needs of the moment, so as not to take an oath from any member of the community. And I do not wish to cite any further argument, since the community may issue any *takkanot* it wishes.[34]

The "utilitarian" arguments of the community representative were rejected, and the scholars of Mainz unequivocally declared the decision null and void on the grounds that the validity of a law rests on the ability of people to comply with it. How could the man be required to give what he does not possess? It is an important principle that God exempts those who, for reasons beyond their control, cannot comply with His laws. Thus, "If the man is really unable to pay, he should be exempt from payment. Can the majority be rogues (*gazlanim*)?" That is to say, the majority, merely by virtue of the fact that it is a majority, cannot unjustly deprive anyone of his money and deny him his basic rights; for no one can require a poor man to pay taxes he cannot afford.

## Protecting the Basic Rights of the Minority

In this same response, the scholars of Mainz established another principle. The principle that the majority can exert its will on the minority applies only when the majority and the minority are on an equal footing—for example, when both have the ability to pay, but the minority objects to the tax as such. But when the economic situation of the minority is such that, were the majority to be in a similar situation, it too could not comply with the law, the principle of majority rule does not apply. Finally, the following principle of public law is stated in this responsa:

If a man is not financially capable of paying, why should he be harassed and fined for lack of means? According to the law, if he has no financial means the community must support him and his family; hence, how can the community demand payment from him? And if his oath is not suspect, why should he not be allowed to swear and be exempt, since he protested the tax from the very beginning?

## Prohibition Against Double Taxation

This fundamental principle of Jewish public law—the majority cannot be rogues[35]—applies not only when the majority acts in such a way as to deprive the underprivileged, but also when the majority unlawfully deprives anyone, even if he is a man of means. This is revealed in the following example: a certain man lived in Community A, while part of his property was in Community B. The leaders of Community A wanted to tax him for the property which was located in Community B, but he protested, arguing that the tax was levied on the property and not on the individual. Community B had already taxed the property owned there, so that were he also to pay taxes on this property in the community in which he lived, he would be paying a double tax on the same property. The leaders of the community, on the other hand, argued that "the community has the power to enact laws which apply to and are binding on everyone." Here, too, Rashba rejected the community's argument: "The argument that the community can enact laws in such matters seems to me to be no more than robbery, and unjust enactments are not valid. . . . .It is not within the power of the community unjustly to deprive anyone of his money and appropriate it for communal use."[36] The community cannot use the legislative authority granted to it and obligate anyone by law—even with the consent of the majority—if such action involves an infringement of justice or law, or involves some form of swindling.

## Payment of Taxes That are Under Dispute—When?

Rabbi Meir (Maharam) of Rothenburg, the greatest halakhic scholar in thirteenth-century Germany, established this same principle in another matter. A number of responsa by various scholars dealt with the fairly common case of disputes between an individual and the community as to the amount of taxes to be paid, where the individual appeals to the court. According to the law, were it to be strictly applied, the person who demands payment must show due cause; thus, the community would be able to collect only that amount on which there was agreement, while the remainder, which was under dispute, could not be collected until a court decision had been reached. Nevertheless, the rabbis ruled—whether on the basis of a special *takkanah* or otherwise—that the individual must pay the entire sum, and only after a court decision in his favor will the money be refunded to him. This decision was based on the following argument: "People cannot be left free to say, 'I will not pay until after litigation,' for then everyone would do so, the tax could never be collected, and cheating would be encouraged."[37] "Whenever the community has a claim against anyone, it is assumed that it is in possession of the claim, for otherwise public affairs could not be conducted. Everyone would act dishonestly, thinking: 'Who will challenge me in court?'"[38] Therefore, the public good is to be upheld over the letter of the law, for this enables the community to maintain services and to pay the sums demanded of it by the government. However, Maharam ruled, the public good is to be upheld over that of the individual only in cases in which there is reasonable doubt as to the amount of tax to be paid. But, "Where it is clear that the public authority is not in the right, it must not be permitted to wrong the individual, for its status as a public authority does not entitle it to be unjust to anyone." The law, then, is as follows: "every person must pay tax on all his property, apart from cases clearly exempted; but if there is some doubt as to exemption and the community claims that he must pay, he must do so and then go to law."[39]

## Elections to Public Bodies—Who Can Vote, and What is the Weight of Each Vote?

Problems in the realm of public law often reflect the social environment of a community. A clear example of this was the preoccupation of the rabbis, at different times and in different Jewish communities, with the nature of the majority. As we have seen, one of the greatest problems in determining the framework of Jewish internal rule was the problem of the majority versus the minority. After the principle of majority rule was established, a fundamental question arose: How is the majority to be composed? Should the vote of every person have equal weight, whether he be rich or poor, educated or ignorant? Perhaps the majority ought to be determined by a combination of these factors? These problems were dealt with extensively within various legal frameworks. Different usages were common under different legal systems, in different eras, and under different forms of government. It is reasonable to say that there was interaction—both positive and negative—between the non-Jewish and Jewish environments. Thus, what emerged from the halakhic discussions on this question is a spectrum of solutions, all guided by the realities of life and all, in turn, regulating life.

At one end of this spectrum, we find, for example, the opinion of Rabbi Elijah Mizrahi, the foremost scholar of Constantinople in the late fifteenth century and early sixteenth, already cited above: "It makes no difference whether the majority are wealthy or poor, men of learning or common people, since each community acts as a court in dealing with its own affairs."[40] A view diametrically opposed to this is that of Rabbi Samuel de Medina, the Maharashdam, one of the great rabbis of sixteenth-century Salonika. He argued that:

The Torah speaks of "By a majority you are to decide" only when both parties are equal; then the opinion of the majority is decisive. But when the two groups are not equal, one man may have the weight of a thousand. . . . .When they are equal, the majority is determined by number; when they are unequal, the majority is determined by personal standing. Accepting the will of the majority, when that majority is composed of ignorant men, could lead to a perversion of justice. For if there were one hundred men in a city, ten of whom were wealthy, respected men, and ninety of whom were poor, and the ninety wanted to appoint a leader approved by them, would the ten prominent men have to submit to him regardless of who he was? Heaven forbid—this is not the accepted way ("the way of pleasantness").[41]

Complete equality, irrespective of wealth or knowledge, according to the Maharashdam, stands in contradiction to both law and the "ways of pleasantness." Hence, when the members of the community are not on an equal footing, the majority is determined not by number but by prestige, by the specific weight of each vote. Between these diametrically opposed positions, there are many shades of meaning and nuance. These include those expressed by: Rabbi Isaac Adarbi of sixteenth-century Salonika, who believed that decisions on fiscal matters should follow the "economic majority" while the "simple majority"—with every vote having equal weight—should decide in all other matters;[42] and Rabbi Abraham di Boton, also of sixteenth-century Salonika, who gave a broad definition of the concept "fiscal matters" in which the "economic majority" was to rule, while only those matters that were in no way related to finance, such as laws determining prohibited behavior, should be decided by a simple majority.[43]

How did the halakhic scholars determine their positions on this issue? Here, too, various analogies, legends (*aggadot*), and so on, were used as sources in the formation of definite halakhic positions on this fundamental question. For example, the following question was posed to Rabbi Menachem Mendel Krochmal, one of the great German scholars of the mid-seventeenth century: in a particular case, several of the notables of the town wished to establish the rule that only those "who paid high taxes or who were learned in the Torah should have the right to vote . . . .since most public matters require an outlay of money; therefore, how could the opinion of the poor be equal to that of the wealthy? Similarly, how could the opinion of the ignorant be equal to that of the scholar?" However, "The masses of the poor cried out: why should our rights be limited if we, too, are taxpayers and give our share. Although the wealthy pay more, it is more difficult for the poor to give their small share than it is for the wealthy to pay much more."[44] Rabbi Menachem Mendel Krochmal decided in favor of the poor, ruling that the majority should be determined by a combination of both factors—wealth and numbers. He based his decision on the last *mishnah* of the tractate *Menahot*[45]:

> Concerning the burnt-offering of an animal or a fowl and the meal-offering (*minha*) it is written: "A sweet-smelling sacrifice" (i.e., all three sacrifices are equally pleasing although they differ in intrinsic value). From this we learn that although there are those who spend much and those who spend little, what is important is that they direct their thoughts to heaven.

From this *mishnah,* Rabbi Krochmal concludes: "Therefore, clearly the small sum which the poor contribute is equal to the large sum which the rich contribute. . . . .The little that the poor man contributes is worth more than the greater amount given by the wealthy." This, too, is derived from the tractate *Menahot*[46] dealing with the meal-offering: "Rabbi Isaac said, 'Why does the word *nefesh* (soul) appear in relation to the *minha* sacrifice?'[47] God said: 'Who generally brings a meal-offering? A poor man (who owns no animals). I therefore regard his sacrifice as though he had offered his very soul.'" Thus, the sacrifice offered by the poor is greater than that offered by the rich, "for the poor man must give of himself in order to obtain what he brings . . . .whereas the rich man brings that which he already possesses without labor."[48] On the basis of this—and other similar references in the Aggadah—Rabbi Menachem Mendel Krochmal concludes that "the argument of the poor is to be accepted, for it is harder for them to give their small share than it is for the rich to give their larger share."[49]

Equally original is the proof that Rabbi Krochmal adduces refuting the argument that sought to distinguish between the weight of the scholar's vote and that of the unlearned. The source cited is the tractate *Hagigah*[50]:

> Rabbi Papa said: On what basis do we today accept the testimony of the unlearned (as opposed to the opinion of the sages in the *baraita* cited in the Babylonian Talmud, Pesahim 49, 2, that the testimony of the unlearned is unacceptable)? This is the opinion of Rabbi Yose, who held that: "We should trust everyone as to the purity of wine and oil, for otherwise they will set themselves apart from the community."

From this, Rabbi Krochmal concludes:

It is clear that even the testimony of ignorant men is to be accepted for fear of animosity—if they are afraid that they are being kept apart they will set up their own forum. This is even more true in the matter under discussion. If we isolate the ignorant to such an extent that we do not include them in the community consensus, they will surely feel animosity towards us and will set up their own forum and separate themselves from the community, leading to dissention among the Jews, heaven forbid! Therefore this is to be avoided.

The manner by which an eminent scholar such as Rabbi Menachem Mendel Krochmal established such a basic principle of election law, within the framework of Jewish law, serves as an additional example of the broad-mindedness and initiative displayed in the formation of fundamental principles of *halakhah*. For, from a logical, formal point of view, the legends telling of the sacrifices offered by the poor have little to do with the fundamental and controversial question of assigning greater weight to the votes of the wealthy members of the community in elections to the communal government. Moreover, it was argued, it was the wealthy citizens who, in the last analysis, financed the public services. What answer could be found to this argument—which is by no means simple—in the Talmudic discussion on the *minha* sacrifice offered by the poor? But this was the method adopted by the rabbis, whose responsibility was proportional to their greatness, when called upon to solve new problems, immersed as they were in the world of the *halakhah,* its aims and its spirit. After they had established a new principle, it was incorporated into the existing *halakhah,* and if there was no appropriate *halakhah,* into an existing *aggadah* in one way or another.

### The Creative Power of the Sevarah (Reasoning) in the Development of Jewish Public Law

The concept of the *sevarah,* that is, the logic on which the reasoning of the halakhic scholars was based, has been discussed at length elsewhere.[51] The *sevarah* served as a special tool for creation in the world of the *halakhah* and as one of its important sources. As a source for the formation of a particular *halakhah,* it is fostered by a logical penetration of the essence of halakhic and legal principles, an understanding of man's behavior in his social relationships, and an examination of the realities of life. An important place was assigned to this creative tool in the development of Jewish public law.

The great changes that occurred in the social-economic-political environment on the one hand, and the lack of real precedents in the existing Talmudic law which could be used to solve the new problems arising from this environment on the other hand, led the rabbis to make extensive use of the creative power of the *sevarah*. Many examples of this can be found in the matters dealt with here. For example, when Rabbenu Asher Ben Jehiel, the Rosh (a leading halakhic scholar, both in Germany and in Spain, towards the end of the thirteenth century) sought to establish the principle that the majority of a community can compel a dissenting minority to comply with a *takkanah* enacted by the majority, his overriding motives were logic and practical necessity. As Rabbenu Asher states, "Were it not so, the community would never agree on any subject, if individuals were able to revoke the consent of the majority," or, as he states elsewhere, "Were it not so, the community would never have any hope of real order, for when is the community ever of one mind?"[52]

Conversely, when it is necessary to revoke an existing *takkanah,* logic demands that the majority be free to do so. Thus, Rabbi Simeon ben Zemah Duran, the leading scholar of Algiers in the fifteenth century, states: "It is unreasonable to say that a single opinion can outweigh the opinion of many, forcing them to consent against their will . . . .for if this were so, the majority would be subject to the individual and might be compelled to act in a manner contrary to the law. This would be a surprising state of affairs."[53]

Another question that arose within the framework of the majority-minority issue is the following: in a court judgment, the minority must be present—they debate with one another[54]—during both the discussion and the decision. If only the majority is present, the decisions of the court are invalid. Were we to apply this ruling to communal decision, the minority, by purposely absenting themselves at the time of the vote, could thwart a decision accepted by the majority. However, the rabbis ruled that the decision of the majority is valid even if the minority is absent from the meeting:

> [The minority] brought it upon themselves, and they must, however reluctantly, accept the decision, for otherwise the maxim "By a majority you are to decide" would be meaningless. Those who object to the majority decision would set themselves apart and refrain from attending meetings and being present at voting, and thus be exempt from the ruling. Such a situation is clearly unacceptable.[55]

The solutions found to other questions of community law were similar. When Rabbi Joseph Colon, one of the foremost halakhic scholars in fifteenth-century Italy, sought to explain why a *qinyan* is not required in order to grant validity to a public agreement—in contradistinction to a private agreement, which is invalid without a *qinyan*—he stated the following: "An agreement made by the public follows in 'the path of pleasantness and all these are paths of peace.' Therefore it was said that the decisions of the public are valid when made in agreement and unity, and no one will be able to change his mind and disturb the confidence in, and peace of, the community."[56] This explanation is based on a *sevarah*—on Rabbi Joseph Colon's view of the meaning of "the paths of pleasantness."[57]

When Rabbi Isaac ben Sheshet Perfet (Ribash), a leading halakhic scholar both in Spain and Algiers towards the end of the fourteenth century, considered the problem of how to make the enactments of the community binding on those categories of people who, according to the fundamental principles of private law, could not be held legally responsible, such as minors, he did so using the following *sevarah*: "Minors must abide by existing enactments when they come of age, for otherwise the people of the city would have to reestablish their enactments daily as the minors came of age. This is unreasonable, hence the enactments are binding on all residents of the city."[58] This decision, too, is based not on any halakhic proof but rather on practical necessity, rooted in logic and reality: if the ruling were otherwise, enactments would have to be reenacted every time a minor came of age—a situation that would be both irrational and untenable. In such cases where the amount of taxes levied on an individual by the community was disputed, this same approach was adopted by Rabbi Solomon ben Aderet (Rashba) and by Rabbi Meir of Rothenburg. The individual who lodged the appeal was to pay the entire sum and would be reimbursed if and when the court decided in his favor. This view contradicts the basic principle that "He who demands payment has the burden of proof." Yet, although here it is the community that is demanding payment, this ruling regarding payment by the individual can be justified on the basis of logic: if the rabbis ruled in favor of the appellant, everyone would argue that he was exempt from payment of taxes, or had already paid his taxes and therefore taxes could never be collected; cheating would be encouraged, and the community would suffer.[59]

In this same way, the Maharashdam, previously quoted, solved one of the most difficult and troublesome problems—also of an outstanding social-communal nature—facing the halakhic scholars after the expulsion of the Jews from Spain. With the increase in the number of Marranos, as they began to return openly to Judaism in Turkey and elsewhere, the question arose as to the validity of legal transactions carried out by them before they returned to Judaism, as these transactions had not been made according to halakhic law—with a proper *qinyan,* witnesses, and so forth. This would have resulted in the reversal of all the business transactions that had been conducted over a period of several decades, and would have created chaos in the socioeconomic order of the Marrano community in particular, and the Jewish community in general. The Maharashdam, and others, decided that all transactions that had been carried out by the Marranos were valid, even after their return to Judaism. His argument is instructive:

> Otherwise the Marranos would be placed in an impossible situation, since those with whom they had done business would now protest that their obligations had been contracted according to the law of the land and not according to the law of the Torah and hence were invalid. This is clearly unreasonable. What is done is done: from now on, they will have to meet all the requirements of Jewish law.[60]

This was the approach of the great scholars when dealing with basic problems concerning the entire public. At the root of their decision lay the consideration of the public needs in general and not only those of the individual in question.

The framework, tools, and principles that served as the basis and the content of the power and authority of the Jewish community during a period of approximately seven hundred years represent one of the most striking phenomena in the history of the Jewish political tradition. The halakhic scholars and communal leaders established a framework for Jewish autonomy under alien sovereign rule, and developed a full range of halakhic norms in the sphere of Jewish public law which granted absolute power and authority to the new form of Jewish internal rule—the *kahal* or the federations of *kehillot.* This authority was even greater than that characteristic of the earlier forms of government under the King or *Nasi.* At the same time, the rabbis shaped, consolidated, and established this authority and granted it spiritual power through a system of regulations and restrictions, so that it would not become arbitrary and dictatorial, but would preserve the basic principles of justice and equity found in the *halakhah* and the *aggadah,* reflecting the spiritual character of Judaism.

## Its Significance Today

With the spread of the emancipation nearly two hundred years ago, the *kehillah,* as an autonomous Jewish entity, came to an end. Both external and internal factors contributed to this termination, but we shall not discuss them here. Owing to this change, which took almost two centuries to come about, we were overtaken by consequences both trying and distressing: this great creation in the spiritual and practical life of the Jews was lost, and its image distorted. Hence, we no longer have recourse—neither in practice nor in theory, neither for the sake of education nor for study—to the great values that were the fruit of that great era; and we make virtually no use of them for the consolidation or enrichment of our spiritual and practical life today.[61]

## Decisions of the Supreme Court and the Rabbinical Courts

Some halakhic cases in the realm of government and administration, from the time of the kehillah, have indeed found renewed practical use today through the decisions of the Supreme Court and the Rabbinical Courts in Israel. A few examples are cited here.[62]

In one case, a city employee was dismissed for improper conduct. The employee appealed to the Supreme Court, sitting as a High Court of Justice, to invalidate the dismissal, arguing that he was not given the opportunity to explain or to answer the charges made against him. The municipality, on the other hand, argued that, according to the existing law, it was under no obligation to grant the employee a hearing before dismissing him—and, indeed, the paragraph concerned so indicated. However, the Supreme Court accepted the employee's argument and invalidated his dismissal, quoting halakhic sources and basing its decision on the following three principles of Jewish law: (a) a person can be dismissed from a public position only if he commits an offense, and not on the basis of hearsay alone; (b) communal leaders are to be considered as judges, and hence they cannot make arbitrary decisions but must consider each matter individually; and (c) the communal leaders, who are regarded as judges, must act in accordance with the basic principles of judicial procedure: it is a fundamental halakhic rule that a person cannot be judged in his absence, and that the accused has the right to appear and to present his case.[63]

In another case, the Supreme Court ruled that a council member elected through a party list is free to express opinions that differ from those of the party he represents, as long as his action stems from serious considerations and not from irrelevant motives. A council member is regarded as a judge, and must base his decisions on his own discretion and understanding, "for he knows only that which his eyes can see."[64] On the basis of this same principle—that a person elected by the community is to be considered as a judge—the Supreme Court ruled that when the election committee appoints the chairmen of the polling committees, it must treat all citizens equally and must not discriminate against any citizen or group of citizens, relying on the power of the majority, for the chairman need not be a member of the majority in order to conduct fair elections; in fact, it is perhaps preferable that he represent the minority.[65]

Another interesting problem was brought before the Rabbinical District Court (acting as arbitrator) involving three political parties that stood for election to the municipal council under a joint list. The parties had made a written agreement that if only two out of the first three candidates on the list were elected, the second would resign in favor of the third. Indeed, as they feared, only two were elected, but the second candidate refused to resign. He argued before the Rabbinical Court that the agreement had no legal validity, for several reasons: the obligation to resign had been made before the elections took place, and was therefore invalid because it concerned a presumed future event ("a matter as yet nonexistent"); moreover, the agreement was invalid owing to the defect of *asmakhta* because it was based on the conviction—common to all candidates before election—that more than two would be elected and there would be no need for any resignation. Furthermore, it was argued, there had been no proper *qinyan* as required by Jewish law. The court rejected all these arguments, basing its decision on the responsa cited above, which indicates that any communal act is fully valid even if there is no *qinyan,* even if it involves such defects as a presumed future event, *asmakhta.*[66]

This decision was appealed in the Rabbinical High Court of Appeals. The appellant argued that the decision should not be based on the *halakhah* that states that communal acts do not require a *qinyan,* for this *halakhah* applies only to communal leaders—town leaders and representatives—whereas here the agreement was between political parties and their representatives and hence, like partnerships, it is subject to private law in which a *qinyan* and other provisions are required. The High Court rejected this argument and, in addition, made an important contribution to Jewish public law:

> If the *halakhah* is such that there is no need for a *qinyan* in communal affairs, and the community has such authority that the restrictions placed on individuals do not apply to it (such as the restrictions placed on presumed future events, *asmakhta,* etc.), there is nothing more clearly communal in nature than the case under consideration—the selection of the communal leaders.[67]

The Rabbinical High Court reaffirmed the decision of the Rabbinical District Court that the second representative must resign in accordance with the prior agreement, adding, in conclusion, the following significant remarks:

> In conclusion, we must add and say to the litigants that, as public servants, and when acting in this capacity, they should not argue that the obligations which they undertook are not binding because their validity can be disputed under law. Promises and obligations, especially in communal affairs, are holy and must be fulfilled to capacity, in accordance with their original intent, wording and spirit. Public servants shall not go back on their word and bring ruin on the public by insisting on the strict letter of the law.[68]

From the examples given, it is clear that the significance of the achievements of the halakhic scholars in the sphere of public law during the period of Jewish autonomy has retained its value for today's problems. There is, of course, an essential difference between the political sovereignty of Israel today and the internal rule of the medieval *kehillah* which lacked such sovereignty. But there is also an important similarity between the Jewish historical reality today and the historical reality in the heyday of the *kehillah.* Both are based on a conception of autonomy and sovereignty in which the people and the community, and not the king, or the single ruler, are central. Therefore, the issues and principles of Jewish public law that emerged during that era can also serve as a basis for the solution of problems arising out of the rebirth of Jewish sovereignty. The spirit and the force of these principles can help us continue to solve the many new problems that arise.

## Where are These Historical Realities to be
## Found in the Curricula of Studies?

This is precisely the problem. We have not as yet benefited from the creative process described above in the solution of the many and varied problems related to revived Jewish sovereignty, as a process that represents a further phase in the great legal-halakhic activity of Jewish autonomy in the *kehillah*. This fact stems from many factors, but principally from a lack of knowledge and awareness, which is, indeed, painful.[69] But what is more painful is the fact that not only has the legal-halakhic material that formed the power and authority of the *kehillah* failed to serve as a real source of creativity and inspiration for us today, but knowledge of this historical fact is disappearing, as though it had never existed, from the hearts and minds of the educators and their students. We feel compelled to pose the following simple but penetrating question: where is this historical reality to be found in the Jewish history curricula that determine what our children will learn? Is it not time that we placed these great periods of the Middle Ages in their full and proper historical perspective?

These were, of course, also difficult times, with pogroms, plagues, both black and white, crusades, and massacres. But these were not the outstanding features of this era. The central phenomenon was the life and creativity of the community and the individual within the framework of Jewish internal rule, based entirely on Jewish law, its principles and sources. This led to tremendous creativity in all areas of law—public and private—and in the various branches of the philosophy of law. Of course, life was not a bed of roses, and there were not a few negative incidents involving both individuals and the leadership as a whole, as has been noted above. But these were only a part of an almost "normal" reality, a reality that comprised both animation and social tension, reflecting life and not an abstract, theoretical study of the good versus the bad, the just versus the unjust. An accurate, objective description of the history of this great era can reveal to us and our young people a living, breathing community coming to grips with the problems of its time and overcoming them. Through such study and knowledge, our youth will become proud of its past, will become proud of the *galut* that has been so denigrated. It will become proud of the community whose scholars and courts, in the most adverse circumstances and despite continued persecution, maintained a social structure in which, while the majority ruled and the minority had to submit, the majority could not, and moreover was not entitled to, exploit this privilege in order to rob the minority of its basic rights.

This same youth will know not only what happened, or what could have happened, to Baruch of Mainz as related in the poem by Saul Tchernichovsky, but also, and more importantly, about Rabbi Baruch ben Samuel,[70] one of the judges of Mainz, who fiercely defended the right of a person not to pay taxes beyond his means, and transformed the Talmudic saying "The majority cannot be rogues" into a cornerstone of Jewish democratic theory. The majority, merely by virtue of the fact that it is a majority, cannot arbitrarily violate the basic rights of the minority. This was true not only in Mainz but in all the communities of the Jewish diaspora, and particularly in Spain, North Africa, Turkey, and the Balkan countries. Most of the legal-halakhic material that served as the basis of Jewish public-administrative law was found in the thousands of responsa of the rabbis of Spain and the Oriental countries, and it was they who stood at the head of its development and advancement. We should do well to bring before our children this spiritual, social, and practical reality that is part and parcel of medieval Jewish history.

Yehezkel Kaufman showed great perception in noting this in his book *Golah ve-Nechar*.[71]

> The common denominator between autonomy in the diaspora and in Eretz Israel was the desire to live according to Jewish law. Throughout the generations of exile, this desire served as the basis of Jewish autonomy. This desire, as we have seen, grew out of the ideal of living according to the Torah. Judaism, which recognizes only religious law, did not recognize pagan-secular law. An integral part of the desire to live according to the Torah was the desire to live according to the legal system laid down by the Torah. Hence, throughout the generations of exile, the Jews longed for legal autonomy. Legal self-rule was, in effect, what distinguished the Jewish community from a religious community and transformed it into a national-political entity. This recognition by the alien state of the right of the Jews to be judged according to their own legal system was of tremendous significance. First of all, as a result of this recognition, the Torah remained a kind of political constitution, even in the diaspora. The study of the Torah had great social value, its scholars were viewed as leaders, and the houses of learning were respected by the people. In addition, the Jewish community was recognized as a special political entity. Legal autonomy is what actually made the Jewish people in the diaspora a "state within a state."

## A Clarification of Relations between Religion and State

This reexamination of Jewish history in the diaspora and of Jewish law as it continued to be applied throughout the centuries has had a direct impact on the vast and complex network of relations between religion and state today. It is a fact that the movement of national renaissance could not have arisen, nor could it have endured and struck roots among the people, had it not been for the prayers and the longing of the Jews throughout all centuries for a future redemption, for Eretz Israel—the Land of Israel—and for Jerusalem, both the "physical" and "spiritual." The source of all these lay in the Torah and its commandments. This is true despite the fact that a number of the observant Jews and religious leaders refused to participate in the early stages of the Zionist movement. But it is also a historical fact that the Zionist movement arose within a Jewish reality which, for nearly a century, had not enjoyed any form of autonomy. Jewish autonomy had come to an end after the emancipation, when the Jewish community ceased to exist as a body ordering the lives of its members and was reduced in scope to become the Jewish community as we know it today, dealing with matters of man's relationship to God—centered around the synagogue and the rabbi—and with matters among men, centered around philanthropic, charitable, and communal aid institutions. The Jewish community lacked any autonomous character, and its public life was integrated into the life of the public at large. The Zionist movement, which aspired to Jewish independence, viewed the Jewish environment from which it arose as the negation of this basic object, and assumed this state of affairs to have been typical of the Jewish community throughout its existence in the diaspora. It therefore rooted itself in the early periods of Jewish independence and sovereignty in Eretz Israel, and all the generations that followed were presented in a negative light, characterized by persecution, pogroms, and massacres.

Perhaps, in order to do them justice, we should try to understand those who presented generations of Jewish history in this manner and who believed that what was required was revolution and conflict, which are inherent in, and lead to, radical change; but this rejection of entire periods of Jewish history led to dissociation from the past, to a lack of roots, to obliteration of earlier periods and creation of an interim almost totally void of belief in the Torah and *mitzvot*, and of a proper appreciation of the spiritual heritage of those generations. This reality had a strong impact on the religious Zionist movement. Religious Jewry did indeed preserve the continuity of Torah and *mitzvot* in relations between man and God. However, in the light of the post-emancipationist reality in which the observant Jews lived, a reality centered around prayer, the Sabbath, *kashrut;* the entire religious struggle within the Zionist movement was confined solely to these. The vast portion of halakhic life intrinsic to autonomous communal life—problems of majority versus minority, the freedom of the individual, ethics and law (not to mention halakhic jurisdiction and judicial systems)—was almost totally discarded as being irrelevant to contemporary conditions. This explains the startling fact that, throughout the period of religious Zionism, almost until the establishment of the State of Israel, virtually no thought was given and, in any case, no action was taken, to introduce Jewish law and jurisdiction in the pre-state Jewish community in Eretz Israel nor, in fact, after the establishment of the State. As a result, the confrontation between religion and state has been limited to the narrow sphere of family law and to the observance of the Sabbath and *kashrut,* as if *halakhah,* throughout its history, had had nothing to say on matters of law and justice, leaders and leadership, taxation and elections, basic rights and the freedom of the individual, possession and ownership, criminal responsibility and laws of torts, methods of punishment and the treatment of offenders, to mention only a few. This fact added significantly to the strained atmosphere surrounding the entire question of the proper relation between religion and state.

A practical consideration of social and ethical values in daily life would have had a tranquilizing and unifying effect on the various camps in Israeli society and would have imbued that society with the spirit of the Torah, thus helping to create mutual understanding on the many controversial issues. The law of the Jewish state and halakhic law come into contact only in matters of family law, the Sabbath, *kashrut,* and autopsies—matters in which there is an almost unlimited range of personal standpoints and in which everyone not only vehemently defends his own position but views it as something that is both inviolable and a matter of conscience. We can state with near certainty that there is a close relationship between this regrettable and distorted restriction of the contact between spiritual and social life in Israel and the limitation and distortion of the study of history and *halakhah* in the schools. The correction of these flaws in the field of education would have a salutary effect on social and communal life in Israel.[72]

# Notes

1.  Y. Baer, *"Ha-Hathalot ve-ha-Yesodot shel Irgun ha-Kehillot ha-Yehudiot be-Yemei ha-Benayim"* (The Beginnings and the Foundations of the Organization of the Jewish Communities in the Middle Ages), *Zion* 15 (1950): 1.
2.  *Tosefta Bava Mezia,* 11, 23; Babylonian Talmud, *Bava Batra* 8, 2. See Menachem Elon, *Jewish Law: History, Sources, Principles,* translated from the Hebrew by Bernard Auerbach and Melvin Sykes, (Philadelphia: Jewish Publication Society, 1994), vol. 2, p. 679 (hereafter *Jewish Law*).
3.  On this see *Jewish Law,* vol. 1, p. 36ff.
4.  B. Akzin, *Torat Ha-Mishtarim* (Jerusalem, 1968), p. 104.
5.  Ibid., pp. 104–105.
6.  *Piskei HaRosh, Bava Batra,* ch. 2, par. 11.
7.  For details see *Jewish Law,* vol. 2, pp. 682ff, 715ff.
8.  That is, in a contractual obligation, or when the obligation stems from the actions of another, such as the obligations of him who causes damage to recompense the injured party, see *Jewish Law,* vol. 2, p. 587.
9.  On the methods of creation in Jewish law, using these legal sources, see *Jewish Law,* vol. 1, pp. 228ff, 275ff; vol. 2.
10. See, for example, Responsa of Maharam of Rothenburg, cited in *Mordekhai, Bava Mezia,* 457–58.
11. See *Jewish Law,* vol. 2, p. 704, note 99.
12. *Tosefta Bava Mezia,* 11, 23; Babylonian Talmud, *Bava Batra,* 8, 2.
13. Maharam of Rothenburg, cited in the Responsa of Rabbi Judah Minz, 7.
14. Responsa of Rosh, Klal 6, par. 5 and 7.
15. *Tashbetz,* part 1, 123.
16. Responsa of Rashba, part 3, 411.
17. Responsa of Rashba, part 3, 417; part 7, 490.
18. *Tashbetz,* part 1, 133; compare with: *Tashbetz,* part 1,123.
19. Babylonian Talmud, *Moed Katan,* 16, 1. See Responsa of Rashba, part 3, 411, 417; part 7, 490; *Tashbetz,* part 1, 123.
20. Responsa of Rabbi Elijah Mizrahi, 53 (Jerusalem Darom edition, 1938, pp. 145–146).
21. Ibid., 57, p. 186.
22. Compare this with the view of Rabbi Menahem ben Solomon Meiri who believed that the approval of a "distinguished person" was required only for a *takkanah* enacted by tradesmen, but "the entire population of the town can issue ordinances without this approval, for they can revoke his appointment." (*Bet ha-Behirah, Bava Batra,* 9, 1). See also *Jewish Law,* vol. 2, p. 754 and note 283.
23. *Hazon Ish, Bava Batra,* par. 4, sub-par. 8. The author of *Hazon Ish* used similar reasoning to justify the authority of the trade unions over their members:

> The authority of craftsmen is comparable to that of townsmen, and just as townsmen have the authority of a court, so do the craftsmen have the authority of a court with respect to their fellow craftsmen. *Takkanot* enacted by them have the validity of the *takkanot* of a court, for according to these *takkanot* a man can obtain a lien on his fellow's property and can sell this property in order to receive what is due to him. There is no need for a *qinyan;* rather, the *takkanah* of the court serves in place of a *qinyan.* Thus, all craftsmen, acting together, have the same authority as townsmen. This may have been a *takkanah*

of the sages designed to grant the townsmen the authority of a court, and to grant all the members of a single trade the authority of a court.

And further on (sub-par. 10): "and if all the craftsmen agreed, their decision is as significant as a *takkanah* enacted by the entire community, which has the same power as a *takkanah* of the scholars of the generation over all of Israel."

24. On the extent of the parallel between the status of the communal leaders and that of the court, see the subsequent discussion and note 31. Another interesting argument, based on a *severah,* in favor of public, as opposed to private, agreement is to be found in the statement of Rabbi Joseph Colon (Maharik) quoted in connection with note 55.

25. Indeed, several of the sages also based the authority of the *kahal* on the similarity of this form of rule to that of the King or *Nasi.* See Elon, *Jewish Law,* vol. 1, p. 55ff., as well as *Hatam Sofer,* cited on p. 61, note 37 (Elon, *Jewish Law*). See also Elon, *Jewish Law,* vol. 2, p. 679, note 1, and p. 700, note 88.

26. See *Jewish Law,* vol. 2, p. 685ff; p. 700, note 88; pp. 715, 736–51.

27. Rabbi Elijah ben Hayyim, Responsa *Mayyim Amukim,* 63; *Jewish Law,* vol. 2, p. 704ff.

28. Responsa of Rashbash, 566, 112.

29. *ewish Law,* vol.2, p. 706. With regard to the concept of *asmakhta,* see *Jewish Law,* vol. 1, p. 301, note 51; *The Principles of Jewish Law* (ed. M. Elon, 1975), pp. 171–74. The power of the *kahal* was sometimes greater than that of the court—*Jewish Law,* vol. 2, p. 706, note 110. See also the subsequent discussion.

30. Rabbi Israel Isserlein, *Teruman ha-Deshen,* Pesakim u-Ketavim, 214.

31. *Shulhan Arukh, Hoshen Mishpat,* 37, 22, according to Rabbi Moses Isserles (Rema). Of course, the parallel between the elders of the *kahal* and the judges holds true only for those powers granted to them as leaders of the community. See *Jewish Law,* vol. 2, p. 703, note 97.

32. Responsa of Rashbash, 566. In this respect, the power of the *kahal* is greater than that of a court, for if a court errs in its assessment, its sale is void. For a detailed discussion, see *Jewish Law,* vol. 2, p. 706, note 110.

33. Responsa of Rashba, part 2, 279.

34. Responsa of Maharah, *Or Zarua,* 222.

35. This principle is cited in the Babylonian Talmud, *Bava Batra,* 100, 1, with regard to an entirely different matter: If a majority choose a site for a public road, their choice stands, because, in so doing, they rob someone of his property or rights, because they have no right of way over that land. Here the expression is used to signify that the majority is limited in its decision-making power in that it cannot infringe on the basic rights of the minority. See *Jewish Law,* vol., 2, p. 764, note 321.

36. Responsa of Rashba, part 5, 178.

37. Responsa of Rashba, part 3, 398.

38. Responsa of Maharam of Rothenburg, Prague, 106, etc.

39. Ibid.

40. Responsa of Rabbi Elijah Mizrahi, pp. 145–46.

41. See Proverbs 3:17; Responsa of Maharashdam, *Orakh Hayyim,* 37; *Hoshen Mishpat,* 421.

42. Responsa *Divrei Rivot,* 68; 224.

43. Responsa *Lehem Rav,* 2; also Responsa of Maharshah to Rabbi Solomon Ha-Kohen, part 2, 95; part 3, 76. It seems to have been commonly accepted that only those who paid some tax had the right to vote. See Responsa of Maharam of

Rothenburg, Berlin, 865, and the Responsum of Maharam cited in the Responsa of Rabbi Judah Minz, 7.

44. Rabbi Menachem Mendel Krochmal, Responsa *Zemah Zedek,* 2.

45. Mishnah, *Menahot,* 13, 11.

46. Babylonian Talmud, *Menahot,* 104, 2.

47. In Leviticus 2:1 it is written: "When a person [*nefesh*] presents an offering of meal to the Lord." The word *nefesh* (soul) does not appear with regard to the other sacrifices. See, for example, Leviticus 1:14: "If his offering to the Lord is a burnt offering of birds. . . ."

48. Compare this with the statement by Rabbi Joseph Trani (Responsa of Maharit, part 1, 69): "all those who pay taxes are equal—the rich man who gives of his wealth, and the poor man who gives of the little he possesses—for the poor man is as careful with his penny as the rich man is with his pound, because payment is according to the amount of money each possesses."

49. In the course of his argument, Rabbi Menachem Mendel Krochmal has difficulty in reconciling his conclusion with the statement of the Rosh (Responsa of Rosh, Klal 7, par. 3) that "If a community imposes an ordinance (ban) in fiscal matters, the "economic majority" rules. . . . .It is illogical that a simple majority composed of those who contribute only a small portion of the taxes should impose a ban on the wealthy." In order to reconcile his own conclusion with that of the Rosh, Rabbi Krochmal explained the opinion of the Rosh through a restrictive interpretation, similar to that of Rabbi Joshua Falk Katz (S'ema on the *Shulhan Arukh, Hoshen Mishpat,* 163, sub-par. 13):

> It may be said that the decision of the Rosh that the "economic majority" should rule applies only to those cases in which the majority of the people who contribute the smaller share of the money wish to enact ordinances against the will of the minority which contributes the greater part, but he did not state that the few wealthy men are to be considered a majority with the authority to impose ordinances on the majority of the community. It could also be that he believes both sides to be of equal weight in such cases and that they must come to a compromise among themselves on such matters. This requires further examination.

Therefore, Rabbi Menachem Mendel concludes that the majority must be composed of both an "economic majority" and a simple majority. The opinion of *"Hazon Ish"* is instructive. He, too, was surprised at the decision of the Rosh, and believed that a simple majority alone should rule. He says (*Hazon Ish, Bava Batra,* 5, 1, p. 154):

> If for the purposes of tax assessment, the community chose seven city elders and the majority of the community agreed upon these seven, and the wealthy members agreed upon seven different men, it appears that the decision of the majority of the community is to be accepted, and there can be no distinction between rich and poor, for they are all taxpayers . . . .and Rabbi Asher's argument that the poor cannot enact ordinances binding on the rich is invalid, for the poor would not base their decision on their own interests but rather on truth and justice in the public interest. If they are to be suspected of increasing the burden of the wealthy and lightening that of the poor, then, were the wealthy to have the power of majority, they, the wealthy, would be open to suspicion.

From this it follows that the statement of the Rosh does not refer to tax assessment, and his intention in this matter needs to be further examined.

See also the opinion of *"Hazon Ish"*, p. 154, explaining the view of Rabbi Israel Isserlein cited in *Terumat ha-Deshen*, 344.

50. Babylonian Talmud, *Hagigah*, 22, 1.
51. See *Jewish Law*, vol. 2, p. 987ff.
52. Responsa of the Rosh, 6, 5; 6, 7. See also the opinion of Rabbi Samuel De Medina (Responsa of Maharashdam, *Yoreh Deah*, 117) on the decision of the Rosh:
In my humble opinion, it seems that we can say that even the Rosh, who uses the Torah sentence "By a majority you are to decide," does not think that we are bound by the Torah to follow the majority in general public affairs but uses the sentence as an indication only: Since the Torah states that we should follow the majority in matters of precepts and Torah, it follows logically that in all matters in which there is a disagreement we should follow the majority.
53. *Tashbetz*, part 1, 123.
54. See *Mishnah Sanhedrin*, 5, 5.
55. Responsa *Lev Sameah* of Rabbi Abraham Aliggeri, *Hoshen Mishpat*, 5.
56. Responsa of Maharik, 179 (first response, Lemberg edition; Warsaw edition, no. 181). There, Maharik cites the verse (Proverbs 3:17) as follows: "The ways of God (*darkei ha-Shem*) [instead of 'her ways' (*darkeha*)—the ways of wisdom] are ways of pleasantness, and all her paths are peace." This is not a printing error, for the same text appears in the original edition of the Maharik, Venice, 5279 (1519).
57. See, for example, Maharashdam, *Orakh Hayyim*, 37, and *Hoshen Mishpat*, 421 (quoted above, referred to in note 41), which among other things, explains his view that the vote of a wealthy man carries more weight than that of a poor man, for otherwise "we would not be following the ways of pleasantness." Other sages, as we have seen above, do not agree with Maharashdam on the weight of a poor man's vote; we must assume that they disagreed in their interpretation of the expression "ways of pleasantness." Compare the opinion of Maharik with that of Rashbash, quoted above, referred to in note 32.
58. Responsa of Ribash, 399.
59. See above, referred to in note 37.
60. Responsa of Maharashdam, *Hoshen Mishpat*, 327. This was the rulng of Maharival, Maharit, and others. See M. Elon, *The Principles of Jewish Law* (Jerusalem, 1975), "Conflict of Laws," p. 717ff.
61. For a full-length discussion of this see *Jewish Law*, vol. 4, p. 1576ff.
62. Cited here are several examples of cases in which the principle adopted was that communal leaders are to be viewed as judges. Here are also judgments which rely on Jewish legal sources to establish other principles of administrative law. For example: on the right to plead one's case, see the judgments cited in the following note; on the administrative authority's obligation to give grounds for its decision and the citizen's right to have access to the files of the public authority, see H.C. (High Court of Justice), 142/70. *Shapira vs. The District Committee of the Bar Association, Jerusalem*, P.D. *(Piskei Din)* 25 (1), p. 325, pp. 333–35.
63. H.C., 290/65. *Altagar vs. the Mayor and the Municipality of Ramat-Gan*, P.D. 20(1), p. 29. In the judgment, among others, is cited (pp. 39–40) the opinion of Rabbi Moses Isserles, who wrote the *Mappah* on the *Shulhan Arukh* (Responsa of Rema, 108):

Therefore it is clear that we cannot judge a matter without hearing the argument of the accused, for the Bible (Deuteronomy 1:16) states: "Hear out your fellow men." And although this is a simple matter, we can also derive it from the ways of God, for all His acts are just and His ways are pleasant and His paths are peaceful. First he asked Adam: "Who told you that you are naked?" then He asked Cain: "Where is your brother Abel?"—in order to hear their arguments. So much the more so should this apply to simple men. Therefore our sages ruled: "I will go down and see" (Genesis 18:21) to teach the judges not to rule before they hear and understand, and from this we learn that even if it is clear to the judges that the defendant will be found guilty, they must listen to his arguments first.

See also H.C., 3/58, 9/58. *Berman vs. The Minister of the Interior,* P.D. 12, p. 1493, p. 1507; H.C., 295/72. *Bachar vs. the District Rabbinical Court of Rehovot,* P.D. 27(1), p. 568, pp. 572–73.

64. H.C., 24/66. *Malkah vs. Sari Levi,* P.D. 20(1), p. 651, p. 657.
65. II.C., 311/65. *Marziano vs. the Polling Committee-Local Council of Ofakim,* P.D. 19(3), p. 393, pp. 396–98.
66. File 1390/5726, *The Federation of Agudat Israel and Poalei Agudat Israel, Rehovot vs. NRP, Rehovot Branch,* P.D.R. (*Piskei Din Rabbaniim*), 6, p. 166.
67. Apeal/5727/96. *The National Religious Party in Rehovot vs. the Federation of Agudat Israel in Rehovot and the Federation of Poalei Agudat Israel in Rehovot,* P.D.R. 6, p. 173, p. 176. at the bottom of the page.
68. Ibid., p. 181.
69. See *Jewish Law,* vol. 4, p. 1588ff.
70. One of the three judges who signed the judgment in the Responsa of Maharah *Or Zarua,* 222, cited above, referred to in note 34.
71. *Golah ve-Nechar,* part 1, p. 518.
72. See *Jewish Law,* vol. 4, p. 1576ff, 1605ff. M. Elon, *"Mi-Baayot Ha-Halachah ve-ha-Mishpat be-Medinat Israel"* ("Problems of *Halakhah* and Law in the State of Israel"), Publications of the Society for the Study of the Jewish People in the Diaspora, under the auspices of the President of Israel, published by the Institute for Contemporary Jewry, The Hebrew University, Jerusalem, 1973, Series 6, No. 7, p. 9ff.; M. Elon, *"Baayot u-Megamot be-Yahasei Halakhah u-Medinah"* ("Problems and Trends in the Relationships between *Halakhah* and the State"), *Amudim* (publication of the religious kibbutzim), 1974, pp. 202–207, 256–64.

# 11

# Individual and Community in the Middle Ages: *Halakhic* Theory

*Gerald J. Blidstein*

The subject of the present discussion is the relation of the individual to the community in Jewish public law during the Middle Ages. What I would like to examine is the nature of the authority of the community over the individual, its sources and its limitations; and, from the point of view of the individual, what is the nature of his relationship to the community; what is the basis of his willingness to accept its rule; how does he view himself as part of the whole?

Our discussion of these basic issues will derive from halakhic, legal sources for, as Ullmann put it, "Law in the Middle Ages is one of the indispensable gateways to the recognition of governmental principles and ideology."[1] This is especially true if we wish to penetrate the Jewish *weltanschauung*.

Many of the sources that shed light on these questions deal with the problem of "majority vs. minority"—with the right of the majority of the community to impose its authority on the minority—while trying to define the limits of this authority and examine its origins. But the expression "minority vs. minority" is no more than a legal formula for defining the status of the *individual* within the community, as the individual invariably constitutes a minority.[2] And just as the term "minority" can be seen to denote the individual, so does the term "majority" denote the community, which, apart from any other authoritative basis (e.g., Torah scholarship), owes its authority to the fact that it is a community.

## A Constitutional Responsum

At this point, it is worthwhile stressing the interrelationship between two factors: (1) the presence of aristocratic-authoritative elements in communal government; and (2) the fact that even these elements functioned only by virtue of communal sanction. The medieval halachists therefore sought to legitimatize the authority of the *community,* with those benefitting directly from this being the elders of the community who required this support despite their status as scholars. It was only natural that the ideas expressed should consolidate communal government as such, regardless of the nature of the leadership in question. But this is only a one-dimensional presentation which (for reasons inherent in juridical problems) ignores the fact that neither the reality nor the theory were quite so arbitrary.

It appears that the Jewish community was characterized by a synthesis of aristocratic leadership and communal sovereignty, although this synthesis may not be easy to define. As early as the tenth century, Rabbi Meshullam ben Kalonymus granted the "leaders of the community" the prerogative of a court to appropriate money.[3] Rabbenu Gershom claims a similar right for the *kehillot,* that is to say, for the communal leaders appointed as *parnasim* of the community.[4] But although it is clear in both cases that the decisive fact is the dependence of the leader upon his constituents (from the legal point of view), the question of who, in fact, these leaders were, remains unanswered. It is reasonable to assume that they were not chosen from among the commonest of men; and although Rabbenu Gershom cites the Talmudic maxim, "Even the most worthless of men, once appointed chief, should be respected as the most eminent," it should not be forgotten that this *baraita* is quoted in the Talmud in order to establish the authority of Rabban Gamliel (!),[5] and that the Talmud knows very well who is worthy of being a leader and who is not. Rabbenu Gershom himself emphasizes the fact that what was new in his teaching was the granting of the right to appropriate money (and consequently to enact *takkanot*) not only to "important" courts but to any court set up by the community.[6] The question of the identity of the communal leadership also arises in the writings of Rashi. Rashi's attitude towards the community, as expressed in his rulings that "he who vows to exclude himself from the laws of the community is like he who breaks a law of the Torah," is well-known.[7] But it seems that we should note here (with M. Frank and S. Zeitlin[8]) that Rashi assumes that the leaders of the community were in fact its elders and scholars. Among the arguments he brings in support of the need to conform with communal *takkanot* is the verse: "Listen to the words of the wise (*hakhamim,* i.e., scholars)."[9] Moreover, Rashi states[10] that the communal leaders in his day were none other than "his [Rabbenu Gershom's] students who sustain the next generation"—and it is reasonable to assume that the "students" of Rabbenu Gershom were, in fact, themselves scholars. Nor is Rashi's choice of R. Gershom as signifying the communal leader *(parnas) par excellence* without significance. We do not know, on the other hand, the nature of the "important men of the city *(hashuvei ir)*" to whom Rashi grants the status of an "important court,"[11] a decision that strengthened the authority of the local community. Did their "importance" derive from their social standing alone, or perhaps from other, ethico-traditional characteristics? Rashi claims that they constitute an "important" court in their own community, "even if there are more important (leaders) elsewhere"; thus, leaders were identified by specific qualities by which they could be compared objectively with others (e.g., scholarship)[12] and not by their socio-political status alone.

It seems, then, that we should adopt the schema suggested by Agus: the community *(kahal)* ought to choose scholars to lead them, but the authority of the scholars in communal affairs stems from the sovereignty of the *kahal.*[13] The elders do in fact rule, but the authority by which they rule is actually the authority of the *kehillot,* for the authority of the leadership grows out of the community that grants it legitimacy.

A similar dynamic is revealed in the famous responsum of Rabbi Judah Ha-Cohen and Rabbi Eliezer ha-Gadol (eleventh century), a responsum that establishes at length and in detail the authority of the community in various spheres.[14] On the right of the members of the community to refuse to abide by the *takkanot* enacted by their "elders," they wrote:

It is a general rule that lesser men obey their elders[15] in all that they may decree, and certainly when they were silent and accepted the decrees of their elders, they cannot later protest: but even had they cried out, their outcry would come to nought, for their elders are greater than they. And if you say that the lesser men are more numerous than their elders and therefore refuse to obey them—since they were silent at the time and did not refuse to comply with the decree nor protest against it, they cannot do so now. Although the lesser men are more numerous than the greater, they should obey those who are older and wiser than they, for we have seen . . . that God treated the elders with respect.

Thus, in the case before them, the authors of the responsum argued that the members of the community had no right to refuse to obey their leaders, for although they constituted a majority, they had agreed to the *takkanah* at the time it was enacted; indeed, this was only proper, for the common men should accept the authority of those who are wiser than they. However, the wording used in the responsum seems to imply that had the "lesser" men, who constitute the majority, refused to accept the opinion of their leaders from the outset—an act that undoubtedly runs counter to the desired attitude towards the elders of the community—such refusal would have prevented the implementation of the *takkanah*.[16] The text does indeed oscillate back and forth, but the final impression is that it is the community itself that has the final say in the implementation of a *takkanah* (as the *baraita* states: "Public affairs are conducted only on condition that the majority of the community accepts the decisions made"[17])—although it is only "proper" that the community should accept the decisions of its elders.

Up until this point, this is a theory that balances the authority of the community with that of its leaders. But the question was put to the rabbis in a particular social context, or more precisely, on the basis of a deviation from the accepted norm. The appellants noted that, until the incident that had led to dissension, the "lesser" members of the small community had accepted the authority of the "elders," and "had never protested against any of their *takkanot* but rather accepted them." The communal leaders now ask:

When we issue a decree, are we to ask each and every one if he agrees with our decision? And if we do not ask and he remains silent and does not protest, can someone then say that the decree was issued without his knowledge and, as he was not asked, will not comply with it (even though he did not protest either at the time the decree was issued or afterwards)?

This then, is the context of the discussion on the right of the majority to oppose their elders, and it becomes apparent that the elders generally did as they wished, while the community accepted their decisions. Theoretically, authority was based on the will of the community but, in fact, the "elders" governed them. Only now do we ask: what is the proper relationship between the leaders of the community and its members who grant them their authority, and to what extent can the leaders assume that the silence of the community signifies consent?[18]

## Sources of Communal Authority

Granting broad powers to the community and its representatives called for a conceptual-juridical development of the sources available to the rabbis, a step that was also necessary in order to meet the exigencies of time and place. The rabbis of the Middle Ages seem to have utilized two basic approaches in their efforts to increase the authority of the community.

The first approach grants authority to the community without bothering to explain or substantiate it. Rabbi Judah Ha-Cohen and Rabbi Eliezer Ha-Gadol (who adopted this method) do indeed declare that "every Jew must compel his neighbor to follow truth and justice and the laws of God," but they do not use this principle, which emphasizes the responsibility of every man for his fellow, as a source for the authority of the majority, and there is no organic link between this statement and the subsequent argument.[19] For, in the discussion that follows, they found it sufficient to demonstrate that the community's right to impose its authority on the individual members is a *biblical fact*. The evidence for this extends from the covenant made on the plains of Moab to the ban issued by Joshua at Jericho, the ban issued by Saul, and the decree issued by the tribes of Israel after the incident of the concubine in Gibeah, cases in which those who had not agreed to the decree (see Deuteronomy 29:18, and the story of the people of Jabesh-Gilead) or had not even known of it (Jonathan) were found guilty or condemned.[20] These cases serve as proof of the community's authority right down the line, including the right to appropriate money and to inflict punishment. What the rabbis added in their responsa, then, was the fact that these powers, which had been granted in the Bible to central figures or bodies fulfilling national functions, were now granted to a local community over its constituents.[21] Here, Rabbi Judah and Rabbi Eliezer base their opinion on the *baraita,* which authorizes the "citizens" to stipulate measurements and rates,[22] seeing this as a basis for broad legislative action in civic matters. But they did not feel themselves obliged to demonstrate *from* where the citizens derived such authority—and the implication is that it is derived from the authority of the community, to which the Torah and the Prophets bear witness. Moreover, the *baraita* is cited only in order to establish the right of the local community to enact laws in matters of optional behavior; this implies that in matters of religious duty *(mitzvah),* the local community possesses the same right as the entire biblical collective, a fact that requires no proof.

The community—even the local community—is a virtual reservoir of power: Jewish history and law attest to this. Is this power based on consent, on a moral-legal principle? Perhaps the fact that the authors of the responsa do not argue that the majority bound the minority by the covenant at Sinai hints at the legal-moral basis of the Torah—that the authors of the responsa wanted to imply that the covenant was in fact accepted by each and every person. But if this hint is inherent in the argument, it cannot outweigh the national-historical element. The overwhelming evidence, therefore, is *biblical* not only with regard to the proof cited by the rabbis above,[23] but also with regard to the basis of their argument. The Bible does not clearly distinguish between the different elements of the covenant idea—legal-moral on the one hand, and religious-existential on the other. This organic synthesis is repeated in this exposition of the authority of the community, which can perhaps be thought of as a "charismatic community."[24]

The second approach to communal authority is based on a clustering of ideas around the concept and the institution of the *bet din* (court).[25] However, we should be wary of the wholesale and comprehensive use of this term which, in its original meaning, denoted a special arm of the social organism.

There are a number of sources that grant the "heads" of the community, its leaders, the status of a *bet din* with the right to appropriate money—both in order to carry out punishments and to enact *takkanot.*[26] The former principle (using the power of the *bet din* to appropriate money as a tool for imposing fines) is easier to establish, for Talmudic law grants every *bet din* the right to confiscate property. There are nevertheless two new elements here:

1. The Talmud authorizes the *bet din* to confiscate property as punishment for contempt of court,[27] but judgment in civil cases is based on its legal authority to condemn or acquit. Therefore, the cancellation of the official authorization of judges (or its absence in Babylonia) had already caused a major crisis in the Talmudic period, and the sages in Babylonia and the Gaonim who succeeded them tried to fill this gap in order that the courts might nonetheless pass judgment.[28] The present solution broadened the scope of the power of the *bet din* to confiscate property. From a tool designed to uphold the honor of the *bet din* itself, it was transformed into one that could be used for the application of judgments,[29] or even for settling disputes between people.[30]

2. The leaders of the community are to be viewed as a *bet din.* Talmudic law does indeed allow for the authorization of "unordained" judges to act as "agents" of their predecessors, and, more importantly—it grants legal authority to a *bet din* composed of laymen when these laymen are accepted by those under their jurisdiction.[31] Formally speaking, there is perhaps no significant difference between an appointment of this kind and the ordainment of a communal leader to serve as a judge over his fellow citizens. But, in their discussion of this matter, the rabbis of the Middle Ages make no use whatsoever of the sources dealing with the appointment of laymen as judges, and the tone that they adopt is totally different from that which would be used in the appointment of laymen. A *bet din* made up of laymen is clearly limited from the outset and is dependent upon the consent of each and every person under its jurisdiction; the public law established by the rabbis of the Middle Ages did not follow along these lines.[32]

In all likelihood, then, authorizing the leaders of the community to judge by virtue of the principle of confiscation *(hefker bet din)* heralds and reflects the second step—the use of this principle to sanction the enactment of *takkanot* by the local institutions. In Talmudic law, the power to enact laws is granted only to a national, central *bet din,* a body that can be assumed to have been composed of men with appropriate qualifications.[33] Here, for the first time (and this step was taken as early as the Gaonic period when the elders of the community were authorized to enact *takkanot* for the members of their community), this authority was applied to a local, municipal institution. Much research has been done on the authority of the *kehillah* as expressed in the responsa of the great rabbis of Germany and France in the tenth and eleventh centuries. In effect, their major aim was to justify the right of a local body to enact laws,[34] where the identity of this body is not altogether clear—the important members of the community, its *parnasim,* or a *bet din*—and where this institution derives its authority from its relation to the community at large. Therefore, we will now turn to the community, the *kehillah* as legislator.

What is the theoretical basis of this evolution? L. Finkelstein argued, some fifty years ago, that the documents of the tenth and eleventh centuries reveal that the authority of the leading members of the community was derived from the community itself.[35] This argument was extended by I. Agus to include the idea that the Ashkenazic community termed itself a *bet din*—that is, a body that has the right to judge and obligate its members—and, for this purpose, the community transferred its authority to its representatives-leaders. S. Albeck makes a similar claim for the Sephardic community of the same period.[36] Actually, a community that in fact functions as a court is a rare phenomenon. We can indeed find cases in which the community is considered a sovereign entity, but the status of a *bet din* is usually reserved only for its leaders—and it is generally the leaders who inflict punishment and enact laws. This holds true in the responsa of Rabbenu Gershom, Rabbi Meshullam, and Rashi. But the idea is at times implied; and an idea that is implied even more strongly is that the right of the leaders to serve as a *bet din* derives from the authority of the community which empowers its leaders.[37] It is possible to speak of the community as court on two levels—the juridical and the legislative. For the juridical, Agus has already pointed to the custom whereby a man who feels that some wrong has been done him may interrupt the service and address the congregation—an institution that is derived from the concept that the community is required to pass judgment on its members.[38] Evidence that this was indeed related to the concept of legal jurisdiction can be found in the anonymous response that states that "this custom is not known" in Babylonia. *"For there the community does not have control over law and justice; rather, this power is granted to the courts."*[39] From this we can infer that the Gaonim in Babylonia thought that the Ashkenazic community viewed itself as a legal body. Recently, on the basis of a case in a Sicilian court (1020), which was presented as "a case which was put before us, the community of Sarcossa, sitting as a court," S. D. Goitein has inferred that the institution of a community sitting as Ashkenaz as well.[40]

Certainly, "interrupting the prayers" signifies more than an appeal to public opinion. But it does not necessarily imply that the community so addressed functioned as a court. The community saw itself as responsible for justice, and as the creator and sustainer of the court appointed to determine what was just in each particular case.

Albeck does indeed maintain, as regards the Spanish communities before the mid-thirteenth century, that the elders or *community itself* passed verdicts in the absence of an established court; but his citations indicate the opposite, for we read therein of "elders of the community," "students of the yeshivah," or "court."[41] Nor ought we to be surprised—societies generally deposit the judicial task with a specialized group, and do not (except in cases of emergency) act themselves as courts. There is no need, therefore, to claim that the community is a "court" (except in cases such as the Sicilian village cited above) in order to discover in it a necessary link in the process of justice, for it is the community that appoints those men possessing the qualifications thought necessary (by the community itself!) to act as its judges.

Did the idea that the community serves as a *bet din* meet with any opposition? Were there rabbis who explicitly refused to recognize the community's status as a *bet din*? The answer to this question will, of course, shed light on the opposition to the idea and its conceptual sources, but also on the extent and scope of its dissemination. We find that Rabbi Joseph Ibn Migash (1077–1141) denies the community the right (which is granted to certain *batei din*) to inflict punishments that go beyond those prescribed by normative *halakhah* because "the community cannot be compared in such cases to an 'established' judge."[42]

R. Joseph's correspondent did, it would appear, think that the community could function as court vis-à-vis its members, but R. Joseph disagreed. His opinion is brief and general; R. Joseph might even agree that the community could function as a court in more modest and standard procedures.[43] In any case, this exchange does indeed indicate a claim that the community does possess broad juridical powers, and the opposition to this idea in twelfth-century Spain.

With regard to the legislative level, the authority of the community expresses itself, primarily, in its ability to enact *takkanot* and in the assertion that *takkanot* be endorsed by the entire community. We have seen in the responsum of R. Judah Ha-Cohen and his colleagues, and will see again in the discussion by *Rabiah* of the "consent of the townspeople" (*ma'amad benei ha-'ir*) that it is no easy matter to define this "endorsement." Albeck shows, indeed, that R. Isaac Al-fasi and R. Me'ir HaLevi Abulafia do stress active participation of the entire community, and both Albeck and Agus note the grounding of the community's right to legislate on the court's right to expropriate property. We shall see in what follows that this analogy to a court—even when the entire community, and not its leadership is compared to a court—was not always understood (as by Rashba, thirteenth century, for instance) simplistically.

In any case, it is important to note the central role of the elders and the leadership even in the Sephardic documents treated by Albeck. It is true, perhaps, that halakhic theory sees the community legislating with the consent of its leadership. But the semantic structures reveal a more varied reality: sources emanating from R. Al-fasi and R. Me'ir Abulafia do describe the community as legislating with the consent of its leaders, but the documents collected by R. Judah Al-Barzeloni describe the leaders as legislating with the agreement of the community: "we the elders and heads of the community . . . joined with all the members of our community . . . and decided in the presence of the entire community" and so on.[44]

## The Community as Court

For reasons inherent in the nature of medieval Judaism, centered as it is around the Talmud, it was natural that the Jewish community should prefer to be integrated on an institutional basis within some religious structure or, alternatively, to identify itself with a central-historical authority. Therefore, it preferred to base its right to enact *takkanot* on a concept such as "confiscation by the court" and to anchor it in the biblical sources of this institution that are to be found in the books of Joshua and Ezra and Nehemiah—rather than on those rights granted in the Talmud to "citizens" (the right "to stipulate measurements, rates, and wages").[45] On the contrary, in the writings of the Makiri family, we can already detect an attempt to base the Talmudic authority of the "citizens" on the concept of "confiscation by the court"[46]—and this not only because the status of "citizens" (from a legal point of view) is one of partnership, a structure lacking broad scope and powers. What was more important was that this concept was not deeply rooted in Talmudic Judaism; it is not a Jewish value, and does not bestow an authority based on the values and mission of Judaism. To be a "citizen" is not a Jewish (but rather a Hellenistic) ideal. Thus, many rabbis treated this concept as a secondary tradition, an institution that must seek appropriate axiological support.

It seems to me that this holds true as well for Rabbi Judah ha-Kohen and Rabbi Eliezer ha-Gadol despite the fact that they based their opinion on the *baraita* which sets forth the rights of "citizens." They cite this *baraita* only after a long, comprehensive list of references to biblical sources that grant authority to the community, surrounding it with a charismatic-ethical halo. Only then do they turn to the problem of "authority in such matters as taxation and other *takkanot* which the community itself issues," where they find the solution in the "citizen" model. Thus, the stress is placed on the authoritative value of the community—a value *expressed* in the people's rights as "citizens" but not *derived* from it. In saying that the members of the community should not be disqualified from enacting *takkanot* dealing with one of its members for fear of "ill-feeling and rivalry, as this restriction applied only to a *bet din*," the authors of the responsa do not intend to equate the status of the community with that of partnership.[47] It seems more likely that they wished to recognized the community as a focus of authority (after all, the object was to broaden the powers of the community, not to deny it the status of a *bet din*) without imposing upon it any particular model, with the limitations any model entails.

There are other examples of cases in which powers that were not granted to the *bet din* were granted to the community—for example, the right to appropriate money and to determine responsibility without being subject to the rule that "the burden of proof rests with the claimant."[48] On the other hand, the community can at times profit from a parallel to the *bet din*. However, this parallel is not always exact and it appears that the comparison of a community to a *bet din* was primarily used as an analogy and as a precedent for deviating from the norms that govern the actions of the individual.[49]

The use of analogy is particularly striking in the writings of the Rashba. He wrote:[50] "Each community, in its own locality, can be compared to the Gaonim when they issued *takkanot* which applied to all of Israel"; "The majority in every city is to the individuals within it as the high court is to all of Israel"; "The relationship between them and their fellow citizens can be compared to that between all Israel and the high court or the king." It should be noted that, in these examples, the Rashba does not confine himself to the argument that every community is equivalent to a *bet din*: in each case, he identifies the community with a different central focus of power—the Gaonim, the high court, the king.[51] The Rashba was certainly aware of the fact that an ordinary court did not have the right, according to Talmudic law, to issue *takkanot,* and he therefore did not use this analogy. But neither did he maintain that the community functions as a high court *per se.* This is an indication of the fact that what was important to him was the authoritative status of the institution, a status that in each case required a central authority; hence, he chose the high court and the king as examples. The Rashba would undoubtedly agree that there are not insignificant differences between the laws enacted by the high court and those issued by the king—but what was important to him was their common denominator, namely, the authority to legislate.

The problematics entailed by the description of the community as court are reflected in yet another area. Are communal enactments in fact considered enactments of a court? This question has important implications for the process of enacting a *takkanah,* but even more for the process of revoking one. This topic is discussed, in one fashion or another, from gaonic times on. It appears—as Finkelstein has pointed out—that communal enactments are described, in this context, on the basis of two distinct models: the model of the vow, and the model of the court-enactment. It may well be that different concepts of community underlie the use of these two models. Yet even where the "court" model is used, the major intent may be to assert that rules deemed fair and responsible for a court (such as: "all matters decided by vote must be revoked by vote," "one does not enact legislation that the majority of the community cannot abide by") will also control legislation and decision making by a community.[52]

## Representation

The idea that the *bet din* is a representative body of the community was, perhaps, not an innovation of the rabbis of the late Middle Ages, although it was only then that this view was given explicit expression. There are many historians who view the Sanhedrin of the Second Temple period as a representative body in the broadest sense of the term.[53] This is not merely a sociological datum. The Sanhedrin was in effect considered "the eyes of the community," and, from a purely halachic point of view, the community was required to offer sacrifices for a Sanhedrin that had erred in its decisions.[54] Maimonides wrote that: "The high court . . . is the community of Israel as a whole."[55] The statement that the *bet din* "conducts public affairs only on condition that the majority of the community accepts its decisions" is similar in meaning.[56] It has been argued that the concept "confiscation by the court" is derived from the view that personal property belongs to the collective as a whole, which therefore has the right to expropriate such property through the proper organs.[57] It has also been claimed that the "seven city elders" *(tovei ha'ir)* represent their fellow citizens—they do not rule over them.[58] It is interesting that Rav, one of the *amoraim,* suggests that the principle "the sender is responsible for his agent's actions" (the Talmudic norm that provides the basis for representation) is derived from the division of the land of Israel by the heads of the tribes[59] (an act that is cited as proof of the principle *"hefker bet din hefker"*—confiscations made by the court are valid"!).[60] According to Rav, the head of the tribe served as its delegate. This idea was indeed rejected in the course of the Talmudic discussion, but appears with slight modification in Rashi's commentary on the Bible.[61] Maimonides (the Rambam) was familiar with a similar idea,[62] and Nahmanides (the Ramban) explicitly stated that "the *bet din* takes the place of the community."[63] But only in the sixteenth century was this idea fully formulated and discussed:

> This was the power which was granted to the high court in Jerusalem and to every court in every generation . . . because the high court in every generation is recognized by all members of that generation . . . and it is for this reason that they were granted the power to issue decrees and ordinances. And although it was not explicitly chosen and no specific conditions were agreed upon, it is a fact that everyone recognized it . . . and although someone may object, it is as if he explicitly gave his consent and then changed his mind.[64]

However, we should be careful not to oversimplify the concept of representation. This concept admits considerable complexity, and it is reasonable to assume that this was true in the case of the *kehillah.* We have already seen that the important members of the community served as its leaders—and its representatives. There is no contradiction between the idea of representation and the desire of the constituents to choose as their representatives only men of a certain caliber. This approach was particularly characteristic of the Middle Ages, when even monarchs claimed that they sat on the throne by the grace of both their subjects and God. A delegate must represent the "real" interests of his constituency, and not everyone is capable of doing this.[65] Even the communes, which equalized the status of all citizens, appointed their leaders only from certain strata of the population.[66]

This reference to the monarchic ideology of the Middle Ages should also serve as a warning to us. We must not forget that the king's claim that he represented his people, that he sat on the throne with their consent, was a double-edged sword. It can imply that the authority of the king is derived from his subjects, who can dismiss him at will— and this approach has had its proponents. But the idea of representation can serve an opposite purpose as well, in which the monarchic party maintains that, as the king is, in fact, the embodiment of his people, his will is their will.[67] Kern has already suggested that it was precisely the Roman legal model, according to which the citizens chose their emperor, that gave rise to the absolute rule of the late medieval period. As a well-known *midrash* states, "Moses is Israel . . . the leader of the generation is the whole generation"; and Rashi adds, "For the *nasi* is all."[68] The idea of representation is interpreted in the real world, and it is in this context that it must be examined. Do the people reserve the final say, the casting vote for themselves? Or can the "representative" leaders act without any regard for the will of their constituency because the collective identity has been transferred irrevocably to them and is expressed by them alone? Several sources that raise this question have already been cited.[69]

## The Organic Community

One of the problems involved in granting such authority to the community is that of community attendance at the enactment of a *takkanah*. Is someone who was absent at the time subject to the majority decision? Were this the case, there would be a clear loophole in communal rule, as anyone who desired to be exempt from a particular *takkanah* with which he did not agree could simply absent himself at the time of its enactment and thus release himself from the obligation to abide by it. A common solution to this problem is to assume that failure to appear signifies tacit designation of those present to serve as representatives of those absent, since the latter, in so doing, forfeit the right to voice their opinion on the matter at hand.[70] However, the halachic problem is more complex than appears from this short summary.

The medieval *takkanah* comprised, in effect, two elements: (a) the *takkanah* itself, which either required or prohibited a certain action; (b) the ban or curse placed on those who refused to comply with the *takkanah*.[71] These two elements are closely related—both sociologically and conceptually. Let it suffice to note that the well-known Talmudic maxim that "No decree should be imposed upon a community unless the majority can comply with it" is based on the verse: "Ye are cursed with the curse, yet ye rob Me, even this whole nation" (Malachi 3:9), which Rashi explains (in the light of the medieval enactments?) as follows: "You accept these rules with curses and imprecations." In the framework of Jewish public law in the Middle Ages, the ban was understood as an oath made by the community and each individual within it that they would comply with the *takkanah,* incurring the prescribed punishment if they failed to do so.[72] Thus, if we take into consideration the oath-like nature of the ban, the following question arises: Can a ban be imposed on someone who opposes the *takkanah* or who was not present at the time of the decree? For we are now no longer dealing with a norm applied to an individual as a member of a particular community, with a norm that requires a specific act; here we are dealing with the taking of an oath, that is to say, we are attributing to an individual a voluntary decision, a mental state, that does not exist. The fact that the majority did make such a decision is, of course, irrelevant here. The Talmud does indeed empower the court to compel someone who has been excommunicated to take an oath, as Maimonides notes: "The judge should administer an oath to him against his will that he will not or has not done so."[73] But his statement is not sufficient in the present context for two major reasons: first, it speaks of an oath imposed on a man who had already been found guilty of an offense; and second, it was a court that imposed the ban. These two conditions are lacking here, where the rabbis of the Middle Ages chose to use the ban in a different manner, imposing it on a guiltless community as security for the observance of a *takkanah*.[74] In light of this, we can understand Maimonides' ruling that a ban imposed by the community does not apply to those who did not actually accept it.[75]

We can trace the discussion of this question by referring to a number of sources: the responsum of Rabbi Judah ha-Kohen (eleventh century), the writings of Rashi, the responsum of Rabbi Eliezer ben Joel ha-Levi of Bonn (Rabiah, twelfth century), and Ramban's treatise (thirteenth century) on the laws governing the ban in general. In the early Ashkenazic responsum, the question of the ban-as-oath was not seen as particularly problematic. On the contrary, the biblical passages cited in support of the inclusion of the individual within the community deal, in fact, with curses and bans that the community imposed upon itself as security for the carrying out of a particular decree, thus serving as proof that the individual cannot "dissociate himself from the community." The right of the majority to "administer an oath" is its primary right, from which follow, in order of decreasing significance, the right to appropriate money and to set restrictions of all kinds. The emphasis thus placed on the right to administer oaths clearly testifies to its importance since the possession of this right was seen as sufficient to confer more limited rights (and also points to the direct biblical reference to this problem).[76] But there is no discussion here of the special nature of the ban and the oath, as opposed to the *takkanah* or the decree.

Rashi did not deal with the specific issues raised by the *herem* (as distinct from the *takkanah* itself), but he did address himself to the broader problematics. He thought, on the one hand, that no individual might exempt himself from the enactments of the community, and that a vow to this purpose was void; it is likely that the same would apply to the *herem*. But, on the other hand, Rashi inferred from "those who make enactments and from their custom that they do not intend to punish the unwary (violators) who do not know of the decree, but rather curse whoever knows of the enactment and rejects it."[77] He who rejects the *herem* is under the curse, not he who is ignorant of it. It is possible that this decisive statement is directed against an opposing opinion, an opinion held by those so fearful of the power of the *herem* (or so desirous to utilize it) that they felt it obtained even upon the unwary. Be this as it may, Rashi's ethical-legal theory is clear: no Jew may evade communal enactments deliberately, but he who is ignorant of them is not to be penalized by the ban.

Later centuries see a more explicit discussion of our topic. The question is specifically raised, first, by Rabiah.[78] He was aware of the special problematic nature of imposing a ban on an entire community, for the laws governing a ban are the same as those governing an oath, namely: "Anyone who responds 'amen' to an oath is considered to have pronounced the oath himself,"[79] whence we may infer that an oath is binding only upon the consent of he who takes the oath. Here Rabiah raises, in halakhic terms, the issue of the right of the individual to oppose the community under the special conditions created by the ban. However, he accepts the earlier opinion of Rabbi Judah ha-Kohen, including its biblical basis, relying on cases in which the community imposed a ban or an oath on individuals: "Even if they do not find it satisfactory and do not know of it—it still applies to them."[80] Therefore, Rabiah has no choice but to infer that the community has the right not only to enact *takkanot*, which are binding on its members, but even to bind them by oath against their will. He does find a solution for the problem of individual consent, but this solution is no more than a formal one: the consent of the individual is required in order to exact a sacrifice from him, but an oath is valid even without such consent. This formal solution (which has its roots in early Ashkenazic tradition[81]) nevertheless has far-reaching implications from a conceptual point of view.[82]

Ramban,[83] on the other hand, integrated this phenomenon into his general treatment of *herem* in all its aspects. It ought be said, by way of introduction, that Ramban is particularly sensitive to the *distinction* between a normal oath and the *herem,* for the purpose of his work is to explain how a community is allowed to revoke an enactment accompanied by herem, though ordinary vows are not so easily revoked.[84] The solution of Ramban (and here he follows in the footsteps of others, such as R. Abraham b. David of Posquieres) involves a distinction between a *herem,* which is considered the act of a court that derives its authority from the community and can therefore be revoked by that same communal institution, and a vow.

In effect, Ramban accepts the importance of the biblical tradition on this issue and even reinforces it. In addition to the verses quoted by Rabbi Judah ha-Kohen, the Ramban adds further evidence from the Torah; the verse "No human being who has been proscribed can be ransomed: he shall be put to death" was interpreted as referring to communal bans, and authorized the proscriber (when he is "a king of Israel or the Sanhedrin in the presence of the majority of Israel") to put the transgressor to death. Ramban thus provided a biblical source to support this general norm which allows the death penalty to be imposed on someone who violates the will of the community and its leaders.[85] But what was more important was the combining of the biblical tradition with the categories of public law: "but when the *bet din* makes such a pronouncement on a man, that is to say, when they say anyone who does such and such will be proscribed, we did not derive this from the Torah of Moses until this was revealed to us by the prophets."

> The ban is like the vow and the curse mentioned in the tractate *Mo'ed Katan,* and has an element of severity which is absent in oaths, in that he who is adjured by another but did not respond "amen" is not bound by a spoken oath, but in the case of the ban, although he did not accept it and was not even present at the time it was decreed, because the *bet din* has the right to impose a ban, as it is written, "I will adjure them and curse them in God's name," the ban applies to him and he is forbidden to violate the decree, just as if he had pronounced the oath himself. And this rule applies to the citizen of a town if all or a majority of them agreed in the presence of the town elders to impose a ban on someone. Since they have the right to enforce decrees and to pronounce bans in this matter, their ban is binding upon all those who must follow their laws, and if anyone violates these laws, thus violating the ban, he is as one who has broken an oath, and the ban applies to his entire person, including his trees and stones . . . and he should be ostracized from his fellow townsmen who must treat him as one who is excommunicated and avoid him. They must see that he should not derive benefit from their property . . . and he who is banned must refrain from those things that are forbidden to he who is placed under a ban . . . and not derive benefit from the property of those who have proscribed him. And it was said that a ban cannot be declared when there are less than ten men for they constitute neither a community nor a court serving in place of a community and they do not have the power to impose a ban but can only require each person separately to take a spoken oath.
>
>   And if it was a king of Israel or a Sanhedrin sitting before a majority of Israel, he who violates the ban deserves death and the king or Sanhedrin has the right to put him to death by whatever method they choose, and this is the ruling of Joshua who judged Achan. . . . And with regard to spoken bans, we find the example of Saul who said "Jonathan shall die" and that of Israel in the days of the concubine at Gibeah when they killed the people of Jabesh Gilead, for it is written: "For they had made a great oath concerning him that came not up to the Lord to Mizpeh, saying, he shall surely be put to death" and it has been taught in the name of Rabbi Akiva: was an oath taken there? But in order to teach us that a ban is an oath and an oath is a ban, we learn that the people of Jabesh Gilead did not go up and therefore incurred the death penalty. . . . Four differences were found between the ban and the oath or the vow: the ban need not be pronounced by each individual, it is binding even against one's will and in one's absence, and he who violates it must separate himself from the community as prescribed by the laws of excommunication and even beyond that.[86]

As for the content of the ban, it seems that Ramban identifies two stages: (1) the vow to uphold the *takkanah;* (2) the undertaking to suffer excommunication, expressing dissociation from the community, as punishment for having separated oneself from the community and its *takkanot*. The death penalty imposed on one who violates a national ban may, in fact, reflect his dissociation from the nation as a whole to the point of physical annihilation.[87] But the individual, for his part, must also behave as one who has been isolated and ostracized, for the concept of excommunication is based on the consent— both internalized and actualized—of he who is thus excluded from society. His acceptance of the ban includes an agreement to behave in the prescribed manner.

Here we return to our original question, which was posed by Ramban as well: what gives the community the right to impose a ban, which is like an oath in nature, on an individual and this even against his will and in his absence? The biblical evidence does indeed show that this was the case in practice but does not explain or justify it.

It seems that the crucial sentence here is: "But in the case of a ban, even if he did not accept it . . . [it is binding] because the *bet din* has the right to impose a ban."[88] What the Ramban meant to say, first and foremost, was undoubtedly that the right of the citizens of a town to impose a ban is meaningless if it is dependent upon the consent of the very person who is himself to be placed under a ban. But Ramban most likely meant to use this argument in the broadest sense, hinting that this question should be dealt with within the framework of the laws governing oaths in general. It thus becomes clear that an individual cannot in all cases refuse to accept an oath imposed on him. A *bet din* (or an individual in the presence of a *bet din*) may impose an oath on a witness concerning testimony or deposits, even if the witness refuses to take the oath, and then charge him with violating this oath.[89] From this we can infer that someone who is required to take an oath cannot evade it, even if he does not agree with it. This applies to the ban as well (the *gaonim* may perhaps[90] have already drawn an analogy between the laws governing oaths and those governing bans imposed by a *bet din*); since the *bet din* is entitled to administer oaths and enact *takkanot,* no individual can argue that the oath is not binding upon him simply because he does not agree to it, and this even though Ramban admits that communal *herem* differs from an oath.

However, we are still dealing with sources and formulae. The essence of the ban, and of the right of the community to impose the ban on its members, is revealed in several conditions and definitions that the Ramban appends to his statement. He declares that "A ban cannot be declared where there are less than ten men for they do not constitute a community or a *bet din* serving in place of the community."[91] This implies that the ban can only be imposed by a community, and a *bet din* that imposes a ban does so only by virtue of the fact that it represents the community. And even the Sanhedrin (and apparently the king as well) imposes a ban only "in the presence of the majority of Israel."[92] It seems that the reason for this lies in the fact that the ban signifies a threat to dissociate the offender from the community (as the Ramban often states) and, therefore, only the community has the right to impose a ban. The right to lift a ban imposed by a king or Sanhedrin is reserved for "all," that is, for the entire nation.[93] The Ramban goes so far as to require[94] that the ban be imposed on the entire community. "But a *bet din* or community that declares: "we swear that no (specified) individual shall do such and such"—that individual is not bound except with his consent; this implies that that which binds the individual is the fact that he constitutes a part of that community which imposes the ban on itself as a community. The broadly ethical thrust of this notion, which prevents the community from selective use of the *herem* against specified individuals, is also clear.

It thus emerges that the ban is imposed on someone who refuses to accept it by virtue not only of the legal right of the community and its institutions, but also of the organic participation of the individual in the community. And, as in all organic theories, the individual submits himself to the general will.[95] In this context, it can almost be said that an individual who refuses to be included in the ban has already dissociated himself from the community and, paradoxically, in so doing, brings the full weight of the ban to bear upon himself. It therefore appears that the Ramban would also include under the ban someone who was not present at the time it was decreed (as his membership in the community does not depend on physical presence at any single moment), even if he was not aware of it. Nevertheless, it seems reasonable to assume that no one would be found guilty of violating the ban if he did so unwittingly, that is to say, if he was not informed of the existence of the *takkanah* and of the ban reinforcing it. For, according to the Ramban, the people "rescued" Jonathan from death having violated his father's ban, arguing that he had eaten of the honey unwittingly.[96] These last arguments are important not only with regard to the theory of the ban, but also in that they establish legislative procedures for the community and relate to the discussion of the real relationship between the elders of the city, for example, and its citizens.

In this context, it is worthwhile to note the discussion—although I will not be able to go into it in depth here—that developed around the concept "the elders of the city in the presence of the citizens" during the Middle Ages, and to list several important phenomena.[97] The concept appears in the Talmud with regard to public property and the cancellation of its sacred status; inferences are then drawn to decisions that concern the entire community, even if the case in point involves *private* property. (The gap between the two is not necessarily that large: since each individual is a partner in public property in Jewish law, its disposition by the majority implies the right to dispose of private property, too.) The term *ma'amad* seems to imply that the elders of the city acted in the presence of the citizens.[98] Rabiah interprets this as meaning that they acted with the knowledge of the citizens—and this need not have been positive knowledge; it was sufficient that they should have had an opportunity for possessing such knowledge, that is, that the elders did not behave secretively. Rabiah will infer that there are elected leaders, but that there are also such who are not elected but whose decisions are legitimated by their acceptance by the townspeople, who always possess the right to object. To translate this position into contemporary terminology, we would speak of community participation through the accountability of its leadership, a theory that is considered elitist.[99] Yet these safeguards should not be dismissed lightly, particularly in view of the difficult period in which these leaders functioned, and the need for effective and firm leadership. Whatever the nature of the hermeneutic applied to this Talmudic source, it is clear that the medieval sages found therein one of the few sources for descriptions of the partnership of leadership and the public in conducting the affairs of the community.

Rabiah also argued that it were enough if a majority of the community supported its leaders for their decisions to be considered to have been taken in the "presence of the townspeople." The status of the majority is given further expression in the phrase "the majority is like the whole."[100] On the surface, this is no more than a quotation from the Talmudic passage[101] that establishes the link between the biblical verse "Ye are cursed with the curse. Even this *whole* nation" and the concept of "a decree which the *majority* of the community can obey" by saying: "The majority is like the whole.[102] But it seems that, here, this phrase was given an additional and stronger meaning—for the sages of the Middle Ages were not merely trying to substantiate the Talmudic interpretation (and the expression is not used in the Talmud to explain the fact that a *bet din* decides according to the majority view). The saying (and it is now translated into Hebrew) is used to establish the right of the majority of a community to impose their opinions and decisions on the minority, where the whole and the majority are viewed as identical. Thus, there is no place for a minority as such in the public organism.

A straight line can be drawn connecting the biblical *edah* in which the individual realized his existence to the fullest, the Tannaic *zibbur* which "did not die"[103] and which appeared primarily in the sacred realm,[104] and the midrashic *knesset israel* which personified the entire nation in all generations. The innovation of the *kehillah* lay in the fact that a small and partial community inherited the cloak of charisma that had previously been worn by the Sanhedrin, the king, and the people of Israel as a whole. Similarly the ban, too, regained its biblical significance in the period of the *gaonim;* it was transformed from a means of implementing a verdict to a means of incorporating the individual into a community in such a way that he is bound by its laws—only now the ban was imposed by the local community. As in the biblical period, the legitimacy of the ban grew out of the organic position of the individual within the whole. It is interesting that Rashi, in denying the individual the right to release himself by an earlier oath from the ban of the community, argues that "he was already under oath at Mt. Sinai";[105] that is to say, the primary loyalty, from which the community draws its power and which cancels that of the individual, is the loyalty to the historical, national covenant at Sinai. Does he mean to say that the covenant at Sinai not only bound the nation to God but also each member of the nation to one another?

Yitzhak Baer has already dealt at length with the organic-corporative elements in the popular-legendary perception of the city-community in the Talmud. He has even suggested that the *kehillah* of the Middle Ages inherited this perception and was founded on this basis.[106] The *kehillah* did indeed flourish in medieval Europe, but it is my guess that its rise was based in the legal treatments, at least) not on the corporative elements, which, according to Baer, inhered in the institution of the "townspeople" but on the comparison of the *kehillah* to other authoritative institutions of the Jewish people, namely, the

Sanhedrin, the king, and the *gaonim*. I would go so far as to argue that these institutions were not merely models for an ethical-legalistic analogy. The *kehillah* had to fall back on them because they—and not the local community—possessed the power to legislate in the Talmudic period; and this power goes hand in hand with the charismatic forces that are present in the consciousness of the nation. In the last analysis, the *kehillah* does not seek to view itself as a society of partners but as a *kehillah kadoshah* (holy community), an organic unit within the Jewish people that can assure its members a place in the world to come: *knesset israel.*

It should be noted that the success of the *kehillah* was not the result of a struggle against its sages. To the contrary, the responsa and *takkanot* of the rabbis empowered the community to run its affairs. Of course, we must not regard these sources naively—much of their content deals with the social-religious elite. But they also speak of the rule of the majority. The picture that emerges is very different from that of Christian society divided between the church and the secular authorities. The Jewish sources echo a faith in the legitimacy of the Jewish polity, an urge to be integrated within it, an organic fusion of sages and folk. It is likely that this situation is rooted in the deepest levels of Jewish reality, and is not merely a sociological phenomenon.

### R. Tam: The Limited Community

Let us now turn to the minimalistic approach to this question, which we can define simply as that of Rabbenu Tam.[107] But here the discussion becomes much more speculative; not only is the available material limited from a quantitative point of view, but it is difficult to determine the scope and the spheres within which Rabbenu Tam sought to apply his views.

Rabbenu Tam[108] argued that the power of the community over its members was limited—at least in secular matters. The citizens of a town constitute only a partnership[109]—they do not represent a *bet din* with the power to appropriate money and enact *takkanot*. The fact that a group constitutes a majority does not grant it authority: "Even if ninety-nine say thus and one says otherwise . . . we heed the one who spoke in accordance with the law."[110] The *baraita* stating that "Citizens have the right to establish measurements and rates and wages and to enforce them" deals, according to Rabbenu Tam, with cases in which all members of the community had already unanimously agreed to fix a particular rate or price: only then does the community have the right to enforce a decision that is contested—that is to say, to compel the individual to comply with a decision to which he was a party. Rabbenu Tam is indeed prepared to grant the majority the authority to legislate on "public needs," but this category was limited to the needs of the entire community, such as a city wall or a Torah scroll—excluding fixing of prices (as not everyone buys a particular product) and even the collection of charity (as not all are poor).

As for the freedom of the individual to act contrary to public needs, it appears that here, too, Rabbenu Tam did not recognize the authority of the community over the individual merely by virtue of its status as a majority. He wrote: "The citizens of a town do not have the power to compel one of their fellows to do as they wish"; the individual need not subject his will to theirs. He sometimes expresses this approach in an interesting manner. For example, "Rabbenu Tam says[111]: If a nobleman imposed a tax or contribution on the citizens of a town and some of them fled and were therefore exempt, those who remain cannot force those who fled to pay the tax together with them." Morally, one could argue that they should all bear the burden together, as they all share the same lot and are members of the same community, and everyone who evades payment increases the burden on his neighbor. Here we are reminded of the censures leveled against anyone who does not participate in misfortunes of the community. But Rabbenu Tam ruled otherwise: if an individual succeeded in escaping, his responsibility ends there. Those who remain must bear the burden. Rabbenu Tam only exempts, it is true, those who escape *post facto;* he does not state that the individual may do so *a priori.* Nevertheless, this ruling does shed light on his attitude towards the relationship between the individual and the community.

It may also be that Rabbenu Tam's stand on the issue of individual vs. community stems in part from the feeling that a community made up of ordinary men is not worthy of government. Government, in effect, implies the right to decide on matters of law and justice, and a community as such does not possess the necessary scholarly attributes; its rule would be based merely on its status as a majority. But this is no more than a legal formula for power, and lacks any moral-ethical weight. The denial of power as the basis for rule is perhaps expressed by Rabbenu Tam in another case—in his refusal to grant any Jewish government (whether in Eretz Israel or in the diaspora) any authority on the basis of the principle *"dina demalkhuta dina"*—the law of the land is the law. His reasoning was: "The kings of Israel and the kings of the House of David cannot steal." In so ruling, he indicated that in ruling that "the law of the king is law," "the sages appropriated money. . . . for the public good," that is, they legalized robbery where foreign kings were concerned (with certain limitations, of course). Such authority, however, was not granted to the kings of Israel.[112]

It is not clear whether Rabbenu Tam recognized the representative option that allows the communal leadership to act effectively in both decision making and execution while preserving (to a certain degree) the principle that the entire community must agree to fiscal *takkanot*.[113] In fact, this option virtually nullifies the importance of Rabbenu Tam's approach and would only require that the elders be elected unanimously. It is interesting that the students of Rabbenu Tam, who quote the teachings of their master, do not suggest this option. On the other hand, the *takkanot* issued by Rabbenu Tam grant certain powers to "the elders of the city,"[114] and it is clear that he expected the community to function on the administrative plane—and it is hard to imagine that the entire community could have been responsible for this day-to-day activity.[115]

The general impression that emerges, then, is that Rabbenu Tam did not grant the majority the right to rule over the minority. As many have already pointed out, Rabbenu Tam viewed the local community as a partnership of many individuals.[116] The community does not constitute an entity entitled to powers that reflect a special legal status, and is certainly not a charismatic authority. The Talmudic sources that describe the actions of the "cities" are rooted, from a literary point of view, in the framework of partnership;[117] and this fact has conceptual significance as well. However, the question remains: was Rabbenu Tam prepared to relinquish the social stability that would be lacking in a community solely dependent upon trust and reciprocity?

## R. Tam: Individual Rights, or Rabbinic Authority

Finkelstein[118] has suggested that Rabbenu Tam aspired to establish a central rabbinic authority in Western Europe. Rabbenu Tam wrote, "The citizens of a town do not have the authority to force one of their fellows to do as they wish. And, as for the principle *'hefker bet din hefker,'* only a court such as that of Rabbi Ammi and Rabbi Assi is suitable for appropriating money."[119] *Takkanot* (in fiscal matters) can be enacted only on the basis of *"hefker bet din,"* and this right is therefore granted to a *bet din* and not to the citizens of a town—and only to a *bet din* of the status of Rabbi Assi and Rabbi Ammi, "for there were none greater than they in their generation." From this last statement, we can infer that the high court of a generation—and the high court alone—has the right to enact *takkanot*.[120]

However, it is hard to imagine that the affairs of every community could be conducted by a single central authority. It seems that Rabbenu Tam's view on this question underwent a certain evolution. At first, he felt (as reported by Rabbi Asher in the thirteenth century)[121] that "The *prosbul* (a legal formula whereby a creditor could still claim debts after the Sabbatical year, despite biblical injunction against doing so) should not be used today, for we are not as expert as Rabbi Ammi and Rabbi Assi"; but Rabbenu Tam later relented and he himself wrote a *prosbul,* "for he said that the only requirement was that it be written by an important court of the generation." However, his *Sefer ha-Yashar* (Book of Righteousness) indicates that Rabbenu Tam believed every *bet din,* "even if it is not the high court in its generation," has the right to write a *prosbul* and only laymen were considered unfit to do so.[122] Perhaps we can see a development from Rabbenu Tam's earlier view that no *bet din* could function as a high court to his later view that every local *bet din* has the right to function in fiscal matters pertaining to its local residents. What is important here is the disqualification of "laymen." Rabbenu Tam also distinguishes in the matter of judicial authority between "judges appointed by the local residents" who, collectively, hold the titles of *bet va'ad* (committee) and *"arkaot"* (court of law), and "laymen" who serve as judges with the consent of the local residents.[123]

In fact, then, Rabbenu Tam offers an alternative to government by the local community—the authority of the local rabbis as opposed to the laymen. It is interesting that Rabbenu Tam issued his own *takkanot* together with his colleagues, "the sages of the Rhineland and the rabbis of Paris . . . and the sages of Milan . . . the great ones of our generation"; there is no mention here of the fact that *kehillot* have the right to enact *takkanot*. He cites "Rabbenu Shelomo" (Rashi) as the enactor of *takkanot* ascribed by others to "the residents of Troyes and the surrounding communities."[125] He introduces his own *takkanot* with the phrase "And the law is the true law"; we are dealing here with a directive and not with a covenant. If this assumption is correct, we have found that Rabbenu Tam did indeed offer an alternative to the rule of the local community—the leadership of the sages. They are authorized to conduct the affairs of the community, or at least to issue *takkanot* that are binding upon it. In light of this assumption, we can now reevaluate Rabbenu Tam's position on the individual and his rights. He does indeed protect the rights of the individual, but it now becomes apparent that this protection is not absolute. What is of primary importance is that the authority to rule over the individual—and such authority does exist—be given to the proper body.[126]

Therefore, Rabbenu Tam was prepared to compromise on the pragmatic level, so long as he remained faithful to his conceptual structure. According to one tradition, Rabbenu Tam agreed that the citizens of a town had the right to compel the individual members to comply with "a takkanah of the town."[127] This concept was interpreted by him in a very limited sense, as he excluded from it charity, the fixing of rates, and so forth; it appears then that he defined "a *takkanah* of the town" as including only those essential matters that concerned all the citizens equally. Here Rabbenu Tam was obliged to accept the authority of the community, for the Mishnah had already ruled that "He is forced to build a wall and doors and bolts for the city." Recourse to the authority of the citizens is acceptable to Rabbenu Tam for the individual is being forced to comply with the community decision only in those matters specifically mentioned in the Talmud; that is, the community is merely carrying out a decision already made in the Torah. Therefore, remaining true to his stated position Rabbenu Tam does not grant the community authority beyond that granted in the Talmud.

Where does this approach, emphasizing the polarity of the community and its scholars in matters of government, originate? And, in posing this question, I am referring to imminent factors in Jewish history. It seems that we should recall the dual nature of the views expressed by a considerable number of Rabbenu Tam's predecessors. On the one hand, they authorized the *kahal* to act and to legislate. On the other, it becomes apparent that those who fulfilled these functions were, in fact, the sages. This authority, then, was complex, growing out of both the community and the Torah. Rabbenu Tam, as the heir of this ambivalent tradition, saw the Torah and not the community as a reliable source of authority, and he drew the logical conclusions as to the positions of leadership. And, if we accept Baer's statement, this can be seen as a return to the Talmudic model. For Baer has argued that the institutions based on the "citizen" model were not recognized by the sages of the Talmud. This fact, as we have already surmised, reflects the tendency towards central authority, a tendency that has a moral-ethical aspect; that is, the central authority draws on a super-social existence and commands by virtue of this power. But the "citizens" remained fixed in the bedrock of human society. If we recall that Rabbenu Tam denies the community even the authority to subject the individual members to its will, we will realize that he (as an interested party!) did not simply advocate the rule of the religious scholars, but argued that only this leadership could serve as a guarantee for the protection of the rights of the individual against the power of the majority.

## Notes

My thanks to Sarah Lederhendler for her translation of a most difficult manuscript.

1. W. Ullmann, *Law and Politics in the Middle Ages* (Cambridge University Press, 1975), p. 28. Y. Baer pointed out the parallels between medieval Jewish legal thought and Roman and Germanic patterns in his seminal "The Bases and Origins of Medieval Jewish Communal Organization," (Heb.) *Zion* 15 (1950): 1–41. It might also be useful to examine patterns of village organization and behavior; cf. W. Ault, "Village By-Laws by Common Consent," *Speculum* 29 (1954): 378–94. Ault collects information testifying to the importance of common consent in village decision making, but also notes the problems involved in giving an exact definition to the terms and descriptions conveying "common consent." Similar problems may exist in our sources.

2. Special awareness of this point was displayed by S. Albeck, "Sources of the Authority of the Kehillot in Spain until R. Me'ir Abulafia (1180–1244)," *Zion* 25, no. 2 (1960): pp. 85–121; S. Morell, "The Constitutional Limits of Communal Government in Rabbinic Law," *Jewish Social Studies* 33, nos. 2–3 (July 1971): 87–119. The discussion was of course opened by I. A. Agus, *R. Meir of Rothenburg* (Philadelphia, 1947); Agus argues throughout that in examining the halakhic sources, attention should be given to their political significance.

3. *Teshuvot Ge'onim Kadmonim,* par. 125. See note 29 below.

4. *Responsa of Rabbenu Gershom Me'or ha-Golah,* edited by S. Eidelberg, no. 7, pp. 154–58.

5. Rosh ha-Shanah, 25b. Note, in any case, the use of this *sugyah* in circles deriving from Rashi in *Sefer Rashi* (Jerusalem 1957), p. 362.

6. See nn. 21, 34.

7. *Responsa of Rashi,* edited by Elfenbein, no. 247, pp. 288–89. This notion is also attributed to R. Yehuda'i Gaon; cf. Hagahot Maimoniyyot to Laws of Oaths, chap. 1, n. 2; R. Moses of Coucey, *Semag,* Negatives, 238, 69a. Whatever the

authenticity of this attribution, it may be pointed out that the use of an oath to avoid accountability to a court is already known in gaonic times: see the responsum of R. Hay in *Geonic Responsa,* edited by Harkaby, no. 180; *Ginzei Schechter,* vol. 2, pp. 62, 462.

8.  M. Frank, *The Kehillot of Ashkenaz and their Courts* (Heb.) (Tel-Aviv, 1938), pp. 1–19; S. Zeitlin, "Rashi and the Rabbinate," *Jewish Quarterly Review* 31 (1940–41): 36ff.

9.  *Responsa of Rashi;* but compare mss. cited by editor. In a similar case Rashi believed that one should not take an oath against a communal decree, for, in so doing, "they would be taking an oath to transgress the commandment and not obey the laws of the Jewish religion which require them to heed their elders who set limits and restrictions" (*Responsa of Rashi,* par. 70, pp. 83–84), but an "elder" is not necessarily more than a leader. In any case, we learn that the *takkanot* of the community owe their authority to the authority of its elders.

10. *Responsa of Rashi,* no. 70, p. 84. As regards the assertion that the students of R. Gershom lead their generation, it ought to be noted that the context is one of revoking a ban *(heter niddui),* a privilege reserved for scholars; the significance of this statement for our purposes is of course minimized thereby. Rashi had also stated that all men "of the dispersion of Ashkenaz" are the disciples of R. Gershom's disciples" (*Responsa of Rashi,* p. 83), but that does not completely nullify the significance of our passage.

11. *Responsa of Rashi,* no. 238, p. 266; and cf. A. Grossman, "The Attitude of the Early Sages of Ashkenaz to the Community" (Heb.), *Annual of Jewish Law* 2 (1975): 189–90.

12. Cf. Rashi Ketubot 103b, s.v. *ha-hu: hashuv* as a comparative term designating superior wisdom.

13. Agus (note 25 below), pp. 202–3, 210. Zeitlin (note 8 above, pp. 43, 58) already made an attempt to reach a formula that would reflect this interrelationship.

14. The responsa is quoted in *Kol-Bo,* sec. 142. The date (eleventh century) is according to Agus. Baer ("Bases") has disputed this date, arguing that the responsa was written in the thirteenth century. Recently, Grossman ("Attitude," pp. 181–87) reaffirmed Agus' opinion. See Agus (note 2 above), pp 71–83; "Democracy in the Communities of the Early Middle Ages," *Jewish Quarterly Review* 43 (1952): 153–76). We can also trace the penetration of concepts used in this responsa over the centuries; see notes 18, 80 below.

15. The expression appears in Rosh Ha-Shanah 25b; also in the statement of R. Joshua B. Levi and Rabbi Isaac, Deut. Rabbah 1,10; see also the opinion of Rabbi Isaac, Shabbat 119b. The Talmudic sources will be discussed elsewhere.

16. My approach here is close to that of Morell (note 2 above), p. 96, n. 76. Compare this with Agus, *R. Meir,* pp. 82–83.

17. Tosefta Sanhedrin, 2, 13. See note 56 below.

18. Compare this with Agus (note 2 above), p. 73, n. 89. This problem—which can reveal a great deal about the real political situation in the *Kehillot*—arises on many occasions. See note 69 below, and nn. 97–99. It almost sounds as though these respondents knew of Rabiah!

19. This statement does indeed play an important role in this responsum because, "If the citizens of a town transgress the commandments of the Torah, the citizens of another town may compel them and ban them in order to correct them. And they cannot say that 'we live in our town and you in yours,' but rather all of Israel must compel them."

20. Deuteronomy 29:13–20; Joshua 6:17; I Samuel 14:24–44; Judges 21:10.

21. Indeed, Agus argues (note 2 above, pp. 79–80) that the authors of the responsa emphasize the role of the community in such cases and not the role of the leader.

22. "The citizens may stipulate measurements and rates and wages and may enforce them."—Bava Batra 8b.

23. See Agus (note 14 above), pp. 163–65.

24. This expression, whose source escapes me, is used in a number of discussions on the special significance of the society or nation in certain religions: see, for example, W. M. Watt, *Islam and the Integration of Society* (Northwestern University Press, 1961), pp 54–63; A. Lichtenstein, "Brother Daniel . . ." *Judaism* 12, no. 3 (Summer 1963): 270.

25. See Agus (note 2 above), pp. 60–61, p. 65, n. 53, and p. 91; M. Elon, *Jewish Law* (Hebrew) (Jerusalem, 1973), vol. 2, p. 569ff; A. Grossman, "Attitude," pp. 177–78; I. Agus, *The Heroic Age of Franco-German Jewry* (New York, 1969), pp. 203–205. A. Nahlon, "The Body that Enacts *Takkanot* According to the Tashbetz," *Annual of the Institute for Research in Jewish Law* (Hebrew) 1 (1974): 161 n. 89, finds that the perception of the *kahal* as a high court is already present in the responsa of Rav Sar Shalom Gaon (ninth century). We should also add the statement of Rabbi Judah ha-Kohen: "The citizens of the other town may compel them . . . for we found . . . that those who sat in the Stone Hall [the Sanhedrin] compel them and judge them." What then is the significance of this parallel? Does it imply identity? (Cf. below, at nn. 50–52.) Rabbi Judah ha-Kohen's statement seems to imply that the high court functions in order to carry out the responsibility that in fact rests on "all of Israel" (see note 19 above), that is, as the representatives of the community; cf. n. 62 below.

26. Rabbi Meshullam ben Kalonymus, tenth century *(Teshuvot Gaonim Kadmonim,* no. 125); Rabbenu Gershom; Rashi; Rabbi Hananiah, tenth century *(Sha'arei Zedek* 4, 4, 4, 16) and others.

27. Moed Katan 17a. On the different uses made of the principle *hefker bet din,* see G. Blidstein, "Notes on *Hefker Ben Din . . .* " *Dinei Yisrael,* vol. 4 (Tel-Aviv, 973), pp. 35–50.

28. See, for example, the Talmudic passages Baba Kamma 84a-b, Sanhedrin 2b on the efforts of the *gaonim* in this matter, see B. M. Lewin, *Ozar ha-Gaonim,* Bava Kamma, part 1, pp. 56–60; H. Tiktinski, *Takkanot ha-Gaonim,* pp. 70–74.

29. The Gaonim did indeed use the ban in order to subdue the defendant and appease the plaintiff (cf. Bava Kamma 15b), but this is still only a ban, and not the direct appropriation of money. See J. Mann, *Jewish Quarterly Review* 10 (1920): 357–58; A. Aptowitzer, *I.Q.R.* 4 (1913): 46–7. Agus notes in *Urban Civilization in Pre-Crusade Europe* (Leiden, 1965), vol. 2, p. 425 that, according to the responsa of Rabbi Meshullam, the individual had the right to appeal a verdict pronounced by the communal leaders, and might even succeed (in this case only partially) in his appeal.

30. From the responsa in T.G.K. (n. 26 above) we learn of a "fixed fine" for injuries; the responsum cited by L. Ginzberg, *Ginzei Schechter,* vol. 2, p. 274, speaks of a payment of "10 dinar for every injury, according to what is written in your *takkanah,*" and this, too, seems to refer to the responsa of Rabbi Meshullam. Despite the delicate situation involved in judging cases of physical injury, (see n. 28 above), there seems to have been a tendency to fix penalties in such cases. See the *baraita* in Bava Kamma 27b, providing a different list of punishments from that which appears in the Mishnah, the same *baraita* is cited in the Palestinian

Talmud, Bava Kamma 8:6 in the name of "Rav Karni" (Karna), and this is therefore a Babylonian *takkanah*. Later, Rabbi Asher (Rosh) noted that the loss of official authorization did not prevent the sages of the generation from fixing and collecting fines: Rosh on Gittin, chap.4, par. 41. See also n. 44 above. R. Tam also fixed fines; cf. Finkelstein, pp. 177, 194. See also the comment of R. Hayyim Hefez-Zallav, *Responsa of R. Meir of Rottenberg* (Prague), no. 383; Mann (n. 29 above), and Baer, "Bases," p. 32, n. 13.

31. Bava Kamma 84b; Gittin 88b; Sanhedrin 24a-b, etc.

32. In other cases, the Talmudic concepts continued to fill the vacuum, but this is not the place to examine this phenomenon. However, compare with Finkelstein (n. 35 below), pp. 8–9, who sees the *"bet din* of laymen" as the model for authority in the *kehillot* of the Middle Ages.

33. Talmudic *takkanot* are generally assumed to be national in scope. In some cases it is specified that a sage instituted a *takkanah* (or a practice—*hinhig)* in (and for) his locality; see, e.g., Sanhedrin 19a, Sukkah 55a, Rosh HaShanah 34a, p. Bezah 61c, p. Shekalim 46a. These enactments may be treated (by Maimonides for example) as normative for all, probably by virtue of their inclusion in the Talmud. Tosafot (Gittin 36b, s.v. *'elah,* end) acknowledge (characteristically?) that various sages did enact local *takkanot.* In effect, the *minhag* (custom) served as a local *takkanah (minhag ma-makom)* in Talmudic times, and the significance of this point should not be overlooked; for in a *minhag* the center of gravity is shifted to the consent and practice of the local population (whatever the point of origin of the *minhag* in question), as we find is the case with the medieval local *takkanah.* See the interesting comments of W. Ullmann, *Individual and Society in the Middle Ages* (Johns Hopkins, 1966), pp. 59–61. I believe that the local *takkanah* is mentioned in Maimonides' *Mishneh Torah* only in the introduction (edited by Y. Cohen, Jerusalem, 1964), lines 116–21, which deals with a post-Talmudic court (or sage) that enacts *takkanot* for the local population; something that is called for in the context as a whole. (Incidentally, Rambam's comments there imply that a *takkanah* of a local court which spreads throughout "all of Israel" is equivalent to a *takkanah* enacted by a high court; acceptance by the nation is decisive.) Nor does Maimonides find the central "tribal" court to have any distinction; cf. H. Sanhedrin 5:1, and especially *Sefer haMitzvot, Aseh,* 176. R. Sa'adiah had a similar attitude; cf. M. Zucker, *The Torah Translation of R. Saadiah* (Heb.), p. 475. For both, authority is to be centralized; cf. Blidstein, "Maimonides on Oral Law," *Jewish Law Annual* 1 (1978): 120–21. Ramban, on the other hand, asserts (in his comment to Deuteronomy 16:18; cf. also Numbers 25:5) that the court of the tribe is superior to the local courts, "and if an enactment must be passed to govern the tribe, it does so, and this enactment is for the tribe what the decree of the Great Sanhedrin is for the entire people Israel." He does not, however, specify the scope of these enactments: are they concerned with civil law or even with religious matters? On the relationship of the terms *minhag* and *takkanah,* see Elon, *Jewish Law,* p. 404.

34. Rabbenu Gershom ( n. 4 above) argues for the authority of the *"parnasim";* and their actions are called "the *takkanot* of the *kehillot"* because their authority stems from the *kehillot* in whose name they act. Similarly, for Rabbi Joseph Bonfils (Tov Elem—eleventh century), the major problem is to justify the authority within the community and to reject the attempts of another community to enact *takkanot* for it. He is not concerned with identifying the competent institutions:

and we have seen that the sages granted each and every community the power to enact *takkanot* for themselves . . . for we learned that the citizens of a town may stipulate measurements etc., and Rabbi Isaac asked: From where do we know that *hefker bet din hefker* etc., and Rabbi Elazar says: I have heard that the *bet din* inflicts punishments not specified in the Torah. From this we learn that the *bet din* (!) in each and every *kehillah* has the right to pass decrees for its own *kehillah* as it sees fit according to the needs of the time. (*Responsa of Maharam bar Baruch,* Lemberg ed., no. 423).

Cf. also at n. 45. *infra.*
35. L. Finkelstein, *Jewish Self-Government in the Middle Ages* (New York, 1920), pp. 9–10, 33–34.
36. See nn. 2, 25 above.
37. For a slightly different perception among the *gaonim* of Babylonia, see the opinion of Rabbi Samuel ben Hophni (based on a Tannaic *midrash*) cited by Haim Hillel Ben-Sasson. "The Place of the City . . . in Jewish History," *Ha-ir ve-ha-Kehillah* (Jerusalem, 1968), pp. 165–66. Agus in *Urban Civilization* (n. 2 above, p. 83, n. 119) has already pointed out the exclusive authority of the "elders" in the responsa of Rav Hananiah Gaon (see also p. 94, n. 145, ) In any case, this was not the only view held by the *gaonim*. Cf. the opinion of Rav Hay in *Sha'arei T'shuvah,* no. 86; and even in the responsum of Rav Hananiah Gaon, the authority of the elders expresses the right of the "citizens of the country" to compel one another by means of the takkanah.
38. See nn. 2, 52. Finkelstein (n. 33 above, p. 15) argued, on the other hand, that addressing the congregation has no legal significance and is not more than a useful tactic for bringing the complaint before the entire community.
39. According to S. Assaf, *T'shuvot ha-Gaonim* (Jerusalem, 1952), p. 108. Agus (n. 22 above, pp. 206–207) has already noted this responsum, but his purpose in citing it was to point out the Babylonian custom, and not the Ashkenazic position.
40. S. Goitein, *A Mediterranean Society* (University of California Press, 1971), vol. 2, pp. 40–41, 56–57. N. Golb, "A Judaio-Arabic Court Document of Syracuse A.D. 1020," *Journal of Near Eastern Studies* 32 (1973): 116–21, gives the Hebrew original (I am grateful to Dr. Reuven Bonfil for having referred me to this article). Even the phrase "to seat a *kahal*" (which is to be found in the *takkanot* of the Rhine communities; see Finkelstein, p. 228) gives the impression that the *kahal* functioned as a legal forum; cf. Gittin 5,6; Eduyyot 8,3; Sanhedrin 5,4; cf. Finkelstein, p. 184. But from A. Aptowitzer, Introduction to "*Sefer Ra'abiah,*" p. 436, it would appear that the true translation of this phrase is "to stop the prayer of the community," in its origin at least (as in *lehoshiv sheliah zibbur*—to stop the prayer-leader). The question of the prevalence of the custom of interrupting the service (did it exist only in Western Europe?) does not concern use here. On the meaning of the term *"kahal"* in the responsa of the rabbis of Western Europe, see Agus' comments in his book on the Maharam, p. 65, n. 53, and in his latest book (n. 25 above), pp. 203–204. As to the legal basis of this practice it is worth noting the opinion of R. Isaac b. Asher (a younger contemporary of Rashi) that "if one of the disputants refuses to adjudicate at all, he may be forced by any three—even laymen *(hedyotot)*—to appear before them" (*Or Zaru'a,* beginning of Sanhedrin; *Temim De'im,* no. 207; cf. also Tosafot, Sanhedrin 5a), an opinion accepted by Rabiah (Mordekhai, Sanhedrin, sec. 675). One wonders as to the

historical relevance of this ruling; cf. Frank, p. 75 n. 2, and Albeck (n. 2 above), pp. 114–21. R. Jonah of Gerona and Ramban, too, ruled according to Riba. Most medievals would also find this view implied in R. Alfas (Sanhedrin, sec. 965, 1021) and Maimonides *(Commentary to Mishnah Sanhedrin* 3,1), who allow a single *mumheh larabbim* (public expert) to impose himself on disputants. (The Maimonidean situation is quite complex: see also H. Sanhedrin 4,14 and 7,1; Tur, H. M.13 and *Bah ad loc.* Generally speaking, Maimonides avoids recognition of communal authorization, e.g., "Syrian tribunals.") All in all, the legal basis for a "people's court" is clearly present here. These discussions do not assume organized public authorization, which might be implied by Sanhedrin 23a and phrases like *mumheh larabbim* (sources developed in Ra'aban, ed. Ehrenreich, II 224b, and *Sefer Halttur,* repr. New York, 1955, ii, la) but derive rather from the moral and religious authority of each individual. But traces of an opinion that denied even the *mumheh* jurisdiction unless by appointment or consent may perhaps be detected: see R. Hanan'el at Sanhedrin 3a (though compare R. Alfas sec.968 and *Ittur,* i,78a and n. 4); *Sefer VeHizhir,* ed. Freimann, p.100; *Halakhot Gedolot,* ed. Warsaw, 113b; ed. Berlin, p. 463. This opinion may even be at the heart of Rashi, Sanhedrin 5a, s.v. *ve'i;* Tosafot, consistent with their view on the authority of three laymen, disagree (ad loc.).

41. Albeck (n. 2, above), p. 120, and see also p. 106. I wonder whether the use by *Sefer HaShetarot* of the *baraita* "a court may punish in excess of Torah law" as a basis for the authority of "a congregation or a community or . . . the men of a *yeshiva*" (p. 9:3), does not refer especially to the use of the ban, a communal punishment par excellence; the same applies to the citation from R. Isaac Al-fasi (p. 106). The meaning of the term *Kahal* in these sources (the gaonic responsum cited on pp. 106–107, for example) ought also to be clarified; is the entire community, or its leadership, meant? Cf. n. 40, above.

42. *Responsa of R. Joseph Ibn-Megas,* no. 161; Albeck, "Sources of the Authority," p. 93. On the relationship of the court and the "seven best men of the city." Cf. also Finkelstein, *Jewish Self-Goverment,* p.121, and n. 49, below.

43. Albeck, "Sources of the Authority." We do find, in the literature emanating from the Makhirite clan, use of the *baraita* on extraordinary punishment as a basis for the practice of "the townspeople" in imposing financial and physical punishment (n. 46, below), and the *baraita* is also used as the basis for communal enactments (Albeck, "Sources of the Authority"; note also R. Joseph Bonfil, n. 34 above and in I. Agus, ed., *Responsa of the Tosafists* [Heb.], no. 1, pp. 41–42, though it is unclear whether he refers to the entire community or to its leadership). But ibn Megas is not objecting to either of these claims here. As for Rabbi Isaac Al-fasi (Spain, 1013–1103; teacher of Rabbi Joseph ibn Megas), Rabbi Jacob ben Asher (Tur, Hoshen Mishpat, chap. 2) states in his name that either "the great man of the generation . . . or the city elders have the right to impose fines." But this statement is not to be found in the *Halakhot* of Rav Al-fasi in the place indicated (Bava Kamma sec. 174), and it seems that its source is Rosh, Bava Kamma, IX, par. 5. The practice of the "seven best men" sitting on cases of fines is found in thirteenth-century Normandy *(Mordekhai, Gittin,* sec. 384), and cf. n. 30 above and nn. 114, 119 below.

44. Agus, n. 25 above; Albeck, "Sources of the Authority," pp. 114–15. Cf. also Goitein, *Mediterranean Society,* pp. 1–68. A further example of the prominence of the leadership: from *Sefer haShetarot* (R. Judah al-Barzeloni), p. 132, it would appear that "the community . . . agrees to pass an enactment," but on p. 136 we

read that "the elders of the city or its court have made . . . the document of enactment . . . and have written it." Are we to say that the latter passage refers only to the writing of the enactment agreed upon by all? Or does the former passage really refer to the actions of the elders described later? Cf. n. 1 above.

45. Cf. Baer, "Bases," p. 8.

46. See *Ma'aseh HaGa'onim* (Berlin, 1910), p. 70, no. 81: "We adjudicate according to the local custom, which is to impose punishments either financial, the ban, or flogging . . . for the townspeople may flog or impose the ban and use compulsion, for they can cite Biblical authority."

47. Cf. Grossman, "Grossman," p. 186, who stresses the practical significance of this opinion.

48. Cf. Elon, *Jewish Law,* vol. 2, pp. 603–607.

49. Compare with Elon, *Jewish Law,* vol. 2, pp. 571–74. Despite the explicit comparison with a *bet din* in one of the responsa of R. Me'ir of Rothenburg (n. 60, *Jewish Law*), it seems more likely that what is truly important in going surety is definitive consent (*gemirat da'at*), and the mention of *bet din* (in conjunction with other arguments) serves only as evidence for the principle that *gemirat da'at* is possible without a *kinyan* in special cases. See Elon, *Jewish Law,* n. 68. It seems that this explanation also applies to Rabbenu Tam's statement that the entire community is equal to an important *bet din* in cancelling a conditional *asmakhta* (Tosafot Nedarim 27b s.v. *ve-hilkhetah*) here, too, it is a matter of an act that is invalidated because of a flaw in consent (a different explanation can be found in Agus, n. 25 above, p. 202, n. 47); cf. n. 104 below. The same applies to the seven city elders: cf. *Ra'aban* (ed. Ehrenreich) no. 100 (cited in the *Responsa of the Maharam* of Rothenburg, [Prague] no. 392; *Mordekhai* Sanhedrin sec. 679–81).

50. Responsa cited by Elon, 569ff.

51. Cf. Morell (n. 2, above), p. 89. Cf. also n. 33, above.

52. Finkelstein, p. 197, n. 3; Albeck, pp. 101–103. I hope to treat this problem in the future.

53. G. Alon's study of "The Position of the Pharisees Toward Roman Rule," *Mehkarim be-Toldot Yisrael* (Tel-Aviv, 1957), vol. 1, pp. 24–47, is based, for example, on this assumption; see also M. Stern in H. H. Ben-Sasson, ed., *The History of Israel in Ancient Times* (Heb) (Tel-Aviv, 1969), vol. 1, p. 242.

54. Leviticus 4:14, and *Sifra ad. loc.;* Horayot 1, 5. In general, it should be noted that many communal concepts are lodged in the laws of this tractate.

55. *Commentary to the Mishnah,* Horayot 1,6 (trans. Yosef Kafah).

56. Tosefta Sanhedrin, 2, 13. This *baraita* does not allude to "the decision of the community as a particular legal body" (Baer, "Bases," p. 7, n. 18), but it does allude (contrary to the wording in the *baraita* in Avodah Zarah 36a) to the community as a body which grants authority in the legal sense.

57. H. Cohen, *"Hefker Bet Din Hefker,"* Proceedings of the Fourth World Congress of Jewish Studies (1967), vol. 1, pp. 185–88.

58. A. Gulak, *Yesodei ha-Mishpat ha-Ivri* (Berlin, 1922), vol. 1, p. 52. Gulak apparently bases his opinion on the Jerusalem Talmud, Megillah, 3:2; 74a, "Seven of the townspeople are as the city. What does this mean? If the townspeople accept [his] authority, even one can represent the city. If not, even several do not have this authority." See also S. Albeck, *Dinei ha-Memonot ba-Talmud* (Civil Law in the Talmud) (Tel-Aviv, 1976), pp. 506–16.

59. Kiddushin 42a.

60. Yevamot 89b.
61. See Rashi's commentary, Numbers 34:17: "Every chieftain is the guardian of his tribe . . . as if they had appointed them their agents." According to Rashi, Numbers 3:18, the Levites are the agents, as it were, of the Jewish people; this despite Numbers 3:12.
62. See n. 55 above. Further examples: in *Hilkhot Terumot* 1,2–3, the phrases "according to the opinion of the majority of Israel" and "according to the high court" are used interchangeably (as I learned from Rabbi J. B. Soloveitchick). Other examples might be cited; cf. H. Milah, 1,1–3; 3,1; and *Commentary to Mishnah Shabbat,* chap. 19, end. Maimonides requires "the consent of the populace" for the appointment of the Exilarch, who acts "as a king," and this may parallel the function of the Sanhedrin in the appointment of a king (*Commentary to M. Bekhorot* 4,4; H. Sanhedrin 4,13; H. Melakhim 1,3). This is apparently the understanding of *Ridbaz,* H. Melakhim, 3,8.
63. We will return to this statement, quoted from a treatise by the Ramban on the laws governing the ban, in greater detail below.
64. *Responsa of Rabbi Elijah Mizrahi* (Turkey), no. 57. On other "democratic" tendencies in the rulings of R. Elijah Mizrahi; cf. A. Shohat, *Sefunot* 11 (Heb.) (1977): 324.
65. A. Carlyle, *A History Of Medieval Political Theory in the West,* vol. 2, pp. 56–76; vol. 3, pp. 41f, 160f; vol. 1, pp. 86–112, 45ff; vol. 6, pp. 13–64, 89f; O. Gierke, *Political Theories of the Middle Ages,* pp. 61–67; F. Kern, *Kingship and Law in the Middle Ages,* pp. 187–94; 74.
66. H. Pirenne, *Early Democracy in the Low Countries,* pp. 54–55. See also C. H. McIlwain, *Growth of Political Thought in the West,* pp. 303–15.
67. See E. H. Kantorowicz, "Kingship Under the Impact of Scientific Jurisprudence," in M. Clagett, ed., *Twelfth Century Europe . . .* (University of Wisconsin, 1966), pp. 89–114, as well as the bibliography given there.
68. *Tanhuma, Hukkat,* 22; Rashi to Numbers 21:21; cf. *Midrash HaGadol,* Numbers (ed. Z. Rabinowitz), p. 391. For discussion of issues of relevance, see H. Pitkin, *The Concept of Representation* (Berkeley, 1967); H. C. Mansfield, "Modern and Medieval Representation," *Nomos* 10 (1968): 58–83.
69. See Elon, *Jewish Law,* vol. 2, pp. 584–87. However, he concentrates on a different problem from that which will be examined here, and on different sources.
70. The responsa of the *gaonim* of Babylonia attests to the custom of accepting a *takkanah* or the custom of "imposing the ban with Torah scrolls and curses." (See the responsa in *Sefer Ha-Eshkol,* ed. Albeck, vol. 2, pp. 152–54, and the notes of the editor). This evolution signifies a return to biblical models. It is interesting that Rav Hananiah Gaon (n. 26 above) recommends that someone who disobeys a *takkanah* should be banned, but does not say that the ban should be imposed at the enactment of the *takkanah*.
71. Avodah Zarah 36a. This biblical basis is absent in the Tannaic parallels, and is found only here, cited in the name of Rav. For us, Rashi's statement is of course important because the Talmudic exegesis is somewhat unclear.
72. Attention should be drawn, if only briefly, to the "biblical" nature of these medieval patterns. The outstanding phenomena in the Bible, for our purposes, are: (a) the public-general use of the ban; (b) the inclusion of a curse in the oath. In fact, the ban, the oath, and the curse constitute a single unit. In the Talmudic period, on the other hand, the halakhic range became narrower; the oath was perceived more as an obligation and was not, in general, imposed on someone,

and certainly not on a community; the oath did not include a curse (although many sources contain threats of a death penalty for anyone who broke the oath); the ban was not viewed as an oath, and it was generally imposed as a punishment and not as a means to guarantee the observance of a decision. In the Middle Ages, greater use was made of the biblical model; this development is based on hints that can be discovered in the Talmud and midrashim (it ought to be pointed out that "he heard the curse . . . ." (Leviticus 5:1) is understood by the rabbis to refer to the oath concerning testimony—*Sifra, ad.loc.;* Shevu'ot 35b-36a; M. Shevu'ot 4,13; Abaye at Shevu'ot 35a. Cf. A. Nahlon, *Annual* 3 (1967–68): 313–14, for a different interpretation. But the phenomenon is apparent from the period of the *gaonim* on. This is the picture that arises out of an examination of various studies: H. C. Brichto, *The Problem of "Curse" in the Hebrew Bible* (Philadelphia, 1968), pp. 22–71; L. Ginzberg, *An Unknown Jewish Sect* (New York, 1976), pp. 398–402: B. S. Jackson, *Theft in Early Jewish Law* (Oxford, 1972), pp. 218–23; H. Albeck, "Halachah Hizonit be-Targumei Eretz Israel u-va-Aggadah," *Sefer ha-Yovel lichvod B. M. Lewin,* pp. 63ff. For a "Juridical" explanation of the nature of the ban in the Middle Ages, see Agus (n. 25 above), 290–99.

73. Mo'ed Katon 16a. Rambam, H. Sanhedrin 24,8.

74. This discussion also serves as evidence (though marginal) for the Ramban; in principle, the oath is administered against the will of one who is compelled to take the oath.

75. *Responsa of the Rambam,* edited by Y. Blau, II, no. 183, pp. 334–35: "The ban is no more than an oath . . . and the rules which govern it are those which apply to someone who takes an oath . . . but anyone who did not respond 'amen' to this ban is not bound by it because the ban does not close a breach." Cf. also no. 329, pp. 596ff. In conclusion, Rambam distinguished several kinds of bans and *takkanot,* and was careful to indicate that an individual cannot exempt himself from a ban intended to "close a breach." For a discussion of this expression and its meaning, see Morell, "Constitutional Limits," pp. 94ff; on Ramban, see p.95, n. 73. 76. Several of these references are used by the Talmud, Shevu'ot 36a.

77. Rashi, *Responsa,* p. 86, 288–290. Perhaps the anonymous ruling in *Mahzor Vitri,* I, p. 25 sec. 45, attempts to prevent the penalizing of someone unwary of the ban.

78. In his responsum given in R. Hayyim 'Or Zaru'a, *Responsa,* no. 222; *Mordekhai,* Baba Bathera, sec. 482.

79. The statement of Samuel, Shevu'ot 29b.

80. Compare *Seder HaTeshuvah* of R. Eliezer of Worms (1160–1237): "No man may say: I did not hear the ban and did not include myself in it. This we learn from the example of Jonathan, the son of Saul, who did not know of the ban imposed by his father. Nevertheless, Saul wanted to put Jonathan to death because of the oath and the ban of which he was ignorant" (*Mordekhai* Shevu'ot, sec. 755). The biblical basis of this argument appears again in the responsa of Rabiah and in the writings of Ramban; see below. Does this not reflect the influence of the responsa of Rabbi Judah ha-Kohen and his associates? Cf. n. 96 below.

81. See the opinions of Riba (beginning of eleventh century) and Ra'aban concerning the irregularities in the communal oath of testimony. Ra'aban (*Mordekhai,* Shevu'ot sec. 760) argued that these were deliberate, "so as to enable the court to pursue the truth without risking the penalties entailed by a true oath," that is to say, to compel people to testify without endangering them. Be this as it may, this type of ban did not win universal assent; see *Or Zaru'a* to Shevu'ot, published by

Freiman in the Jubilee Volume for 1. Levi (1911), p. 10.

82. The seriousness of the matter is revealed in the fact that Rabbi Meir of Rothenburg refused (according to one tradition) to confirm a ban imposed by the community against the will of an individual although he was willing to agree that the *takkanah* applied to all: *Semak,* par. 81 (Agus, n. 2 above, pp. 110–11, has already pointed this out). There is an interesting discussion in the *Responsa of the Gaonim* (Harkabi), no. 333 (p. 161): "Shimon cannot be forced to appear in the synagogue while Reuven calls out the ban but Shimon cannot prevent Reuven from imposing the ban, and if he leaves (and he has the right to do so), we can ask him: 'Why do you leave?' But to force him to sit there against his will, this we have no authority to do." See the responsum of the sages of Mainz (twelfth century) who say that we cannot deduce this from the case of Saul and Jonathan for "We are sure that, were he there, he would have accepted the decree," which is not true in the case where an individual protests against the application of the ban (*Responsa of Rabbi Hayyim Or Zarua,* no.222); but in that case there were several reasons to invalidate the decree.

83. The major portion of Ramban's statement is to be found in his *Mishpat ha-Herem* ("The Law of the Ban"); Rashbaz (1, 123, near the beginning) calls the essay: *Igeret Hatarat Ha-Herem* (A. Nahlon, "The Body that Enacts," p. 167). References are to *Hiddusei Ramban* published by the Institute of the Complete Jerusalem Talmud (Jerusalem, 1976), edited by H. Sha'anan.

84. See n. 83.

85. Leviticus 27:19, and his interpretation of the verse; *"Mishpat Herem,"* pp. 296–97. For objections to this view, see n. 95 below.

86. Ibid., pp. 294–98.

87. Cf. Rambam's statement in H. Talmud Torah 7,4: "And if someone dies while under a ban issued by the *bet din,* we place a stone on his coffin, that is to say, he is stoned because he is separated from the community." This explanation, provided by the Rambam, perhaps reflects the fact that, in light of the increased number of causes for excommunication, the subject of the ban can no longer be identified with the rebellious scholar who must be put to death for not accepting the authority of the *bet din.* A different explanation for the attitude of Ramban can be found in Albeck (n. 72 above), p. 101.

88. Ibid., p. 295.

89. Ramban is of the opinion (*Novellae* to Shevu'ot 31b) that he who is called to testify is considered bound by the oath even if he refuses to answer, "Amen." In this he follows Maimonides (H. Shevu'ot 9:1,10), who apparently follows R. Joseph ibn Megas, *Novellae* to Shevu'ot 32a, 35b. This can also be inferred from Mishpat HaHerem, p. 294, bottom.

90. Cf. R. Menahem Me'iri, *Beit ha-Behirah,* Shevu'ot, p. 94.

91. *Hiddusei Rambam,* p. 295. The idea that a ban requires the presence of ten men can be found in *Tanhuma Va-Yeshev,* 2. (Indeed, we find already in the Mishnah that oaths are taken "in the *bet ha-knesset"* (Shevu'ot 4,10), but this is only one out of many possibilities. But compare this with Lev. Rabbah 6,2 (ed. Margaliot, I, p.130), line 3 according to mss. DT.) With the disuse of the oath in the name of God and its substitution by the ceremony of the ban, we hear of a ban "before the community" (see for example the responsa of Rav Natronai, Shaarei Zedek, 4,4,72). Rashi, as we know, said that "the people's custom is to proclaim the ban in the presence of ten men" (Responsa, par. 244, p. 285).

92. *Hiddusei Rambam,* p. 296. This echoes the fact that with regard to sale of sacred

property, the seven city elders act only "in the presence of the townspeople" (Megillah 27a); the king and the Sanhedrin = the city elders, as we have seen in note 62 above. Similarly, Ramban requires that a king be appointed "in the presence of the people" (*Commentary* to Numbers 27:19; drawn from *Sifra, Millu'im* 1, 4 (40d), and *Midrash HaGadol,* to Leviticus 8:3), though he would seem to understand this requirement differently than his Talmudic sources.

93. *Hiddusei Rambam,* p. 299.
94. Ibid., p. 300.
95. *Neziv* (R. Naphtali Berlin, d. 1893) took exception to Ramban's approach, and particularly to his interpretation of Leviticus 27:29, and all it implies, in *Ha'amek She'alah* 142, 9:

> I pondered and tried to understand how someone who is banned can be killed. Can anyone who is under a curse be slain? What about the curses in the Torah of Moses; can it be that anyone who was under a curse could actually be put to death? [And] it seems to me that the high court in Jerusalem had no more power over Israel than a *bet din* in any city has over the townspeople. And in the case of Achan, he was killed because the incident took place during a time of war and caused God to forsake Israel . . . thus he endangered the people (i.e., *rodef* and could be killed in self-defense).

*Neziv* must, of course, find halakhic justification for what happened to Achan and Jonathan, but he refuses to grant the Sanhedrin special powers; no human authority has the right to put a man to death except for those offenses cited in the Torah as requiring this penalty. In this, he expresses his opposition to the granting of unlimited power to the community and its leaders, and cites the already familiar parallel between the local court and the high court, but his aim is to limit the power of the Sanhedrin and not to broaden the power of the local institution. His reasoning is clear: the individual is subject to a given authority only if such authority is already granted in the Torah to a human institution—to any human institution. For a contrasting nineteenth-century view, see R. Moses *Sofer, Resp. Hatam Sofer,* O.H. no. 208

96. *Hiddusei Rambam,* p. 299; and see the opinion of R. Saadiah Gaon cited in Kimhi to I Samuel 14:45. In his discussion of the operation of the ban, the Ramban ruled that "even if he was not there when it was decreed . . . the ban applies to him" (p. 295); the acts of the city elders are binding on the townspeople "who were silent or did not hear" (*Novellae* to Megillah 25b). It would appear that the point of all this is to obligate the man who refuses to hear the ban, with the penalizing for actions taken before the ban is known being secondary. This squares with the comment of Ramban (with the exception of his reference to Jonathan); cf. also Rabiah (!) as cited by R. Me'ir of Rothenberg, *Responsa* (ed. Cremona), no. 165. See also the opinions of Rashi and R. Eliezer of Worms, nn. 77, 78 above. The use of Jonathan and Saul as paradigms is already found in the responsum of R. Judah HaKohen, and see n. 76, above. See also Ramban to Deuteronomy 29:28.
97. See Rabiah, n. 78, above, and his responsum in *Sefer Rabiah,* II, pp. 316–17; Ramban to Megillah 25b; R. Hayyim Or Zaru'a, *Responsa,* no. 65. See also A. Nahlon, *Annual,* III, pp. 285–6. It ought be noted that in contrast with Rashba, who wrote that "the seven best men need not be distinguished by wisdom or wealth but need merely be the seven men chosen by the community to manage its

affairs" (Responsa, I, 617)—Maimonides wrote that "the bestmen are scholars, men of Torah and good deeds" (*Responsa,* edited by J. Blau, II, no. 271, p. 519); see as well his *Commentary* to M. Berakhot 4,7. It is questionable whether lack of these characteristics would disqualify in his view; cf. H. Tefillah 11,17–19, where no qualifications are given. (This subject warrants investigation from the perspective of historical practice; see Elon, *Jewish Law,* p. 590, n. 166.) Maimonides also wrote, in connection with the appointment of the Exilarch, that "we are not concerned with wisdom but with his descent and that the appointment should be with the consent of the populace" (n. 62, above), thus giving the people a free hand.

98. Cf. nn. 18, 69, 80, above. It is to be noted that Rashi (Megillah 26a, s.v. *elah*) had already interpreted "ma'amad" as "consent."

99. Pitkin, *Concept of Representation,* 55ff; P. Bachrach, *The Theory of Democratic Elitism* (Boston, 1967), p. 8.

100. Rabiah, n. 78 above; *Responsa of Rashba,* 2, 279; *Responsa of Rashba* (Pseudo-Ramban) no. 280, and others.

101. Horayot 3b; cf. *Dikduke Soferim.* The expression is missing in the parallel version in Avodah Zarah 36a but it seems to have been present in Rashba's text. In any case, it is more appropriate to the discussion in Horayot, dealing with the expression "the whole."

102. Indeed, Rav Huna uses the expression to indicate the status of the minority in the *bet din.* In our discussion, of course, the minority plays a double role: it is the minority of the members of the *bet din* dealing with the problem, and it is also the subject of the discussion itself.

103. Temurah 15b, see ps.-R. Gershom, ad loc.; Rambam's commentary on the Mishnah, Temurah 2,2 (ed. Kafah); and *Halakhot P'sulei ha-Mukdashim* 4,1. See M. Kadushin's instructive discussion in *Worship and Ethics* (1964), pp. 131ff., although it seems to me that he erred in his explanation of this source.

104. Statistically speaking, the expression *"zibbur"* appears most often in the sources dealing with the laws governing sacrifices and the Temple; the expression *"rabim"* (many, or majority) appears in "secular" contexts in rabbinic literature. In the laws on sacrifices, the difference between a sacrifice offered by partners and one offered by the *zibbur* is emphasized; *zibbur* = great Sanhedrin (*Sifra, Hobah* 2:5); and the *karet* punishment does not apply to the *zibbur,* that is to say, to the entire nation (*Sifra Kedoshim* 4:5 according to the interpretation of Rabbenu Hillel—another interpretation can be found in *Rabad, Sifra Zav* 13:9 and in parallel versions); the uncleanness of the majority of the nation was also permitted *"be-zibbur."* Ramban was particularly aware of this phenomenon—see his commentary on the Bible, Leviticus 1:2, as well as his interpretation of the discussion on "There is no public fast in Babylonia" in his comment on Ta'Anit 15a. Perhaps we should also interpret Rabban Gamliel's comments (Rosh Ha-Shanah 4,9) that "the delegate of the community absolves the *rabbim* of their duty" as indicating the relationship between majority = individuals together, and (the delegate of the) community = (the man who represents these) people as a holy unit. See S. Lieberman, *Yerushalmi Kifshuto,* p. 504, and in *JBL* 71 (1952): 201, 3. I do not intend, of course, to include here the terms found in the Judean Desert Scrolls.

105. *Responsa of Rashi,* par 247, p. 289. However, this sentence does not appear in all versions of this responsum.

106. Baer, "Bases," pp. 10ff. Gulak has already discussed the development of the legal character of the *kehillah,* n. 58 above. However, it should be noted that,

already in the Talmud, precedence was at times given to the "city" rather than the individual; see Baba Batra 2:7,11. See also M. Elon, *Encyclopedia Judaica,* vol. 13, p. 1354.

107. Part of this discussion is drawn from an article by S. Albeck, "Rabbenu Tam's Relation to Contemporary Problems," *Zion* 19 (1954): 104–41. I repeat his comments in order to present a more complete picture.

108. The opinion of Rabbenu Tam on this matter can be found in several sources. In one responsum (cited in Mordekhai Baba Kamma, sec. 179), Rabbenu Tam responded to a question concerning the collection of taxes from funds that were half-deposit, half-loan, and denied the community the right to collect these sums. (For the history of the problem, see *Responsa* of Rashi, ed. Elfenbein, pp. 266ff; Finkelstein, pp. 37–38, 148–49; *Hagahot Asheri* Bava Batra, ch. 2, par.11). Rabbenu Tam here ruled that no *takkanah* should be enacted charging the depositary against his will:

> And if someone wishes to enact such a *takkanah* . . . from now on, and another disagrees—the latter view prevails. . . . When we say that "the townspeople have the right to compel payment," it means: the townspeople have the right to impose upon and tax he who violates the assessment made with the agreement and knowledge of all, and to which the individual agreed at the time the *takkanah* was implemented and now refuses to fulfill. . . . But it is forbidden to appropriate money without the knowledge of the owner, except through a public confiscation—*hefker zibbur*—or by a court, and I have in the past so instructed all who consulted me.

Thus, Rabbenu Tam rules here on the basis of his interpretation of the abovementioned discussion in Bava Batra, and even informs us that he so ruled (?) in other cases, although we do not know the nature of those cases. In another responsum (cited by Maharam of Rothenburg, *Teshuvot Maymoniyyot, Shoftim,* No. 10) Rabbenu Tam again deals with the enactment of *takkanot* detrimental to one of the members of the community; if the individual did not protest at the time, the *takkanah* is binding on him—but if he did protest, it is not binding. "When a decree is made by the *Kahal* . . . if it was made by the city elders and if the person in question did not appeal the decree when he heard it, his later protests have no basis." And the explanation: "For it is said, the *bet din* has the right, etc., for the imposition is made with his knowledge and without his protesting it." In a responsum dealing with the addition of a monetary condition to a marriage contract (see *Teshuvot Maymoniyyot Ishut,* no. 17), Rabbenu Tam again argues that "he who thinks that the local custom is sufficient to require additional payment is an utter fool, if the town did not make a special *takkanah* . . . and everyone agreed to it. But it does not automatically apply." It should be noted that all these cases deal with the cancellation of already existing rights, or with the questioning of established practices; they do not deal with the fixing of a new practice or collection where there was no previous tradition. Even Rabbenu Tam's statement that "The impositions are made with the knowledge of the city elders, and the city elders are as a city council" (*Mordekhai,* Bava Batra, par. 480) does not mean that the decision of the city elders is sufficient to obligate the townspeople (although the presentation in *Mordekhai* may perhaps seem to imply this). What it means is that, in *addition* to the consent of the entire community, the consent of the city elders is required as well, where the new element here was the viewing of the city elders as a "town sage" (*hever ir*), i.e., they function in place of the sage of the city. Albeck has already so explained this passage (Rabbenu Tam, p. 30, n. 46), and this interpretation is confirmed by Rabbenu Tam's statement in the responsa attached to *Hilkhot Ishut* (above), where he determines those areas in which the city elders can function as a town sage and those areas in which it cannot. Moreover, it is explicitly stated there that if a decree was issued by the city elders and was not disputed at the time, no one can later contest it. From this we can infer that the city elders did, in fact, function as a body with the right to enact *takkanot,* but the individual reserved the right to appeal their decisions. The final citation is found in *Or Zarua, Zedakah,* sec. 4 (cf. Tosafot Baba Bathera 8b, s.v., *akpei*):

> R. Tam would explain that the townspeople could certainly not compel payment of charity nor anything else which is not necessary for the city. And when Rava compelled R. Nathan, this was because there had been a prior agreement upon assessments among the townspeople, and R. Nathan then refused to honor the assessment, so he compelled him to do so. Sometimes R. Tam would explain that the townspeople . . . had agreed that the charity-warden might use compulsion against them.

From the last sentence it appears that R. Tam argued that no compulsion could be used unless it had been consented to in advance.

109. It is ironic that Rabbenu Tam did compare the status of all the townspeople together to that of a *bet din;* compare with n. 479 above.

110. *Pe'ah* 4,2. Rabbenu Tam's statement is well-known: "There are customs which are not to be trusted even though we say that we follow the custom of the land," for "the custom may be a boorish custom" (Tosafot Baba Bathera 2a). E. E. Urbach, *The Tosafists* (Heb), p. 79, points to R. Tam's position on the right of settlement *(herem hayisshub)* as another instance of his defense "of the rights of the individual against the powerful men of the community."

111. *Mordekhai,* Baba Bathera, sec. 476. R. Isaac disagrees violently.

112. I. Agus, *Teshuvot Ba'alei HaTosafot,* no. 12. Since the problem is rooted in the flawed nature of the "law of the kingdom," it is appropriate that R. Tam will emphasize the ethical side of the matter rather than the territorial; cf. S. Shiloh, *Dina DeMalkhuta Dina* (Jerusalem, 1975), p. 100. On the use of this principle to establish the authority of Jews over Jews, see Shiloh, pp. 101ff. It is possible that this principle was used to strengthen the authority of the *kehillah,* and perhaps Rabbenu Tam (and in this he is cited as being in disagreement with others) sought to prevent the development of this view, even though it seems remote.

113. See Albeck (n. 107 above), p. 30, n. 46 (end). On the other hand, Agus (n. 2 above, p. 94) believes it to be "self-evident" that the community can authorize the majority to act in all matters concerning it, but he does not support this assumption. In any case, Rabbenu Tam agrees that the community has the right to accept the authority of its *gabbayim* (see n. 108), but the scope of their authority is not clear.

114. Finkelstein, *Jewish Self-Government,* p. 168: "And no man may tarry without the knowledge of his wife unless he has the permission of seven city elders." Does this imply that "city elders" is also a description and not just an institution? See also at p. 153, *Responsa Maharam* (Cremona) no. 230. R. Tam also legislated the defense of the "bestmen" against hostile informers (p. 153); the distinction be-

tween these officials and the town court is clear (pp. 176, 121). Rashi and other respondents of his time also speak of "seven of the important men of the town" rather than of a formalized body (see his *Responsa, no.* 207, p. 234; no. 231; no. 238, p. 266).

115. Rabbenu Tam, for example, is of the opinion that "a community can alter" the purpose of money donated for charity (cited in R. Asher Baba Batra 1, 29, and in other sources). However, in Tosafot Bava Batra 8b it is stated that "Rabbenu Tam [himself!] used to give the money of the treasury to the guards of the city in fulfillment of the wishes of the townspeople." Can we infer from this that the scholarly figure was the real representative of the "townspeople" (see below)? Or is this identical to R. Ashi, B.B. 9a?

116. This does not imply that "the rule of unanimity reflected the feudal disintegration of the sense of community" (E. Lewis, *Medieval Political Ideas* (1954), vol. 1, p. 203). On the contrary, Pollack and Maitland (*History of English Law,* 2nd ed., vol. 2, p. 626) have argued that the requirement that the twelve jurors should reach a verdict unanimously expresses the communal principle.

117. M. Baba Batra, chap. 1; Tosefta Baba Mezia, ch. 11.

118. Finkelstein, *Jewish Self-Government,* p. 50ff.

119. Mordekhai Baba Batra, par 480. And Rabbenu Tam continues there, "That is to say that, in their generation, there is no one as great as he. But if there is in their generation someone as great as he, he does not have the right to appropriate money." This statement is appropriate to the second stage below.

120. Baer ( "Bases and Origins," p. 39) sees the problem of a *bet din* like that of Rabbi Ammi and Rabbi Assi as "irrelevant to the reality of the Middle Ages." But it seems that Rabbenu Tam did find it relevant. Compare with S. Albeck, *The Attitude of Rabbenu Tam,* pp. 140–41, who cites several of the sources that will be noted below, although his presentation is somewhat different. See also R. Chazan, *Medieval Jewry in Northern France* (Johns Hopkins Press, 1973), pp. 60–61.

121. R. Asher, Gittin 4, 13.

122. *Sefer ha-Yashar,* Hiddushim, Sec. 270: "Samuel wished to exclude two laymen only." Albeck, n.2 above, does not view this source as a third stage, and argues that Rabbenu Tam continued to hold the view that only the great sage of the generation may write a *prosbul,* but "He did not want to say explicitly that all must turn to him as the great sage of the generation." In any case, his statement does not imply this. Moreover, from the statements of the rabbis of Mainz (*Responsa of Rabbi Hayyim Or Zarua,* no. 222) that Rabbenu Tam ruled that "everyone" can appropriate money, it seems that, at this stage, he no longer required that this necessarily be done by a great sage of the generation. (Cf. Albeck, n. 2 above, p.133, n. 51.) However, it is interesting that the rabbis of Mainz understood Rabbenu Tam's statement as supporting a decision of the communal leaders—i.e., laymen! Later the authors of the responsa retreated from this solution. Cf. Morell, p. 97, n. 82. In any case, Y. Gilat (*Sefer Baruch Kurzweil,* 1975, p. 111) has already pointed out that there was no practical follow-through of this method which authorized a local *bet din* to write a *prosbul.*

123. *Sefer ha-Yashar, Hiddushim,* sec. 668. It is possible that Rabbenu Tam adopted several positions here as well: cf. R. Asher, Sanhedrin ch. 3, par. 41; Tosafot Bava Kamma 112b s.v. mazi. In *Or Zarua* Baba Kamma, sec 436, Rabbenu Tam questions the status of the *bet din* in our city, but it is clear that he does not agree with the responsum of Rabbi Samson cited there that the local court is equivalent to the high court.

124. Albeck, n. 2 above, has already pointed out this view, but he emphasizes other sources. The *takkanah* can be found in Finkelstein, *Jewish Self-Government,* p. 152ff.

125. Finkelstein, pp. 36, 148. As we know, this statement is not always attributed to Rashi.

126. It ought be pointed out that R. Tam mandates the agreement of the "important scholar" to communal enactments not only to protect his honor, but for substantive reasons: "since there is no *kinyan* (act of conveyance) . . . the presence of the 'town scholar' *(hever 'ir)* is necessary" *(Mordekhai,* Baba Kama, 179). It would almost seem as though such consent is a *sina qua non,* though it is clear in the Talmud (B. B. 9a) that where no scholar is in residence the enactment is binding in his absence. Cf. Baer, "Bases and Origins," p. 39, n. 34; Elon, *Jewish Law,* p. 581, n. 110, and 607ff.

127. *Or Zarua* Hilkhot Zedakkah, par. 4. Cf. Agus (n. 2 above), p. 112, n. 199.

128. Cf. Agus (n. 2, above), p.112, n. 199. Similarly, the rights of the gentile kingdoms *(dina demalkhuta dina)* are based, according to R. Tam, on *hefker bet din,* that is to say, on the will of the sages, not on the consent of the people (see his responsum n. 112, above; Shiloh, p. 61). It is also characteristic of him to state (Tosafot Sanhedrin 5a, s.v. *hakha,* though cf. Tosafot Hullin 18b) that the preeminence of the Exilarch (as compared with the Palestinian Patriarch) reflects his superior descent and not popular consent, as Rashi had claimed.

# 12

# Patterns of Political Organization and Leadership in Modern Jewish Communities and Their Contemporary Implications

*Peter Y. Medding*

Earlier in this century, Western Jewish communities outside of Israel were confronted by common internal and external challenges. These gave rise to intense and deep community conflicts that severely tested the capacities of existing Jewish communal leaders and resulted in new patterns of Jewish communal leadership. The similarities in these communities' responses to major issues of conflict are significant in explaining their contemporary functioning, and provide a sense of unity and continuity that extends beyond the boundaries of individual communities.

## Anti-Zionism, Non-Zionism and Zionism

One major issue in the first half of this century was the degree to which the leadership of a community should support the Jewish national enterprise in Palestine. Those who strongly opposed it, and those who wanted support moderated and kept within the Jewish community feared that involvement in the Jewish national effort would create dual loyalties—political commitment to, and identification with, a "foreign" political body which infringed their citizenship loyalty. In addition, there was some apprehension that this would adversely affect their social acceptance by non-Jews, emphasize their distinctive differences from the rest of society, and, by making Jews conspicuous, engender anti-Semitism. In the countries of the British Empire these apprehensions were compounded as Britain and the *Yishuv* in Palestine came into conflict; for many, to support the Zionist effort did not arouse the tensions associated with dual loyalty, but constituted outright disloyalty.

Neutrality or antipathy to Zionism as a political ideology were shared in these societies by those who opposed the nationalistic solution to the Jewish problem, and sought some form of internationalist or universalist solution, namely, communists, socialists, and Bundists. They were joined from completely different directions by the traditionalist religious elements who opposed secular Zionism and waited for some kind of Messianic solution, and by the more extreme Reform groups who were concerned with Judaism's universal mission, not its national aspirations.

If we examine some of these countries more closely we find that particularly in Britain and Australia, many outstanding Jewish personalities and leaders and key organizations were at the forefront of the anti-Zionist campaign. A split in the "establishment" and careful organization by the Zionists, however, saw the resolution of the issue via the capture of key communal bodies by leaders committed to the Zionist cause. This generally coincided with a rise to power of the immigrants (mainly from Eastern Europe) who had arrived since 1900.[1]

In South Africa, by the way of contrast, Zionism was the official communal ideology and that of the communal leadership and major institutions from very early in this century. In fact the Zionist Federation, founded in 1898 pre-existed the Board of Deputies and performed general communal and representative functions until it handed them over to the Board of Deputies in 1912. The anti-Zionists, although present, constituted a very minor element. This arose partly from the Eastern European pre-twentieth-century Lithuanian origins of the community, but mainly because South African national identity in the context of the country's racial divisions became increasingly Afrikaans-dominated and did not offer a viable alternative citizenship loyalty pattern or model for Jewry. At the same time, Afrikaans political leaders such as Botha, Hertzog, and Smuts were highly sympathetic to

Zionism.[2] Similarly in Canada, the Zionist movement developed earlier than the countrywide representative organizations, and when the latter developed in the form of the Canadian Jewish Congress their leaderships integrated easily, and Zionism was accorded a central place in communal endeavor and identification. Opposition to Zionism seems to have been at a low level.[3] (The examples of Canada and South Africa suggest that Zionism for Jewry had an easier transition to communal centrality in societies where monolithic citizenship ideals were not dominant and where there was a multiethnic or multicultural society.)

In the United States, the Zionist movement throughout its development—and in keeping with the nature of the Jewish community—was loosely organized. Early opposition came from leaders of Reform Judaism and the CCAR, on the one side, and from the East Europeans involved in the Socialist movement who sought universal solutions to Jewish problems. But whereas in other societies there were accepted, recognized, and authoritative communal representative bodies, in the United States there were none—except perhaps the German patrician, elitist, wealthy, and self-appointed American Jewish Committee (AJC). Its attitude is far better described as non-Zionism rather than anti-Zionism, although some of its actions at various times and some of its leaders better fitted the latter designation. It accepted the Zionist Organization and Zionism as representative of those Jews concerned with Palestine particularly after the Balfour Declaration, but strongly opposed the Zionist group in American Jewry and their efforts to gain greater mass support and influence in American Jewry. It strongly resented all attempts at Zionist (and later) Israel's "interference" in the internal affairs of American Jewry, although it eventually made "formal peace" with the State of Israel, as seen in the Blaustein-Ben Gurion exchange. Its attitude to Zionism stemmed partly from concern over the effects that a Jewish state would have on the integration of Jews into American society and their acceptance by their non-Jewish neighbors (thus, it supported Zionist efforts more when the state seemed unlikely and moved to a much more ambivalent, independent and anti-state position when partition moves become a reality), and partly from the threat that American Zionism and beyond them world Zionism (and Israel) represented vis-à-vis their claims to lead and speak for American Jewry. As an elitist organization, it could operate successfully if the Jewish masses were unorganized; the moment, however, they became mobilized, its claims to unquestioned leadership based on elitist criteria were in question. In this context it is interesting that after it had come around to accepting the state, particularly after it was established, it sought to retain its leadership role by direct negotiations with the prime minister of Israel almost as if it felt it occupied a position of equal status.

After the AJC had become fully committed to the State of Israel, even though it had not become Zionist in a formal sense, the main opposition to Israel came from the American Council for Judaism, and from various ultra-Orthodox, Hasidic elements.[4]

In France, the official and recognized bodies of the Jewish community remained either reserved or hostile to Zionism right up until 1945, reflecting clearly the views of their native-born French Jewish leadership. Insofar as Zionist organizations developed between the wars they were mainly confined to Eastern European immigrants. After 1945, Zionism became a central element in the French Jewish ideology, and the intensity of its commitment increased over time, reaching its height during the wars of 1967 and 1973. According to one of French Jewry's leading spokesmen, Guy de Rothschild, "Our passionate interest comes from the identification with Israel as part of our personality."[5]

Latin America presented another pattern again. Here, by and large, there were no "established" Jewish communities or groups when the immigrants began to trickle in mainly from Eastern Europe from the mid-1800s and arrived in increasing numbers after 1880. The pattern of communal life was, therefore, in many ways a transplantation of the Eastern European pattern, and Zionism was no exception. From the very outset the Zionists and the Jewish communal authorities cooperated closely, so much so that later in Argentina the elections for the *Kehilla* were contested and won by Zionist parties that were replicas of the early Eastern European parties later institutionalized in Israeli politics. Similarly the patterns of opposition are those of Eastern Europe—the Yiddishist, Bundist, Socialist and Communist opponents of independent Jewish nationalism, and statehood in the name of either integration into the local scene, or of the promise of universal brotherhood.[6]

In recent years with the issue resoundingly resolved in favor of Zionism, Israel has become the focal point of Jewish life and political organization in the communities outside it, and today constitutes the core of Jewish peoplehood and ethnic identification. Anti-Zionism in the Jewish community hardly exists.

## Established and Patrician Elements and Immigrants and Masses

This second issue—leadership and social conflict—revolved around the issue of leadership of the Jewish community, and its representation in the outside world. It was also directly connected with the first conflict, in that the established and patrician elements tended to be opposed to Zionism while the immigrants and the masses tended to support it. It was also often accompanied by ethnic overtones; the former tended to be either of native origin over a number of generations, or of German stock, while the latter tended to be Eastern Europeans. It was compounded by marked residential disparity, with the former living in prestigious areas in conditions of great affluence and splendor; while the latter lived in crowded conditions, sweat shops, ghettoes, and densely populated slums. The leadership issue was one of representativeness—whether the established and patrician leaders were sufficiently attuned to the values and aspirations of the Jewish masses to be able to represent them faithfully, particularly as in many areas of Jewish life, such as religious observance, Jewish education, language and culture, as well as Zionism, the latter took strong and intense Jewish survivalist positions while the former adopted more integrationist outlooks in keeping with their social situation. The established and patricians were particularly concerned lest association with the masses endanger their hard earned acceptance into the larger society. This fear also often led to cold, patronizing, and tactless attempts to Americanize, Anglicize, and Australianize the immigrants as quickly as possible, side by side with concern for their social and economic welfare in their new societies as expressed in philanthropic endeavor.

The issue was eventually solved by the immigrants' rapid upward social mobility and acculturation, by the patricians stepping aside or being pushed aside; by a slow process of immigrant organization gaining strength and support and eventually prestige; by the obvious need to stand united against the common enemy anti-Semitism in its many forms, which eventually led to various forms of merger and integration based on common values and interests. Other patricians simply followed their continuing process of integration and ended up outside the Jewish community either as a result of conversion or intermarriage.

These patterns of conflict and integration were particularly pronounced in the United States (especially New York), England, Australia, and South Africa. There seems to be less evidence of it in Canada, while in Latin America Eastern European patterns of communal organization and goals seem to have been dominant from the outset. There the boot seemed to be on the other foot: it was not the established who were made uneasy by the immigrants, but it was the mass of immigrants who were embarrassed by wealthy Jewish "White Slave" traffickers. In fact the whole community ostracized them socially and organized against this traffic until it succeeded in eradicating it.[7]

In Britain and Australia the struggle was focused mainly on the battle for control of major communal representative bodies such as the respective Boards of Deputies, and in conflict between the broad representative bodies and Zionist bodies.[8] This was also the case, but in lesser degree, in South Africa and Canada.

In the United States, with its pluralist and noncentralized Jewish communal structure, there was conflict in the area of religion and religious worship, which led to the establishment of the Conservative movement, providing Eastern European Jews with an acculturated form of Jewish worship, far more traditional and more in tune with their general concerns, than German-dominated reform. In the political sphere, the American Jewish Committee was an elite body seeking to represent American Jewry, whose membership of a few hundred was handpicked and dominated by a central core of New York patricians. The struggle in this area took place directly with the establishment of mass-supported parallel bodies, seeking to represent their own broader membership, and to undo the AJC's monopoly. These included initially the American Jewish Congress, the various Zionist bodies, and here too ought to be included the synagogues and labor and veterans groups that developed.

## Leftist Orientation and Community Interest

The unity of the Jewish communities and, therefore, their political influence was weakened by conflict between those swayed by ideologies of the Left and those who concentrated on Jewish concerns. Those committed to the Left operated in two different directions. Some took a universalist, and anti-national and anti-particularist position often mixed with a strident secularism. The result was that they either denied the need for Jewish community survival or thought it a matter of little importance; by tying their hopes to radical social change they sought a solution to anti-Semitism in socialism. In it, true equality would exist for all men; the most fruitful path for Jews, therefore, was to throw in their lot with the progressive forces and their problems would be solved. Many looked to the Soviet Union as their ideal society. As Fascism and Nazism developed, this kind of analysis gained considerable influence in the liberal democracies which promised equality yet could not eradicate prejudice. The other basic position was to seek to amalgamate the Jewish struggle with the socialist struggle, and in doing so to subordinate the former to the latter.

The impact of the socialist cause upon the Jewish community was generally to weaken the Jewish community by diverting its members away from Jewish values and aspirations. The entry of the Soviet Union into the war against the Nazis enabled the communists to establish front organizations within the Jewish community, which in some cases actually sought to take over Jewish organizations and causes and to divert their energies to fight the universal battles to which their ideology and party directed them. Their analysis of Fascism and Nazism as the enemy not only of the Jews but also of democracy enabled them to disguise their political struggle against the Right as a battle to eradicate prejudice and to free society of anti-Semitism. This gained the support of Jewish organizations and leaders, among others, many of whom did not realize that they were being used in the service of the Soviet Union and the Communist International.

This was particularly critical in Australia in the late 1940s and early 1950s when these front organizations succeeded for a time in capturing control of the major representative Board of Deputies, although eventually they were removed from influence.[9] Similar conflicts, though on a smaller scale, took place in South Africa (particularly in the 1930s). They were of lesser significance in Britain and in the United States, although there is some evidence to suggest that various Jewish community bodies were subjected to attempts at control by front organizations. This occurred at the national level via the attempt of the large Jewish section of the Communist-front organization, the IWO, to gain admittance into the various councils of the Jewish community by muting its traditional antagonism to Zionism in the name of "unity." It also sought to participate in the American Jewish Conference of 1943, and on being refused entrance on the grounds that it was international and not distinctively Jewish, it reorganized and renamed itself to remove such obstacles to participation.[10]

Historical and autobiographical works document the inroads made by such elements into various local communities including Buffalo and Los Angeles. In both communities the struggle was strongly fought from the 1920s to the late 1940s. Thus, for example, the Los Angeles chapter of the American Jewish Congress adhered faithfully to the party line and was finally expelled by the national organization. Again in Los Angeles an active fight had to be waged to prevent the Communist front organizations from gaining control of the Community Relations Committee of the Jewish Community Council.[11]

The cold war, the conversion of the Soviet Union from supporter of Israel's establishment to the Arab States' main arms' supplier, the treatment of Jews in the Soviet Union, and the general spread of information about freedom and equality in Russia, reduced this threat to the Jewish community.

## Religious Leadership and Nonreligious Leadership

Who speaks in the name of the Jewish community is directly related to concepts about the nature of the Jewish group. If it is conceived of as a religious group then the authority of the group will be vested in its religious leaders, and religious organizations will take precedence over others. If it is conceived of as an ethnic group, essentially secular in character, despite a religious component, then authority will be vested in nonreligious Jewish leaders and their organizations. One way of analyzing this problem is briefly to trace the significant common elements in the development of the Jewish communities in the countries of immigration in the nineteenth and twentieth centuries. One can distinguish six stages in their development (some of which also occurred in the older established communities such as Great Britain and France).

Stage 1: Establishment of synagogues, burial societies, *shechita,* and provision for circumcision. This stage is more or less concerned with the *rites de passage* and with terminal aspects of honor that separate Jews from Christians. It is also accompanied at a slightly later stage by Hebrew and religious teaching.

Stage 2: The development of various social welfare and philanthropic enterprises, old age homes, mutual loan societies, widows' aid, and various other communal charities. This stage is clearly social and economic, drawing on Jewish sources of tzedaka, and ensures that

Jews do not become distinctive by their refusal or inability to assist their own who are in need. These bodies were often but not always closely linked to the synagogues, and in many cases their emergence was barely separated in time from those that preceded them.

Stage 3: This was characterized by the development of organizations for the fulfillment of social, cultural, and recreational purposes outside the rabbinical and religious welfare and philanthropic or charity frameworks. They were established by members of the community to give expression to their needs, accustomed patterns of behavior, and their aspirations.

Up to this stage, it would probably be correct to suggest that the rabbis in particular, often backed by their synagogal leadership counterparts, were the recognized spokesmen of Jewry. They were in fact Jewry's only professionals. This was particularly evident in the United States at the local community level, and in the societies in which the total Jewish community was small and embryonic, such as Australia and South Africa. It was also true of Britain and France which had officially recognized Chief Rabbis.

Stage 4: This stage witnessed the establishment of bodies to represent the Jewish community to the outside world and to governmental authorities. Initially it dealt with defense of Jews against prejudice and discrimination and with securing the rights of persecuted Jews in other countries. Often synagogue leaders and religious authorities had a significant voice in these bodies, some of whose main spokesmen were patrician and established elements. Another common pattern was for them to be set up by Jews who were particularly successful and prominent in the outside world. The characteristic approach was behind-the-scenes negotiations in a dignified manner; public demonstrations and pressure were regarded as undignified, too conspicuous, and likely to cause anti-Semitism.

Stage 5: Here Jews sought greater internal representativeness of those who represented them outside. In addition, the proliferation of bodies and groups fulfilling various purposes within the community, all making financial, social, and temporal claims upon its members, demanded greater internal organization and coordination. The result was a marked increase in the strength of the nonreligious organizations and their leaders both internally and externally. They were greatly assisted by their access to financial resources, and by the urgent and extreme nature of the external problems facing Jewry, which necessitated the united and concerted support of all sections of the community. The process was reinforced by the rapid socioeconomic mobility of large numbers of Jews, recognition of which some desired to express via community leadership. Their wider goals and aspirations could not be expressed within the confines of the local synagogues whose pattern of activity and concerns were often too parochial for their taste, and too narrow and limited for their energies and abilities. It also meant potential leadership and prestige competition and conflict with the rabbis.

This stage was also often accompanied by a marked degree of coordination of internal activities: the formation of local roof bodies, the uniting of welfare institutions into federations and the growth of national confederations, in all areas of Jewish life—community relations, welfare, education, and also in religious affairs.

The result was the rise to prominence and dominance in Jewish community affairs of independent large-scale nonreligious community organizations, operating on their own or in various federative or representative patterns of coordination in which the nonreligious spokesmen of the community control their own organizations and the more general ones as well. Rabbis may be prominent, but usually more in an individual capacity or as the representatives of nonreligious organizations in which they are involved.

A general distinction can be made between the more centralized Jewish communities (Britain, Australia, South Africa, France) and the pluralistic and decentralized ones, such as the United States. In the former, the authoritative representative community organizations provided an umbrella beneath which religious affairs take place at the synagogal level, but rabbinical leadership was displaced by or incorporated within the leadership of the nonreligious. In the United States, due to the role of religion in American society, to the size and strength of the organized rabbinical associations and their affiliated synagogue bodies, and to the outstanding qualities and capabilities of individual leading rabbis, they continued to play a more prominent public spokesmanship role. This is seen, for example, in the presidency of the American Jewish Congress or in the membership and chairmanship of the Conference of Presidents of major American Jewish Organizations.

Nevertheless, it must be noted that at the leadership level rabbis operated more as leading Jewish individuals than as representatives of faith groups or of the "Jewish religion." Their role, then, downgraded religious authority by incorporation. It permitted rabbis to share in the leadership mainly at the representational level, not by virtue of their religious authority, but by virtue of either their individual talents or the fact that they happen to speak in the name of a rabbinical association joined with other nonreligious organizations in a secularized organizational framework. In this context the development of a large cadre of Jewish professionals in the welfare, community relations, and educational spheres was also most significant.

In some societies—for example, Australia and France—there was considerable conflict involved in displacing religious (synagogal and rabbinical) spokesmanship. In the United States there was less open and direct conflict—the uncoordinated, fragmented pluralistic environment provided ample scope for the development of varied parallel forms of leadership and laid the ground for integration and coexistence. On the local plane, rabbis continued to play a prominent leadership role representing the Jewish community to its Christian neighbors both in specific interfaith activities and in more general community relations.

The contrast between Britain and France is also instructive. In Britain the Chief Rabbi and the Board of Deputies seemed to develop a *modus vivendi* at an early stage with the Board attaining a recognized representative spokesmanship function in the nineteenth century, without in any way derogating from the clear areas of authority of the Chief Rabbinate. In fact, the Board's constitution binds it to regard the Ashkenazi Chief Rabbi and the Sephardi Hacham as their rabbinical authorities on questions of Jewish law.

In France, the Chief Rabbi and his centralized consistorial synagogue framework were regarded as the official spokesman of the Jewish community via the CRIF, which they founded and consequently controlled. The CRIF operated out of the Consistoire's offices and its president was always either the president of the Consistoire or his delegate. This was challenged only in the late 1960s by the welfare, educational, and Zionist bodies, led by the Fonds Social, and the issue was specifically who should speak in the name of the Jewish community.

According to the Consistoire and its leaders it had to be the Chief Rabbi of France, the traditional head of French Jewry. According to its opponents, only a community leader representing all the various tendencies, religious and irreligious, could speak in the name of all French

Jews, and not just in that of the Jewish religion. As Alain de Rothschild, representing the Consistoire, put it:

> In matters having to do with representing the community before the government, it is certain that the government and the local or departmental authorities for Jewish questions, consider the community as one of the spiritual and religious families among other spiritual and religious families in France. Therefore they see in religious institutions or in their emanations their preferred negotiating partners, rather than representatives of many other institutions, whose political meaning they do not always grasp. . . . But what counts are the statements of the Chief Rabbi of France.[12]

Eventually the issue was settled by a greater degree of integration between a newly constituted CRIF and the Fonds Social. The offices were removed to the Fonds Social premises and the director was a Fonds Social official. Although the name was kept, and the president of the Consistoire retained the formal right to name the president, power and authority had moved, as seen in the fact that the first president was a former member of the executive committee of the Fonds Social and had never been a Consistoire leader. On the other hand the central role of the Chief Rabbi was consciously maintained, although in conjunction with the president of the CRIF. Of vital significance in providing the basis for the new cooperation was the strong common interest in a united policy on Israel. Both aspects were symbolized when during the 1973 war, the Chief Rabbi was accompanied by the CRIF president when he visited the French premier to protest French policy towards Israel.[13]

This process continued during the mid-1970s and strong cooperation between the two bodies was evident, especially with regard to Israel and the French government's policy towards it. Further representations by the Chief Rabbi and the CRIF president to the French president were made in 1975, for example, to protest French government policy on the PLO.

From the internal point of view, the most interesting development in France has been the success of the Fonds Social in becoming the umbrella organization for all Jewish communal activity, except the narrowest and strictest religious activity, which remained the province of the Consistoire. It changed from a fund-raising body to an integrated and inclusive framework covering all areas of Jewish communal activity, belief, and ideology. On the other hand, it sought in a sense to turn the clock back and to reestablish a form of *kehilla* with direct individual membership and democratic elections. But in this it failed; its membership drives to enroll individual members attracted only a small proportion of the community (17,000 in 1975) and its elections gained even less support and participation. Despite its failure to "democratize," the Fonds Social's significance in all areas of Jewish communal life was steadily increasing. Its failure to enroll individual members lay not in the fact that its work was not valued, but more in the fact that it did not control that one area of Jewish life of which individuals had most need and which could not be supplied elsewhere—the immediate, religious, ceremonial, and official functions in relation to the *rites de passage,* prayers, and dietary observances, all of which remained with the Consistoire.

We should also take note of the different pattern of development in Argentina in relation to these stages. In Argentina, stages 1–4 were telescoped and tended to occur almost simultaneously. The community developed a nonreligious representational pattern of community organization in which various political parties and cultural groups were represented via elections. Even though it grew out of the religious community, broadly conceived, it developed more out of community burial activities than out of its performance of religious practices for the living. In this pattern, then, there was never an established and prominent religious leadership to be displaced or even integrated, as Argentinian Jewry was established almost from the beginning on a secular representative basis within an ethnic rather than a religious framework. This was facilitated by the Argentinian view of ethnic group organization expressed in the concept of *madre patria.*[14]

By the mid-1970s it seemed that this form of communal organization in Argentina was unable to cope with the political and economic crises in which the Jewish community found itself. It was widely reported that the community's institutional structure was falling apart at the seams and facing rapid disintegration due to social instability, direct political violence, and the tremendous inroads of massive inflation of nearly 600 percent and, above all, due to deep communal apathy. Thus, teachers, administrators, and other communal workers participated in strike movements, and at one stage it seemed as if the whole Jewish educational structure was in jeopardy. In such a situation continuing elections on Israeli political party lines, in which only about 15 percent of those eligible voted, seemed anachronistic. Jewish school enrollment dropped 11 percent between 1975 and 1976, despite more coordinated administration. The synagogue, and the Jewish religion in general, seemed far removed from the lives of Argentinian Jewry and of little significance. In 1975 it was reported that only 25,000 Jews out of an estimated 250,000 Jews in Buenos Aires attended synagogue on the High Holy Days, which was one of the lowest proportions, if not the lowest proportion in the Jewish world (outside the Soviet bloc). Under such conditions Jewish youth were becoming even further removed from all forms of Jewish existence and had little contact with forms of Jewish organization, even of the nontraditional variety.

Stage 6: This stage was one of increasing significance in, and dominance of, Jewish communities by fund-raisers. This has come about partly through the widely accepted and increasing financial needs of Israel, but in addition the internal needs of the Jewish communities and the provision of educational, welfare, and other facilities have also played their part. The power and influence of the fund-raisers is greatest where fund-raising is unified or federated, and at that point it takes on some of the characteristics of the taxation function, and the power and influence that such functions command, even if both the community and its fund-raising are organized on essentially voluntary lines. The importance of fund-raisers may also be radically increased by the connection with Israel, and the power and prestige which for its purposes it accords to those who raise significant sums on its behalf, and which then carries on in internal community affairs (see below).

Coordinated communal fund-raising began much earlier in the United States than elsewhere and has reached its highest achievements there, both in the sums raised and the degree of coordination of local and overseas interests. In the United States the general rule is one major appeal in each community, the proceeds of which are then allocated for both overseas and local needs. However, streamlining, coordination, removal of competition and overlap, and planned budgeting have not been confined to the United States. Over the years there have been concerted efforts to maximize results, minimize costs, streamline and coordinate fund-raising, and achieve a degree of equitable and rational budget allocation in South Africa, Canada, Argentina, Brazil, France, and Australia. However, most communities have not followed the U.S. example, and have kept local and Israeli fund-raising separate, often because of strong and vested local Zionist and Jewish Agency interests and views.

## The Structure of Leadership:
## External Representation and Spokesmanship

Within these various organizational frameworks two patterns of leadership and representation seem to have developed: one was a centralized and recognized external representation together with noncoordinated fund-raising; the second was dispersed external representation with no recognized or authoritative framework together with centralized and coordinated fund-raising. The first tended to be the pattern of the British Commonwealth with officially recognized representative roof bodies, having grown out of an initial pattern of coordination among synagogues, and then been accepted by governments and by Jews (often in that order) as being in "control" of the community's external affairs. This status was reinforced by activity on behalf of Israel and by the representatives of Israel who have tended to work with these official communal bodies rather than invest legitimacy in the Zionist organizations. (South Africa is an exception in this context; the Zionist Federation's official task is to represent the community in all matters relating to Israel.) External communal policy is a matter of bargaining, negotiation, discussion, and agreement at the executive and plenary levels of the roof bodies; internally the tendency is for each separate body and institution to determine its own policies and to find the funds to match them. Such noncentralized fund-raising and policy-making sometimes resulted in overlapping, inefficient distribution of scarce resources, poor planning and coordination, and in the spreading of the available professional and administrative talent too thinly.

The second pattern of community control developed in the more pluralistic setting of the United States. There many competing organizations represented the community externally, in areas of civil rights, church and state, fighting discrimination, and so forth. Over the years there was a rapid rise to greater prominence and leadership by fundraisers, through their federated and coordinated fund-raising structures. Their capacity to fund the budgets of the various institutions in the community gives them potential influence in the setting of internal goals and policies. This pattern was distinguished therefore by coordination and control at the fund-raising level growing out of the earlier unification of welfare bodies into federations, and by representational disunity, except on the question of Israel.

In the 1950s an overall representational body with regard to Israel developed in the United States in the form of the Presidents' Conference, which consisted of the various competing public affairs bodies and other important religious and nonreligious organizations. Its powers of mobilizing concerted Jewish community action in support of Israel were greatly assisted by its direct and frequent connections with leading Israeli officials both in the United States and in Israel. Through its more than thirty member organizations, particularly the synagogue bodies, it could quickly mobilize both subleaders and the Jewish masses in support of Israel's policies, while its national spread also ensured maximum pressure via individual congressmen and senators. Both facts were clearly demonstrated during the Yom Kippur War. Its central mobilizing and representative role was also emphasized in its close involvement with the Conference on Soviet Jewry over the Jackson Amendment, and their agreement that both had to approve policy. Although there was a tendency among some Presidents' Conference leaders to tread lightly with the administration on this issue in order not to jeopardize support for Israel, it was eventually overridden by the Conference on Soviet Jewry's militant support for the Jackson Amendment. The latter's approach was strongly backed up at the grass roots in the United States and by Soviet Jewish activists who sent cables reminding American Jewish leaders of world Jewry's previous historic mistakes in failing to save Jews in danger.[15]

There were critics, on the other hand, who claim that the Presidents' Conference was a rather weak body, lacking in power, prestige, or respect, often overridden by its constituent organizations and held in contempt by their professionals.[16]

After the election of the Begin government in Israel in 1977, the Presidents' Conference seemed to increase in importance and status. While it had little influence on Israeli policy, it acted as the main public body maintaining support for Israeli policies, even when there was considerable disquiet among other leading American Jews at Begin's seeming inactivity and intransigence at various stages of the peace process. The Conference was handsomely repaid for its loyal support by Mr. Begin who reported to it regularly and seemed to consult with it on his frequent trips to the United States. Whatever the final verdict, the recent record makes it clear that the Presidents' Conference has provided a coordinated but not authoritative framework for enabling American Jewry to represent the most vital contemporary

Jewish interests with much greater unity than has hitherto been the case in the United States.

## Jewish Pursuit of Political Interests:
## The Recurrent Dilemmas of Representation

In developing these patterns of representation and authoritative spokesmanship, these Jewish communities have had to grapple with and resolve certain basic dilemmas that confront Jews in their political activity as a community in these societies.

### Individual or Group Participation

The first recurrent political dilemma has been whether Jews should be involved in politics as individuals or as a group. The first view was that Jews as a group do not have corporate political interests to be pursued collectively, and therefore Jews should participate in politics only as unorganized individuals. It sometimes was argued, further, that internal Jewish political organization was not sufficiently pervasive to permit taking a representative Jewish stance on issues.

The proponents of the group view assert that given the nature of the political system, the realistic pursuit of political interests demands group organization. They also have been more attuned to the existence of Jewish interests in politics. The development of pluralistic group-based political systems were seen either as an advantage for the pursuit of Jewish interests or, at the very least, as a reality to be exploited. In their view, the problems of Jewish unity and divisiveness should not stand in the way of group political activity; to the contrary, group political activity should be based only upon what is commonly agreed, it being the function of interested organizations within the group to create sufficient unity to enable the public statement of political positions.

An intermediate political stance developed after World War II, as seen in the changes that have taken place in the implications of the classic statement of the individualist position that "there is no Jewish vote," intended to affirm that Jews are not expected either by religious values or by communal membership or organization to support any particular political party, ideology, policy, or candidate. It should be noted that this view is still commonly put by representative and authoritative Jewish community spokesmen when elections are fought, even though the same bodies take strong group stances on basic Jewish interests such as Israel. This suggests a distinction between group pursuit of clear Jewish interests, on the one hand, where coordinated group activity is regarded as legitimate by Jewish leaders and organizations, and the individual citizenship obligations which demand that citizens play a more independent role in politics, assessing candidates and policies according to their own political views and attitudes, among which Jewish ethnic interests may be one factor among many, on the other hand. The classic individualist position goes one step further suggesting that there were no separate distinctive Jewish ethnic interests in politics in liberal societies which demanded either individual or group action qua Jews.

*Citizens or Minority Ethnic Group*

The second recurrent political dilemma, closely connected with the first, is whether strong Jewish political activity detracts from citizenship and national loyalties. Generally speaking, those who promote the individual position above emphasize citizenship, while those who take the group perspective view Jews as an ethnic group and see no necessary conflict between citizenship and minority ethnic group membership nor any diminution of citizenship status by group activity. Those who wish to be perceived solely as citizens whose religion happens to be Jewish believe that group political activity will expose their minority status, and create a fundamental inequality between Jews and other citizens. The way to maintain equality is not to act as an independent political group pursuing particularistic interests, as this merely serves to focus attention upon that which divides Jewry from the rest of society, rather than emphasize that which unites them. Those who adopt this position are concerned that Jews are not fully accepted socially by non-Jews and are accorded lower prestige, and they do not wish to accentuate this situation by emphasizing independent Jewish political interests.

Their view is that the organized group pursuit of Jewish political interests cuts across the individual citizenship loyalty to the state and threatens the uneasy coexistence of Jewish and national loyalties. Ethnic group political activity, they believe, intrudes into and disturbs the direct relationship of the citizen to the government so clearly expounded in liberal democratic theory. According to this classical theory the citizen should be motivated by individual and independent rational assessment of the collective good, not by permanent ascriptive noncompromisable primordial loyalties, not subject to rational argument and which reflect partial or particular, not collective or universal, goals.

Those who support ethnic group participation and conscious ethnic group attribution take the view that in the modern society a citizen has many loyalties and ties, an important one being the ethnic tie. The citizen is, moreover, generally able simultaneously to maintain these various ties and loyalties. From this perspective the ethnic tie does not derogate from, or even diminish, the uninterrupted tie connecting the citizen to his government, if for no other reason than that this simply does not exist.

In political terms, then, this outlook attempts to synthesize the individual and the group approaches as being consistent with the reality of modern society. It suggests that the individual will get little in society unless he is organized on group lines, and if there are Jewish interests in politics, a view that it affirms, then the only way to pursue them is in collective group activity. What is more, the proponents of this view argue that citizenship is enhanced by the diversity and cultural pluralism that stem from recognition of the varied ties and loyalties of the individual in the modern society. Nor, in their view, will Jewish behavior, by and large, have a great impact upon the way in which society perceives Jews. If society's ethnic prestige ladder places Jews in a subordinate position, Jewish political action will not affect this prestige ranking, which is more deeply rooted in the prejudices of the society's culture and values. To the contrary, the only way to alter negative ethnic esteem and to improve the ranking is by group political activity. Thus, a paradoxical result of the individual citizenship position is to maintain the negative ranking it sought to avoid, and to neglect Jewish political interests that might otherwise have been protected.

*Intervention in Politics—Particularist or Universal?*

The particularist view encompassing both the individual and the group orientations argues for narrow, self-concerned Jewish activity in politics confined to immediate and clear Jewish interests, such as anti-

Semitism and discrimination and, of course, Israel. It sees no benefit, and potential disadvantages, in engaging in political activity beyond this immediate almost private Jewish sphere. In this view, every group must protect its own interests, and Jews bear no responsibility for any other group or for the society as a whole. Such concerns would dissipate Jewish energies, lead to neglect of Jewish interests, or would attract additional opposition and antagonism to Jewry. It is safer, wiser, and more secure for Jews, who have enough problems and battles of their own to contend with, not to fight the battles of others.

The universalist conception is broader, other-oriented, and more public-minded. It consists of ideological and pragmatic components. The ideological argument appears in many forms and guises; its essence is that Jews, especially, ought to assist other less privileged groups, because Jews have been the persecuted people par excellence. Because of their history and experiences, and guided by the universalistic aspects of the prophetic tradition, Jews should fight persecution, discrimination, prejudice, injustice, inequality, and the like, against whomsoever it is directed. The pragmatic argument contends that only when prejudice, injustice, inequality, and so forth, are completely eliminated, will Jewry be really safe and secure, and accepted as equals, and it therefore benefits Jews, if only indirectly, to fight the battles of other underprivileged and persecuted groups. Jews must therefore be involved in the general and universal struggle for human rights and justice because this is, in the long run, the only way in which they can guarantee their own human rights and equality as individuals and as a group. The pragmatic argument thus directly contradicts the pragmatic assumption for Jews not fighting the battles of others, the view that it will engender additional opposition and antipathy to Jews among those who oppose the causes and groups Jews support.

*Nonvisibility and Conspicuousness*

One of the underlying themes of the previous three dilemmas bears individual mention: whether Jews should try to be as nonvisible as possible, or whether they should accept conspicuousness as an unavoidable consequence of public and political prominence. The argument is asymmetrical: the positive side does not contend that as a matter of principle Jews ought consistently to seek to play a prominent role. The argument is one of unavoidability—that there seem to be no other ways to protect Jewish political interests. Thus, both views share the basic assumption that lack of prominence and inconspicuousness are preferable.

This psychological predisposition stems directly from Jewry's minority status, a state of mind that wherever possible seeks to avoid drawing attention to Jewry as a distinctive group with values and interests that differ from those of the rest of society. The fear is that visibility as a distinctive group may lead to increased discrimination, prejudice, anti-Semitism and the like. Nonvisibility makes discrimination more difficult to apply and justify, it being assumed that Jewish behavior will directly affect their treatment. This apprehension, in whatever form, whether lightly or acutely felt, is part of the unavoidable heritage and inescapable implications of minority status, as Kurt Lewin pointed out in the 1930s.

This disposition, however inescapable, is subject to a process of waxing and waning in different societies and under different historical conditions, but it never disappears completely. The history of Jewry in the last thirty to forty years in Western pluralist societies provides strong evidence of a decline in the compelling power of this argument and its steady abandonment, combined with greater willingness to accept the consequences of conspicuousness. But this is only a recent development, coming earlier and going further in some societies than in others. But even in the former, the fear of visibility still places limits on Jewish public intervention in politics. For example, all the previous arguments in favor of individual, not group pursuit of political interest, in support of citizenship identity rather than independent minority ethnic group identity, in support of either complete nonintervention in politics or a self-regarding, Jewish centered, particularistic intervention, rather than a universalistic, public-minded interventionism, are all partly motivated by, and partly influenced by this psychological disposition.

### Structural Characteristics of Jewish Communities:
### A Brief Outline

These developments suggest a recent degree of convergence in world Jewish patterns of community organization, regardless of their historical origins, and the specific issues over which representational unity has been achieved. In all cases we deal with Jewish communities that are *organizations of organizations,* not organizations of individuals or organizations of citizens, believers, or a single community of members. The recognized and authoritative community roof body or spokesman does not enjoy unmediated or direct contact with the individual members or families in the Jewish community, but has contact with, and authority over them only through other organizations to which they belong, and little influence over them if they belong to no organization. One direct result of this pattern of community organization is that the views, ideas, goals, and aspirations of the Jewish grass roots and rank and file reach the top, if at all, only as interpreted and presented by various subleaders who, presumably, have their own personal and institutional interests to promote, which must clearly influence their transmission of the views of their constituencies.

There are limits to the degree of possible unification. The pattern of arrangements we described suggests that the top bodies of the Jewish communities are "peak associations," similar to the top bodies of industry in the various societies in which the Jews are living, such as the Federation of British Industry, or the United States Chamber of Commerce, or the National Association of Manufacturers. Such associations often encounter problems through seeking to include all the relevant organizations within their structures, on the one hand, and once they do, of having to adopt policies that do not disaffect members, on the other. The result is often a watering down of policies in order to ensure maximum unity. Peak associations, including federations or umbrella organizations derive their strength from member organizations and their continued willingness to cooperate, and not from a relationship of loyalty and commitment of individual members. In loosely organized federative bodies, such as the Presidents' Conference, affiliates are often jealous of their independence, distinctive character, and autonomy, and perceive these to be threatened by any increase in the peak association organizational capacity or strength, and they therefore tend to prevent unification proceeding beyond a very loose umbrella. Much, of course, depends upon the nature of the external threat: if this is considered great and affects all Jews and organizations equally, there will be a greater inclination to cede some autonomy and distinctiveness to the common cause.

Even in countries with representative roof bodies the situation is not very different. Although the authoritative single external spokesmanship role is accepted as legitimate, and it is recognized, these representative boards are able to function in this way precisely because they keep out of the path of the organizations in the internal sphere. There they allow the latter to pursue their own goals as private, voluntary, and autonomous organizations.

The general organizational picture of the Jewish communities, then, is of a large variety of organizations each operating in its own particular sphere of interests and concern, with varied degrees of local, regional, national, or functional coordination, and the top bodies being loosely organized peak associations coordinating various other coordinating bodies. These umbrella bodies coordinate existing activities and create a free space for organizations, but few plan, direct, or undertake community-wide policy initiatives. Each organization does its own planning and policy initiation. Thus, it would be wrong to conceive of the Jewish community as a government in the conventional sense, instituting policies that will be effective over the whole community and which has final authority in particular federal, state, or local areas. Each body in the Jewish community can act independently if it wishes, because the community has no formal or legal coercive power to enforce its decisions, and rests entirely on a foundation of voluntary subordination and agreement. The only test for a Jewish organization is whether it can get sufficient leadership and financial resources to carry out its program and goals and maintain its institutions.

These structural arrangements have produced a number of distinctive institutional characteristics. Given the nature of Jewish community organization, membership of the Jewish community is formally established by affiliation to some Jewish organization or by donation or subscription to some Jewish cause, provided of course that the person is born Jewish. (Membership of the Jewish people, by way of contrast, is by birth.) Membership of Jewish organizations is formally voluntary, although in many instances the psychological and social consequences of nonaffiliation may be quite high, as in Argentina where Jewish burial will not be provided for those who do not belong. In most communities intense social pressures are brought to bear on individuals to affirm their natural membership of the Jewish people by contributing to Jewish causes or by joining some body. Membership of synagogues fits into the same pattern, insofar as it is closely related to the *rites de passage,* which in many cases will not be administered to nonmembers, and to the provision of Jewish education, which is often restricted to the children of synagogue members.

The second major distinctive organizational characteristic of contemporary Jewish communities is that there exist no democratic or representative integrative mechanisms for joining rank and file members to their leaders. In most communities there are no elections for those who represent the community and are its authoritative spokesmen. At best, organizations send representatives to broader bodies and these elect their leaders. Often this process of leadership selection can be repeated at three or four levels, which removes it considerably from the average rank and file member of the Jewish community. In some communities there are direct elections for the membership or part of the membership of the roof body, but even here this excludes the membership of its leadership group which is chosen by the elected delegates. What is more, these elections are marked by very low levels of participation of the eligible. In Argentina only 28 percent participated in the elections in 1969, while in France in the same year only 15 percent turned out to vote and in Australia at its peak less than 20 percent voted.[17]

Neither are there devices for enabling the masses to participate in policy formulation, for expressing views on policy matters, nor for binding their leaders to follow any particular policy line. Most important issues are decided at executive levels and, even where there are public debates on issues in more or less open forums like the various Boards of Deputies, they strike very few echoes in their communities. The latter tend to be ignorant of the activities of these bodies, apathetic towards them and completely uninvolved in what they do.[18]

In communities where fund-raisers are prominent if not dominant in communal governance, government is developed via fund-raising, which is the opposite of the usual political processes. In the latter the governing authority or those that seek its control first set a series of goals and adopt a set of policies, and then use their political power to find the resources to allocate to these programs in accord with their priorities. In the fund-raising-dominated Jewish communities the tendency in the past has been *first* to collect the funds and then allocate them to the various affiliated projects. Overall community needs, planning, long-range plans, and priorities have in this process often been neglected. Governmental decision making and resource allocation encourages public input and feedback both at elections and between them when they can express their views on these matters. In the Jewish community there is little scope for the average community member or contributor to express to the fund-raisers views on how to disburse the money contributed to comprehensive Jewish appeals.[19]

In the United States, the process of fund-raising federation and centralization now seems to be entering a new phase, under the influence and guidance of its professionals, with an increasing emphasis upon communal planning, budgeting, and coordination. There has been a move away from the provision of welfare and health services such as hospitals, which served non-Jews as much as if not more than Jews, to overall community goals for both cultural and external Jewish purposes. The communities, therefore, are becoming more centralized in their planning. The federations are now setting goals first, budgeting for them, and collecting and distributing the resources to fulfill these goals, in a more coordinated communal framework and orientation. Community planning sections and committees are becoming increasingly important—side-by-side with fund-raising campaign committees.

Nevertheless, while these processes are now more tailored to community need and interests, they still lie in the domain of the fund-raiser and the professionals and their community planning advisers, often academics, and are still not closely integrated with nor attuned to the grass roots in a direct representational sense (see below).[20]

There is a marked degree of elite control in contemporary Jewish communities. One must be able to assess the quality of its rule by showing how it controls the affairs of the community or society, and how it exercises its dominance so that its views always or nearly always prevail against those of others. Finally, one must examine the substance of its decisions, to ask: Who benefits? In whose interests are the decisions? While the establishment of these criteria is very difficult in larger complex societies with many decision areas, many sets of competing leaders, many interests, and with a myriad of formal institutions and organizations at all kinds of levels, not to speak of the countless informal connections and behind-the-scenes influentials, to examine this problem in terms of the Jewish community is somewhat easier.

Three fundamental facts suggest that contemporary Jewish communities are run on elitist lines. First, there is a screen of wealth which generally, although not always, determines who will become a leader. The major figures on the fund-raising scene are generally also major donors who set an example, and to be a major donor requires wealth. At the very least one must give according to one's means. At a lesser

perceive problems and understand Jewish interests differently from the rest of the community. Leaders may act according to their particular interests or attitudes, for example, to preserve their social position, to enhance their integration or to earn general societal prestige, rather than promote the views of the community or its needs, of which they may be unaware. In the United States, but not elsewhere, this was reflected in the specific social welfare and health orientations of the various federations, and particularly the vast expenditures on medical and health services and hospitals, much of which were of greater benefit to the general, rather than the Jewish, community, and the relative neglect of Jewish education and activity to promote Jewish values and survival. In recent years there have been strong challenges to this orientation and significant changes in it. It is also reflected in the differing responses to the current problems of liberalism and radicalism in the United States of the upper-class Jews and the Jewish leaderships, who have been generally more favorable to the black than have been the Jewish lower middle class who are directly threatened.[22]

Jewish leadership selection processes tend to follow the classic elitist tactic of co-optation. Those deemed suitable by the current leadership are co-opted, and it is the former who determine what, and who, is "suitable." Generally they will be of similar social status and of similar attitudes and will in all likelihood carry on similar policies. Without elections it is difficult for potential leaders of different views, outlooks, and policies to become members of the community's leadership group or to redirect the community's energies. The talented and the motivated can rise into the leadership only insofar as the entrenched incumbents permit them, and not through mobilizing wider community support. The test for leadership then is highly personal and in no way democratic.

The third element of elitism in contemporary Jewish community leadership is that most decision making is conducted in private and not through discussion in any public forum joining community leaders and members. The leaderships make crucial political decisions on behalf of the communities behind closed doors. Even the representative Boards, despite open meetings, do little to involve the public. Key issues are discussed in camera by executive bodies; any open public discussions tend to be the final ratifications of policies already made or approval of actions already taken or the discussion of noncontroversial issues. One specific reason for such in camera decision making in the contemporary period is the Israeli connection. Leading Jewish community bodies undertake activity in support of Israel, following official Israeli policy in conjunction with the Israeli authorities and diplomatic representatives, which is of its nature highly secret and out of the public eye. Secrecy, of course, maximizes leaders' control over their communities.

Jewish community leaderships therefore seem to constitute an elite which is not accountable to the community members, or a series of unaccountable elites which often coalesce rather than operate separately to form what Elazar has called a multi-element oligarchy, rather than a single-element oligarchy,[23] representing the various major organizations and institutions in the community. But a multi-element oligarchy, even though representative in a functional sense, is no less an oligarchy.

There are also certain counter-tendencies in contemporary Jewish community structure and leadership that point in a nonelitist direction. One is the aspect of incentive: few members of the community seem to have the incentive to become highly involved, and thus leaders often evolve by default. It is therefore often suggested that anyone wishing to become involved in Jewish community affairs will be accepted and integrated into the leadership if he has sufficient talents, time, and leisure. While this may be so it still leaves leadership the preserve of the wealthy: it does not answer the question of how someone who does not have the time, leisure, and means can become a community leader. So long as there are no salaried top representative and policy-making positions in the community there will be no answer to this question.

Second, it is often argued that there is no demand within the Jewish communities to develop more accountable and responsive representative and democratic institutions, and to enable the Jewish public to participate in leadership selection and policy making, because the latter do not utilize the currently available avenues of institutional participation. This is taken as an indication that individuals are either satisfied with the way things are, or their incentive for involvement is irreversibly low, for otherwise they would be involved in the existing structures. While this may be factually correct, without the experience of truly representative institutions one can never assume with certainty that nonparticipation in unsatisfactory present forms would necessarily imply nonparticipation in new ones.

The strongest counter-elitist tendency is the fact that, by and large, Jewish organizations are representative of the basic views of the majority of the Jewish community on the fundamental issues of Jewish interest—Israel, anti-Semitism, Soviet Jewry, and so forth. Historically speaking, as we saw, the leaderships of Jewish communities moved in consonance with the expectations of the Jewish masses. For example, as the communities became more Zionist and more willing publicly and actively to promote Jewish interests, the leaderships fell into line. Where they failed to do so they were pushed aside, as in the case of the various anti-Zionist leaderships. In this sense the leaderships represent widely shared community attitudes and act as their "trustees."

Unresponsive and unrepresentative leaderships generally lead to the rise of internal protest movements, which are either co-opted into the leaderships, or get their point of view and the intensity with which they hold it taken note of in altered policies, or they just fade out. Different examples of this protest phenomenon are the Jewish Defense League, the Jewish student protest movement, and its offshoot, the Jewish radicals. The latter were specifically concerned with a radical reorientation of Jewish priorities back to Jewish survivalism and "authentic" Jewish values. In the initial stages they were also involved in the campaign to focus public attention on Soviet Jewry, before this was taken up by the top leaderships. The radical student movement has also taken a different line on Israel, being more sympathetic to Left and radical views on the Palestinian question. They are not content to follow official Israeli policy unquestioningly as do all the main Jewish leadership bodies, but have sought to find room for Palestinian claims within their overall support for Israel.[24]

The elitist argument hinges upon the implicit assumption that participation in both the associational and the value aspects of Jewish life could be higher. Of this there is no doubt. And it is also true that normatively some believe it should be higher. The question, however, is whether it is low in comparison with patterns of participation in other voluntary organizations. In other words, how realistic is the demand for greater participation? In general the rate of affiliation to organizations in the Jewish community roughly parallels that in most industrialized societies. In industrialized countries about 60 percent of adults belong to some voluntary organizations and among the higher educated and the middle classes participation rises to about 80 percent while active membership among the latter group is about 60 percent.[25] No definitive figures are available for the Jewish communities, but Sklare's findings in Lakeville suggest that membership in some kind of Jewish organization (including synagogues) reaches 88 percent.[26] Similarly Elazar estimated that 5 percent of the Jewish community were hard core, 10 percent were involved participants, 30 percent were members, 30 percent were contributors and consumers, and only 25 percent were either peripherals or quasi-Jews.[27] A similar pattern exists in other Jewish communities.[28] In comparison, then, with rates of participation in other voluntary organizations, that within the Jewish community seems *high rather than low*.

The problem, however, is not the extent of membership, but the quality of the participation. Compared with the past there has been a decline in authentic Jewish values and their embodiment in independent or autonomous self-governing communities whose leaderships related to the value system of the Jewish community and not to external criteria, and where Jews were more fully Jewish in every sense of the word and in every aspect of life. Now the element of Jewishness occupies a much smaller part of their life space and time, and contemporary Jewish community life pales in comparison.[29] The Jewish community, moreover, is not the same kind of political entity as a sovereign state with all the coercive power and national goals that characterize the latter. At very best, it is a partial community—a series of voluntary organizations serving the interests of Jews. It is perhaps not appropriate, therefore, to judge it by the representative and democratic standards of sovereign states, but more fitting to compare it with the patterns of leadership and authority in voluntary organizations, which tend to be more oligarchical. Yet even here the Jewish communities suffer by comparison. Within voluntary organizations it is commonly possible to present differing views, contest elections, and so forth. But in contemporary Jewish communities as a loose series of independent and overlapping organizations, even this possibility is for the moment closed. Whether Jewish communities, organized as they currently are, and without more responsive and representative leadership and executive bodies, will continue to be able to mobilize the vast majority of members of Jewish communities and command their loyalty is an open question.

These processes are accelerated by the fact that contemporary Jewish communities are *acephalous*: they have no single head, no single or final source of leadership and power, and they have not devised mechanisms that will provide them with legitimate authority. In terms of what one might expect from such an acephalous situation, one ought perhaps to express wonder at the extent of common Jewish effort rather than criticize the absence of representative and democratic mechanisms. Yet even if one grants that their applicability to voluntary organizations is somewhat limited, the fact is that the available possibilities have not been fully explored, nor is there much inclination to do so. From this perspective, therefore, one might seek improvement, unless, of course, one took the view that these mechanisms work only where individuals and groups know what they want. It is by no means certain that the average Jew knows what he wants out of Jewishness and from the Jewish communities and their various affiliated organizations, or that the Jewish leaderships know what the communities want. Nor is it certain that what the leaderships desire corresponds to what the communities want, or need, if they are to survive.

## Notes

1.  See Chaim Bermant, *Troubled Eden: An Anatomy of British Jewry,* (London, 1969), pp. 101–6; On Australia, see P. Y. Medding, *From Assimilation to Group Survival* (Melbourne, 1968).
2.  See Steven E. Ascheim, "The Communal Organization of South African Jewry," *Jewish Journal of Sociology* 12 (December 1970): 201–34; and *Encyclopaedia Judaica,* entries under "South Africa" and "Zionism in South Africa."
3.  See Moshe Davis, "Centres of Jewry in the Western Hemisphere: A Comparative Approach," *Jewish Journal of Sociology* 5 (June 1963): 4–26, and *Encyclopaedia Judaica,* "Canada" and "Zionism—In Canada."
4.  See Samuel Halperin, *The Political World of American Zionism* (Detroit, 1961); *Encyclopaedia Judaica,* "United States" and "Zionism—In the United States"; on the American Jewish Committee, see Naomi W. Cohen, *Not Free to Desist: The AJC 1906–1966* (Philadelphia, 1972).
5.  M. Salzberg, "The Organized Jewish Community in France," Ph.D. thesis (University of Paris, 1975); *Encyclopaedia Judaica,* "France" and "Zionism—In France."
6.  See H. Avni, "A Profile of Contemporary Argentinian Jewry," unpublished manuscript; M. Davis, *Centres of Jewry*; and *Encyclopaedia Judaica,* "Latin America."
7.  Avni, "A Profile"; Davis, *Centres of Jewry* and *Encyclopaedia Judaica.*
8.  Bermant, . *Troubled Eden*; Medding, *From Assimilation.*
9.  Medding, *From Assimilation.*
10.  P. Selznick, *The Organizational Weapon* (Glencoe, 1960), pp. 117–8.
11.  See S. Adler and T. E. Connolly, *From Ararat to Suburbia: The History of the Jewish Community of Buffalo* (Philadelphia, 1960), pp. 385–9; M. Vorspan and L. I. Gartner, *History of the Jews of Los Angeles* (Philadelphia, 1970), pp. 201–202; and P. E. Jacobs, *Is Curly Jewish?* (New York, 1965).

12. Quoted in Salzberg, "The Organized Jewish Community," pp. 154–55.
13. Ibid.
14. See Davis, *Centres of Jewry.*
15. On the Jackson Amendment, see W. D. Korey, "Struggle Over Jackson-Mills-Vanik" *AJYB* 75 (1974/75): 198–223.
16. See G. Strober, *American Jews: Community in Crisis* (New York: Doubleday, 1974), p. 30.
17. See Avni, "A Profile," p. 175; Medding, *From Assimiliation,* pp. 41–42; and Salzberg, "The Organized Jewish Community," p. 193.
18. See H. Avni, "A Profile"; J. Gould and S. Esh, *Jewish Life in Modern Britain* (London: Routledge & Kegan Paul, 1964), p. 22; and Bermant, *Troubled Eden*; and Medding, *From Assimilation.* See also P. Y. Medding, ed., *Jews in Australian Society* (Melbourne, 1973), p. 25.
19. For a very critical approach to the fund-raisers, see Judah J. Shapiro, "The Philistine Philanthropists: The Power and Shame of Jewish Federations," in J. N. Porter and P. Dreier, *Jewish Radicalism: A Selected Anthology* (New York: Grove Press, 1973), pp. 203–7.
20. On these developments see D. J. Elazar, *Community and Polity: The Organizational Dynamics of American Jewry* (Philadelphia, 1976).
21. On professionals, see Shapiro, "The Philistine Philanthropists"; Elazar, *Community and Polity*; and C. S. Liebman, "Dimensions of Authority in the Contemporary Jewish Community," *Jewish Journal of Sociology* 12 (June 1970): 19–38.
22. For an elaboration of this theme, see my chapter in this volume, "Towards a General Theory of Jewish Political Interests and Behavior."
23. Elazar, *Community and Polity.*
24. On Jewish radicalism, see Porter and Dreier, *Jewish Radicalism.*
25. See S. Verba and N. Nie, *Participation in America* (New York: Harper & Row, 1972), pp. 174–80.
26. M. Sklare, *Jewish Identity on the Suburban Frontier* (New York: Basic Books, 1967), pp. 252–53.
27. Elazar, *Community and Polity.*
28. See Medding, *From Assimilation.* See W. M. Lippmann, "Profile of Melbourne Jewry," in Medding, ed., *Jews in Australian Society,* pp. 24–26.
29. I have elaborated on this theme at greater length in "Equality and the Shrinkage of Jewish Identity," in M. Davis, ed., *World Jewry and the State of Israel* (New York: Arno Press, 1977), pp. 119–34.

# IV

# Contemporary Implications

# Introduction: Judaism and Jewish Communities in the Contemporary World

The Jewish polity has undergone many changes since its inception somewhere in the Sinai Desert but none have been more decisive than those that have affected it in the past three centuries.[1] The inauguration of the modern epoch, born out of the revolution in science, technology, politics, economics, and religion that caused the Western world to take a radical turn in the mid-seventeenth century, initiated a process of decorporatization of Jewish communal life that gained momentum for the following two centuries.[2] Jewish corporate autonomy, a feature of diaspora existence in one way or another since the Babylonian settlements, is the product of the modern epoch. World War I brought down the last remnants of that kind of autonomy in Europe, where it had been on the wane for two centuries. Only in certain of the Muslim countries did the old forms persist until the nationalist revolutions of the period after World War II eliminated them.

Decorporatization—perhaps denationalization is a better term—brought with it efforts to redefine Jewish life in Protestant religious terms in western Europe and North America and socialist secular ones in eastern Europe and, somewhat later, in Latin America. In Europe the process was promoted from within the Jewish community and without by Jews seeking wider economic and social opportunities as individuals and by newly nationalistic regimes seeking to establish the state as the primary force in the life of all residents within its boundaries. In the Americas, it came automatically as individual Jews found themselves in the same position as other migrants to the New World.

Out of decorporatization came new forms of Jewish communal organization in the countrywide and local arenas: (1) the *consistoire* of postrevolutionary France which spread to the other countries within the French sphere of influence in Europe and the Mediterranean basin—an attempt to create a Jewish "church" structure parallel to that of the Catholic church; (2) the nineteenth-century Central European *kehillah* or *cultesgemeinde,* essentially a religious and social agency chartered and regulated by the secular government to provide an official framework for all Jews parallel to the frameworks binding Christians in the state; (3) the united congregational pattern of Britain and its overseas settlements by which Jews voluntarily banded together to create a board of notables ("deputies") to represent Jewish interests to the government of the host country; (4) the radically individualistic "congregational" pattern of the United States by which individual Jews voluntarily banded together, principally in the local arena, to create whatever kinds of Jewish associations they wished without any kind of supralocal umbrella organization even for external representation; and (5) separate communal associations based on the *Landsmannschaft* (country of origin society) principle, which became the basis for voluntary affiliation of the Jewish immigrants to Latin America. The common denominator of all these different forms was their limited scope and increasingly voluntary character.

While these organizational changes were taking place, a two-pronged demographic shift of great importance began: the live birth and survival rate among Jews rose rapidly, causing the number of Jews in the world to soar, and the Jews began to migrate at an accelerating rate to the lands of the Western world's great frontier (the Western Hemisphere, southern Africa, and Australia in particular but also in smaller numbers to East Asia), thus initiating a shift in the balance of Jewish settlement in the world (see table IV.1).[3]

Finally, the modern epoch saw Jewish resettlement of the Land of Israel. The first settlers to come as founders of new settlements began to arrive in the seventeenth century and continued regularly thereafter, pioneering new communities of a traditional character within the framework of the Ottoman Empire's *millet* system.[4] They were followed by the Zionist pioneers who, beginning in the last decades of the nineteenth century, created new forms of communal life as part of the latest stage in the transformation of the Jewish people.[5]

Table IV.1
Jewish Population and Distribution by Continent
(in thousands)

| Continent | 1840 | | 1900 | | 1939 | | 1982 | |
|---|---|---|---|---|---|---|---|---|
| | Total | % | Total | % | Total | % | Total | % |
| Europe[1] | 3,950 | 87.8 | 8,900 | 80.9 | 9,50 | 56.8 | 2,843 | 21.9 |
| Asia | 300 | 6.7 | 510 | 4.6 | 1,030 | 6.2 | 3,417 | 26.3 |
| Africa | 198 | 4.4 | 375 | 3.4 | 625 | 3.7 | 172 | 1.3 |
| North America | 50 | 1.1 | 1,200 | 10.9 | 5,540 | 33.1 | 6,478 | 49.9 |
| & | | | | | | | | |
| South America | | | | | | | | |
| Oceania | 2 | * | 15 | 0.2 | 33 | 0.2 | 79 | 0.6 |
| Total | 4,500 | 100.0 | 11,000 | 100.0 | 16,728 | 100.0 | 12,989 | 100.0 |

\* less that 0.1%
1. Including Russia
*Sources*: Jacob Lestschinsky, *Tfutzot Yisrael ahar haMilhamah*, Tel Aviv, 1958. *American Jewish Year Book,
1968* and *1984*.

## Beginning a New Epoch

World War II marked the culmination of all the trends and tendencies of the modern epoch and the end of the epoch itself for all peoples. Sometime between 1946 and 1949, the postmodern epoch began. For the Jewish people, the Holocaust and the establishment of the State of Israel provided the pair of decisive events that marked the crossing of the watershed into the postmodern world. In the process, the entire basis of the Jewish polity was radically changed, the locus of Jewish life shifted, and virtually every organized Jewish community was reconstituted in some way.

Central to the reconstitution was the reestablishment of a politically independent Jewish commonwealth in Israel. The restoration of the Jewish state added a new factor to the *edah,* creating a new focus of Jewish energy and concern precisely at the moment when the older foci had reached the end of their ability to attract most Jews. As the

1967 crisis demonstrated decisively, Israel was not simply another Jewish community in the constellation but the center of the world for Jews.

The Jewry that greeted the new state was no longer an expanding one that was gaining population even in the face of the attrition of intermarriage and assimilation. On the contrary, it was a decimated one (even worse, for decimated means the loss of one in ten; the Jews lost one in three), a Jewry whose very physical survival had been in grave jeopardy and whose rate of loss from defections came close to equaling its birthrate. Moreover, the traditional strongholds of Jewish communal life in Europe (which were also areas with a high Jewish reproduction rate) were those that had been wiped out.

At the end of the 1940s the centers of Jewish life had shifted decisively away from Europe to Israel and North America. By then, continental Europe ranked behind Latin America, North Africa, and Great Britain, as a force in Jewish life. Its Jews were almost entirely dependent on financial and technical assistance from the United States and Israel. Except for those in the Moslem countries that were soon virtually to disappear, the major functioning Jewish communities all had acquired sufficient size to become significant factors on the Jewish scene only within the previous two generations. In many cases, the original shapers of those communities were still alive, and many were still the actual community leaders. The Jewish world had been willy-nilly thrown back to a pioneering stage.

This new epoch is still in its early years, hardly more than a single generation old; hence, its character is still in its formative stages. Nevertheless, with the establishment of the State of Israel in 1948 the Jewish polity began a constitutional change of revolutionary proportions, inaugurating a new epoch in Jewish constitutional history. For the first time in almost two millennia, the Jewish people were presented with the opportunity to attain citizenship in their own state. Israel's very first law (*Hok Ha-Shevut*, the Law of Return) specified that every Jew had a right to settle in Israel and automatically acquire Israeli citizenship.

To date, only a fraction of the *edah* have taken advantage of Israel's availability. Most continue to live in the lands of the diaspora of their own free will. Hence, the dominant structural characteristic of the *edah* continues to be the absence of a binding, all-embracing political framework, although it now has a focus. The State of Israel and its various organs have a strong claim to preeminence in fields that touch on every aspect of Jewish communal life. The Israeli leadership have argued consistently that Israel is qualitatively different from the diaspora and hence its centrality must be acknowledged. The American Jewish leadership, in particular, have taken the position that Israel is no more than first among equals. Nevertheless, the reestablishment of a Jewish state has crystallized the *edah* as a polity, restoring a sense of political involvement among Jews and shaping a new institutional framework in which the business of the *edah* is conducted.

The diffusion of authority and influence, which continues to characterize the structure of the *edah* and its components, has taken various forms in the new epoch. The *keter malkhut* has been transformed into a network of single and multipurpose functional authorities, most of which do not aspire to do more than serve their particular functions, but all of which acknowledge the place of the State of Israel at the fulcrum of the network. The *keter kehunah* has become a conglomeration of synagogue movements and their rabbinates, who are mainly responsible for ritual and pastoral functions. Each manages—independently—various ritual functions in a manner it deems appropriate to its own traditions, perspectives, and environment. That each of these movements has established a framework with worldwide aspirations, such as the World Union for Progressive Judaism and the World Council of Synagogues, merely underlines the new organizational character of the *edah*.

Sectoral segmentation is most pronounced in the *keter torah*. Contemporary Jews take their cues in this domain from a kaleidoscopic spectrum of authorities. Their range stretches from the Jewish professors and scholars who influence contemporary Jews' understanding of what is expected of them as Jews to the rabbinical leadership of the Orthodox, Conservative, and Reform camps, who may use the traditional devices for ruling on matters of Torah but often in untraditional ways; to the heads of very traditional *yeshivot* and the *rebbes* of various emigré Hassidic communities who have reestablished themselves in the principal cities of Israel and the United States from which they have developed multicountry networks.

The fragmentation of the *keter torah* is both a reflection and an expression of the absence yet of a clear-cut, commonly accepted constitutional basis for the entire *edah*. The tendency toward a wide variety of interpretations of the Torah (traditionally referred to in Hebrew as *Torat Moshe,* the teaching of Moses) which emerged during the modern epoch has now become exacerbated. It is a sign of the times that if the Torah is to be included in the definition of the constitution, it has to be reinterpreted for a majority of Jews. The reality is that the norms by which Jews live their lives are interpreted through various prisms, of which the traditional prism is now only one. Still, it seems that most Jews perceive the Torah to be a constitutional referent in some way.

This fragmentation is further reflected in the multiplicity of camps and parties that exert influence on the life of the *edah* and its constituents. Broadly speaking, the principal camps can be termed: the Orthodox and the *Masorati* (traditional) who see themselves as continuing the ways of the Pharisees, the Liberal religious, and the Neo-Sadducees. The last includes Israelis seeking to express their Judaism through Israeli Jewry's emerging civil religion—Zionists—and those diaspora Jews who find their best means of Jewish expression in the Jewish communal institutions. These camps are separate but not mutually exclusive. Presented diagrammatically, they ought to be viewed as a triangle, a device that stresses their points of overlap as well as their distinctiveness. The Mizrahi Party, for instance, straddles the Zionist and the Orthodox camps, viewing its Zionism as one expression of its Orthodoxy. Increasingly, too, do the Conservative (Masorati) and Reform (Liberal) movements find themselves linked with Zionism. At the same time, the Neturei Karta, the secular Zionists, and the surviving classical Reform elements remain separated in their respective camps.

Whatever its form of organization, the primary fact of Jewish communal life today is its voluntary character. Although there are differences from country to country in degree of actual freedom to be Jewish or not, the virtual disappearance of the remaining legal and even social or cultural barriers to individual free choice in all but a handful of countries has made free association the dominant characteristic of Jewish life in the postmodern era. Consequently, the first task of each Jewish community is the learn to deal with this freedom. This task is a major factor in determining the direction of the reconstitution of Jewish life in this generation.

The new voluntarism also extends into the internal life of the Jewish community, generating pluralism even in previously free but relatively homogeneous or monolithic community structures. This pluralism is increased by the breakdown of the traditional reasons for being Jewish and the rise of new incentives for Jewish association. This pluralistic Jewish polity can best be described as a communications network of interacting institutions, each of which, while preserving its own structural integrity and filling its own functional role, is connected to the others in a variety of ways. The boundaries of the polity, insofar as it is bounded, are revealed only when the pattern of the network is uncovered. The pattern stands revealed only when both its components are: its institutions and organizations with their respective roles and the way in which communications are passed between them.

The pattern is inevitably dynamic. There is rarely a fixed division of authority and influence but, instead, one that varies from time to time and often from issue to issue, with different entities in the network taking on different "loadings" at different times and relative to different issues. Because the polity is voluntary, persuasion rather than compulsion, influence rather than power, are the only tools available for making and executing policies. This, too, works to strengthen its character as a communications network because the character, quality, and relevance of what is communicated and the way in which it is communicated frequently determine the extent of the authority and influence of the parties to the communication.

The reconstitution of the *edah* is only in its beginning stages; its final form for this epoch cannot yet be foreseen. At this writing, the Jewish people is in the buildup period of the second generation of the postmodern epoch and is actively engaged in trying to work through a new constitutional synthesis, both political and religious. It is likely that the constitution for the new epoch will find its source in the traditional Torah as understood and interpreted in traditional and non-traditional ways. The continued reliance on the Torah as a constitutional anchor could not have been forecast during the first generation of the new epoch, when the late modern trend of secularization was still alive. But it is now fair to conclude that for most Jews, the Torah continues to serve as a constitutional foundation even though they no longer feel bound by its commandments as traditionally understood.

A second element in the new constitutional framework is the commitment to Jewish unity and peoplehood as embodied in the network of institutions serving the *edah*. This commitment is basically founded on a people-wide consensus. However, it is also acquiring a documentary base through congeries of quasi-covenantal constitutional documents generated in the new institutions of the *edah*. These may develop into a comprehensive postmodern constitutional supplement to the *edah*'s historic constitution, following the patterns of earlier epochs.

# Notes

1. Howard M. Sachar's *The Course of Modern Jewish History* (New York: Dell Publishing, 1958) is a comprehensive source of the history of Jewish life in this period. The changes themselves are discussed by Jacob Katz in *Tradition and Crisis* (New York: Free Press of Glencoe, 1965) and Michael A. Meyer, *The Origins of the Modern Jew: Jewish Identity and European Culture in Germany 1794–1824* (Detroit: Wayne State University Press, 1967). See also Louis Finkelstein, ed., *The Jews: Their History, Culture, and Religion* (Philadelphia: Jewish Publication Society of America, 1960), 3d ed., 2 vols.; Salo W. Baron, "The Modern Age," in Leo W. Schwarz, ed., *Great Ages and Ideas of the Jewish People* (New York: The Modern Library, 1956), pp. 315–484.

2. For a brief exposition of this definition of the modern epoch, particularly as it applies to the United States, see Daniel J. Elazar, *Cities of the Prairie* (New York: Basic Books, 1970), Introduction and Appendix; and, by the same author, *Toward a Generational Theory of American Politics* (Philadelphia: Center for the Study of Federalism, 1968). The writer has discussed this periodization of Jewish history in "A Constitutional View of Jewish History," *Judaism* 10, no. 3 (Summer 1961): 256–64.

3. Cf. Jacob Lestichinsky, *Tfutzot Yisrael Ahar haMilhamah* (The Dispersions of Israel After the War) (Tel Aviv, 1958) (Hebrew); Aryeh Tartakower, *HaHevrah haYehudit* (Jewish Society) (Tel Aviv: Massada, 1957–59) (Hebrew).

4. Yitzhak Ben-Zvi, *Toldot Eretz Yisrael beTekufah haOtomanit* (History of the Land of Israel in the Ottoman Period), (Jerusalem: Yad Itzhak Ben Zvi, 1955) (Hebrew); Robert Sherevsky, Avraham Katz, Yisrael Kolatt, and Hayim Barkai, *Meah Shanah ve'od 20* (One Hundred Years and Another 20) (Tel Aviv: Ma'ariv 1968) (Hebrew).

5. It should be noted that most, if not all, of the first colonies were founded by covenants or articles of agreement, thus continuing the classic Jewish pattern. Cf. Daniel J. Elazar, *Israel: Building a New Society* (Bloomington: Indiana University Press, 1986).

# 13

# The Jewish People and the Kingdom of Heaven: A Study of Jewish Theocracy

*Ella Belfer*

In the present chapter I shall examine one aspect of the Jewish political tradition, namely, the dimension of metaphysical sanctity within the political system. Through a structural review of Jewish history I hope to demonstrate the continued interaction between the heavenly and the earthly in the Jewish political conception.[1] The recognition of the existence of such a continuity will help us to understand the fundamental problems of the Jewish polity in general, and the Israeli polity in particular, not as independent phenomena but as a single edifice whose basic structure is the dialectic encounter between these two components.[2]

The roots of this political-metaphysical encounter lie, in my opinion, in the overall approach of Judaism, which views the existential dichotomy of existence between the human and the Divine as the two dialectic components of a single system.[3] Politically, this approach is reflected in the perception of the political phenomenon as existing on two planes—both as an earthly phenomenon of territorial existence and as a heavenly phenomenon represented by the Temple Mount—the mountain of God, of the Divine presence. Thus, Judaism recognizes the meaning of political existence while relating it to the world of the sacred, to which metaphysical criteria are applied. Thus, while the state is in fact a polity, one of many, it is also located in the Holy Land, whose existence is an integral part of the Divine order.

This interpolation of the sacred in the institutions of government is known in political language as theocracy. I shall in the following pages try to trace the extent of theocracy[4] present throughout Jewish political history, while discussing the continuousness of the encounter between the two component elements of this form of government: *theos* and *kratos*. The term *kratos* here comprises everything related to the political phenomenon—not only government, but also the political entity and territorial sovereignty, not only policy but also polity. The concept *theos* will be understood as comprising the entire system of beliefs with a sacred dimension, not restricting it merely to the religious conception in its traditional sense. However, despite the broadness of this definition, it shall not include those ethical-social or historical-theological ideas that do not possess the binding nature of an absolute value. Neither will I refer to the different varieties of atheistic religions, which, like the "civil religion" of Rousseau,[5] grows out of *kratos* alone.

The subject of the present article is thus to elucidate the duality of the Jewish political conception, tracing the continuous encounter between *theos*, as a supreme system of absolute values,[6] and *kratos*, as the independent entity of the political system.

This encounter can in fact be divided into two parts: the positive encounter, which, remaining true to the two-dimensional approach,[7] strives to achieve a dialectic harmony between *theos* and *kratos*; and the negative encounter, which seeks a way out of the fundamental imbroglio of dialectic unity to achieve a unidimensional political way of life and ideology. The theo-political essence of Judaism is therefore a source of constant struggle between opposing attitudes.

## Constant Trends in Jewish Theocracy

It is my contention that there are three constant trends in Jewish theocracy: (1) conflict; (2) unity; and (3) priority, namely, a synthesis that accords greater weight to the theistic element. I shall briefly define the nature of these three trends and then present them chronologically in a historical survey.

*Conflict*

The approach that views *theos* and *kratos* as two opposite poles finds support in the logical-conceptual dissimilarity between them, as Nathan Rotenstreich notes: "In religion, man relates to God, and this relationship of man, as a human being, to God has a universalist meaning, and its nature and validity are independent of time and place. In a state, man relates to man, and this relationship is by its very nature limited, fragmentary, and lacking in universal scope."[8]

In light of the basic dissimilarity between these two substances, the unidimensional political approach calls for a monolithic rather than a dual definition of life:[9] either an independent political-national existence, or a fusion with the sacred, waiving physical-political existence. Josephus Flavius[10] renounced Jewish political existence (undoubtedly partly in justification of his betrayal, as did Philo Judaeus.[11] Spinoza, on the other hand, chose an existential policy, and saw the attempt to achieve a political-metaphysical encounter as the very cause of Israel's political destruction.[12]

These approaches are aware of the existence of the theo-political encounter in Jewish history but try to evade it through an absolute decision on the essence of Judaism either as political nationalism or as a religious-spiritual value.

*Unity*

As opposed to this, there also exists within Judaism a central school of thought that maintains an integrated view of the state and Divine sacredness, according to which one cannot exist without the other. Judaism, according to this view, is no more than metapolitical realization through political fulfillment. The anomaly of this synthesis is perceived as the part that is indicative of the whole, as the singularity which is the essence of Judaism. To this school belong—with varying definitions of sacredness—such personalities as Moses Mendelssohn,[13] Uri Zvi Greenberg,[14] Maimonides,[15] and Ben-Gurion[16] (whose philosophies will be discussed below).

*Priority*

As opposed to these two is the approach that does not reject the encounter, but does renounce the attempt at unity; it recognizes the body politic, but only as the basis of Divine worship. Despite the differences between the spiritual-sacred outlooks of Abravanel,[17] Ahad Ha'am,[18] Buber,[19] and Borochov[20] (to be discussed below), they all share a minimalistic approach to the state as the basis for realizing the sacred goal.

## Three Stages of Jewish History

I shall try to prove that these three approaches—the perception of the political goal as legitimate in and of itself or as the basis of sacred values or, alternatively, the yearning for a dialectic fusion between the two—have characterized Judaism throughout its history, and the present generation is no exception.

In this respect, Jewish history can be divided into three broad units: (1) the generation of the wilderness and the First and Second Temple periods; (2) the diaspora and messianism; (3) Zionism and the State of Israel. The generation of the wilderness, the diaspora, and Zionism, especially spiritual Zionism, represent the heavenly theistic aspect, while the period of the kings of Israel and the Hasmoneans, messianism, and the sovereign existence of Israel as a state, with their political-"kratic" emphasis, serve as a counterweight.

*The Generation of the Wilderness*

I will not try to present a factual historical analysis of the generation of the wilderness; rather, I shall refer to the imprint that it left on our historical consciousness, in which the controversy between the historical-archeological and biblical-fundamentalist approaches is irrelevant. The generation of the wilderness, as it appears in Jewish tradition, serves as a symbol of the pre-state period in the life of the Jewish people, based on a highly developed relationship between man and God, during which social relations were formed and institutionalized. However, despite the existence of a political community, the generation of the wilderness lacked the essential political element— territorial-political life. This, then, was a period of *theos* without *kratos*—in the sense of polity. The Jewish people and God were engaged in preparing themselves to receive the land—the body politic. In contrast to this reality of exclusive *theos,* the generation of the wilderness was confronted with two examples of "kratic" existence: Egypt, with its affluence and plenty, which served as a temptation and a trap; and the Land of Israel, which represented both a destination and a challenge. Their task was to free themselves from the negative effect of the Egyptian *kratos* in order to be worthy of attaining the desired positive *kratos.* Like the two political models, they were confronted with two types of temptation: the attraction to exaggerated worldliness, from the golden calf to their craving for meat—the "Egyptian" mentality of their past; and the attraction to absolute spirituality, as fitting for a people which has always maintained a dialogue with God.

The generation of the wilderness is thus an ambivalent phenomenon in Judaism, as the generation that was closest to God but which was at the same time found unworthy to enter into the Promised Land. While R. Akiva (in accordance with his personal adherence to the idea of political sovereignty) believed that the generation of the wilderness has no portion in the world to come,[21] kabbalistic literature[22] attributes the separation between the generation of the wilderness and the Land of Israel and the "sin of the spies" to its excess sacredness, as a generation which did not want to be defiled by the worldly life of state and government after having been privileged to witness the revelation at Sinai. But even according to this interpretation, which praises the exclusive spirituality of the generation of the wilderness, it does not serve as an ideal model for the Jewish people. The historical challenge—even in light of the admiration of the *theos* of the wilderness—remains the achievement of a "kratic" existence. Thus, while Jewish life can be elevated even without territory, the peak of Jewish life is a combination of sacredness and sin.

The biblical account of the generation of the wilderness—with its conflicting interpretations—also reflects the dialectic attitude of the Jewish tradition towards political *kratos*; purely physical political existence as in Egypt is one of the "forty-nine gates of uncleanness" from which the people can to be purified over a period of forty years before reaching the level of true political life, which is not the converse of Divine worship but its fullest realization. Thus, without *kratos,* there can be no existence; but *kratos* alone has no value.

This approach became part of the Jewish heritage, and the generation of the wilderness has come to symbolize the motif of exclusive *theos,* with the elevation and the destruction inherent in it. This motif was not expunged even after the transition to territorial existence within the Land of Israel, but it was offset by constant conflict with the opposite tendency towards overemphasis of the political-human dimension.

It is common practice[23] to view this period in Jewish history as a theocratic period (beginning with the affirmation of the state, and ending with the Pharisaic position of anti-political theocracy). However, it is hard to find factual support for this view. The Bible itself, while "theistic" in character, tells of a *dual system* of two parallel authorities: the ruling establishment represented by the king, versus the prophet, as the agent of God. The traditional views of this duality vary: Abravanel, in accordance with his overall meta-political approach,[24] rejected the very existence of the monarchy as an attempt to create an "empty" *kratos* in the Egyptian style, a situation that runs counter to the goal of the Divine Promised Land.

This approach also finds support in modern interpretations. According to Abraham Heschel,[25] prophecy and monarchy are mutually incompatible, both ideologically and historically: political prosperity has always led to a neglect of the Divine goal, while political-territorial decline has led to a recognition of theistic truth.[26] This view of the conflict between prophetic *theos* and political *kratos* also implies the rejection of this *kratos* as a decadent phenomenon within Judaism.

In contrast to this is the positive attitude of Maimonides[27] towards political manifestations, an attitude supported by the fact that prophecy flourished precisely during the height of the monarchic period, indicating that they complement one another.

However, despite these differences of opinion, there is no question that the relationship between prophet and king—*theos* and *kratos*— was not one of identity but rather encounter, either harmonious or conflicting, according to one's point of view.

As for the Second Temple period, the priests indeed represented *kratos,* and thus would seem to have constituted a theocratic government in the *literal* sense of the term; however, in a patent adulteration of content, although they performed the religious rituals, they did not represent the fundamental Jewish *theos.* They were Hellenizers at the beginning of the period and Sadducees at the end. While the first

Hasmoneans truly embodied the identity between *theos* and *kratos,* at the end of the period Alexander Yannai personified the independent "kratic" aspect in its extreme sense, with no trace of the prophetic *theos* that had characterized the Maccabees. Similar anti-"theistic" phenomena also emerged in the golden age of the Davidic monarchy: although David was called the servant of God and became the symbol of Jewish independence and the father of the Messiah, he was not found worthy to build the Temple, for his hands had been contaminated by the blood of his many enemies.[28] Solomon, who did in fact build the Temple, sinned by possessing many horses and wives,[29] like the gentile kings, and in the time of his son Rehoboam, the kingdom was divided. Subsequently, neither the kingdom of Judah nor the kingdom of Israel corresponded to the criteria of political existence established by the prophets. Thus, the prophetic voice became a "voice calling in the wilderness"—in the name of the generation of the wilderness, as opposed to the Egyptian and Canaanite phenomena of Jewish *kratos.*

Thus, in its territorial metamorphosis, the internal tension of the generation of the wilderness was repeated: the development of a political existence, "like all the nations," as reflected in treaties with Egypt and Aram, versus the theistic-prophetic yearning for the wilderness,[30] for the closeness with God that had existed prior to the establishment of the monarchy in Israel. The government naturally leaned towards the creation of a political center of gravity, often even to rebellion against the oppressive presence of Divine power. This was paralleled by the protests voiced by the prophets with the full weight of their authority, by means of which God was involved in the life of the Jewish state even when the representatives of the political *kratos* sought to deny such involvement.[31]

Thus, while theocracy was not actually implemented as a form of government in the First and Second Temple periods, the encounter between *theos* and *kratos* was a decisive political factor of the entire period. It was not the government but history itself which was theopolitical; political phenomena were measured by clearly metapolitical criteria, and as such were accepted as an integral part of the nation's relationship with God; just as the building of the capital city was equated with the sanctification of God's name in the time of David, so was religious transgression equated with an aborted political act in the case of Saul and the Amalekites. Thus, general political ruin was perceived as a manifestation of religious sin and punishment; the loss of Jewish political-sovereign existence was equated with the destruction of the Temple.

Thus, exile, which is a purely political phenomenon, is also considered a religious phenomenon, as a period of alienation and remoteness between God and the Jewish people. Our historical consciousness thus reinforces Maimonides' approach by negation: in the absence of a sovereign *kratos,* the "kingdom of Israel," *theos,* too, became remote, and we were deprived of the "kingdom of heaven." In the same way, Divine involvement in political existence was a source of its vitality; the remoteness of God and the destruction of the political entity were thus reciprocal causes.

## The Diaspora and Messianism

With its political destruction, the Jewish people returned for the second time in its history to life in the wilderness: in other words, it had to fortify itself within political-communal patterns in the absence of any territorial foundation—without a polity. In his book *Jerusalem,* Mendelssohn provides a good description of this semi-existence:

> And even today, no better advice than this can be given to the House of Jacob: Adopt the mores and constitution of the country in which you find yourself, but be steadfast in upholding the religion of your fathers, too. Bear both burdens as well as you can. True, on the one hand, people make it difficult for you to bear the burden of civil life because of the religion to which you remain faithful; and, on the other hand, the climate of our time makes the observance of your religious laws in some respects more burdensome than it need be. Persevere nevertheless.[32]

In contrast to Mendelssohn's solution of "be a Jew at home and a man outside," the Jews developed a way of life based on the home alone, isolating themselves within the spiritual kingdom of heaven while renouncing any contact with the external world of *kratos.* In establishing the academy of Jabneh following the destruction of the political center in Jerusalem, Johanan ben Zakkai established a refuge for the Jewish spirit, which succeeded in protecting it for almost two thousand years. While this institution belonged to the wilderness of the nations, Judaism found consolation in it and drew strength from its spiritual life.

By consciously exploiting historical necessity, Judaism renounces the problematic encounter between *theos* and *kratos,* thus deriving certain benefits: it freed itself from internal tensions, from the temptation to deteriorate into an existential political structure, as had Yeroboam and Alexander Yannai. Now, without a body politic, it was easier to ascend to heavenly heights, to be a chosen people—as Leibowitz notes:

> It was an easy matter from a religious point of view to be a good Jew in the diaspora. While such an existence required courage—the spiritual capacity to suffer and even die in the name of values . . . the Jew in the diaspora was freed from responsibility for some of the most difficult human tasks and obligations—problems of government and constitution, of war and peace, the welfare of the people, and social reform. It is much harder to be a religious Jew and to observe the Torah while fulfilling the political obligations of a state and providing people with their social needs. The justification for the easier nature of religious observance in the diaspora lay in the historiosophy which postponed political independence and responsibility to the time of the messianic redemption in the indefinite future.[33]

Again we find, this time as the result of bitter historical experience, the recoiling from political existence characteristic of the wilderness, as a land that "devours its settlers." This recoiling was accompanied by a reconciliation with the phenomenon of the diaspora, through an ideological rationalization according to which the national existence of the Jewish people is based not on territorial factors but on its metaphysical source embodied in the Sinai covenant.[34] The Jew can therefore fulfill his obligations as a citizen in the country of his dispersion, while at the same time maintaining and observing the covenant between God and His people, which was loftier and more exalted than the life of the state.[35] However, this phenomenon of "love" of the diaspora cannot be understood without the messianic belief that counterbalanced it.[36] Despite the variety of interpretations of the nature of the messianic age—the degree of its spirituality or corporeality, its universal or naturalness—it is generally accepted in Jewish tradition that the coming of the Messiah also (according to Abravanel)[37] or primarily (according to Maimonides)[38] signifies the return to Zion and the establishment of a Jewish state, namely, a return to the existence of a Jewish polity. While full Jewish existence as a people, serving its God in its own state, was transformed from a realistic aspiration to a messianic dream, the dream itself was designated as an integral part of the system of *theos,* one of the fundamental tenets of faith. Hence, the diaspora without the belief in the coming of the Messiah and without the yearning for Zion is also a diaspora without prayer and without the belief in God.

This messianic belief demonstrates that the *post factum* affirmation of the diaspora never became—except for rational arguments in favor of assimilation—an ideal, doctrinal affirmation. Ultimately, Jewish thought viewed the diaspora as a distorted situation produced as the result of sin, which will be terminated with the coming of the Messiah. Judaism never renounced *kratos,* even in the diaspora, but rather elevated it to the level of *theos*; in accordance with the spirituality of life, the longing for political territorialism became a messianic-metaphysical principle.

The anomaly of Jewish existence through the thousands of years of exile is epitomized not by nonterritorial existence but by the internalization of this territory, preserving it as part of its spiritual life. An extreme expression of this can be found in Jabotinsky's explanation of the miracle of Jewish life in the diaspora:

> A small group of people is huddled together, assaulted on all sides by many enemies who are demanding something of them; the small group does not surrender, and apparently prefers to suffer unending torture, so long as it can preserve something, not surrender something to the enemy. . . . If the history of the diaspora is the self-protection of a group of people—what is this sacred treasure which they are defending with such obstinacy, so that their adherence to it would appear to constitute the basic motive of the entire history of this nation without a land? This sacred treasure is its religion. . . . However, Judaism is not developing, Judaism does not yield to the law of evolution. Since the Jewish people lost its land, Judaism has ceased to change and evolve. It became frozen in place, remaining at the same level as when the Jewish people lost its homeland. This dead corpse is certainly not the sacred treasure itself, but only the cloak or the shell of that treasure. Judaism has died; anything that does not develop is considered dead. . . . It died, in effect, at the very hour when Israel became a people without a land. . . . It is not the Jews living in the diaspora who protected the religion, but the religion which protected something else. . . . It is not its religion but its uniqueness which our people has preserved. . . . The Jewish religion is mighty, a religion which contains many grains of eternal truth. Nevertheless, the role which the Torah fulfilled in the diaspora was not that of the treasure itself, but only of that which preserves and protects this treasure. . . . What is the uniqueness of Judaism?—The true kernel of our national uniqueness is the pure fruit of the Land of Israel.[39]

This reflects, of course, Jabotinsky's personal definition of the essence of Judaism, from his evaluation of the stagnation of the Jewish religion to his view of the national axis as the sole axis of Judaism. But despite this subjectivity, his radical view of the diaspora as a "theistic" shell to a "kratic" kernel serves as a counterweight to the view of the diaspora as a period of theistic exclusivity that utterly rejects the political idea.[40]

The key to the question of the balance between *theos* and *kratos* in Jewish thought throughout the diaspora lies in the essence of messianism, according to which the return to a political existence in the Holy Land is viewed as the basis for the return of the Divine Presence, or as identical to it. Thus, Judaism displayed a clearly passive attitude—except for the tragic exception of false messiahs—towards the actual realization of the messianic era.

This passivity was derived to no small extent from their acquiescence to their condition in the diaspora and from their contenting themselves with realizing the goal of undisturbed spiritual life—and perhaps also from their inability to cope with political reality. But it was also caused by the ideological perception of the ideal political existence: while the future redemption will be political in nature, it is utterly dependent upon spiritual redemption. Hence, while there has been no renunciation of the "kratic"-political dimension, the possibility of its neutral existence has been completely negated. The Land of Israel—in the diaspora as in the wilderness—is God's Promised Land, for the fulfillment of metapolitical goals. The longed-for realization of such a state, which is also in a sense the kingdom of heaven, requires a metaphysical miracle; even if a Jewish political entity should be established in the Holy Land through independent human action without direct Divine intervention, it will lack metaphysical content and will therefore also be valueless.[41]

## Zionism and the State of Israel

The revolt of Zionism against the diaspora phenomenon was first and foremost a protest against passivity, against human paralysis with regard to the historical aspirations of the Jewish people. If we add to this the elements of secularization, the revolt against God, and the true impetus for the Zionist awakening—the persecution of the Jews and not their ideal destiny—one would have thought that the continuing dialectic of the adherence to *theos* as a part of "kratic" existence or as the major element in the yearning for its reestablishment would have come to an end. The Zionist perception of life without territory as the root of all evil should have finally upset the balance in favor of *kratos,* creating an emotional identity between metapolitical life based on sacred values and extinction, adversity, destruction, and anti-Semitism, all of these having been the fate of the Jews in the diaspora. The revolt against the diaspora should therefore also have been the revolt against the metaphysical content of messianic yearning.

But despite this logical reasoning, the theocratic encounter continued even in the political thought of Zionism. While the traditional belief in Torah and the religious commandments had disappeared (except for the exception of religious Zionism), the belief in the unique sacred Jewish mission remained. While the Jewish *theos* lost its permanent framework and content, it still found expression in the yearning for some form of sacredness, in the motif of the Jews as the Chosen People,[42] and in the desire, as such, to establish a political existence. Thus, despite its revolt against the values of the diaspora, Zionism did not renounce its right to fulfill the aspirations of the diaspora, namely, the embodiment of the messianic phenomenon, without passively waiting for metaphysical aid, but also without renouncing the self-fulfillment of a metaphysical goal. Thus, it remained necessary to find justification for political existence in a goal that went beyond this simple existence, anchoring it in a world of sacred values.

The revolutionism of political ideology in the Zionist philosophies is expressed not in the repudiation of the traditional encounter between *theos* and *kratos,* but in the refutation of the traditional content of *theos* and in the search for a new sacred content that accords with individual beliefs. Hence, the great divergence of theistic goals which Zionist thought defined for the political entity: for Borochov, an idealistic-Marxist goal; for Bergman, a humanistic-universalist goal; for Buber, a mystical-Jewish goal; for Joseph Salvador, the creation of an ideal society; for David Ben-Gurion, the reestablishment of harmony between state and prophecy. But despite this great divergence of views, all were united in their attitude towards sacredness, which is the essence of religious Judaism.

Even Herzl himself, who was divorced from the traditional Jewish values of sacredness and motivated primarily by his desire to put an end to Jewish suffering, referred to the uniqueness of the Jewish mission. Although he formulated the idea of the return to a political-sovereign existence as a nation among nations, he nevertheless saw the need to invest this independent political entity with special content. According to *Altneuland,*[43] Jewish political existence in the Land of Israel would form an ideal society, which, in its content, progress, culture, and moral values, would serve as a banner to the nations. Thus, even the father of the Jewish state was afflicted by the diaspora approach of not being able to accept Jewish political existence as a self-evident fact that did not have to be legitimized by its uniqueness. While this is a form of traditional apologetics directed towards the non-Jewish world, it can also be viewed as a response to an internal Jewish need for an extra-existential justification for the political phenomenon—if not a wheel in the Divine Chariot, then at least an example to the nations.[44]

Although he viewed political *kratos* as his central goal (to the point of proposing the Uganda plan), Herzl did not renounce, in principle, the idea of Jewish uniqueness, and viewed political revival not only as a means of restoring the body, but also as a way to achieve the flourishing of the spirit, as his statement before the Second Zionist Congress indicates: "Our culture is like a miser who places his inventions and discoveries in a box. Rather, it is in order to be used by man that they came into this world."[45] From a condition of nonpolitical isolation, Herzl called for the restoration of an open political existence, not at the expense of the Jewish spirit, but in order to achieve its fullest realization, as a light unto the nations.

The theistic aspect of political Zionism becomes the center of gravity in spiritual Zionism and in the philosophy of Ahad Ha'am. Despite the secular nature of his teaching, despite his renouncement of the transcendental dimension of Judaism, Ahad Ha'am does not renounce the ethnocentric sacredness of the values of Jewish tradition, and continues to believe, if not in the God of Israel, then in the immanent spirit of Israel and its universal mission as the spiritual center of the world. The essence of Judaism, according to his worldview, is the constant following of this spirit; he viewed the Land of Israel as the territorial-geographical nest for the spirit. He therefore affirms the return to Zion, while restricting the political dimension to communal autonomy in the historical territory of the Jewish people. His minimalist approach to the political phenomenon can be viewed as the continuation of the recoil from the "kratic adventure" characteristic of the wilderness and the diaspora. It is not by chance that Nordau argued: "Ahad Ha'am is one of the secular rabbis of protest." In fact, the latter's political ideology can be summed up as Zionist fulfillment with a theistic substance and a "kratic" vessel, tempering the significance of each: a *theos* without God, resting on a *kratos* without sovereignty.[46]

In contrast to this was the ultra-political Zionist approach. Those who adhered to this approach, known in Zionist literature as "territorialists,"[47] viewed the establishment of the Jewish state as the pinnacle of achievement and rejected any extra-territorial or metapolitical goals. Any search for a moral-religious-historical goal to justify political existence is to perpetuate the Jewish anomaly of the diaspora, while self-justifying political revival would be a sign that the Jews had recovered from the deformity of the diaspora and were becoming part of the global political system.

The storm raised by the Uganda affair was essentially the eruption of this basic controversy over the aims of Zionism: the realization of the exclusivity of the Jewish people in its land, or the ultimate liberation from this exclusivity and from the suffering inherent in it—acceptance or rejection of political existentialism and of the traditional Jewish values of sacredness.

Unlike Herzl who recommended Uganda as a realistic compromise between concrete adversities and historical desires, the extreme territorialists identified Zion with the Jewish prayer book[48] and with the messianic yearnings of the diaspora. For them, divorce from the past also required a divorce from the myth surrounding geographical Zion: They therefore preferred Uganda over Zion as a matter of principle. For the very same reasons, the "Land of Israel" Zionists clung to Zion—the land—which they viewed as the basis of the traditional values, desires, and rights of Jewish history, as stated by Heinrich Rosenbaum at the Sixth Zionist Congress:

> On what basis did the Zionist executive take it upon itself to enter into negotiations on the question of East Africa? Since when has Zionism begun to see its role as the creation of places of refuge for the Jewish people? . . . We shall continue to wait! We shall continue to fight! Our fathers gave their lives on the pyre, crying "Hear O Israel" and we, their sons, shall not cease to fight for the country which is so dear to us, and which symbolizes redemption for us and for all humanity. We shall continue to fight through suffering and with patience, and so long as breath remains within us, we shall say: we have not yet lost hope.[49]

The Uganda affair ended with the overwhelming identification of the Zionist movement with *Zion,* but not so the controversy in the area of political ideology—the perception of the state as an independent system, or as rooted in a higher normative sphere.

## Approaches to the Theocratic Dilemma

The theocratic dilemma was extended to the State of Israel itself, and finds expression in three traditional approaches: (1) synthesis, with a preference for the metapolitical goals; (2) the dichotomous approach, choosing an existential policy; and (3) the desire to realize the biblical idea of the harmonious union of the two.

### The Theistic Synthesis

The view of the state as the basis of spiritual values, the search for a "spiritual center" as proposed by Ahad Ha'am, also finds expression today, receiving even greater force in the search for a counterweight to the excessive worldliness of a purely political existence. The writings of S.H. Bergman, for example, express the fear of the thickening of Israel's political shell as an independent, atheistic value, and the need to strengthen its spiritual heritage as the true goal of the Jewish state:

> We have over the past two generations witnessed the growing secularization of our people. The Jewish people can be likened to a man who until now thought that he had only a soul and suddenly discovered his body—thus has the Jewish people discovered the terrestrial world. This was perhaps the greatest revolution which our people has experienced since its dispersion. For the generation which created the national movement, it was clear that its transient life in this world was the decisive fact which required all the nation's strength. But the time has come to note the limits of this approach. The time has come to recall that we also have a soul which demands to be heard: the soul of the Jewish people is its faith; no one would disagree with the fact that Zionism has drawn its strength from this source; it was a simple matter to muster this great strength which had been accumulating for centuries. . . . But we must ask: what will happen after us? . . . Are we not in the dangerous situation of a man who lives off his capital but does not add to it? I doubt whether the secular ideal can gather such strength over a long period of time, for this ideal, though lofty, does not embrace the Jew as a whole, for the Jew is first and foremost a man of faith, for the seed of the father of all beliefs lives within us. All the ideals of the various currents within Judaism, whether social, national or conservative, are derived from the overriding ideal of the Jewish people: to reform the world in the kingdom of heaven; the time has come to recall this ideal in its fullest scope.[50]

In contrast to the reality of the diaspora which Herzl described as the hoarding of spiritual treasure without using it, Bergman warns against the waste of this treasure in political life which does not hark back to the spiritual life, which is declining. In a metamorphosis of the prophetic call, he, too, proclaims:

We seek to renew the old meaning of the Holy Name: The ethical movement known as Zionism will show us the way today. Put aside all half-measures, all compromises and all conveniences, and be whole in your paths; renew yourselves in the spirit of unbiased strictness, and God will be for you what he was for Moses: a consuming fire.[51]

A similar attitude towards the Jewish state can be found in Buber's philosophy. While in his *Kingship of God*[52] he foresees total unity between Divine worship and the political institutions, as a "covenant between power and faith," this ideal of the absolute synthesis between political existence and the worship of God, which he believes existed in the time of David, did not yet apply to the Israeli political reality.

Thus, any high statism is in the meantime a form of false messianic pretentiousness of "power without faith."[53] Buber's fear of the false messianism of the Israeli state contains something of the fear of Jewish law and of the reaction of Hasidism to Sabbateanism; indeed, Buber's Zionist view is similar to R. Nahman of Bratslav's love of Israel, referring not to the concrete land but to the heavenly Jerusalem. While he recognizes the sovereign-political existence of Israel (in contrast to his mentor, Ahad Ha'am, who was content with territorial autonomy), the theocratic encounter which he proposes in this context is a "kratic" foundation for a theistic essence. Hence, he calls for a spiritualization of the political reality in Israel.

A similar reservation with regard to excess *kratos* and a demand for greater *theos,* out of a similar recognition of the fundamental necessity for *kratos,* emerges from Soloveitchik's teaching:

> The state is the property of the entire people, given to them by God in His great kindness. There is an absolute identity between the Holy Land and the state. The commandment to inherit and settle the land is expressed not only in the concrete development of the Land of Israel—the construction of houses, the planting of parks and forests, the settling of the land . . . but also in political conquest and the occupation of the Land of Israel. . . . The very fact that Israeli political sovereignty exists and that Jews rule over the land is the fulfillment of the major aspect of the commandment to inherit and settle the land. . . . The sacredness of the land with which the land is invested cannot be uprooted.[54]

But:

> Just as I differentiate between government and state as between sacred and profane, so do I differentiate between a state which is cloaked in the holiness of the land and the Jewish community, identified with the eternal Torah, as between one holiness and another. Higher than all is the God of the universe, who revealed

Himself to His people and outlined a special way of life for them. This link between people and God is the ultimate purpose and the foundation. The holiness of the land is also derived from the Divine inspiration which shone on the people when they entered into a relationship with their Creator. Outside of this extraordinary framework, a small country surrounded by enemies has no value. God made two covenants with Abraham—a national covenant and a territorial covenant. . . . The territorial covenant is not independent. . . . Hence I view its greatness, value and importance only within the framework of the uniqueness of the Jewish people and its unity with God. As a historical-secular entity that is not guided by its covenantal mission, the state does not arouse any enthusiasm in me, nor does it ignore a burning fire in my heart.[55]

While the theological content of Soloveitchik's philosophy is not identical to that of Buber or Bergman, the political tone is the same: the minimizing of the value of the political system, because of the uniqueness of the spirit and the mission of the Jewish people.

## The Dichotomous Approach

In contrast to this perpetuation of the theistic approach to Jewish political life, we find the political-existentialist approach, which in its most extreme form is known as the Canaanite philosophy.[56] Its basic premise is that the State of Israel is not an immanent continuation of historical Jewish existence—although it is rooted in Zionism, which is an integral continuation of the diaspora-messianic-metapolitical Jewish heritage. However, this has nothing to do with the new Hebrew nation in Israel:

As for the revival of the Hebrew nation which is emerging before our eyes in its own land, still only half-consciously; this nation is not a continuation of that "eternal people," scattered and dispersed, whose traits, which are foreign to us, are constantly presented as the "Jewish consciousness." This national revival is a new beginning and not the outgrowth of Zionism. . . . Rather it sprouts from new roots in the same ancient land. . . . Just as the profoundest layer is Hebrew-Canaanite, so does the new Hebrew nation tend to develop in the Canaanite direction.[57]

According to this view, the Israeli political adherence to Jewish theism is anomalous, both according to comparative logical criteria, and in relation to the developing reality of the state. In place of "Jewishness," the Canaanites sought to base themselves on purely "gentile" Israeliness, limited to life and no more, a state whose political myth is not historical-metaphysical but historical-territorial—from the land of Canaan and the Hebrew language to a pan-Hebrew geo-political dream.

Thus, the Canaanite values are atheistic values, as Yonathan Ratosh wrote:

> A national purpose, unlike a religious-ethical-ideological purpose, does not leave any room for a superstructure. The purpose of a nation, like the purpose of every living organism, is simply to life: to fight for independence if enslaved, to nationalize its land, and to become a nation within it. Our people and our leaders are afraid to alter the Jewish communal purpose. They and their leaders do not grasp that the communal mission is not national; rather, it is fundamentally contrary to such a purpose, for the national purpose, as noted, is the purpose of every living organism: simply to be.[58]

According to this approach, the Jewish heritage of the diaspora, to which the State of Israel clings, is the root of all evil in the Israeli political context: so long as Israel continues to identify itself with the worldwide Jewish diaspora, while hermetically closing itself off from the peoples of the region, it will continue to be a foreign body in the Eastern Mediterranean, and its existence will be in constant danger.

It is ironic that the Canaanite philosophy in its very revolutionism and criticism of the over-Jewishness of the State of Israel is the reembodiment of an immanent phenomenon of the Jewish political tradition: the flight from *theos* to an existential political condition rooted in the geographic environment has reoccurred periodically in Jewish history from the first attempt to return from the wilderness to Egypt, through the Egyptian-Aramaic orientation of the kings of Judah and Israel, to the expansionist tendencies of Alexander Yannai. The view of *theos* and *kratos* as two mutually destructive, conflicting components is not new. Josephus, whose definition of the essence of Judaism is purely theistic, viewed the development of *kratos* as the central cause for the problems of the Jews; while for Spinoza, it was exactly the opposite—the essence of political life must be existential-independent—it is the excess of *theos* in Judaism which brought about its political destruction and exile. Thus, the polarity of the political aspect is reflected in the various interpretations of Jewish history. The Canaanite approach is no more than a modern manifestation of the territorial-Egyptian motif which competed with the prophetic-wilderness motif over the true essence of the Jewish political entity.

> It is strange—states the Canaanite historian A.G. Horon—that the State of Israel, which from the point of view of scientific and technological development clearly belongs to the 20th century, professes an identity between religion and nationality.

This is only because of the claim that the "Jewish people" is unique. Once we abandon this approach, as has been done by the Hebrew movement, there is no reason why there should not be a clear and absolute separation between religion and state.[59]

The polarity implied here is clear—state versus religion, political doctrine versus the apolitical approach of the "Jewish people."

These views emerged with similar sharpness in the teaching of Leibowitz, who serves as an extreme example of the other side of the spectrum. In contrast to Horon's call for "a state which belongs to the 20th century," Leibowitz is seeking only the national-historical-unique aspect of the state:

The State of Israel, unlike any other state, is not the state of an "Israeli people" living within it at the present time; it is the state of the Jewish people defined not territorially but historically. The state belongs to the people, and not the people to the state. The state was established as the state of the Jewish people, and only as the state of the Jewish people is there any justification for its existence, in spite of all the complications and conflicts which this entails. If it is not the state of the Jewish people, I doubt whether it can survive for long. From the point of view of accepted political theory, this may be an anomaly, but the history of the Jewish people is also an anomaly.[60]

The overemphasis on this anomaly brings Leibowitz to underestimate the political component, approaching a virtual negation of its value:

I do not know whether the historical Jewish people will continue to exist, but if the state is not the framework for the continued history of the Jewish people—it is utterly superfluous; then this state is only a ruling-sovereign mechanism, a framework of coercion and violence; this is the nature of the state under every regime. The justification for the existence of this mechanism is that it serves as an existential framework for a people which is an empirical, historical given, whose existence does not require explanation.[61]

In accordance with the dialectic laws of logic, a common denominator can be found between these two poles of the theo-"kratic" approach: between the ultra-theistic approach of Leibowitz and the Hebrew-atheistic approach of the Canaanites. First, there is an interesting convergence of interpretations: the ideal of the Canaanites, in the name of which they criticize the existing situation, is in the eyes of Leibowitz, our present image—and it is against this that he is protesting. According to the former, the state still suffers from the anachronism of the diaspora, while according to the latter it is already afflicted with

Canaanite existentialism, for example:

> The character of Israeli society and its political framework is determined by the fact that three million members of the Jewish people have here formed themselves into a new nation which has no history and no tradition—neither a tradition of ideas nor a tradition of a way of life; all this is lacking in this nation, which is increasingly composed of Jews, the majority of whom . . . have severed their links with the essential content of the historical Jewish people, which is Judaism. A new, synthetic nation is being formed here, with no specific original content, a people whose national uniqueness is merely its political framework. Not the Jewish people building a state for itself, but a state which is creating a people for itself. Instead of serving as a tool for realizing the values latent in the national existence, the state itself is becoming an end, a supreme value.[62]

Starting with an opposite analysis of the Israeli political reality, both these approaches arrive at the same conclusion: the need for a decision. Like the Canaanites, Leibowitz wants a clear and open confrontation "between this state which is ours, and which is at present secular, and religion which calls for a totally different substance for the national organization of the Jewish people."[63]

*The Unified Approach*

*The statist approach.* The actual patterns of the State of Israel are interpreted as an "absurd national-religious symbiosis,"[64] so long as it is based on a fundamental conflict between political existentialism and a metapolitical Jewish existence. From Abravanel to Leibowitz, there has existed in Judaism an approach which views all manifestations of full political existence as a form of idolatry. To this category of dichotomous approaches we may also attribute the Canaanite parallel which views all manifestations of spiritual Judaism in politics as morbid and anomalous.

In contrast, however, the central current in Judaism and in Israel today is interested in just such a "symbiosis." The political ideal accepted by the Israeli governmental system is rooted in the myth of the kingdom of David—not the historical reality which brought with it disintegration and collapse, but rather the harmony that it embodied in our historical consciousness between a strong polity and sacred apolitical content. Although this content has today become bereft of the religious patterns of the historical past, it still comprises the element of uniqueness and of mission, the belief that the Jewish people has been chosen as a universal, moral spearhead. These elements are integrated into the overall structure of political existence. Thus, the essence of Jewish existence in a state is measured in two ways—as a political-territorial-historical phenomenon, and also as a spiritual-universal-eternal value.

In his statist aspirations, Ben-Gurion's philosophy took on the characteristic pattern of the unified approach: the proud and sovereign realization of political existence as one of the most radical of the Jewish "political" approaches, alongside the development of Israel as a spiritual center. Ben-Gurion's belief[65] in the spiritual mission of the State of Israel is the result of a theism similar to that of Ahad Ha'am, namely, the recognition of the immanent-Divine sacredness of the Jewish people, embodied in the Bible and the prophetic vision:

> In the teaching of the prophets of Israel—the prophets of truth, purity and absolute justice—one finds the secret of the spiritual strength of the Jewish people in all generations. One senses in every page of these eternal books a moral and conceptual striving for unity: the unity of man, the unity of the human race, the unity of the cosmos, the unity of matter and spirit, the unity of the Creator and the creation. This striving can be traced from the time of Abraham, Moses, the prophets, the medieval sages, to the great thinkers of recent generations such as Spinoza and Einstein. In the Bible, one finds intertwined the historical uniqueness of the Jewish people and its universal mission to all humanity. It expresses something more than history, than poetry, wisdom, philosophy, or revelation. In the Book of Books, one discovers the prophecy of the future—the future of the Jewish people and the future of the human race.[66]

As a member of the People of the Book, Ben-Gurion views the nation living in Zion as the legitimate heir of the Chosen People, with the obligations inherent in this status:

> The belief in and the devotion to the supremacy of the spirit have characterized the Jewish people throughout its long historical journey from the revelation at Sinai to the present wars of Israel. This belief was the legacy of all those men of Israel who formed the character of the Hebrew nation from its beginnings to the present, who created and cultivated its philosophy, its poetry, its prophetic teaching, its literature, its laws, its vision of the end of days, and its messianic belief; those who strove to fulfill its national and world mission, who waged its struggle for political and spiritual independence, and who died as martyrs during the Crusades, the Inquisition, the massacres of Chmielnicki, and the Nazi Holocaust, and who created and fostered the settlement movement which led to the establishment of the State of Israel.[67]

Thus, Jewish history appears in the eyes of Ben-Gurion as a continuum of conceptual uniqueness which every generation coped with in its own way and with its own courage. The State of Israel, as part of this continuum, must embody this uniqueness in its political life, hence his declaration:

> Israel was never promised that it would rule over the nations, but rather it would be a covenant of people, a light of nations, and today, more than any time in the past, the Jews will understand that the redemption of Israel is related to the redemption of the world, and that the world's hope of salvation from the threat of destruction and annihilation lies in just government and peace, mercy and truth, and precious is man who was created in God's image, as the prophets of Israel taught. . . . The Jewish state, which incorporates within it the Jewish people, both its distant past and its recent history, is destined to discover and to express the traits latent in the Jewish people, to be a light unto the nations and to pave the way to a new world order which will not betray the vision of messianic redemption.[68]

Ben-Gurion's attachment to the prophetic myth reflects the full depth of the dialectic of the unity between *theos* and *kratos* in his view. The land, in which he himself was the head of the "kratic" system, is in his eyes the land of the prophets—the direct representatives of *theos,* for which there is no longer any metaphysical, metapolitical, and at times even anti-political manifestation.

Ben-Gurion himself was aware of the apolitical ideal inherent in the prophetic vision,[69] and his statist approach therefore contains a dialectic synthesis between national political sovereignty and Divine orientation as expressed by Jeremiah or Isaiah. As he himself summed up in his book *The Eternity of Israel*: "Zionism is the faithful striving for the eternity of Israel, and the eternity of Israel is embedded in these two things: *the State of Israel and the Book of Books*" (my emphasis).[70]

*The messianic approach.* Ben-Gurion's "State of Israel" is an eminent expression of Jewish sovereign *kratos,* but without a king, without the glory of the past, without the promised borders; and his "Book of Books," the embodiment of his credo, is the prophet without his Sender, the Bible without the giving of the Law.

In view of these fundamental changes in content, the statist approach defines itself as the legitimate heir of the biblical theo-political conception, but it does not pretend to embody the Orthodox fulfillment of messianic belief.

On the other hand, there exists a higher unified approach in Israel with real messianic aspirations, for which the vision of the end of days is being fulfilled in the political revival, and the State of Israel must therefore function as the Promised Land—with the maximum of political power and the perfection of Divine worship. *Kratos* shall be the kingship of the House of David; *theos*—the heavens, in the manner of ancient Israel; and the political goal—the establishment of the Third Commonwealth.

The poetry of U.Z. Greenberg, for example, is a strong literary expression of these messianic-political aspirations, as in the following appeal to God:

> We want eternity in body, eternity in our land,
>     eternity in the crown of majesty,
> And not eternity in wandering, eternity in spirit,
>     eternity in the misery of exile.[71]

This messianic approach shares much in common with the statist approach: both maintain a unified conception of the kingdom of Israel as its political form of existence and the kingdom of heaven as our eternal goal, and both are identified as a historical fulfillment of age-old longing. But given the significant differences of content between them, they are also mutually critical: from the point of view of the compromising approach, the fundamentalist messianic aspirations seem more like dangerous fanaticism, while the statist approach is viewed by the extremist as the commercialization of a vision, as the depreciation of the act of fulfillment.[72]

In fact, this convergence of contrast and similarity is present in the theocratic encounter in Judaism, in all its forms—not only in the dichotomous approach which distinguishes between exclusive-existential *kratos* and *halakhic*-wilderness *theos,* not only in the unified approach which combines statism and messianism, but also in the theocratic syntheses with an explicitly theistic bias. Particularly noteworthy in this regard is Buber's approach: his ideal of the end of days, like his historical myth, is similar to the messianic ideal of the unified approach. In both these visions, the kingdom of heaven represents the true glory of the kingdom of Israel. But, for Buber, the political reality in Israel is a false messianism, and he views every unified approach (which contains real *kratos*) as an essentially mistaken messianic pretension.

From all this, what emerges is the relative nature of all definitions and the relative nature of any understanding of the political phenomenon in Israel: the same political reality is interpreted both as a *halakhic* state and as a Canaanite state; the same political ideology is interpreted both as a false messianism and as a form of pragmatism which intentionally destroys the vision.

The primary reason for this lies in the roots of Jewish political life, namely, in the adherence in principle to a political outlook that is essentially dialectic in nature. No position or period in Jewish history can be defined as being free of this problematic dialectic. The essence of theocracy as a vision of fulfillment and as an arena of conflict remains unchanged: hence, the criticism and accord among the different approaches is derived from their contact with the two opposite axes of the Jewish polity.

Figure 13.1 will help clarify the political system in Israel, in its theocratic ramifications. (The horizontal line denotes dichotomy, and the three intersecting points between the two poles represent the three approaches of theocratic synthesis):

**FIGURE 13.1**

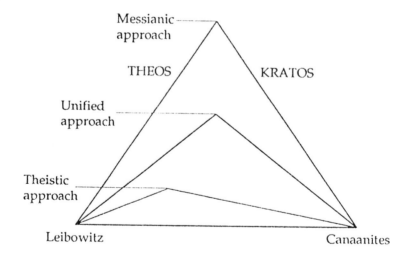

level, because so much of Jewish activity is voluntary and time-consuming, the time, leisure, energy, and resources devoted to this pursuit demand a significant level of economic security. Prestige is also significant. Jewish organizations often seek as leaders individuals who have high prestige in the non-Jewish community, and in contemporary industrial societies this will tend to focus on individuals who have achieved marked success in business or in the professions. Conversely, successful individuals particularly those of recent immigrant origins, will seek prestige from involvement at the top level of Jewish affairs, particularly if the avenues to leadership in the general community are more difficult to traverse. The result then is that universally the leadership of the Jewish communities is predominantly comprised of men of wealth and prestige in business or in the professions, particularly in law.

One aspect needing close examination is the relationship between the various organizational professionals, including the rabbis, and the top organizational leaderships.[21] Employed professionals (owing their livelihood to the organization and removable by the board), who are able to leave their imprint and influence upon an organization's policy, are the exception rather than the rule. The Jewish professional ranks have traditionally been avenues of upward mobility for Jews from the working and lower middle classes. As such those who enter them have often lacked the independence of the organizations' leaders, and often these professional choices take place after the independent and prestigious professions have attracted the most talented. Only a rare professional has the independence of mind and means, and the will, to stand up to extremely determined organizational leaders who seek to ensure that they get what they want, even though they may not always know what that is. Moreover, the prestige of the Jewish professions has in the past been low, which further deters the best talent. There are of course notable exceptions, which occur, for example, when the professional can demonstrate skills that the organization's leaders lack, or when organizational leaders are particularly oriented towards acceptance and promotion of the professional's role and status. One prominent organization in this category is the American Jewish Committee. Similarly, while leaders may steal the limelight, the effective policy decisions may be heavily influenced by their professional bureaucrats on whom they may become dependent for advice.

The greater wealth and leisure of Jewish leaders may lead them to

Another factor contributing both to the convergence between the various approaches and to the sharpness of the mutual criticism is undoubtedly the unifying recognition that all are a reflection and a realization of the Jewish *Weltanschauung* and a decisive statement on the essence of Jewish existence. Political ideology (in both its unidimensional approach which seeks abrogation or exclusivity, and in its two-dimensional approach which views the polity as an actual historical phenomenon and as an abstract value) is therefore reflected in every important chapter of Jewish history, and is related to the fundamental questions of the essence of Judaism, as expressed in its myths, in the messianic longings torn between deterministic restraint and initiative, in our historical consciousness, and in our present existence.

## Conclusion

The development of the present political reality provides a new perspective on the basic questions of the essence of Judaism. It also serves as a touchstone for the whole range of Jewish political ideologies: an inevitable gap has been revealed in all sectors between the political ideal and the actual reality. Bergman or Buber would find it hard to identify the State of Israel with the universal mission of sanctifying God's name, just as Borochov would find it hard to discover in it the society moving towards the egalitarian-socialist age. Ben-Gurion would have had to admit the steady retreat from the ideal of the land of the prophets; and U. Z. Greenberg, despite the spirit of Judah ha-Levi which animated him, would have had to come to grips with the fact that, notwithstanding all the signs of redemption, we are still far from the messianic age, while the Canaanites would have to recognize the continuing involvement of the Jewish people of the diaspora in the fate of Israel,[73] as well as in such objective difficulties as the existence of the Palestinian entity, which refutes the vision of the Hebrew Canaan within a homogeneous geo-political bloc.

In fact, if we add here the objective conditions of siege and isolation in which the State of Israel finds itself today, we can infer not only that the eternal Jewish mission is striving to establish itself in the renewed national Jewish existence, but also that it reflects the eternal affliction of the Jewish people[74]—that their state, today as in the distant past, is "the heritage of all the nations."[75] The Jewish political anomaly is thus transferred from the realm of the internal spiritual struggle with the idea of the kingdom of heaven, to the realm of historical-actual phenomena in which the world political system is reluctant to accept the existence of a Jewish political entity.

This view is related to such external issues as anti-Semitism, the Jewish persecution complex, and the like, which go beyond the bounds of the present study. To return to the subject under discussion here, which is in the realm of Jewish self-examination: over and beyond the problematic comparison between real and ideal, the difficulties of the political attitudes in Israel today can be viewed as being derived from three basic factors: the pluralism of the definition of *theos*; the controversy over the place of the present in the historical evolution towards the messianic age; and, as opposed to these, the continued revolt against the tradition of the diaspora and the attempt to build a new independent Israeli existence.

Despite the novelty of these phenomena, they continue to find expression within the traditional framework of the theocratic continuum. Despite the revolution that has occurred in the system of beliefs and opinions, the basic structure of the political ideologies remains unchanged. Then as now, there exist within us extremists on both sides of the fence: the existential political voices as opposed to the prophetic voices of the wilderness. While the former tried, and are still trying, to free themselves from the Jewish destiny to become "like all the nations," the latter strive for a particularist realization of a uniqueness which distinguishes Judaism from the historical-political world around it. The proponents of existential *kratos* bestowed their blessing on both the worship of Ba'al and on the Uganda plan, while the advocates of exclusive *theos* applauded the loss of territory. From the point of view of the overall Jewish outlook, both are exceptions. We can conclude that, while the central current in Judaism never renounced political existence, the value of the state was never perceived as an independent normative system. The political goal remained neither to be "like all the nations" nor "not reckoned among the nations," but rather to be a light unto the nations, as expressed in the prophetic vision: "For out of Zion shall go forth the law, and the word of the Lord from Jerusalem."

In his book on Jewish theocracy, G. Weiler criticizes this phenomenon:

A central tenet of popular Zionism, which has today been adopted by the entire Jewish people, is that the Jewish state must be a shining example to others. For some reason they think that a Jewish state designed to deal only with those needs with which states generally concern themselves is beneath the dignity of the Jewish people.[76]

However, such criticism cannot alter the facts. I therefore return to my point of departure: the dialectic continuum of Jewish history in which the political and metapolitical are intertwined has not been broken. The aspiration of Judaism, except for one-dimensional exceptions, is to be part of the political world but not to be assimilated within it, to cling to eternal life but without relinquishing the reality of territorial existence. Its goal is to achieve a "federalist" covenant between the *political reality,* with borders, trade, security, economy, and civil law, and the *worship of God* which sanctifies the land, the people, and life.

It is because of this dialectic duality that theocracy, in the literal-ecclesiastical sense of the term as the *actual rule of the representatives of God,* has never been realized in Israel; on the other hand, the political system has never been severed from the theistic system of thought expressed in, "Render unto God those things that are God's and unto Caesar the things that are Caesar's." The kingdom of Israel—terrestrial Jerusalem—has constantly been faced with the challenge of realizing the kingdom of heaven—celestial Jerusalem.

History has yet to prove whether this challenge constituted the true course and the essence of Judaism, or whether it is a hopeless, obstinate quest for the impossible.

## Notes

1. In contrast to the Christian Augustinian approach which views the state as the antithesis of the kingdom of heaven. On this see C. H. McIlwain, *The Growth of Political Thought in the West, from the Greeks to the End of the Middle Ages* (New York, 1932), ch. 5, pp. 154ff.

2. The opposite approach views the history of the State of Israel not as a new chapter in Jewish history, but as a *new nation,* and any connection between this nation and the "eternal people" or the wandering Jew is artificial. A good example of this is B. Bettelheim, "Survival of the Jews," *The New Republic* (July 1, 1967): 23–30. The struggle for self-determination in Israel as opposed to the historical Jewish consciousness finds expression in G. Weiler, *Theocratia Yehudit,* "Jewish Theocracy," (Tel Aviv, 1976), especially pp. 281ff. See also A. Rubinstein, *Lihiyot Am Hofshi* (To Be a Free People) (Jerusalem, 1977).

3. See *Zohar*, I, 44b. S.H. Bergman has enlarged upon this in his book *Faith and Reason: An Introduction to Modern Jewish Thought* (Washington, D.C., 1961), pp. 81–121; and in *BaMishol*, ed. N. Rotenstreich (Tel Aviv, 1976), pp. 182–85.

4. Despite my reservations with regard to the accepted definitions of *theocracy*, I nevertheless find it useful to discuss the idea of the kingdom of heaven in Judaism in terms of theocracy, first because this is the accepted term, and second because in this way I will be able to highlight the profound differences between the *rule of religion* as literal theocracy and "theocratic" ideologies, and their historical applications in Jewish history.

5. J. J. Rousseau, *The Social Contract*, book 1, ch. 8. See also J. N. Shklar, *Men and Citizens: A Study of Rousseau's Social Theory* (Cambridge, 1963), pp. 1–33.

6. In the words of S. H. Bergman:

> The State of Israel is faced with the choice, whether it wishes to be a state like all other states, with all the intrigues of politics—but then the State of Israel will be without any importance and its foundation will be an ordinary historical event which is of no interest to humanity as a whole. Or does this small state, quantitatively insignificant, wish to serve as the true fulfillment of the messianic longings of the Jewish people throughout the generations, as the beginning of the redemption of the world in the kingdom of God. . . . If the State of Israel views itself and its deeds as the beginning of the kingdom of God, then "all the families of the earth" will be blessed by this state. (*BaMishol*, pp. 57–58)

A similar view is expressed by Y. Leibowitz in *Yahadut, Am Yehudi u-Medinat Yisrael* (Judaism, the Jewish People and the State of Israel) (Jerusalem-Tel Aviv, 1975), p. 71.

7. Moses Mendelssohn provides a good definition of this two-dimensional approach to political existence in Judaism. See M. Mendelssohn, *Jerusalem and Other Jewish Writings*, trans. and ed. Alfred Jospe (New York: Schocken, 1969), p. 99.

8. N. Rotenstreich, "Mendelssohn's Approach to the Understanding of Judaism," introduction to the Hebrew translation of Mendelssohn's *Jerusalem. Yerushalayim, Ktavim Ktanim be-Inyenei Yehudim ve-Yahadut* (Tel Aviv, 1947), p. 17.

9. G. Weiler wrote:

> *Halakhah* cannot be the law of the state. *Halakhah* knows only slaves. It does not recognize the national will. . . . It runs totally counter to the principles which animate the state and the life of its citizens. Perhaps the attitude of *halakhah* is that man need not be a citizen at all. This is the problem of *halakhah*. The problem of the state is that man cannot be a citizen and the slave of one whose representatives claim supreme authority. (*Theocratia Yehudit*, p. 291)

10. E.g., Josephus Flavius, *Jewish Antiquities*, XIV, 3:2; and *The Jewish War*, I, 4:3.

11. E. R. Goodenough, *The Politics of Philo Judaeus: Practice and Theory* (New Haven, 1938), p. 32.

12. B. Spinoza, *Tractatus Theologico-Politicus*, pp. 8, 183, 192, 193.

13. Mendelssohn, p. 132.

14. See, for example, U. Z. Greenberg, *Sefer ha-Kitrug veha-Emunah* (Jerusalem, 1936), p. 37.

15. *Guide for the Perplexed,* part III, ch. 12. See also *Mishneh Torah,* Hilkhot Bet ha-Behirah, 6:16.

16. D. Ben-Gurion, *Nezah Israel* (The Eternity of Israel) (Tel Aviv, 1964), p. 186.

17. Don I. Abravanel, *Commentary on the Torah* (Jerusalem, 1955), p. 39. See also his commentary on the minor prophets, pp. 53–54, 211–14.

18. See, for example, his articles "Moses" (Hebrew), *Al Parashat Derakhim* (At the Crossroads), collected articles (Berlin, 1904), vol. 3, p. 221; and "Flesh and Spirit" (Hebrew), ibid., vol. 3, pp. 222–32.

19. As he wrote: "Die Selbstbehauptung muss mit einer Hingabe an eine uberselbstische Sache verkupft sein, um deren willen dieses Selbst erhalten wird," in "Rede auf dem XVI Zionisten-Kongress in Basel," *Der jude und sein judentum* (August 1, 1929): 521–22.

20. B. Borochov, "The Elements of Proletarian Zionism" (Hebrew), *Kitvei B. Borochov* (Writings of B. Borochov), ed. Z. Abramovitz and I. Yitzhaki (Tel Aviv, 1934), p. 172.

21. "The generation in the wilderness hath no portion in the world to come, as it is written, 'In this wilderness they shall be consumed and there they shall die.'" *Sanhedrin* 110b. See also Ezekiel 2:1–28.

22. See *Etz Hayyim, Sha'ar He'arat Ha'mochin,* ch. 1, or *Likkutei Torah, Parashat Shalah,* 38a. See also B. Spinoza, *Tractatus Theologico-Politicus,* p. 178.

23. See, for example, G. Weiler, *Theocratia Yehudit,* pp. 111–26. He bases himself primarily on Y. Kaufman, *Toledot ha-Emunah ha-Yisraelit* (The Religion of Israel) (Jerusalem-Tel Aviv, 1953), vols. 3–4.

24. Abravanel, *Commentary on minor prophets,* pp. 211–14 and 234–35. See also *Mashmia Yeshu'ah* (from *Sefer Rosh Amanah;* Koenigsberg, 1861), pp. 37–39.

25. A. J. Heschel, *The Prophets* (New York, 1962), pp. 103–40, 474–83. See also D. Daiches, "The Prophets, by Abraham J. Heschel," *Commentary* 35, no. 6 (June 1963): 538.

26. This is Heschel's interpretation to Isaiah 9:1: "The people that walked in darkness have seen a brilliant light; on those who dwelt in a land of gloom light has dawned." See Heschel, *The Prophets,* p. 171, and pp. 162, 167.

27. *Mishneh Torah,* Hilkhot Melakhim, 1:9, and the comments by R. Abraham b. David there. See also *Guide of the Perplexed,* part I, ch. 54.

28. II Samuel 7:1–18.

29. I Kings, chs. 8, 9, 11.

30. E.g., Isaiah 40:3; Jeremiah 2:2 and 31:1–2.

31. E.g., the open conflict between King Ahab and Elijah the prophet. See I Kings, chs. 17–21.

32. M. Mendelssohn, *Jerusalem,* p. 138. See also D. Ben-Gurion, "Israel Among the Nations" (Hebrew), *Nezah Israel,* pp. 126, 127.

33. Y. Leibowitz, *Yahadut Am Yisrael uk-Medinat Yisrael,* p. 76.

34. See *Yalkut Shimoni,* Nitzvim, on the three covenants. See also *Berakhot* 48b, and Rashi's commentary there.

35. S. R. Hirsch, *Horeb—Essays on Israel's Duties in the Diaspora,* trans. I. Grunfeld (1962).

36. See G. Scholem, *The Messianic Idea in Judaism* (New York, 1971).

37. Abravanel, *Yeshuot Meshiho* (cited in *Sefer Rosh Amanah*), ch. 7, pp. 57–62. See also his *Commentary on minor prophets,* p. 401.

38. *Mishneh Torah,* Hilkhot Melakhim, 12:1.

39. Z. Jabotinsky, "Zionism and the Land of Israel" (Hebrew), *Ktavim Zionim Rishonim* (Early Zionist Writings) (Jerusalem, 1949), pp. 128–29.

40. Quite consistently, rabbinic Judaism never found anything to say in condemnation of Josephus Flavius, the priest from Jerusalem who was prepared to become a Roman slave. This is not surprising. Rabban Johanan b. Zakkai is credited with having laid the foundations for the continued survival of Judaism after the fall of Jerusalem. According to tradition, he saved his life by being smuggled out of besieged Jerusalem in a coffin to Titus' camp. There he asked that the Roman general grant him Jabneh and its sages—this against the background of the destruction of the holy city, where its residents were faced with the alternative of choosing between death and bondage. Rabban Johanan b. Zakkai was accorded his request. He and Josephus must be judged in the same manner—guilty, condemned, or praised. Both made a choice, and they knew what they were choosing. G. Weiler, *Theokratia Yehudit,* p. 32.

41. On the fear of messianic activism, see L. Strauss, "Abravanel's Political Tendency and Political Teaching," *Isaac Abravanel: Six Lectures,* ed. J.B. Trend and H. Loewe (Cambridge, 1937), p. 108. See also Ahad Ha'am, "In the Footsteps of the Messiah" (Hebrew), from *Yalkut Katan,* cited in *Al Parashat Derakhim,* vol. 4, pp. 87–90. Hence also the rejection of Zionism and the State of Israel by the ultra-Orthodox. On the question of whether "the State of Israel divested the Land of Israel of its sanctity," see J. D. Soloveitchik, *BeSod haYahid vehaYahad,* ed. P. Pelli (Jerusalem, 1976), pp. 422–24.

42. As for the motto for the Jews' "uniqueness and mission," Ben-Gurion chose Deuteronomy 7:7–8: "It is not because you are the most numerous of peoples that the Lord set His heart on you and chose you—indeed, you are the smallest of peoples; but it was because the Lord loved you." Quoted in *Nezah Israel,* p. 7.

43. T. Herzl, *Altneuland* (1902). Trans. English P. Arnold (1960), pp. 47, 64, 73–74, 80, 82, 87, 131, 151, 170, 271, 282, 288, 293.

44. This in contrast to the criticism of Ahad Ha'am, who viewed *Altneuland* as merely an imitation of the gentile states: "There is really no impression here of the special national spirit of an ancient people, and it is merely an imitation which testifies to the enslavement of the spirit." But despite his criticism of the severance from the source, Ahad Ha'am admits that "there is also a temple in *Altneuland,* though it is not on the Temple Mount." "Sin and Punishment" (Hebrew), from *Yalkut Katan,* cited in *Al Parashat Derakhim,* vol. 3, p. 162.

45. *Stenographisches Protokoll der Verhandlunger des II Zionisten-Congresses* (Wien, 1898).

46. Ahad Ha'am, "The First Zionist Congress" (Hebrew), from *Yalkut Katan,* cited in *Al Parashat Derakhim,* vol. 3, p. 56: "The salvation of Israel will be brought about by prophets and not by diplomats." See also B. Kurzweil, "Ahad-Ha'amism: The Group Will to Survive," *Judaism* 4 (1955): 213; and A. Herzberg, *Introduction to the Zionist Idea* (New York, 1973), pp. 51ff.

47. See Ahad Ha'am, "Those Who Cry" (Hebrew), *Al Parashat Derakhim,* vol. 3, pp. 200–209. See also Z. Jabotinsky, "On Territorialism" (Hebrew), *Ktavim Zionim Rishonim,* pp. 134–36.

48. Jabotinsky, "On Territorialism," pp. 137–38:

> As for those who fear that "we are liable to transfer to Palestine too many ancient laws which have become obsolete"—to them I do not even wish to respond, for it is impossible to argue seriously whether or not our intelligentsia in the Land of Israel will grow side-curls or wear a fringed garment. All this—excuse me for the sharpness of the expression—is pure nonsense.

49. Quoted by A. Bein in *Theodor Herzl* (1940; latest ed. 1970), p. 373.
50. S. H. Bergman, *BaMishol,* p. 93.
51. Ibid.
52. *Koenigtum Gottes* was written in 1932. The third German edition (1956) was translated into English as *Kingship of God* (1967).
53. M. Buber, *On Zion: The History of an Idea,* trans. Stanley Goldman (London, 1973), p. 142.
54. J. D. Soloveitchik, *BeSod hayahid vehaYahad,* pp. 424–25.
55. Ibid., p. 430.
56. B. Kurzweil, "The Nature and Sources of the 'New Hebrew' ('Canaanites')" (Hebrew), *Sifruteinu haHadasha—Hemshekh o Mahapekha?* (Modern Hebrew Literature - Continuation or Revolution?) (Jerusalem-Tel Aviv, 1960), pp. 280–83.
57. A. G. Horon, "The Canaanite Heritage—Its Burial and Resurrection" (Hebrew), from "The Hebrew Past," quoted by Y. Ratosh in *MiNizahon leMapolet* (From Victory to Defeat) (Tel Aviv, 1976), p. 259.
58. Ibid., p. 105.
59. Ibid., p. 375.
60. Y. Leibowitz, *Yahadut Am Yehudi u-Medinat Israel,* p. 147.
61. Ibid., p. 243.
62. Ibid., pp. 429–30.
63. Ibid., pp. 241–42.
64. Ibid., p. 183.
65. With the closing of the Bible, prophecy came to an end, but the Divine Presence did not depart. The people were severed from their land and went into exile, and the messianic vision accompanied them throughout their wanderings, and the voice of God continued to ring in their ears. Their hope in a future of independence and justice was not shaken and did not die. This Divine voice speaks to man today just as it did three thousand years ago. There are those who believe that the voice comes from heaven, and those who say that it comes from the heart. What is important is the voice, and not the debate over its source. (D. Ben-Gurion, *Nezah Israel,* p. 174)
66. Ibid., p. 185.
67. Ibid., p. 27.
68. D. Ben-Gurion, *Kokhavim veEfer,* "Stars and Dust" (Ramat-Gan, 1976), p. 196.
69. Ibid., pp. 176–77.
70. Ben-Gurion, *Nezah Israel,* p. 186.
71. U. Z. Greenberg, *BeKez haDerakhim Omed Rabbi Levi Yizhak miBerdichev veDoresh Teshuvat Ram* (Rabbi Levi Isaac of Berdichev Stands at the End of the Roads and Demands an Answer from God), *Ha'aretz,* May 3, 1946; also in U. Z. Greenberg, *Rehovot haNahar* (1951).
72. B. Kurzweil, "The Essence of the Poetry of U.Z. Greenberg" (Hebrew), *Bein Hazon leVein haAbsurdi* (Between the Vision and the Absurd) (Jerusalem-Tel Aviv, 1966), p. 49. See also D. Ben-Gurion, *Nezah Israel,* p. 125.
73. On the subject of the diaspora in Zionist ideology, see Daniel J. Elazar, "Towards a Renewed Zionist Vision," *Forum* 26, no. 2 (1977): 52–69.
74. The State of Israel is isolated today, just as the Jewish people was isolated during the thousands of years of its existence. And perhaps the isolation of the state today is even more striking than in the past, for it is clearly revealed in the international arena. . . . The Jews of America cannot remain silent and in repose

until the danger in which the State of Israel finds itself should pass. Those living in the Holy Land cannot speak nonsense about the "new Jew" being created there. (J. D. Soloveitchik, *BeSod hayahid vehaYahad,* pp. 395–96)

75. Genesis 1:1, and Rashi's commentary on this verse.
76. G. Weiler, *Theokratic Yehudit,* p. 283.

# 14

# The Jewish Political Tradition as a Vehicle for Jewish Auto-Emancipation

*Dan V. Segre*

Twenty-eight years after the establishment of the State of Israel, Jews and non-Jews alike are divided on its role. Its viability is still questioned and the Arabs are not the only ones to express doubts about its right to exist. Extreme Jewish Orthodoxy and leftist radicalism join in asking this question—though, of course, for entirely different reasons. The Zionists themselves, though certain the answer is in the affirmative, cannot always quite say why; the fact that any decent person must agree that the UN resolution equating Zionism with racism is a libel does not help Zionism to define itself as a nonracist, national movement acceptable to a "progressive," anti-Western ideologically dominated world. Russians and Chinese may call each other "Zionists" in their propaganda broadcasts, but Zionists are still uncertain whether their movement is one that creates a refuge for persecuted Jews, for interested Jews, or for all Jews. If the ideal is a refuge, then it makes sense to argue that there is one ideal Zion in Israel and another in America—or Australia—like the two temples of Jerusalem and Leontopolis in Egypt. If the ideal is to have concerned Jews, then perhaps there are more concerned Jews in America than in Israel. Moreover, for every American Jew who has emigrated to Israel there are seven Israelis who have emigrated to the United States.

There is even more confusion about Zionism as a political, contemporary movement: Is it really secular, or crypto-religious? Is it national or nationalistic? If it is national, what is a Jewish nation? How does one deal with a people which is also a pigmentation of world culture, living within Christianity and Islam, like Buddhism in so many Eastern religions? What happens to a civilization—such as the Jewish civilization—when it manifests itself in the often parochial behavior of the new, sovereign Israeli state? How is it possible to analyze the behavior of this new political entity now that it has changed, in one single generation, from a shaky home in a colonial territory to a major power factor in the Middle East, increasingly and unwillingly involved in the crisis created by the still unfilled imperial vacuum left by the disappearance of the Ottoman Empire after World War I?

These questions are as political as they are moral, touching on that universal dilemma posed by Machiavelli to Western civilization: that a Christian prince has to choose between being a Christian or being a prince. In the view of Isaiah Berlin,[1] this choice between Christian and pagan morality split "the rock on which Western beliefs and lives have been founded." The ultimate logic of Machiavelli's doctrine is indeed that ends equally ultimate and equally sacred may contradict each other, and that entire systems of values may come into collision without any possibility of rational arbitration.

In as much as Jewish monotheism is one of the sources of the monistic pattern of Western civilization, it is both part of and confronted by the Machiavellian dilemma: *part of,* since time immemorial; *confronted by,* not for the first time but with dramatic force, since the emergence of a Jewish state and the success of the political, Western, national ideology—Zionism—which gave birth to it. The question as to whether the Jews can allow themselves to follow pagan political morality and still remain Jewish is the central ideological question facing the state of Israel and splitting the "rock" upon which its political legitimacy rests. If tactics are not to be confounded with strategies, this is what people mean when they claim, with Professor Yaakov Talmon of the Hebrew University of Jerusalem,[2] that not by the sword alone can the State of Israel live, a wise statement indeed, but then, if Israel cannot survive by the logic of *realpolitik*, why should it be able to do so by any other standard of Western political morality, paralyzed as we have seen by the Machiavellian dilemma? None of the modern critics of Israeli politics has tried to elaborate a Jewish policy for a modern Jewish state. The noncritics have usually chosen an existentialist stand: we have succeeded and therefore we have the right to exist, even if our existence surprises you. Or, as General Rabin put it in his speech of acceptance of the degree of Doctor of Philosophy Honoris Causa for having won the 1967 war: Jews are not used to being winners; it is still a shock for them to have won such a victory.

The purpose of this chapter is to investigate some of the factors that have so far hampered the development of a Jewish political thought, and to speculate on the chances that such a thought might be elaborated in a modern Jewish polity, not in opposition to, but as a possible link between tradition and modernism. The topic is far from being new. The need for such a link has been in the forefront of the preoccupation of many Israeli thinkers. But the idea that the political problems of modern Israel may be understood better when analyzed according to non-European rather than Western models is not accepted, probably because of the fear that such an approach might lead to a kind of Jewish "Black Studies," endangering the monopoly that traditional Judaica scholarship has held on every aspect of Jewish Studies. This is an important methodological aspect of the research into Jewish political thought on which I shall not dwell here: I mention it because of the growing relevance I believe it will have for the study of Israeli politics.[3]

Let us stick to the subject and return to the problems of the Jews in a modern world. Professor Nathan Rotenstreich, of the Department of Philosophy in the Hebrew University, said in a symposium on Zionism almost twenty years ago that "the face of world history changed completely at that point when it felt prepared, knowingly or unknowingly, for good or ill, to receive the Jewish people in its midst."[4] To him, the fact that the Jewish people once again took its place in the history of mankind, that it was given a place in the ordinary daily course of historical events, meant that at this—unspecified—time, two or three generations ago, the face of history "ceased to be *Christian* history in the specific meaning of that term and became the *political* history of nations and of political blocs." But, asks Rotenstreich, how was it now possible to reconcile "Jewish existence among the forces of the world with the specific character of the Jewish people and with its heritage which is the crystallization of generations? Can Judaism become a power capable of shaping our human existence while meeting the challenge posed by the problems and ideologies of our time, even when it does not strive to expand beyond the limits of the historical Jewish group?"

In Rotenstreich's view, Israel must

> take an Archimedean point, intellectually, which will be faithful to its own principles on the one hand, and open-minded to the world on the other. Such an Archimedean point can be derived from the basic Jewish outlook that man's life does not belong to himself...man is not master of the world, and yet his attitude to the world is not a passive one.

If I understand correctly, Rotenstreich tends to believe that traditional Jewish *halakhah* can be revived through activation of the Jews on the World Historical Stage, as Hegel would say. In other words, it matters not to what end we act, but on what *stage*. It could be called a Sisyphean activation of Jewish tradition in a historico-political framework.

Another, quite different, type of preoccupation with the coexistence of Jewish tradition with modern politics is that of Professor Isaiah Leibowitz. For Professor Leibowitz,[5] Judaism is embodied in the religion of Israel in a unique form: a way of life of the Torah and the Commandments, whose formulated expression is the *halakhah*. "It is impossible," he says, endorsing the traditional claim of Jewish orthopraxis, "to erect Judaism on the basis of the Bible, nor is it possible to base it on ethics or on Messianism." The current Israeli "Biblioloatry" is not Judaism in his view.

> Jews have not contributed anything to world culture. There is no such thing as Jewish philosophy or Jewish ethics or a specific Jewish political or social idea, specific Jewish artistic or aesthetic values, or Jewish science. The only specifically unique Jewish creation that actively appeared in history is *halakhah,* that is, the attempt to organize the rules of human life against a background of law, the aim of which is the service of God. The world did not accept this from us. It rejected it clearly and emphatically, and at the time when this Jewish thought was gaining considerable influence, the world launched a successful counterattack against us. This counterattack was Christianity....We cannot contribute anything of our own to the solution of the problems which confront the world today, for our peculiar approach to the world and man is that of the Torah and the Commandments alone, and this the world has not accepted and is not likely to accept. Anything else that we may have to say is nothing but a paraphrase of what others have said in a more original form. The non-Jewish world does not need us to preach to them the philosophy of Jefferson and Lincoln—they preach that themselves. They do not need to learn liberalism from us, nor humanism nor the rights of man. It is they who proclaimed the rights of man and it is they who preach them.

There is no point, asserts Leibovitz, in talking about being a "Light to the Gentiles": It is not possible to extract from Judaism guidance for a secular way of life. It is about time, he claims, that Jews forgot the pyrotechnics of being a light to the gentiles and took a closer look at themselves.

So much for the examples: Berlin, who does not deal specifically with the Jewish political problem but who obliges us to think of the relevance of the Machiavellian dilemma for the State of Israel; Rotenstreich, who sees the Jewish revival in terms of a constant labor against existence; and Leibovitz, who feels that Judaism has nothing to look for, outside *halakhah*. The trouble with the *halakhah*, namely, the Jewish rabbinical code of life, both as understood through what Rotenstreich calls the Archimedean approach, or what Leibovitz calls a unique Jewish creation, is that in matters pertaining to politics it is far less developed than in other fields. A rabbi can define a kosher chicken; he cannot define a kosher state. And the central factual observation is that in political thought, both Orthodox and secular Judaism are impoverished by their own choice. Any student of politics can find a list of books dealing with French, British, American, Chinese, Islamic political thought; he will certainly have difficulty finding books about Jewish political thought, not because they do not exist (although there are relatively few, compared to some other civilizations) but because they are not readily available or recognized for what they are.[6] In the *Encyclopedia Judaica* there are forty-five entries under the heading "Politics," but only four deal with political theory,[7] and even these do so in an erratic and chronicle-like way. Concepts such as "power" and "diplomacy" do not appear in the monumental Judaica index as independent items. A "power"[8] is mentioned only in connection with a "power of attorney" and a reference to "diplomacy" relates to the Diplomat Hotel in Jerusalem. There is no mention of a Jewish theory of political opposition, although this has been a central idea in Judaism throughout the centuries, and although the oldest Jewish parliament (the Great Knesset) was pre-Christian. Nobody, of course, would take the index of the *Encyclopedia Judaica* as a final reference, but its omissions on political subjects are too numerous and too obvious to be mere editorial oversights, especially in view of the Encyclopedia's preoccupation with Jewish history, ethics, economics, and, of course, religion—as expressed, for instance, in the entries on *War and Peace*.[9]

That Jewish Orthodoxy should have difficulty in distinguishing between religion and politics is not surprising. Any anthropologist or sociologist will admit that the political element does not spring from nothingness, but is an integral part of the religious culture and kinship organization of any society. But one would expect that at a time when Jewish statehood was being revived, both religious and secular elements would be interested in the study of the process of political differentiations and developments in Judaism. Yet the contrary seems to be the case. In most Israeli universities, political theory is taught, from Plato to Marcuse, but any mention of Maimonides or Abarbanel, or of political ideas in the Bible or the Talmud, is carefully avoided. (Several years ago the Department of Political Studies at the religious University of Bar-Ilan introduced a course in Jewish Political Thought into its curriculum, as part of a field of specialization in Jewish political studies which it now offers. It did so against considerable opposition on the part of the various factors within the university.) Although the political components of Jewish culture and tradition are perceptible even in the stories of the Patriarchs,[10] they are ignored in the curricula.

Why is this so? When one starts investigating the matter, one meets with many curious and complementary answers. Let us marshal a few. First, Jewish political studies sound suspiciously like a Jewish version of "Black Studies." Jews seem to be fundamentally different from, say, Zulus, whose political society can be investigated by a political anthropologist in a standard manner with the aid of his standard professional tools.

A second objection to the existence of a specific body of Jewish political ideas is that Jewish political thought has little to offer because it has not developed sufficiently due to the long absence of sovereignty within Judaism. This objection is not reasonable, at least from the point of view of Jewish rabbinical literature. The aim of *halakhah* was, inter alia, to keep alive, even if only in a purely academic way, those parts of Jewish life destroyed through the loss of political independence. One-third of the Talmud, for instance, deals with sacrifices, which obviously had no practical application after the destruction of the Temple.

A third objection is that Jewish political ideas may, in fact, exist, but they have remained so scattered and fragmentary over the whole vast Jewish literature that they could not produce the minimum of essential accumulation of knowledge necessary to make them signify.

So much for the standard objections. Put together they already offer us a picture of Jewish culture through the ages "sine" politics. This picture obviously contradicts the normal development of Jewish culture, at least as it has come down to us through the traditional literature. As long as the Jews lived in communities run by religious rabbinical tradition, their terms of reference were the Written and the Oral Law. This is what gave basic, actual interconnectedness to the Jewish culture of the diverse and dispersed communities, and continuity through many centuries. Political thought is no exception here: it may have been exposed to widely different situations, different in terms of place and time; it may have been expressed in widely differing terms; but as long as it remained linked, however tenuously, to the interpretation of the Law, it developed in an interconnected and continuous manner, and thus exhibits consistency—even if incoherently. It is well known that each of the works of the most important Jewish thinkers was quickly distributed among the widespread Jewish communities; that correspondence between scholars was intense at all periods and was rapidly published and incorporated into the tradition. The language—Hebrew—and the traditional values were kept in common: even if as mere fiction, they were still kept in common. What has passed relatively unnoticed by religious or secular Jewish scholarship is the intensity, the originality and the relevance of this tradition of Jewish political thought. These qualities become evident when the relevant political passages in the biblical and postbiblical literature are collected and classified according to political questions, such as sovereignty, legitimacy, political institutions, and so on.[11]

Turning back then, to Jewish polity, my examples will be two: the idea of *legitimacy of power,* and the idea of *opposition to power.* With regard to the idea of legitimacy of power, one of the leitmotifs of Jewish biblical and postbiblical literature is the idea of a covenant regulating the relationship between the ruler (whether God or man) and the ruled. There are the early pacts between God and the Patriarchs[12] in which, though for all practical purposes they seem not to possess a political meaning, some authoritative Jewish rabbinical interpreters already found a distinct, extra-religious meaning.

The political content of the "covenant" is no longer doubted, we are told, after the Exodus from Egypt, whether it relates to the right of the people to inherit the Land of Canaan,[13] or to the legitimacy of the House of David as rulers.[14] Conversely, it is because the "covenant" has been broken, we are told, that political disaster befalls the people of Israel.[15] King Josiah of Israel reinterprets the covenant between God and the people as a politico-religious measure to restore popular unity.[16] The same procedure is followed by Nehemiah the Scribe to mobilize the people for the reconstruction of Jerusalem after their return from the Babylonian Exile.[17]

Procedures of this kind must be understood in the terms through which Jewish Orthodoxy looks at the sovereign power of the Lord. His power is, of course, supreme, but He, Himself, once the Covenant is signed, is voluntarily subject to its rule. The power of "God in Parliament"—to speak metaphorically—is the only aspect of the Divine power that is limited. "By the customs of men," says the Talmud,

> a human King takes a decision which, if he wants, he fulfills; if he does not want—others fulfill; but the Holy One, Blessed be His Name, does not behave like this, but when He takes a decision He fulfills it first. Why is this so? (Because it is written) Keep my guard, I am the Lord, I am the One who has respected the commandments of the Law from the beginning.[18]

This concept of "God in Parliament" might be considered as an *a posteriori* interpretation of the Talmudic approach to the problem of the limitation of the power of God as King, through covenant. This may be so, but I am not the first to think so. Bossuet, teacher of King Louis XIV and defender of the rights of the Absolute Monarchy, could not find a proper answer to the limitation of power of the ruler by biblical covenant. For him, at least, the problem was as much political as religious.[19]

For Spinoza, the only way to overcome the problem of true democracy (insoluble, for instance, to Rousseau) was the transfer of the legitimacy of power to a body outside the body politic, such as God. "None of the Jews had renounced his rights," he wrote, "but all had democratically cried: 'Here we are (without any mediator) to do what the voice of God will tell us': they could keep unaltered their reciprocal equality, all having equally the right to consult God, to receive and interpret the laws, and to provide with equal and absolute authority the needs of Government."[20]

Spinoza's legitimation of power is by no means unusual. In this case Spinoza is a typical Jew. Because of its limitation by virtue of agreement, the power of the ruler is restricted both by the covenant he signs with the people and by the transfer of absolute sovereignty—as distinct from absolute rule—to God. But this is democratic only because God, too, is restricted by Covenant. The Talmud is quite right when it states that contrary to the habits of the world in earthly politics, in which a ruler makes and unmakes his own laws at his own pleasure, God first establishes a rule and then acts accordingly. It is stated that God has to comply with the judgement of a Rabbinical judgment: the Torah, once given, applies to everyone.[21]

A second illustration of Jewish polity is that of opposition to power. Opposition is a central concept in Jewish political culture. It is founded on the biblical commandment—"Reprimand your brother when he is wrong,"[22] reinforced by many additional injunctions. The prophet Ezekiel, for instance, cries out: "When I say to the sinner that he will die (for his sin) and you have not warned him to change his ways, he, the sinner, will die, but his blood will be on your head."[23] In the Talmud we hear Rabbi Jochanan proclaim: "Why has Jeroboam obtained the Kingdom? Because he criticized (King) Solomon."[24]

The concept of opposition develops along many lines: as a confrontation of Divine and human political logic between the Prophet Samuel and King Saul, for instance.[25] One demands the complete destruction of the Amalekite enemy; the other wants to prevent the destruction of the booty which could only increase the economic and military strength of the victor—as a criticism of the leader's personal conduct, as in the case of King David and court prophet Nathan,[26] as criticism of the system of government, as in the case of the clash between King Ahab and Elijah.[27] Isaiah, on the other hand, could fit the Leninist model of the political propagandist (a man who puts many ideas into many heads) when he shouts at the great of Judea: "Shame on you! You make unjust laws and publish burdensome declarations, depriving the poor of justice, robbing the weakest of my people of their right."[28] Amos as seen by Amazia, the priest at Beth-El, fits the model of the agitator better (the man who puts many ideas into one mind) in his alleged attempt to organize opposition to the ruler.[29] Jeremiah speaks more like the leader of the opposition: "If you do not listen to my words....Although you are dear to me as Gilead or as the heights of the Lebanon, I swear I will make you a wilderness, a land of unpeopled cities."[30]

The postbiblical talmudic literature is full of instances of political opposition within and without the Jewish establishment. A typical case is that of Raban Gamliel and Rabbi Joshua, Nassi (president) of the Sanhedrin established in Yavneh by Rabbi Yochanan Ben Zakkai after the destruction of the Temple. A powerful religious and political leader in a period of incredible difficulties, Raban Gamliel was deposed and reestablished as Head of the Sanhedrin in the wake of his clash with Rabbi Joshua. The issue, as reported in the Talmud,[31] was the obligation to recite the main daily prayer (the eighteen Blessings) three times a day and in the order laid down by Raban Gamliel, as opposed to the views of Rabbi Joshua and Rabbi Akiva, who wanted to make this prayer optional in the evening and shorter in form. The talmudic passage relating the dispute, which is in effect a record of a palace—or rather an academic Senate (the Sanhedrin)—revolution, is a classic description of a religious infight full of implicit political information.

Many other examples could be cited, and the question remains: why is so much of this absent from, say, the *Encyclopedia Judaica,* or from any open and accessible relevant literature?

The answer may be partly technical: passages like the one I have just mentioned about the revolt at the Sanhedrin in Yavneh[32] give the full measure of the filigree—like political evidence that transpires from the talmudic literature through the careful censorship of its compilers. The censorship was inspired by the political views of the rabbis (their stand in the fight between Pharisees and Sadducees) as well as the infighting within their own rabbinical elite. Rabbis in talmudic times often had divergent opinions about the policy to be followed vis-à-vis the powers that be. Many of the views of the more militant and politically minded rabbis were not recorded, or were recorded by allusion only, or were recorded and later deleted. One must remember the permanent state of suspicion in which the Jews as a people lived in the Roman Empire, both in its pagan and later in its Christian phases. If one recalls the ordeals the Jews had to endure in order to maintain their religio-cultural identity, the fact that they could and did find the time, the courage, and the ingenuity to record—even if sometimes in cryptic fashion—their political opinions in times of persecution, dispersion, and destitution, greater in every sense than that of any colonial dependence, is perhaps indicative of the vitality of Jewish political thought.

But the answer cannot be technical only. One is entitled to look for some explanation of a more substantive character, and one could be the price which the Jews repeatedly paid in antiquity for their attempts at self-preservation, and for their unsuccessful attempts to restore political independence by military means. The rabbis did not oppose the dismembering of Judaism as a body politic. Yitzhak Baer dates the last manifestations of a warlike spirit among the Jews to the seventh century, when they took part in the struggle for the control of Palestine between Rome and Persia, and again between Rome and Islam, which they interpreted in eschatological terms. From then on the nation definitely submitted to the admonitions of its teachers: that love cannot be prematurely aroused, that the Kingdom of God cannot be set up by force, that one cannot rise in rebellion against the overlordship of the nations. At that moment, says Baer, "the Jews left the ranks of warring nations and put their fate altogether in the hands of God—a unique historical fact to which no historian has yet given its proper importance."[33]

Yet the rabbis did guarantee the survival of the nation through a series of institutions, seemingly disjointed politically and thus less liable to be the object of political repression by the oppressive authority. The result was an enormously flexible, decentralized polity—the very first in history. The central idea behind the creation of the first Talmudic Academy at Yavneh by Rabbi Yochanan ben Zakkai was to transfer the emphasis of Jewish efforts to survive from political to utterly nonpolitical (i.e., academic) channels. In actual fact the academic center was also a center of the sensitive coordination of a highly decentralized polity.

But in spite of this decentralization, political life and discussion continued and flourished within the dispersed Jewish communities, and in all circumstances the opposition party found sufficient evidence in the Bible to legitimize its oppositional stand. *Midrash Tanchuma* states:

> Whosoever could reprimand the members of his house and has not done so, will be held responsible for it: who (could reprimand) the people of their town (and did not do so), will be held responsible for them; who (could reprimand) the world (and did not do so), will be held responsible for the whole world. Rabbi Hanina said: Which is the reference? The Lord will come to the (place of) judgment with the Elders and with the Ministers of His people [Isaiah, 3:14]. If the Ministers are culprits, why are the Elders (culprits) as well? Because the elders did not protest against the Ministers.[34]

In fact the decentralization institutionalized by the rabbinical establishment could not have existed without a very strong social, religious, and political culture pervading all the scattered communities. The interplay of Jewish authoritarian centripetal forces and opposition centrifugal trends is a constant reminder to the political scientist of the horizons of research open to him if he applies his tools to the analysis of the highly refined Jewish political society. Samuel Morell's study on the institutional limits of communal government in rabbinical law[35] is an example of what a politically minded student of Jewish communities can do in his field. It also entitles the student of Jewish political thought to ask to what extent the traditional cultural heritage of the Jews can influence the political behavior of a modern Jewish polity, and to what extent Jewish political culture can contribute to what Levi-Strauss calls "the practice of playing as a syndicate" with other cultures, while retaining its own characteristics which obviously work against the uniformity needed by a peaceful and efficient international society.[36]

Before attempting to answer this question in principle, I must go back to the question raised by Berlin, Rotenstreich, and Leibovitz, and query whether the constant labor of a reborn Jewish polity over-against existence, over-against the actual world, affords a possibility of returning to the sources of Judaism: of understanding historically—as Rotenstreich claims—the Jewish *halakhah* and thus its political meaning. Can a modern Jewish political *halakhah* avoid the Machiavellian dilemma of the confrontation between monotheistic and pagan virtues underlined by Berlin?

To try and discover some specific, ethical Jewish values by virtue of which a new political *halakhah* could be developed and adapted to modern times, seems to me a vain effort. Leibowitz is certainly right when he claims that there has never been such a thing as Jewish ethics, but he implicitly admits that there must be a certain way of thinking proper to the elaboration of the *halakhic* way of life. If so, this way of thinking must be equally applicable to political problems and would underline the originality of a Jewish approach to politics. It seems that it is this peculiarly Jewish way of thinking, and not always or necessarily the *halakhic* values that it has produced, which has been the major obstacle to an understanding of the Jewish *halakhah* by non-Jews, and even by many Jews who are not conversant (as is the case today) with traditional Jewish culture.

Here, however, we come up against two factual obstacles to the understanding of Jewish traditional thought. One concerns the type of concept currently used by rabbinical scholars to convey their ideas;

the other the methods that they employ. Rabbi Adin Steinsaltz has noted[37] that while modern thought tends to use abstract concepts and a general, abstract terminology, Jewish thought, from its beginnings in the Bible and right down to some of the latest creations, such as Hasidism, shies away from abstractions. It is of course difficult to manipulate complex ideas without general concepts, but those employed in the Jewish sources are of a more pictorial type. For instance, when the Jewish scholar of *halakhah* wishes to convey certain general principles inspiring activities that are forbidden on the Sabbath, as in the case of extracting food from a container, he does not resort to abstract definitions or even to any abstract term: he calls this activity "threshing" ("ladush").[38] An operational word becomes a general, abstract concept. A person who milks a cow on the Sabbath thus transgresses the prohibition of "threshing." The process has a technical name. It is called "undressing," transforming a complex abstract idea into a concrete one.

This type of reasoning, notes Steinsaltz, has its advantages and its disadvantages, but when compared with abstract European conceptual thinking it cannot be said to be more advanced or more backward: it is simply parallel. Yet it is clear that a culture based on this type of reasoning and requiring a constant effort of translation and interpretation of concepts, cannot easily be understood by outsiders. The matter is further complicated by the fact that almost every great talmudic scholar had his own method of interpretation. These differ profoundly in essence, but have one common element: they all follow a dialectic, nonsystemic pattern of discussion and reasoning, which is quite different from that which has produced the great modern systems of thought in Western civilization, including the Hegelian dialectics. These patterns have not been created artificially in the rabbinical academies for didactic purposes, although these methods have undoubtedly contributed to the refinement of the Jewish mind. They are capable of meeting the scientific challenges of modern times despite the noninterest for science of traditional Judaism. They seem to be rooted in a much older, metaphysical conception of the world, understood as a complex of fundamental opposites which man cannot and must not try to combine.

The Jewish dislike for abstract systems would appear to go back a very long way. When we look at the text of the Written Law and at the interpretation of the Oral Law—the Talmud—with its commentaries, we are struck by what seems to be a general taboo in the Jewish tradition on the *hybrid*. There are precise prohibitions on "mixing" things which nature, so to speak, has set apart. Jews must not, for example, plough a field with two different types of animal yoked together; they may not wear clothes made of fibers from both plant and animal or sow two types of seed in the same plot.[39] If mixing is the antithesis of purity, the list can easily be multiplied: there is an entire tractate in the Talmud dealing with *Kilaim*—Mixtures.

The above may help one to understand why Jews were regarded by the rationalists of the eighteenth century as being incapable of contributing to political theory. It was not that they were incapable of thinking in terms of modern politics but that modern Western politics, insofar as they proclaimed the eternal values of human myths, remained alien to the traditional Jewish way of thinking.

Jews, of course, have their own myths—for instance, that of the "Chosen People"—but they are not overly dogmatic about it, nor were they ever asked to believe in it as other people have been asked to believe in dogmas—such as that the real world starts after death, that all men were born equal, that history is fulfilled by and through the state, or that society develops through the class struggle. Jews are bound, by an agreement with God, to *act* on the presumption that God is one. This is certainly the foundation of a system, of a wholeness; but its very unity and totality does not leave place for other systems or political *wholes or entities* of the type of "collective souls," "national spirit," "popular will," "thinking class," or "achieving race." All political ideas of this type look like idols to Judaism, and for idols the traditional mode of Jewish thought has no kind words.

M. de Bonnal, who had to defend the rights of the Kings and of the Church in France after Napoleon, understood this quite well. Speaking of the Jewish hate of idolatry he said: "Idolatry begins by making a man out of God and ends by making gods out of men."[40] A separation of ends and means, such as the separation between spirit and letter of the revelation, between ideal and application, or between spiritual and temporal, can only result in the final separation of Heaven and Earth, leading the gods of the one totally detached from man, and the evils of the other as a permanent human lot. In western society, the Machiavellian dilemma has been amplified by the divorce between faith and science. The new idolatry is due to the fact that science, once deprived of the element of faith, seeks to become inhuman—like politics when divorced from morality—and penetrates faith in order to destroy it. To this, Judaism opposes the unity of a people which is a family, a nation which is a religion, a faith constantly transformed in practice, of an identity formed not on a common credo but by a "veritable organic cell in which the spiritual and the physical domain are welded into one unity."[41] This is what has kept Judaism afloat in history in the past.

But what about modern Judaism? Can it produce a political behavior strong enough to overcome the Machiavellian dilemma and yet remain original and faithful to its own heritage? Can Judaism produce what could be a political counterpart to the Jewish religious contribution to civilization, namely, a political monotheism?

One cannot here do more than pose the question, and conclude by summing up the argument in favor of the need for greater consciousness of the relevance of traditional Jewish political thought for modern politics.

The study of Jewish traditional literature shows that such a thought exists, that it is consistent, that it is part of Jewish traditional culture. It shows that the *halakhic* way of expression makes it difficult for this thought to be understood by people who are not conversant with it. It seems also to indicate that it stands in basic opposition to some current political ideologies because of its aversion to abstract intellectual systems.

Modern Jewish nationalism—Zionism—is one of these systems. It has been brought into Judaism from outside and, as a result, it has brought about a Jewish state, for which Jews had been longing, but without waiting for the Messiah, for whom the Jews were equally longing. For in the process the state caught by surprise rabbinical political *halakhah* which relied on the Messiah to find the proper solution for the problems of the restored independence of the Jews.

This event split Judaism no less than Machiavelli split western conscience with the dilemma of coexistence between pagan and Christian political morality. On the one side there is today a religious minority that still rejects the state because it is not Messianic, without being able to formulate the idea of a "kosher state." On the other side there is a majority of religious and secular Jews who believe that *halakhah* and state can coexist on the basis of a compromise which allows the religious Jew to live according to his godly way of life in a state which lives according to its worldly way of life. This, at all events, is the way religion and state have coexisted in Israel for the past twenty-eight years.

Both approaches seem lacking: traditional Judaism can no longer survive without a Jewish polity and must admit its failure to provide a political *halakhah*; but a Jewish state cannot thrive on a non-Jewish culture in politics and must admit the failure of an approach which Professor Leibowitz rightly defines as biblical pyrotechnics. As we all know, the Zionist revolution has meant a break with Jewish tradition. But in its contradictory nature it has also meant a return to the sources of that Jewish tradition—the language, the land, the physical detachment from Western and Islamic society, and so forth—and has therefore contributed to the revival of Jewish traditional culture. The fact that this is not always recognized, especially in the field of politics, should not surprise us. Modern Jews, Zionists or not, are probably the most Westernized, non-Western community in the world. Like many emerging colonial societies they have developed a deep complex of inferiority and admiration for the West. In the field of politics and science they tend to believe that there is nothing better than the Western heritage although, curiously enough, Israeli prestige in the underdeveloped countries rests on the recognition of the vital importance of the native culture for development.

But traditional Judaism is something quite different from negritude. It therefore seems only natural to believe that it will continue to play a central role in molding the images and the behavior of the modern Israeli, *inter alia* in the political field. It also seems quite rational to assume that by uncovering the political content of traditional Jewish culture one might contribute to the reactivation of global *halakhic* thinking in contemporary Jewish society.

In *halakhah*, after all, there is no such thing as a Jewish unbeliever: there are only different levels of faith, and the final aim of the *halakhah*, let us not forget, is not to make Jews out of men, but men—including political men—out of Jews.

## Notes

1.  Isaiah Berlin, "The Question of Machiavelli," *The New York Review of Books,* November 4, 1971.
2.  Yaakov Talmon, "Is Force an Answer to Everything?" *Dispersion and Unity—Journal on Zionism and the Jewish World* 17/18 (Jerusalem, 1973): 7–42.
3.  A notable contribution in this field has been made by Professor Daniel Elazar, regularly through the Center for Jewish Community Studies and most immediately through the International Seminar of the Institute for Judaism and Contemporary Thought held yearly at Bar-Ilan University. The 1975 meeting of the

Seminar under Professor Elazar's direction was devoted to the subject of this volume. The 1976 Seminar continued this theme by focusing on the impact of statehood on the Jews of Israel and the diaspora.

4. Nathan Rotenstreich, "Judaism in the World of Our Day," Forum IV, *Proceedings of the Jerusalem Ideological Conference,* World Zionist Organization (Jerusalem, 1959), pp. 41–50.

5. Isaiah Leibovitz, "The World and the Jews," ibid., pp. 83–90.

6. Philo, Josephus, Maimonides, Abravanel, Spinoza, Mendelssohn, and Buber have all written books on Jewish political thought which, except among certain specialists, are not even recognized to be such. Take the case of Josef-Salvador (*Histoire des Institutions de Moise,* 3rd ed., 1862), a major and little known writer in the field. Although much of his work is pervaded by strong Jewish-Christian apologetic syncretism, his interpretation of Moses as a political rather than a religious prophet is original. Nahum Sokolow rightly included Salvador among the significant proto-Zionist thinkers. As for this century, the only book I know on the subject is Hans Kohn: *Die Politische Idee des Judentums* (Munich: Meyer & Jessen, 1924).

7. *Encyclopedia Judaica*: (a) 26 lines on Abrabanel's politics (2:103) and 3 on his political philosophy (13:450); (b) 11 lines on the politics of Philo (13:427); (c) 46 lines on the politics of the Prophets, containing a detailed list of the political interventions of each prophet with no attempt to establish a rational link among them or draw any political conclusion (13:1157–58); (d) 50 lines on theocracy, of which 14 about theocracy in the State of Israel (15:1099).

8. Ibid., 2:352 ff.

9. Ibid., "Peace"—2:7, 964; 10:1481; 11:148; 12:1365; 13:194–9; 14:1356,180; 15:716. "War"—5:709; 6:851; 10:868; 11:510; 13:197; 16:266,273, 278.

10. See, for instance, A. Shohat, "Megamot Politiot Besipurei Ha'Avot," *Tarbiz,* 24 (1955): 252–67.

11. Some preliminary work has been carried out in this direction at Haifa University. It consists of the collection of passages with obvious political significance from the Bible and the Babylonian Talmud, followed by their classification according to standard political questions. Although it is still too early to draw any definite conclusions, this simple preliminary work has clearly underlined the strong consistency of many political ideas in biblical and talmudic literature. One should also note that no comprehensive study has ever been made of Jewish diplomacy, although extensive records exist of diplomatic activities carried out by Jewish leaders on behalf of their own countries (communities) or of Gentile states.

12. For instance, Rabbi Ovadia Sforno (1475–1550), who saw the covenants with the Patriarchs as a prelude to the time when the Jews would be "a large enough people to make a political group." *Kavvanot Hatorah* (The Intentions of the Law), Introduction. Genesis 8:17; 7:21; 17:1–4; 19:22; 28:13–15; Exodus 3:17; Numbers 33:50–56; 31:1–15.

13. Joshua 24:12–13.

14. II Samuel 7:12–13; Chronicles 17:14.

15. II Kings 17:21–23.

16. II Kings 23:1–3.

17. Nehemiah 10:1–3.

18. Jerusalem Talmud, Rosh Hashanah, Ch. 1, Halakhah 3, p. 57b.

19. Politique Sacree 1, Art. IV, p. 6.

20. Benedetto de Spinosa, *Trattato Teologico Politico* (Italian translation by C. Sarchi), 1875, p. 303.

21. Babylonian Talmud, Baba Metzia, p. 59b.
22. Leviticus 19:17.
23. Ezekiel 33:8.
24. Babylonian Talmud, Sanhedrin, p. 101b.
25. I Samuel 15:10–30.
26. II Samuel 12:1–14.
27. I Kings 18:18.
28. Isaiah 10:1–4.
29. Amos 7:10–15.
30. Jeremiah 22:1–8.
31. Babylonian Talmud, Berakhot, pp. 27b, 28a.
32. The supreme court organized at Yavneh by Jochanan Ben Zakkai not only gradually dealt with the whole range of legislative problems formerly invested in Jerusalem, but kept the chairmanship open until a scion of the royal house of David—Raban Gamliel—could once again come into the open and become the Nassi (president) of the Academy. While descent from the royal family was a condition for becoming Ethnarc in Babylon, and possibly elsewhere, Palestine remained the "eternal center" of Judaism. The material and symbolic politico-religious expression of this geographical centrality and prominence of Palestine (quite independently of, and frequently in spite of the dwindling influence of the Jewish community there) was expressed in many ways. One was the fixing of the Festivals and the intercalation upon which all Jewish public life depended. The Romans were quick to grasp the importance of this, as evidenced by their chasing the messengers carrying the announcement of the New Year. This practical affirmation of the preeminence of the Land of Israel over all other Jewish centers of the diaspora lasted until the middle of the fourth century c.e. It was, in fact, in the wake of the crushing of the Jewish Revolt against Emperor Gallus (351–2) and the consequent destruction of many Jewish communities in Palestine, that Patriarch Hillel II agreed to limit his functions as *Nassi* in connection with the proclamation of the New Moon, and published the *Sod Ha-Ibbur* (The Secret of the Intercalation) and the *Keviuta de-Yarha* (The Fixing of the New Moon) in 358, on which the Jewish calendar is based. The calendar itself was accepted not because of its utility but because of the legitimacy of the authority of Hillel II.
33. Yitzhak F. Baer, *Galut* (New York, 1947), p. 19.
34. Babylonian Talmud, Sanhedrin, p. 17a.
35. S. Morell, "The Constitutional Limits of Communal Government in Rabbinic Law," *Jewish Social Studies* 33, nos. 2–3 (April-July 1971): 87–119. See also Louis Finkelstein, *Jewish Self-Government in the Middle Ages,* 1924, and H. H. Ben Sasson, *Toledot Am Yisrael,* 3 vols., 1969–70, pp. 260–86.
36. Claude Levi-Strauss, "Race and History," in *Race and Science,* UNESCO 1961.
37. Adin Steinsaltz, "Imagery Concepts in Jewish Thought," *Reshafim* (Jerusalem, 1960).
38. A whole tractate of the Mishna—the fourth—deals with these matters, providing, *inter alia,* one of the oldest studies in botany and agriculture ever recorded.
39. M. de Bonnal, *Oevres Completes Publiees par L'Abbe Migne* (Paris, 1859), vol. 1, ch. 4, p. 277.
41. Baruch Litvin, *Jewish Identity, Modern Responsa and Opinions, etc.,* edited by S.B. Hoenig (Jerusalem, New York, 1970): reply of Prof. H. Baruch to Prime Minister D. Ben-Gurion, p. 169ff.

# 15

# Towards a General Theory of Jewish Political Interests and Behavior

*Peter Y. Medding*

Since the Emancipation, Jews in the West have been citizens of many states embracing various forms of government. According to the conventional wisdom about Jewish political behavior, Jews, regardless of differences in social structure and regime, have been consistently liberal or Left in their political responses and attitudes, rather than conservative or Right. Most theorizing about Jewish political behavior, therefore, has attempted to explain this supposedly universal phenomenon. In fact, the conventional wisdom about Jewish political behavior was based upon the assumption that the "natural" Jewish political response was liberal and Left, and that this was anomalous given the class position of Jews in Western societies.

This chapter seeks to develop a more general theory of Jewish political behavior based upon a broader view of Jewish political interests. It will demonstrate that the political liberalism of Jews is a particular variant of Jewish political behavior, occurring only under specific historical and societal conditions, rather than a universal phenomenon.

## A Note on Concepts

It should be recognized from the very outset that we are dealing with highly ambiguous terms and concepts, and with vague and often contradictory sources of evidence, and sets of facts. The Left/Right distinction is a relative one, depending upon the situation of the Center, and the Center itself often moves. What is Left in one society may be Center or even moderate Right in another. Similarly, liberalism and conservatism are historical movements that are constantly changing. Thus, there are major differences between important manifestations of the same movement in different societies and continents (e.g., the differences between continental and Anglo-American liberalism). Moreover, what was liberal yesterday may be conservative today, because liberalism affirms the desirability of change, reform, and progress. By the same token, what conservatives opposed yesterday they may accept today as part of an accepted status quo. Even more confusing is the absence of complete overlap between the terms Left and liberal, on the one hand, and Right and conservative, on the other. To begin with, radical and socialist are also commonly associated with the Left, and these, clearly, are not synonymous with liberal. Similarly there may be aspects of liberalism on the Right, and it is also commonplace by now to recognize a radical Right.

Determining what constitutes Left or liberal political behavior is also extremely difficult. This is usually done by examining support for various political entities, such as parties, candidates, policies and programs, orientations to issues involving change or reform, and general views of societal organization. The problem is that political reality often does not correspond with the demands of theoretical consistency. The same party takes on different images in different parts of the country; liberal parties may offer illiberal candidates for election and vice versa; general programs and orientations may be liberal, but specific policies and responses of particular candidates, politicians, party bodies, and governments may be illiberal, and so on. With so many liberal and Left criteria and so many varied aspects of political reality, contradictions and inconsistencies are bound to occur. Nevertheless, there is sufficient evidence of consistency and a common core to both liberal and Left politics, on the one hand, and conservative and Right politics, on the other, to suggest that the political scientist proceed with caution, rather than abandon the exercise completely.[1]

## The Conventional Wisdom

Let us begin by examining the empirical evidence that provides the basis for the theory that constitutes the conventional wisdom. Survey research and other forms of electoral analysis have shown that in the past in a number of countries—the United States,[2] Britain,[3] Australia,[4] and Austria[5]—Jews have overwhelmingly supported parties to the Left of the political Center. In these countries and also in others in Eastern and Central Europe, Jews who were actively involved in politics at the parliamentary level were more numerous and prominent in Left parties.[6] What is more, Jews in these and other countries have been disproportionately prominent in the leadership of radical and revolutionary left-wing political parties.[7] Jewish political attitudes, too, have been found to be overwhelmingly liberal on such matters as social justice, economic welfare, civil liberties, anti-discrimination, and internationalism.[8]

Had Jews in these societies been predominantly working-class the data would have aroused little wonderment. However, their pattern of voting and political attitudes seems to be contradictory to their class situation and to the voting and attitude patterns of *all* other groups in similar socioeconomic situations. This problem is heightened when it is recalled that other immigrant ethnic groups moved Right and became more conservative with upward mobility.[9] Jews clearly did not. The discrepancy is so marked in the case of the Jews that they have sometimes been singled out as being especially altruistic and "public-regarding" in their political choices.[10]

The intellectual history of the problem, therefore, has always been to account for this seeming paradox of Jews voting against their class and socioeconomic interests. This is clearly seen in the major attempts to explain Jewish voting behavior and political attitudes. There are four major explanations of this phenomenon, all of which, with the possible exception of the last, accept the anomaly of Jewish liberalism and Left voting as the universal norm to be explained.

The *value theory* propounded by Fuchs suggests that Jews vote democratically because they are liberal in their attitude, which, in turn, stems from traditional Jewish cultural values, of charity, education, and nonasceticism.[11] This theory suffers from a number of difficulties. It has been shown that those most identified with the traditional Jewish values specified by Fuchs are often among the least liberal in their political attitudes and more likely to vote Right than Jews less identified with these values, who have been found to be the most liberal.[12] Moreover Fuchs omits to show how these values give rise to liberal responses, which is a serious omission because similar values held by others (e.g., certain Protestant groups) do not result in liberal responses.

The *sociological theory,* associated in various ways with the work of Michels,[13] Lipset,[14] and Lenski,[15] emphasizes the discrepancy between the economic achievements of Jews and their social status and acceptance. Inferior or discrepant status positions lead to various forms of protest, such as Left voting and political liberalism, and in other cases to radical and revolutionary political activity. The lack of social acceptance and the conferring of inferior status by the dominant groups in the society create a sense of marginality which permits the questioning of accepted patterns of behavior and prevents the development of the same pattern of vested interests and their promotion that characterizes other socioeconomically advantaged groups.

The *historical approach,* mainly associated with the work of Werner Cohn,[16] suggests that after the Emancipation and the Revolutions of 1789 and 1848, and despite all the high ideals of civic and political equality, Jews were not accepted fully or granted equality. The main forces opposing their full entry into society in France, Germany, Austria, and even England were to be found on the conservative, nationalist, Christian Right. They were, however, accepted much more fully on the Left, and relied on the Left to win for them the full application of civil liberties and egalitarian principles in political, civic, and legal practice. As the Right became more openly anti-Semitic, Jewish support for and dependence on the Left increased.[17]

The *socio-cultural* theory is the theory of estrangement proposed by Liebman. It sees liberalism as the response of Jews who seek the "options of the Enlightenment but rejected its consequences." It is the search for a universalistic ethic which removes the differences imposed by the older conservative traditions (both Jewish and non-Jewish) but permits Jews to retain their nominal identification as Jews. It is being "accepted into the traditions of the society without adapting to the society's dominant tradition."[18]

I wish to argue that a more broadly conceived view of Jewish political interests than the conventional wisdom suggests that the question is not why are Jews universally liberal and altruistic in spite of their socioeconomic interests, but rather what are Jewish political interests? How have Jews in different societies behaved politically in pursuit of their political interests? What would a comparative examination suggest with regard to supposed universal norms or traditions of Jewish political behavior? Or put in another way, given these political interests, under what conditions are Jews liberal? And is such liberalism particularly altruistic or public-regarding?

## Jewish Political Interests

The outstanding political characteristic of Jews in the Western world has been their vulnerability as an identifiable, conspicuous, and permanent political minority group. As such, their political interests can be separated into a set of immediate, micro-political interests, and longer-term macro-political interests.

Jewry's first political interest is for the survival of the Jewish group, not only of those Jews in the same society, but of Jews everywhere. Among other ways this manifests itself in the sheer "instinct for survival"[19] of Jews as an independent people, and in intense concern with all aspects of physical security, the certainty of which is never, as with other interest groups, taken for granted, and in an ever-present need to replace psychological insecurity with a sense of security and well-being. Feelings of unease and insecurity are a given fact of minority existence and are not restricted to societies such as Eastern Europe or Germany in the 1930s. They are very real in all societies in which Jews live, as Norman Podhoretz made clear in an important article in *Commentary* magazine in 1971 entitled "A Certain Anxiety."[20] Similarly a survey in the United States comparing levels of trust and distrust among seven ethnic groups showed that on a scale ranging from +4 to -4, Jews were by far the most distrustful. Irish Catholics, the most trusting, scored 2.506, Italian Catholics (fifth) scored 0.502, WASPS (sixth) scored 0.242, while Jews, who were seventh, scored -3.106.[21]

Jewish concern with sheer physical survival and security as a basic and primordial political interest has, in recent years, been strikingly manifested in actions in support of Israel, particularly those seeking to ensure its continued physical existence. Throughout Jewish history, threats to the survival of Jews in any place, and their actual persecution and destruction, made Jews everywhere apprehensive about their physical security and survival. This century differs only in the enormous magnitude of the threat, stemming from the unspeakable Nazi Holocaust in the past, and the position of Israel in the present, at least until recently. Israel represents a two-edged sword with regard to Jewish security. On the one hand, it offers the security of majority existence and the physical and military capacity to defend Jewish survival and political interests, and has therefore acted as an enormous psychological boost to Jewish political and psychological security. It has, on the other hand, engendered marked apprehensions and insecurity, and once more conjured up the specter of mass destruction of Jews, to the extent that fears are held for its ability to survive given the forces and resources ranged against it both in the Middle East and worldwide. Because of Israel's contemporary role as the central element in Jewish identity and sense of peoplehood and as a self-explanatory focus of ethnic self-worth, providing a reason for survival which nourishes the "instinct for survival," its destruction would mean far more to Jews everywhere than the physical liquidation of a large number of Jews, however horrendous that would be. It would strike at the very core of Jewish existence in such a way as to cast serious doubts upon the ability of the Jewish people to continue to survive.

The second immediate or micro-political interest of Jewry, closely connected with the issue of survival, seeks for Jews the capacity to participate fully and freely in the societies in which they live. Put negatively, it consists of opposing anti-Semitism specifically in all its forms, and of attempting to combat prejudice and discrimination in general. Jewry seeks to ensure that conditions do not arise which again threaten its physical existence, with the implicit assumption that discrimination and anti-Semitism, if unopposed, may easily degenerate into a threat to Jewish physical survival. Bearing in mind the lessons of Jewish history many Jews in secular pluralist societies are simply not prepared to trust that "their society is different," often believing deep down, however unpleasant and troublesome they find this, that every Christian society has untapped potential for anti-Semitism which could, under certain social and economic conditions, produce catastrophic results for Jews. The result is constant vigilance and both public and private opposition to anti-Semitism.

Jewry's third immediate micro-political interest is the quest for social and political conditions that will permit the free exercise of Jewish religious and national values and allow a distinctive pattern of Jewish social organization and affiliation, without in any way infringing upon Jewish participation in the larger society, and without requiring Jews to conform to any particular manner of participation. In other words, it seeks for Jews the freedom and opportunity to pursue as intensely as they desire all forms and manifestations of Jewishness and Jewish life, for whichever reason this may occur, be it a belief in ethnic self-worth, a commitment to the values of the religio-cultural tradition and their perpetuation, or a quest for the social support, solidarity, intimacy, and group warmth that are conferred by participation in the community's informal and formal social networks. By way of contrast with other religious groups, Jewry does not seek to universalize its values and interests, and it rarely makes claims upon society to have it follow Jewish values, goals, and aspirations. Rather it seeks a more negative and limited goal—the achievement of a form of permissive consensus which will give it the freedom to pursue its own ends, although it does sometimes justify such an open-ended approach as being of benefit to society as a whole.

A fourth and often neglected set of Jewish micro-political interests, although Nathan Glazer has drawn attention to them,[22] are the economic interests of Jews. In the past, particularly in Eastern Europe, Jewish communities were often divided along class lines with a significant urban working class. But in recent years and particularly in the countries of the new world, there has developed a characteristic Jewish pattern of occupational concentration in the middle and above middle sectors, particularly in the professions, in managerial and administrative positions, and in independent business. An even distribution over the occupational and socioeconomic class hierarchies would be divisive for Jewish political interests. Concentration unifies because it enables Jews to pursue their other interests without being cross-cut and weakened by class differences and antagonisms. It also adds complications. What might under other circumstances be seen merely as economic matters to be settled quickly on instrumental grounds, may become suffused with ethnic connotations of identity and group honor, not so easily given to compromise, and often leading to an intensification of conflict, as occurred, for example, in the New York teachers strike of 1967. In general, where there is high concentration, economic interests become ethnic interests, Jewish interests.

Jewish middle-class economic concentration has important consequences. There is the direct and immediate sense in which middle-class concentration, which reflects achievement and is often accompanied by an accumulation of economic resources and social position, leads to the development of a vested interest in maintaining the societal arrangements which made these possible, legitimatizes them, and facilitates their perpetuation.

Middle-class concentration also provides the leisure, skills, and financial opportunities for influencing political activity. Jews have the time and the means to devote to political activity. Their various and abundant professional skills are highly valuable in politics. And if money is directly needed, it too is available. Middle-class urban residential concentration—a direct offshoot of their occupational distribution, historical traditions, and communal and social needs for propinquity—often produces crucial electoral concentration, thereby adding additional weight, bargaining power, and "access" to politicians. In sum these immediate micro-political interests constitute one overriding immediate political interest in order, stability, and predictability, and in whatever conditions maximize these factors—in particular, the maintenance of constituted political authority. This is particularly so where there is an intense preoccupation with security and survival. Whenever security is tenuous or thought to be so, and whenever survival is in doubt (a given of the Jewish situation) the issue of political interests is transformed into a very immediate short-term calculation of how best to ensure survival. Particularly in such circumstances political activity tends to proceed with the utmost caution, maximizing whatever possibilities of predictability exist, and refraining from political actions that seem to threaten and endanger whatever security, predictability, and constituted political authority exist. A common reaction in such bad situations is to do nothing which might disturb the status quo and undermine constituted political authority, however undesirable and unacceptable it may be, because this may simply make things worse. Things are rarely so bad that they cannot be made worse, and the almost instinctive reaction therefore is to avoid this at all costs.

The first and overriding emphasis, then, is upon immediate issues of survival and security, and upon doing what is necessary to secure these in the short term. The tendency therefore is to make immediate compromises and concessions in the hope that these will head off further threats to security and survival.

In addition to these immediate micro-political interests, Jewry also has a *longer-term macro-political interest* in that type of legislation and that form of societal organization and governmental structure which both makes possible the achievement of its micro-political interests, and promises to guarantee these permanently and unquestionably.

This is an interest in a liberal or open society where Jewry is not at the mercy of dominant groups for its rights, freedoms, and liberties. These are constitutionally guaranteed and cannot easily be removed. In this society, the rights of citizenship in the broadest sense are more or less automatically maintained by various checks and balances, by self-correcting mechanisms, by the existence of plural centers of power, and by the intense form of political competition and seeking of public and group support that characterize its decision-making processes. Once granted, these rights tend to be maintained by the momentum of the workings of the system. No single group is powerful enough to be able to threaten or have removed the rights of weaker groups. (It is of course possible that a constellation of a number of groups could, if it so desired, remove the rights of other groups. But this possibility is one of the oldest problems of democratic societies: how to avoid the possibility of majority tyranny, and how to ensure that democratic majorities in a procedural sense will make "right" decisions in a normative and substantive sense.) What we can say, however, is that the chances of majority tyranny are less in this type of society.

It therefore seems to be in the political interests of Jewry to ally itself with all groups which support and uphold the liberal society and to oppose all threats to its political and constitutional structure. Conversely, it is in the interests of Jews to oppose all forms of society in which they would be at the mercy of dominant groups, in which their security was always in question by being subject to the whims, wishes, or goodwill of the ruler or rulers.

In actual practice micro-political interests take precedence over macro-political interests, and only insofar as the former have been satisfied do Jews turn to the latter. Conversely, if immediate micro-political interests are threatened, Jews concentrate first upon securing these. The need for constant concern with immediate micro-political interests may, in both the short- and the long-term, divert attention away from their macro-political interests. It means that often they may have to accept, acquiesce in and refrain from opposing unpleasant and barely palatable forms of constituted political authority providing *relative* order, stability, and security. Actively to promote and seek the establishment of liberal constitutional regimes may, in certain situations endanger further and already precarious political, economic, and physical security, because it directly challenges constituted political authority.

If this is true in practice it is not necessarily so in logic or theory. The radical political reformer may simply argue that all short-term compromises and solutions are self-defeating, and in the long run endanger security further by inviting additional pressure. The only solution, therefore, in this view, is a complete and radical restructuring of society. Unfortunately, as we shall see below, in many historical cases the pessimistic view of the radical reformer that compromise was inevitably followed by further pressure turned out to be the grim reality. But it was only partly right. If compromise did not work for Jews neither did the radical restructuring of society, which in many cases proved no better for them. In others, it proved somewhat worse because restructured societies conferred an enormous capacity for direct and effective political and administrative control on their highly centralized leaderships.

On the basis of this analysis we can develop specific generalizations and expectations about Jewish political behavior and responses that can then be examined in the light of historical experience.

In general, Jews will first seek to secure their micro-political interests, and only then their macro-political interests. The major concern will be to achieve a maximum degree of stability and security, irrespective of the nature of the regime.

The specific Jewish political response will be inversely related to the direction from which the greatest perceived threat to Jewish micro-political interests is seen to come.

We shall examine these generalizations by separately analyzing the historical experiences of liberal and nonliberal societies.

## Nonliberal Societies

*Moderately Right-wing Forces*

Where the dominant political and social forces maintaining order, security, and stability are moderately right-wing, Jews will support and co-operate with them rather than seek to upset the status quo by strong open support for left-wing and socialist forces. This will hold true even where the moderate Right is anti-Semitic, but less so than the extreme Right which represents the source of the greatest threat to Jewry.

It will also hold true even where the Left is generally sympathetic to Jews (even if not as unreservedly sympathetic as the previous scholarly model of a liberal Left and an anti-Semitic Right suggested.[23] This generalization fits closely the historical experiences of Jews in Romania and Poland between the two world wars.

*Romania.* In Romania between the wars, the less extreme right-wing political parties and organizations, in spite of their intense nationalist views, were not closed to Jews. For this reason, the extreme Right questioned the nationalist and rightist bona fides of their more moderate allies. Thus, the National Liberal Party (NLP), the main ruling party which was outspokenly nationalist and rightist, formed an electoral alliance with the largest Jewish political organization in Romania, the anti-Zionist, assimilationist and integrationist Union of Romanian Jews (UER). UER leaders entered Parliament on NLP lists, as did other Jewish politicians who were not members of the UER. Other rightist parties such as the people's party and the pro-Axis "neo-liberals" also gained some Jewish support, as did the reactionary Transylvanian Hungarian Party.

During the interwar period the politics of the Right in Romania were characterized by a consistent broadening of the base of anti-Semitism from the extreme Right until it overcame all elements of the Right including the more moderate, as the latter felt forced to compete with the anti-Semitism of its rightist counterparts in order "to take the wind out of their extremist sails." Thus, a rift between the UER and the NLP came with the elections of December 1937, the last in interwar Romania, when the NLP concluded a nonaggression pact with the rabidly anti-Semitic Iron Guard. Even then the NLP continued to nominate candidates of Jewish origin in constituencies with large concentrations of Jewish voters.

Romanian Jewry was divided into three main political camps: the "Romanian Jews" opposed Zionism and the establishment of the separate Jewish political party in order to speed the integration of Jews into Romanian political and cultural life; the Zionists and other nationally inclined Jews sought national minority status and independent Jewish political organization; while the third and smallest group supported the communists and socialists. Although Jews were highly prominent in the latter—comprising, according to one estimate, 50 percent of the Communist party—they totalled only about 1,000 Jews out of a Jewish population of 800,000.

The case of Romania is significant because there were no liberal or radical parties of the kind common elsewhere in Europe, yet in these circumstances the bulk of Romanian Jewry supported various rightist and anti-Semitic bourgeois parties, and gave little support to the more sympathetic Socialist Left. Similarly in the elections of 1931 and 1932 when the majority of Jews supported the Jewish party (which in 1933 and 1937 gained no parliamentary seats), the Jewish party immediately made alliances with the bourgeois parties and leaders. If Jewish Left and liberal preferences were universal they should nowhere have been more apparent than in majority Jewish support for the socialist camp in Romania, but instead it allied itself firmly with a nonliberal and anti-Semitic Right, while support for the Socialist Left was marginal.[24]

*Poland.* Poland between the wars is particularly significant because the Jewish population of some 3.1 million represented nearly 10 percent of the Polish population. They were divided politically into a number of national and Zionist groups led by the bourgeois General Zionists; the Orthodox *Agudat Yisrael*; and the socialists, mainly in the Jewish Bund but with some supporters of the Polish Socialist parties. Both in the national elections and in the internal Jewish community elections the bourgeois centrist and right of Center groups enjoyed the preponderant political support of Polish Jewry throughout most of the period. In the external sphere this means that "a considerable section of Polish Jewry went on supporting the rightist anti-democratic and authoritarian ruling bloc," until late in the 1930s.[25]

The political activities and relations with the regime of the leaders of both the Zionists and the *Aguda,* the most powerful single organization, are particularly significant. The Zionists negotiated with the government in the mid-1920s to improve the lot of Jewry in Poland, and in doing so "pledged Jewish support for an openly anti-Semitic government, in return for vague promises which they had no guarantee would be fulfilled," and in fact they were not, with the result that the Jewish condition continued to deteriorate.[26]

The basic strategy of the *Aguda* was to come to terms with the Pilsudski government and to accommodate to it publicly, despite increasing anti-Semitism, in order to improve the lot of Jewry through behind-the-scenes negotiations. In 1928 this relationship was formalized with the entry into Parliament on the government list of a leading *Aguda* politician. Here too results were minimal; in fact the *Aguda* politicians spent much of their time attempting to explain the obvious deterioration in the Jewish condition and the increase in anti-Semitism. The statement of the Aguda president in 1934 is characteristic of their view, and expresses their dilemma succinctly:

> No matter how many demands we have of the present regime, which has not fulfilled our just demands, it remains obvious that any other regime consisting of the present opposition would be incomparably worse for the Jews and for the country in general. . . . .We remain firm in our belief that the present regime, which maintains order in the country with a firm hand, strongly and firmly protects the security of the Jewish population and prohibits all anti-Semitic outbursts.[27]

Only in 1937 when government directed anti-Semitism intensified to utterly untenable and unacceptable levels did the *Aguda* sever its political alliance with the regime, but by then it was too late to have any effect upon the fate of Jewry. In fact it was only in 1939 that the Jewish Left gained a majority among Polish Jewry, but events soon made this irrelevant.

Thus, the general political experience of Polish Jewry until very late in the interwar period was similar to that in Romania: "The Jewish masses tended toward the bourgeois Center; a large section of the Jewish voters even backed the ruling rightist forces rather than the Left. Only a minority supported the non-Jewish Socialist Left."[28]

*Extremely Right-wing Forces*

Where the dominant forces of order and stability are extremely anti-Semitic right-wing, the majority of Jews will be to the left of them. In the face of a rabidly anti-Semitic Right, if the political spectrum offers three options—Right, Center, and Left—Jews will seek to maximize security and stability by adopting a position least threatening to the status quo, that is, Center and moderate Left rather than more extreme Left. In a bipolar Left-Right situation, given the complete capture of the Right by rabid and extremist anti-Semitism, Jews will support the Left. The first case approximates the situation in interwar Hungary, while the second that of interwar Austria.

*Hungary.* The Right in Hungary was divided into a number of different groups whose anti-Semitism ranged from extreme to rabid and proto- and pro-Nazi. As in Romania they competed among themselves over the purity of their prejudice against Jews, but unlike Romania, apart from a few isolated instances, even the less extreme Right was uninterested in Jewish support and cooperation.

Jewry was also politically heterogeneous. Some were prominent in the leadership of the Communist party, many of whose supporters were Jewish. Similarly, they were active in the leadership and membership of the Social Democrats, and among its intellectuals, journalists, and trade unions. A politically conscious and prominent bourgeois liberal and radical element was highly involved in the Center bourgeois democratic parties. In addition a small upper-class group sought to assimilate politically into the most moderate section of the reactionary rightist ruling groups. The largest group by far, however, were the "politically passive mass of hundreds of thousands of petit-bourgeois-minded, conservative, mostly observant Jews."[29]

A brief examination of their voting preferences finds a slight majority of Jewry supporting the moderately Left centrist bourgeois liberals and radicals, and most of the remainder supporting the Social Democrats.[30]

*Austria.* Here the situation was much less complicated than elsewhere. The nonsocialists were Christian and ultra-nationalists who on principle refused to have anything to do with Jews politically (although this did not prevent some Jews lending political and financial support to these defenders of "established interests"). Before the elimination of the Social Democrats in 1934, therefore, the vast majority of Austrian Jewry supported them.[31]

In all these cases the greatest perceived threat to Jewish security and survival was from the more advantaged groups in society, from above, from the superior groups in class terms, from the groups on the Right who either were the dominant forces maintaining order and stability by virtue of their control of constituted political authority and the wielding of the key political symbols of nationalist and religious purity and virtue, or were under pressure from more extremist groups. The masses, the politically disadvantaged classes, the groups below the Jews in class terms, the workers and peasants, while not generally thought or known to be sympathetic to Jews and often recognized as infected with a vicious and primitive anti-Semitism, which represented an incipient threat to Jews, and which always made them available for mobilization by the dominant groups, were not usually perceived as the immediate threat to Jewish security and survival. Yet despite the egalitarianism and liberalism of the socialist and Communist parties and the disproportionate prominence of Jews in their leaderships, the majority of Jews reacted to the immediate perceived threat from the dominant groups on the Right in a way which least threatened the status quo, disturbed order and predictability the least, and was least likely to make their condition worse. Thus, in seeking to guarantee security and survival, the majority of Jews adopted the most moderate and least extreme solution inversely related to the source of the greatest perceived threat, that is, the solution closest to the Center, to the status quo, and to constituted political authority. If the threat was from the extreme Right, they were Center and moderate Right; if the threat was the whole Right, they were Center and moderate Left; if the threat was Right and there was no Center, they were Left.

## Authoritarian and Racist Right-wing Forces

If the dominant forces of order and stability are right-wing, authoritarian and racist, although not specifically anti-Semitic, and where there is an obvious incipient or potential, if not immediate threat from both above and below, the majority of Jews will support those more moderate and liberal political forces permitted to exist by the dominant nonliberal repressive constituted political authority. There will be a significant element of support for the dominant forces of the regime itself, which will tend to increase as long as its threat to Jewry remains incipient or becomes less apparent, or if the threat from below begins to loom larger. Jews will generally not openly espouse or join in radical opposition to the dominant forces, and will, rather, remain silent or be acquiescent to the main contours of the regime, while separating themselves politically from the underclass. The emphasis is upon moderate support for the status quo represented by the constituted political authority or for slow moderate changes to the situation which do not threaten or endanger the status quo. A good example is South Africa under *apartheid.*

*South Africa.* Here *apartheid* represented white supremacy and Afrikaner dominance. It was not only the dominant value, it also was the very structure of the society. To oppose *apartheid* as racial inequality, therefore, was not just to oppose an abstract set of values or an ideology on theoretical grounds, it was to propose the radical restructuring of society. This left its political marks on Jewry. South Africa was probably the only society in the contemporary Western world in which the dominant concepts of citizenship and national identity did not either act as a challenge to Jewry, or exert an attraction competing with the Jewish sense of peoplehood. Jews simply did not identify with Afrikaner national identity, nor was this expected of them by the ruling Afrikaner and Calvinist groups. To speak of identification with the blacks was simply not meaningful. The political results of such a society organized along ethnic lines further emphasized Jewry's precarious separateness as a permanent minority in search of security and survival.

*Apartheid* more or less foreclosed for Jews the liberal option of racial equality, characteristically supported by Jews in other Western societies. What in other societies would be moderate and even mainstream liberal responses in matters of race became in South Africa radical threats to the system. It was moot whether the restructuring of society would be regarded by Jews as in their long-term interests (apart from the immediate need to avoid repressive action by the Afrikaner-controlled government following upon such demands). In any event over time there developed in South Africa the recognition that Jewish interests were best served by the maintenance of the status quo, and that the interests of Jews as an economically advantaged and successful group in society depended upon the continuance of white domination. To openly promote racial equality therefore appeared to many Jews to threaten their political and economic security, and would have involved sacrificing themselves on behalf of another group, which, it seemed, was not particularly well disposed to Jewry.[32]

Before 1934 the organized Jewish community acted on the principle that they had a collective political interest only in seeking to combat anti-Semitism and anti-Jewish discrimination. Accordingly it insisted that "there was no Jewish vote" and that in all other areas of politics, including race, Jews acted as individuals not as an organized community. The majority supported the Smuts-Botha line of cooperation between the English and the Afrikaner, and their more moderate position on the racial question and not the narrow Nationalist line of Hertzog and Malan.

After 1934 the situation changed when the Nationalist party, then in opposition, first officially opposed Jewish immigration and later adopted a general anti-Semitic program, capped with declarations of neutrality when South Africa went to war against Nazi Germany. During this period the organized Jewish community openly supported Smuts' party, and strenuously opposed the Nationalist party with its anti-Semitism, totalitarian and fascist views, and its Nazi-like racist theories.

The year 1948 marked a significant turning point, for in that year the Nationalist party came to power, a position which it maintained until it led the way to a regime change in the early 1990s. On coming to power the Nationalist party officially repudiated anti-Semitism. Consequently the official organization of the Jewish community, the Board of Deputies, reverted to the position that there is "no Jewish vote," and no collective political outlook among South African Jewry, and that Jews behave in politics as individuals.

There is no firm data on Jewish voting behavior since 1948. However, it seems commonly agreed that the Nationalist party, though steadily gaining support, is still the least supported among Jewry, with the major support being given to the more moderate parties. The latter served as a "legitimate" opposition generally committed to segregation, but came to support federal solutions rather than separate development.[33] A minority of Jews were also prominent in the integrationist parties which sought to establish a multiracial society, including the African National Congress and the South African Communist Party.

There was a long debate in the Jewish community over its attitude to racial equality. While many on the Left, students, and an occasional religious leader took the position that on moral and ethical grounds Jewry should officially be in the forefront of the liberal camp, the Board of Deputies clearly rejected official involvement until the National party's shift. While emphasizing the ethical and moral dimensions of the problem and the question of justice, bearing in mind the diversity of opinion on racial and political questions in the Jewish community, it called upon Jews individually to promote these ends according to the teachings and tenets of Judaism.[34]

The Board thus rejected the argument that Jews for their own self-protection should identify with the black man's struggle. It believed that the average Jew wished to separate the question of Jewish rights and Jewish security from the black man's struggle, because to identify the Jew with the black man's struggle would be to endanger the security of Jews.

Jewry's political position in South Africa seemed to be dictated by the belief that its political fate is inseparable from that of the white man, and that Jews had nothing to gain and everything to lose by openly opposing *apartheid*. Either they would be destroyed politically and economically by the regime, or if the black majority came to power their position would be no different from that of other white men. They recognized that they must either support the status quo actively, or at the very least not oppose it publicly.

### Right-wing, Authoritarian Forces Dependent on Military Support

If the dominant forces of order and stability are right-wing, authoritarian, and dependent upon direct military support, and where there is incipient anti-Semitism from both above and below, the majority of Jews will support the various legitimate and recognized elements of the dominant groups upholding the status quo, particularly those promising economic stability. This is by and large the situation of the large Jewish communities of Latin America before the 1980s.

*Latin America.* There are considerable differences between Latin America and the other Western societies currently host to large concentrations of Jews (the Left/Right distinction is less meaningful; the weakness, underdevelopment, and instability of the economy; and the weakness of the middle classes). Nevertheless there is sufficient, common ground to enable us to deal briefly with Jewish political responses in Latin America.

Political conflict in Latin America is basically between those whose prosperity depends on the maintenance of the status quo, and those whose disadvantaged condition stems from it. Among the former are the landowners, industrialists, and those in commerce and in the provision of services—which covers most of the middle class. These groups have till now been strongly supported by the Catholic church, and their dominance rests upon the support of the armed forces. On the other side are the trade unions, the mass of unorganized workers, and the peasants, often strongly supported by left-wing intellectual circles, university professors, and students . Jewry, as elsewhere, is heavily concentrated in the middle classes, which in general, in Latin America, only recently have become a strong force for democracy in itself. Many of them follow upper-class behavior and conventions, and they fear that entrusting power to the lower classes would jeopardize their future. Moreover, "legality is not sacrosanct in Latin America; constitutional 'illegitimacy' rather is the political norm, and the middle class is unwilling to make sacrifices for democracy if that entails basic changes in the social structure."[35]

The political reactions of Jewry to the situation in Latin America are aptly summed up by Haim Avni:

> Since throughout the continent the Jews are largely in the middle class, their response to economic and political developments is like that of other elements in this class. For a considerable number of the Jews this essentially conservative reaction may clash with the socialist beliefs of their youth, and others find themselves in conflict not only with themselves but with their children, particularly university students. But whether they like it or not, economic and social realities seem to impose on them the need for political identification with the status quo.[36]

He goes on to point out that Jews, because of their occupational structure, are particularly vulnerable to prolonged economic crisis, especially rapid and prolonged inflation. Of significance is the extremely apprehensive reaction of many middle- and upper-middle-class Jews to the Allende regime in Chile in leaving the country, many of them to return with its overthrow. The essentially conservative reaction of Jews and their political identification with the right-wing upholders of the status quo, despite the existence of some strong anti-Semitic sentiments on the extreme Right fed by nationalist views and pro-German and pro-Nazi activities, have now been further reinforced by the development of anti-Semitic, anti-Zionist, and anti-Israel sentiments on the extreme and not so extreme Left.

## Liberal Regimes

### The Threat from the Socially and Economically Advantaged

Where the greatest perceived threat to Jews comes from above, that is, from dominant (and right-wing) socially prestigious and economically advantaged upholders of the established order and the status quo, Jews will be liberal in their political attitudes and outlooks. This will also manifest itself in support for liberal parties either of the Center or of the Left depending upon the particular circumstances and the options available. Typical examples are the United States, Britain, Australia, France, and prewar Czechoslovakia.[37]

In those societies Jewish micro-political interests have been relatively well satisfied, and Jewish security and survival are hardly an issue, and are less in doubt here than elsewhere. In meeting instances of discrimination and prejudice Jews have taken a militant public liberal position, thereby availing themselves of the system's liberal and egalitarian ideals and calling on it to put them into practice. Jews are therefore directly encouraged to pursue their macro-political interests.

Where the dominant social and political values are basically liberal, and fundamentally egalitarian, historically the threat to Jews has generally come from the established advantaged groups discriminating against Jews in housing, university admissions, civil service appointments, club memberships, and executive positions in large corporations. Where there is such social and economic discrimination or fears among Jews of religious tests and establishment of religion as a social category which either confers advantages or confirms disadvantages, Jews strongly promote the liberal view of society and politics *because this represents their political interests in the situation.* To that extent, such a reaction is neither particularly altruistic nor public regarding, but is basically self-regarding except in the sense that all support for a liberal regime is public-regarding because it seeks to confer equal benefits upon all.

In liberal societies, therefore, the macro-political view of society dealt simultaneously with both their micro- and macro-political interests. More specifically, because the greatest perceived threat came from the Right and from conservative groups either less committed, or not committed, to the liberal view of society, Jews found their political allies among liberals and on the Left. The latter were also both more accommodating and more accepting of Jews, and themselves fully committed to the liberal view of society.

In nonliberal regimes, in order to gain a minimum of their micro-political interests and ensure their security and survival, Jews had to compromise with a status quo which was unpleasant and unpalatable, and collaborate with social forces and dominant political groups which were often extremely anti-Semitic. In liberal regimes by way of contrast, they could seek the assistance of the free operation of the system in order to achieve their ends and better their lot, and simultaneously seek to improve society. This was an ideal situation for Jews—they could utilize the advantages of the system and exploit the protections it afforded to both serve their own micro-political interests, and as well offer public-regarding benefits and advantages for all members of the society. The evidence for liberal attitudes and Left voting in liberal societies has been well documented elsewhere with regard to the United States and Australia, and we shall not repeat this here.[38] We shall instead briefly examine the lesser known instances of Britain and France.

*Britain.* There is no survey evidence with relation to Britain (except for some very recent work), but it appears that in the first half of this century, Jewish support for the Labour party was predominant, although since then there have been some dramatic changes. In the early period, according to Geoffrey Alderman,

> most Jews were Liberal. The Tory party was, after all, the party of the Established Church; the High Tory majority in the House of Lords had acted as a barrier to the advancement of Jewish emancipation for more than a decade; and some of the arguments put forward against the Jews, both in and out of Parliament, reflected the traditional Tory view that Church and State were part of an inseparable entity, in the promotion of which Jews ought to play no part.[39]

While the established and wealthy Anglo-Jewish leadership had moved into the Conservative camp, the Jewish masses at the turn of the century were solidly Liberal, particularly in view of Conservative support for the anti-immigration laws and its open espousal of anti-Semitism.

With the rapid entry into English society of the European Jewish migrants, many with socialist experience and traditions and an apprenticeship in the British trade union movement, and with the decline of the Liberal party as an electoral force, the major Jewish political support swung solidly behind the Labour party. This reaction was further reinforced by some Conservative support for the British Union of Fascists, by the appeasement policies of the Munich era and by the 1939 Conservative Government's White Paper restricting Jewish immigration into Palestine. "The children of the immigrants educated in the ways of British democracy, were determined to build a better life. Entry into the Conservative Party was unthinkable, entry into the Liberal Party seemed pointless."[40] Before 1945, and the complete turnabout of the Attlee-Bevin Labour government on Palestine, this resulted in many Jews joining and supporting the Labour party, and some were prominent as Labour M.P.s. From then on there was a decline in support for Labour as we shall see below.

*France.* In France, too, there was a similar pattern. In the nineteenth century the political emancipation of the Jews was opposed by the established conservative and often reactionary Catholic forces. Jews were therefore more closely associated with the secular and radical elements in French politics, in particular those on the moderate and constitutional Left and in the Center. Such relationships were reinforced in the aftermath of the Dreyfus affair which highlighted the anti-Jewish opposition on the Right, and made it clear from where Jews were gaining their political support and where they were socially and politically welcome. In the early part of this century and later, Jews became active and prominent in various branches of the socialist movement.[41]

These relationships do not persist unchallenged even in liberal regimes. A change in the direction from which the greatest threat to Jews is perceived to come will produce changes in Jewish political responses. Where the threat comes from the Right and from above, and where support for the liberal society is concentrated on the Left, then Jews are liberal and Left. But what happens if the greater (or the only) threat to Jews is perceived to emanate from the Left, and from socially and economically more disadvantaged groups, from forces challenging the status quo and the established order? In such circumstances, according to our previous analysis we should expect the following reaction.

### The Threat from the Socially and Economically Disadvantaged

Where the greatest perceived threat to the status quo providing Jewish stability and security is from below, from the socially and economically disadvantaged and from the radical Left, Jewish political behavior will move in a conservative direction. Movement will be a function of the differential degree of perception of threat. Evidence supporting this expectation can be found by examining developments in the United States.

*The United States.* An extremely instructive example of changes in Jewish political attitudes is afforded by developments in approach to the American blacks among Jews in the United States. Until the mid-1960s Jews were among the staunchest supporters of the blacks' civil rights struggle. When the claim was for equal opportunity for the black to enjoy constitutional rights previously denied him, the Jew supported him, and disproportionately so. This was in keeping with the Jewish view of the liberal or pluralist society as providing the greatest security for Jews, particularly as the civil rights struggle till then sought merely the same universal opportunities as had facilitated the upward social and economic mobility of Jewry. The extent of the ideological commitment of American Jews to liberalism and liberal ideals can be gauged from the results of a survey in the late 1950s which found that one-third of the respondents thought it essential if one wanted to be a good Jew to be liberal on political and economic matters, and another third thought it desirable.[42] These proportions are so high that it has been suggested that for these Jews the meaning of Jewishness was to be liberal.[43]

As black claims came to be made in ascriptive terms, seeking societal advancement on the basis of color and membership of a historically disadvantaged group, and as quotas were applied, Jewry became divided in its attitude to them. Jewish opposition to these claims derived first from the fact that such claims—the antithesis of achievement and universalistic criteria of merit—threaten the individual basis of citizenship in terms of which the Jewish group sees its interests and its future. They carry the implicit threat that Jewry, too, will be judged as a group, which Jews, having learned the bitter lessons of Jewish history, reject.

It stems secondly from the direct threat to economic and occupational positions and advantages previously gained. To support such black claims, therefore, is to ignore Jewish economic security, because Jews currently occupy many of the occupational positions to be gained by blacks on the basis of quotas.

Some of the political alliances of black militants have also been perceived by many Jews as threats to their own security, and to Jewish survival. There was strong (and unexpected) black anti-Semitism in a number of conflict situations which was often exacerbated as blacks ran into Jewish opposition. Moreover, blacks were often supported by radical and New Left elements, which were distinctly cool to Jewish issues and interests and generally supported Israel's adversaries, including the terrorists.

Perhaps most threatening of all to Jews was their seeming desertion by established liberal groups, previously supportive of Jewish interests. Now radicalized, many of them supported black claims and interests, even when this meant opposing those of Jewry. Jews became keenly aware of such desertion by their former liberal and Left allies, and began to feel hemmed in from both above and below:

> If the crunch ever comes between the "haves" and the "have nots," the "haves" are perfectly willing to sell out the Jews to the blacks to save what they have. . . . .The truth is that both Jews and blacks are marginal to the power structure of the United States. The goyish world looks at Jews as a pool of brains to be used and at blacks as a pool of backs to be used. The WASP world would be perfectly willing to let the brains and the backs fight it out.[44]

There is also survey evidence to suggest that urban Jews interpreted racial conflict as being directed specifically against them[45] and, what is more, in a 1973 poll during the New York City Democratic primary, 49 percent felt "that anti-Semitism was a very important problem," with 44 percent blaming blacks as the group chiefly responsible.[46]

The net result of these changes is that many are beginning to ask whether American Jewry is moving Right, becoming conservative, deserting liberalism, and supporting the Republicans rather than the Democrats. In fact, liberalism, previously so important to Jews, has declined in ideological significance. Thus, a survey of Reform Jews in 1970 found that half of the respondents thought that "it made no difference" whether one is or is not a liberal, and only 15 percent thought it essential.[47] On certain specific issues of conflict Jewish responses also tended to oppose the liberal position: in 1973 in New York City, only 19 percent supported the use of quotas to ensure that minority group members were adequately represented in college admissions and civil service hirings while 58 percent endorsed the strict merit system only. Over 60 percent approved the 1968 strike by the predominantly Jewish New York City teachers union to protest school decentralization, 61 percent supported the school boycott undertaken by Brooklyn parents to protest a school bussing program; and 65 percent thought that active demonstrations by Jewish groups in Forest Hills to protest construction of a low-income housing project in their neighborhoods was justified.[48]

Various elections and referenda confirm these trends. In the 1966 struggle to establish a Civilian Review Board to oversee police actions in New York, which was supported by Mayor Lindsay, Senators Javitz and Kennedy, various civil rights and Jewish organizations, endorsed by the Liberal party, and opposed by the Patrolmens' Benevolent Association and an assortment of conservative groups, approximately 60 percent of Brooklyn Jews and 55 percent of all Jews in New York voted against the proposal.[49] Perhaps even more significant is the Jewish vote against Mayor Lindsay (formerly strongly supported by Jews) in the New York mayoralty election of 1969. In that year 42 percent of New York Jews voted for Lindsay standing on an avowed liberal ticket and program, whereas 49 percent of Jews voted for the conservative Democratic candidate and 9 percent for the conservative Republican.[50]

The 1972 presidential elections reflected these concerns. Nationally, Nixon received 34 percent of the Jewish vote and McGovern 66 percent which represented a gain for Nixon of 19 percent while in New York State the gain by Nixon was 23 percent, and in Brooklyn it was 27 percent.[51]

These findings signalled a modest move to the Right among American Jewry in line with our original expectations, and our analysis gains further reinforcement as we discover that this move does not affect all groups in American Jewry equally. In fact, Jews whose security is most directly threatened by the mooted changes in society, for whom instability looms largest, are more likely to move Right and become conservative because their perception of the threat from below (aided and abetted from above) is more salient and acute. Jews whose security is more protected and who feel little, if at all, affected by the proposed changes in society, in short, those who do not perceive an acute threat to their security, remain liberal and continue to support the Democrats nationally.

To see the vote for McGovern in proper perspective it should be noted that the proportions voting Democrat among Jewry had rarely been higher than in the previous two elections. Thus, while Stevenson polled 64 percent in 1952 and 60 percent in 1956, Kennedy polled 82 percent in 1960, Johnson gained an estimated 90 percent of the Jewish vote in 1964, and Humphrey 83 percent in 1968.[52] This meant that any Jewish class differentials in voting which may have existed previously[53] had probably disappeared.

The effect of the McGovern campaign was, however, not to reinstate the previous pattern of class voting, but to reverse it nationally, maintaining a trend that had earlier appeared in New York City. In general the wealthier Jews voted for McGovern, and in fact, the upper middle classes, the professionals, and the suburbanites were the mainstay of the McGovern Jewish vote. Thus, figures that relate voting to income show that the Democratic loss between 1968 and 1972 ranged from 3 percent to 11 percent in the income range $22,000 to $36,000, but ranged from 17 percent to 27 percent in the range $6,000 to $19,000.[54] These trends had first been noticed in New York, where, for example, Lindsay received 42 percent of the votes of all Jews, but when broken down into class, he received 55 percent among the wealthy, 39 percent of the middle class, and 36 percent of the working class.[55] An analysis of the vote on the Civilian Review Board by occupation also found that in Brooklyn where 40 percent of Jews overall supported the Board, among those in clerical occupations the figure was 20 percent, among blue collar 31 percent, among business people 46 percent, and among professionals 63 percent.[56]

Despite these changes, Jews are still more liberal and more Democrat than equivalent groups of non-Jews. Thus, the vote for Nixon in 1972 among nonmanual Protestants was over 75 percent (in fact, of the major groups, only Jews and blacks gave McGovern a majority).[57] Similarly, whereas 55 percent of New York Jews opposed the Civilian Review Board, this compares with 70 percent among Protestants, and 84 percent of Catholics.[58] That the Jewish reaction was more against the McGovern candidacy, rather than against the Democrats in general, in support of whom they were among the strongest in the country can be seen in the fact that in the congressional elections of 1972 the Democratic party was supported by 85 percent of Jews.[59]

The change in attitudes among Jews arose over a new political agenda; on the older liberal agenda of social and economic issues Jews still retained their liberal attitudes:

> It is not fair to say that this is a conservative trend. In terms of traditional definitions of conservative, this is not a conservative shift. The people want federal action. They want mass transportation. They want medical care. They want all the things that used to be called "liberal". . . . .It's liberalizing on the economic and programmatic issues, and it's conservative or hard line or tough on the social issues.[60]

How is one to put some semblance of intellectual order into this mass of conflicting data and trends; the retention of the old liberalism and the rejection of the new; the decline in the Democratic presidential vote; the greater support for both liberalism and the Democrats among the better off and suburbanites; and the decline in liberalism and Democratic support among the less comfortable and urbanites, all of which go against the norm? In our view, as indicated above, the explanation lies in two differing views of Jewish interests, two differing perceptions of threat, and a differential incidence of the price to be paid for the changes in society. Both views operate out of concerns of self-interest.

Those who feel directly threatened from below, and that not only are they going to be faced with social disruption and instability, but in addition they themselves are going to pay either the whole price or a disproportionate share of it,[61] move to the right because their micro-political interests are threatened. These then take precedence over their macro-political concerns. (For some, of course, particularly the ideologically aware and the intellectually committed, opposition to the new liberal agenda is differently explained. For these it is right to oppose the new social demands not, or not only, because they threaten the stability of the established status quo and undermine Jewish security, but because fundamental liberal societal values of merit, achievement, universalism, and equality are threatened.)[62]

Those insulated against the threat from below by virtue of their social, occupational and residential situation, who thus do not perceive the new social demands as threatening Jewish security or undermining the stability of a status quo upon which their situation rests, remain with their previous macro-political position. They still see the greatest threat to Jewish security emanating more from above, from the dominant and established forces maintaining order and stability, from those determining societal evaluations of prestige, those who, in short, maintain executive discrimination, residential closure and demonstrate social distance, by exclusion from private social clubs.[63] In order to protect and maintain their interests and position in society they remain committed to the liberal view of society and to the liberal camp and seek to retain the support of key liberal groups and individuals.

At the ideological level, while recognizing that affirmative action and quotas may threaten fundamental liberal principles, they argue that there is a difference between quotas used as a means of holding down people which must be rejected in favor of merit as the correct principle, and quotas used to help minority groups sometimes in disregard of the merit principle and sometimes in order to realize the merit principle. In short, merit is a major principle but not the only one; justice, equity, recompense, and minority rights also count. This is particularly relevant where people on top find and use merit as a social convenience, so that the formal defense of the equality of opportunity perpetuates extreme inequalities of condition because of different starting points.[64]

In general, therefore, the Jewish political response, stemming from its minority situation, is to oppose policies which are perceived to threaten Jewish security, *even if these are put forward in terms of liberal principles*. If they perceive their interests to be directly threatened, or believe that they will have to pay the price for these changes, the logical expectation is one of self-interested opposition in order to maintain the status quo. More generally Jews may tend to oppose change even if put forward in liberal terms because the results are an unknown and are therefore feared likely to be worse than the known status quo. For Jews who live in a relatively high state of permanent insecurity, whether their situation is good or bad, it can always be made worse.

### A Concluding Speculation and a Note on the Impact of Israel

It follows that in liberal societies where the threat to Jewry is perceived so to decline that it has no impact or influence upon Jewish security and political interests, then Jewish voting and political behavior will be more directly influenced by socioeconomic interests. This means that the majority of Jews in middle- and upper-middle-class socioeconomic situations should vote overwhelmingly for the Right. There is some evidence for this contention in the case of Britain. Geoffrey Alderman has established that in certain London suburbs with heavy concentrations of Jews (accounting for nearly 40 percent of London Jewry) the majority of Jews vote Conservative. In one such electorate (comprising 5 percent of the total Jewish vote in Great Britain), of those who voted in 1970, 55 percent supported the Conservatives, 26.5 percent Labour, and 18.4 percent the Liberals. The intended vote for 1974 gave the Conservatives 59.1 percent, Labour 15.9 percent, and the Liberals 25.0 percent, and these figures were very much in line with those of the equivalent non-Jewish socioeconomic groups.[65]

In Britain Jews did not differentiate between the major parties on the basis of their support for Israel; since 1948 they had felt disappointed with both parties. The absence of such differentiation adds to the significance of the socioeconomic variables. On the other hand, the influence of attitude to Israel was not completely irrelevant to Jews in determining their support for individual candidates, irrespective of party. In all parties, candidates who supported Israel strongly and publicly were rewarded, while those who did not polled less well in Jewish areas.[66]

In view of the centrality of Israel for Jewish political interests and for their sense of security, the attitude towards Israel of candidates, parties, and governments will significantly influence Jewish political behavior. This will hold whether or not the internal threat to Jewry is perceived to continue or is seen to decline. Where the perceived internal threat continues, Israel will be one of many factors; where it is perceived to decline Israel will take on a more central role. Also of great relevance will be the strength and intensity of the candidate's or party's attitude to Israel, on the one hand, and their capacity for assisting (or conversely harming) Israel, on the other. One should perhaps also make a distinction between those in power and those seeking power. The former can be judged by their acts, the latter only by their promises, and, in general, acts, even if not as positive as those sought, will be more convincing than the strongest promises and undertakings.

There is already some evidence regarding the influence of Israel on Jewish political behavior. This issue was prominent during the 1972 presidential elections in the United States. It was commonly suggested that Jews moved to the Right because of Nixon's support for Israel which as president he had made tangible in various ways, and out of fear that McGovern would even reverse or weaken American support for Israel. Previously there had been some pressure upon Jewry to support unpopular American overseas commitments (Vietnam and Taiwan) on the grounds that Jews needed to do so in order to ask for an American overseas commitment to Israel. Jewish apprehensions about McGovern derived from his association with the radical coalition and the New Left, both of which were in the main regarded as anti-Israel. Whether McGovern as president would have been less sympathetic to Israel is unknowable, but the fact remains that attempts to gain Jewish votes for Nixon played on these apprehensions in contrast to the proven support of those who had demonstrated friendship for Israel, as, for example, in Ambassador Rabin's controversial intervention in the campaign on the side of Nixon.

There can be no doubt that the question of Israel played some role in the 19 percent swing to Nixon among Jewish voters, but it was not crucial or decisive. Thus, in New York where Nixon received 35 percent of the Jewish vote and McGovern 65 percent, another survey found that 44 percent of Jewish voters thought Nixon had the best policy on Israel, 21 percent thought McGovern did, 11 percent both, 7 percent neither, and 17 percent didn't know.[67] Those who believed that Nixon was better for Israel outnumbered those who thought McGovern was by a ratio of more than two to one. If we divide the other categories in proportion, Nixon was thought to be better on Israel by about 64 percent of the Jewish voters, yet he received only 35 percent of their votes.

In Australia the evidence suggests that the adoption by the Labor government under Mr. Whitlam of an "even-handed" policy on the Middle East and subsequent condemnations of Israel at the UN together with various votes in favor of the PLO at the UN (despite opposition to the resolution declaring Zionism to be racist) made Jews quite certain that the Whitlam government was opposed to Israel's interests. The result was, as far as can be ascertained, a very marked swing away from Labor in the 1974 and 1975 elections. Thus, whereas probably more than half and possibly as high as two-thirds of Melbourne's Jewish voters supported the Labor return to power in 1972 in line with the national mood, their disillusionment was such that by 1975 analysis of polling booths in areas of heavy concentrations of Jews suggests Jewish support for Labor was cut in half, which was far in excess of the national swing against Labor. It is also relevant that in 1975 it was known that the Liberal leader, Mr. Fraser, was strongly pro-Israel and not afraid to state it publicly. (It should also be noted that the Labor government's economic policies and management affected business conditions and profits, and also therefore Jewish economic interests, and this, too, must have influenced their voting response.)

If the effect of Israel upon Jewish voting patterns and political attitudes in these liberal societies has been to move Jewry to the Right and to make them conservative, in France the opposite has occurred. France was Israel's staunchest ally and main supplier of arms between 1956 and 1967, and although the policies had been initiated under a Socialist-led coalition in the context of the Algerian crisis, and in the shadow of the ill-fated Suez invasion, they were carried on and developed under the De Gaulle regime which was clearly on the Right. Prior to the 1967 Six-Day War, De Gaulle counselled Israel not to strike the first blow under any conditions under the threat of losing French backing. When war began De Gaulle attacked Israel strongly in what were regarded as anti-Semitic terms, and French policy took an about face. From then on France opposed Israel and sided with the Arabs. The result for French Jewry was not only outspoken opposition to the government's policies and public protests against them (for the first time in French Jewish history), but the propulsion of the vast majority of French Jewish voters clearly and directly into the Left camp, from the more central position that they previously occupied.[68]

Israel remains a primordial Jewish political interest, and concern about its security will have a real impact upon Jewry in liberal societies above and beyond their party loyalties. This will be particularly so where governments have the capacity directly to affect Israel's security, either positively or negatively. Even countries unable to supply tangible support in the form of foreign aid or weapons will be judged by Jews according to the degree of political support they give Israel's position in world bodies.

But just as the Jewish interest in Israel's security and its effect upon Jews everywhere rests above party, so too is there, in liberal societies, no direct connection between party and policy to Israel. Parties and governments on both the Right and Left can be and have been in favor of or opposed to Israel, and there is no logical or necessary ideological or principled connection between their political stance and their attitude to Israel. But that there is not a logical or necessary connection should not blind us to the fact that where there is a relationship to Israel, either positive or negative, it will have a direct and meaningful impact upon Jewish voting behavior and political attitudes. As a general rule, where there is little difference between parties or candidates in relation to Israel, Jews' traditional voting patterns will be maintained; where there is support for Israel on one side, and opposition to it on the other, Jewish voters will be under strong pressure to register their support of Israel in their voting preference.

## Notes

1. For a useful analysis illustrating such a position, see David Spitz, "A Liberal Perspective on Liberalism and Conservatism," in R. A. Goldwin, ed., *Left, Right and Center* (Chicago, 1965), pp. 18–41.

2.  See L. Fuchs, *The Political Behavior of American Jews* (Glencoe, Ill., 1956); E. Litt, "Status, Ethnicity and Patterns of Jewish Voting in Baltimore," *Jewish Social Studies* 23 (1961): 159–64; M. Guysenir, "Jewish Vote in Chicago," *Jewish Social Studies* 20 (1958): 198–214; M. Levy and M. Kramer, *The Ethnic Factor: How America's Minorities Decide Elections* (New York, 1973).

3.  See G. Alderman, "Not Quite British: The Political Attitudes of Anglo-Jewry," in I. Crowe, ed., *British Political Sociology Yearbook,* vol. 2 (London, 1975), pp. 188–211.

4.  See P. Y. Medding, *From Assimilation to Group Survival* (Melbourne, 1968); P. Y. Medding, "Factors Influencing the Voting Behaviour of Melbourne Jews," in P. Y. Medding, ed., *Jews in Australian Society* (Melbourne, 1973), pp. 141–59. For evidence that Jews in Sydney did not share this Left preference as long as those in Melbourne, see S. Encel, B. Buckley, J. Sofer Schreiber, *The New South Wales Jewish Community: A Survey* (mimeo) (School of Sociology, University of New South Wales, 1972), pp. 114–15.

5.  See S. M. Lipset, *Political Man* (New York: Anchor, 1963), p. 256.

6.  While this is true of all these countries, the most outstanding example is Britain, where by 1974 there were 46 Jewish MPs of whom 32 were on the Labour side (about 10 percent of the Labour members). Interestingly in view of our later analysis the number of Jewish Conservative MPs rose from two in 1955 through 1966, to nine in 1970, and twelve in 1974. See Alderman, "Not Quite British," pp. 197–99.

7.  See R. Michels, *Political Parties* (Glencoe, Ill., 1915), pp. 275–76; and W. Cohn, "The Politics of American Jews," in M. Sklare, ed., *The Jews: Social Patterns of An American Group* (Glencoe, Ill., 1959), pp. 614626.

8.  See Fuchs, *The Political Behavior of American Jews,* pp. 100–11; Medding, *From Assimilation to Group Survival,* 254–63.

9.  See R. Dahl, *Who Governs?* (New Haven, 1961), pp. 23–25; R. Wolfinger, "The Development and Persistence of Ethnic Voting," *American Political Science Review* 59 (1965): 896–908; and M. Parenti, "Ethnic Politics and the Persistence of Ethnic Identification," *American Political Science Review,* 61 (1967): 717–26.

10  See E. Banfield and J. Q. Wilson, *City Politics* (Cambridge, Mass., 1963), p. 234.

11. Fuchs, *The Political Behavior of American Jews,* pp. 171–203.

12. See Medding, *Jews in Australian Society,* and C. S. Liebman, *The Ambivalent American Jew* (Philadelphia, 1973), pp. 135–68.

13. Liebman, *The Ambivalent American Jew.*

14. Ibid.

15. G. Lenski, *The Religious Factor* (New York, 1961).

16. Ibid.

17. Ibid.

18. Ibid., pp. 156–57.

19. The term is used by Leonard Fein, "The New Left and Israel," in M. Chertoff, ed., *The New Left and the Jews* (New York, 1971), p. 144.

20. Norman Podhoretz, "A Certain Anxiety," *Commentary* 52 (August 1971): 4–10.

21. This is a survey by the NORC organization for Dr. Melvin Kohn of the National Institute of Mental Health, quoted in S. D. Isaacs, *Jews and American Politics* (New York, 1974), p. 148.

22. N. Glazer, "Jewish Interests and the New Left," in M. Chertoff, ed., *The New Left and the Jews,* pp. 152–65.

23. On this point see Bela Vago, "The Attitude towards the Jews as a Criterion of the

Left-Right Concept," in Bela Vago and George L. Mosse, eds., *Jews and Non-Jews in Eastern Europe 1918–1945* (New York, 1974), pp. 21–50.

24. Vago, "The Attitude towards the Jews," pp. 22–26, 35–38.
25. Ibid., p. 42.
26. Ezra Mendelsohn, "The Dilemma of Jewish Politics in Poland: Four Responses," in Vago and Mosse, . *Jews and Non-Jews in Eastern Europe 1918–1945,* p. 208.
27. Ibid., p. 213.
28. Vago, "The Attitude towards the Jews," p. 40.
29. Ibid., p. 39.
30. Ibid., pp. 38–40.
31. Ibid., pp. 43–44.
32. E. Feit, "Community in a Quandary. The South African Jewish Community and Apartheid," *Race* 8 (1967): 402.
33. On the racial policies of the various South African political parties, see C. P. Potholm, *Four African Political Systems* (Englewood Cliffs, 1970), p. 100.
34. It has made many statements in this vein over the years. See for example, *South African Jewish Board of Deputies Report,* 1970–72, p. 6.
35. Haim Avni, "Latin America," in Louis Henkain, ed., *World Politics and the Jewish Condition* (New York, 1972), p. 251.
36. Ibid., p. 261.
37. As we shall not examine the case of Czechoslovakia in any depth, reference should be made to Vago, "The Attitude towards the Jews," pp. 30, 42–43.
38. See notes 2 and 4 above.
39. Alderman, "Not Quite British," pp. 189–90.
40. Ibid., p. 195.
41. See W. Cohn, "The Politics of American Jews," and B. Wasserstein, "Jews, the Left and the Elections in France," *Midstream* 19 (August/September 1973):41–54.
42. M. Sklare and J. Greenblum, *Jewish Identity on the Suburban Frontier* (New York, 1967), p. 322.
43. N. Glazer, "The Crisis in American Jewry," *Midstream* 16 (November 1970): 5.
44. Arthur Hertzberg, President of the American Jewish Congress, and an "old liberal" quoted in Isaacs, *Jews and American Politics,* p. 166.
45. L. Harris and B. Swanson, *Black-Jewish Relations in New York City* (New York, 1970), pp. 104–107, quoted in W. Schneider, M. D. Berman and M. Schultz, "Bloc Voting Reconsidered: 'Is there a Jewish Vote?'" *Ethnicity* 1 (1974): 345–92.
46. Schneider et al., "Bloc Voting Reconsidered," p. 364.
47. L. Fein, "Liberalism and American Jews," *Midstream* 16 (October 1973), p. 8. This compares with the Sklare figure above where nearly two-thirds thought it essential or desirable.
48. Schneider et al., "Bloc Voting Reconsidered," pp. 384–85.
49. Levy and Kramer, *The Ethnic Factor,* p. 110; Isaacs, *Jews and American Politics,* p. 163.
50. Levy and Kramer, *The Ethnic Factor,* p. 117.
51. Ibid., p. 119.
52. See the table in Levy and Kramer, *The Ethnic Factor,* p. 100.
53. Guysenir, "Jewish Vote in Chicago," found that the Republican vote among Jews increased as socioeconomic status improved. By way of contrast, Litt, "Status, Ethnicity and Patterns of Jewish Voting in Baltimore," found that Jews with the

highest SES were more likely to be Democrats than those with lower SES.
54. Levy and Kramer, *The Ethnic Factor,* p. 243.
55. Ibid., p. 117.
56. Ibid., p. 110.
57. See the graph in Schneider et al., "Bloc Voting Reconsidered," p. 348.
58. B. Rosenberg and I. Howe, "Are American Jews Turning to the Right," *Dissent* (Winter 1974), p. 40.
59. Levy and Kramer, *The Ethnic Factor,* p. 244.
60. Ben Wattenberg, quoted in Isaacs, *Jews and American Politics,* p. 181.
61. As Arthur Hertzberg put it:

> It's in the interests of Jews and Blacks to work this out together. Let's put it this way. I didn't ship any blacks over here as slaves. I never owned any slaves, but I feel a common responsibility for slavery. If prices ought to be paid, and I believe they should be—I just want [the Gentiles'] children to have to pay as well as mine. (Isaacs, *Jews and American Politics,* p. 166.

Similarly, Ben Wattenberg, in affirming that Jews want "all the things that used to be called 'liberal,'" goes on to say, "But they are not prepared to pay the price of social disruption for it," in Isaacs, *Jews and American Politics,* p. 181.
62. Views of this kind have been strongly stated by Glazer (see above) and by Podhoretz, "A Certain Anxiety," and also in "Is it Good for the Jews?" *Commentary* 53 (February 1972): 12–14. See also S. M. Lipset, *Group Life in America* (New York, 1972).
63. There is evidence for this in Harris and Swanson, *Black-Jewish Relations in New York City,* pp. 122–30, cited by Schneider et al., "Bloc Voting Reconsidered," p. 389.
64. This ideological view is taken from Rosenberg and Howe, "Are American Jews Turning to the Right," pp. 1–2.
65. Alderman, "Not Quite British," pp. 204–206.
66. Ibid.
67. Levy and Kramer, *The Ethnic Factor,* p. 243.
68. Wasserstein, "Jews, the Left and the Elections in France," and L. Abrams, "France Votes," *Midstream* 21 (January 1975).

# 16

# The Application of Jewish Public Law in the State of Israel

*Menachem Elon*

What is the role of the impressive Jewish legal creation—produced in the context of the Jewish internal autonomy that began in the tenth century—in the legal system of the State of Israel, especially withh respect to public and constitutional law?

### Incorporation in Court Rulings without Binding Legislation

Jewish public-constitutional laws are incorporated into the legal system of the Jewish state in two ways: through court decisions, particularly those of the Supreme Court, and through Knesset legislation and subsequent case law that applies the legislation.

The difference between the two methods is that in the first case, rulings based on Jewish law are given at the desire of the judge, who is not *required* by law to take the system of Jewish law into account; in the second case, the court is *required* to refer to Jewish law under an express legal provision. Let us first consider the first method by reviewing several examples.

In chapter 10 of this volume we have already explored—although with great brevity—several examples in which the Supreme Court based rulings in matters of regulatory administrative law on the provisions of Jewish law.[1] We now examine two other examples in a more comprehensive and exhaustive manner.

### Delegation of Powers: The Goldberg-Sherman Case

In one case,[2] a question arose concerning the delegation of discretionary powers. That is to say, when the law grants a power or powers to the chairperson of a local council, is he or she entitled to delegate this power where the law does not explicitly permit this? It is clear that purely *technical* powers may be exercised by another; the question that arose pertained to the exercise of *discretionary* powers.

In the opening section of the opinion, the Court[3] discussed previous case law that relied on the following statement of the learned de Smith:[4]

> A discretionary power must, in general, be exercised only by the authority to which it has been committed. It is a well known principle of law that when a power has been confided to a person in circumstances indicating that trust is being placed in his individual judgment and discretion, he must exercise that power personally unless he has been expressly empowered to delegate it to another. (De Smith, *Judicial Review of Administrative Action,* 3rd ed., 1973, p. 263)

Subsequently, however, the Supreme Court preferred to base its decision on Jewish administrative law. The opinion continues:[5]

> Notably, we have encountered this principle in Jewish administrative law since time immemorial. The rules of administrative law experienced extensive development and efflorescence in Jewish law ever since the tenth century, when the Jewish community gained in strength and status. The Jewish community, in its various countries of dispersion, benefited from far-reaching internal and judicial autonomy and, because of the ramified activity of its public leadership in various public and administrative domains, a lengthy series of principles in Jewish administrative law took shape and developed. . . .
>
> In one of his responsa, R. Isaac b. Sheshet Perfet—"the Rivash," a principal halakhic authority in Spain and northern Africa in the late fourteenth and early fifteenth centuries—adjudicated a question that leaders of the Barcelona community had presented him. The essence of the question concerned the delegation of authority in matters of municipal management, much as in the case at hand (*Responsa of Rivash,* 228). The question itself was this: A community in Catalonia province had enacted a regulation that empowered three of the community leaders (known as trustees), together with the community rabbinical court, to elect a thirty-person team that would supervise various community affairs, particularly the apportionment and collection of tax revenues. As it happened, "The trustees and the court negotiated with each other in selecting the aforementioned thirty [administrators], and, unable to arrive at a consensus, they asked two men to choose the thirty

men and agreed to honor the thirty selections that these two would make." Several members of the community objected to this delegation of power by the three trustees and the court, arguing that "The trustees and the court are not empowered to appoint others to make the choice, because the discretion and prerogative to choose was given to them . . . .and for this reason, even if the two men were appointed to make the selection, their selection is void."

In his lengthy and detailed responsum on the rules of agency (*shelihut*) and delegation of powers in Jewish law, the Rivash accepted this objection and adduced:

"Although an agent ordinarily may name someone else as his agent where his principal is presumed not to object, it would seem in this matter that the trustees and the court, the community's agents in appointing the thirty administrators, should not have appointed others in their stead to make this choice, because the regulations contained no explicit provision allowing them to delegate their authority to others.

"This is because the matter at hand is of extreme public concern; the fate of the entire community's affairs rests on the choice of the thirty administrators, and those who select them must ascertain, through evaluation and thought, that they are indeed wise and sagacious men, learned in community affairs in their rulings, practices, and regulations, lovers of justice and pursuers of peace, and men acceptable to the majority of the community. The question of the electors' identity is undoubtedly a matter of concern . . .and since the community is concerned that the electors be important, excellent people, it is not the community's intention to allow the electors to appoint others in their stead, even if said others are their equals in wisdom and numbers. . . .

"For this reason, the original electors may not appoint others in their stead unless they have express permission to do so, in which case it would be as though the community itself had selected the two" (see also *Shulhan 'Arukh, Hoshen Mishpat* 182:8; and M. Elon, "Public Authority and Administrative Law," *The Principles of Jewish Law,* 1975, pp. 645 and 648–49).

A function and a power that a public appointee is given by law and that entails "evaluation and thought" must be exercised by the appointee personally unless an express provision allows delegation to others.

Needless to say, an empowered person, in exercising his function and power, may avail himself of others by transferring a purely technical function to them, for many different actions must ordinarily be performed before the power is exercised, and it does not stand to reason that the appointee must perform all of them personally. Nor is it easy to determine in advance when a given action is only of assistance in the exercise of the power, in which case it may be performed by another, and when it is actually part of the power itself.

*Behavior and Trustworthiness of Public Leaders: The Lugasi Case*

In various decisions the Supreme Court, sitting as the High Court of Justice, has discussed the behavior and reliability required of public leaders. These rulings rely heavily on sources of Jewish law; we shall now consider one of them and, in an additional decision by the Court, we will see how the matter is taken further. In the Lugasi case,[6] the issue was the essence of the *legal* requirement for the litigants to act in *good faith,* which is found in various provisions of law. With respect to the actual meaning of the term in the *legal* sense, I stated, inter alia:[7]

> The term "good faith," according to its Hebrew-language sources and the conventional usage of our time, is a synonym for "uprightness of heart"—and it constitutes an integral part of an overarching norm in the world of *Halakhah,* which is manifested in the phrase "And you shall do what is right and good" (Deut. 6:18). This overarching norm has served our Sages as a guiding principle, a kind of "royal command" in the entire world of *Halakhah.* This is the meaning of acting in "good faith," both in contract law and in public administrative law. The meaning of this general, universal concept/term cannot be defined *a priori*—in much the same way as the meanings of other terms, such as justice, public policy, and the like cannot be so defined—and it is given content by case law, case by case. The principle of good faith must be applied with a maximum of care, not by the prior formulation of general rules but on a case-by-case basis until, over time, several guidelines and rules in the use of this principle may crystallize. For if this is not done, legal stability will be impaired, and no person, even a person of good faith, will know exactly what good faith is and where its limits lie. We may acquire some assistance in understanding this expression from a telling and pungent expression coined by the Ramban (R. Moshe b. Nahman, a leading halakhic authority in late twelfth-century Spain) to define behavior that lacks the element of "doing what is right and good." One who conforms to Torah law in the technical and formal sense only, i.e., one who is punctilious only in matters expressly stated but not in other matters that, although not mentioned, are implicit in its general spirit is, in the words of the Ramban, "a scoundrel within the bounds of Torah" (Commentary of Ramban on the Torah, Lev. 19:2[b]). Thus, the absence of good faith in fulfilling a contractual obligation is the behavior of a "scoundrel within the bounds of the contract." Similarly, absence of good faith in fulfilling an undertaking by a public authority is the behavior of a "scoundrel within the bounds of public activity."

Subsequently, the Supreme Court[8] discussed the essence of the legal requirement of good faith in *public* law and asked whether this imperative is equivalent and similar to the requisite behavior in the field of *private* law, e.g., contract law. In its ruling, the Supreme Court established that a public authority must display a *greater* degree of good faith than an individual in the field of private law must exhibit. I reached this conclusion on the basis of a protracted discussion[9] in Jewish public law that has developed since the tenth century. At the outset of my deliberations I noted, as discussed above,[10] that by the thirteenth century it had become accepted that a legal transaction performed by a public agency is valid even if unaccompanied by *qinyan,* formal public confirmation of the transaction, contrary to the Talmudic rule that requires *qinyan* as a prerequisite for the validation of a transaction. Later on in the discussion, it was stated that additional principles in Jewish public law are integrated into this principle:[11]

A public authority must exhibit a greater measure of seriousness, honesty, and probity in the discharge of its duties than that required of an individual in his undertakings within the confines of private law. For this reason, when a representative of a public authority acknowledges that a certain citizen is exempt from a particular payment, such an acknowledgment is legally binding and fully valid. It is true that such an acknowledgment given by an individual would not be valid unless made in the presence of two witnesses whom he requested to act as witnesses. The *halakhah* assumes that an acknowledgment made in the presence only of the two litigants does not meet the test of full intention, because the person who gave the acknowledgment may say "I was jesting" (Sanhedrin 29a). However, such is not the case with an acknowledgment given by a public authority, because "Although we say this about an individual who makes an acknowledgment, we do not say so with respect to a public that makes an acknowledgment, for *it is not the way of the public to jest" (Responsa of Rivash,* 476).[12]

Another principle, related to the previous one and discussed later in the Lugasi opinion, states that a public authority cannot renege on an agreement it has made, even though such an agreement if made by an individual in the field of private law may be breached if there is a mistake in the price, for reasons of "overreaching." A ruling to this effect was made as far back as the fifteenth century in Algiers: "See for yourselves how all Jewish communities conduct themselves in this matter; *they never renege [on their agreements]* . . . .because it is beneath their dignity to say that they were mistaken."[13]

There is yet another aspect to Jewish public law, as we pointed out in the Lugasi case.[14]

A public authority that has made an undertaking must therefore fulfill it with greater uprightness and probity beyond the requirements of the law than an individual would have to display with respect to such an obligation in the field of private law. On the other hand, under certain circumstances an individual, in his legal relations with another individual, must display greater uprightness and probity than a public authority. For example, when the public authority has made no undertaking, and the question at issue affects public entitlements such as public property or funds, this entitlement must be upheld and safeguarded from infringement with greater stringency than that applied in the matter of an individual in the field of private law. This, too, is a major principle in Jewish law, as we learn in the . . . .responsum of R. Eliyahu b. Hayyim as to the extra concern for and protection of every right of the public, whether significant or inconsequential. In protecting the rights of the public, a public authority must itself be exacting and must assert the letter of the law.

We may exemplify this additional rule with a matter that approximates that of the petition before us. As is known, there is a duty in Jewish law to act, under special circumstances, *lifnim mi-shurat ha-din*—beyond one's strict legal duty—in order to meet one's requirements vis-à-vis God, even where the law may absolve one of having to behave thus (see, for example, Bava Metsiya 83a and Bava Qama 55b-56a). This duty, which exists in relations between two individuals, does not exist regarding a public authority. Why is this? Because the individual is obliged, under certain circumstances, to carry out the general principle expressed in Hulin 134a as "You are in the right, but yield what is yours . . . .." A public authority, in contrast, is not so obligated, for it is not allowed to pay any individual *out of public funds* beyond its strict legal duty *(lifnim mi-shurat ha-din)*. In such a case, the public authority would be favoring one individual at the expense of the entitlements of many anonymous others—because the public authority is a trustee for the money and rights of the entire community and is enjoined from behaving thus. The rule is this: You are in the right but yield what is *yours—yours,* not *the public's.*

## Incorporation by Adjudication via Legislation

As stated, the second way in which Jewish public law may be incorporated into the legal system of the State of Israel is through parliamentary legislation, which may *require* the court to avail itself of Jewish law in order to solve a problem that it encounters. Israeli law embodies this principle in two basic acts: the Foundations of Law Act, 5740–1980, and a pair of Basic Laws—Human Dignity and Freedom and Freedom of Occupation—enacted by the Knesset in 1992 and amended in 1994.

### The Foundations of Law Act, 5740–1980

We first consider the Foundations of Law Act, which states the following:

1. Where a court finds that a legal issue requiring decision cannot be resolved by reference to legislation or judicial precedent, or by means of analogy, it shall reach its decision in the light of the principles of freedom, justice, equity, and peace of the Jewish heritage (*moreshet Yisra'el*).

2. *Repeal of Article 46 of the Palestine Order in Council, and Saving Clause.*
   a. Article 46 of the Palestine Order in Council, 1922–1947, is repealed.
   b. The provision of subsection (a) shall not impair the effectiveness of the law that was accepted in this country before the effective date of this statute.

Article 1, which creates the obligation to rule in accordance with the principles of the Jewish heritage (*moreshet Yisra'el*), applies in cases where there is a lacuna in the law, i.e., the issue at hand has been addressed neither in legislation nor in case law, and cannot be adjudicated by means of analogy to another topic or decision. Everyone accepts that this *obligation* does not exist where the *subject* has been discussed in a statute or in case law but the court finds it difficult to reach a decision on *a particular issue.* According to the law in effect until that time, the court was required in cases of lacuna to avail itself of the principles of the common law and the rules of equity in British jurisprudence, under the provisions of Article 46 of the Palestine Order in Council. Article 2 of the Foundations of Law Act repealed this article and replaced the *obligation* to turn to English law with an *obligation* to turn to Jewish law, as stated. In the Supreme Court, Justices Barak and Elon disagreed about the *nature* of a lacuna and *when* it exists. We elaborate on this below.

The principles of freedom, justice, equity, and peace mentioned in the Foundations of Law Act are fundamental rules and guidelines in the Jewish heritage, and courts of law have invoked them to solve various problems presented to them.[15] Here we explore two examples, out of thousands, of Supreme Court decisions based on Jewish public law—in light of the Foundations of Law Act—with respect to basic issues in the field of public law.

*Behavior expected of a possessor of public authority: The Dekel Case.* In *Dekel vs. Minister of Finance,*[16] the issue was the conditions under which a public authority may appoint an employee to the public service, and the type of behavior required of a public authority. The Court quoted from a previous ruling that stated:

A private authority is not comparable to a public one, because the former deals with its own property, dispensing it or withholding it as it chooses, whereas the sole *raison d'être* of the latter is to serve the public. It has no property of its own; all it has is that granted it in trust. It has no entitlements or liabilities that are additional to or different from those deriving from this trusteeship or granted it or imposed upon it by law.[17]

The decision continues:[18]

> This basic principle that the sole *raison d'être* of public authority is to serve the public, and that it has no property of its own, has been given special expression in the principles of Jewish heritage (the Foundations of Law Act, 5740–1980) since time immemorial. The guideline for those appointed to public positions is: "In the past, you were independent; from now on, you are public servants" (*Sifrey* [Finkelstein], Deuteronomy, A, paragraph 16, p. 26). Therefore: "Do you think that I am giving you authority? I am giving you servitude!" (*Horayot* 10a-b). This is "because authority is slavery for the person in whom it is vested, for he must bear the burden of the community" (Rashi, *ad loc.*, explaining the word *'avdut—*servitude). This is why the Sages harshly criticized people who "assumed authority in order to benefit from it" (*Pesiqta Rabati* 22, *parasha taninuta*, Ish Shalom edition, p. 111), and "public official[s] who treat the community arrogantly" (Hagiga 5b; see also Maharal of Prague, *Netivot 'Olam*, Jerusalem edition, 1972, part 2, and *Netiv ha-'Anava,* Chapter 5, p. 12, second column).
>
> *Before* one becomes a public figure, one is independent, once one becomes a public figure, one is the public's servant. A public official serves the public, not the reverse. The authority such an official assumes is for the public's benefit, not his or her own. Community leaders are duty-bound to sustain the community rather than be sustained by the community and treat it condescendingly.
>
> The basic quality required of a public official is, as stated, trust. This quality was attributed to Moses, sustainer of the Israelites. Proverbs 28:20—"A faithful man will abound with blessings," was attributed by the Sages to Moses, "because everything he oversaw was blessed, for he was *trustworthy*" (*Midrash Rabba*, Exodus, *Piqudey* 51a. See ibid. for further examples of Moses's trustworthiness; he made sure that two "other men" should audit his expenditures from public donations for work on the Tabernacle. See also Ramban, Gen. 47:14; Sforno, Gen. 47:14, and R. Naftali Zvi Yehuda Berlin ["Ha-netsiv"], *Ha`ameq davar,* Gen. 47:14). With the great advances in Jewish administrative law from the tenth century on—a consequence of the community's enhanced power and status in the context of Jewish internal autonomy . . . .this concept of *public trustee* to denote the essential function of a public *servant* was also used instructively in the terminology of Jewish public administration. Community leaders and public officials in various spheres of community life were called *trustees* (see, for example, a responsum by R. Yosef Tuv Elem, cited in *Responsa of Maharam of Rothenburg,* Lvov edition, 423; *Responsa of Rashba,* part 3, 398; part 4, 112; part 5, 259; and part 7, 353; Responsa of Rivash, 33, 61, 198, 228; *Tashbets,* part 1, 33), *public trustees (Responsa of Rivash,* 399; *Responsa of Rashbash,* 287), or *trustees of a given community (Responsa of Ran,* 65, near the end. See also *Index of the Responsa of the Sages of Spain and North Africa—Legal Index* [J. L. Magnes, ed. M. Elon, vol. 2, 1986], pp. 414–415). These appellations for Jewish community leaders and figures of authority expresses the essence of their competence as trustees, i.e., persons entrusted with the authority vested in them, with all that this entails, according to the principles of justice and equity in the Jewish heritage . . . . .
>
> The statements made . . . .are based on the aforementioned sources of Jewish law and others of similar nature. This was vastly important in the past and is vastly important today, now that the Foundations of Law Act has gone into effect and the principles of equity and justice in Jewish heritage have become complementary

legal sources and part of the basic principles that form the infrastructure of the country's legal system.[19]

*Legal validity of a political agreement: The Zarzewski Case.* The Zarzewski case dealt with a basic question in the field of public law—one that found no answer in legislation, case law, or analogies. The question concerns the extent to which a political agreement is legally valid. The decision begins with the following remarks:[20]

> What is the legal status of a political agreement concluded between two parties in the Knesset before the formation of a new government? Does such an agreement have legal validity, and, if so, what are the legal sources that support this validity? What rules and legal standards may be used to review such a political agreement? These issues lie at the heart of the petition before us and evoke many additional questions, such as how to treat a breach of such an agreement and what remedies are available in the case of a breach. The major aspects of these questions have not yet been dealt with in this Court.

After a lengthy exploration and analysis, my opinion went on to state: "The problems of the legal validity of a *political* agreement, such as that before us, have not been dealt with before by this Court on their merits,"[21] and no decision can be reached in this matter on the basis of legislation, case law, or analogy. Therefore, in respect of reaching a decision in this case, there is a *lacuna* in Israeli law, which should be resolved in the following way:

> An explicit and clear answer is presented in the Foundations of Law Act: if a legal issue cannot be resolved in the listed sources of law—legislation, case law, or analogy—the court should resolve the issue "in the light of the principles of freedom, justice, equity, and peace of the Jewish heritage." These principles serve the courts as "complementary sources of law" in reaching decisions, and the thrust of this legislation, and its purpose, is that where a lacuna exists and no answer can be found in legislation, case law, or analogy, then, according to all opinions, the Court must fill the lacuna in the case at hand by availing itself of the aforementioned principles of the Jewish heritage. . . .[22]

In view of this guideline, and after extensive analysis of Jewish law, I reached the conclusion[23] that

> Political agreements are binding upon the parties thereto, and I have reached this conclusion based upon the Foundations of Law Act, 5740–1980, and the principles of equity, justice, and peace of the Jewish heritage.[24]

In the Zarzewski case, I reviewed many of the provisions of Jewish law of which we had availed ourselves (see above) in the cases of Lugasi[25] and Dekel:[26] the validity of a legal transaction of a public authority in the absence of *qinyan* (formal public confirmation of the transaction); the validity of an acknowledgment given by a public official, even if not given before witnesses, since "it is not the way of the public to jest"; the general principle that public officials "cannot renege [on their agreements] . . . .because it is beneath their dignity to say that they were mistaken"; the guiding principle under which "a public authority must exhibit a greater measure of seriousness, honesty, and probity in the discharge of its duties"; and the fundamental quality required of a public official, that is, trustworthiness, as borne out particularly by the fact that community leaders and public officials in various areas are called "trustees"—all as discussed above.

In addition to the above statements in this extensive opinion, we stated the following in the Zarzewski case:[27]

> An instructive rationale for the legal validity of a public agreement is found in the words of R. Joseph Kolon ("the Maharik"), one of the great authors of responsa in fifteenth-century Italy:
>
> "In regard to a public agreement, all of its ways are ways of pleasantness and all of its paths are paths of peace. This is why [the Sages] said that [matters agreed upon] are effective when all have agreed and are united and no one may rescind his consent and destroy the state of truth and peace" (*Responsa of Maharik,* Lemberg Press, 1798), 179 [first responsum], and ibid. [Warsaw Press, 1870], 181).
>
> This principle, based by the Sages on Prov. 3:17—"Its ways are ways of pleasantness and its paths are paths of peace," which literally refers to wisdom but was applied by the Sages to describe the virtues of Torah and those who study it—was established in Jewish law as a canon of interpretation and a guiding principle for judicial decision-making (see Elon, *Jewish Law,* p. 387ff; Elon, *Index of Responsa of the Sages of Spain and North Africa, Index of Sources,* 1981, Introduction, p. 25). On the basis of this principle, it was established that an agreement involving the public or its representatives was legally binding even in the absence of a *qinyan,* and that none of the parties thereto could retract and "destroy the state of truth and peace." The ways of pleasantness, paths of peace, and the state of truth require that the parties to a public agreement not renege on their promises.

In the matter of the validity of a political agreement in Jewish law, we also based our opinion in the Zarzewski case on an instructive decision in the Israeli rabbinical courts. Both the rabbinical district and Supreme Courts, in their function as arbitrators (pursuant to the laws of the state), bestowed full legal validity on a political agreement concluded between representatives of parties in municipal elections who had asked the rabbinical court to adjudicate their case. The decision is accompanied by instructive and detailed explanations based on the sources of Jewish law that we discussed in detail above.[28]

Thus, on the basis of all these aforementioned sources of Jewish public law from the twelfth century to the present day, we reached the following conclusion:

> The legal validity of a political agreement, according to the principles of the Jewish heritage is firm, and these provide a source for the legal validity of such an agreement in our legal system.[29]

*Basic Law: Human Dignity and Freedom; the Values of the State of Israel as a Jewish and Democratic State*

In 1992, the Knesset adopted two Basic Laws: Human Dignity and Freedom, and Freedom of Occupation. About two years later, the legislature amended them in certain ways. The Basic Laws introduced a radical change in the Israeli legal system as to the nature of the basic principles enumerated in them. The proscription of injury to a person's life, body, or dignity and the duty to protect them; the prohibition against depriving an individual of personal freedom through imprisonment, detention, quarantine, or any other method; the right of every Israeli citizen to leave and re-enter the country; an individual's right to privacy and confidentiality; the proscription of entering a person's private property without his consent; the prohibition against searching one's private property, body, and belongings; freedom of vocation—all of these have become basic principles having constitutional force. The Israeli legal system embodied these basic principles before these Basic Laws were adopted, mostly by virtue of Supreme Court decisions, that is, through "judicial legislation," and some by virtue of ordinary legislation, such as the Protection of Privacy Law and the Eavesdropping Law. The basic change wrought by the aforementioned Basic Laws is that they codified these basic principles in Basic Laws—gave them constitutional force—and not principles that are based only in Supreme Court rulings or ordinary legislation.[30] Each of the aforementioned Basic Laws contains a balancing clause that fully expresses the constitutional nature of these basic principles:[31]

> Rights under this Basic Law must not be infringed, except by a Law appropriate to the values of the State of Israel which has a valid purpose, and then to an extent that does not exceed necessity, or under an aforesaid Law by virtue of an express authorization included in it.

Therefore, infringement of basic rights may take place under a statute that meets three conditions: that it be appropriate to the values of the State of Israel, that is, the values of a Jewish and democratic state (see below); that it have a valid purpose; and that it not exceed necessity.

The two aforementioned Basic Laws include another provision which constitutes a cultural-value laden innovation in the *interpretation* of the provisions of Basic Laws. I am referring to the paragraph entitled "Purpose," which reads as follows:[32] "The purpose of this Basic Law is to protect human dignity and freedom in order to anchor in a Basic Law *the values of the State of Israel as a Jewish and democratic state.*" From now on, when the Court wishes to interpret or introduce content into the meaning of the basic principles in these two laws, it must contend with the exegetic task imposed upon it in the paragraph entitled "Purpose": it must entrench the values of the State of Israel as a *Jewish and democratic* state in each of the basic rights. This has brought about a radical, revolutionary change in the Court's interpretative approach. Until these Basic Laws were passed, the Court considered itself duty-bound to interpret basic rights according to the values of a freedom-loving democratic state, as manifested in a series of Supreme Court rulings.[33] The Court was not required to anchor its interpretations in the values of the State of Israel as a Jewish state, although several justices, chiefly in the Supreme Court, customarily did so of their own volition and according to the credo articulated in an earlier document, the Declaration of Independence. From now on, the Court is bound by this dual-value goal, "the values of a Jewish and democratic state," in interpreting and providing content in every basic principle enumerated in the two aforementioned Basic Laws. Furthermore, this interpretative requirement is a *sine qua non* even with respect to the balancing clause that permits infringement of rights on the condition—inter alia—that such infringement is appropriate to the values of the State of Israel, that is, the values of a Jewish and democratic state, and that it is meant for a valid purpose and does not exceed the bounds of necessity.

I explored the method of interpretation flowing from this dual-value goal in a series of decisions and articles,[34] but this is not the place to elaborate on them. Here I merely wish to mention several major points that should guide interpretation in view of this dual-value goal.

Needless to say, the Court is bound, when asked to decide on the nature of a basic principle, to examine sources that illuminate the Jewish values, and the democratic values that enlighten the thinking of freedom-loving democracies, in order to anchor, through them, the values of the State of Israel as a Jewish and democratic state. By means of such an examination, the Court should arrive, first of all, at a synthesis of the values of a Jewish and democratic state, "so that the two be mutually inferential and complementary, until they become as one in our hands."[35] The question that arises, one that requires discussion and study, is the nature and essence of the synthesis effected from this dual-value goal—the values of a Jewish and democratic state—and how it functions and is used. As we have stated elsewhere, this synthesis is manifested in various ways, as, for example, with the very concept of democracy. As we have seen, this concept has undergone instructive development in the Jewish world since the tenth century, and this development may provide a solid foundation for a synthesis of Western democratic values and Jewish values exemplified in the field of Jewish law, with the diverse attitudes that it embodies, that would be compatible with these democratic values. Occasionally, this synthesis may be the product of a reverse process, that is, through the adoption of a democratic value compatible with Jewish values. At times, we will have to give preference to a conclusion warranted by the values of a Jewish state—the set of values mentioned first in the Law—and interpret the term "values of a democratic state" in light of the values of a Jewish state. In this context, it is worth adding and emphasizing that, in the world of the Jewish heritage, the concept "human *rights*" is but one facet, one side of the coin; the obverse of the coin and, in fact, its *primary* facet is expressed in the term "human obligations," on which the world of human rights rests. I have discussed these and similar matters elsewhere, and this is not the place to elaborate.[36] However, several remarks about the meaning of the term "values of a *Jewish state*" are in order.

The term "Jewish values" includes, first and foremost, basic principles, philosophy, laws, and discussions within the vast legal heritage of Judaism. This heritage is a product of the Jewish nation, compiled and developed over generations, against the social and historical background of various periods, with controversies in thought and custom, in the manner of the Jewish heritage since time immemorial.

A clear and explicit exposé of the meaning of "values of a Jewish state" was provided by Uriel Lynn, chairman of the Knesset Legislative Committee, when he submitted the Basic Law, Human Dignity and Freedom, for second and third readings in the Knesset. Let us bear in mind that the *draft* of this Basic Law made no reference whatsoever to the values of a Jewish state; it referred only to the values of a democratic state.[37] When the Legislative Committee amended the text of the Basic Law to include the expression "The values of the State of Israel as a Jewish and democratic state," the chairman of the committee saw fit to call his colleagues' attention to this change and explain the background and significance of such a radical modification, as follows:[38]

> This bill was drafted with the understanding that we should create a broad consensus of all factions in this House. We were aware that we cannot pass a Basic Law that anchors the values of the State of Israel as a Jewish and democratic state unless we achieve a broad consensus of all factions. . . . .The bill begins with a declarative statement, a declaration that it is meant to protect human dignity and freedom in order to anchor in law the values of the State of Israel as a Jewish and democratic state. In this sense, the bill states in its very first paragraph that we consider ourselves *bound by the heritage of Israel and Judaism* because this statement was made as an affirmative statement: the values of the State of Israel as a Jewish and democratic state. The bill stipulates some of the individual basic freedoms, none of which are contrary to the Jewish heritage or the value system that is prevalent and accepted today in the State of Israel by all Knesset factions [my emphasis—M.E.].

In this study of the values of the State of Israel as a Jewish state, we should bear in mind what we have often reiterated concerning the nature of our recourse to sources of the Jewish heritage according to the Foundations of Law Act, 5740–1980—sources that acquire considerable importance in our current effort to interpret basic principles in order to create an anchor for this dual-value goal of a Jewish and democratic state.[39]

> It is well known that Jewish thought, throughout the generations, including even the halakhic system itself . . . .is replete with differing views and conflicting approaches. Each party to a dispute can easily find in the multifarious halakhic sources some support for his cause and his arguments. This is true with respect to

all matters, including freedom of speech and of expression. . . .

It goes without saying that all views and opinions have contributed to the depth and richness of Jewish thought throughout the generations. Nevertheless, the scholar and researcher must distinguish between statements made for a particular time only and statements intended for all times, and between statements reflecting the accepted view and those expressing aberrant views. Out of this vast and rich treasure, the researcher must extract the ample material to be applied so as to meet the needs of his time; and the new applications will then themselves be added to the storehouse of Jewish thought and the Jewish heritage. Such an approach and the making of such distinctions are essential to Jewish thought and to the *Halakhah*— as they are, because of their very nature, to every philosophical and theoretical system.[40]

Elsewhere, we added the following:[41]

> Proliferation of views is a virtue in any philosophical cultural system, and is a great virtue in the world of the *Halakhah*. Remarks by the most recent codifier of the *Halakhah*, R. Yehiel Michal Epstein, author of *'Arukh ha-Shulhan*, in his preface to the *Hoshen Mishpat* section, are exceedingly appropriate in this context: "All the different points of view among the *tannaim*, the *amoraim*, the *geonim*, and the later authorities are, for those who truly understand, the words of the living God. All have a place in the *Halakhah*, and this is indeed the glory of our holy and pure Torah. The entire Torah is described [in the Bible] as a song, and the beauty of a song is enhanced when the voices that sing do not sound alike. This is the essence of its pleasantness. One who travels the 'sea of the Talmud' will hear a variety of pleasant sounds from all of the different voices."
>
> The *Halakhah* is a mighty symphony made up of many different notes; therein lies its greatness and beauty. In every generation, it needs a great conductor, blessed with inspiration and vision, who can find the interpretation of its many individual notes that will please the ear and respond to the needs of the contemporary audience.

Needless to say, any exploration of Jewish values embodied in the Jewish heritage should take place through study of the sources and literature of the Jewish heritage and should contend with these sources, amid which these values took shape and from which they emanated.[42]

A further point should be made clear: the phrase "the values of a Jewish state" in a law passed by the legislature of a Jewish state also includes, of course, values that acquired special significance in the period of national revival that led to the re-establishment of the Jewish state, that is, the values of Zionism with its various factions. Examples of such values are the provision in the Law of Return entitling every Jew to immigrate to Israel, designation of Hebrew as the national language, the national anthem and flag, and the like.[43]

Moreover, the significance of this provision in the balancing and purpose clauses of the Basic Law, which anchor the values of the State of Israel as a Jewish and democratic state, greatly transcends the interpretation of the basic principles in the aforementioned Basic Law. I touched upon this in the Shefer decision:[44]

> This probe into the values of the State of Israel as a Jewish and democratic state, and of the thinking behind this purpose with its interlocking values, is of extreme importance. Basic rights, the provisions and guidelines in the Basic Law: Human Dignity and Freedom, not only exist in their own right but also have implications for the entire Israeli legal system, because they constitute the basic values of the Israeli jurisprudential approach with everything this implies (see remarks by Justice Barak in High Court of Justice 953/87, 1/88, *Poraz vs. Mayor of Tel Aviv-Yafo et al.,* 42[2], P.D. 309, 329–331). In view of the constitutional stature and importance of the Basic Law: Human Dignity and Freedom, the provisions of this law are not merely basic values of the legal system in Israel but constitute the basic infrastructure of the Israeli legal system, whose rules and laws will be interpreted in accordance with the stated goal of this Basic Law—that is to say, to embody the values of a Jewish and democratic state.

Summing up, the enactment of the two Basic Laws has created a broad and *mandatory* opportunity to discuss and decide questions of public law that will be submitted to the courts, through a synthesis of the values of a Jewish and democratic state. The great edifice of Jewish public law, as constructed since the tenth century—a small portion of which we have explored in this article—should and must serve as an inexhaustible source for the study of Jewish history, the relationship between religion and state, and the Jewish character of the State of Israel as *a Jewish and democratic state.*

## Notes

This chapter may be viewed as a continuation and updating of my article, "On Power and Authority: The *Halakhic* Stance of the Traditional Community and Its Contemporary Implications" (chapter 10 of this volume). Since that article was written, research on the public constitutional power and authority of the kehilla (medieval Jewish community) has expanded substantially in regard to the issues discussed in the article and other matters. Such matters include the majority's right to decide and basic minority rights that are inalienable even under legislation (i.e., enactments) adopted by the majority; the right to freedom of movement and of association; valid and invalid motives in the adoption of enactments and the like. These issues are discussed in Menachem Elon, *Jewish Law, History, Sources, Principles,* translated by Bernard Auerbach and Melvin J. Sykes (Philadelphia: Jewish Publication Society, 1994), p. 678ff (hereinafter *Jewish Law*). See also my article "Democracy, Basic Rights and Sound Administration in the Rulings of Oriental Halakhic Authorities After the Expulsion from Spain" (Hebrew), in Eliav Shochetman and Shmuel Shilo, eds., *Shenaton ha-Mishpat ha*

*Ivri,* vol. 18–19 (1992), pp. 9–63.

The number of scholars who are delving into this subject has multiplied. A list of them is provided in *Jewish Law* (see above), p. 778, n. 363.

This is the place to note that in my article published in the previous edition of *Kinship and Consent,* the notes to my book *Jewish Law* were cited as they appeared in the Hebrew in its first edition (see n. 2 and thereafter). When the book appeared in its English translation (see above), the note references in my article (see chapter 10 of this volume) were modified to correspond with the pages and notes in the *English translation* for the reader's and student's convenience.

1.  *Jewish Law,* text at nn. 62–65.
2.  High Court of Justice 702–79, *Goldberg v. Sherman,* chairman of Ramat Hasharon Council *et al.,* 34 (4), P.D. 85.
3.  Decision handed down by Justice Menachem Elon, with Justices Yitzhak Kahan and Miriam Ben-Porat concurring.
4.  Ibid., p. 88.
5.  Ibid., pp. 89–90.
6.  High Court of Justice, 376/81, *Lugasi et al. vs. Minister of Communications et al.,* 36(2), P.D. 449.
7.  Ibid., p. 466.
8.  With Justices M. Shamgar, M. Ben-Porat, and M. Elon sitting.
9.  Ibid., pp. 467–70.
10. See text at nn. 27–29.
11. The Lugasi case, ibid., p. 468.
12. *Responsa of Rivash,* by R. Isaac b. Sheshet Perfet of the fourteenth century, one of the leading rabbinical authorities in Spain and Algiers, 476. The Rema ruled accordingly in *Shulhan 'Arukh, Hoshen Mishpat* 81, 1 [f] (Rema *ad loc.*).
13. *Responsa of Rashbash* (R. Solomon b. Simon Duran, the spiritual leader of the Jewish community in Algeria in the fifteenth century), 5166; see the Lugasi case, pp. 468–69. See also ibid., pp. 469–70, *Responsa of Ra'anah* (R. Eliyahu b. Hayyim, one of the leading authorities in sixteenth-century Turkey) in the matter of community representatives who had reached an agreement with one Reuven concerning the level of tax he had to pay on his father's estate. Subsequently they argued that the agreement should be revoked because they had erred in evaluating the estate. R. Eliyahu b. Hayyim ruled that although public representatives had to exhibit extreme caution so as not to misappropriate public funds, "all actions taken by community leaders who are entrusted with community affairs are valid and the community cannot retract them, even if they see that the leaders have erred" (*Responsa Mayim 'Amuqim* 63).
14. Lugasi case at ibid., p. 470.
15. For details, see *Jewish Law,* part 4, pp. 1827–1897.
16. High Court of Justice, 4566–90, *Dekel v. Minister of Finance and others,* 45(1), P.D. 28.
17. Ibid., pp. 33–34.
18. Ibid., pp. 34–35. The decision was written by the Deputy President, Justice M. Elon, with Justices S. Netanyahu and Y. Meltz concurring.
19. High Court of Justice, 1635/90, *Zarzewski vs. Prime Minister and others,* 45(1), P.D. 749.
20. Ibid., p. 760; three opinions were given in the case—the opinion of the Deputy President, Justice M. Elon, and by Justices A. Barak and A. Goldberg.

21. Ibid., p. 776; see also p. 778.

22. Ibid., p. 779.

23. Ibid., p. 778.

24. Justice Barak also arrived at a conclusion affirming the legal validity of a political agreement, but he did so using a method that he termed "legal development," that is, development of "the basic principles *of the method*" (ibid., p. 859) with respect to "a public servant's duty to be trustworthy, his corollary duty to be fair, and other duties derived therefrom" (ibid., p. 87). Therefore, Justice Barak found no lacuna here and saw no need to invoke the principles of freedom, justice, equity, and peace of *the Jewish heritage* (ibid., p. 859). In the Zarzewski case (ibid., pp. 826–28), I took exception to Justice Barak's method, which denied *the existence of a lacuna* by declaring it possible to adduce anything through "legal development from the basic principles of the method"—but this is not the appropriate place to elaborate. Justice Barak's method "closed the door on recourse to the principles of Jewish heritage, and in so doing it drained the main thrust and purpose of the Foundation of Law Act of its worth" (see my article, "Law and Constitution: The Values of a Jewish and Democratic State in View of the Basic Law: Human Dignity and Freedom" [hereinafter: "Law and Constitution"], *Eyuney Mishpat* [Legal Studies] Law Review, Tel Aviv University, vol. 17, 659, pp. 671–72 and p. 688).

25. See above, text at nn. 7–15.

26. See above, text at nn. 17–19.

27. Zarzewski case, pp. 780–81.

28. Text at nn. 66–68.

29. Zarzewski case, p. 785. See ibid., pp. 786–813, concerning the laws that apply to different types of public agreements and the political agreement at issue in the Zarzewski case. See also ibid., pp. 813–35, for a detailed discussion and critique of Justice Barak's attitude and criticism.

30. The justices of the Supreme Court and the community of jurists have disagreed about the constitutional nature of the two Basic Laws, but this is not the place to elaborate. For details, see Menachem Elon, "Law and Constitution," n. 25 above, pp. 659–88, and see Menachem Elon, "The Basic Laws: Their Enactment, Interpretation and Expectations," Bar-Ilan Law Studies (hereinafter: "Basic Laws"), vol. 12, 5756–1995, pp. 253–307, and decisions and articles cited there.

31. Paragraph 8 of the Basic Law: Human Dignity and Freedom. The last words were added to this Basic Law in the course of amending the Basic Law: Freedom of Vocation. A similarly phrased balancing clause, with a slight and insignificant difference, is found in Paragraph 4 of the Basic Law: Freedom of Vocation, as amended.

32. Paragraph 1a of the Basic Law: Human Dignity and Freedom, and Paragraph 2 of the Basic Law: Freedom of Vocation.

33. See, for example, President Landau, High Court of Justice 243/62, and *Israel Film Studios, Ltd. vs. Gary,* 16 P.D. 2407, 2425ff.

34. See "Law and Constitution," p. 663; Civil Appeal 506/88, *Shefer vs. State of Israel,* 48(1), P.D. 87, 105 and the decisions cited there; and "Basic Laws" (n. 30 above), pp. 10–35.

35. Civil Appeal 294/91, *Kehillat Yerushalayim Burial Society vs. Kastenbaum,* 46(2) P.D. 464, 511; "Law and Constitution" (n. 24 above), pp. 666–72.

36. See n. 34 above.

37. See "Law and Constitution" (n. 24 above), pp. 665–66.

38. See *Proceedings of the Knesset* 125 (5752–1972), pp. 3782–83.

39. See the recent Shefer case (n. 34 above), pp. 106–107, and other sources cited there.

40. See also "R. Avraham Isaac Hacohen Kook, Chief Rabbi of Palestine," *Adar ha-Yekar,* Mossad Harav Kook (Jerusalem, 1967), pp. 13–28.

41. Menachem Elon, "Human Dignity and Freedom in the Jewish Heritage," the Beit Hanassi Group for Bible and Jewish Sources, issue no. 2 (1995) 27; and Menachem Elon, *Jewish Law,* p. 1452.

42. See "Law and Constitution" (n. 24 above), pp. 669–70, 684–88; and my criticism of Justice Barak's attitude.

43. See Menachem Elon, "Human Dignity and Freedom: Jewish Studies and the Values of the State of Israel as a Jewish and Democratic State," *Jewish Studies* 34 (1994) 17; and Elon, *Jewish Law,* p. 1839.

44. See n. 34 above.

# 17

# Moral and Symbolic Elements in the Politics of Israel-Diaspora Relations

*Charles S. Liebman*

There is an inherent asymmetry in the political relations between Israel and the various diaspora communities and subcommunities. Israel is a state. The diaspora communities, whether organized territorially, ideologically, or socially, are voluntary organizations. Statehood means that Israel has mechanisms, formal and informal, for the establishment of public policy—mechanisms embedded in the constitutional and political system of Israel. They are relatively closed to pressures from diaspora Jewry which are generated from outside the political system and have no domestic counterpart. This is not to say that diaspora Jewry has never influenced Israel in the adoption of public policy. It has. But it does suggest that a diaspora organization must generate a great deal more pressure to influence Israel than would be required by an organization or community within the Israeli political system. In other words, diaspora Jewry has no voice in shaping Israeli policy precisely because the mechanisms of policy formation are relatively speaking rather structured. The diaspora can only hope to influence one or more of the participants in the policy-making process. In the less structured, more fluid situation of diaspora decision making, Israel can exercise a direct voice because no "rules of the game" exclude it.

There is another side to statehood that does not operate in Israel's favor. Precisely because diaspora communities are voluntary and relatively unorganized they are less subject to controls and pressures. Whereas the formal leadership of American Jewry, for example, has invariably supported Israel and Israeli policy since its establishment, the same leadership cannot control all groups in American Jewish life. The American Jewish Committee represented a distinct minority of American Jews and yet was quite critical of Israel in the 1950s and exercised a good deal of pressure on Israeli policy. Israel was unable to control the American Jewish Committee through its ostensible control over the leadership of the American Jewish community. Orthodox Jewry successfully influenced Israel to change its policies on at least two occasions in the 1950s precisely because Orthodox Jewry was not subject to the discipline of the American Jewish community. Whereas the Orthodox objections to Israeli policy and certainly the tactics used by the Orthodox surely reflected a minority point of view among American Jews, it was a minority whom Israel could not control.

Also, the fact that diaspora communities, at least in the West, are loyal to their own nation-states, limits Israeli control. Israeli policy with respect to South Africa in the late 1950s and early 1960s was limited by anticipated South African responses to South African Jewry but also by the fact that this Jewry was loyal to South Africa. In cases of conflict between Israel and Western nations, Israel cannot always depend on the support of the diaspora community in question. It depends on the circumstances and the diaspora's perception of the conflict. In the case of the 1956 Sinai War the American Jewish community offered little support to Israel and some of its leaders came close to openly siding with U.S. efforts to force Israel to withdraw. Had Israel continued to refuse to withdraw, it is not clear what the outcome would have been.

In summary, however, Israeli statehood confers distinct advantages to it in its political relationships with diaspora communities. This is evident, I believe, if we contrast Israel-diaspora relations with their pre-state counterpart. The closest analogy to Israel-diaspora relations before 1949 would be the relationships between the World Zionist Organization or the Jewish Agency executive (as the government counterpart) and various diaspora organizations and communities. In one respect one might have anticipated that the Jewish Agency executive, which included leading diaspora Zionists (between 1929 and World

War II it included non-Zionists as well), might have carried even more weight than the government of Israel.

In fact, of course, it did not. There is simply no comparison in the relative influence and deference accorded to the government of Israel by Jews all over the world, by Jewish communal leaders or by such organizations as the American Jewish Committee and the respect and deference accorded to, or the influence of, the Jewish Agency executive, much less the leadership of the pre-1949 *Yishuv*. While there are a number of reasons for this shift in relative influence, I suggest that one major reason is the fact of Israeli statehood.

In general, because Israel and the diaspora confront and interrelate as two significantly different entities, the symbolic status and moral claims of each on the other are of particular importance in determining the politics of their relationships. By political relationships I mean the capacity and willingness of one side to influence another to take action which the latter would not otherwise undertake. Symbolic status and moral claims are of special importance because Israel cannot impose its authority on the diaspora and necessarily has recourse to moral and symbolic suasion. The diaspora, or more properly speaking, various Jewish organizations and communities outside Israel, are committed to Israel not because of their own material interests, but rather because Israel and activity on behalf of Israel represents a symbolic affirmation of their Jewish identity.[1] Thus, their attitude toward Israel is only affected in a small measure by what Israel does. It is affected far more significantly by how diaspora Jews view themselves in relation to Israel. The consequence is that the diaspora, rather than pressing demands upon Israel with threats of sanctions, limits its demands or raises them in the context of requests or advice. This, in turn, provides Israel with great latitude. Acceptance or rejection of diaspora demands depends more on Israel's self-image vis-à-vis the diaspora or the symbolic status of the diaspora than on the physical resources that each side might bring to bear on the other in the case of conflict.

## Israel's Moral and Symbolic Claims

Regardless of how awkward the issue is, and how cautious Israelis have become in expressing themselves, the fact is that any claims by the diaspora upon Israel are measured by Israelis, consciously or unconsciously, against the moral right of diaspora Jews to live in the diaspora. This is separate and apart from the feelings prevalent among Israelis in the 1950s that the diaspora was doomed to physical and/or spiritual extinction and it was, therefore, pointless to consider their needs beyond encouraging them to come to Israel. Many view Soviet Jewry in these terms; but hardly anyone thinks about Western Jewry, American Jewry in particular, in this light. Israelis are not especially sanguine about the future of Western Jewry. But at least their leaders do believe that it is both their responsibility as well as in their own interest to promote diaspora survival. The question, however, is not one of survival but of the moral authority that lies behind the claims that one side raises against the other. The diaspora has and perforce will continue to have a negative symbolic resonance as long as Israel perceives of itself as a Jewish State. To Israelis the diaspora communities of the free world, and increasingly of the Soviet Union as well, represent that community of Jews who choose, for whatever reason, not to live in Israel—that is, not to fulfill their Jewish obligations, not to live a "full" Jewish life.

As a consequence, Israelis did not think it amiss for them to ask American Jews to restrain their opposition to the war in Vietnam or to support Richard Nixon in 1972. On the other hand, their leaders acted to suppress criticism of Israeli economic policy by the editor of a Zionist publication in Britain and expressed indignation at his criticism or the criticism of an American Zionist leader who, while in Israel, questioned its policy of military reprisals.[2]

The symbolic status of the diaspora is not entirely negative. The economic and political support of diaspora Jewry and the courage of Soviet Jewry coupled with their aspiration for *aliya* has had the indirect result of raising the symbolic status of the diaspora by reassuring Israel that it is not alone.

Isolation has serious cultural consequences and Israel fears these consequences quite apart from their political and economic implications. Diaspora Jewry's support provides a bulwark against the sense of isolation. It is difficult to document this phenomenon. It is not always apparent or readily expressed in daily life but is somewhat more evident in a time of crisis. This is perhaps the best explanation for the reportage in the Israeli press in the period of the Six-Day War. Between June 1 and June 12, the period immediately surrounding the war, *Ha'aretz* devoted 45 stories and 510 column centimeters to world reaction to the Israeli crises. Obviously, many of these stories also included hostile reactions. Of the total, 22 items covering 224 column centimeters concerned the reaction of world Jewry.[3] In other words, almost half the material in the Israeli press concerning world reaction, was devoted to Jewish reaction.

Israel Kolatt has pointed out that Israel's reevaluation of the importance of the diaspora was strengthened precisely in that period after 1956 when it felt most isolated—when the Soviet Union on the one hand and Eisenhower and Dulles on the other were unsympathetic to her needs.[4]

The Israelis' sense of moral superiority by virtue of living in Israel is buttressed by a second claim: that Israel carries the moral authority of Zion; that those sentiments traditionally associated with Eretz Israel and Zion are legitimately transposed to the State of Israel.

## The Diaspora Perspective

Most diaspora Jews involved in activity on behalf of Israel recognize that living in Israel bestows a certain moral authority on Israelis. This does not stem from any conscious recognition on their part that as Jews they are obligated to live in Israel. Rather, it stems from a sense that Israelis are called upon to make sacrifices and endure hardships incomparably greater than diaspora Jews are asked to suffer. This, alone, limits their right to make demands of Israel and, as I have heard it expressed, even their right to criticize Israel. In the last analysis, however, there is a common element in the Israelis' sense that the diaspora Jew is obligated to live in Israel and the diaspora Jews' sense of guilt about how little he is asked to do compared to the Israeli. After all, what the Israeli does he does for himself. His army service, his tax load, his sacrifice of life is undertaken to defend his own life. Diaspora support for Israel, on the other hand, is done on behalf of somebody else. Nonetheless, no one has as yet suggested that all Israelis leave the country thereby relieving both sides of their burden. Obviously, the diaspora Jew not only wants to save the lives of three million Jews in Israel, but he has a commitment to the continued existence of a Jewish state. In other words, there is a measure of self-interest in Israel's survival. But if one has such a commitment it follows that those living in Israel are honoring that commitment more than those who live abroad. What Israelis sometimes forget is that this commitment in the last analysis is to Israel as a Jewish state, not to Israel qua Israel.

This, too, must be qualified. Even Israel's existence as a state, regardless of the quality of its Jewish life or Jewish commitment, has important implications in the politics of Israel-diaspora relations. The fact that Israel is a state, with all the recognition accorded a state, provides it with an arsenal of status symbols which it distributes and confers upon those whom it favors. This operates directly, for example, in an invitation to meet with the Israeli ambassador or a minister, an autographed photo taken together with the prime minister, a briefing by an Israeli general at a military installation; these are the kinds of symbols which a state can confer and from which diaspora Jews derive great satisfaction.[5]

Diaspora Jewry acquiesces in Israel's claim to moral authority, although, as we have seen, it interprets that claim differently than Israel. Israel's claim to authority by virtue of its position as the legitimate inheritor of the symbols of Zion is also interpreted somewhat differently by Israelis and diaspora Jews. Nevertheless, here as well, there is an element common to both groups. From a religious point of view, Israel's claim is questionable.[6] I suggest that it could only be offered in a period where religious claims are no longer examined seriously or in a period where the ability of religious symbols to mobilize and motivate Jewish behavior has declined but not disappeared. Not only has the resonance which Jewish symbols traditionally evoked declined, but equally significant, their referent is less clear than ever before.

Traditional Jewish symbols no longer possess clear "religious" referents to most Jews, nor is it at all clear what claims these symbols make upon them beyond evoking a diffuse emotionalism. Israel has entered the vacuum with its claim that the symbols refer to it. This claim has found resonance among many Western Jews—at least up to a point, and it is by no means clear whether that point has been reached. The reasons are not hard to find. Activity on behalf of Israel provides options for Jewish activity in a period where religious activity has lost its resonance. Israel, as a referent for Jewish symbols, evokes uniform clear and specific responses. It mobilizes Jews for meaningful activity. One doesn't wonder, anymore, what exactly the symbols mean.[7]

Whatever hesitation some diaspora Jews, the Orthodox in particular, may have about Israel's claims in this regard, special significance does attach to the fact that Israel represents the Jewish community of Eretz Yisrael, the Holy Land. Elsewhere, I have written about the consequences of this for Orthodoxy's relationship to the State of Israel.[8] The territory over which Israel exercises hegemony has a special sanctity quite apart from one's attitude to the state. The traditional Jew has special obligations and responsibilities to the Land and to Jews living in the Land of Israel. Indeed, it was argued quite forcefully by religious leaders in the last century (and of course earlier) that the prayers of Jews all over the world could only reach God via the prayers of those in the Land of Israel. Thus, there must be a special significance to the government which rules over the Land. The fact that the personnel of such a government is Jewish and that this government not only permits Jews access to the Land but encourages the restoration of holy places is not without significance. This attitude is not, I believe, confined only to Orthodox Jews but extends to broader circles of traditionalists. Related to this is that Israel has become the repository for a host of emotions associated with physical and historical survival, the responsibility toward those who perished in the Holocaust, guilt feelings about what Jews ought to have done and did not do, and nostalgia for a style of Jewish life associated with what Americans call "the old country" and Yiddish-speaking Jews call the *heim*. In short, Israel has enormous emotional and symbolic import. It stands for the Jewish past, present, and future. Given the kind of meaning that Israel has for diaspora Jews there is very little of a specific nature that the diaspora wishes Israel to do. In other words, the diaspora is relatively indifferent to Israeli policy and the nature of its leadership because this is not what makes Israel important to the diaspora. Israel is, on the one hand, a most inappropriate object of pressure. But it, in turn, is a most forceful subject or instrument of pressure on the diaspora.

As already suggested, Israel's preeminent importance to the diaspora is as a symbol. Most diaspora Jews don't know, or if they know aren't conscious of Israel's role in providing direct educational and cultural assistance to diaspora communities. Israel's symbolic importance makes it an inappropriate object of influence and also obviates the necessity of influencing it. What must also be stressed, however, is that as a symbol Israel evokes only positive resonance. The diaspora, in turn, is also a symbol to Israel but as such its effect is more negative than positive.

The consequences for mutual political influence favor Israel. Given the ambiguous symbolic import of the diaspora for Israel there is something denigrating about Israelis yielding to diaspora pressure—

surrender of any kind to diaspora influence carries emotional overtones of a lack of faithfulness to one's ideology and a "selling out." The diaspora, on the other hand, can yield to Israeli influence without the negative emotional overtones.

## The Impact of the Political Relationships on the Internal Communal Structure[9]

We have noted that the imbalance of moral claims and symbolic statuses between Israel and the diaspora contributes to the imbalance in the relative influence which each party exercises on the other. It is not surprising that this imbalance is also reflected in the relative impact which the presence of each has on the internal structure of the other.

The American Jewish community—and probably other Jewish communities in the free world as well—have witnessed a shift in the relative status of communal leaders in recent years.[10] One reason for this shift is the increased importance that Israel has assumed in the eyes of the diaspora. This means that those communal leaders engaged in activity of direct relationship to Israel have benefited at the expense of those leaders not so engaged. The benefits have accrued because the Jewish community at large places a higher value on the services which they perform and because Israel has conferred its symbols of prestige primarily on those leaders who are of greatest benefit to it.[11] Thus, for example, no diaspora rabbi or educator will receive the kind of reception in Israel that is accorded to the large financial contributor. Israeli ministers in their trips abroad make it a point to visit with leaders of the Council of Jewish Federations, not outstanding Judaica scholars.[12] But the primary changes result from the diaspora communities themselves devoting more and more of their Jewish life-space to matters connected to Israel—which necessarily increases the prestige of those who are most active on Israel's behalf. This helps explain the growth in prestige of the Presidents Conference and the Council of Jewish Federations and the decline in prestige of many other voluntary organizations, of rabbis or the Synagogue Council of America. It also helps account for programming changes within national Jewish organizations who have increased their stress, in terms of personnel and budget, on Israel-related activity.

The existence of diaspora Jewry for Israel has had less noticeable consequences on the structure of Israeli politics. It was probably one factor (less important today than twenty years ago) in the feeling of the then-dominant Labor party that the National Religious Party ought to be part of the government coalition—the feeling that this would please diaspora Jewry or that their presence in the government moderates the pressures and attacks on Israeli policy by religious elements in the diaspora. In the early 1950s the General Zionist party sought to capitalize on the prestige of American Zionist leaders Abba Hillel Silver and Emanuel Neumann. Election campaign material stressed the alignment of the American Zionist leaders with the General Zionists in Israel. Ben-Gurion also feared that American Zionist leaders would utilize their prestige and resources to influence Israeli policy and this is one reason he sought to strengthen the non-Zionist leadership of American Jewry at the expense of the Zionist. Such fears and hopes, however, are today a matter of historical curiosa.

Within the Foreign Office, the recognition of diaspora Jewry's importance has, other things being equal, led to the appointment of people who are considered more knowledgeable and sensitive to diaspora needs. Within the prime minister's office a unit on diaspora affairs has functioned under one name or another since the 1950s. In some instances, the example of Yaacov Herzog is probably the outstanding one, belief that the bureaucrat in question possessed ties to and an understanding of diaspora Jewry led to greatly increased influence. However, the importance of this factor ought not to be overstated.[13]

In conclusion, the political interrelationships and effects of Israel-diaspora relations are likely to be affected far more by the symbolic and moral claims of each side then by the usual mechanisms of political pressure that we are accustomed to seeing in the political arena.

## Notes

Many of the observations recorded here are based on my own sense of what Israeli and diaspora Jews feel. I offer little evidence to buttress my position. Even if I were to quote from this or that spokesman, one could argue that I was presenting the views of individuals on matters that were highly personal. Since I also maintain that many of the positions that I ascribe to Israelis are held subconsciously, it becomes virtually impossible to demonstrate the truth or falsity of my argument. The only real test is whether what I say strikes a chord among those readers who are both interested and involved in the problems of Israel-diaspora relations.

1.  I have developed this notion more fully in chapter 4 of my book, *The Ambivalent American Jew: Politics, Religion and Family in American Jewish Life* (Philadelphia: Jewish Publication Society, 1973).

2.  These incidents are treated in greater detail in my book, *Pressure without Sanctions: The Influence of World Jewry in Shaping Israel's Public Policy* (Cranbury, N.J.: Fairleigh Dickinson Press, 1976).

3.  Ibid.

4.  Israel Kolatt, "Changing Relations Between Israel and the Diaspora," *Hebrew Study Circle on Diaspora Jewry,* Series 6–7 (Jerusalem: The Institute of Contemporary Jewry, The Hebrew University, 1968–1969), pp. 17–18.

5.  The importance of the symbols of statehood in achieving political objectives was brought home to me very vividly in 1967—although in that instance it served the purposes of Israel-diaspora cooperation rather than conflict. This was the period when Israel was anxious to arouse public opinion concerning the plight of Soviet Jewry. It was considered important to bring the message of the agony of Soviet Jews to the attention of Sovietologists. Whereas many of these scholars were themselves Jews, they tended to be indifferent to the special problems of Soviet Jews. It is highly unlikely that any Jewish organization could have reached most of these scholars individually, much less brought them together collectively, in order to present the factors of Jewish oppression and the need for assistance. But the experts were assembled together through the initiation of the Israel Consul-General in New York to meet, in his home, with his excellency, Joseph Tekoah, former Israel ambassador to the Soviet Union. Tekoah was able to present his impressions of Jewish life in the Soviet Union to a group of about thirty leading experts on Soviet life and later engage them in an extended question and answer period to further clarify the condition of Soviet Jewry.

6.  American Jews, glorying in the Zionised expressions of Chanukah would be no less shocked than Israelis to realize that Yeshayahu Leibowitz has a fairly strong case in arguing that there is a paradox in the fact that Jerusalem in 1967 was reunified, and the Temple Mount brought under Israeli dominion by the modern day *mityavnim* (Hellenizers), not modern day *chassidim* (pietists).

7.  The other side of the coin is that the symbols now became highly parochial by virtue of their very specificity. If the prayer ". . . may our eyes see Your return to Zion . . ." is fulfilled by a visit to the Western Wall, then many Jews will search for additional symbols to express their yearning for a "totally other" kind of existence. If Israel is the ultimate referent for the most sacred of Jewish symbols, many sensitive Jews will look beyond Judaism for symbols of ultimate meaning. Furthermore, statehood and political authority can never point to more than partial answers to an individual's quest for identity and understanding in the twentieth century.

8.  Yesha'yahu (Charles) Liebman. "The Role of Israel in the Ideology of American Jewry," *Dispersion and Unity* 10 (Winter 1970): 19–26.

9.  I touch on these briefly—the field has not been researched at all despite its obvious importance and I am too far removed from the diaspora scene, where most of the changes have taken place, to make more than some very general observations.

10. Daniel J. Elazar, "Decision-Making in the American Jewish Community," in David Sidorsky, ed., *The Future of the Jewish Community in America* (New York: Basic Books, 1973), pp. 271–316.

11. Israel has sought to confer prestige on other types of Jewish leaders as well.

There is, for example, an annual award by the president of Israel to outstanding Jewish schools in the diaspora. But the relative neglect of, say, Jewish educational leaders compared to major philanthropists is quite striking.

12. Israeli leaders, politicians, and generals probably feel more comfortable with American Jewish millionaires, professional administrators, and communal leaders than they would with Jewish scholars, educators, and rabbis.

13. When Louis Pincus, Jewish Agency chairman, died in the summer of 1973, Yitzhak Rabin was one of the people mentioned as a possible successor. Rabin, however, was considered unacceptable to diaspora leaders because of his rather standoffish attitude toward American Jewish leaders during his tenure as Israeli ambassador to Washington. This, in turn, had absolutely no bearing in his subsequent selection as prime minister.

# 18

# *Halakhah* as a Ground for Creating a Shared Political Dialogue Among Contemporary Jews

*David Hartman*

Zionism in the twentieth century has created a framework for Jewish political activism. It expresses the revolutionary thrust of the Jewish people to become politically autonomous and responsible. It reflects the will of the Jewish community to determine, as far as this is possible, its own historical destiny. Zionism has provided a cause around which Jews with different ideologies and life-styles have forged a minimum basis for community. The yearning for liberation from exile, however these terms are understood, is a vital source of Jewish self-understanding and collective action.

Joseph Ber Soloveitchik, in his article "Kol Dodi Dofek," utilizes traditional covenantal categories to illuminate the religious significance of a community forged by a common political destiny.[1] Soloveitchik views the resurgence of Jewish political autonomy as an expression of *brit goral,* covenantal destiny. The attempt of a great *halakhist* to understand the Zionist revolution and the State of Israel in traditional, covenantal categories indicates, in itself, how deeply Israel's political existence has permeated the spiritual consciousness of contemporary Jews. However, Soloveitchik is not satisfied merely with community based upon *brit goral,* a common historical and political fate. He argues that the Jewish people should again strive to become, as they were in the past, a community of shared spiritual goals. His article reflects the hope that beyond shared political destiny, the soil of the Israeli reality may nurture a renewal of *brit ye'ud,* covenantal meaning.[2]

One can appreciate the pathos of Soloveitchik's yearning that *brit goral* be consummated with *brit ye'ud.* But while the shared values of a Jewish society were quite clear during long periods of history, today, unfortunately, there is no consensus as to how the Jewish people should give expression to *brit ye'ud.*[3] Given the contemporary breakdown of traditional Jewish society, is it possible to create a shared community of values? Or will the sense of Jewish community be limited to the struggle to maintain our political autonomy?

One may understandably question how any community of meaning is possible between Jews who subscribe to the normative structure of *halakhah,* however understood, and those who do not feel bound to organize their pattern of living by those norms. Furthermore, can those who seek to live within the *halakhic* framework understand and spiritually appreciate life-styles whose values are not grounded in Revelation and traditional *halakhic* authority?

A strong current within contemporary religious education tends to negate the possibility of a shared dialogue with Jews who lack faith in God and belief in Revelation. There are, however, religious educators who are aware that we must meet upon the common ground of the larger society. Yet even among them we often hear the argument that, ideally, Judaism can best sustain itself and thrive in a climate of insulation. These educators recognize, however, that given the potency of modern communications media, we cannot hope to achieve this insulation. Modernity is forcibly imposed upon us; we cannot escape its impact and challenges.[4]

One who sincerely believes in insulation and yet is forced to react to the modern world, will often enter the confrontation in a spirit of polemicism. He will try to prove that what is different from the tradition is wrong or, if recognized to be of value, that the tradition had it first and in a better form! Forced confrontation of this nature often leads to exaggerated spiritual arrogance.

The approach suggested in this essay is not that of a polemical confrontation with the modern world. On the contrary, we believe that the experiential and intellectual encounter with modern values and insights can help deepen and illuminate one's commitment to the tradition.

It is not accidental that the first *aggadah* that Maimonides chose to comment on was "God only has in His world the four cubits of the *halakhah*" (T.B. Berakhot 8a). A literal understanding of this aggadic statement would suggest that Judaism's approach is one of insulation from other intellectual disciplines. This *aggadah* is a succinct statement of a worldview which would negate any attempt to construct a synthesis between philosophy and *halakhah*. In fact, Leo Strauss utilizes this text to show that Judaism has no interest in philosophy.[5] However, in order to undermine the mistaken notion that *halakhah* is intellectually self-sufficient, Maimonides interprets this *aggadah* as referring to an individual who has mastered both *halakhah* and philosophy. The *hasid* who represents the ideal *halakhic* man is, according to Maimonides, an individual whose *halakhic* practice has been illuminated by general philosophic knowledge.[6]

Maimonides was not satisfied merely with indicating that philosophy had autonomous value. In the *Mishneh Torah* he showed how the *mitzvah* of *ahavat hashem,* love of God, can only be realized to the extent that one appropriates intellectual disciplines that are not particular to the Jewish tradition.

> This God, honoured and revered, it is our duty to love and fear; as it is said "Thou shalt love the Lord, thy God" (Deut. 6:5), and it is further said "Thou shalt fear the Lord, thy God" (Deut. 6:13). And what is the way that will lead to the love of Him and the fear of Him? When a person contemplates His great and wondrous works and creatures and from them obtains a glimpse of His wisdom which is incomparable and infinite, he will straightway love Him, praise Him, glorify Him, and long with an exceeding longing to know His great Name; even as David said "My soul thirsteth for God, for the living God" (Ps. 42:3). And when he ponders these matters, he will recoil affrighted, and realize that he is a small creature, lowly and obscure, endowed with slight and slender intelligence, standing in the presence of Him who is perfect in knowledge.[7]
>
> It is known and certain that the love of God does not become closely knit in a man's heart till he is continuously and thoroughly possessed by it and gives up everything else in the world for it; as God commanded us, "with all thy heart and with all thy soul" (Deut. 6:5). One only loves God with the knowledge with which one knows Him. According to the knowledge, will be the love. If the former be little or much, so will the latter be little or much. A person ought therefore to devote himself to the understanding and comprehension of those sciences and studies which will inform him concerning his Master, as far as it lies in human faculties to understand and comprehend—as indeed we have explained in the Laws of the Foundations of the Torah.[8]

When Maimonides wanted to educate his student to the love of God, he included as part of the curriculum logic, mathematics, astronomy, physics, and metaphysics.

In our generation, when Soloveitchik attempts to illuminate the complex dimensions of *halakhic* experience, he uses the insights and categories of modern religious existentialism. Just as Aristotle aided Maimonides, so does Kirkegaard help Soloveitchik plumb new depths in the *halakhic* experience. An important aspect of Soloveitchik's article, "The Lonely Man of Faith," is his treatment of the implications of *halakhic* man's confrontation with technology. Although emphasizing that there are dimensions of the religious life that extend beyond the values of technological man, he nonetheless presents a sympathetic religious appreciation of technology. Soloveitchik shows his reader how modern scientific knowledge enlarges the scope of *halakhic* man's moral responsibility. The dignity of man, a *halakhic* category, is enriched by the new-found power that technology makes possible.[9]

These are two illustrations of the type of approach that I am suggesting. Such an approach seeks to help students value, and therefore learn from, what is different from them. It encourages the selective integration of other values rather than polemical debate with an enemy.

This essay will argue against the claim that an educational system grounded in total commitment to *halakhah* must of necessity educate toward the spiritual isolation of its students from "secularists." We do not deny the existence of many elements in the tradition which appear to validate a separatist philosophy of Jewish education. In fact, one often has difficulty finding support within the tradition for tolerance of non-*halakhic* positions held by Jews![10] This chapter will suggest, however, that possibilities exist within the tradition to educate toward a sensitivity to other viewpoints and an openness to dialogue. A willingness to confront ideas that are in conflict with one's own tradition can be nurtured within an educational system committed to *halakhah*. Dedication to a particular spiritual system does not require insulation from other intellectual outlooks. Pluralistic sensibility can contain deep particularistic passion.

In our attempt to develop grounds for a shared spiritual language between many sectors in the Jewish community, we will focus upon the following points. First, we will explore the possibility of developing and encouraging spiritual openness within the framework of traditional *halakhic* education. We will consider how a *halakhically* committed student can find support within his tradition for the appreciation of values that are not based upon his own sources of authority. We will suggest ways to mitigate the rigidity and harshness that is at times mistakenly identified with the inculcation of passionate love for the *halakhah*.

Second, we will suggest philosophic approaches to *halakhah* and God that may help create a shared universe of discourse between *halakhic* and non-*halakhic* Jews. We will try to show that religious language need not create a private world of meaning that bars men of faith from dialogue with those who do not share their commitment.[11]

Finally, we will argue for an approach to *mitzvot* that stresses the urgency of realizing one's individual spiritual aspirations within the matrix of community. We will show that the *halakhic* system requires that sensitivity and commitment to the spiritual needs of the community precede and provide the framework for personal fulfillment.

In addressing this essay to all those concerned and involved in traditional religious education, we do not wish to give the impression that the responsibility for carrying on a shared dialogue is to be shouldered by this group alone. The difficulties involved in building bridges of understanding must be faced by all men of good will in our society. All groups within the Jewish people must free themselves of stereotyped opinions and be willing to listen to the deepest convictions of the other.[12] However, intellectual honesty demands that we begin with ourselves and seek to refine that which we know best.

Let us now examine some of the complexities involved in seeking to create a community of meaning among Jews. Any creative encounter changes all those who are involved. The "other" invades one's sense of self. One's previous position must be reevaluated in the light of new awareness and insights. In his introduction to *The Guide,* Maimonides is fully conscious of the fact that once his student has encountered other philosophic positions he cannot maintain a vital relationship to the tradition while ignoring the challenges they present to Judaism. Intellectual repression is not conducive to spiritual joy.[13]

In suggesting that students of our traditional educational system engage in dialogue with Jews who follow various life styles, and become intellectually involved with different value systems, we are aware that they will be deeply affected by the encounter. They will not emerge without doubts and questions. They will be forced to rethink previously accepted certainties. Recognizing this, we must help the student overcome his potentially paralyzing doubts, and provide him with tools to sustain him through periods of intellectual struggle.

What educational approach will help the student realize that conflict and doubt can exist within a religiously committed person? What insights does he need in order to turn the turmoil of the encounter with others to creative use? How can we make him aware that his most painful doubts can contain the seeds of new insights to illuminate the untapped depths of the tradition?[14]

First, students must be taught to realize that insulation from differing views and experiences does not, of necessity, characterize the spiritual life of those who ground their faith in the certainty of Revelation. It is essential that the student be shown how religious men in our tradition confronted, and often welcomed, challenges that forced them to rethink their own beliefs and practices. Instead of viewing the tradition as immune to novelty, the student must be taught to appreciate the profound dialectic between continuity and change that is present within it. In the form of commentary, masters of the *halakhic* tradition respectfully expressed their intense loyalty to the past, while exploring the new insights made available by their own generation.

Professor Gershom Scholem's two essays, "Religious Authority and Mysticism" and "Revelation and Tradition as Religious Categories in Judaism," brilliantly illuminate the orientation of a traditional mind to novelty. These essays reveal that intellectual boldness is not antithetical to acceptance of *Torah mi-Sinai*.[15] A religious education that provides an appreciation of the thought processes of the traditional mind, and focuses on the dynamic tension between continuity and novelty present in our sources, would encourage today's students to continue in the tradition of bold yet loyal *parshanut*.[16]

A generation that will have to grapple with significant intellectual challenges and grow spiritually within a society often indifferent to its deepest commitments must be provided with models that exemplify the creative possibilities that can emerge out of doubt and uncertainty. Too frequently in traditional education, men of religious convictions are portrayed as models of dedicated, unquestioning, simple faith. Too seldom do we indicate the dark nights of the soul that often precede the illuminating certainty of faith. Can one, however, imagine Maimonides' *Guide of the Perplexed* written other than by a sensitive spirit who had struggled with profound religious issues? It is inconceivable to think that his *Guide* was written only for others and not for himself. One cannot illuminate the perplexed without having first tasted the pain of doubt oneself.

The price we pay for our neglect to show how religious men struggled with their faith is heavy indeed. The "dropout" rate among those who move from religious circles into the open and pluralistic society reflects the weakness of an educational approach that does not prepare its students to face and grow from religious confusion.

We must also correct the mistaken perception that religious men of the past were of one cloth. We must give due recognition to the variety of religious sensibilities expressed in the tradition. Our students, therefore, should be exposed not only to the formal patterns of *halakhic* practice, but to the vital, inner spiritual life of *halakhic* man as well. Our students must be made aware of the variegated approaches to *ta'amei hamitzvot* that are reflected in the tradition. We provide them with an incomplete understanding of the nature of *halakhic* practice if we divorce the *description* of an action from the *intention* of the actor. The observer who has access only to the external features of an act lacks a proper understanding of what he is observing. In the eyes of the observer, the Kabbalists and Maimonides are performing the same *mitzvah*. However, one who understands their respective approaches to *ta'amei hamitzvot* cannot continue to believe, in the fullest sense, that they are really doing the same thing. To do so is to reduce the observance of *mitzvah* to external, mechanical behaviorism.[17]

Exposure to the multiple aggadic approaches to *mitzvot* lends emphasis to the important traditional concept that although the Torah was given once, it is received differently in each generation.[18] Men who create their own *aggadah* within the discipline of a common *halakhah* give expression to their individual religious sensibilities.

What happens when an educational system emphasizes the variety of spiritual options expressed within the tradition? The student becomes aware that the tradition asks for more than shared practice and behavioral obedience. It also encourages man to bring the fullness of his personality to his practice of *halakhah*.

An educational system that encourages its students to confront the variety of rhythms present in modern society will have to face the reality that those it educates will not necessarily be of one cloth. Our educators must present a broad range of authentic religious models with which their students can identify. The multiplicity of models provides breathing space for the variety of psychological sensibilities present among the students.

In an attempt to achieve religious certainty, however, contemporary *halakhic* education tends to emphasize one model of authenticity. It attempts to gloss over and harmonize the teeming variety of religious sensibilities and approaches contained in our tradition. The religious security that a monolithic approach hopes to achieve is often hollow and atrophying. Religious monism often excuses the student committed to *halakhah* from developing his own *ta'amei hamitzvot*, a responsibility one must shoulder even in a system that has a detailed *Shulhan Arukh*. An education that ignores the complex emotional dimensions of spiritual man inhibits the growth of a religious personality capable of engaging seriously and totally in the creative adventure of discovering new-yet-old vistas in one's religious life.

When one is exposed to the playful mythic imagination of the mystics, the sober, rational passion of Maimonides, the love of imagery in Halevi, one recognizes that the tradition is able to accommodate many different spiritual sensibilities. In the tradition, *aggadic* teleology was never normative.[19] A fuller understanding of Judaism must, therefore, contain an appreciation of the interaction between pluralistic *aggadot* and uniform *halakhic* practice. It must reflect the interplay between obedience and conformity to imposed authority, on the one hand, and a spontaneous, personal, freely chosen spiritual teleology, on the other.

Emphasis upon the subjective elements within *halakhah* will help mitigate the monistic harshness that frequently accompanies a well-ordered and objective spiritual system. The mistaken claim that the goal of *halakhah* is to provide objective certainty and religious security will be corrected when one realizes that one cannot understand *halakhic* practice without appreciating the inner experience of the *mitzvah*.[20] The student whose understanding of *halakhah* contains an awareness of the variety of *ta'amei hamitzvot* will be educated to find security in his spiritual life even as he recognizes that others will draw meaning for their *halakhic* practice from different spiritual sources.

Thus far I have suggested how important it is to show that *halakhah* never freed the individual from the need to develop his own spiritual worldview. Emphasis on the broad *aggadic* options available within the tradition may be helpful in developing a pluralistic sensibility; one who is secure in his approach to religious practice while recognizing that there are other perceptions of *halakhah* is well on the way to developing an appreciation of religious pluralism. I would now like to indicate briefly how such a sensibility may also be nurtured by the study of the logic of *halakhic* argumentation.[21]

What is the relationship of *halakhic* argumentation to Revelation? What are the logical tools needed to understand the rational basis for legal disagreement in the Talmud? How can two opposing views both be considered "the words of the living God"? What is the cognitive status of minority opinion? Is Divine truth revealed in the opinion of the majority, or is majority rule merely a procedural, juridical principle which in no way claims identification with the truth?

A serious study of these crucial questions may help the student realize that *halakhic* argumentation never provided the cognitive certainty of a deductive syllogism. Legal decisions are not necessary inferences drawn from premises. Appreciation of facts and the context in which one wishes to apply the law do not flow necessarily from the law itself. Decision making in a legal system is not a mechanical process.[22] Emphasis placed on certain principles, weight given to specific values, appreciation of the historical situation and its needs, are all constitutive elements of a *halakhic* decision. In applying the law to a living situation, the judge expresses an entire philosophy of life. Judges, as distinct from logicians, are responsible for their decisions.[23]

A traditional understanding of *Torah mi-Sinai* cannot be divorced from the way in which talmudic scholars applied Torah to life. The *halakhic* process clearly shows that there was more than one road that led from belief in a literal Revelation to *halakhic* decision making.

One who has a deep appreciation of the logic of the *halakhic* system can never be certain that his actions represent the only possible cognitive response to the Torah of God. Alternate ways of practice are present in a system that applies *Torah mi-Sinai* to its everyday life. "These and these are the words of the living God" is an enduring description of *halakhic* thinking. *Halakhic* masters did not confuse the absoluteness of law grounded in Revelation with the claim that *halakhic* decisions reflect the only logical response to Divine law.[24] In the tradition, the ultimate source of *halakhic* authority is God; the application of *halakhah* to life is multiple and human. *Knesset Yisrael* also was, and will remain, responsible for the way of life it developed.

An awareness that *halakhic* practice is never based, logically, upon the cognitive claim to certainty, contributes a rational foundation for the development of a pluralistic sensibility. For pluralism, as distinct from tolerance, cannot be achieved unless one's epistemology provides a cognitive basis for validating multiple ways of practice. Both the *halakhic* and *aggadic* components of the tradition can help us find support for the possible development of a pluralistic spiritual sensibility. Total commitment and passion for action need not be grounded in an epistemology that provides absolute certainty.

I would ban the teaching of *mitzvot* based upon the *Kitzur Shulhan Arukh,* as it distorts the complexity and richness of the *halakhic* experience. It is a far-reaching educational mistake to teach laws from a text that does not include different *halakhic* arguments and a variety of *ta'amei hamitzvot.*[25] Learning based on the *Kitzur Shulhan Arukh* has a quality of rote catechism. In contrast to the Talmud, the *Kitzur Shulhan Arukh* is like a bath tub as against an ocean. When swimming in an ocean, multiple strokes in various directions are possible. In a bath tub you immerse yourself and passively soak in water without having much maneuverability. There is a spiritual adventure and diversity in the ocean of Talmud. There is limiting spiritual monism and religious passivity in the study of the *Kitzur Shulhan Arukh.*

We appreciate the concern to educate towards the importance of *halakhic* practice. However, it should not be achieved at the expense of denying the rich adventure of being exposed to multiple points of view. Students who are encouraged to practice a common *halakhah* should use study texts which inspire them to choose their own *aggadah.* This is crucial to a religious system that wishes to sustain itself and grow within the complexities of the modern world.

Let us now consider ways in which a shared language may be achieved between the *halakhic* and non-*halakhic* society. Any discussion between two parties requires agreed-upon criteria of meaning, as well as shared values that provide a common universe of discourse. With reference to our discussion, we must explore the question of whether *halakhah* and religious faith of necessity create a private world of meaning which is unintelligible to those who do not understand or share the presuppositions of the tradition. Is it possible to translate a way of life based upon belief in Revelation into categories intelligible to one who does not share this belief?

What approach to *ta'amei hamitzvot* can effect such a translation? A mystic, theocentric orientation immediately rules out any common language between a believer and a nonbeliever. An approach that insists that duty to God's law must be the sole motivation for observance of the commandments similarly creates an insurmountable barrier to dialogue. The statement "I do this solely because I believe" usually blocks discussion between believer and nonbeliever. However, the tradition provides other approaches to *halakhic* practice which open up possibilities for a shared language of appreciation between individuals who do not participate in a common *halakhah*. One approach is suggested by Maimonides in *The Guide*.

> There is a group of human beings who consider it a grievous thing that causes should be given for any law; what would please them most is that the intellect would not find a meaning for the commandments and prohibitions. What compels them to feel thus is a sickness that they find in their souls, a sickness to which they are unable to give utterance and of which they cannot furnish a satisfactory account. For they think that if those laws were useful in this existence and had been given to us for this or that reason, it would be as if they derived from the reflection and the understanding of some intelligent being. If, however, there is a thing for which the intellect could not find any meaning at all and that does not lead to something useful, it indubitably derives from God; for the reflection of man would not lead to such a thing. It is as if, according to these people of weak intellects, man were more perfect than his Maker; for man speaks and acts in a manner that leads to some intended end, whereas the deity does not act thus, but commands us to do things that are not useful to us and forbids us to do things that are not harmful to us. But He is far exalted above this; the contrary is the case—the whole purpose consisting in what is useful for us, as we have explained on the basis of its dictum: *For our good always, that He might preserve us alive, as it is at this day. And it says: Which shall hear all these statues (huqqim) and say: Surely this great community is a wise and understanding people.* Thus it states explicitly that even all the *statutes (huqqim)* will show to all the nations that they have been given with *wisdom and understanding.* (*Guide*, III, 31)

In this chapter, Maimonides argues against an approach to the commandments which insists that religious passion must be nurtured by a private language. According to this worldview, *mitzvot* must isolate one cognitively from those who do not believe in Revelation. Without this sense of isolation, one does not appreciate the unique significance of *mitzvot*. The greater the separation of oneself from nonbelievers, the more deeply does one experience the full meaning of *halakhah*.

One may call this religious sensibility the *akedah* consciousness. For an important element of the *akedah* is its total unintelligibility.[26] If the *akedah* model symbolizes the highest rung of spiritual development, then those *mitzvot* which make one's actions unintelligible to others will be seen as the supreme expression of one's religious faith. No shared language is possible if the nonrational and the sense of isolation feed the religious passion.

Maimonides sought to correct this religious "sickness." He insisted that belief in Revelation does not require man to dissociate himself from rationally communicating the values of his religious life to others who are not committed to *Torah mi-Sinai*. Maimonides uses the proof-text of "for it is your wisdom and your understanding in the sight of the peoples" (*ki hi hakhmatkhem u'vinatkhem l'eyney ha'amim*) to demonstrate that the Torah informs us that other nations can recognize the wisdom of a way of life which they themselves do not obey. Appreciation by others, however, is only possible if one is able to explain the purpose of one's actions in categories that can be generally comprehended. Maimonides seeks to cast the particularist *halakhic* Jew into the world, and informs him that he can explain his spiritual life to others. He offers his reader universal criteria for understanding the purpose of the *halakhah*.

> Rather things are indubitably as we have mentioned: every commandment from among these six hundred and thirteen commandments exists either with a view to communicating a rule of justice, or to warding off an injustice, or to endowing men with a noble moral quality, or to warning them against an evil moral quality. Thus all (the commandments) are bound up with three things: Opinions, moral qualities, and political civic actions. (*Guide,* III, 31)

Given these criteria which are universally intelligible, a *halakhic* can begin to communicate with others.

In *Helek,* Maimonides again uses the proof-text quoted above with regard to the cognitive claims of the tradition.[27] Here he argues against those who do not subject the truth claims of *aggadic* teachers to universal criteria of rationality. The knowledge claims of the *aggadah* and the behavior patterns of *halakhah* need not isolate one from participating within a universal culture. To Maimonides, commitment to tradition is not fed only by nonrational leaps of faith. Cognitive isolation need not be the price one pays for commitment to a particular way of life.

The educational implications of Maimonides' orientation to religious experience are of utmost importance. Education in his spirit would not allow the student to *revel* in his distinctiveness and separation from the world. He would be taught to discover *ta'amei hamitzvot* which are grounded in values that can be understood by all men, Jew and non-Jew alike. He would find it valuable and necessary to construct a teleology of his own system that could be appreciated by others. He would be trained to speak intelligibly without having to validate the significance of his actions solely by an appeal to faith. Exclusive reliance on faith, *emunah,* can easily serve as an escape for one who does not want to be troubled to consider the human implications of his way of life.

The comfortable security that habit provides, and the psychological and intellectual support gained from living only with those who think and behave similarly, are shaken when one recognizes the important spiritual orientation that Maimonides applies to the commandments. One must constantly oscillate between two powerful poles, the universal and the particular, always striving to find a way of integrating both claims upon one's life. One must evaluate one's spiritual growth not in terms of the *akedah* model, but in terms of Abraham's passionate prayer for the people of Sodom. Abraham demands that God make Himself intelligible within universal criteria of morality. The model of Abraham at Sodom corrects the one-sided notion that religion creates a private language. At Sodom, God does not demand that Abraham sacrifice his sense of morality.

*Mitzvah* takes on deeper dimensions when *halakhic* man is capable of sharing his spiritual life with others. Maimonides' methodological approach to *ta'amei hamitzvot,* filled with a philosophic content that is significant for today, would provide a bridge leading from behavioral separation to cognitive communication.

In exploring the possibility of a shared language for believer and nonbeliever, we must also consider the following serious question. Can the *halakhic* Jew recognize in non-*halakhic* behavior those aspirations which his own system is attempting to realize? If he could do so, he could share with non-*halakhic* Jews a common teleology, even though the ways to implement those aspirations might differ. Again, let us turn to Maimonides.

Before discussing the teleology of many *halakhot,* Maimonides begins chapter 4 in *Shmonah Prakim* with a discussion of the ethical theory of Aristotle. He indicates the nature of virtue based upon moderation, the relationship between action and the formation of character, and then shows that *halakhah* aims at realizing those virtues which are also present in the Aristotelian system. Aristotelian ethics and the *halakhic* system share a common approach to the nature of virtue. Although the two systems do not have a common *halakhah,* Maimonides indicates that, to a great extent, they do share a common teleology.[28]

We find the same approach in chapter 1 of *Hilkhot De'ot*. Maimonides again follows the pattern he set in *Shmonah Prakim*. He begins by establishing the concept of virtue based upon moderation; he does not derive this approach from any authoritative source of his tradition.

> To cultivate either extreme in any class of dispositions is not the right course nor is it proper for any person to follow or learn it. If a man finds that his nature tends or is disposed to one of these extremes, or if one has acquired and become habituated to it, he should turn back and improve, so as to walk in the way of good people, which is the right way. The right way is the mean in each group of dispositions common to humanity; namely, that disposition which is equally distant from the two extremes in its class, not being nearer to the one than to the other. (*Hilkhot De'ot* 1:3, 4)

In *Shmonah Prakim* Maimonides shows how the specific details of *halakhah* aim at the formation of healthy character traits. In *Hilkhot De'ot* he identifies God's attributes—being merciful, gracious, etc.—with the virtuous actions of a healthy soul.

> We are bidden to walk in the middle paths which are the right and proper ways, as it is said, "and thou shalt walk in His ways" (Deut. 28:9). In explanation of the text just quoted, the sages taught, "Even as God is called gracious, so be thou gracious: Even as He is called merciful, so be thou merciful; even as He is called Holy, so be thou holy." Thus too the prophets described the Almighty by all the various attributes "long-suffering and abounding in kindness, righteous and upright, perfect, mighty and powerful," and so forth, to teach us, that these qualities are good and right and that a human being should cultivate them, and thus imitate God, as far as he can. . . . .And as the Creator is called by these attributes, which constitute the middle path in which we are to walk this path is called the Way of God and this is what the patriarch Abraham taught his children. (*Hilkhot De'ot,* 2:5–7)

In Judaism, one arrived at the ideal of a healthy soul through *halakhic* prescription, or by imitating the moral attributes of God.

What is important for our purpose is that both in *Shmonah Prakim* and *Hilkhot De'ot*, Maimonides enables the *halakhic* student to recognize many similarities between the goals of his religious practices and the teleology of other systems. *Halakhah* and the imitation of God aim to develop character. These goals are perceived to be religious commandments by the *halakhic* Jew. But that perception does not prevent Maimonides from making *halakhic* practice intelligible within categories that are not grounded in Revelation and *mitzvah*.

If one follows in the spirit of Maimonides, it would be correct to show that individuals can share *halakhic* aspirations even though these are not concretized through *halakhic guidelines.* A student trained in this perspective will find it possible to participate meaningfully with others who do not share the presuppositions upon which his own life-style is based. *Halakhah* taught in this fashion will enable the student to forge a worldview that accepts the possibility of aggadic discourse independent of *halakhah.*

We have thus far attempted to show how *halakhic* practice need not isolate one from sharing common goals with those not committed to the behavioral prescriptions of the *halakhah.* A much more difficult question is whether a shared theological language is possible between the believer and the agnostic or atheist.

We suggest that such discourse is possible if the believer has a clear understanding of what constitutes—in modern terms—the battle against the seductive powers of *avodah zarah,* idolatry. I use the evocative term "seductive" intentionally, so as to indicate that the rejection of idolatry is important only if what is rejected has a luring power.[29] To negate can be a moving experience and be deeply meaningful, if what is negated has a powerful attraction. Our convictions gain vitality when we understand what is not compatible with them. The negative illuminates the force of the positive. If our belief in God sometimes appears to be a hollow and superficial gesture, it may be due to our limited understanding of what constitutes modern idolatry.

Do educators really believe that the story of Abraham in the idol shop of his father has meaning to anyone beyond the age of three? Abraham as the iconoclast of history is a weak figure if the only idols he smashes are the ones found in his father's shop.

Maimonides sees the rejection of idolatry as one of the primary goals of *halakhah.*

> The precept relating to idolatry is equal in importance to all the other precepts put together, as it is said, "And when ye shall err and not observe all these command-ments" (Num. 15:22). This text has traditionally been interpreted as alluding to idolatry; hence the inference that acceptance of idolatry is tantamount to repudiat-ing the whole Torah, the prophets and everything that they were commanded, from Adam to the end of time, as it is said "From the day that the Lord gave command-ment and onward, throughout your generations" (Num. 15:23). And whoever de-nies idolatry confesses his faith in the whole Torah, in all the prophets and all that the prophets were commanded, from Adam to the end of time. And this is the fundamental principle of all the commandments. (*Hilkhot Avodah Zarah,* 2:4)[30]

In a talmudic discussion on why Mordechai was called *Yehudi,* when he came from the tribe of Benjamin, R. Johanan answered: He was called a Jew because he rejected idolatry. "For anyone who repudiates idolatry is called a Jew" (*Megillah* 13a).

If our students are to appreciate their role as iconoclasts in history, it is important that we educate them to understand how the *yetzer hara* of idolatry is still alive.[31]

In his book *The Morality of Law,* Lon Fuller raises the following issue.[32] Can we know what is bad, without knowing the perfectly good? Fuller argues that we can know what is plainly unjust without committing ourselves to declare with finality what perfect justice would be like. In terms of our concern, we can ask whether rejection of idolatry is possible without a positive affirmation of God. If we can assume that it is possible for individuals to agree on what they reject, without acknowledging what they affirm, we may be able to create a shared theology of the repudiation of idolatry, without demanding a clearly defined commitment to belief in God. The believer can share common aspirations with the atheist and the agnostic, if all three strive to reject idolatry. This striving can have great significance and far-ranging consequences if the idolatry that is combatted is luring and constitutes a vital problem to be eradicated.

Ephraim Urbach, in his article "The Rabbinical Laws of Idolatry," develops insights that can be helpful to our discussion.[33] He notes that although the Talmud records differing approaches to idolatry, "one thing is certain—neither the Tannaim of the second century nor the Amoraim of the third showed any tendency to compromise or to concede to anything connected with emperor worship." Evidently the worship of idols was not luring to the Jews of that period, but the worship of the emperor had a power of attraction that had to be combatted as forcefully as possible. Urbach writes:

> According to the Jerusalem Talmud, the Tannaim were divided in their opinions about the generality of images, but if it was certain that they were images of kings, all agreed in forbidding them. . . . .In the ancient world there were—on the evidence of Pliny—more gods than human beings . . . .but in that same world, there was only one emperor whose sovereignty and power were felt daily.

The power of Rome, as distinct from pagan idolatry, impinged upon the daily life of the community. It was a felt reality. Emperor worship had to be combatted because its attractiveness and power could lure man away from his religious commitment.

As Urbach develops his thesis, he notes that from the time of Antoninus onwards, the cult of the emperor became "the religion of absolute political power. It was not an individual that was worshipped, but the more than human power of which he was the personification. . . . .Everything connected with this cult was absolutely forbidden (by the Sages)."

The idolatry of absolute power has not been destroyed. The urge for political power and control present in the twentieth century is a flagrant rejection of the sovereignty of God. The demand for total and uncritical allegiance to a political state is idolatrous. Any political figure or party which considers itself beyond criticism has, in a very important sense, denied the reality of God. Insisting on criticism, demanding accountability, limiting the dangerous hunger for power, building political structures that create balances of power, may be important ways to implement the *halakhic* struggle against idolatry.

The *yetzer hara* of idolatry need not, however, manifest itself solely in the political longing for absolute power. Its seductiveness may also be evident in the personal realm. It is interesting to observe the rabbis' use of the term "as one who worships idols," *Ke'ilu oved avodah zarah*, and similar references to idolatry, with regard to specific behavioral traits.

> Rabbi Johanan said in the name of R. Simeon B. Yohai: Every man in whom is haughtiness of spirit is as though he worships idols. . . . .R. Johanan himself said: He is as though he had denied the existence of God, as it is said, *Thine heart be lifted up and thou forget the Lord thy God* (*Sotah* 4b). R. Eleazar also said: Every man in whom is haughtiness of spirit is fit to be hewn down like an *asherah* (an object of idolatrous worship) (*Sotah* 5a). R. Hisda said, and according to another version it was Mar Ukba: Every man in whom is haughtiness of spirit, the Holy One blessed be He declares, I and he cannot both dwell in the world (*Sotah* 5a). R. Simeon B. Eleazar said in the name of Halfa B. Agra in R. Johanan B. Nuri's name: He who rends his garments in his anger, he who breaks his vessels in his anger, and he who scatters his money in his anger, regard him as an idolater, because such are the wiles of the Tempter: Today he says to him, "Do this," tomorrow he tells him, "Do that," until he bids him "Go and serve idols," and he goes and serves (them). R. Abin observed: What verse (intimates this)? *There shall be no strange god in thee; neither shalt thou worship any strange god;* who is the strange god that resides in man himself? Say, that is the Tempter. (*Shabbat* 105b)

One may claim that there is no actual relationship between idolatry and arrogance and uncontrolled anger. One may argue that the rabbis' evocative language is simply persuasive. Perhaps in order to stress the importance of guarding oneself against arrogance and the loss of temper, the rabbis used such phrases as "I and he cannot both dwell in the world" and "as if he had denied the existence of God." This may be true. However, the choice of these terms, with all their associations and overtones, may be *literally* significant, and indicate a goal far more profound than the need to persuade. Perhaps the Rabbis wished to suggest that one may perceive the ugliness of idolatry in the character structure of man. Perhaps our Sages sought to educate us to recognize that one who is subject to rage so intense that he loses self-control, or one who is swollen with arrogance, manifests character traits that are incompatible with the worship of God.

The capacity for self-transcendence is an essential element in the faith experience. The believer is conscious of his creatureliness and finitude when he stands before the Infinite. This awareness should enable him to appreciate the dignity of others and be responsive to realities beyond his own self. The man who says, wholeheartedly, "Blessed art Thou," *Barukh Atah,* is a human being who has broken out of the prison of egocentricity. In states of rage, however, the person is trapped within his own hate. In moments of arrogance, the individual is imprisoned within his own inflated sense of self. Arrogance and rage prevent the full appreciation and confirmation of a reality beyond oneself; they inhibit man from transcending himself, a condition that is essential for the encounter with God.

In this sense, there is an important similarity between these character traits and the longing for absolute power in the political realm. Hunger for power, arrogance, and rage all prevent the individual from seeing and appreciating the dignity of others. Not to respond to others as persons is, in fact, a denial of one's creature consciousness. Arrogance and the urge for absolute power are states of consciousness in which the individual does not recognize the human implications of God's dwelling in the world.

The translation of idolatry into behavior patterns and character traits is a mode of thought inherent to the spirit of normative Judaism. *Halakhic* man always translates belief into behavior. Just as the rabbis recognized that an acceptance of the kingdom of Heaven is incomplete if it does not lead to the acceptance of the commandments, they may have also recognized that belief in God is void of significance if it does not lead to the shaping of character.[34]

The insistence that faith be expressed in behavior patterns and the shaping of character, creates a realm of common categories which makes possible a fruitful discussion between believer and nonbeliever. The importance that Judaism ascribes to practice makes possible the creation of a shared language. If faith alone were the major focus of the spiritual life in Judaism, this attempt at translation would be far more difficult.[35]

If our educational system would emphasize the character traits that emerge from faith in God, and educate toward a full appreciation of what constitutes the contemporary struggle against idolatry, we might alleviate the sense of value-isolation that frequently oppresses the student committed to *halakhah,* and begin to create a theological language that is intelligible to and usable by broad sectors of the community.

The significance given to practice within Judaism not only makes the creation of a shared language a logical possibility, but also provides the sense of urgency to make that attempt. *Mitzvah* illuminates the *centrality of community* within Judaism. *Halakhah* is a way of life of a community, and serves to develop a collective consciousness within the individual Jew. Systems of thought in which the individual is dominant cannot do justice to a worldview where law, which is vital to community, plays a central role. Existentialism, which focuses primarily on individual self-realization, cannot illuminate sufficiently the communal depths of *halakhic* Judaism. *Halakhah* can best be understood through the categories of political philosophy, for example, law, community, and authority.

Maimonides, the master *halakhist,* perceived the *halakhic* system in political terms.[36] For Maimonides, the legal category of *mitzvah* did not exist prior to Moses. Only after the exodus from Egypt, with the formation of a community, did *halakhah* become the dominant and organizing principle within Judaism. Abraham is described by Maimonides as a teacher who convinces through rational argumentation. Moses, who brings the law to the people, addresses the community in the name of God's legislative authority.[37] Prior to Sinai, man sought God through reflection upon His power and wisdom, as revealed in nature. That spiritual way, based upon philosophy, is individualistic. The authority of *mitzvah* becomes central to Judaism only when the collective community stands before God at Sinai. *Halakhah,* therefore, guides man to realize his longing for God within the context of community. As the "I" becomes a "we" consciousness through the collective covenant, it must seek a communal language, the language of *mitzvah.*

According to Maimonides, the *halakhic* Jew who has travelled the individual road of philosophy never abandons his collective consciousness. Community and practice are central even for the Jew who seeks contemplative love of God.[38] The profound longing for community is intrinsic to a worldview in which *halakhah* is the dominant organizing principle. *Halakhah* cannot respond to man's yearning for self-realization if he does not first feel the urgency of building a covenantal community.

Unfortunately, however, rather than serving as a catalyst for the building of community, *halakhah* is often used as an instrument for divisiveness, subtle aggression, and spiritual isolation. Instead of *mitzvah* awakening the individual to embrace *klal yisrael*, it is often, and mistakenly, viewed as calling for the isolation of the individual from the community. The performance of the *mitzvah* becomes exclusively an expression of man's striving for personal excellence.

One who hears a collective call in *mitzvah* is pained by the sectarian isolationism prevalent today. One who seeks to receive the Torah everyday within community feels the urgency to build shared spiritual meanings within our society.

Undeniably the attempt to build a shared community of value is a lengthy and difficult process, requiring enormous patience and spiritual courage. But inherent in Maimonides' approach to Revelation is an appreciation of the importance of patience. Process and stages, rather than instant transformations, characterize the educational philosophy of *halakhah*. The Revelation of the law gives expression to the way the Divine teacher patiently works over long periods of history. The *mitzvot* reflect the Divine acceptance of man as he is, with all his limitations. The Revelation of the law, as distinct from the Creation, is anthropocentric. The word of Creation expresses the overflowing power of Divine self-sufficiency. The word that emanates from Sinai reflects God's loving awareness of the human capacities of His students. In Revelation, God, the teacher of Torah, listens before He speaks. In addressing man, He speaks in the language of man—*dibrah torah bil'shon bnei adam*.

The recognition of the importance of process in the spiritual growth of the community, the love required to accept man as he is and to speak in categories that he can understand and appropriate, should be central to the *halakhic* approach to education. This is profoundly illustrated in Maimonides' treatment of Revelation in the *Guide*. I quote at length because of the suggestive power of this text as a model for Torah education.

> For a sudden transition from one opposite to another is impossible. And therefore man, according to his nature, is not capable of abandoning suddenly all to which he was accustomed. . . . .at that time the way of life generally accepted and customary in the whole world and the universal service upon which we were brought up consisted in offering various species of living beings in the temples in which images were set up, in worshipping the latter, and in burning incense before them— the pious ones and the ascetics being at that time, as we have explained, the people who were devoted to the service of the temples consecrated to the stars: His wisdom, may He be exalted, and His gracious ruse, which is manifest in regard to all His creatures, did not require that He give us a Law prescribing the rejection, abandonment, and abolition of all these kinds of worship. For one could not then conceive the acceptance of (such a Law), considering the nature of man, which always likes that to which it is accustomed. At that time this would have been similar to the appearance of a prophet in these times who, calling upon the people to worship God, would say: "God has given you a Law forbidding you to pray to Him, to fast, to call upon Him for help in misfortune. Your worship should consist solely in meditation without any works at all." Therefore He, may He be exalted, suffered the above-mentioned kinds of worship to remain, but transferred them from created or imaginary and unreal things to His own name, may He be exalted, commanding us to practice them with regard to Him, may He be exalted. . . . .What was there to prevent Him, may He be exalted, from giving us a Law in accordance with His first intention and from procuring us the capacity to accept this? . . . .[T]he text of the Torah tells a quite similar story, namely, in its dictum: *God led them not by the way of the land of the Philistines, although it was near, and so on. But God led the people about, by the way of the wilderness of the Red Sea.* Just as God perplexed them in anticipation of what their bodies were naturally incapable of bearing—turning them away from the high road toward which they had been going, toward another road so that the first intention should be achieved—so did He in anticipation of what the soul is naturally incapable of receiving, prescribe the laws that we have mentioned so that the first intention should be achieved, namely, the apprehension of Him, may He be exalted, and the rejection of *idolatry.* For just as it is not in the nature of man that, after having been brought up in slavish service occupied with clay, bricks, and similar things, he should all of a sudden wash off from his hands the dirt deriving from them and proceed immediately to fight against *the children of Anak,* so is it also not in his nature that, after having been brought up upon very many modes of worship and of customary practices, which the souls find so agreeable that they become as it were a primary notion, he should abandon them all of a sudden. . . . .[S]o did this group of laws derive from a divine grace, so that they should be left with the kind of practices to which they were accustomed and so that consequently the belief, which constitutes the first intention, should be validated in them. . . . .What was there to prevent Him from causing the inclination to accomplish the acts of obedience willed by Him and to avoid the acts of disobedience abhorred by Him, to be a natural disposition fixed in us?
>
> There is one and the same general answer to all these three questions and to all the others that belong to the same class: Though all miracles change the nature of some individual being, God does not change at all the nature of human individuals by means of miracles. Because of this great principle it says: *O that they had such*

*an heart as this, and so on.* It is because of this that there are commandments and prohibitions, rewards and punishments. We have already explained this fundamental principle by giving its proofs in a number of passages in our compilations. We do not say this because we believe that the changing of nature of any human individual is difficult for Him, may He be exalted. Rather is it possible and fully within capacity. But according to the foundations of the law, of the Torah, he has never willed to do it, nor shall He ever will it. For if it were His will that the nature of any human individual should be changed because of what He, may He be exalted, wills from that individual, sending of prophets and all giving of a Law would have been useless. (*Guide*, III, 32)

One must not forget that the master *halakhic* judge of the *Mishneh Torah* perceived and understood Revelation within these profound educational categories. *Halakhah*—as understood by Maimonides—expressed the sober passion of a wise teacher who begins the spiritual process from where his students stand. A teacher who has internalized the power and strength provided by tradition and knowledge should manifest the loving patience reflected in Maimonides' theory of Revelation. An educational philosophy following this spirit, will seek to develop in its students patience, and an ability to listen and respond to the other in terms of his worldview—in other words, it will educate men to imitate the Divine qualities that God exhibited at Sinai.

The risks implicit in many of the suggestions presented in this essay cannot be denied. There are dangers in suggesting that religious education deal with issues that may weaken the student's loyalty to the *halakhic* tradition. There are risks in encouraging intellectual openness, in exposing the student to views and life-styles that do not conform to, or confirm, his community's pattern of life. This is why one is invariably greeted with words of extreme caution when suggesting that we encourage our students to confront the modern world. We are told that we must wait until filled sufficiently with *lechem ubasar,* "the knowledge of what is permitted and what is forbidden" before entering into such a potentially dangerous enterprise.[39] But how is one to judge when one is sufficiently strong and learned to withstand the challenge of new ideas?

There is an attractive simplicity in the isolationist approach to religious education, but one must also recognize the very severe risks involved in waiting to be sufficiently strong before engaging in encounter. We may find that when we are ready to speak, there is no community willing to listen.

The opportunity to begin the process of creating a *brit ye'ud* for our people does not come often in history. The presence of a living Jewish society in Israel, with its dedication to *brit goral,* constitutes a fruitful soil for the creation of such a community of meaning. The danger in a separatist religious philosophy of education today, is that Judaism may turn into a sect and cease being a way of life for the total community. An educational philosophy that ignores the challenge of the present opportunity takes a great risk indeed. Single-minded concern with saving the Torah for the few may entail losing the people as a whole. *This should not be the response of a halakhic Jew to history.* The centrality of *mitzvah* demands that we feel the urgency of concretizing norms within the public domain of *klal yisrael.*

There is no authentic life choice that is risk-free. Any important decision entails dangers and uncertainties. The choice before us is not between an educational philosophy that is certain of its results, and one that is filled with risks—but rather, to which risks one chooses to be exposed.

Religious education must develop a philosophy which equips its students to respond responsibly, but also courageously and effectively, to the challenges of our new historical reality. The Zionist revolution created a people willing to accept responsibility for its collective actions within history. The *halakhic* community must now express a spiritual boldness commensurate with the enormous courage reflected in the Zionist revolution.

## Notes

1.    J. B. Soloveitchik, "Kol Dodi Dofek," *Ish HaEmunah* (Jerusalem: Mossad Harav Kook, 1968), pp. 65–106. Soloveitchik perceives *brit goral* as creating the *halakhic* ground of collective responsibility. The law that derives from *brit ye'ud* requires that individual members of Israel sense their collective responsibility. Common historical fate has a normative significance in Soloveitchik's philosophy. (See pp. 89–91.)

      Soloveitchik is also careful to distinguish between theodicy and the human response to suffering. He does not pretend to offer a solution to the metaphysical problem of evil. His approach is practical, i.e., he is concerned with developing a *halakhic* response to events in history. His theology of history is a logic of response and not a logic of description. Action, not metaphysical truth, is his concern, and it is in this light that one must appreciate his theological approach to the State of Israel. See as well the opening remarks in "The Lonely Man of Faith," *Tradition* 7, no. 2 (Summer 1965): 9.

2.    Soloveitchik, "Kol Dodi Dofek," pp. 103–107.

3.    For approaches to the loss of tradition and its possible renewal, as reflected in the

Israeli reality, see Natan Rotenstreich, *Tradition and Reality* (New York: Random House, 1972); Gershom Scholem, "Zionism, Dialectic of Continuity and Rebel Lion," in *Unease in Zion,* Ehud Ben Ezer, ed. (Jerusalem and New York: Quadrangle Press, 1974); Eliezer Schweid, *Israel at the Crossroads* (Philadelphia: Jewish Publication Society, 1973).

4. It is unfortunate that certain educational approaches guiding many *halakhic* Jews appear to be blind to the complexity of this question and, even worse, deaf to the urgency of creating a community of meaning among Jews. They frequently reflect an isolationist mentality that seeks to develop religious passion by emphasizing exclusively those *mitzvot* which encourage religious isolation. Indeed, the "burning" *halakhic* issues often discussed serve to discourage large sectors of the Jewish community from considering the tradition as a significant spiritual option. Even among religious groups which express a deep concern and involvement with the larger Jewish community, one does not sense recognition of the spiritual values which may be inherent in behavior that is not grounded in Divine Revelation. Instead of communication and dialogue with other Jews, one witnesses the attempt to convince the others of the validity of *halakhic* categories of thought and patterns of behavior. They speak to others, but often do not listen.

   All of us, *halakhic* and non-*halakhic* Jews alike, realize that the exigencies of life force different sectors of our society to meet. The battlefield awakens our sense of *kol yisrael haverim*; political isolation on the world scene brings us together to fight the battle of *goral.* Nonetheless, in the land of *ye'ud,* we continue to walk separate paths and live in total value-isolation from one another. This is a potentially explosive reality that must be faced by all thinkers and educators concerned with the Jewish content of Israeli society.

5. Leo Strauss, *Persecution and the Art of Writing* (Glencoe, Ill: The Free Press, 1952), pp. 19–21. See also Abraham S. Halkin, "The Attitude of Normative Judaism to Philosophy," *Perspectives in Jewish Learning,* vol. 4 (Chicago: Spertus College of Judaica, 1972).

6. Introduction to the *Commentary to the Mishnah,* pp. 21–24, Kafih edition. See *Mishneh Torah, Hilkhot Yesodei haTorah,* chap. 5, hal. 11, where the characteristic approach of the *hasid* is to act, always, *lifnim mishurat hadin.* See *Guide,* II, 51, for the way the *hasid* utilizes the *halakhah* for training in contemplative love of God. On the relationship between philosophy and *halakhah,* see Isidore Twersky, "Some Non-*Halakhic* Aspects of the Mishneh Torah," in *Jewish Medieval and Renaissance Studies,* Alexander Altman, ed. (Cambridge, Mass.: Harvard University Press, 1967), pp. 95–119.

7. *Hilkhot Yesodei HaTorah,* chap. 2, hal. 1–2. In contrast to Maimonides' description of *yir'ah* and *ahavah* in chapter 10 of *Hilkhot Teshuvah,* where *yir'ah* is a stage to be overcome by love, here *yir'ah* is an outgrowth of love. In *Hilkhot Teshuvah, yir'ah* is a motivating principle for action; here *yir'ah* is a description of a state of consciousness in which man feels the enormous difference between human and Divine perfection. The felt impact of one's creature consciousness is an outgrowth of intellectual love of God. The *yir'ah* dimension in *Hilkhot Teshuvah* expresses the self-interest of the "child" who can only be motivated to act by promises of external reward. Growth in philosophy, i.e., growth in intellectual love of God, leads to the healing of man's egocentric needs and enables him to act out of a sense of pure love. See my *Maimonides: Torah and the Philosophical Quest* (Philadelphia: Jewish Publication Society, 1976), chapter 2.

8. *Hilkhot Teshuvah,* chap. 10, hal. 10–11. Compare this with Maimonides' state-

ment in *Commentary to the Mishnah, Makkot,* chap. 3, mishnah 17, where it would seem that love of God also expresses itself through one's attitude toward practice.

9.  Soloveitchik, "The Lonely Man of Faith," pp. 14–15:

> The brute is helpless, and, therefore, not dignified. Civilized man has gained limited control of nature and has become, in certain respects, her master, and with his mastery, he has attained dignity, as well. His mastery has made it possible for him to act in accordance with his responsibility. . . . .There is no dignity without responsibility, and one cannot assume responsibility as long as he is not capable of living up to his commitments. Only when man rises to the heights of freedom of action and creativity of mind does he begin to implement the mandate of dignified responsibility entrusted to him by his maker.

There is an important relationship between Soloveitchik's approach to technology and the *halakhic* concern for understanding God in terms of models of action. To Soloveitchik, man is called upon not only to imitate the moral attributes of God, but also to imitate God the Creator,

10.  See Jacob Katz, *Exclusiveness and Tolerance* (New York: Schocken Books, 1962), especially chapter 10. Even the Meiri, who reinterpreted the talmudic attitude toward the non-Jew, expresses an intolerant attitude toward deviant behavior manifest by the Jew. See Hameiri on *Horayot,* p. 11a. 11. One should contrast the approach suggested in this essay with MacIntyre's interesting critique of all Christian theological attempts at translation.

With regard to the dilemma of contemporary moral theology, MacIntyre writes, "Either it will remain within the theological closed circle in which case it will have no access to the public and shared moral criteria of our society. Or it will accept those criteria: in which case it may well have important things to say, but they will not be distinctively Christian." Alasdair MacIntyre, *Against the Self-Images of the Age* (New York: Schocken Books, 1971), p. 23.

In *The Religious Significance of Atheism* (New York: Columbia University Press, 1969), MacIntyre argues the stronger claim that not only have the translations of Bultmann, Tillich, etc., failed, but that every translation must fail. "Any presentation of theism which is able to secure a hearing from a secular audience, has undergone a transformation that has evacuated it entirely of its theistic content" (p. 26). "Thus the abandonment of theistic content in favor of secular intelligibility leads away from even the remnants of theistic practice" (p. 29). See also his book *Secularization and Moral Change* (London: Oxford University Press, 1967).

12.  Eliezer Schweid, "Shabbat in the State of Israel," *Petahim* 31 (December 1974): 38–47. For an important attempt at enabling one to understand the spirit of the Shabbat without going into a detailed elaboration of the laws of the Shabbat, see A. J. Heschel, *The Sabbath* (New York: Farrar, Strauss and Young, 1951). Heschel's writings reflect the work of a dedicated Jewish teacher who speaks to a generation where large sectors manifest a spiritual numbness and deafness because of the loss of Jewish tradition. He speaks to an audience which has forgotten how to feel within Jewish rhythms. His evocative language is an attempt to cultivate a religious sensibility.

13.  Maimonides' Introduction to *Guide,* pp. 5–6. All references to *Guide* in this

article use the Shlomo Pines translation and edition (Chicago: University of Chicago Press, 1963).

14. See the suggestive remarks by Soloveitchik in "Sacred and Profane," *Gesher* (June 1966): 23–28. Throughout Soloveitchik's writings, one discerns how struggle, doubt, and failure can be utilized to deepen one's religious commitment. One senses at times a romanticization of the darker side of man in the creation of new religious energy. See *Al HaTeshuvah* (Jerusalem: World Zionist Organization, 1974), pp. 175–87.

15. Gershom Scholem, "Revelation and Tradition as Religious Categories in Judaism," *The Messianic Idea in Judaism* (New York: Schocken Books, 1971); "Religious Authority and Mysticism," *On the Kabbalah and its Symbolism* (New York: Schocken Books, 1965). In the former essay, Scholem sees the achievement of the biblical scholar as an example of "spontaneity in receptivity." He writes that "out of the religious tradition (these scholars) bring forth something entirely new, something that itself commands religious dignity: commentary. . . . .Commentary thus became the characteristic expression of Jewish thinking about truth, which is another way of describing the rabbinic genius." Scholem is sensitive to the profound dialectic which is expressed in commentary. "There is . . . .a striking contrast between the awe of the text, founded on the assumption that everything already exists in it, and the presumptuousness of imposing the truth upon ancient texts. The commentator, who is truly a biblical scholar, always combines both attitudes" (pp. 289–90).

   Scholem believes that the mystic understanding of Revelation illuminates the boldness reflected in Rabbinic commentary. Because the mystic confirms and perpetuates authority, he is able to express unlimited freedom in his exegesis ("Religious Authority and Mysticism," pp. 12–13, 22).

16. For a discussion on the possibility of continuing in the tradition of commentary without the ancient belief in Revelation, see Gershom Scholem, "Reflections on the Possibility of Jewish Mysticism in Our Time," *Ariel* 26 (1970): 49–50. Guttmann claims that commentary is not possible for a generation that has lost faith in a literal Revelation. He therefore attempts to clarify essential principles in the tradition which can act as a framework for continuity within change. See "The Principles of Judaism," translated from the Hebrew by David W. Silverman, *Conservative Judaism* 14, no. 1 (Fall 1959): 1–24.

17. For different approaches to the significance of sacrifices, see Halevi, *Kuzari*, II, 26; Rambam, *Guide*, 111, 32; and commentary of the Ramban to Leviticus 1:9. On the contrast between mythic and rational sensibilities, see G. Scholem, *Major Trends in Jewish Mysticism* (New York: Schocken, 1961), pp. 28–37. Contrast the approach to the Shabbat taken by Maimonides, *Guide*, 11, 31, with the mystic approach discussed by Scholem in "Tradition and New Creation in the Ritual of the Kabbalists," *On the Kabbalah . . . .*, pp. 118–58.

18. The need to find new ways to understand and apply the Torah to one's generation is a vital way of realizing the Rabbinic attitude toward *kabbalat hatorah*. "Let the Torah never be for you an antiquated decree, but rather like a decree freshly issued, no more than two or three days old. . . . .But Ben Azzai said: Not even as old as a decree issued two or three days ago but as a decree issued this very day." (*Psikta d'Rab Kahana*, piska 12, section 12). "When you study My words of Torah, they are not to seem antiquated to you, but as fresh as though the Torah were given this day" (Piska 12, section 21). "R. Judah spoke further in honor of the Torah, expounding the text. *Attend (hasket) and hear, O Israel: this day thou*

*art become a people unto the Lord thy God.* Now was it on that day that the Torah was given to Israel? Was not that day the end of the forty years (of the wandering)? It is, however, to teach thee that the Torah is as beloved every day to those that study it as on the day when it was given from Mount Sinai" (Berakhot 63b). See also Sifre, 33, 6.

19. See B. M. Levin's *Otzar HaGeonim, IV, Hagigah,* p. 60; Maimonides' Introduction to *Guide,* pp. 18–20.

20. Soloveitchik is concerned with showing how the detailed, objective prescriptions of the *halakhah* do not exhaust the full richness of the *halakhic* experience. He does this by showing the relationship between the inner realization *(Kiyyum shebalev)* and the outward act *(Ma'aseh)* of a *mitzvah.* In examining the writings of Soloveitchik we note the lengthy treatment he gives to the *mitzvot* of prayer, repentance, joy, and mourning. These *mitzvot* illuminate the relationship of internal experience and objective form in *halakhah.* See Soloveitchik, "Lonely Man of Faith," pp. 34–43.

For a discussion of the way autonomy and spontaneity may be expressed within *halakhah,* see the chapter on *mitzvot* in Ephraim Urbach's *The Sages* (Jerusalem: Magnes Press, 1975), pp. 317–42. See also J. Heschel, *God in Search of Man* (New York: Farrar, Strauss and Cudahy, 1955), pp. 281–348, for a modern attempt at integrating *halakhah* and *aggadah.*

21. See my "Torah Mi-Sinai BeDoreinu," *Petahim* 33 (June 1975): 10–16; and *Maimonides: Torah and Philosophic Quest,* chapter 3.

22. See Benjamin N. Cardozo, *The Growth of the Law* (New Haven: Yale University Press, 1963), pp. 64–70; H. L. A. Hart, *The Concept of Law* (London: Oxford University Press, 1964), chapter 7; Chaim Perelman, *Justice* (New York: Random House, 1964), pp. 91–110; Julius Stone, *Legal Systems and Lawyers' Reasoning* (London: Stevens and Sons, Ltd., 1964), chapter 8.

23. Julius Stone, *Social Dimensions Of Law and Justice* (London: Stevens and Sons, Ltd., 1966), chapter 14; Chaim Perelman, *The Idea of Justice and the Problem of Argument* (New York: Humanities Press, 1963), pp. 98–134.

24. See the fundamental disagreement between the Rambam and the Ramban regarding the relationship between authority based upon Revelation and the content of Revelation. *(Sefer Hamitzvot,* first and second principles, and the comments of the Ramban.) See also Menahem Elon, *Mishpat Ivri* (Jerusalem: Magnes Press, 1975), pp. 223–32.

25. See comments of the Rabad to Maimonides' Introduction to the *Mishneh Torah.* Jewish history did not allow Maimonides to realize his search for simplicity in *halakhic* formulation. The multiple commentaries on Maimonides and the complicated legal discussion centering around a code which was supposed to simplify man's knowledge of *halakhah* seem to indicate that the Jewish legal mind does not respond comfortably to the quest for *halakhic* simplicity. One cannot fully appreciate what Maimonides attempted to do with the *Mishneh Torah* without relating this to his general understanding of the relationship between philosophy and *halakhah.* See *Guide,* III, 51, 54, on the religious implications of the difference between legal and philosophic knowledge. See also Isidore Twersky, "The Beginnings of Mishneh Torah Criticism," in *Biblical and Other Studies,* A. Altman, ed. (Cambridge, Mass.: Harvard University Press, 1963), pp. 161–82.

26. Yeshayahu Leibowitz's exaggerated claim that if the *mitzvot* reflect any human value they are empty of religious significance, is a modern application of the *akedah* consciousness. To Leibowitz, anything that deviates from the model of

the *akedah* is self-worship, i.e., idolatry. It is doubtful whether his understanding of Judaism can illuminate a tradition which recognized stages of growth in man's religious development, and allowed for a variety of motives in the performance of *mitzvot*. Given the tradition's uncompromising attitude toward idolatry, this tolerance toward practice is not understandable within Leibowitz's categories. See his *Yahadut, Am Yehudi U'Medinat Yisrael* (Jerusalem: Schocken Press, 1975), p. 26.

27. *Helek,* pp. 136–37.
28. On some of the possible differences between Aristotelian and Maimonidean ethics, see Eliezer Schweid, *Iyyunim beShmonah Perakim* (Jerusalem: Jewish Agency, 1969), p. 63. See also the comment of Leo Strauss, "Notes on the Book of Knowledge," *Studies in Mysticism and Religion,* presented to G. Scholem (Jerusalem: Magnes Press, 1967), pp. 277–78.
29. See Emil Fackenheim's profound treatment of what constitutes modern idolatry in "Idolatry as a Modern Possibility," *Encounters Between Judaism and Modern Philosophy* (New York: Basic Books, 1973).
30. It is interesting to observe that Maimonides introduces the laws relating to idolatry with a long statement regarding both the historical origin of idolatry and how the philosophical way of Abraham leads to the *halakhic* way of Moses. Possibly, Maimonides wanted us to understand that only within the context of the struggle against idolatry is man best able to appreciate the relationship between philosophy and law. For a further understanding of Maimonides' approach to idolatry, see *Guide,* 1, 36; III, 29, 30, 37, 41.
31. Although the Talmud speaks of the destruction of the evil instinct toward idolatry, Soloveitchik nevertheless describes how modern idolatry may manifest itself in unconditional allegiance to family or state. See Yoma 69b, *Sanhedrin* 63b, 64a and Soloveitchik, *Al HaTeshuvah,* pp. 140–43.
32. Fackenheim's remarks are germane to this question. "Whether or not idolatry could be possible if there were no God, or if He were not jealous, idolatry in any case achieves its full religious meaning only in the context of a covenant with a jealous God." Emil Fackenheim, *Idolatry as a Modern Possibility,* p. 176. See also, E. Urbach, *Sages,* pp. 21–23; Fuller, *The Morality of Law,* pp. 10–13.
33. E. Urbach, "The Rabbinical Laws of Idolatry, part II," *Israel Exploration Journal,* no. 4 (1960): 238–45. See Saul Lieberman, "Rabbinic Polemics Against Idolatry," *Hellenism in Jewish Palestine* (New York: Jewish Theological Seminary, 1950), pp. 115–27.
34. See Sifre, 48; *Berakhot* 2, mishnah 1; *Kiddushin* 30b, 31a, 40a; *Yebamot* 78b, 79a; *Hilkhot Teshuvah,* chap. 2, hal. 10; *Hilkhot Issurei Bi'ah,* chap. 12, hal. 22, 23, 24.
35. Seminal for our discussion is the following remark:

> R. Huna and R. Jeremiah said in the name of R. Hiyya B. Abba: It is written, *They have forsaken Me and have not kept My Law* (Jer. 16:11)—i.e., would that they had forsaken Me but kept My law, since by occupying themselves therewith, the light which it contains would have led them back to the right path. R. Huna said: Study Torah even if it be not for its own sake, since even if not for its own sake at first, it will eventually be for its own sake. R. Joshua b. Levi said: Every day a *bat kol* issues from Mount Horeb, declaring "Woe to mankind for slighting Torah!" (*Midrash Rabbah, Lamentations,* Soncino edition, pp. 2–3)

See *Pesikta d'Rab Kahana,* piska 15, 5; *Yerushalmi Hagigah,* chap. 1, hal. 7. This statement would be unintelligible if faith were the exclusive and primary focus of the tradition. Similarly, the discussion in *Rosh Hashannah* 29a, about whether *mitzvot* require *kavanah,* would also be unintelligible.

MacIntyre's critique of modern Protestant theology does not fit a theology where *halakhah* is central. "Injunctions to repent, to be responsible, even to be generous, do not actually tell us what to do. And about the content of the moral life Christians in fact have no more to say than anyone else. Christians behave like everyone else but use a different vocabulary in characterizing their behavior, and so conceal their lack of distinctiveness (*Against the Self-Images of the Age,* p. 24). MacIntyre sees partial significance in the work of Bonhoeffer because there was a social context which affected practice.

> One gets from Bonhoeffer's writings no clear picture of what type of action he would actually be recommending now, but one gets the clearest picture of what Bonhoeffer means if one sees it in the context out of which he wrote. For in Nazi Germany, and in the Europe of the 1930s, the Christian role was at best one of suffering witness. The Nazi regress to gods of race made relevant a Christian regress to a witness of the catacombs and of the martyrs. There was available then a simple form in which to relive Christ's passion. Bonhoeffer lived it. And in all situations where nothing else remains for Christians, this remains. But what has this Christianity to say not of power-lessness, but of the handling of power? Nothing; and hence the oddity of trying to reissue Bonhoeffer's message in our world. (Ibid., p. 19)

MacIntyre's critique of modern theological attempts at translations, i.e., to create general intelligibility of religious language, is related to his strong claim that "urbanization and industrialization produced a new form of social life, in which religious utterance and activity were necessarily contextless gestures" (*The Religious Significance of Atheism,* p. 43). MacIntyre's important critique may, however, not be applicable to Judaism which defines the cultural life of a community. The living Jewish community in the State of Israel seeks cultural forms to give expression to its collective life. The attempt to see if Judaism can be concretized within the political structure of the community provides a social context for the meaning of religious language. The important place that peoplehood, land, history, and law occupy in Jewish theology may provide the modern framework for the renewal of faith in God. See Ernst Simon, "The Way of the Law," in *Tradition and Contemporary Experience,* Alfred Jospe, ed. (New York: Schocken Books, 1970), pp. 221–38; G. Scholem, "Some Reflections on Jewish Theology," *The Center Magazine,* 1973.

36. See *Guide,* I, 54; II, 36–40; III, 34, 41, and the introductory comments of S. Pines, lxxxviii-xcii, cxx-cxxiii; L. Strauss, *Persecution and the Art of Writing,* pp. 7–21; Julius Guttmann, *Philosophies of Judaism,* trans. David W. Silverman (New York: Anchor Books, 1966), pp. 203–205 and n. 125; and J. Guttmann, "Pilosofia shel hadat o pilosofia shel hahok?" *Proceedings of the Israel Academy of Sciences and Humanities* 5, no. 9 (1975): 188–207.

37. See Maimonides' Commentary to the *Mishnah, Hulin,* chap. 7, mishnah 6; *Hilkhot Avodah Zarah,* chap. 1, hal. 3; *Hilkhot De'ot,* chap. 1, hal. 7; *Guide* I, 63, II, 39. Notice the repeated emphasis in Maimonides that the patriarchs only teach.

38. See *Guide,* III, 51, 54, and my book, *Maimonides,* chapter 5.

39. See *Hilkhot Yesodei HaTorah,* chap. 4, hal. 13 and comments of the Kesef Mishneh, *Hilkhot Talmud Torah,* chap. 1, hal. 12. Maimonides never intended that one must first be a master of talmudic thought before engaging in philosophic reflection.

# Afterword: Future Directions

*Daniel J. Elazar*

If this book has served its intended purpose, it should have demonstrated to the reader that there is a Jewish political tradition that has never ceased to influence the political and communal life of the Jewish people, even in periods when it was half-forgotten and expressed subliminally more than overtly. In the past two generations, historians who have attended seriously to the matter have rediscovered the extent to which Jewish communities of the premodern diaspora remained vehicles for the expression of an autonomous Jewish existence on the political as well as other planes. Students of the Jewish legal tradition have enriched and deepened the exploration by showing how the very constitutional foundations of those communities reflected the continuing Jewish political tradition. For contemporary Jewish communities, the issues has been less well explored, perhaps because most of those who explore contemporary Jewry are not sufficiently rooted in classical Jewish sources to draw the connections. This volume has made an effort to bridge that gap. Nevertheless, many questions remain to be explored regarding the transmission of the tradition across the fault line represented by emancipation and modernization.

The foregoing chapters also should have established at least two points regarding the character of the Jewish political tradition and several others regarding its content. It should be clear that a political tradition is compounded out of the interaction of political thought, political culture, and political behavior and that it is possible to study the Jewish political tradition only by examining all of those dimensions. It should also be evident that political tradition is not expressed through a single doctrine or an ideological "line." Rather, it is compounded from a number of currents that relate to each other as parts of the same stream—that share common questions and engage in common dialogue. One of the best ways to learn about the Jewish political tradition is through examining the differences of opinion that have been expressed within it and the conflict that has occurred between exponents of those differences in the effort to hammer out agreed lines of action. This book has focused to no small degree on those differences of opinion. The authors have tried assiduously to avoid the "Judaism says" approach, but the book also should have revealed how these differences of opinion function within a common framework. Hence, if there was a sharp disagreement over whether or not medieval Jewish communities should be governed by the principle of majority rule, the dispute was not between exponents of majority rule as opposed to some kind of absolutism but rather majority rule versus unanimity. It need hardly be said that both principles functioned within the same republican and democratic cultural parameters.

This volume has tried to provide initial answers for a number of these questions and, by doing so, has reshaped the questions themselves. It began by suggesting that the covenant provides the framework or backbone of the Jewish political tradition. How it does so and to what extent certainly remain to be explored more fully. What are the various strands which together form the Jewish political tradition? What are the basic questions which that tradition raises repeatedly? Necessarily those questions must be universal ones, but to what extent are they expressed in a particularly Jewish way? Here it should be made clear that the Jewish political tradition does not stand independent of other political traditions. No political tradition does. The way in which all humans have had to grapple with the same questions precludes anything like total originality or autonomy in matters political or in any others. Even what we have suggested here as the central idea of the Jewish political tradition, the covenant, is not the exclusive invention of the Jewish people. What counts is the original way in which the Jewish political tradition developed the concept and became the central source of its transmission to the rest of the world. Thus, a great part of the study of the tradition must focus upon how Jews offer their own forms of expression of universal political concerns or their own conceptualizations of universal political ideas.

There remains the task of focusing on specific problems of the Jewish political tradition, such as the structure of Jewish politics, the founding of Jewish polities, the character of Jewish political interests, matters of Jewish political leadership, the handling of power and community conflict, the relationship between the individual and the community, the basis for authoritative decision making, the problem of relations between different Jewish communities and between Israel and the diaspora.

On another level, we need to explore anew the Jewish language of politics. A major part of the Zionist argument was that the revival of Jewish culture was predicated on the revival of the Hebrew language as the living language of the Jewish people. This is as much true for the Jewish political tradition as it is for any other aspect of Jewish civilization. There is, indeed, a Jewish language of politics, a vocabulary of terms, most of which date back to the Bible itself, which convey their own special meanings with regard to matters political. Many of these terms were reinterpreted as part of the revival of the Hebrew language to be Hebrew imitations of modern European political ideas, regardless of how much violence that reinterpretation may have done to their original meaning. In the process, those original meanings have frequently been lost and with them the great chain of tradition has come unlinked. One of the best ways to restore the chain, to refasten the links, is through a rediscovery of the original terminology and a revival of original usages where appropriate. Jews should be additionally encouraged to do this since, in most cases, the original usages are even more appropriate to the postmodern era than their adaptations. In any case, this endeavor is not an arid theoretical exercise by any means.

The Jewish political tradition, then, is embodied in the chain of thinkers about things political, actors in the political realm, and concepts derived "from Sinai" that surface and resurface from time to time, tied together by a common vocabulary. Earlier, we said that the Jewish political tradition involves the interaction of texts and behavior. One of the reasons that texts are so important is because the law is a central factor in the Jewish political tradition. The covenant creates relationships that are embodied in law and the law, which becomes their primary formal manifestation, becomes a principal institution of the tradition. Given the fact that the Jews had to survive so long in exile, dispersed and without a state of their own, it was natural for them to turn even more fully to the law as the institutional embodiment of their autonomy and separateness, not merely as the handmaiden of their political society but as much, much more—as a substitute for the spatial dimension of that political society. The significance of this for the Jewish political tradition can hardly be overestimated.

Nevertheless, those who would suggest that a legal or halakhic tradition can replace the political tradition also err. *Halakhah* is indeed central, but it is not sufficient, for the same reason that law in any society is not enough but requires politics to make it meaningful, just as politics requires law to make it legitimate. The matter is further complicated today by the fact that a majority, no doubt the great majority of Jews in the world, no longer consider *halakhah* binding in the traditional way, whereas they consider the association of Jews with one another in some formal manner to be a *sine qua non* of Jewish identification. This emphasis on association is inevitably political in character as are the acts that inevitably flow from it, namely, the emphasis on organizational activity and, increasingly, political action on behalf of perceived Jewish interests. Thus, the Jewish political tradition has a capacity to serve as an integrating factor in the life of the Jewish people across boundaries and within communities.

The results of the consent were to create a situation in which *kol Israel arevim ze la-ze*—all Israel are guarantors for one another. Thus, Sinai bound the Jews not only to God, but to one another, creating *arevut*. To this day, the Jewish political tradition does not dictate to Jews what form of regime they must have but it does dictate that the regime must be based upon this *arevut*, upon the covenant from which it flows, and must be what Professor Goitein has termed a religious democracy. Whatever the value of these immediate goals, the major language goal of the Jewish political tradition must be to perfect the political life of Jews, of the Jewish polity as a whole, and, most particularly, of the Jewish state.

Finally, as the outlines of the Jewish political tradition become clarified, it will be possible to explore the impact of that tradition on the gentile world, particularly the West. Modern democratic theory and practice are based on two great classical sources, the Greek and the Hebrew. While the two are at least as mutually reinforcing as they are contradictory, there are important differences between them. At one time, both received equal attention at the hands of political theorists and the political leaders who learned from them. This was true as late as the seventeenth and eighteenth centuries when both contributed mightily to the shaping of modern democracy. Since the secularization of modern political thought, the Hebraic elements have been neglected. It has come to be assumed that no systematic political theory inheres in what is essentially a theologically based approach to politics and that the political institutions of the Israelite polity are merely particularistic, confined in meaning to their time and place. As Eliezer Schweid pointed out, Spinoza was the author of this viewpoint at the very outset of the modern era.

The end of World War II brought with it the end of the modern era. We are now completing the end of the first generation of the postmodern era. With the coming of the postmodern era, many of the assumptions of modernism are being challenged. Spinoza's assumption is one of them. To date, that challenge has been muted and sporadic, perhaps because the sense of the Jewish political tradition which was available in previous epochs has been lost, making it difficult to challenge today's conventional wisdom. Thus, the revival of the understanding of the Jewish political tradition along with the revival of the tradition in its fullness as a result of the reestablishment of the Jewish state may mark another turning point in the impact of the tradition on humanity as a whole.

# Contributors

*Ella Belfer* is a fellow of the Jerusalem Center for Public Affairs and professor of political studies at Bar-Ilan University. She has written extensively on religion and political thought, and is the author of *The People of Israel and the Kingdom of Heaven—Studies in Jewish Theocracy*.

*Gerald J. Blidstein* is a fellow of the Jerusalem Center for Public Affairs and M. Hubert Professor of Jewish Law at Ben-Gurion University in Beersheva. He has written extensively on Jewish political thought, including *Political Concepts in Maimonidean Halakhah* (Hebrew), which was awarded the Jerusalem Prize in Jewish Studies (1985), and *Prayer in Maimonidean Halakhah* (Hebrew).

*Stuart A. Cohen* is professor of political studies at Bar-Ilan University and a fellow of the Jerusalem Center for Public Affairs. His books include *The Jewish Polity* and *The Three Crowns: Structures of Communal Discourse in Early Rabbinic Society*.

*Eliezer Don-Yehiya* is an associate of the Jerusalem Center for Public Affairs and professor of political studies at Bar-Ilan University. He is the author of *Religion and Politics in Israel* and *Religious Institutions in the Political System: The Religious Councils in Israel* (Hebrew).

*Daniel J. Elazar* is president of the Jerusalem Center for Public Affairs, Senator N.M. Paterson Professor of Intergovernmental Relations at Bar-Ilan University, and professor of political science and director of the Center for the Study of Federalism at Temple University in Philadelphia. He is the author of numerous books, including *Community and Polity: The Organizational Dynamics of the American Jewish Community, The Jewish Polity: Jewish Political Organization from Biblical Times to the Present,* and *Covenant and Polity in Biblical Israel,* and is the founder and editor of the *Jewish Political Studies Review.*

*Menachem Elon,* Vice President Emeritus of the Supreme Court of Israel, is professor of Jewish law and the founder of the Institute for Research in Jewish Law at the Hebrew University of Jerusalem. Among his many works is the monumental *Jewish Law: History, Sources, Principles.*

*Gordon M. Freeman* is an associate of the Jerusalem Center for Public Affairs, adjunct assistant professor at the Graduate Theological Seminary, and rabbi of Congregation B'nai Shalom, Walnut Creek, California. He is the author of *The Heavenly Kingdom: Aspects of Political Thought in the Talmud and Midrash.*

The late *Shlomo Dov Goitein* was director of the Hebrew University's School of Oriental Studies and professor of Arabic at the University of Pennsylvania. The bibliography of his writings contains 548 items, including the three-volume magnum opus *A Mediterranean Society: The Jewish Communities of the Arab World as Portrayed in the Documents of the Cairo Geniza.*

*David Hartman,* senior lecturer in Jewish Philosophy at the Hebrew University of Jerusalem, is the founder and director of the Shalom Hartman Institute for Judaic Studies in Jerusalem. He is the author of numerous books including *A Living Covenant.*

*Charles S. Liebman* was vice chairman of the Jerusalem Center for Public Affairs' Center for Jewish Community Studies and is professor of political studies at Bar-Ilan University. He is the author of *The Ambivalent American Jew: Politics, Religion and Family in American Jewish Life, Aspects of the Religious Behavior of American Jews,* and *Pressure Without Sanctions: The Influence of World Jewry in Shaping Israel's Public Policy.*

*Peter Y. Medding* was a fellow of the Jerusalem Center for Public Affairs and is professor of political science and contemporary Jewry at the Hebrew University of Jerusalem. He is the author of *From Assimilation to Group Survival: A Political and Sociological Analysis of an Australian Jewish Community* and *Mapai in Israel.*

*Eliezer Schweid* is vice president and a fellow of the Jerusalem Center for Public Affairs, professor of Jewish philosophy at the Hebrew University of Jerusalem, and recipient of the 1994 Israel Prize for his contributions to Jewish thought. He is the author of numerous works, including *Jewish Thought in the Twentieth Century—An Introduction, Wrestling Until Day-Break: Searching for Meaning in the Thinking on the Holocaust,* and *Democracy and Halakhah.*

*Dan V. Segre* is a fellow of the Jerusalem Center for Public Affairs and Professor Emeritus of Political Science at Haifa University. His numerous books include *Israel: A Society in Transition, The High Road and the Low: A Study in Authority, Legitimacy and Technical Aid,* and *Zionism and Israel: A Study in Self-Colonisation.*

*Bernard Susser* is an associate of the Jerusalem Center for Public Affairs and associate professor of political studies at Bar-Ilan University. He is the author of *Existence and Utopia: The Social and Political Thought of Martin Buber* and various articles on political theory.

*Moshe Weinfeld* is Professor Emeritus of Bible at the Hebrew University of Jerusalem and served as visiting professor of Bible at the Jewish Theological Seminary of America and at Brandeis University. He is the author of *Deuteronomy and the Deuteronomic School, Social Justice in Ancient Israel and the Ancient Near East,* and various monographs and articles, such as "Covenant in the Bible and in the Ancient Near East," "Theological Trends in Pentateuchal Literature," "Jeremiah and the Spiritual Metamorphosis of Israel," "The Period of Conquest and the Judges as Seen by the Earlier and Later Sources," "The Qumran Sect—Its Organization and Liturgy."

# Index